MO

D1154919

The Papers of
George Washington

The Papers of
George Washington

W. W. Abbot and Dorothy Twohig, *Editors*

Philander D. Chase and Beverly H. Runge, *Associate Editors*

Beverly S. Kirsch and Debra B. Kessler, *Assistant Editors*

Presidential Series

4

September 1789–January 1790

Dorothy Twohig, Editor

UNIVERSITY PRESS OF VIRGINIA

CHARLOTTESVILLE AND LONDON

Barry University Library
Miami, FL 33161

This edition has been prepared by the staff of
The Papers of George Washingon
sponsored by
The Mount Vernon Ladies' Association of the Union
and the University of Virginia
with the support of
the National Endowment for the Humanities,
the Andrew W. Mellon Foundation,
and the J. Howard Pew Freedom Trust.

THE UNIVERSITY PRESS OF VIRGINIA
Copyright © 1993 by the Rector and Visitors
of the University of Virginia

First published 1993

Library of Congress Cataloging-in-Publication Data
(Revised for volume 4)

Washington, George, 1732–1799.
   The papers of George Washington. Presidential series /
Dorothy Twohig, editor.

   Includes indexes.
   Contents: 1. September 1788–March 1789 — 2. April–
June 1789 — [etc.] — 4. September 1780–January 1790.
   1. Washington, George, 1732–1799—Correspondence.
2. Presidents—United States—Correspondence. 3. United
States—Politics and government—1789–1797. I. Twohig,
Dorothy. II. Title: Presidential series. III. Title.
E312.72 1987b   973.4′1′092   87-410017
ISBN 0-8139-1103-6 (v. 1)
ISBN 0-8139-1407-8 (v. 4)

Printed in the United States of America

Barry University Library
Miami, FL 33161

E
312.72
1987 b

220141

Administrative Board

John T. Casteen III   Mrs. Clarence Morton Bishop
                    Nancy C. Essig

Editorial Board

Stuart W. Bruchey   Richard H. Kohn
Noble E. Cunningham, Jr.   Jackson Turner Main
Emory G. Evans   Jacob M. Price
Jack P. Greene   Norman K. Risjord
Don Higginbotham   Thad W. Tate

Editorial Staff

W. W. Abbot   Beverly S. Kirsch
Philander D. Chase   Charlene M. Lewis
Frank E. Grizzard, Jr.   Beverly H. Runge
Candace Harrison-Caraco   Susan C. Thompson
Debra B. Kessler   Dorothy Twohig

Consulting Editor

Robert Stewart

Contents

Contents

ix

Contents

Contents

Illustrations

following page 285

Portrait of Washington by Edward Savage (Harvard portrait)
Portrait of Washington by Edward Savage (Adams portrait)
Portrait of Washington by Christian Güllager
Portrait of Washington by Madame de Bréhan

MAP
following page 199
Tour of the Eastern States, 15 October–13 November 1789

Editorial Apparatus

Transcription of the documents in the volumes of *The Papers of George Washington* has remained as close to a literal reproduction of the manuscript as possible. Punctuation, capitalization, paragraphing, and spelling of all words are retained as they appear in the original document. Dashes used as punctuation have been retained except when a period and a dash and another mark of punctuation appear together. The appropriate marks of punctuation have always been added at the end of a paragraph. When a tilde is used in the manuscript to indicate a double letter, the letter has been doubled. Washington and some of his correspondents occasionally used a tilde above an incorrectly spelled word to indicate an error in orthography. When this device is used the editors have corrected the word. In cases where a tilde has been inserted above an abbreviation or contraction, usually in letter-book copies, the word has been expanded. Otherwise, contractions and abbreviations have been retained as written except that a period has been inserted after an abbreviation when needed. Superscripts have been lowered. Editorial insertions or corrections in the text appear in square brackets. Angle brackets < > are used to indicate illegible or mutilated material. A space left blank in a manuscript by the writer is indicated by a square-bracketed gap in the text [   ]. Deletion of material by the author of a manuscript is ignored unless it contains substantive material, and then it appears in a footnote. If the intended location of marginal notations is clear from the text, they are inserted without comment; otherwise they are recorded in the notes. The ampersand has been retained and the thorn transcribed as "th." The symbol for per ℔ is used when it appears in the manuscript. The dateline has been placed at the head of a document regardless of where it occurs in the manuscript. All of the documents printed in this volume, as well as other ancillary material usually cited in the notes, may be found in the CD-ROM edition of Washington's Papers (CD-ROM:GW).

During both of Washington's administrations, but particularly in the period shortly before and after his inauguration, he was besieged with applications for public office. Many of the applicants continued to seek appointment or promotion. The editors have usually printed only one of these letters in full and cited other letters both from the applicant and in support of his application in notes to the initial letter. When GW replied to these requests at all, the replies were generally pro forma reiterations of his policy of noncommitment until the appointment to a post was made. In such cases his replies have been included only in the notes to the original application and do not appear in their chronological sequence. Letters to or from GW that, in whole or in part, are printed out of their chronological sequence are listed in the table of contents with an indication of where they may be found in the volumes.

Since GW read no language other than English, incoming letters written to him in foreign languages were generally translated for him. Where this contemporary translation has survived, it has been used as the text of the document, rather than the original which Washington did not read. If no translation has been found, the text in the original foreign language will be used. Both the original and the contemporary translation will appear in the CD-ROM edition of the Washington Papers.

During the first months of the new government, the executive sent out large numbers of circular letters, either under Washington's name or that of one of his secretaries. Circular letters covered copies of laws passed by Congress and sent to the governors of the states. They also covered commissions and announcements of appointment for public offices sent to individuals after their nominations had been approved by the Senate. In both instances, the circulars requested recipients to acknowledge receipt of the documents. The circulars and the routine acknowledgements of these circulars, usually addressed to Washington but sometimes to one of his secretaries, have been omitted unless they contain material of other interest or significance. In such cases the letters are either calendared or printed in full. The entire text of the documents is available in the CD-ROM edition.

Individuals mentioned in the text are identified usually at their first substantive mention and are not identified at length in subsequent volumes. The index to each volume indicates where an identification appears in an earlier volume of the Presidential Series.

During the first months of Washington's first administration, he had the services of several secretaries: Tobias Lear and David Humphreys, who had been in his service at Mount Vernon, went with him to New York, and his nephew Robert Lewis of Fredericksburg joined the staff at the end of May. William Jackson and Thomas Nelson arrived later in the year. Relatively few drafts in GW's hand of letters for these months have survived, and the sequence in which outgoing letters and documents were written is often difficult to determine. In Record Group 59, State Department Miscellaneous Letters, in the National Archives, there are numerous documents that appear to be the original retained copies of letters written by Washington shortly before he became president and in the first months of his first administration. Much of this correspondence is in the hand of Lear or Humphreys. Occasionally the frequency with which the secretary's emendations and insertions appear suggests that the document was a draft prepared by him for GW. More rarely there are changes and corrections on a document in GW's own writing. On other occasions the documents appear to be simply retained copies either of GW's original draft or of the receiver's copy. For most of the letters found in Miscellaneous Letters, there are also letter-book copies in the Washington Papers at the Library of Congress. Some of the letters for this period probably were copied into the letter books close to the time they were written, but others obviously were entered much later. Occasionally Thomas Nelson's writing appears in the letter-book copies for the summer of 1789, as does Bartholomew Dandridge's, although Nelson did not join the staff until October and Dandridge was not employed until 1791. Finally, a few are in the handwriting of Howell Lewis, Washington's nephew, who did not assume his duties until the spring of 1792. When the receiver's copy of a letter has not been found, the editors have generally assumed that the copy in Miscellaneous Letters was made from the receiver's copy or the draft and have used it, rather than the letter-book copy, as the text, describing the document either as a copy or a draft, depending on the appearance of the manuscript.

Symbols Designating Documents

AD	Autograph Document
ADS	Autograph Document Signed
ADf	Autograph Draft
ADfS	Autograph Draft Signed
AL	Autograph Letter
ALS	Autograph Letter Signed
D	Document
DS	Document Signed
Df	Draft
DfS	Draft Signed
LS	Letter Signed
LB	Letter-Book Copy
[S]	Signature clipped (used with other symbols: e.g., AL[S], Df[S])

Repository Symbols and Abbreviations

Arch. Aff. Etr.	Archives du Ministère des Affaires Etrangères, Paris (photocopies at Library of Congress)
CD-ROM:GW	*see* Editorial Apparatus
CSmH	Henry E. Huntington Library, San Marino, Calif.
CStbKML	Karpeles Manuscript Library, Santa Barbara, Calif.
Ct	Connecticut State Library, Hartford
CtHi	Connecticut Historical Society, Hartford
CtY	Yale University, New Haven
DLC	Library of Congress
DLC:GW	George Washington Papers, Library of Congress
DNA	National Archives
DNA:PCC	Papers of the Continental Congress, National Archives
DSoCi	Society of the Cincinnati, Washington, D.C.
DT	U.S. Department of the Treasury, Washington, D.C.
IaU	University of Iowa, Iowa City
InHi	Indiana Historical Society, Indianapolis
IPB	Bradley University, Peoria, Ill.
KyLoF	Filson Club, Louisville, Ky.
LNHT	Tulane University, New Orleans
MB	Boston Public Library
MdHi	Maryland Historical Society, Baltimore
MH-Ar	Harvard University Archives, Cambridge, Mass.
MHi	Massachusetts Historical Society, Boston
MHi: Knox Papers	Henry Knox Papers, owned by the New England Historic Genealogical Society and deposited in the Massachusetts Historical Society
MiU-C	William L. Clements Library, University of Michigan, Ann Arbor
MnMAt	Minneapolis Athenaeum, Minn.
MSaE	Essex Institute, Salem, Mass.
MWalJFK	John F. Kennedy Library, Waltham, Mass.
Nc-Ar	North Carolina State Department of Archives and History, Raleigh

NcD	Duke University, Durham, N.C.
NCoxHi	Greene County Historical Society, Inc., Coxsackie, N.Y.
NhD	Dartmouth College, Hanover, N.H.
NhHi	New Hampshire Historical Society, Concord
NHi	New-York Historical Society, New York
NHpR	Franklin D. Roosevelt Library, Hyde Park, N.Y.
NIC	Cornell University, Ithaca, N.Y.
NjMoNP	Washington Headquarters Library, Morristown, N.J.
NjP	Princeton University, Princeton, N.J.
NN	New York Public Library, New York
NNC	Columbia University, New York
NNS	New York Society Library, New York
OHi	Ohio State Historical Society, Columbus, Ohio
PEL	Lafayette College, Easton, Pa.
PHC	Haverford College, Haverford, Pa.
PHi	Historical Society of Pennsylvania, Philadelphia
PP	Free Library of Philadelphia
PPAmP	American Philosophical Society, Philadelphia
PU-L	University of Pennsylvania, Biddle Law Library, Philadelphia
PWacD	David Library of the American Revolution, Washington Crossing, Pa.
R-Ar	Rhode Island State Library, Rhode Island State Archives, Providence
RG	Record Group (designating the location of documents in the National Archives)
ScCA	South Carolina Department of Archives and History, Columbia
Vi	Virginia State Library and Archives, Richmond
ViHi	Virginia Historical Society, Richmond
ViMtV	Mount Vernon Ladies' Association of the Union
ViU	University of Virginia, Charlottesville
WHi	State Historical Society of Wisconsin, Madison

Short Title List

Abernethy, *Western Lands and the American Revolution.*   Thomas Perkins Abernethy. *Western Lands and the American Revolution.* New York, 1959.

Alexander, *Princeton College.*   Samuel Davies Alexander. *Princeton College during the Eighteenth Century.* New York, c.1872.

Allen, *Massachusetts Privateers.*   Gardner Weld Allen. *Massachusetts Privateers of the Revolution.* Collections of the Massachusetts Historical Society, vol. 77. Cambridge, Mass., 1927.

American Book-Prices Current.   Edward Lazare, ed. *American Book-Prices Current. A Record of Literary Properties Sold at Auction in the United States during the Season of 1946–1947.* New York, 1947.

Annals of Congress.   Joseph Gales, Sr., comp. *The Debates and Proceedings in the Congress of the United States; with an Appendix, Containing Important State Papers and Public Documents, and All the Laws of a Public Nature.* 42 vols. Washington, D.C., 1834–56.

Archives Parlementaires.   M. J. Mavidal, ed. *Archives Parlementaires de 1787 à 1860.* Paris, 1877.

ASP.   Walter Lowrie et al., eds. *American State Papers: Documents, Legislative and Executive, of the Congress of the United States.* 38 vols. Washington, D.C., 1832–61.

Ballagh, *Letters of Richard Henry Lee.*   James Curtis Ballagh, ed. *The Letters of Richard Henry Lee.* 2 vols. New York, 1911–14.

Bartlett, *R.I. Records.*   John Russell Bartlett, ed. *Records of the Colony of Rhode Island and Providence Plantations in New England.* 10 vols. Providence, 1856–65.

Bentley, *Diaries.*   William Bentley. *The Diary of William Bentley, D.D.* 4 vols. Salem, Mass., 1905–14.

Bowling, *Creation of Washington, D.C.*   Kenneth R. Bowling. *The Creation of Washington, D.C.: The Idea and Location of the American Capital.* Fairfax, Va., 1991.

Bowling and Veit, *Diary of William Maclay.*   Kenneth R. Bowling and Helen E. Veit, eds. *The Diary of William Maclay and Other Notes on Senate Debates.* Baltimore, 1988.

Boyd, *Jefferson Papers.*   Julian P. Boyd et al., eds. *The Papers of Thomas Jefferson.* 22 vols. to date. Princeton, N.J., 1950–.

Brigham, *American Newspapers.*   Clarence S. Brigham. *History and Bibliography of American Newspapers, 1690–1820.* 2 vols. Worcester, Mass., 1947.

Britt, *Nothing More Agreeable.*   Judith S. Britt. *Nothing More Agreeable: Music in George Washington's Family.* Mount Vernon, 1984.

Burnett, *Letters.*   Edmund C. Burnett, ed. *Letters of Members of the Continental Congress.* 8 vols. Washington, D.C., 1921–36. Reprint. Gloucester, Mass., 1963.

Calendar of Virginia State Papers.   William P. Palmer et al., eds. *Calendar of Virginia State Papers and Other Manuscripts.* 11 vols. Richmond, 1875–93.

Carter, *Territorial Papers.*   Clarence E. Carter et al., eds. *The Territorial Papers of the United States.* 27 vols. Washington, D.C., 1934–69.

Caughey, *McGillivray of the Creeks.*   John Walton Caughey. *McGillivray of the Creeks.* Norman, Okla., 1938.

Clark, *Naval Documents.* William Bell Clark et al., eds. *Naval Documents of the American Revolution.* 9 vols. to date. Washington, D.C., 1964—.

Coleman, *Georgia Biography.*   Kenneth Coleman and Charles Stephen Gurr, eds. *Dictionary of Georgia Biography.* 2 vols. Athens, 1983.

Cullen and Johnson, *Marshall Papers.*   Charles T. Cullen, Herbert A. Johnson, et al. *The Papers of John Marshall.* 6 vols. to date. Chapel Hill, N.C., 1974—.

Dahlinger, *Fort Pitt.*   Charles W. Dahlinger. *Fort Pitt.* Pittsburgh, 1922.

Decatur, *Private Affairs of George Washington.*   Stephen Decatur, Jr. *Private Affairs of George Washington, from the Records and Accounts of Tobias Lear, Esquire, His Secretary.* Boston, 1933.

DeMarce, *Canadian Participants in the American Revolution.*   Virginia Easley DeMarce. *Canadian Participants in the American Revolution: An Index.* Arlington, Va., 1980.

DHFC.   Linda G. De Pauw et al., eds. *Documentary History of the First Federal Congress of the United States of America.* 6 vols. to date. Baltimore, 1972—.

Diaries.   Donald Jackson and Dorothy Twohig, eds. *The Diaries of George Washington.* 6 vols. Charlottesville, Va., 1976–79.

Eisen, *Portraits of Washington.*   Gustavus A. Eisen. *Portraits of Washington.* 3 vols. New York, 1932.

Elias, *Letters of Thomas Attwood Digges.*   Robert H. Elias and Eugene D. Finch, eds. *Letters of Thomas Attwood Digges (1742–1821).* Columbia, S.C., 1982.

Evans, *Holland Land Company.*   Paul Demund Evans. *The Holland Land Company.* Buffalo Historical Society Proceedings, vol. 28. Buffalo, N.Y., 1924.

Executive Journal.   *Journal of the Executive Proceedings of the Senate of the United States of America.* Vol. 1. Washington, D.C., 1828.

Fairchild, *Francis Van Der Kemp.*   Helen Lincklaen Fairchild. *Francis Adrian Van Der Kemp, 1752–1829: An Autobiography.* New York and London, 1903.

Few, *Autobiography.*   William Few. "Autobiography of Col. William Few of Georgia." *Magazine of American History,* 7 (1881), 343–58.

Flick, *History of the State of New York.*   Alexander C. Flick, ed. *History of the State of New York.* 10 vols. New York, 1933–37.

Ford, *Washington and the Theatre.*   Paul Leicester Ford. *Washington and the Theatre.* New York, 1899.

Ford, *Writings of Washington.*   Worthington Chauncey Ford, ed. *The Writings of Washington.* 14 vols. New York, 1889–93.

Goebel, *History of the Supreme Court.*   Julius Goebel, Jr. *History of the Supreme Court of the United States: Antecedents and Beginnings to 1801.* New York, 1971.

Griffin, *Boston Athenæum Collection.*   Appleton P. C. Griffin, comp. *A Catalogue of the Washington Collection in the Boston Athenæum.* Cambridge, Mass., 1897.

Gwathmey, *Historical Register.*   John H. Gwathmey. *Historical Register of Virginians in the Revolution.* Richmond, 1938.

Harris, *Eleven Gentlemen of Charleston.*   Ray Baker Harris. *Eleven Gentlemen of Charleston.* Washington, D.C., 1959.

Heads of Families (Massachusetts).   *Heads of Families at the First Census of the United States Taken in the Year 1790* (Massachusetts). Washington, D.C., 1908. Reprint. Baltimore, Md., 1964.

Heitman, *Historical Register.*   Francis B. Heitman. *Historical Register of Officers of the Continental Army during the War of the Revolution, April, 1775, to December, 1783.* Washington, D.C., 1893.

Hening.   William Waller Hening, ed. *The Statutes at Large; Being a Collection of All the Laws of Virginia from the First Session of the Legislature, in the Year 1619.* 13 vols. 1819–23. Reprint. Charlottesville, Va., 1969.

Historic Places.   Western Pennsylvania Historical Survey. *Guidebook to Historic Places in Western Pennsylvania.* Pittsburgh, 1938.

Hough, *Proceedings of the Commissioners of Indian Affairs.*   Franklin B. Hough, ed. *Proceedings of the Commissioners of Indian Affairs Appointed by Law for the Extinguishment of Indian Titles in the State of New York.* 2 vols. Albany, N.Y., 1861.

Janvier, *In Old New York.*   Thomas A. Janvier. *In Old New York.* New York, 1894.

JCC.   Worthington C. Ford et al., eds. *Journals of the Continental Congress.* 34 vols. Washington, D.C., 1904–37.

Jenkins, *Bronx.*   Stephen Jenkins. *The Story of the Bronx.* New York, 1912.

Journal of the House, 1.   *Journal of the House of Representatives of the United States, Being the First Session of the First Congress: Begun and Held at the City of New York, March 4, 1789.* Washington, D.C., 1826.

Journal of the House of Delegates, 1789.   *Journal of the House of Delegates of the Commonwealth of Virginia; Begun and Holden in the City of Richmond . . . on Monday, the Nineteenth Day of October, in the Year of Our Lord One Thousand Seven Hundred and Eighty-nine.* Richmond, 1828.

Journal of the House of Delegates, 1790.   *Journal of the House of Delegates of the Commonwealth of Virginia; Begun and Held at the Capitol in the City of Richmond . . . on Monday, the Eighteenth Day of October in the Year of Our Lord One Thousand Seven Hundred and Ninety.* Richmond, 1828.

Journals of the Council of State of Virginia.   H. R. McIlwaine, Wilmer L. Hall, and Benjamin Hillman, eds. *Journals of the Council of the State of Virginia.* 5 vols. Richmond, 1931–82.

JPP.   Dorothy Twohig, ed. *Journal of the Proceedings of the President, 1793–1797.* Charlottesville, Va., 1981.

Kappler, *Indian Treaties.*   Charles Joseph Kappler, ed. *Indian Affairs: Laws and Treaties.* 7 vols. Washington, D.C., 1903–41.

Kinnaird, *Spain in the Mississippi Valley.*   Lawrence Kinnaird, ed. *Spain in the Mississippi Valley, 1765–1794.* 3 vols. Annual Report of the American Historical Association for the Year 1945. Washington, D.C., 1946.

Ledger B.   Manuscript Ledger in George Washington Papers, Library of Congress.

Letters to John Langdon.   *Letters by Washington, Adams, Jefferson, and Others, Written during and after the Revolution, to John Langdon.* Philadelphia, 1880.

Mason, *John Norton & Sons.*   Frances Norton Mason, ed. *John Norton & Sons, Merchants of London and Virginia, Being the Papers from Their Counting House for the Years 1750 to 1795.* New York, 1968.

Mathews, *Andrew Ellicott.*   Catharine Van Cortlandt Mathews. *Andrew Ellicott, His Life and Letters.* New York, 1908.

Miller, *Treaties.*   Hunter Miller, ed. *Treaties and Other International Acts of the United States of America.* Vol. 2. Washington, D.C., 1931.

Minutes of the Common Council of the City of New York.   *Minutes of the Common Council of the City of New York, 1784–1831.* 19 vols. New York, 1917.

Morris, *Diary of the French Revolution.*   Beatrix Cary Davenport, ed. *A Diary of the French Revolution by Gouverneur Morris.* 2 vols. Boston, 1939.

Mulkearn, *George Mercer Papers.*   Lois Mulkearn, ed. *George Mercer Papers: Relating to the Ohio Company of Virginia.* Pittsburgh, 1954.

Murchie, *Saint Croix.*   Guy Murchie. *Saint Croix.* New York, 1947.

Nasatir, *Before Lewis and Clark.* A. P. Nasatir, ed. *Before Lewis and Clark: Documents Illustrating the History of the Missouri, 1785–1804.* 2 vols. St. Louis, 1952.

Naugle, *Virginia Tax Payers, 1782–87.* Augusta B. Fothergill and John Mark Naugle. *Virginia Tax Payers, 1782, Other Than Those Published by the United States Census Bureau.* Baltimore, 1974.

N.C. State Records. Walter Clark, ed. *The State Records of North Carolina.* 26 vols. Raleigh and various places, 1886–1907.

New Jersey Archives. William A. Whitehead et al., eds. *Archives of the State of New Jersey.* 1st ser., 42 vols. Newark and various places, 1880–1949.

New-York Historical Society Collections. *Collections of the New-York Historical Society for the Year 1905.* Vol. 38. New York, 1906.

Odell, *Annals of the New York Stage.* George C. D. Odell. *Annals of the New York Stage.* New York, 1927.

Parsons, "The Mysterious Mr. Digges." Lynn Hudson Parsons. "The Mysterious Mr. Digges." *William and Mary Quarterly*, 3d ser., 22 (1965), 486–92.

Pennsylvania Archives. Samuel Hazard et al., eds. *Pennsylvania Archives.* 9 ser., 138 vols. Philadelphia and Harrisburg, 1852–1949.

Petitions, Memorials, and Other Documents Submitted for the Consideration of Congress. *Petitions, Memorials, and Other Documents Submitted for the Consideration of Congress, March 4, 1789, to December 14, 1795.* A Staff Study Prepared for the Use of the Committee on Energy and Commerce, U.S. House of Representatives. Washington, D.C., April 1986.

Polishook, *Rhode Island and the Union.* Irwin H. Polishook. *Rhode Island and the Union, 1774–1795.* Evanston, Ill., 1969.

Reardon, *Edmund Randolph.* John J. Reardon. *Edmund Randolph: A Biography.* New York, 1974.

Records Relating to the Early History of Boston: Boston Marriages. *Records Relating to the Early History of Boston: Boston Marriages, 1752–1809.* Boston, 1903.

Robertson, *Debates and Other Proceedings of the Convention of Virginia.* David Robertson. *Debates and Other Proceedings of the Convention of Virginia, Convened at Richmond, on Monday the Second Day of June 1788 . . . .* Richmond, 1805.

Rosenbloom, *Biographical Dictionary of Early American Jews.* Joseph R. Rosenbloom. *A Biographical Dictionary of Early American Jews: Colonial Times through 1800.* Lexington, Ky., 1960.

Rutland, *Madison Papers.* William T. Hutchinson, Robert A. Rutland, J. C. A. Stagg, et al., eds. *The Papers of James Madison.* 19 vols. to date. Chicago and Charlottesville, Va., 1962—.

Scharf, *History of Delaware.* J. Thomas Scharf. *History of Delaware, 1609–1888.* 2 vols. Philadelphia, 1888.

Seilhamer, *American Theatre.* George O. Seilhamer. *History of the American Theatre: During the Revolution and After.* 3 vols. Philadelphia, 1888–91.

Seitz, "Thomas Paine, Bridge Builder." Don C. Seitz, "Thomas Paine, Bridge Builder," *Virginia Quarterly Review,* 3 (1927), 571–84.

Shepherd, *Statutes at Large.* Samuel Shepherd. *The Statutes at Large of Virginia, from October Session 1792, to December Session 1806, Inclusive.* 3 vols. (new series). Richmond, 1835–36.

Smith, *New York City in 1789.* Thomas E. V. Smith. *The City of New York in the Year of Washington's Inauguration 1789.* 1889. Reprint. Riverside, Conn., 1972.

Smith, *St. Clair Papers.* William Henry Smith, ed. *The St. Clair Papers.* 2 vols. Cincinnati, 1882.

Sparks, *Writings.* Jared Sparks, ed. *The Writings of George Washington: Being His Correspondence, Addresses, Messages, and Other Papers, Official and Private, Selected and Published from the Original Manuscripts.* 12 vols. Boston, 1833–37.

Sprague, *Annals of the American Pulpit.* William B. Sprague. *Annals of the American Pulpit.* Vol. 2. New York, 1969.

Stat. Richard Peters, ed. *The Public Statutes at Large of the United States of America.* Vol. 1. Boston, 1845.

6 *Stat.* Richard Peters, ed. *The Public Statutes at Large of the United States of America.* Vol. 6. Boston, 1848.

Syrett, *Hamilton Papers.* Harold C. Syrett et al., eds. *The Papers of Alexander Hamilton.* 27 vols. New York, 1961–87.

Thomas, *History of Printing in America.* Isaiah Thomas. *The History of Printing in America.* Ed. Marcus A. McCorison. New York, 1970.

Thornbrough, *Outpost on the Wabash.* Gayle Thornbrough. *Outpost on the Wabash, 1787–1791.* Indiana Historical Society Publications, vol. 19. Indianapolis, 1957.

Tousey, *Military History of Carlisle and Carlisle Barracks.* Thomas G. Tousey. *Military History of Carlisle and Carlisle Barracks.* Richmond, Va., 1939.

Trumbull, *Autobiography.* John Trumbull. *The Autobiography of Colonel John Trumbull.* Ed. Theodore Sizer. 1953. Reprint. New York, 1970.

Tyler, *Letters and Times of the Tylers.* Lyon G. Tyler. *Letters and Times of the Tylers.* 2 vols. Richmond, 1884–85.

Wagstaff, *Steele Papers.* H. M. Wagstaff, ed. *The Papers of John Steele.* 2 vols. Raleigh, N.C., 1924.

Wallace, "Sketch of John Inskeep."　　Henry Edward Wallace, Jr. "Sketch of John Inskeep, Mayor, and President of the Insurance Company of North America, Philadelphia." *Pennsylvania Magazine of History and Biography*, 28 (1904), 129–35.

Warren, "History of the Federal Judiciary Act of 1789."　　Charles Warren. "New Light on the History of the Federal Judiciary Act of 1789." *Harvard Law Review*, 37 (1923–24), 49–132.

Watlington, *Partisan Spirit.*　　Patricia Watlington. *The Partisan Spirit: Kentucky Politics, 1779–1792.* New York, 1972.

Williams, *Lost State of Franklin.*　　Samuel Cole Williams. *History of the Lost State of Franklin.* New York, 1933.

Williamson, *History of Belfast.*　　Joseph Williamson. *The History of Belfast, Maine.* 2 vols. 1877. Reprint. Somerset, N.H., 1982.

The Papers of George Washington
Presidential Series
Volume 4
September 1789–January 1790

To James Craik

Dear Sir,   New-York September 8th 1789.

The letter with which you favored me on the 24th ultimo came duly to hand, and for the friendly sentiments contained in it, you have my sincere and hearty thanks.

My disorder was of long and painful continuance, and though now freed from the latter, the wound given by the incision is not yet closed [1]—Persuaded as I am that the case has been treated with skill, and with as much tenderness as the nature of the complaint would admit, yet I confess that I often wished for your inspection of it—During the paroxysm, the distance rendered this impracticable, and after the paroxysm had passed I had no conception of being confined to a lying posture on one side six weeks—and that I should feel the remains of it for more than twelve—The part affected is now reduced to the size of a barley corn, and by saturday next (which will complete the thirteenth week) I expect it will be skinned over—Upon the whole, I have more reason to be thankful that it is no worse than to repine at the confinement. The want of regular exercise, with the cares of office will I have no doubt hasten my departure for that country from whence no Traveller returns; but a faithful discharge of whatever trust I accept, as it ever has, so it always will be the primary consideration in every transaction of my life be the consequences what they may. Mrs Washington has, I think, better health than usual, and the children are well and in the way of improvement.

I always expected that the Gentleman whose name you have mentioned [2] would mark his opposition to the new government with consistency—Pride on the one hand, and want of manly candor on the other, will not I am certain let him acknowledge an error in his opinions respecting it though conviction should flash on his mind as strongly as a ray of light—If certain characters which you have also mentioned should tread *blindfold* in his steps it would be matter of no wonder to me—They are in the habit of thinking that every thing he says and does is right, and (if capable) they will not judge for themselves.

It gives me pleasure to hear, and I wish you to express it to them that my Nephews George and Lawrence Washington are attentive to their studies, and obedient to your orders and admonition. That kind of learning which is to fit them for the most useful and necessary purposes of life—among which writing well, arithmetic, and the less abstruse branches of the mathematics are certainly to be comprehended, ought to be particularly attended to, and it is my earnest wish that it should be so.[3]

The Gazettes are so full of the occurrences of public, and indeed of private nature, which happens in this place that it is unnecessary (if I had more leisure than falls to my lot) to attempt a repetition: I shall therefore refer you to them or to the Alexandria paper, through which they may, if pains is taken, be retailed—Mrs Washington and the rest of the family join me in every good and friendly wish for Mrs Craik, yourself, and the rest of your family—and with sentiments of sincere regard and friendship, I am dear Sir, Your affectionate

G. Washington

LB, DLC:GW.

1. For GW's illness in the summer of 1789, see James McHenry to GW, 28 June 1789, n.1.

2. GW is referring to George Mason. Craik had commented on Mason's dissatisfaction with the Constitution in his letter to GW of 24 August.

3. For GW's concerns regarding the education and behavior of his nephews, see Francis Willis, Jr., to GW, 24 Sept. 1788, source note, Samuel Hanson to GW, 2 Oct. 1788, and GW to George Steptoe Washington, 23 Mar. 1789. In his letter to GW of 24 Aug., Craik had commented favorably on the boys' progress.

Letter not found: from the inhabitants of Kentucky, 8 Sept. 1789. On 18 Nov. 1789 Tobias Lear submitted to Henry Knox a letter from "a number of respectable Inhabitants of Kentuckey recommendg the Mountain leader [Piomingo] a Chickasaw Chief."[1]

1. Although Lear indicates that the letter was received by GW, it is possible that it was not addressed to him. It is undoubtedly the letter described in GW's Memoranda on Indian Affairs, 1789, as a letter from "George Muter, Saml McDowell, Caleb Wallace, Harry Innes, George Nicholas, Christophr Greenup, Benja. Sebastian, James Brown, William McDowell, Thos Barber & Wm Kennedy." These residents of Kentucky "Recommend Piemingo or Mountain Leader as a Chief of the Chicasaws applying for supplies of Ammunition for the use of his Nation; who from its friendly conduct towards the People of the United States, are at enmity with, and expect an attack from the Creeks. The Chicasaws they say are at present unconnected with both Spaniards & English, & have no chance ⟨*illegible*⟩ supplies from either, without becoming dependent on the Spaniards, or joining the Creeks, and thence for-

ward more than probably enemies to the U. States. They add, that they are daily suffering from the Incursions of the Creeks; and have every reason to expect that they will be continued—that they have further reason to believe, if the Chicasaws can obtain a supply of Amn, they will cut out work for the former at home—and submit whether this will not be the most effectual, as well as the cheapest mode of retaliating—They are decidedly of opinion that some change should take place in the manner of conducting Indian Affairs in the Western Country." On 15 Dec. Knox reported to the Kentucky citizens who signed the letter: "The President of the united States has directed me to acknowledge the receipt of your letter dated at Danville on the 8th of September last.

"You will probably have learned that Piamingo, the chickasaw chief did not proceed to new York, but that he was furnished with certain articles at Richmond by the Legislature of Virginia.

"I am further directed to inform you that such measures as are within the power, and consistantly with the general duties of the President of the united States will be adopted for the protection of the frontiers, and for the purposes of conciliating the chickasaws and choctaws, and if necesssary to avail the public of their assistance" (InHi).

To James Madison

[New York, c.8 Sept. 1789][1]
Confidential

The points which at present occur to me, and on which I wish your aid, are brought to view in the enclosed statement—I give you the trouble of receiving this evening that you may (if other matter do not interfere) suffer them to run through your Mind between this and tomorrow afternoon when I shall expect to see you at the appointed time.

Besides the enclosed [2]

Would it do *now* that Mr Barton has declined the Judges Seat (western Territory) to nominate Col. Carrington for that Office?[3] If not, can you think of any other that would suit him, of new creation—by this I mean, which has not an actual occupant or one who from similarity of Office may have better pretensions to it.

Can you bring to mind any fit character for the vacancy just mentioned (west of New Jersey)—as Virga has given & may furnish characters, for important Offices probably it would be better to exclude her also on this occasion.

What sort of a character in point of respectability and fitness for this office has Majr Turner late of So. Carolina now of Philadelphia.[4]

Have you any knowledge of the character of Mr Laurence?— a practising Attorney and Son in law to General St Clair.[5]

What can I do with A—L——he has applied to be nominated one of the Associate Judges—but I cannot bring my mind to adopt the request—The opinion entertained of him by those with whom I am most conversant is unpropitious and yet few men have received more marks of public favor & confidence than he has. These contradictions are embarrassing.[6]

Should the sense of the Senate be taken on the propriety of sending public characters abroad—say, to England, Holland & Portugal—and of a day for thanksgiving.

Would it be well to advise with them before the adjournment, on the expediency and justice of demanding a surrender of our Posts?

Being clearly of opinion that there ought to be a difference in the Wages of the Members of the two branches of the Legislature would it be politic or prudent in the President when the Bill comes to him to send it back with his reasons for non-concurring.[7] Yrs sincerely

                                        G. Washington

ALS, PPRF.

1. This letter has been dated on the basis of GW's appointment of George Turner as a judge of the Northwest Territory on 11 Sept. 1789.

2. The enclosure has not been identified.

3. William Barton was appointed a judge of the Northwest Territory by GW on 18 Aug. 1789. For Barton's letter of application for a post, see his letter to GW, 3 Sept. 1789. Barton's uncle, David Rittenhouse, had also approached Madison in relation to an appointment for him. Barton declined the appointment as judge but hoped to secure a treasury post. See Rutland, *Madison Papers*, 12:286, 357–58. GW had already mentioned Edward Carrington to Madison for a federal appointment in a letter of 9 Aug. 1789. For Edward Carrington's solicitation for an appointment, see his letter to GW, 11 May 1789. His inclinations, however, did not lie in the direction of the Northwest Territory. As he wrote Madison, 9 Sept., the "Office of District Marshall for Virginia is thought to be important from its extent, & not altogether unhonorary from the powers & Trusts it involves; it is also thought it will be productive of compensation not contemptible. Viewing the subject thus some of my Freinds have expressed a desire that I should signify my readiness to accept the appointment. . . . Any disposition in me to accept, will depend altogether

on your opinion. Should you deem the appointment eligible & not derogatory in its Nature upon a view of all circumstances, I shall be willing to accept it. General Knox has written me on this subject—in my answer I have left my choice dependent on the circumstances here mentioned to you. . . . I have not written, nor shall I write to any other person about it" (Rutland, *Madison Papers*, 12:391–92). GW appointed Carrington to the post on 24 Sept. (*DHFC*, 2:44).

4. For George Turner's application for office, see his letter to GW, 18 Aug. 1789. On 11 Sept. GW appointed Turner one of the judges for the Northwest Territory (*DHFC*, 2:38). A letter to Turner from Tobias Lear, 14 Sept. 1789, informed him of his appointment. "If you accept this appointment, you will give due notice thereof to the President of the United States who will cause your commission to be forwarded to you at Philadelphia, and whose wish it is that you should proceed to the western Territory and enter upon the duties of your Office without delay" (DNA: RG 59, Miscellaneous Letters).

5. Later in life Madison inserted an asterisk at this point and wrote "Mc-Dougal meant," a reference to the fact that Alexander McDougall's daughter Elizabeth married New Yorker John Laurance. However, GW was undoubtedly referring to John Lawrence (1751–c.1799) who had served as a captain during the Revolutionary War and was married to Gov. Arthur St. Clair's daughter Elizabeth.

6. Madison later inserted an asterisk at this point and wrote at the bottom of the page "Arthur Lee." For Lee's application for a position as a justice of the Supreme Court, see his letter to GW, 21 May 1789.

7. GW is referring to the impending legislation on the salaries of members of the Senate and House of Representatives. It had been suggested that salaries for senators should exceed those for members of the House, and Madison had already spoken in the House of Representatives in support of a discrimination, contending that "it had been evidently contemplated by the constitution to distinguish in favor of the senate" in order to induce outstanding men to serve (Rutland, *Madison Papers*, 12:293). For the debates on the bill, see *Annals of Congress*, 1:676–84, 701–5, 706–10, 712–14. "An Act for allowing Compensation to the Members of the Senate and House of Representatives of the United States, and to the Officers of both Houses," approved by GW, 22 Sept. 1789, provided that the members of both houses should receive $6 per day while in attendance and an allowance of $6 for every 20 miles from their place of residence to the capital. After 1795, however, the compensation for senators would be raised to $7 per diem (1 *Stat.* 70–71).

To Edmund Randolph

Dear Sir,   New York September 8th 1789
Your favor of the 2d Ultimo came duly to hand. A tedious and painful disorder which deprived me for many Weeks of the use of my pen,[1] and which consequently required the greater exer-

tion of it when I was able to set up, is the best apology I can make for not having acknowledged the receipt of the above letter sooner.

The list of associates who purchased 100 Tickets in the lottery of the deceased Colo. Byrd is all the memorandom I have of that transaction[2]—To the best of my recollection Mr Thomson Mason (deceased) was one of the associates and was either authorised, or assumed (I do not know which) the management of the business—He did it so effectually it seems as to monopolize the whole interest. Some of the prizes it has been said, are valuable—but whether there is any Clue by which Mr Masons conduct in this business can be developed I am unable to say. Your Uncle (The Honorable Peyton Randolph) was one of the ten associates—But if neither Mr Fitzhugh nor any of the others who are living can give such information as would avail in an enquiry we must, I presume, set down with the loss of the money and prizes.

With respect to Mr Powells application[3] I can only repeat to you what I say to all others upon similar occasions—that is—I leave myself entirely free until the office is established and the moment shall arrive when the nomination is to be made—then, under my best information and a full view of all circumstances I shall endeavor to the best of my judgment to combine justice to individuals with the public good making the latter my primary object. My best wishes attend Mrs Randolph and your family and with sentiments of sincere regard and friendship I am— Dear Sir, Your Most Obedient and Affectionate Servant

George Washington

LB, DLC:GW; ALS, sold by John Heise, item 31, 11 Dec. 1925. A copy of this letter is listed in *Calendar of the Miscellaneous Letters Received by the Department of State* (Washington, D.C., 1897), 316. The copy, however, is not presently (1992) in its chronological position in DNA: RG 59, Miscellaneous Letters of the Department of State, 1789–1906.

    1. See James McHenry to GW, 28 June 1789, n.1.
    2. For William Byrd's lottery, see Randolph to GW, 2 Aug. 1789, n.1.
    3. For Benjamin Powell, see Randolph to GW, 2 Aug. 1789, n.2. In his letter to GW of 2 Aug., Randolph had recommended Powell for public office.

From Richard Bland Lee

Sir, N. York September 9: 1789
At the request of Mr Roger West I take the Liberty of forwarding the inclosed letter:[1] at the same time I beg leave to present to you the most respectful regards of Mr Francis Corbin, who requests me to inform you that Mr John Segar, would be happy to be appointed Surveyor in the place of Mr Stage Davis, who has or will resign, and to assure you that he is well fitted to execute the duties of the office.[2] I have the honor to be with the most profound respect and veneration your most ob: hum: Servant

Richard Bland Lee

ALS, DLC:GW.
1. The enclosure was probably Roger West's letter to GW, 30 Aug. 1789.
2. Staige Davis (d. 1815) had replaced his brother George Davis as collector at Urbanna in late 1788 (*Journals of the Council of State of Virginia*, 5:10). In his 3 Aug. appointments, GW named him surveyor of the port, but he declined the appointment. John Segar (b. 1730) of Middlesex County, Va., did not receive the appointment; Peter Kemp rather than Segar replaced Staige Davis (*DHFC*, 2:16, 21, 38).

Ratification of the Consular Convention with France

[New York, 9 September 1789]
George Washington President of the United States of America.
To all to whom these Presents shall come—Greeting.
Whereas a Convention for defining and establishing the Functions and Privileges of the respective Consuls and Vice Consuls of his most christian Majesty, and of the said United States, duly and respectively authorised for that purpose, which convention is in the form and words following.[1]
Now be it known that I having seen and considered the said Convention, do, by and with the advice and consent of the Senate accept, ratify and confirm the same, and every article and clause thereof. In testimony whereof I have caused the seal of the United States to be affixed to these Presents, and signed

the same with my hand. Given at the City of New York the 9th day of September in the year of our Lord 1789.

G: Washington

LB, DLC:GW.

In the letter book this document is headed "Form of Ratification." For information on this treaty, see *DHFC*, 2:251–351, Moustier to GW, 1 May 1789, and GW to the United States Senate, 11 June 1789. On 29 July the Senate consented to the treaty and advised "the President of the United States to Ratify the same" (*DHFC*, 2:12).

1. The text of the treaty was to be inserted at this point. For the text, see Miller, *Treaties*, 2:228–41.

From Abraham Bancker

Castleton[,] Staten Island [N.Y.]

Sir.   10th Septemr 1789.

I, for some time past, have had it in Contemplation, immediately on the Organization and Establishment of our new Government, to sollicit for some Office of Emolument, for which I might be deemed capacitated and deserving of; but when I considered, how many Competitors I might have to contend with, whose Abilities might be accounted superior to mine, and whose Claims to Preferment, might be better founded; there appeared so much Presumption, in the Attempt, that I felt a reluctance to prosecute my Intention.

Upon farther deliberation, however, I have flattered myself, that an Application of this Nature might, probably, receive some degree of Attention from Your Excellency; by reason, that some part of the Services, I rendered my Country, in the course of the late Contest, have come to Your Excellency's Knowledge and Observation—In order to elucidate the above Suggestion, permit me to advert to Facts. In the Campaign of the Year 1780, a Correspondence was established with certain communicative Characters, within the British Lines, (friendly to the American Cause,) for procuring and transmitting to Head Quarters, from time to time, such political Intelligence, as tended to facil[it]ate the Operations of the Army.

In this Business, I took an early and active part, as the Certificates herewith presented, as well as a Variety of Vouchers, that can be obtained, will bear ample Testimony to the Authenticity of this Assertion.

Your Excellency I trust will recollect that you received Sundry Papers of that Nature, under the Signature of *Amicus Reipublicae*, and many other anonimous Productions penned by the same Hand;[1] and likewise Plans of Fortifications, and other Communications of an interesting and important Nature, forwarded through the same Channel.

I beg leave farther to represent, that independent of this, I corresponded with several Gentlemen, in public Service, at different Periods, in the War; who, can, I trust, bear Witness to the honest Zeal, by which I was actuated in the Undertaking as well as to the imminent Hazards I ran of being detected in the prosecution of it.

For those Services I have not received any Compensation, nor was it my Intention to have Sought it—My Breast was fired with that Ardor for Liberty, and detestation of Slavery which, at that time, pervaded the honest Citizens of America. My Motives for engaging in so arduous and hazardous an Attempt, were pure and disinterested; as they flowed from a cordial Regard for the true Interests and Welfare of my Country. I was not permitted from Situation & Circumstances, to draw the Sword in her defence—and the voice of Reason, and the impulse of Duty pointed out to me this, as the only method, within my Power, of being at all serviceable.

This Application proceeds merely from a reverse of Fortune. My Situation previous to the War, and at the present day affords a Striking Contrast—I was born to good Prospects, and was, at the Commencement of the War, going through a Course of Study; being intended for one of the learned Professions—But that, unhappily intervening, crushed all my hopes, as it not only diverted me from my Pursuits; but has divested my Parents of large and valuable Possessions, and reduced them to Distress.

Thus situated, I conceive it my Duty to use the means, which are afforded me, of advancing their Interests, as well as my own, from a full Persuasion, that Your Excellency will not reject any Applications, that are made by Servants of the Public, without having well weighed their Import and Merits.

I must acknowledge, that from my Ignorance of the Offices,

which remain vacant, I can have no particular Object in view. I wish to leave my Cause with your Excellency, and to submit entirely to Your Excellency's Judgment; referring Your Excellency to Governor Clinton, for any Information, you may wish to have respecting my Family, Situation and Abilities.

If Your Excellency, therefore, has any Office to bestow, sufficiently productive to enable me to live in Character, and to contribute towards the Support of my dearest Connections in Life, and shall compliment me with it, I will endeavor to discharge my Duty therein with Fidelity and Attention, and shall ever esteem myself under peculiar obligations to Your Excellency's Beneficence.[2] I have the honor to be, with Sentiments of the highest Respect & Esteem, Your Excelly's most obedt & very humble Servt

Abrm Bancker

ALS, DLC:GW.

Abraham Bancker (c.1760–c.1832) reportedly attended King's College before the Revolution. He was the county clerk (1781–84) and sheriff (1784–88) for Richmond County, which included Staten Island. In addition to service on the New York board of regents, he served in the New York assembly (1788–90) and attended the New York Ratifying Convention. Bancker did not receive a federal appointment. In 1804 he was clerk of the New York chancery court.

1. See, for example, Bancker's report, under his alias Amicus Reipublicae, 6 July 1780, claiming that Ethan Allen was collaborating with the British in New York (DLC:GW).

2. Bancker enclosed this letter in a second letter, dated 12 Sept., in which he stated that the "tedious Length" of his first letter demanded an apology: "The Nature of the Affair, it was out of my Power fully to relate in concise Terms—I crave Your Excellency's forgiveness for having So much trespassed on Your Patience, and even for taking up any part of your Time with my Concerns. Perhaps from the advanced State of the Session, and the Number of Appointments already made, there may be few Offices left to be conferred which are not either engaged, or have suitable Characters waiting for them. If So, I must rest Satisfied with my Attempt, and if at a future Day, I may be considered deserving of some small Mark of Public Favor, as a Gratuity for past Services, I Shall be well pleased, if Your Excellency will be pleased to hold me in Remembrance" (DLC:GW). Bancker enclosed certificates in his favor from the following individuals: from Elias Dayton, 3 Nov. 1783; from Asher F. Randolph, 29 Nov. 1783; and from John Vanderhooven, 14 Nov. 1788. Two certificates from Joshua Mercereau, 22 Nov. and 1 Dec. 1788, were also enclosed. These documents are all in DLC:GW and appear in CD-ROM:GW.

From George Cornell

[10 September 1789]

The Memorial of George Cornell of Portsmouth On Rhode Island—Your Excellency Humble Memorialist is the first of all this State that yet appears To Congratulate your Excellency Too the Appointment of Their President—and he Thinks Himself forever Happy Now under Your Excellencys Reign and Good Government, and To whome with a faithfull heart he wishes Long life and all Happiness—and your Memorialist Looks up To your Excellency as a father To his people—and he as One of the Children, who have Been Ever faithfull[1] Begs Leave To inform Your Excellency that Our State will Soon Be Joined To the union—and as there Must Be Custom House Officers appointed within the State—he would Most Humbly Beg your Excellency To Confer the Collectorship of the Customhouse of Newport upon him, Or any Other appointment as your Excellency in his Clemency will Be Graciously Pleased To appoint Beleave him On the word of a man that your Excellency will find none More faithfull Through all his america then your Excellencys Humble Memorialist[.] He also Begs Leave to acquaint your Excellency, that he went into the Canadia war in 58 as an Ensign, and then at the Age of 16 years and Soon obtain a Company in the Rhode Island Corps, and Continued in the field untill 65 and his Conduct was Such as To Merit the Esteem of sir Jeff. Amhast who Treated him with that Respect Due to a faithfull Soldier—But the war Being Over he Left the Army and Betook him Self To the Seas—a poor Exchange—as he has been Amazing unfortunate in being Taken in the Late war—and as there is places of Appointments wholy in your Excellencys Own Disposial he Begs your Excellencys Clemency—He flatters himself that as Some person Must be appointed To the Customhouse that if your Excellency will be Graciously pleased To Confer that Honor on him that his Steady Conduct will be always Such as To Merit Esteem—He Begs Leave To Take the Liberty thus Early To Recommend himself to your Excellency Protection—Hopeing your Excellency in his Great Goodness, will Be pleased to Signify his Pleasur—for which Your Excellencys Most Humble Memorialist will be in Ever Duty Bound[2]

Geo. Cornell Son of Clarke

ADS, DLC:GW.

During the French and Indian War George Cornell (1736–1799), the son of Clarke Cornell (b. 1714), served as an ensign in 1758, a second lieutenant in 1760, and a first lieutenant in 1761. By 1763 he had apparently risen to the rank of captain with Rhode Island forces.

1. At this point in the MS Cornell wrote "faith," followed by "faithful." He neglected to delete the first word.

2. On 5 Nov. 1789 Cornell again wrote to GW asking for an appointment. In his earlier memorial he "did then Open his Simple and most faithfull Heart To Your Excellency as to his father, and as there is appointments To be Made he could wish your Excellency could find the freedom To help the widows Son, who is forever faithfull. . . . Your Excellencys Memorialest Could Make a Good Clerk and Steward To One of Your Excellencys Hospittles Or Clerk To Your Dockyards. . . . May it Please Your Excellency if Our State Does Not Come into the Union Dont Cast of Your faithfull Memorialest and Subject for he will Move Out of the State to fall river in the Massachusetts State Immediatly and God bless Your Excellency Due Give him Some Small appointment To Enable him To Maintain his famerly he will Move in 10 Day from this Date and there wate your Excellencys Benevolence and Goodness." Receiving no appointment, Cornell wrote GW on 1 June 1790 asking for a post in the customs or as keeper of a lighthouse in Rhode Island. In a letter dated July 1790 Cornell reminded the president that he was "as Good an Enginear and Draughtsman as is in your Amarica" and suggested himself for the command of the fortress at West Point. Both letters are in DLC:GW.

From the Rhode Island Legislature

[10–19 September 1789]
State of Rhode Island and Providence Plantations
In General Assembly September Session A.D. 1789.

The critical situation in which the people of this State are placed, engage us to make these assurances on their behalf, of their attachment and friendship to their sister States, and of their disposition to cultivate mutual harmony and friendly intercourse. They know themselves to be a handful, comparatively viewed; and although they now stand, as it were, alone, they have not separated themselves, or departed from the principles of that Confederation, which was formed by the sister States in their struggle for freedom and in the hour of danger; they seek by this memorial to call to your remembrance the hazards which we have run, the hardships we have endured, the treasure we have spent, & the blood we have lost together, in one common cause and especially the object we had in view—

the preservation of our Liberty. wherein, ability considered, they may truly say they were equal in exertions with the foremost, the effects whereof in great embarrassments and other distresses consequent thereon, we have since experienced with severity, which common sufferings, and common danger, we hope, and trust, yet form a bond of union and friendship not easily to be broken.

Our not having acceded to, or adopted the new system of Government, formed and adopted by most of our sister States, we doubt not hav[e] given uneasiness to them. That we have not seen our way clear to do it, consistent with our idea of the principles upon which we all embarked together, has also given pain to us; we have not doubted but we might thereby avoid present difficulties but we have apprehended future mischief. The people of this State from its first settlement have been accustomed and strongly attached to a Democratical form of Government. They have viewed in the Constitution an approach, though perhaps, but small towards that form of Government from which we have lately dissolved our connection, at so much hazard and expence of Life and treasure they have seen with pleasure the administration thereof from the most important trust downwards committed to men who have highly merited and in whom the people of the United States place unbounded confidence: yet even in this circumstance, in itself so fortunate, they have apprehended danger by way of Presedent—can it be thought strange then that with these impressions they should wait to see the proposed system organised and in operation? to see what further checks and securities would be agreed to and established, by way of amendments, before they could adopt it as a Constitution of Government for themselves and their posterity? These amendments we believe have already afforded some relief and satisfaction to the minds of the people of this State And we earnestly look for the time when they may with clearness and safety be again united with their sister States, under a Constitution and form of Government, so well poised as neither to need alteration, or be liable thereto, by a majority only of nine States out of thirteen, a circumstance which may possibly take place against the sense of a majority of the people of the United States. We are sensible of the extremes to which Democratical Government is sometimes liable, something of

which we have lately experienced, but we esteem them temporary and partial evils compared with the loss of Liberty and the
rights of a free people, neither do we apprehend they will be
marked with severity by our sister States, when it is considered
that during the late trouble, the whole United States notwithstanding their joint wisdom and efforts fell into the like misfortune. That, from our extraordinary exertions this State was left
in a situation nearly as embarrassing as that during the war; that
in the measures which were adopted Government unfortunately had not that aid and support from the monied interest
which our sister States of New York and the Carolina's experienced under similar circumstances, and especially when it is
considered that upon som⟨e⟩ abatement of that fermentation in
the minds of the people whic⟨h⟩ is so common in the collision of
sentiments and of parties, a disposition appears to provide a
remedy for the difficulties we have laboured under on that
account. We are induced to hope that we shall not be altogether
considered as foreigners, having no particular affinity, or connection with the United States; But that Trade and Commerce
upon which the prosperity of this State much depends will be
preserved as free and open between this and the United States,
as our different situations at present, can possibly admit, earnestly desiring and proposing to adopt such commercial regulations, on our part, as shall not tend to defeat the collection of the
Revenue of the United States, but rather to act in conformity to,
or co-operate therewith, and desiring also to give the strongest
assurances that we shall, during our present situation, use our
utmost endeavours to be in preparation, from time to time, to
answer our proportion of such part of the interest or principal
of the foreign & domestic debt as the United States shall judge
expedient to pay, and discharge.

We feel ourselves attached by the strongest ties of friendship,
kindred, and of interest, with our sister States & we cannot
without the greatest reluctance look to any other quarter for
those advantages of commercial intercourse which we conceive
to be more natural and reciprocal between them and us. I am, at
the request, and in behalf of the General assembly, your most
obedient humble Servant

John Collins Govr

Copy, DNA: RG 46, First Congress, Records of Legislative Proceedings, President's Messages; copy, R-Ar; LB, DNA: RG 59, George Washington's Correspondence with His Secretaries of State, 1789–96; LB, DLC:GW. The heading of the document reads: "To the President, the Senate, and the House of Representatives of the eleven United States of America in Congress Assembled." The address at the closing is to "his Excellency The President of the United States." The letter was sent to GW who enclosed it in his letter of 26 Sept. 1789 to the Senate. See also *DHFC*, 1:193–94.

From Pierre L'Enfant

Sir   New york Septmr the 11th 1789.
The late determination of Congress to lay the Fundation of a City which is to become the Capital of this vast Empire, offer so great an occasion of acquiring reputation, to whoever may be appointed to conduct the execution of the business, that your Excellency will not be surprised that my Embition and the desire I have of becoming a usefull Citizen should lead me to wish a share in the Undertaking.[1]

No Nation perhaps had Ever before the opportunity offerd them of deliberately deciding on the spot where thier Capital city Should be fixud, or of Combining Every necessary consideration in the choice of Situation—and altho' the means now within the power of the Country are not such as to pursue the design to any great extant it will be obvious that the plan Should be drawn on such a Scale as to leave room for that aggrandisement & embellishment which the increase of the wealth of the Nation will permit it to pursue at any period however remote— viewing the Matter in this light I am fully sensible of the extant of the undertaking and under the hope of a continuation of the indulgence you have hitherto honored me with I now presume to sollicit the favor of being Employed in this Business.

and now that I am addressing your Excellency I will avail myself of the occasion to call to your attention an object of at least equal importance to the dignity of the Nation, and in which her quiet and prosperity is intimately connected I mean the protection of the Sea Coast of the united States—This has hitherto been left to the Individual States and has been so totally neglected as to endanger the peace of the Union for it is certain that any insult offered on that side (and there is nothing to prevent it) however immaterial it might be in its total Effect, would degrade the nation and do more injury to its political interests than a much greater depradation on her Inland frontiers from these considerations I Should argue the necessity of the different Bays and Sea ports being fortified at the expence of the Union, in order that one general and uniform System may prevail throughout, that being as necessary as an Uniformity in the discipline of the Troupes to whom they are to be Intrusted.

I flater Myself your Excellency will Excuse the freedom with which I impart to you my ideas on this subject indeed my Confidence in this Business arises in a great measure from a persuasion that the Subject has already engaged your attention. having had the honor to belong to the Corps of Engineer acting under your orders during the late war, and being the only officers of that Corps remaining on the Continant I must Confess I have long flattered myself with the hope of a reappointment a hope which was encouraged by several individuals of the former Congress—and now when the Establishment of a truly fœderal Gouvernment renders every post under it more desirable, I view the appointment of Engineer to the United States as the one which could possibly be most gratifying to my wishes and tho' the necessety of such an office to superintend & direct the fortifications necessary in the United States is sufficiently apparent the advantages to be derived from the appointment will appear more striking when it is considered that the sciences of Military and civil architeture are so connected as to render an Engineer Equally serviceable in time of peace as in war by the employment of his abilities in the internal improvemen⟨ts⟩ of the Country.

Not to intrude any longer on your patience and without entering on any particular relating to my private circumstances of which I believe you are sufficiently informed I shall conclud by assuring you that ever animated as I have been with a desir to merite your good opinion nothing will be wanting to compleat my happiness if the remembrance of my former services connected with a variety of peculiar circumstances during fourteen years residence in this Country can plead with your Excellency in support of the favour I sollicite. I have the honor to be with a profound respect Your Excellency Most humble and obeident servant

P. C. L'Enfant

ALS, DLC:GW.

Pierre Charles L'Enfant (1754–1825) was born in Paris. He apparently received some private instruction in art and architecture in France before he was solicited by Silas Deane for service in the Continental army. L'Enfant was appointed a first lieutenant of engineers by the Continental Congress in December 1776 and sailed for America in February 1777, spending the winter at GW's headquarters at Valley Forge. During the war he served as a captain of engineers with GW's army in the north and by 1779 had joined the southern army. L'Enfant was wounded at Savannah in October of that year and was taken prisoner at Charleston in 1780. He ended the war as a major. During the 1780s he designed the medal for the Society of the Cincinnati and Gen. Richard Montgomery's tomb in St. Paul's Chapel in New York and converted New York City's old City Hall into Federal Hall. Appointed by GW early in 1791 to survey the site for the new Federal City, L'Enfant arrived at Georgetown in March 1791 to embark on his brief and troubled tenure as designer of the new city.

1. L'Enfant is referring to the discussions in Congress concerning the establishment of a permanent seat of government. The controversy over the site for the new government in the fall of 1789 was a continuation of the negotiations that had started in the Confederation Congress in the summer of 1788. The resolutions of the Federal Convention submitting the Constitution to Congress, 17 Sept. 1787, specified that after nine states had ratified, electors should be appointed and senators and representatives elected and that the senators and representatives should convene at the time and place assigned. See the report to the Confederation Congress, signed by GW, 17 Sept. 1787. By the early part of July 1788, all of the states except New York, North Carolina, and Rhode Island had ratified the Constitution, and Congress moved to set up the new government. Setting up procedures for the first election moved smoothly, but the decision on the meeting place for Congress was postponed, partly because the delegates hoped the expectation of receiving the plum of the capital would push New York toward ratification. Delegates to the Ratifying Convention from strongly Federalist New York City eventually reached a compromise with Antifederalists, exchanging support for the location of the temporary capital in New York City for approval of a circular letter from the New York Ratifying Convention calling for a second federal convention to amend the Constitution. Between July and September a vigorous and sometimes acrimonious debate in Congress and in the newspapers over the seat for the new government took place, with New York and Philadelphia as the leading contenders. For an account of congressional maneuvering on this issue during these months, see Bowling, *Creation of Washington, D.C.*, 87–96. By August 1788 public pressure and the fear that further delay in arranging the temporary capital would jeopardize the new government led the supporters

of Philadelphia to surrender their ambitions for the moment, and on 13 Sept. 1788 the Confederation Congress agreed that New York would be the meeting place for the new Congress. The question whether New York would remain the temporary capital until a permanent capital could be chosen was left open.

During the summer of 1789, while Congress dealt with other matters, behind-the-scenes maneuvering among various congressional delegations with regard to the future location of the capital continued. When the question was again raised in Congress in late August support was voiced not only for New York but also for such sites as Philadelphia, the Potomac, the Susquehanna, the falls of the Delaware, and Germantown. On 27 Aug. the House of Representatives agreed "that a permanent residence ought to be fixed for the general government of the United States, at some convenient place, as near the center of wealth, population, and extent of territory, as may be consistent with convenience to the nagivation of the Atlantic ocean, and having due regard to the particular situation of the western country" (*DHFC*, 3:171–72, 181, 182). On 7 Sept. a second resolution was introduced proposing to locate the permanent seat of government "at some convenient place on the east bank of the river Susquehanna, in the state of Pennyslvania, and that until the necessary buildings be erected for the purpose, the seat of government ought to continue at the city of New-York." A subsequent motion to amend this resolution by striking out the words "east bank of the river Susquehanna, in the state of Pennsylvania," and substituting the words "north bank of the river Potowmac, in the state of Maryland" was defeated 29 to 21. Successive motions to amend the resolution to locate the seat of government at Wilmington, Del., at "Potowmac, Susquehannah, or Delaware," on the "banks of either side of the river Delaware, not more than eight miles above or below the lower falls of Delaware," and to insert the words "or Maryland" after Pennsylvania were all defeated. Finally the House "RESOLVED, That the President of the United States be authorised to appoint three commissioners to examine and report to him the most eligible situation on the banks of the Susquehannah, in the state of Pennsylvania, for the permanent seat of the government of the United States; that the said commissioners be authorised, under the direction of the President, to purchase such quantity of land as may be thought necessary, and to erect thereon, within four years, suitable buildings for the accommodation of the Congress, and of the officers of the United States; that the secretary of the treasury, together with the commissioners so to be appointed, be authorised to borrow a sum not exceeding one hundred thousand dollars, to be repaid within twenty years, with interest not exceeding the rate of five per cent. per annum, out of the duties on impost and tonnage, to be applied to the purchase of the land, and the erection of the buildings aforesaid; and that a bill ought to pass in the present session in conformity with the foregoing resolutions."

The House finally agreed to the resolution, with the proviso that Pennsylvania and Maryland remove all obstructions in the river between the seat of government and the mouth of the river, and ordered a bill to be brought in

(*DHFC*, 3:182–94). Although there was considerable pressure to have Philadelphia made the capital, the Senate on 25 Sept. amended the bill to authorize a district not exceeding ten miles square in the area of Germantown for the seat of government (ibid., 1:191). On 26 Sept. the bill was given a third reading, passed with amendments, and was sent to the House. The House considered the bill with the Senate's amendments on 26 Sept., and on 28 Sept. it agreed to the amended bill, added an amendment of its own, and sent the bill back to the Senate. At this point the Senate voted to hold the bill over to the next session (ibid., 203). Those members of Congress who hoped a postponement would give them time for extensive additional lobbying for their favored locations for the capital were to be disappointed. The debate on the seat for the new government was to be almost the first order of business when Congress reconvened in January 1790. For a description of the involved and occasionally Machiavellian tactics of the congressional delegations on the seat of government bill, see Bowling, *Creation of Washington, D.C.*, chapter 5. A colorful contemporary account of the maneuvering of individual members of Congress appears in Sen. William Maclay's diary (Bowling and Veit, *Diary of William Maclay*, 144–48, 150–67).

To the United States Senate

Gentlemen of the Senate,   New York September 11th 1789.
   I nominate for the Department of the Treasury of the United States—
   Alexander Hamilton (of New York) Secretary.
   Nicholas Eveleigh (of So. Carolina) Comptroller.
   Samuel Meridith (of Pensylvania) Treasurer.
   Oliver Wolcott Junr (of Connecticut) Auditor.
   Joseph Nourse (in office) Register.
For the Department of war—
   Henry Knox.
For Judge in the Western Territory, in place of William Barton who declines the appointment.
   George Turner.
For Surveyor in the District of Rappahannock, State of Virginia, in place of Staige Davis who declines the appointment—I nominate Peter Kemp.
For Surveyor of Town-Creek in the District of Patuxent, State of Maryland, in place of Robert Young who declines the appointment—I nominate Charles Chilton.
And, in case the nomination of Samuel Meridith should meet

the advice and consent of the Senate—I nominate as Surveyor
of the Port of Philadelphia—
William McPherson.[1]

                                                        Go: Washington

LS, DNA: RG 46, First Congress, Records of Executive Proceedings, Presi-
dent's Messages—Executive Nominations (on deposit at the Truman Library,
Independence, Mo.); LB, DLC:GW. This message was delivered to the Senate
by Tobias Lear (*DHFC*, 2:38).
    1. On 11 Sept. the Senate considered these nominations and confirmed
Hamilton, Eveleigh, and Meredith. Discussion of the remaining names was
"postponed until to Morrow," when the rest of the nominations, except for
Macpherson, were confirmed. Macpherson was confirmed on 18 Sept.
(*DHFC*, 2:38–40, 42).

From John Taylor Gilman

Sir   Exeter New Hampshire Septr 12th 1789.
    On the 12th Ulto I received a Letter from Mr Secretary Lear,
wrote by your Excellency's direction in answer to one from me
of same date—By that Letter I was informed that it was Expected Mr Kean and General Irvine would be in New York in
Three weeks and should have Concluded to Stay until their
Arrival had not the State of my Health been Such as that I was
advised by my Physician and others to make a Journey to the
Northward.
    The State of my Health is such that I cannot well return to
New York at this time, or if I were there should not be able to pay
that attention to the business which it's Importance requires.
    I have been almost the whole of my time for Thirteen Years
past Employed in public Service: when I Accepted of the Appointment as One of the Board of Commissioners of which I am
now a Member, I resigned the Office of Treasurer of the State of
New Hampshire, which Office I had held almost Six Years.
    I am in Hope that I shall be able to return to New York in few
Weeks, but this must depend on my Health, no other Consideration would detain me here a day.
    I could wish to hold my Appointment as One of the Board of
Commissioners, if I may without Injury to the public service, but
not otherwise.
    If the other Commissioners are waiting for me, or any other

Circumstances in your Excellency's Judgment should make it
Necessary that another person should be now Appointed in my
place, be pleased Sir to Consider this as my Resignation of the
Appointment as One of the Board for Settling Accounts between the United States and Individual States. I have the Honor
to be With the Highest Respect Your most Obedient and most
Humble Servant[1]

John Taylor Gilman

ALS, DNA:PCC, item 78.

For background to this letter, see Gilman to GW, 12 Aug. 1789, n.1.

1. On 28 Sept. GW wrote Gilman: "I am sorry to learn, from your letter of
the 12th instant, that the state of your health is such as will, in all probability,
prevent your attendance on the business of your commission.

"The ordinance of the late Congress instituting the Board of which you are
a member, made it necessary for all the Commissioners to be present when
their business commenced—and likewise required the attendance of the
whole when any final adjustment took place. As the business has already commenced agreeably to the ordinance, Genl Irvine informs me that it is pro-
gressing under his inspection, and that the presence of the whole Board will
not be absolutely necessary 'till some final settlement ⟨of⟩ accounts is about to
take place. I shall therefore de⟨lay⟩ making any new appointment until circumstances may render it necessary, in hopes that you will yet so far reco⟨ver⟩
your health as to be able to attend the duties of your office in time; for I
should be very unwilling that a temporary illness should deprive a man of his
office unless the public good rendered a new appointment absolutely necessary.

"Mr Kean has not yet arrived, but by a letter which I received from him
yesterday he may be daily expected" (Df, DNA: RG 59, Miscellaneous Letters).

By mid-December Gilman had still not arrived in New York, although the
other two commissioners were in the city and ready to begin their work. At
GW's request Tobias Lear wrote Gilman on 14 Dec. that his presence could no
longer be delayed. "The two Commissioners now in New York, for settling the
Accounts between the United States and individual States, having informed
the President of the United States that the business of their commission is now
retarded, and will very shortly be at a stand without the presense of the other
Commissioner; I am therefore directed by the President of the United States
to give you notice thereof, and to inform you that your attendance cannot be
well delayed beyond the first, and certainly not beyond the middle of January,
without injury to the public. Should the state of your health be such as to
prevent your being in New York by the middle of January, the President
wishes you to give him immediate information thereof, that another person
may be appointed and the public business not be unnecessarily retarded"
(DNA: RG 59, Miscellaneous Letters). Gilman wrote GW on 28 Dec. that he
had received Lear's letter and "It is with the greatest regret I Consider that

my return to New York has been so long prevented, and public business delayed on my account, although it is my misfortune not my fault. I was in full
Expectation of being able to sett out for New York the last of October, but
about the 25th of that Month I took Cold and was Confined to my Chamber
for several Weeks. I am now so well as that I purpose to sett out on Monday
Next, to proceed as fast as the State of my Health will admit and Hope I may
be in New York by the Middle of the Month" (DNA:PCC, item 78).

From John Parker, Jr.

Sir   Charleston So. Carolina 12th Sepr 1789
    The apprehension of intruding on your excellency engaged
as you are in the great and weighty Concerns of the Union and
my not having the honor of your acquaintance which renders
an application in my own favor particularly awkward, have
detained me from addressing this letter to your attention at an
Earlier period, The request which I have to make to you Sir is
that should there be any appointment under the federal Goverment undisposed of, for which the delegates from this State in
Congress may think me Qualified, Your Excellency will be
pleased to Notice their recommendation in my behalf and on
receiving satisfactory information of my principles, Character
&c. to Nominate me to the same; And I trust that my Conduct in
office will do no discredit either to my friends who may recommend, or to my Country that may Employ me.
    A Large Family to support and very great Losses, Occasiond,
principally, by the late war have induced me to make this application an application Sir as painful for me to make as it may be
troublesome to your Excellency to receive, although I have no
right to advance any pretensions on acct of the Services which I
have endeavor'd to render this State in the respective Stations of
Representative & Senator in their Legislature, of a member of
the Privy Council and a delegate to the Genl Assembly of the
States in Congress, yet my Election to those trusts may operate
towards Satisfying your Excellency that I have been thought
favorably of by this my Native Country. I take the liberty of
referring Your Excellency to Colo. Grayson, Dr Johnson, Mr
Wingate, Mr King & Colo. Few, Gentlemen who know me well
while residing at N. York and who can answer any Enquiries of
my Character & which it may be thought expedient to make,

wishing Sir that your Exertions to fulfill the arduous duties of your high station to which the General Voice of America has Called you may be Crowned with the Merited Success, I have the honor to be with great respect Sir Your Excellencys Most obedt & Most humb Servt

John Parker

ALS, DLC:GW.

John Parker, Jr. (1759–1832), came from a politically prominent South Carolina family. Educated at the Middle Temple in London, he had returned to South Carolina by 1778 and served briefly in the Charleston militia, before returning to London in 1781. After his return to the United States, he was admitted to the South Carolina bar in 1785, served in the South Carolina legislature and in the Confederation Congress during the 1780s, and advocated ratification of the Constitution in the South Carolina convention in 1788.

Parker's application was supported by a letter to GW from Pierce Butler, 24 Sept. 1789, who testified that Parker was an "Old, Respectable Citizen, of good Family, who, by the devastation of the late War is reduced from a good fortune to a very moderate One. He is a Strict honest Man and I doubt not woud prove grateful for any mark of kindness" (DLC:GW). Parker received no federal appointment, and in 1790 Butler made a second unsuccessful attempt to secure federal employment for him, noting that before the Revolution Parker "was possessed of a Considerable Estate; By the Devastation of the British Army He is with a large Family reduced to slender Circumstances— He is a just Man; and if You shall think proper to notice Him I have no doubt but He will discharge the trust with fidelity and honor. I am not Connected with Mr Parker either by blood or Marriage; Neither am I intimate with Him, yet I shall as a Citizen of Carolina, feel myself much obliged by any attention that You may be pleased to shew to Him" (Butler to GW, 30 July 1790, DLC:GW).

To the Pennsylvania Legislature

Gentlemen, [New York, c. 12 September 1789]

When the representatives of a free people, delivering the sense of their constituents, give such marks of affectionate attachment to an individual as are contained in your address to me, it must call forth the warmest acknowledgements of a grateful heart.[1] Under this impression, I beg you to believe that your favorable opinion of my past conduct, and kind congratulations on my elevation to the high station which I now fill, are indelibly marked on my mind.

The early and decided part which the Citizens of Pennsylvania took in behalf of the present system of government cannot be forgotten by the People of these United States—and, in acknowledging the grateful sense which I have of your assurances of the firm and constant support of your State, in all measures in which its aid shall be necessary for rendering my administration easy to myself, and beneficial to our Country, I trust that I meet the concurrence of all good citizens.

The virtue, moderation, and patriotism which marked the steps of the American People in framing, adopting, and thus far carrying into effect our present system of Government, has excited the admiration of Nations; and it only now remains for us to act up to those principles, which should characterize a free and enlightened People, that we may gain respect abroad and ensure happiness and safety to ourselves and to our posterity.

It should be the highest ambition of every American to extend his views beyond himself, and to bear in mind that his conduct will not only affect himself, his country, and his immediate posterity; but that its influence may be co-extensive with the world, and stamp political happiness or misery on ages yet unborn. To obtain this desireable end—and to establish the government of *laws*, the *union* of these States is absolutely necessary; therefore in every proceeding, this great, this important object should ever be kept in view; and so long as our measures tend to this; and are marked with the wisdom of a well informed and enlightened people, we may reasonably hope, under the smiles of Heaven, to convince the world that the happiness of nations can be accomplished by pacific revolutions in their political systems, without the destructive intervention of the sword.

Your wishes for my personal happiness, and fervent prayers for the preservation of my existence have made a grateful impression upon me—and I shall not fail to implore the divine Author of the Universe to bestow those blessings upon you and your Constituents, which can make a people happy.

                                                    G. Washington

LB, DLC:GW.

    1. On 3 Sept. 1789 the Pennsylvania assembly appointed a committee to draw up an address to GW "expressive of the high sense entertained by this House of his distinguished merit, and congratulating him on his appointment to his present exalted station." The address was to be presented to GW by the

U.S. senators from Pennsylvania. GW's reply was read in the assembly on 16 Sept. (*Minutes of the Thirteenth General Assembly of the Commonwealth of Pennsylvania in Their Third Session* [n.p., n.d.], 229, 236, 261–62). The address, signed by Richard Peters, reads: "The Representatives of a free People cannot comply with their duty to their Constituents more to their satisfaction than by paying a just tribute to the merits of One whose important exertions, unexampled perseverance, and distinguished military talents have eminently contributed to the establishment of their liberties.

"Impressed with the most lively sense of your love for your country, invariably evidenced in the course of your past services, and of which you have given a new proof by sacrificing your predilection for private life to the desires of your fellow-citizens, and again appearing on the public stage, we most sincerely congratulate you on your elevation to the high station you now fill.

"The citizens of this State having been among the first to adopt the System of federal Government on which they so much depend for their portion of the national prosperity, cannot but be highly gratified by the progress which has been made towards it's complete organisation, and they have a pleasing addition to their satisfaction by your having been so unanimously placed at the head of it. We are confident that we declare the sense of the People of Pennsylvania, when we assure you of the firm and constant support of this State, in all measures in which its aid shall be necessary for rendering your administration easy to yourself and beneficial to our country.

"We deem it a circumstance which strongly marks the good sense and virtue of our countrymen, that they peaceably and deliberately concurred in a frame of General Government which we firmly trust, will in its operation dignify our character, entitle us to respect among the nations, and ensure happiness to us and our posterity.

"With hearts expanded beyond the limits of our own country, we most ardently hope that the influence of this novel but bright example may be extended until freedom, under government of Laws not of Men, shall bless the oppressed of every climate and country.

"The *old* will then be experimentally taught by the *new World* that reason, virtue, union, moderation, and patriotism, can, under the smiles of Heaven, without the sword, accomplish the happiness of nations by pacific revolutions in their political systems whensoever they require them.

"With the warmest wishes for your personal happiness we fervently beseech the great Author and Supporter of our existence, that he will, by granting you a continuance of health, long preserve a life so dear to your Country and exemplary to mankind" (DLC:GW).

From David Stuart

Dear Sir,   Abingdon [Va.] 12th September—1789
     I meant to have written to you, immediately after the rising of the Chancery Court, respecting the Suit against Alexander[1]—

But as my Lawyers promised me their opinions in writing on the subject, I thought it better to wait, 'till I could lay the matter fully before you—I have written to them since my return, desiring they would comply with their promise, but have recieved no answer—I must therefore endeavour to give you as good a statement of their opinions at present, as I can; since the time, at which, the Court of Chancery will again sit, admits of no longer delay.

A few days before I went to Richmond, Mr Alexander made me the same offer which he had done to Mr Custis, to cancel the bargain and take the land back, leaving the rent to be fixed by indifferent persons, to be agreed on between us—He also wished to put off the trial 'till October—With respect to the first proposition, I informed him, that I did not concieve I had any powers to do such a thing, and that I was also averse to any postponement; but that I would be regulated in the latter, by the opinion of my Council—On going to Richmond, I informed my Lawyers of Mr Alexander's propositions—They informed me, it was a matter of such magnitude, that it ought if possible to be accepted—That the Chancellor as the Guardian of infants might undertake it, if it appeared from the opinions of their friends to be to their advantage.[2] If the Chancellor should not think his powers sufficient, they recommend an application to the Legislature, signed by Mrs Washington & you, and Mrs Stuart & myself—I confess, I never was more astonished, than to find them considering the matter so differently from what I allways understood them—But, I believe, they had never considered the cause, 'till the moment allmost of it's coming on to trial—From my conversation with them hitherto, I understood it to be their opinion, that the twelve thousand pounds, on which the compound interest was calculated, would be scaled—This would have reduced it to two thousand, which with interest for twenty four years would amount to more than four thousand pounds—Tho I allways for my part, considered this as a great price for the land; yet when I reflected on the sum which was contended for, I thought it would be fortunate to get off so well—Their most favourable opinion now; is, that the 48 thousand pounds may be scaled; which by the scale would come to eight thousand pounds hard money—From the experience I have had of the land, I think it more than double its value. But they do not appear even sanguine in obtaining this much; and Alexander's Lawyers speak confidently of their succeeding in the whole sum for which the bond was given—In a matter of such consequence, it is perhaps prudent to recieve a Lesson from an adversary—If judgement should go for the latter sum, the whole family would be ruined, if for the former, the poor girls would be left destitute; while Washington would be left without negroes to work his lands[3]—From these considerations, it is Mrs Stuart's opinion & mine that it will be best to give up the land; or at least signify our opinions to the Chancellor that we concieve it to be to the interest of her children to do it; provided Mrs Washington & you concur in opinion; for I shall take no step without your approbation—I must therefore beg to hear from you immediately, as the time is near at hand when something must be done—If the Chancellor should refuse to do it, and you approve of an application to the Assembly, I beg you will mention it, that I may have a memorial prepared—If the latter should be necessary, it perhaps could not have been done at a more favourable time. Mr Randolph & Mr Marshall being both members, and employed in the cause.

I am just returned from Staunton, where I expected the suit against McClennegan for fourteen negroes would have been tried[4]—To my astonishment when I got there, I found that the cause belonged to the Greenbriar District—So that I have had another proof of the negligence of Lawers. I therefore wrote to the judges requesting it to be put off 'till the Spring—I shall set out in a fiew days for Williamsburg, when I expect the suit against Coll Basset will be tried—I have but little expectations of oversetting his payments.

I have not yet been able to consult the deed you mention, in which you have made a conveyance to Mr Custis for the lands I mentioned;[5] having lodged it with Mr Dandridge for the purpose of having the lands in King William surveyed; there being some disputes about lines, with some of the neighbours—Tho' my information was derived from him, I am pretty certain on recollection, that you are right, as I remember Mr Kenny's applying to me a year or two ago, for your deed to Mr Custis for the land he purchased; and my informing him after consulting the deed, that I could not part with it, as it was included in the deed in which you made a conveyance for the lands in King

William—I did not recollect this at the time I wrote; and besides supposed Mr Dandridge a better judge than myself.

Tho' I have had but little time of late to attend to Politics, yet I think there is but one voice among us now, since the business of titles, that of approbation. The success of amendments will leave but a fiew scattering opponents—Mr Maddison will be a very popular character hereafter on the South side of James river, for his conduct in this business, as Coll Carrington informs me—The same Gentleman informs me, that there has been scarce an instance where the oaths have been refused—It is perhaps somewhat singular, but the Opponents to the Government, appear more generally pleased with the constru[c]tion of the Constitution, which vests the power of removal in the President, than the friends to it—Their satisfaction however, entirely reconciles the latter to it—Mr Kenny is the only one of the party, I have heard of, who disapproves of it—He still thinks too that the single amendment purposed in our Convention respecting direct taxes worth all the rest.

When the plan you have adopted with respect to your family, was first heard of, it was understood to extend to the exclusion of all company whatever—This being considered, as too great a departure from the friendly intercourse, & communion which allways subsisted between the people and their first Magistrates, was viewed as a novelty, and disliked—Since the matter has been rightly understood, I have never heard it condemned—I have heard many members of the former Congress in particular, express their approbation of it.

The people in Alexandria, were lately much disturbed by a regulation in the Naval System—The likelyhood of a repeal has put them into a good humour again—The last Post brought us an account of the vote of the lower House, respecting the permanent seat of Government. The people here say, that their expectations of it's being on the Potowmac, were allways centered in you, and hope that as your opinion has been long known on the subject, it will never pass with your concurrence—For my part, I fear from the majority which have prevailed on the question, that even that will not avail—I am unacquainted with the various steps which have preceded the decision, but it appears to me that some advantage has been taken of the absence of many members from the Southward. A question which involves all the passions and interests of the different parts of the Union, ought not to have been decided on without much previous notice. Perhaps, it ought not to have been decided on at all, in the absence of two States, who will probably soon join the Union. I have no doubt, but the Opponents to the Constitution in those States, and North Carolina particularly, will consider it, as a striking instance of disrespect—A member of that State, tho' a friend to the government, will I think be justifyed in refusing to accede to it, when, a question which is to affect them to the latest ages, has been decided on, without their voice—No possible injury could have arisen, from a suspension of the question for a fiew months—As the arguments of population & wealth seem to have been considered as frivolous, and therefore disregarded, I cannot concieve on what principle the question could have met with such a fate—But, it is too probable, tho' they were not insisted on, that they have had their influence— Upon the whole, it is considered as unfortunate, that a matter of such magnitude should have been agitated at this time, and much more so, that it should be generally considered, that any other circumstance, than that of extent of territory should be supposed to have operated. I am Dr Sir, with great respect Your Affecte Servt

Dd Stuart

P:S: I am just informed that Alexander's friends are dissuading him from the offer he made, as he is so certain of getting more than double the value of his land—I feared this would be the case, and wish I had had power to have closed with him at once—Coll Simms will be in New York the Stage after your receipt of this, who will be able to give you a more particular acct than I have probably done respecting this important matter to the estate. I have begged him to call on you immediately on his arrival.

Dd S.

ALS, DLC:GW.

1. For the legal involvement of Robert Alexander with John Parke Custis, see Stuart to GW, 14 July 1789, n.7.

2. The chancellor of Virginia in 1789 was George Wythe.

3. Stuart is referring to the four children of John Parke Custis and Eleanor

Calvert Custis Stuart: Elizabeth Parke Custis, Martha Parke Custis, Eleanor Parke Custis, and George Washington Parke Custis. The two youngest children made their home with GW and Mrs. Washington.

4. For additional comments on this case, see Stuart to GW, 3 Dec. 1789.

5. See Stuart to GW, 14 July 1789, n.8 and GW to Stuart, 26 July 1789.

From Benjamin Thompson

Morris Town, State of New Jersey
Sir   September 12th 1789

In expectation that, under the present government of the United States, Congress may shortly find it expedient, amongst other commercial regulations, to establish Consuls at foreign Ports—particularly to the Ports of France & french Islands—and having from a long residence with the french nation, acquired a knowledge of their language, Laws & customs, sufficient I flatter myself to discharge the duties of a Consular trust; Beg leave to offer my services to the consideration of your Excellency, as a person who wishes to be viewed as a Candidate for some such Appointment, whenever the commercial interests of the United States, and the arrangement proper on the Ocasion, may render the Same necessary—But as offices of this nature may most probably fall under the immediate Control and direction of the department of Foreign Affairs, an Application to the Head of that department might perhaps be proper, ignorant however on the subject and totally a Stranger to the gentelman who presides over it, I have ventured to Submit my wish & pretensions to your Excellency, to whom in the early part of the late american war, I had the honor to be somewhat known, although at this day not familiar to your Excellencys memory—The following circumstances may, however, enable your Excellency to call me to your mind.

At the commencement of the late american war, I had then been Seven years a resident in Canada and on the entrance of General Montgomery into that province, was one of the first who took an active part in the Cause of America; consequently with many Others I was compelled to take refuge in, & retreat with the american Army in June 1776. on my arrival at New York in July following, I had the honor to be presented to your Excellency as a person who was thought qualified to enter the

British encampment then on Staten Island, with a view to encourage a desertion of the german Troops in the British Service. Afterwards in the same year I was appointed to a command in the Navy, which appearing to afford but little prospect of action at that time, I gave up, for an appointment in the horse Service, in which, in the campaign of Seventy Seven, first as adjutant to Sheldons regiment, and afterwards as acting Brigade Major to Count Pulaski I had sometimes the honor to receive your Excellencys orders—unable to Support my self longer in the Service, in June 1778 I resigned, I have Since held the Office of Commissioner, for Settling the public Accounts between this State & the United States—I have an encreasing young family & but very Slender means for their Support, a circumstance that alone induced me to address your Excellency on this ocasion.

I am well known to the representation in Congress from this State but principally to Messrs Patterson Boudinot, & Cadwallader to whom respecting my qualifications, & conduct in life, I beg to refer your Excellency.[1] I have the Honor to be Most Respectfully Your Excellencys Very Obedient Humble Servant

Benja. Thompson

ALS, DLC:GW.

In addition to the military services described in his letter, Benjamin Thompson served as New Jersey's commissioner of accounts for settling the state's accounts with the Confederation government from 1781 to 1788. He may be the Benjamin Thompson of New Jersey who was a founder and manager of Hibernia Ironworks in that state in 1785 and the Benjamin Thompson who died in Fairfield Township, Cumberland County, in 1814 (*New Jersey Archives*, 1st ser., 42:423).

1. Thompson received no federal appointment in 1789, and in 1790 when consular appointments were being considered he wrote two letters, 30 and 31 Mar., to Thomas Jefferson requesting a post in the consular service (DLC:GW). On 3 April 1790 he reminded GW of his earlier request for a consular appointment. "But I am Still uninformed, sir, of any thing that I may have to hope or expect on the occasion" (DLC:GW). For consideration of Thompson for a consular post, see Boyd, *Jefferson Papers*, 17:253. Thompson was offered a post in the Canary Islands in 1790, "but as these offices have no direct emoluments, depending for indemnification on the consignments and other business they may produce," Jefferson wrote, "he has declined accepting any" (Jefferson to Thomas Mann Randolph, Jr., 3 Aug. 1790, ibid., 298–99). In 1793 Thompson again approached GW. This time, "reduced by a Series of misfortunes, to the necessity of renewing a claim on the United States for a Small pittance due me for a part of my Services during the late Americain War," he requested GW's help in proving his Revolutionary War services

(Thompson to GW, 9 Jan. 1793, DNA: RG 59, Miscellaneous Letters). Papers relating to Thompson's claim are in DNA: RG 217, Miscellaneous Treasury Accounts of the General Accounting Office, account no. 3667. His quest for payment on his Revolutionary claim appears to have been unsuccessful, but in 1801 he received 640 acres of land under the terms of "An Act regulating the grants of land appropriated for the refugees from the British provinces of Canada and Nova Scotia" (6 *Stat.* 42–43 [18 Feb. 1801]).

To Betty Washington Lewis

My dear Sister,　　　　　　　　New York, September 13th 1789
　　Colonel Ball's letter gave me the first account of my Mother's death—since that I have received Mrs Carter's letter written at your request[1]—and previous to both I was prepared for the event by some advices of her illness communicated to your Son Robert.
　　Awful, and affecting as the death of a Parent is, there is consolation in knowing that Heaven has spared ours to an age, beyond which few attain, and favored her with the full enjoyment of her mental faculties, and as much bodily strength as usually falls to the lot of four score. Under these considerations and a hope that she is translated to a happier place, it is the duty of her relatives to yield due submission to the decrees of the Creator—When I was last at Fredericksburg, I took a final leave of my Mother, never expecting to see her more.[2]
　　It will be impossible for me at this distance, and circumstanced as I am, to give the smallest attention to the execution of her will. nor indeed is much required if, as she directs, no security should be given or appraisement made of her estate; but that the same should be allotted to the Devisees with as little trouble and delay as may be. How far this is legal I know not—Mr Mercer can, and I have no doubt would, readily advise you, if asked, which I wish you to do.[3] If the ceremony of inventorying appraising, &ca can be dispensed with, all the rest, (as the will declares, that few or no debts are owing) can be done with very little trouble—Every person may in that case immediately receive what is specifically devised.
　　The Negroes who are engaged in the crop, and under an Overseer must remain I conceive on the Plantation until the crop is finished[4] (which ought to be as soon as possible) after

which the horses, stock of all sorts, and every species of property, not disposed of by the will, (the debts, if any, being first paid) must by law be equally divided into five parts, one of which you, another my Brother Charles, and a third myself, are entitled to—the other two thirds fall to the share of the children of our deceased Brothers Samuel and John. Were it not that the specific legacies which are given to me by the Will are meant, and ought to be considered and received as mementos of parental affection, in the last solemn act of life, I should not be desirous of receiving or removing them, but in this point of view I set a value on them much beyond their intrinsic worth.[5] Whilst it occurs to me, it is necessary it should be known that there is a fellow belonging to that estate now at my house, who never stayed elsewhere, for which reason, and because he has a family I should be glad to keep him—He must I should conceive be far short in value of the fifth of the other negroes which will be to be divided, but I shall be content to take him as my proportion of them—and, if from a misconception either of the number or the value of these negroes it should be found that he is of greater value than falls to my lot I shall readily allow the difference, in order that the fellow may be gratified, as he never would consent to go from me.

Debts, if any are due, should be paid from the sale of the crops, Plantation utensils, Horses and stock; and the sooner an account is taken of the latter and they can conveniently be disposed of, the better it will be for two reasons; first because the Overseer (if he is not a very honest Man) may take advantage of circumstances, and convert part of these things to his own use— and secondly because the season is now fast approaching when without feeding (which would lessen the sale of the corn and fodder) the stock will fall off, and consequently sell to a disadvantage. Whether my Mother has kept any accounts that can be understood is more than I am able to say—If any thing is owing to her it should be received—and, if due from her, paid after due proof thereof is made—She has had a great deal of money from me at times, as can be made appear by my books, and the accounts of Mr L. Washington during my absence—and over and above this has not only had all that was ever made from the Plantation but got her provisions and every thing else she thought proper from thence. In short to the best of my recollec-

Barry University Library
Miami, FL 33161

tion I have never in my life received a copper from the estate—
and have paid many hundred pounds (first and last) to her in
cash—However I want no retribution—I conceived it to be a
duty whenever she asked for money, and I had it, to furnish her
notwithstanding she got all the crops or the amount of them,
and took every thing she wanted from the plantation for the
support of her family, horses &ca besides.

As the accounts for or against the Estate must not only from
the declaration in the will, but from the nature of the case, be
very trifling and confined I should suppose to the town of
Fredericksburg, it might be proper therefore in that paper to
require in an advertisement all those who have any demands to
bring them in properly attested immediately, and those who are
owing to pay forthwith: The same advertisement might appoint
a day for selling the stock, and every thing, excepting Negroes,
at the plantation, that is not devised by the will,[6] as it will be more
convenient I should suppose for the heirs to receive their respective dividends of the money arising from the sales than to be
troubled with receiving a cow, a calf, or such like things after the
debts (which must be the case) have been first paid. It might be
well in fixing the day of sale, to consult the Overseer, to know
when the business of the plantation will admit the Cart, Team,
and Utensils to be taken from it.[7]

As the number of articles to be sold cannot be many and will
be of small value, I think they had better be sold for ready
money and so advertised, for though they would fetch more
on credit, there would more than probable be bad debts contracted, and at any rate delay, if not law suits before the money
could be collected, and besides if there are debts to be paid
money will be wanted for the purpose, and in no way can be so
readily and properly obtained as by a ready money sale, and
from the crops.

If you think this business will be too troublesome for you with
the aid of your sons—Mr Carter[8] and Colonel Ball—who I am
persuaded will give each of us assisstance, and you will let me
know it, I will desire Major George Washington to attend.

As the land at the Little-falls Plantation goes to Mr Bushrod
Washington he should be apprised in time of the breaking of it
up, otherwise there may be injury to the houses and fencing if

left without some person to attend to them. Have particular care taken of her papers, the letters to her &ca.

I should prefer selling the houses and lotts on which my Mother lived to renting of them[9]—and would give a year or two years credit to the purchasers paying interest—and not being acquainted with the value of lotts in Fredericksburg, I would leave the price to any three indifferent and impartial Gentlemen to say what they are worth, and that sum I will take.

If they cannot be sold and soon I would rent them from year to year to any orderly Tenant on a moderate rent—If they are not disposed of on sale or by tennanting before the weather gets cool the paling will, I expect, be soon burnt up.[10]

Give my love to Mrs Carter and thank her for the letter she wrote to me—I would have done this myself had I more time for private correspondencies. Mrs Washington joins in best wishes for her, yourself, and all other friends, and I am, with the most sincere regard, Your affectionate Brother

G. Washington

LB, DLC:GW.

1. Burgess Ball's letter of 25 Aug. had informed GW of his mother's death. No letter concerning this event from Betty Lewis Carter, Betty Lewis's daughter, has been found.

2. See GW to Richard Conway, 6 Mar. 1789, n.2.

3. James Mercer maintained a thriving law practice in Fredericksburg.

4. Presumably these slaves were employed on Mary Washington's Accokeek Run lands and her plantation at Little Falls on the Rappahannock River about two miles from Ferry Farm.

5. See Ball to GW, 25 Aug. 1789, n.2.

6. GW is probably referring to Mary Ball Washington's Deep Run Quarter near Fredericksburg, devised to her in her husband's will in the expectation that she would develop it and leave Ferry Farm to GW.

7. Betty Lewis placed an advertisement in the *Virginia Herald and Fredericksburg Advertiser*, 15 Oct. 1789, announcing that "On Thursday, the 29th instant, will be sold at the plantation, about 4 miles below this town, late the property of Mrs. Mary Washington, deceased, ALL the stocks of Horses, cattle, sheep and hogs, plantation utensils of every kind, carts, hay and fodder. That trouble of collections &c. may be avoided, they will be sold to the highest bidder, for ready money. All persons having claims against the deceased are requested to bring them in properly attested to."

8. Charles Carter (1765–1829) was the son of Edward and Sarah Champe Carter of Blenheim. Since 1781 he had been married to GW's niece, Betty Lewis (1765–1830). The Carters lived in Culpeper County for a time after

their marriage but then moved to Frederick County and later to Pittsylvania County.

9. When Mary Ball Washington moved from Ferry Farm to Fredericksburg in 1771 or early 1772, GW purchased for her use a house and two lots on Charles Street in Fredericksburg close to her daughter's residence at Kenmore.

10. For the settlement of Mary Ball Washington's estate, see Burgess Ball and Charles Carter to GW, 8 Oct. 1789, and Ball to GW, 26 Dec. 1789.

Tobias Lear to Clement Biddle

Dear Sir,					New York, September 14th 1789

I have now before me your several favors of the 15th, 19th and 29th of August, and 2d of September.[1]

The Prayer-Books came safe to hand, and were much approved of by Mrs Washington.[2]

As there is, at present, no opportunity from this place to So. Carolina by water, I have taken the liberty to commit the enclosed letter to your care, requesting that you will be so good as to have it put on board the first Vessel which sails from Philadelphia to So. Carolina with a charge to the Captain to have it delivered immediately on his arrival.[3]

Mrs Washington wishes you to send 25lb. of Chocolate shells to Mount Vernon by the first opportunity, which you will charge to the Acct of the President; and I will thank you for a statement of his Acct from the last rendered in, whenever it may be convenient for you to send it.[4] I am, Dear Sir, with very great esteem, Your most Obedt Servt

Tobias Lear.

ALS, PHi: Washington-Biddle Correspondence; ADfS, ViMtV; LB, DLC:GW.

1. The letters of 19 and 29 Aug. are in PHi: Clement Biddle Letter Book, 1789–92. The letters of 15 Aug. and 2 Sept. have not been found.

2. On 10 Aug. Lear wrote to Biddle asking: "Will you be so good as to send Mrs Washington two handsome prayer books—of the new form, as none of that description are to be had here?" (PHi: Washington-Biddle Correspondence). A week later, at the first lady's behest, Lear sought from Biddle an additional book (17 Aug., PHi: Washington-Biddle Correspondence). Biddle wrote back on 29 Aug.: "The Prayer Books expected having Come to hand I have Order three of them for Mrs Washington to be bound in Morocco & expect them to be ready by Wedsy" (PHi: Clement Biddle Letter Book, 1789–92).

3. Biddle's response to this letter on 16 Sept. (PHi: Clement Biddle Letter Book, 1789–92) reveals that the first vessel to sail for Charleston from Philadelphia was the schooner *Friendship*, commanded by a Captain Welsh, who agreed to deliver Lear's letter of the fourteenth to Nicholas Eveleigh. The letter contained Eveleigh's appointment by GW to the office of Comptroller of the Treasury.

4. Biddle enclosed the president's accounts in his letter to Lear, 16 Sept., and also promised that "the Cocoa Nut Shels shall be sent by first Vessel for Patowmack." On 28 Sept. Lear notified Biddle that the president's account was correct.

To the Rhode Island Society of the Cincinnati

Gentlemen,   United-States September 14th 1789

In returning my grateful thanks for the flattering and affectionate sentiments, expressed in your address of the 3rd instant, I beg you will do justice to the sincerity of my regard, which reciprocates, with great pleasure, the warmest wishes for your happiness, political and personal.[1]

Under a persuasion of the candor and support of my fellow-citizens, I yielded obedience to the voice of my country—and, impressed by a sense of duty, I forsook the pleasures of domestic retirement to promote, if my best exertions can have such tendency, the objects of a dearer interest. Those expectations of support have been amply fulfilled, and my fondest hope of their candor has been gratified by a kind and partial country.

I am much pleased, Gentlemen, with the hope which you entertain that mistaken zeal will give way to enlightened policy—and I desire to repeat to your Society assurances of the most affectionate esteem.

                                                            G. Washington

LB, DLC:GW.

1. The address from the Rhode Island Society of the Cincinnati, signed by Isaac Senter, president, and Robert Rogers, secretary, stated that "Expressions of respect and attachment are a tribute, which the Citizens of America owe to your prudence, your patriotism and valour; to the successful display of which they are already indebted for their freedom; and from a continuance of the exercise of those qualities, they may anticipate a permanent enjoyment of the highest state of political happiness.

"Under these impressions, Sir, we the Society of the Cincinnati of the State of Rhode Island, most sincerely congratulate you upon your appointment to the Chief Magistracy of the union by the unanimous suffrage of more than three millions of free-citizens: an appointment rendered the more dignified by the manner in which it was conferred, and the more pleasing to your fellow-citizens from a conviction that they could no where place the sacred deposit, for which they have so long and arduously contended, with equal safety to themselves and honor to their country. We cannot help expressing, at the same time, the strong obligations we feel for the sacrifice of domestic ease and retirement, to which we are sensible the love of your country alone could have prompted you—And although we are not admitted to a participation of the good effects of the government over which you so deservedly preside, yet we fondly flatter ourselves that the period is not far distant, when the mistaken zeal, which has lately prevailed in this State, will give way to a more enlightened policy.

"We can only add, Sir, our ardent wishes for your health and happiness— Long may the United States be blessed with a life to which they are so highly indebted! and may the close of your days be as peaceful and happy to yourself as the meridian of them has been useful and glorious to your Country" (DLC:GW). See also the *Providence Gazette and Country Journal*, 26 Sept. 1789.

From Arthur St. Clair

Sir.   New York Sept. 14. 1789.

The constant Hostilities between the Indians who live upon the river Wabash, and the people of Kentuckey must necessarily be attended with such embarrassing circumstances to the Government of the Western Territory, that I am induced to request you will be pleased to take the matter into consideration, and give me the orders you may think proper.

It is not to be expected Sir, that the Kentuckey people will, or can, submit patiently to the cruelties and depredations of those Savages. they are in the habits of retaliation perhaps, without attending precisely to the nations from which the injuries are received—they will continue to retaliate, or they will apply to the Governor of the western country (through which the indians must pass to attack them) for redress; If he cannot redress them, (and in present circumstances he cannot) they also will march through that country, to redress themselves, and the Government will be laid prostrate. The United States, on the other hand are at peace with several of the nations; and, should the resentment of those people fall upon any of them, which it is likely enough may happen, very bad consequences will follow; for it must appear to them that the United States, either pay no regard to their Treaties, or that they are unable or unwilling to carry their engagements into effect. Remonstrances will probably be made by them also to the Governor, and he will be found in a situation, from which he can neither redress the one, nor protect the other: they will unite with the hostile nations, prudently preferring open war to a delusive and uncertain peace.

By a resolution of the late Congress the Governor of the western Territory, had power, in case of hostilities, to call upon Virginia and Pennsylvania for a number of men to act in conjunction with the continental Troops, and carry war into the indian settlements.[1] that resolution, it is now supposed, is no longer in force. the revival of it might be of use, as it would tend to conciliate the western people, by shewing them that they were not unattended to; and would in some measure Justify me in holding a language to the indians which might obviate the necessity of employing force against them. The handful of Troops Sir, that are scattered in that country, tho' they may afford protection to some Settlements, cannot possibly act offensively by themselves. I have the Honor to be Sir your most obedient and most humble Servant

Ar. St Clair

Copy, DNA: RG 46, First Congress, Records of Legislative Proceedings, President's Messages; ADfS, OHi: Arthur St. Clair Papers. This letter was submitted by GW to the Senate and House of Representatives with his letter of 16 Sept. 1789.

1. See GW to the U.S. Senate and House of Representatives, 16 Sept. 1789, n.3.

From George Thacher

Sir   City of New York 14th Septemr 1789

I take the liberty of handing to you the names of two Gentlemen either of whom in my opinion will make a respectable District Judge for the District of Maine—viz. the Honourable David Sewal & William Lithgow Junr.[1] The former was appointed one of the Judges of the Supreme Judicial Court, for the Commonwealth of Massachusetts, about the year 1776—which office he has sustained to the present time—He lives at York in the District of Maine.

The latter is a respectable Attorney at Law of about thirteen years standing he lives at Hollowel on Kennebeck River[.] He served four or five years in the Army—where he lost the use of his right arm by a ball he recieved in an engagement with the enemy—He is now Major General of the Militia in the eastern Division of Massachusetts.

Should the former be appointed Judge in Maine District—the latter appears to me the most suitable person in that District for the Attorney to the United States in the said District—But if the latter be appointed Judge, I wish to mention Daniel Davis of Portland as a suitable person for the Attorney in that District.[2]

I further take the liberty of recommending Joshua Bailey Osgood, as a proper person for the Marshall in Maine District[3]—His situation at Portland or Biddeford will accommodate the District—His property, education & general Character, where they are known, I believe, will fully justify this recommendation. I am with the greatest respect Sir, Your most obedient humble Servant

George Thatcher

ALS, DLC:GW.

George Thacher (Thatcher; 1754–1824), a Harvard graduate, studied law with Shearjashub Bourne in Massachusetts and began his law practice in 1782 at Biddeford, Maine. Thacher was elected to the Confederation Congress in 1781 and served in the U.S. House of Representatives from 1789 to 1801 when he became an associate justice of the Massachusetts Supreme Court. In the early nineteenth century he changed the spelling of his name from Thatcher to Thacher.

1. David Sewall (1735–1825) was a 1755 Harvard graduate who practiced law at York, Maine. In 1777 he was appointed a justice of the Massachusetts Superior Court and in 1781 of the Massachusetts Supreme Court. GW named him judge of the U.S. District Court for Maine in 1789; he held the post until 1818. William Lithgow, Jr. (1750–1796), served with Massachusetts militia during the Revolution and on the Massachusetts General Court. GW appointed him U.S. attorney for the district of Maine in 1789.

2. Daniel Davis (c.1762–1835) came to Portsmouth, Maine, from Boston in 1782 and practiced law there until the early nineteenth century. He received no federal appointment in 1789 but served several terms in the state legislature. In 1796 GW appointed him U.S. attorney for the District of Maine to replace Lithgow. In 1801 he was appointed solicitor general of Massachusetts.

3. Joshua Bailey Osgood (1753–1791), a native of Haverhill, Mass., graduated from Harvard in 1772 and settled in Fryeburg, Maine. He did not re-

ceive a federal appointment but was elected to the Massachusetts legislature in 1790.

To Arthur Campbell

Sir,   New York September 15th 1789

Your several favors of the 10th and 16th of May[1] and 22d of August with their enclosures have been received—The information which they communicate claims my thanks, and the personal kindness they express is entitled to my grateful acknowledgments.

Watchful over every interest of the Union, Congress during their present Session, have passed a Law authorising the appointment of Commissioners to treat with the Indians, and providing for the expences attendant on the negociations[2]—In pursuance thereof Benjamin Lincoln, Cyrus Griffin, and David Humphreys Esquires have been appointed Commissioners; and they sailed from New York for Savannah in Georgia fifteen days ago.

Circumstances concur to favor a beleif that the most beneficial consequences will flow from this measure, and that its effects will be extended to every description of Indians within, and contiguous to, the United States.

I accept with pleasure your obliging offers of further communications, and shall at all times be happy to receive such information as you may think interesting to the Government of the United States. I am, Sir, Your Most Obedient Servant

George Washington

LB, DLC:GW.

1. A copy of a letter of 16 May, unaddressed and signed "Your fervent Admirer, A. C.," in DNA:PCC, item 78, is probably the letter referred to by GW. It reads: "If there be many who would rejoice in seeing the civil administration of your Country conducted with the same eclat, that the military operations were lately; yet there are not a few, who are now looking forward with a malignant satisfaction, to see that glory lost, that recently was so nobly won and your own native State, perhaps produces more of these ingrates, than any other. I shall tire you with my hints, and warnings but your goodness will pardon this, with other forwardness, and impute the whole, to an honest zeal—and if found useless, consign this to oblivion. May your Almighty

friend! bless you with his choicest gifts, in every station, and sheild you against all your enemies."

2. See GW to the United States Senate, 20 Aug. 1789.

To George Gilpin

Dear Sir,   New York, September 15th 1789.

I am favored with the receipt of your letter of the 2nd instant, and thank you for the information, which you have been so good as to communicate.[1]

Every circumstance which serves to shew the utility, and which explains the progress of an undertaking so advantageous to the Community, as the navigation of the Potowmack, is at once grateful and interesting.

When your leisure allows an opportunity of making out the draft you mention, I shall be glad to receive it, together with such further observations as may consist with your convenience.[2] I am Dear Sir, Your most obedient Servant

Go: Washington

LS, anonymous donor; copy, DNA: RG 59, Miscellaneous Letters; LB, DLC:GW. The copies of this letter in DLC and DNA are dated 14 September.

1. Gilpin's letter of 2 Sept. gave GW a report of a survey of the Potomac River undertaken on behalf of the Potomac Company.

2. In his letter of 2 Sept. Gilpin promised GW a draft "with the Courses, distance and perpendicular fall of Potomack and of the Allegany mountain where Several of the great waters begin."

Tobias Lear to Clement Biddle

Dear Sir,   New York September 16th 1789

The President has sent to Virginia a German who is to be a Gardener for him there.[1]

As he cannot speak the English Language and is unacquainted with the Country—I have paid his passage in the Stage to Philadelphia; and have written to Mr Inskeep—proprieter of the Stage there,[2] to forward him from thence to Alexandria, and have informed him that the Amount of his Passage to the latter place would be paid by you upon his delivering this Letter—

which I request you to do & charge the same to the Ac[coun]t of the President of the United States. I am Dr Sir, with great esteem, Your Most Obt Servt

Tobias Lear.

P.S. The Man has a trunk which I presume will require to be paid for also.

ALS, PHi: Washington-Biddle Correspondence; ADf, ViMtV; LB, DLC:GW.

   1. For background to this letter, see John Christian Ehlers to GW, 24 June 1789, and *Diaries*, 5:422–23.

   2. See Lear to John Inskeep, 16 Sept. 1789 (DLC:GW). Inskeep (1757–1834), the second son of Abraham and Sarah Ward Inskeep of Marlton, N.J., held several posts in the New Jersey militia during the Revolution before moving in the early 1780s to Philadelphia, where he purchased George Tavern at Second and Arch (Mulberry) streets, from which the stage left for New York and Baltimore. He later became director of the Insurance Company of North America and a partner in the publishing house of Bradford & Inskeep, as well as a founding member of the city's chamber of commerce. Inskeep served Philadelphia as alderman, associate judge of common pleas, and mayor (1800, 1806). As a china and glassware merchant he sold GW a set of china for $22.33 (Household Account Book, 13 Feb. 1797, DLC:GW, and Edward Wallace, "Sketch of John Inskeep," 129–35.

To Margaret Tilghman Carroll

Madam,   New York, September 16th 1789.

   A Person having been lately sent to me from Europe in the capacity of a Gardner, who professes a knowledge in the culture of rare plants and care of a Green-House, I am desirous to profit of the very obliging offer you were pleased some time ago to make me.[1]

   In availing myself of your goodness I am far from desiring that it should induce any inconvenience to yourself—but, reconciling your disposition to oblige, with your convenience, I shall be happy to receive such aids as you can well spare, and as will not impair your collection. Trusting that this will be the rule of your bounty, I have requested General Williams to give you notice, when an opportunity offers to transport the trees or plants in the freshest state to Mount Vernon, and to pay any expence which may be incurred in fitting them for transportation, and to receive them from your Gardner for that purpose. I

have the honor to be, most respectfully, Madam, Your obliged
and obedient Servant

                                        G. Washington

LB, DLC:GW.

Margaret Tilghman Carroll (1742–1817), the daughter of Matthew Tilghman and the sister-in-law of GW's wartime aide Tench Tilghman, was the
widow of Charles Carroll "the barrister" (1723–1783). Carroll's estate Mount
Clare, where his widow was still living, was noted for its greenhouse and its
ornamental plantings. The greenhouse at Mount Clare influenced GW in the
construction of his own greenhouse (see GW to Tench Tilghman, 11 Aug.
1784, and Tilghman to GW, 18 Aug. 1784). GW's letter to Margaret Carroll
marks the beginning of a protracted correspondence between GW, Otho H.
Williams, and Mrs. Carroll over the shipment of ornamental plants for Mount
Vernon from Mount Clare's greenhouse. On 16 Sept. GW wrote Otho H. Williams in Baltimore, requesting Williams's assistance in having the plants from
Mrs. Carroll's greenhouse "conveyed in the freshest state to Mount Vernon—
for the purpose I beg that you would, on agreeing with some careful master
of a vessel that may be going round to land them at Mount Vernon, give Mrs
Carroll such notice of the opportunity as will allow time for putting them
up—and that you would be so obliging as to receive and ship them—the cost
of package, or any other expense attending this matter, I must beg you to
defray, and it shall be repaid with thanks" (LS, sold by Robert F. Batchelder,
item 3, catalog 45, March 1984, quoted from catalog description). In initiating
what appeared to be a modest request, GW had not anticipated either the
enthusiasm with which Williams embraced his assignment or the extent of
Mrs. Carroll's generosity. On 23 Sept. Williams wrote GW that he had delivered the president's note to Mrs. Carroll who "advised me to provide a boat
proper for transporting the trees in about two Weeks from this time. As some
of them are large and bear a good deal of fruit and as their boxes are of
considerable weight, it will be necessary to procure [a] commodious Vessel and
a trusty Navigator" (NjP: deCoppet Collection). Mrs. Carroll responded
warmly to GW's request on 25 Sept., assuring GW that the "Trees shall be
immediately put in order" and shipped as soon as Williams could procure a
vessel. "I have been rather unfortunate in the Shaddocks that were long intended for your Excellency's use, attempting to engraff on them my two other
sorts of Fruit, have fail'd either for want of Skill in my Gardiner or that being
an improper Stock for either of them, you will therefore please Sir to accept
with them a Lemon Tree two yo[u]ng plants and a few Seedlings, those with
two plants of the Aloe and a Geranium, which shall also be sent are all the
kinds my Green-house affords and do not in the least disfurnish it. It will give
me much pleasure to hear they get safe, and should they Succeed Shall think
my Self happy having in the Smallest degree contributed to your convenience
or amusement" (MdHi).

By 2 Oct. GW had received Williams's letter of 23 Sept. announcing his
intention of chartering a vessel to transport the plants. Dismayed, GW replied
that he feared "my request of you, to forward the Plants which Mrs Carroll

had been so obliging as to offer me, was so incautiously expressed as to lead you into a mistake, and myself, consequently, into an expence which I had no intention to incur. More than to embrace the opportunity of the Packet from Baltimore to Alexandr[i]a, or any other *casual* conveyance from the one place to the other, by which the above plants could easily have been sent, I had not extended my ideas; and if a large Vessel should have been employed for this purpose the cost will far exceed the value of the things, if not too late, I could wish to avoid it. I had no expectation of large Trees—or of any plants beyond their infant growth; the first would be a robbery of the good Lady without answering my purposes so well as those which were younger" (ALS [photo-copy], DLC:GW). On 7 Oct. Williams replied: "I regret that my error should give you the trouble of explaining your intentions respecting the fruit Trees." On two visits to Mount Clare to consult with Mrs. Carroll about the plants, Williams had "found her so indecisive, and anxious about their safety, that I indulge myself in the prospect of another visit soon to Mount Clare, which I always find agreeable, and I hope that it will be in my power to gratify all Mrs Carroll's wishes respecting the *small trees*; But there is, at present, very little prospect of sending the larger ones without going to an expence dispropor-tioned to their value. Two careful boat Men have engaged to take, each, a part of the smaller plants this week, But I must wait for an opportunity by some Ship, that may go from here to lade with Tobacco in Patowmac, to send the large ones. Allow me, sir, to explain a word—Mrs Carroll is *indecisive*, only, because she is not quite certain which are the most suitable, and which will be the most fortunate, and acceptable. Her garden contains but one tree which bears both Lemons and Oranges—She thought there were two Was quite dis-appointed! This, she said, must be sent. I presumed to tell her that you would not permit her to make the sacrifice; That its great burden of fine fruit would render a safe conveyance impracticable; That your object, in which we mu-tually wished that you might be long indulged, was to cultivate young trees, and bring them like this, to perfection; The perfection of this fine tree (for she spoke then of no other) was her great reason for wishing it in your collec-tion; Could it not, *possibly*, be conveyed with safety? I expressed my doubts—and her solicitude increased—So I was obliged to sooth it by promising that I would again consult the Boat Men, and provide for the transportation of the small trees, which I have already done. Conceiving, my Dear Sir, that the sat-isfaction which you are to derive from the acceptance of Mrs Carroll's present will be in proportion to the pleasure which you give, by receiving, I have en-deavoured to conduct myself as your agent in the business, with all possible attention and delicacy—But I cannot imagine that Her Compliment will be at all enhanced by unnecessary trouble, or useless expence" (DLC:GW). On 10 Oct. Williams informed GW that "Mrs Carroll prevented my intended visit to Mount Clare, by doing me the honor to call at my House in town. We recapit-ulated all circumstances respecting the fruit trees: and agreed that it is most eligible, at present, to send only the small ones. I expect to Ship half a dozen, for Mount Vernon, tomorrow" (DLC:GW).

On 14 Oct. GW addressed another note to Mrs. Carroll: "I know not how sufficiently to thank you for your polite and obliging compliance with my request—nor, in what manner to express my fears lest those motives should have led you into inconveniences. My Green House is by no means in perfect order, and if it was, it would not have been my wish to have robbed yours of any *grown* or bearing plants. If it is not too late I would again repeat and entreat that this may not happen" (LB, DLC:GW). On the same day GW wrote Williams that although on the point of leaving New York City for his New England tour "I cannot, notwithstanding, depart without again expressing in strong terms—if it is not too late—a pointed wish and desire that Mrs Carroll would not rob her own Green-house of any large & bearing trees especially the one of which she has not a second. It is highly probable that *this* tree, and perhaps *all* large ones would be lost to us both by the act of transportation unless very fine weather—a short passage—and *more* than *common* care are met with" (ALS, MdHi: Otho H. Williams Papers).

Mrs. Carroll, however, wrote again on 26 Oct. assuring GW that "no inconvenience in the least, can arise, from the removal of the Trees. your Excellency rates them too highly, they will not be miss'd in my Green-house, nor will they be such an acquisition to yours, as I could wish; but it has been my intention, ever since I fail'd in buding the Shaddocks, to present you with them, if I could have a conveyance (for such) unfortunately General Williams has not yet procured me one; possibly your cautious Politenes may have prevented. yet mindfull of your Commands, and incapable of deviateing in the Smallest degree from them; he fears to remove, even a plant, without your permission, equally impres'd with a fear of incuring your disapprobation I am at a loss. how Sir shall I convince you, how much 'tis my inclination to furnish your Orangery with a little Fruit, and with what convenience I can do it, you shall judge, when I tell you, mine is rather over Stock'd. allow me then to send them, and I hope it will be pleaseing both to your Self and Mrs Washington to gather of your own fruit on your return. . . . Sensible of the inconvenience such a Correspondence must be to you, I can no longer trespass on your politeness, only be pleased to Say to General Williams that he may inform me when your Green-house is in order" (ALS, DLC:GW).

Williams informed GW on 29 Oct. that "Mrs Carroll sent me five boxes, and twenty small pots of trees, and young plants; among which were two Shaddocks—One Lemon, and One Orange, of from three to five feet in length; Nine small orange trees; Nine Lemon; One fine balm scented Shrub; Two Potts of Alloes, and some tufts of knotted Marjoram; All which, on the 13th Instant, I saw safely Stowed on board the schooner Surprize, Lawrence Lazore Master, which sailed from hence the same day for Alexandria" (DLC:GW). By the time GW returned from his New England tour, he was prepared to surrender to Mrs. Carroll's generosity. "I am overcome by your goodness," he wrote her on 22 Nov., "and shall submit to your decision with respect to the Plants from your Green-house; but I must again declare that, I should feel infinitely more pain than pleasure from the receipt of them, if I thought that for the purpose of increasing my stock, you had, in the smallest degree, done injury to your own. After this declaration which I make, my good Madam, with the utmost truth & candour, such plants as your kindness may have intended for me, Generl Williams will forward when the Season will permit; which will be as soon, as from the alterations which my New Gardener is making at Mount Vernon, as my Green-House will be in complete order for their reception" (ALS, MWalJFK).

1. GW is referring to his recently employed gardener John Christian Ehlers from Bremen. See GW's contract with Ehlers, 24 June 1789, and GW to Henrich Wilmans, 12 Oct. 1789.

From Benjamin Franklin

Dear Sir,   Philada Sept. 16. 1789

My Malady renders my Sitting up to write rather painful to me, but I cannot let my Son-in-law Mr Bache part for New York, without congratulating you by him on the Recovery of your Health, so precious to us all, and on the growing Strength of our New Government under your Administration.[1] For my own personal Ease, I should have died two Years ago; but tho' those Years have been spent in excruciating Pain, I am pleas'd that I have liv'd them, since they have brought me to see our present Situation. I am now finishing my 84th and probably with it my Career in this Life; but in whatever State of Existence I am plac'd hereafter, if I retain any Memory of what has pass'd here, I shall with it retain the Esteem, Respect, and Affection with which I have long been, my dear Friend, Yours most sincerely

B. Franklin

ALS, DLC:GW. This letter has been widely reproduced in facsimile. GW replied to it on 23 September.

1. Franklin was suffering from a number of ailments, among them gout and "the stone," probably bladder or kidney stones. He died in April 1790. James Madison left a description of a meeting with him "in his extreme age when he had been much exh[a]usted by pain and was particularly sensible of his weakness, Mr M. said he, these machines of ours however admirably formed will not last always. Mine I find is just worn out. It must have been an uncommonly good one I observed to last so long especially under the painful malady which had co-operated with age in preying on it; adding that I could not but hope that he was yet to remain some time with us, and that the cause of his suffering might wear out faster than his Constitution. The only alleviation he said to his pain was opium, and that he found it as yet to be a pretty sure one. I told him I took for granted he used it as sparingly as possible as frequent doses must otherwise impair his constitutional strength. He was well aware he said that every Dose he took had that effect; but he had no other

remedy; and thought the best terms he cd make with his complaint was to give up a part of his remaining life, for the greater ease of the rest" (Madison's "Detached Memoranda," n.d., DLC: Rives Papers). For Franklin's son-in-law Richard Bache, see Bache to GW, 21 April 1789.

From Samuel Meredith

Sir   Philada Sept. 16th 1789
The very flattering marks of your attention to me demand my most grateful acknowledgement, which with the utmost sincerity I now offer you; I am afraid you have viewed my Abilities with too friendly an Eye, but depend upon it whatever they are, they will be exerted to the utmost, and that the strictest integrity and attention to the duties of my office shall in some measure justify your choice—I should have thanked you in person this Evening had not Mr Duer delivered me a letter from the Secy of the Treasury desiring me to asist him in a negotiation with the Bank.[1] Mrs Meredith joins me in respectful Compts to yourself and Mrs Washington. Beleive me to be with great truth Sr Your Most obedient humble Servt

Saml Meredith

ALS, DNA:PCC, item 78.
For Samuel Meredith's application for office and his first appointment as surveyor for the port of Philadelphia, see his letter to GW, 23 Feb. 1789. On 11 Sept. GW appointed him treasurer of the United States.
1. Hamilton wrote Meredith in Philadelphia, 13 Sept., stating that Assistant Secretary of the Treasury William Duer was on his way to Philadelphia to procure a loan from the Bank of North America and requesting Meredith's assistance (Syrett, *Hamilton Papers*, 5:369).

To the United States Senate

United States, 16 September 1789. Nominates Lemuel Wyatt as collector of customs for Reheboth, Massachusetts.

LS, DNA: RG 46, First Congress, Records of Executive Proceedings, President's Messages—Executive Nominations; LB, DLC:GW.
This message was delivered to the Senate by Tobias Lear. Wyatt's appointment was confirmed by the Senate on the same day (*DHFC*, 2:40).

To the United States Senate and House of Representatives

[New York] September 16th 1789.

The governor of the western territory has made a statement to me of the reciprocal hostilities of the wabash Indians, and the people[1] inhabiting the frontiers bordering on the river Ohio, which I herewith lay before Congress.[2]

The United States in Congress assembled by their acts of the 21st day of July 1787, and of the 12th of August 1788 made a provisional arrangement for calling forth the Militia of Virginia and Pennsylvania, in the proportions therein specified.[3]

As the circumstances which occasioned the said arrangement continue nearly the same, I think proper to suggest to your consideration the expediency of making some temporary provision for calling forth the Militia of the United States for the purposes stated in the constitution, which would embrace the cases apprehended by the Governor of the Western Territory.[4]

Go: Washington

LS, DNA: RG 46, First Congress, Records of Legislative Proceedings, President's Messages; copy, DNA: RG 233, First Congress, Records of Legislative Proceedings, Journals.

The documents to both houses of Congress are addressed respectively to "Gentlemen of the Senate" and "Gentlemen of the House of Representatives." They were delivered by Henry Knox (*DHFC*, 1:175, 3:210).

1. In the House document this phrase reads "the White people."
2. See Arthur St. Clair to GW, 14 Sept. 1789.
3. The resolution of 21 July 1787 requested the governor of Virginia to order the Kentucky militia to "hold themselves in readiness to unite with the federal troops in such operations as the Officer commanding them may judge necessary for the protection of the frontiers (*JCC*, 33:386). The resolution of 12 Aug. 1788 requested the executives of both Virginia and Pennsylvania to provide militia—1,000 men from Virginia and 500 from Pennsylvania—to unite with federal troops to protect the frontier. The combined military force was to operate under the direction of the governor of the Northwest Territory (*JCC*, 34:412–13). Under both resolutions the militia was to be paid, supported, and equipped by the respective states.
4. The Senate tabled the message. The House referred it to a committee consisting of Elias Boudinot, Jonathan Trumbull, and Aedanus Burke. Boudinot reported for the committee on 17 Sept. and presented a bill for the establishment "of the troops raised under the resolves of the United States in Congress assembled" (*DHFC*, 1:175–76, 3:210, 212).

Tobias Lear to Henry Knox

United States September 17th 1789. "The enclosed Letter was just now received by the President of the United States from the Governor of New York;[1] and I am directed by the President of the United States to transmit the same to you, requesting that you will, after considering the subject, give him your opinion upon the expediency of his making an official or other communication of the information contained therein to the Congress of the United States."

ADfS, DLC:GW; LB, DLC:GW.
   1. Letter from George Clinton not found.

From Andrew Moore

Sir   New York Sepr 17th 1789
   The judicial Bill now before us requires that a martial should be appointed in each district It is with reluctance I mention a person Who I consider as qualified to discharge the duties of that office And would not have presumd to have thus held up to your view—Had I not been informd that you wisht to be informd of such Characters as might have Pretensions—Colo. Jno. Steel of Virginia I consider as well qualified to fill such an office[1] He has been some time engagd in Studying the Law— And has for some Years been Employd in a Clerks office—I expect he has acquird a sufficient legal knowledge for the Discharge of the duties—Colo. Steel early in the War Was appointed an Ensign in the Ninth Virginia Regiment And Servd to the End He has been high in the Estimation of his Acquaintances—not only in the Army But in private life—should you Consider Colo. Steel As worthy your Attention in this Business—I beg leave to refer you to Colo. Grayson—General Matthews and Genl Muhlenburgh for his Character His present Situation is not so Comfortable as I think his Merits Entitle him to—this Sir Was one reason with me for thus Presenting him to View And I hope will plead my Excuse. I have the Honor to be With respt & Esteem your Mt Obt Sert
                                             Aw Moore

ALS, DLC:GW.

Andrew Moore (1752–1821), a Virginia lawyer, was a member of that state's delegation to the House of Representatives. Moore served during the Revolution in the Continental army and the Virginia militia and from 1785 to 1788 was a member of the Virginia legislature. In 1788 he attended the Virginia Ratifying Convention.

1. John Steele (c.1755–1817) of Augusta County, Va., served in the Augusta militia in 1774 and with other Virginia forces to the end of the Revolution. As a delegate from Nelson County, Ky., he voted against ratification of the Constitution at the Virginia convention. In June 1790 GW appointed Steele a lieutenant in the United States Army. He was, however, elected to the Virginia Council of State in November 1790 and therefore declined the appointment (*DHFC*, 2:73, 131; *Journals of the Council of State of Virginia*, 5:405–6). Steele served on the Virginia council until 1796. In 1798 John Adams appointed him secretary of the Mississippi Territory.

To the United States Senate

Gentlemen of the Senate   [New York] September 17th 1789.

It doubtless is important that all treaties and compacts formed by the United States with other nations whether civilized or not, should be made with caution, and executed with fidelity.

It is said to be the general understanding and practice of nations, as a check on the mistakes and indiscretions of ministers or Commissioners, not to consider any treaty, negociated, and signed by such officers, as final and conclusive untill ratified by the sovereign or government from whom they derive their powers. this practice has been adopted by the United States, respecting their treaties with european nations; and I am inclined to think it would be adviseable to observe it in the conduct of our treaties with the Indians: for tho' such Treaties, being on their part made by their chiefs or rulers, need not be ratified by them, yet being formed on our part by the agency of subordinate officers, it seems to be both prudent and reasonable, that their acts should not be binding on the nation untill approved and ratified by the government. It strikes me that this point should be well considered and settled, so that our national proceedings in this respect may become uniform, and be directed by fixed and stable principles.

The treaties with certain Indian nations, which were laid before you with my message of the 25th May last suggested two questions to my mind—Vizt 1st whether those treaties were to be considered as perfected, and consequently as obligatory, without being ratified, if not, then 2dly whether both, or either and which of them ought to be ratified; on these questions, I request your opinion and advice.

You have indeed advised me "to execute and enjoin an observance of" the treaty with the Wyandots &c. You gentlemen doubtless intended to be clear and explicit and yet without further explanation, I fear I may misunderstand your meaning—for—If by my *executing* that treaty, you mean that I should make it (in a more particular and immediate manner than it now is) the act of Government, then it follows that I am to ratify it. If you mean by my *executing it*, that I am to see that it be carried into effect and operation, then I am led to conclude either that you consider it as being perfect and obligatory in its present state and therefore to be executed and observed, Or that you consider it as to derive its completion and obligation from the silent approbation and ratification which my proclamation may be construed to imply. Altho I am inclined to think that the latter is your intention, yet it certainly is best that all doubts respecting it be removed.

Permit me to observe that it will be proper for me to be informed of your sentiments relativ⟨e⟩ to the treaty with the six nations, previous to the departure of the Governor of the Western Territory, and therefore I recommend it to your early consideration.[1]

Go: Washington

LS, DNA: RG 46, First Congress, Records of Executive Proceedings, President's Messages—Indian Relations. This message was delivered by Henry Knox on 17 Sept. (*DHFC*, 2:40). GW's letter to the Senate involved the president's uncertainty concerning the ratification of the Indian treaties concluded by Arthur St. Clair at Fort Harmar in January 1789. See GW to the United States Senate, 25 May 1789. In considering GW's 25 May message on 8 Sept., the Senate had already resolved that the president "be advised to execute and enjoin an observance" of the Fort Harmar treaty with the "Wyandot, Delaware, Ottawa, Chippawa, Pattawatima and Sac Nations" (*DHFC*, 2:38).

1. GW's message to the Senate was committed to a committee consisting of Charles Carroll, Rufus King, and George Read. The committee reported on 18 Sept. that "the Signature of treaties with the Indian Nations has ever been considered as a full completion thereof, and that such treaties have never been solemnly ratified by either of the contracting Parties as hath been commonly practised among the civilized Nations of Europe, wherefore the Com-

mittee are of opinion that the formal ratification of the Treaty concluded at Fort Harmar on the 9th day of January 1789, between Arthur St. Clair . . . and the Sachems and Warriors of the Wyandot, Delaware, Ottawa, Chippawa, Pattawatima and Sac Nations is not expedient or necessary, and that the Resolve of the Senate of the 8th September 1789 respecting the said treaty, authorises the President of the United States to enjoin a due observance thereof.

"That as to the Treaty made at Fort Harmar on the 9th of January 1789, between the said Arthur St. Clair and the Sachems and Warriors of the Six Nations (except the Mohawks) from particular circumstances affecting a part of the ceded lands the Senate did not judge it expedient to pass any act concerning the same" (ibid., 2:42). On 22 Sept. the Senate confirmed the Fort Harmar treaty with the Wyandot and allied tribes, but "It being suggested" that the treaty with the Six Nations "may be construed to prejudice the claims of the States of Massachusetts and New York and of the Grantees under the said States respectively," consideration of this treaty was postponed to the next session of the Senate (ibid., 2:43).

Letter not found: from Bellegard, 18 Sept. 1789. In a letter of 15 Jan. 1790 to the marquis de Bellegard, GW wrote: "I have received your letter dated the 18th of September 1789."

From Clement Gosselin

Du Lac Champlain petitte Riviere Chazy.
Le 18 7bre 1789

J'offre a votre Excellence La situation peauvre, et triste D'une personne Languissante avec toutte sa famille, Qui ne sauroit Dans Cette Occasion, pouvoir vous assurer de ses Respest. Luy même est obligé, d'avoir Recour a la voies Littéral, pour se Dédommager de Ce quil seroit Charmé De faire Luy même, s'il n'etoit Empéché par La maladie, Qui L'accable Annuellement.

Votre Excellence N'est pas En doute, de Ce que L'etat De nouvelle york nous ont Reçus Comme Citoyens Dans Cette province, et quil nous ont Donnée Charitablement Certaine quantité de Tere pour nous y établir, et Que Tous Les frais tant Que De L'arpentage et Des patentes signé par Le Gouverneur De Cette province seroit payée par nous Refugiers Canadiens.

J'ose Représenter a votre Excellence Qu'une partie des Dittes Terres ont Eté mesurée et payée par nous, aux arpenteur, et, Comme il s'en trouve qui sont occupé par L'ennemis, Cela est

Cause Que nous N'en pouvont pas jouir, Entendue Quil nous En est Empechée par L'Ennemis Commun du Canada.

Nous avont Ensuitte été averti qu'il nous falloit au premier de Novembre prochain, aller Chercher nos patentes Chez le Gouverneur Clinton ou a faute De Quoy si nous n'avions pas De Quoy Les Payer, Que Les Terres Qui nous ont Eté promises Nous seroit ôtée.

J'ose dire Quapres avoir vue De meilleur jour que Cela est Tres sensible faute De moyens, et apres avoir perdue moi même mes Biens Du Canada pour Le soutiens Commun Des Etats, helas je ne Demende pas De si grand Biens Que L'on me Lesse La ou je suis avec seuretée, et Que L'on me Lesse Au moins finir En paix, un Restant De Misérable vie, Que jai Toujour Treinée De puis Que jai Eté Blessé a york town En Virginie.

J'ose prier votre Excellence, Comme Connoissant Quil a pour Les affligée un Coeur Remplié De Charitée, De vouloir Dire un mot a mon Egar Au Gouverneur Clinton votre Excellence Connoit Tres Bien Toutte Les peinnes Que jai Essuyée pendant La Guerre pour Donner Les jntelligences Du Canada avec La plus Grande exactitude et fidelité possible je ne Demande Qu'un peu D'Egar pour ma situation présente.

Pour moi qui est Dans une perpetuelle admiration De vos Bontée, je ne sçai aussi Que Garder Le silence Respectueux si Ce n'est que vous me permettiez de Le Rompre pour vous assurer par trois   fois   trois   De La plus profonde soumission avec Laquel je suis De votre Excellence Votre Tres Humble et Tres obéissant Serviteur

Clement Gosselin

ALS, DNA:PCC, item 78.

During the Revolution a number of Canadians, in response to American circulars and appeals to the local inhabitants for aid, supported the Americans with supplies and important military information. When the Canadian expedition failed, many of these residents accompanied the retreating American army from Canada. Some joined the American forces, often serving in James Livingston's lst Canadian Regiment or, as did Clement Gosselin (1747–1816), in Moses Hazen's 2d Canadian Regiment. During the Canadian campaign Gosselin joined Hazen's regiment with the rank of captain and, in addition to acting as recruiting officer at Ste. Anne de la Pocatière, performed valuable service as a spy. He served with the army until 1783. After the war many of the Canadian expatriates settled with their families in various sections of New

York State. Most were impoverished and all expected recompense for their efforts on behalf of the United States during the war. As early as August 1783 Congress voted subsistence for a number of the Canadians and recommended that they be given citizenship in New York State (*JCC*, 24:496–98). Although a committee, ordered to look into the increasing number of petitions for aid, reported to Congress in June 1784 that the United States was not legally obliged to compensate the Canadians for their losses, it suggested that their services "entitle them to the gratitude and attention of these States and that from motives of humanity as well as policy it is advisable to give them such compensation as will relieve their distress" (ibid., 26:75). In October 1788 a committee reporting to Congress on the state of the War Department noted that "It appears by information from the Secretary at War who has directed the business since the year 1785 that the United States for Several years past have been at a great expence in supporting many Canadian families who had taken refuge within the state of New york when the American troops abandoned Canada in the year 1776. That the remnants of the people of this description were transported in 1786 by order of Congress at the public expence to certain lands on Lake Champlain granted to them by the state of New York and there supported with rations of provisions at the expence of the United States until the first September 1787" (ibid., 34:591–92). By mid–1787 Gosselin had settled on the Lake Champlain lands. For a description of the settlement, see Gosselin and others to Congress, 13 Aug. 1787 (DNA:PCC, item 42). On 23 Dec. GW wrote to Gosselin, mistakenly acknowledging his letter of "7th of September, in which you request my interference or assistance to obtain for you a title to Land ceded by the State of New York to the Canadian Refugees. Notwithstanding it is my sincere wish that all those who suffered losses, or rendered services to the American cause, in the late war, should be suitably recompensed & rewarded—yet my present situation forbids any interference, on my part, with the doings of an individual State, unless called thereto by my official duty; I have therefore directed a copy of your letter to be given to Governor Clinton who is undoubtedly acquainted with the circumstances of the case which you have stated" (copy, DNA: RG 59, Miscellaneous Letters). The 130,000-acre tract intended for Canadian and Nova Scotian refugees, located east of New York State's Old Military Tract, later "reverted to the state by reason of nonoccupation" (Flick, *History of the State of New York*, 5:189). A "Map of the State of New York Showing . . . Land Grants[,] Patents and Purchases" indicating the location of the grant is at the end of Flick, *History*. Gosselin returned to Canada in 1802, but from 1815 until his death he was living in Clinton County, N.Y. (DeMarce, *Canadian Participants in the American Revolution*, 121–22).

Letter not found: from William McWhir, 18 Sept. 1789. On 12 Oct. GW wrote to McWhir: "I have received your letter of the 18 ult."

From James Read

Sir,   Philadelphia, September 18, 1789

I am told by my Friend Colonel Biddle, Marshal of our Court of Admiralty, that he has been well informed that it is probable that the appointment of Clerks in the circuit courts about to be established by Congress will be in your Excellency: I therefore humbly offer myself for that Office in this State, in which I am by seven Years the oldest officer living, having been made Prothonotary of the Supreme Court of the Province September 7th 1745, which Commission I resigned in 1752 on being appointed Prothonotary of the Court of Common Pleas & Clerk of the Peace and to several other Offices in the County of Berks, all which I held till the Declaration of Independence. After the settlement of our Government, on a Constitution established by Convention, a commission from the President in Council for the Prothonotaryship in Berks was sent to me at Reading: But, the People of the County soon after unanimously choosing me one of their Representatives in Assembly, my Office, previous to taking my Seat, became vacant. After some time I was unanimously chosen by them a Member of the Supreme Executive Council where I served the Commonwealth three Years, upon the expiration of which term Council, on the Demise of the Register of the Admiralty, in June 1781, unanimously appointed & commissioned me Register of that Court, which Commission I still hold. The kind People of Berks in 1783 chose me one of the Council of Censors, and in 1787 again a Member of the Supreme Executive, though I had lived, not in Berks, but in this City, from the Year 1781—and I am now in Council. Here I humbly beg Leave to remark that these Elections were without my ever once soliciting a Vote from any Man: And I hope I shall be pardoned if I assure your Excellency, that, though under the late Government I held many respectable Commissions, I never used the Mediation of any Gentleman, having always applied in Person to the Governors, several of them, especially Governors Hamilton and Morris, having, on their coming to the Government, spontaneously declared they heartily wished to do me every Service in their Power and accordingly my every Application was successful. This, Sir, I plead as an Apology for not troubling any Friend to solicit your Excellency, by Letter or otherwise, in my Behalf.

I should, Sir, be ashamed to shew any Anxiety for this Appointment, but that Necessity, nigh to Indigence, to which my Steadiness, *at all times*, in the Cause of America has reduced me, obliges me so to do. My Grandfather and my Father were in high Office in Pennsylvania, and 'tis well known that my Love to my Native Country made me sacrifice a very great Interest I had in England to Living here. I shall here make free to mention that Sir Charles Wager, (to whom I had the Honour to be nearly related), when I was in London, in the Year 1741, *entreated* me to accept and depend on his Help to advance me in the Navy, the Army, the Custom House, or the *Church*, and to make my Home at Parsons Green, his Residence when he was first Lord of the Admiralty, till he should demonstrate his Affection for me.[1]

I must pray your Excellency to interpret in an indulgent manner, an old civil officer's, thus intruding on your precious time, induced to it by a due consideration of having fallen from a pleasant unincumbered Situation into Distress. I am, May it please your Excellency, Your most obedient humble Servant

James Read

ALS, DLC:GW.

James Read (1718–1793) was born in Philadelphia but later moved to Reading. While carrying out clerical duties in local courts he also practiced law in Reading. Clement Biddle recommended Read to GW on 18 Sept. as "a steady friend to his Country . . . his knowledge and Experience in the Business of Clerk or Prothonotary and Register is equal to any one I know and his private Life is highly Examplary" (DLC:GW).

1. Sir Charles Wager (1666–1743) was approaching the end of a long and distinguished career in the British navy when Read stayed at his estate Parson's Green. Wager retired from the admiralty in 1742 and was appointed treasurer of the navy.

From Ann Carter Willis

Fredericksburg Septr 18 1789

Mrs Willis presents her most respectfull compliments to the President an Lady and begs there acceptance of four glasses of

Virgin honey. She has not a doubt of that article being plenty in the state of New York but perhaps not wrought in the same manner and of course not so pure. She flatters her self if it has no other recommendation than being sent by an acquaintance from a place near that of his Nativity they will be induce'd to taste it and will be happy to hear of the welfare of the family and that they have made an agreeable breakfast on it.

AL, DLC:GW.

Ann Carter Willis was the widow of John Champe, Jr. (d. 1775), and the wife of Lewis Willis (1734–1813) of Willis Hill near Fredericksburg. Willis was the son of GW's aunt Mildred Washington (1696–c.1745) and her second husband, Col. Henry Willis (c.1691–1740).

From Hugh Williamson

Sir   New York 19th Septr 1789

I took the Liberty some Time ago to mention a Citizen of North Carolina as a Gentleman who might discharge the Duties of a Judge with Honour to himself and Satisfaction to the Public.

Mr James Iredell, who is Brother in Law to Governour Johnston, is the Gentleman to whom I referred.[1] At the Beginning of the late Revolution he held an Office under the Crown, he resigned it immediately and in Order to cut off the Bridge he accepted of a Judge's Gown in the superiour Court. That Office he quitted after some Time and was afterwards for some Years Attorney for the State. He is in the first Practice as a Lawyer, his Abilities and learning are extensive and he seems generally to be measured as the Standard of Integrity; his private Life is amiable and without Reproach; his Diligence is great and I believe there is not a man in the State who does not think him entitled to any Degree of public Trust.

If you should at any Time be disposed to make farther Enquiries concerning Mr Iredell, he is well known to Major Butler and probably to some other Members of Congress. I have the Honour to be with the utmost Consideration Sir Your most obedt servant

Hu. Williamson

ALS, DLC:GW.

1. No earlier letter from Williamson recommending James Iredell (1751–1799) has been found. Iredell studied law under Samuel Johnston and mar-

ried Johnston's sister Hannah in 1773. A prominent figure in North Carolina legal circles since the early 1770s, Iredell served his state as attorney general from 1779 to 1781. At this time he was a member of the North Carolina Council of State and was currently engaged in producing a revised edition of the state's statutes. A strong supporter of the Constitution, he served in North Carolina's first ratifiying convention and wrote a number of essays supporting the new government. Although he could not be considered for a judicial post until North Carolina ratified, when Robert Hanson Harrison resigned as associate justice of the Supreme Court in 1790, GW chose Iredell for the post because, as he observed in his diary, "in addition to the reputation he sustains for abilities, legal knowledge and respectability of character he is of a State of some importance in the Union that has given *No* character to a federal Office. In ascertaining the character of this Gentlemen I had recourse to every means of information in my power and found them all concurring in his favor" (*Diaries*, 6:28–29). GW wrote to Iredell on 13 Feb. 1790, offering him the post (LB, DLC:GW). Iredell's acceptance, 3 Mar. 1790, is in DNA: RG 59, Miscellaneous Letters.

From Edward Archer

Sir   Virginia—Norfolk September 21st 1789

Although I have not the honor of being personally acquainted with your Excellency I have taken the Liberty of addressing you.

I observe a Bill is now pending before the representatives of the United States for establishing Marine Hospitals for Sick and disabled Seamen and preserving regular levies for the Harbours of the United States.[1]

The State of Virginia is now erecting a Marine Hospital which is far advanced in the completion; I doubt not but our Assembly at their next Session will pass a vote offering it for Continental cases;[2] they have done me the Honor to appoint me a Commissioner, for compleating the same; I am hopefull such a mark of their approbation and confidence will operate in my favour with your Excellency, when I declare myself a Candidate for an appointment in this or any other department under the United-States that you may please to Honor me with.

I have long had it in consideration, to solicit your Excellency for an Appointment, but when I reflected how many worthy Characters there were who fought and bled in our late arduous struggle I could not in justice to my own feelings oppose their pretentions.

To the Virginia delagation in Congress I beg leave to refer your Excellency for such information respecting my character and situation in Life, as you may wish to be inform'd of as to most of them I have the honor of being personally acquainted. I have the honor to be Your most Obt Servt

Edward Archer

ALS, DLC:GW.

There were several Edward Archers living in Norfolk at this time. This is undoubtedly the Edward Archer who served as one of the commissioners for the construction of the marine hospital at Washington, Norfolk County, Virginia.

1. On 20 July 1789 the House of Representatives appointed a committee "to bring in a bill or bills, providing for the establishment of hospitals for sick and disabled seamen, and for the regulation of harbours." The committee, consisting of William Loughton Smith, George Clymer, and Daniel Carroll, brought in a bill on 27 August. After two readings of the bill it was postponed until the next session of Congress (*DHFC*, 3:115, 171, 172, 208–9, 210). Provision for the construction of hospitals for seamen was not finally made until the passage of "An Act for the relief of sick and disabled Seamen" in July 1798 (1 *Stat.* 605–7).

2. "An Act for establishing a marine hospital for the reception of aged and disabled seamen" was passed 20 Dec. 1787 and provided for funds to erect a marine hospital for "aged, sick, and disabled seamen" at Washington, Norfolk County (12 Hening 494–95). The commissioners signed a contract with a Norfolk businessman on 8 May 1788 providing that construction of the hospital would be completed before the end of November 1789 (*Calendar of Virginia State Papers*, 5:130). On 24 Dec. 1790 the legislature passed "An act authorising the sale of the Marine Hospital" authorizing the commissioners appointed to superintend the construction of the hospital "to dispose of the said marine hospital to the Congress of the United States, for the purposes of its original institution." The money realized from the sale was to go for discharging expenses for the construction of the hospital, with any remaining funds to be divided between the towns of Norfolk and Portsmouth to support schools for orphans (13 Hening 158–59).

Letter not found: from Ebenezer Hazard, 21 Sept. 1789. In a letter to Jeremy Belknap, 27 Sept. 1789, Hazard stated that he had written to GW on this date.[1]

1. Hazard copied a long extract of his letter to GW of this date into his letter to Belknap. The extract is printed in note 1 to GW to Hazard, 17 July 1789.

From David Humphreys

My dear General   Rock Landing[1] Septr 21. 1789
I did not trouble you with a letter from Savannah, because our public Dispatch to the Secretary at War would inform you of our proceedings to that time.[2] Besides the oppressive nature of the intollerable heat & the exertion we were obliged to make to get forward on our journey, occasioned such a relaxation & consequent sickness as rendered me almost incapable of writing. We are all now well.

After a fatiguing journey through the deep sands which prevail from Savannah to Augusta, we reachd the latter on the evening of the 17th instant. We intended to remain there one day to make arrangements with the Executive for the Negotiation & to take measures for forwarding our Stores, which were expected at Augusta by water in a few days; but upon receiving information from Messrs Pickens & Osborne that the Indians were growing very impatient to return to their homes & that they could not possibly be detained but a few days longer, we recommenced our journey that evening.[3] The next day the iron axtle tree of our Carriage broke at a great distance from any house, which accident occasioned the loss of the whole day. Being determined to arrive at the Rock-Landing the following evening, according to our last letter to Mr McGillevray,[4] General Lincoln & myself took two of the carriage horses, with a guide, & proceeded twenty five miles that night. Yesterday we reached this place at dark, after having travelled a long distance before we reached the Ogechee, and from the Ogechee to the Oconee (between 30 & 40 miles) through a dreary wilderness, in which there was not a single house. Mr Griffin, with Mr Few & Colo. Franks were to come on as soon as the carriage could be mended, for which arrangements were taken before we left them.[5]

We announced our arrival & readiness to proceed to business to Mr McGillevray last night. He is about three miles on the other side of the Oconee with all the Indians & we have not yet seen him. It is but justice to say, that from every thing which we have yet learned, the former Commissioners have conducted themselves with respect to the present negotiations in a very commendable manner.[6] The Executive have resolved to give us every aid & facility in the business. We have not been here long enough to be assured of the prospects of success, or to know the difficulties that may occur. All we can say is that we shall act with all the zeal & perseverance to promote the public service, which may be in our power. It is a favorable circumstance that the present Commission is certainly very acceptable to the whole State, unless a few Land Jobbers be excepted. It is also pretty well ascertained that McGillevray is desirous of Peace—and his word is a Law to the Creeks—With my best respects to Mrs Washington, love to the Children & Compliments to the Gentlemen of the family I have the honor to be My dear General With the purest attachment & respect Your Most obliged & very humble Servant

D. Humphreys

P.S. The number of Indians I believe, does not amount to more than 2000, notwithstanding the exaggerated accounts we had received.

ALS, DLC:GW.

Humphreys was now serving with Cyrus Griffin and Benjamin Lincoln as a United States commissioner to the southern Indians at the council with the tribes at Rock Landing, Georgia. For background to their appointment, see Henry Knox to GW, 7 and 28 July, GW to Benjamin Lincoln, 11 and 20 Aug., to the U.S. Senate, 20, 21, and 22 Aug., to the Commissioners to the Southern Indians, 29 Aug., and Proclamation to the Southern Indians, 29 Aug. 1789.

1. Rock Landing, a frequent location for Indian councils, was on the Georgia frontier between the Oconee and Ogeechee rivers.

2. Humphreys is referring to the commissioners' letter of 12 Sept. to Henry Knox, describing their arrival at Savannah and their preparations to continue their journey (*ASP, Indian Affairs*, 1:69).

3. The letter from Andrew Pickens and Henry Osborne, dated 16 Sept., is in ibid., 71.

4. Alarmed at the possibility of the Indians' leaving the council site before the Americans' arrival, the commisioners wrote the Creek chief Alexander McGillivray on 18 Sept.: "We left New York eighteen days ago, invested with full powers, from the Supreme Executive of the United States of America, to conclude a treaty of peace and amity with the Creek nation of Indians. For the accomplishment of an object of so much importance, we have pressed our journey with uncommon expedition. We arrived here last evening, and, after making the necessary arrangements for our luggage to follow, we propose departing from this place for the Rock Landing this afternoon.

"Being this moment greatly astonished by information from Messrs. Pickens and Osborne, that the Indians would certainly disperse, unless we should arrive within three days after the very day which was originally appointed for the meeting, we shall accelerate our journey as much as possible. We therefore send an express with this letter, to let you know that we shall be at the Rock Landing the day after to-morrow, and to assure you, that, if a lasting peace and friendship shall not be established, between the United States and the Creeks, it will not be owing to the want of the best dispositions on the part of the former" (ibid.).

5. Sen. William Few of Georgia accompanied the party, noting in a later description of his career that "I felt so much interested in the success of those measures that I determined to accompany the commissioners." Few sailed with the commissioners from New York (Few, "Autobiography," 354). For Few's account of the mission, see ibid., 353–54. For an identification of David Salisbury Franks, see his letter to GW, 12 May 1789, source note.

6. Humphreys is referring to Andrew Pickens and Henry Osborne who had carried on negotiations with the Creek earlier in the summer. See their letter to GW, 30 June 1789, and notes.

From William Smith

Sir   College of Philadelphia, Septr 21st 1789

From an Acquaintance and an occasional Correspondence wch I had the Honor & Happiness to commence with You more than *thirty* years ago, & from the indulgent Notice which you have been pleased to take of me, both in my public & private Capacity, on various Occasions since that Time,[1] I am induced to enclose to you my "Proposals for Printing a Body of *Sermons* upon the most important Branches of *Practical Christianity*"—a Subject & a Work, which I well know, stand in No Need of Recommendation to your Protection & Encouragment.[2]

If you will please to peruse the Preface & Titles to the Sermons, and the public Recommendation annex'd to them, by the late *General Convention* of our Church at Philadelphia,[3] and also of the Clergy of all Denominations in this City, as Subscribers, I trust you will permit me to solicit the Honour of your Name and Mrs Washington's next after the printed List of Clerical Subscribers, & before any Application to Members of Congress or others at New York, shall be made.

I have enclosed a Copy of the Proposals to the honble Robt Morris Esqr. of the Senate, and have requested Him to solicit your Name & Mrs Washington's, if you should think proper so far to honor the Work, before he presents it to such Members of the Senate as may be inclined to subscribe—I am, with the most

profound Respect & involable Regard, Worthy and illustrious
Sir, Your most obedient & much obliged humble Servant

William Smith

ALS, DNA:PCC, item 78.

William Smith (1727–1803) was educated at the University of Aberdeen,
Scotland, and came to America in 1751 as tutor to a New York family. In 1753,
largely through the efforts of Benjamin Franklin and Richard Peters, who
were impressed by one of Smith's early pamphlets, he was invited to teach at
what was soon to become the College, Academy, and Charitable School of
Philadelphia. Before beginning his teaching he returned to England to be
ordained in the Episcopal church. By the time the American Revolution broke
out, Smith was one of the colony's most prominent clergymen and educators
and was considerably involved in politics. His support of the Patriot cause was
considered lukewarm in some quarters, and in 1779 he was removed from his
teaching post. He transferred his activities to Chestertown, Md., where he
became rector of Chester Parish and established Kent School. The school was
chartered in 1782 as Washington College, with Smith serving as president. In
March 1789 the college at Philadelphia was reorganized, and Smith resumed
his position in July of that year.

1. As early as 1757 GW had agreed to Smith's request to send him information concerning the French and Indian War and was a subscriber to Smith's
American Magazine or Monthly Chronicle for the British Colonies. See Smith to GW,
10 Nov. 1757. In November 1780, in his capacity as secretary of the American
Philosophical Society, Smith had sent GW his certificate of membership in the
society (Smith to GW, 1 Nov., GW to Smith, 15 Nov. 1780, DLC:GW), and in
1782 the two had exchanged letters concerning Washington College (GW to
Smith, 18 Aug., Smith to GW, 23 Dec. 1782, all in DLC:GW).

2. A copy of the proposal, advocating publication of Smith's sermons and
listing over a hundred of them by name, is in DNA:PCC, item 78. The proposal was published in Philadelphia in 1789 by Benjamin Franklin Bache.

3. Delegates from the clergy and laity of the Protestant Episcopal church
in New York, New Jersey, Pennsylvania, Delaware, Maryland, Virginia, and
South Carolina met in convention in Philadelphia on 29 July 1789. The convention held sessions through early August.

To David Stuart

Dear Sir,   New York Septr 21st 1789

Your letter of the 12th instt came duly to hand. I have given
the subject of it every consideration that time and my situation
would enable me to do. The result is—that if Mr Alexander—
upon your re-conveying of the Land for which the price, &
mode of payment is disputed—and paying rent for it during the

time it has been out of his possession (the latter to be fixed by Men of judgment and impartiality) is disposed to accomodate the Suit which is pending between you—as Administrator of John Parke Custis Esqr. deceased—and himself, that it would, all circumstances considered, be most advisable to accede to it. My reasons for this opinion are many. It is unnecessary I conceive to detail them if I had leisure, which in truth is not the case. I am—Dear Sir Your Most Obedt Hble Servt

Go: Washington

My opinion coincides with the above, and I advise the adoption of the measure accordingly.[1]

Martha Washington

ALS, ViMtV; LB, DLC:GW.

The covering letter for this document, in the writing of Tobias Lear and signed by GW, reads: "I am, at this moment, so much engaged that I have only time to enclose the sentiments which you requested, and to tell you that I am, with great esteem, Your most Obedt Servt" (LS, ViU).

1. The postscript and signature are in the writing of Martha Washington.

From William Grayson

Sir.   New York 22nd Sepr 1789
I do myself the honor to inform you that the Honble John Tyler & Mr [   ] Henry Judges of the late Court of Admy in Virga have signified their desire of serving in the capacity of district Judge of that State.[1]

Mr Innis Atto. Genl of the State of Virga has also expressed his inclination of serving as Atto. general of the district Court; I should also presume that the Office of Atto. general of the supreme Court would not be disagreable. I am with the highest respect Yr Most Obedt & Very Hble Serv.

Will'n Grayson

ALS, DLC:GW.

1. John Tyler (1747–1813) played a prominent part in Virginia's legal and political circles during the Revolution. Both during and after the war he worked closely with Patrick Henry, collaborating with him in opposing the Constitution in the Virginia Ratifying Convention. Tyler received no federal judicial appointment in 1789, but he was appointed by the state a member of the Virginia General Court. An ardent Republican during the 1790s, he

served as governor of Virginia from 1808 to 1811. Tyler was the father of President John Tyler. James Henry of King and Queen County was serving in the Virginia legislature when he resigned during the summer of 1782 to become a judge of the Court of Admiralty.

To Benjamin Franklin

Dear Sir,   New York Septr 23d 1789.

The affectionate congratulations on the recovery of my health—and the warm expressions of personal friendship which were contained in your favor of the 16th instt,[1] claim my gratitude. And the consideration that it was written when you were afflicted with a painful malady, greatly increases my obligation for it.

Would to God, my dear Sir, that I could congratulate you upon the removal of that excruciating pain under which you labour! and that your existence might close with as much ease to yourself, as its continuance has been beneficial to our Country & useful to Mankind—or, if the united wishes of a free people, joined with the earnest prayers of every friend to science & humanity could relieve the body from pains or infirmities, you could claim an exemption on this score. But this cannot be, and you have within yourself the only resource to which we can confidently apply for relief—a philosophic mind.

If to be venerated for benevolence—if to be admired for talent—if to be esteemed for patriotism—if to be beloved for philanthropy can gratify the human mind, you must have the pleasing consolation to know that you have not lived in vain; and I flatter my self that it will not be ranked among the least grateful occurrences of your life to be assured that so long as I retain my memory—you will be thought on with respect, veneration and affection by Dear Sir Your sincere friend and obedient Hble Servant

Go: Washington

ALS, PPAmP: Benjamin Franklin Papers; LB, DLC:GW; copy, DNA: RG 59, Miscellaneous Letters.

1. At this point the words "handed to me by your son-in-law Mr Bache" have been written and crossed out.

To James Madison

[New York, c.23 September 1789][1]

My solicitude for drawing the first characters of the Union into the Judiciary,[2] is such that, my cogitations on this subject last night (after I parted with you) have almost determined me (as well for the reason just mentioned, as to silence the clamours, or more properly, *soften* the disappointment of smaller characters[)]—to nominate Mr Blair and Colo. Pendleton as Associate & District Judges. And Mr E. Randolph for the Attorney General trusting to their acceptance. Mr Randolph, in this character, I would prefer to any person I am acquainted of not superior abilities, from habits of intimacy with him.[3]

Mr Pendleton could not I fear discharge, and in that case I am sure would not undertake, to execute the duties of an Associate under the present form of the Act.[4] But he may be able to fulfil those of the District—The Salary I believe is greater than what he now has; and he would *see* or it might be *explained* to him, the reason of his being prefered to the District Court rather than to the Supreme Bench; though I have no objection to nominating him to the latter, if it is conceived that his health is competent, and his mental faculties unimpaired, by age.

His acceptance of the first would depend in a great measure, I presume, upon the light in which the District Judges are considered—that is, whether superior in Rank to any State Judges.

I am very troublesome, but you must excuse me. Ascribe it to friendship and confidence, and you will do justice to my motives. Remember the Attorney and Marshall for Kentucky, and forget not to give their Christian names. Yours ever

G.W.

ALS, DLC: James Madison Papers.

1. This letter is undated, but Madison, at some later time, wrote "Without date—but it may be inferred from contents—1789–90." The date has been assigned because GW received the Judiciary bill from Congress on 22 Sept. and made his nominations of John Blair, Pendleton, and of George Nicholas and Samuel McDowell, Jr., the attorney and marshal for Kentucky, on 24 September.

2. For background to GW's judicial appointments, see his letter to the Senate, 24 Sept. 1789, source note.

3. In the MS this sentence appears as a note to the letter.
4. See GW to Pendleton, 28 Sept., and to Edmund Randolph, 30 Nov. 1789.

From John Page

Sir   New York Sepr the 23d 1789

That I may not obtrude on you & to the Interruption of other Applicants, I again have Recourse to this Mode of Application in behalf of Gentlemen who wish to be recommended to you for Appointments. The inclosed Letter was left by Mr Andrews with a Friend the Day he set out on his Return to Virginia.[1] I hope you will excuse my troubling you with it as I shall only add respecting him that I think his Knowledge of the Law, as a Justice of James City for several Years & as high Sheriff two Years added to his Study of Law, & his extensive genius leave no doubt with me that he is qualified for the office he solicits. In Justice however to Mr St G. Tucker one of our Judges & to the Gentn whom he recommends I must add that Mr Wm Nelson a Pratitioner of the Law in the General Court for some Years past is warmly recommended by him, & I am requested by Mr Tucker to nominate that Gentleman to you as a proper Person for the same Office[.][2] I am very sorry to be so troublesome, but your Goodness will pardon me I have the Honor to be with the highest Respect & Gratitude your much obliged & most obedient humble Servant

                                              John Page

ALS, DLC:GW.

1. Robert Andrews (c.1747–1804) graduated from the College of Philadelphia and moved from Pennsylvania to Virginia around 1770. For a time he served as tutor to John Page's children. He left Virginia for England in 1772 and was ordained there as a minister in the Anglican church. In 1777 he was appointed by the College of William and Mary as professor of moral and intellectual philosophy. During the war he was a member of the Williamsburg committee of safety and served as chaplain with Virginia forces. In 1784 Andrews was transferred to the chair of mathematics at the College of William and Mary. He attended the Virginia Ratifying Convention in 1788 and during the 1780s was heavily involved in the Dismal Swamp Company. From 1790 to 1799 he represented James City County in the Virginia general assembly. Andrews's letter to Page, 2 Mar. 1789, pointing out his qualifications and request-

ing Page's support for his appointment to the Virginia district court, is in DLC:GW.

2. William Nelson (1754–1813), the son of William and Elizabeth Burwell Nelson, was educated at the College of William and Mary. During the Revolution he rose from the rank of private to lieutenant colonel and served as a member of the Virginia executive council in 1783. No letter of recommendation from St. George Tucker has been found. Nelson was not among GW's first appointments to judicial offices, but on 30 Nov. 1789 the president wrote to him offering the position of attorney for the Virginia district, left vacant by John Marshall's refusal to accept the post (DLC:GW). Nelson wrote a letter of acceptance on 20 Dec. and sent a second letter on 2 Mar. 1790, acknowledging receipt of his commission and explaining the delays involved in its delivery. Both of these letters are in DNA: RG 59, Acceptances and Orders for Commissions.

To Thomas Smith

Sir,   New York, September 23rd 1789.

I have to acknowledge the receipt of your letter of the 24 of July, enclosing a general statement of the monies received for, and paid to my order—and likewise the receipt of a letter from you of the 19th of April last, which has not been acknowledged.[1]

It is unnecessary for me to repeat to you the satisfaction which you have given me in conducting the business that was committed to your hands—as a proof of it I must request your further attention to the recovery of the enclosed bond given by John Stephenson, and Hugh Stephenson on the 22 of August 1765 for seventy pounds ten shillings virginia currency.[2]

I likewise enclose a statement of an account, which relates to the said bond—Colonel John Stephenson, the principal in the bond, lives in Fayette County State of Pennsylvania, and is undoubtedly known to you.

The repeated applications which have been made to Colonel Stephenson for the payment of the bond—and the more than repeated assurances which he has given that he would immediately discharge it, render any further delay not only unnecessary, but improper—and, therefore, if he neglects to pay it upon application, you will not rely upon promises, but put the bond in suit.

Colonel Cannon of Washington county whom I have employed to superintend my property there, and in Fayette was recommended to me as a very active, attentive, and *punctual* man. I wish I could say, from experience, that I have found him so—but it is the reverse—It is now almost three years since he was empowered to take care of my property and collect my rents in that country—during which time I have repeatedly written to him, not only by the post, but by opportunities that must have conveyed the letters to his hands—and so far have I been from receiving regular answers to them, that, I think, I have only had two letters from him since he has conducted my business—the last of which was handed to me in the past winter, in which he mentioned the terms on which he had leased my lands—but I have never heard from him since, or ever received the remittance of one shilling for my rents[3]—I will therefore thank you, Sir, when you are in that part of the country to make some enquiries of Colonel Cannon, relative to the state of my property under his care—and remind him of the necessity there is of his being more frequent in his communications to me, and more punctual in the remittance of my rents.[4] I have enclosed a letter to him, which I will thank you to deliver when you have an opportunity. I am Sir &ca

G. Washington

LB, DLC:GW.

   1. Neither of these letters has been found.

   2. For information on this legal entanglement, see GW to John Stephenson, 13 Feb. 1784, n. 2. By 1783 interest on the original £70.10 owed to GW by the estate of Richard Stephenson had increased the sum to £136.12.11. By 1786 payments by Stephenson's heirs had decreased the sum to £60.6.9 (account with the estate of Richard Stephenson, 22 Aug. 1765–March 1791, NhD). Smith replied to GW's letter on 20 Oct. 1789, stating that he had applied for a writ against John Stephenson and directed the sheriff of Fayette County to serve it at once since Stephenson was reported to be moving to Kentucky.

   3. See GW's letters to John Cannon, 22 Mar. 1789 and 24 Sept. 1789.

   4. For Smith's comments on Cannon, see his letter to GW, 20 Oct. 1789.

From Isaac Stephens

Sirs   Algirs Septr the 23d 1789

   You are not unacquanted of our Long Continueance in a State of Slavery for about four years and more although you Cannot feel for us to Redeem us But have So Much as to allow us a Comfortable Support Whilst we Due Live on the Earth the 13th of September 1789 arrived a Spanish Courier from Spain on the 14th Ditto I wated on the Spanish Consul to Know if any Letters had Com for us americans he Told Me none But Said that he Could not advance any more money to us americans as Mr Carmicheal Could Not pay the money he had advanced for Two years past about 16 hundred Dollars When the Courier Saild from this about Six week ago he wrote to his Banker to Draw the Money and Mr Carmicheal told him that he had Not Received any Support or money for about Two years past and he Could not pay it the Bill was protested and on that account the Consul Said that he Could not advance any more to us as he Could not get his pay it has made a Table talk among all the Consuls in algirs.

We must Suffer greatly for the want of it and be obliged to put up with Many insults and Not only the Charatcer of the grand foederal States Does Suffer greatly I hope this will have a Deep Empression on your minds and give us Speedy Releaf and a Speedy Redemption although it Cannot be Speedy after four years Slavary—Take pattern by the infidels the Empereor of moroco has freed all the mooro Slaves all over Christianity the Spaniard have made three Redeemptions Since We have bin here the first 4 hundred the Next 30 the other Day 14 all taken at Sea the Nepollitens about Two hundred your Souls Cannot Spair the money from your most obedent and humble Servent
Isaac Stephens Slave

My wife wrote me that She was obliged to put hur Children out for their Liveing and hur Self obliged to Work hard for hur bread that is your Liberty in Sweet america I put Confidence in general Washington that he with the help of god may Turn your hard hearts in america for our Redemption Before a Nother year.

ALS, DNA:PCC, item 78. The envelope accompanying this letter is addressed "To His Excellency George Washington Esqr. President of the Continental Congress." At the heading of the document is the address "To the Honorable Continental Congress."

For background to this letter, see Mathew Irwin to GW, 9 July 1789, source note. Stephens was the captain of the *Maria* out of Philadelphia, which was captured by Algerian corsairs in July 1785.

To John Cannon

Sir,   New York, September 24th 1789.

Sometime last winter I received a letter from you by the hands of Major McCormack, giving me a statement of the situation of my lands under your care in the Counties of Washington and Fayette, with the names of the persons to whom they were leased and the terms on which they held them.[1]

You likewise informed me that the Tenants would pay the rents in wheat at your mill, which you would turn to the best advantage for me—In consequence of these arrangements I expected to have received remittances from you before this time, or, at least to have heard from you, in both of which I have been disappointed—you will therefore, Sir, not think it strange that I should express my surprise at your conduct in this respect—and more especially as I was induced to put this business into your hands from the favorable information which I received of your punctuality and attention.[2]

I think I have received but two letters from you since I empowered you to act for me in that country, which is now almost three years—opportunities certainly have not been wanting—for the post affords them from Pittsburg, if private ones should not offer—and I have repeatedly written to you requesting information relative to my property under your care.

Mr Smith will do me the favor to hand this to you, and will be so good as to take charge of, and convey to me any communications you may have to make—and I trust, in future, I shall not have cause to complain of your want of attention in writing.

Any remittances you may have to make can be sent either to me here, or to my nephew Major George Aug. Washington at Mount Vernon as opportunities may make it convenient. I am Sir, your most obedient Servant

                                              G. Washington

LB, DLC:GW.

1. This was John Cannon's letter to GW of 29 Jan. 1789 which has not been found. GW acknowledged receipt of it on 22 March.

2. For GW's difficulties with Cannon's services as land agent, see his letter to Cannon, 26 Dec. 1788, source note.

To Constant Freeman

Sir, New York, September 24th 1789.
Your letter of the 9th of July has been received[1] and, agreeable to your desire, I embrace the opportunity, by the return of Mr Brown to the western country,[2] to inform you that the letter, account &ca, relative to my business in Red-stone came safe to my hands. I am Sir, your most obedient servant

G. Washington

LB, DLC:GW.

Constant Freeman (1757–c.1824) was born in Charlestown, Mass., and served during the Revolution as a lieutenant in Stevens' battalion of Continental artillery in 1776 and as a captain-lieutenant in the artillery from 1778 to 1783. In March 1791 Freeman was appointed a captain in the Second United States Regiment and in July 1793 was made an agent for the War Department to supervise federal military affairs in Georgia, a post he held until 1794. In February 1795 he was promoted to major and in 1802 to lieutenant colonel in the corps of artillerists and engineers.

1. Letter not found.
2. John Brown, United States congressman from the Kentucky district of Virginia, was preparing to return to Kentucky after the adjournment of the first session of Congress on 29 September.

From William Littlefield

Sir Newport [R.I.] 24th Sepr 1789.
I am unacquainted with the mode pursued by Gentlemen of the other States, when they have applied for Offices; therefore hope the President will excuse the Liberty which I've taken in addressing him in this manner; nor should I have presumed so far on the subject had Our present Revenue Officers been such as were approved of by the better sort of people. They took no part in the late Revolution, nor have they been friendly to Federal measures.

If the Contrary Character has any Claim for the Collectors Office in this Town when we Join the Union; would beg leave to Observe; that I served my Country upwards of five years in the Continental line of the Army part of which time was in General Greenes family, and in Matters of business was fortunate enough to have some small share of his confidence—When he went to the Southward left a General Power of Atto. with me to conduct his business here; and his last will was deposited in my hands. I must beg leave Sir to trouble you One moment longer by observing that Indisposition alone obliged me to apply for a discharge from the Army. That altho' I obtained an honorable one, yet forfeited all Claim on the Public for Commutation &c. and that the Notes which I hold against the Treasurer of this State for depreciation of Wages, are forfeited by the Laws of Our present administration.[1]

As I was young in the Line of the Army, perhaps the President may not recollect me, will therefore beg leave to refer him to General Knox, Colo. Wadsworth and my Sister Mrs Greene respecting my Character. I have the Honor to be with Great respect your most Obdt and Very Humble Servant

Wm Littlefield

ALS, DLC:GW. Littlefield's letter to GW was delivered by Henry Knox (Knox to Littlefield, 22 Oct. 1789, MHi: Knox Papers).

William Littlefield (1753–1822), a native of Block Island, R.I., was the younger brother of Catharine Greene, widow of Maj. Gen. Nathanael Greene. Littlefield had served with Varnum's Rhode Island brigade during the early years of the Revolution and in 1779 had become an aide to his brother-in-law. He resigned on 20 June 1780 and returned to Block Island where he fell under suspicion of trading with the enemy although he was later exonerated (Bartlett, *R.I. Records*, 10:45). In 1785 and 1792 he represented Block Island in the Rhode Island legislature. Littlefield received no post in the civil service and later in the 1790s apparently moved to Tennessee.

1. In support of Littlefield's application of office, Jeremiah Wadsworth wrote GW on 15 June 1790, that "I am requested by Captn William Littlefield and his friends to Name him to You as a proper person to be appointed Marshall for the district of Rhode Island. I should not have complied with their request if I had a shadow of doubt of Mr Littlefields fitness for the office" (DLC:GW). Catharine Greene solicited the post of loan officer for Rhode Island for her brother in a letter to GW of 6 Aug. 1790: "Pardon the liberty I take in presuming to address one for whom I have the highest possible respect, and to whom I feel the most perfect homage.

"I have had it on my mind for some time Sir to solicit a favor of you—but timidity has hitherto forbit it. Nor should I have courage to do it now but from the honor of seeing myself and five children reduced to the most humiliating distresses.

"Perhaps Sir you may not be acquainted with the situation of Genl Greenes affairs nor will I presume to take up more of your time than first to tell you that the Laws under the present Government together with Congresses having deferd my memorial places me entirely in the power of my creditors, who are about to seize my Estate—in which case I shall have no possible means of educating my children or of supporting myself.

"My brother Captain Littlefield is the only person whom I could submit to pecuniary obligations his heart is devoted to me and my children, but alas Sir, that heart has been too honorable for his own, or our independe⟨nce⟩.

"The paper money Law of the state in which he lives has impaired his fortune which tho small was sufficient to have allowed some assistance to me, without Embarrassment to himself—but under the present circumstances it would be impossible for me to share with his children, what is bearly sufficient for them. but what his generosity would compell me to do.

"If Sir you should see proper to bestow upon him some office, that of Loan officer, or any other, you see fit, you will sir not only serve an honest and upright man—but preserve from the severest mortification, and perhaps real distress the widow and orphans of a general who by doing more than his du⟨ty⟩ to his country has ruined his family.

"My Partiallity for my Brother may make me see his merits through a false medium but Col. Wadsworth and many other of my respectable friends who know him have the same opinion of his talents and integrity, else I should not dare petition you Sir on this subject.

"Most humbly do I pray you to pardon me Sir for the liberty I have taken and permit me the honor of subscribing myself your most devoted servant" (DLC:GW).

To the United States Senate

United States
Gentlemen of the Senate,   September 24th 1789
    I nominate for the Supreme-Court of the United States
        John Jay of New York, Chief-Justice
        John Rutledge, of South Carolina,
        James Wilson, of Pennsylvania,   Associate
        William Cushing, of Massachusetts,   Judges
        Robert H. Harrison, of Maryland,
        John Blair, of Virginia,
I also nominate for District Judges, Attornies, and Marshalls, the Persons whose names are below and annexed to the Districts respectively—viz.

Districts	Judges	Attornies	Marshalls
Main	David Sewell	William Lithgow	Henry Dearbourn
New-Hampshire	John Sullivan	Saml Sherburne junior	John Parker
Massachusetts	John Lowell	Christopher Gore	Jonathan Jackson

Connecticut	Richard Law	Pierpoint Edwards	Philip Bradley
Pennsylvania	Francis Hopkinson	William Lewis	Clement Biddle
Delaware	Gunning Bedford	George Read junior	Allan McLean
Maryland	Thomas Johnson	Richd Potts	Nathaniel Ramsay
Virginia	Edmund Pendleton	John Marshall	Edward Carrington
South Carolina	Thomas Pinckney	John Julius Pringle	Isaac Huger
Georgia	Nathaniel Pendleton	Mathew McAllister	Robert Forsyth
Kentuckey	Harry Innes	George Nicholas	Samuel McDowell junr

Go: Washington

LS, DNA: RG 46, President's Messages—Executive Nominations; LB, DLC:GW. Except for two first names inserted by Tobias Lear, the body of this document is in the writing of William Jackson.

GW's letter and its enclosed nominations were delivered to the Senate by Tobias Lear on 24 September. On 26 Sept. the Senate confirmed all of the nominations (*DHFC*, 2:43–48).

Appointments to the Judiciary were among the most sensitive of GW's problems in staffing the new government's civil service. The provisions of the Constitution providing for the federal Judiciary had evoked considerable criticism from the beginning. As Joseph Jones wrote Madison in the fall of 1787, there would have been less "repugnance" to the Constitution in Virginia "had the judiciary been less exceptionable" and warned of the variety of objections "which are and may be raised agt. the Judiciary arrangement and the undefined powers of that department. . . . The legislature may and will probably make proper and wise regulations in the Judiciary. . . . But the reflection that there exists in the constitution a power that may oppress makes the mind uneasy and that oppression may and will result from the appelate power of unsetling facts does to me appear beyond a doubt" (Jones to Madison, 22 Nov. 1787, 29 Oct. 1787, in Rutland, *Madison Papers*, 10:255–57, 227–29).

On 7 April 1789 Congress appointed a committee for the organization of the federal Judiciary, consisting of Oliver Ellsworth, Richard Henry Lee, Caleb Strong, William Maclay, William Paterson, William Few, Richard Bassett, and Paine Wingate, and on 13 April Charles Carroll and Ralph Izard were added, insuring that each state would be represented (*DHFC*, 1:11, 14). The committee, led by Ellsworth, Paterson, and Strong, labored for the next two months, attempting to reconcile the differences among the committee members. They quietly buried such antifederalist proposals as designating the state courts to act as inferior federal courts. Following a suggestion made by Hamilton in Federalist 81, they tried to quiet the fears of those who maintained the federal court system would cancel that of the states by arranging a system that largely followed the geographical boundaries of the states. Much of the debate centered on the establishment of the federal district courts which were thought by many to offer a direct threat to the state court system. The committee had sought opinions and advice from many of the new nation's leading lawyers and jurists, and by the time the committee finally brought in a bill on 12 June, most of its provisions were already well known. See Goebel, *History of the Supreme Court*, 479, n.59, 490–94. As Edmund Pendleton warned: "This department is the Sore part of the Constitution & requires the lenient touch of Congress. To quiet the fears of the Citizens of being drag'd large distances from home, to defend a suit for a small sum, which they had better pay however unjust, than defend with success, is as worthy of attention, as to provide for the speedy Admon. of Justice to honest Creditors" (Pendleton to Madison, 3 July 1789, in Rutland, *Madison Papers*, 17:537–39). After considerable and often acrimonious debate for much of the summer, the bill finally went to GW for his signature in September. For a detailed account of the bill's legal implications and its thorny path through both houses, see Goebel, *History of the Supreme Court*, 457–508; Warren, "History of the Federal Judiciary Act of 1789."

The passage of the Judiciary Act did little to quell the controversy. Sen. William Grayson spoke for many opponents when he stated that the act "wears so monstrous an appearance that I think it will be *felo-de-se* in the execution. . . . Whenever the Federal judiciary comes into operation, I think the pride of the States will take the alarm, which, added to the difficulty of attendance, from the extent of the district in many cases, the ridiculous situation of the venue and a thousand other circumstances, will in the end procure its destruction. The salaries, I think, are rather high for the temper or circumstances of the Union, and furnish another cause of discontent to those who are dissatisfied with the government" (Grayson to Patrick Henry, 29 Sept. 1789, in Tyler, *Letters and Times of the Tylers*, 1:169–71).

"An Act to establish the Judicial Courts of the United States," divided the country into thirteen districts, each presided over by a district judge, and holding four annual sessions. The act also provided for the districts to be divided into three circuits, with two courts to be held annually in each circuit, presided over by two justices of the Supreme Court, riding circuit, and one of the district judges. The district courts were given original jurisdiction in "all crimes and offences that shall be cognizable under the authority of the United States, committed within their respective districts, or upon the high seas" where the punishment was limited and the fine did not exceed $100, and in maritime and seizure cases. The circuit courts had original jurisdiction in cases where the matter in dispute exceeded $500, and "the United States are plaintiffs, or petitioners; or an alien is a party, or the suit is between a citizen of the State where the suit is brought, and a citizen of another State." Exclusive jurisdiction belonged to the courts in all crimes cognizable under the laws of the United States. The circuit courts were also given appellate jurisdiction in cases from the district courts. The Supreme Court had exclusive jurisdiction in "all controversies of a civil nature, where a state is a party, except between a state and its citizens; and except also between a state and citizens of other states, or aliens, in which latter case it shall have original but not exclusive jurisdiction." Article 27 of the Judiciary Act provided for the appointment of a marshal for each district for a term of four years, removable at pleasure, to attend the circuit and district courts, and carry out all orders directed to him. A United States attorney was to be appointed for each of the districts "whose duty it shall be to prosecute in such district all delinquents for crimes and offences, cognizable under the authority of the United States, and all civil actions in which the United States shall be concerned, except before the supreme court in the district in which that court shall be be holden." The act further provided for a person "learned in the law" to act as attorney of the United States, who would prosecute all cases brought before the Supreme Court in which the United States was involved, "and to give his advice and opinion upon questions of law when required by the President of the United States, or when requested by the heads of any of the departments" (1 *Stat.* [24 Sept. 1789] 73–93). A supplementary statute, "An Act to regulate Processes in the Courts of the United States," (1 *Stat.* 93–94), was passed on 29 September.

The nominations for the Supreme Court justices and for most of the district court judges and marshals were delivered to the Senate on 24 Sept. by Tobias Lear, and on 25 Sept. Lear brought it the remaining court appointments—those for New York and New Jersey. See GW to the U.S. Senate, 25 Sept. 1789. By 26 Sept. the Senate had confirmed all of the nominations (*DHFC*, 2:43–50). GW indicated in his diary on 5 Oct. that he "dispatched the Commissions to all the Judges of the Supreme and District Courts; & to the Marshalls and Attorneys and accompanied them with all the Acts respecting the Judiciary Department" (*Diaries*, 5:452). The commissions for the appointees under the Judiciary Act were similar to Jay's commission for chief justice: "Know Ye, That reposing special Trust and Confidence in the Wisdom, Uprightness, and Learning of *John Jay* of *New York*, Esquire, I have nominated, and by and with the Advice and Consent of the Senate, do appoint him Chief Justice of the Supreme Court of the United States, and do authorize and empower him to execute and fulfil the Duties of that Office according to the Constitution and Laws of the said United States; and to have and to hold the said Office, with all the Powers Privileges, and Emoluments to the same of Right appertaining, unto him the said John Jay during his good Behaviour.

"In Testimony whereof I have caused these Letters to be made Patent, and the Seal of the United States to be hereunto affixed.

"Given under my Hand the twenty sixth Day of September, in the Year of our Lord one thousand seven hundred and Eighty nine. George Washington" (copy, DNA: RG 59, Miscellaneous Letters).

Among the appointments for staffing the civil service of the new government, GW considered those of the Judiciary—"that department which must be considered as the Key-Stone of our political fabric"—the most important (GW to John Jay, 5 Oct. 1789). As he informed the new judicial appointees, he regarded "the Judicial System as the chief-Pillar upon which our national Government must rest, I have thought it my duty to nominate, for the high Offices in that Department, such men as I conceived would give dignity and lustre to our national character" (GW to William Cushing, 30 Sept. 1789). In making his judicial appointments it was necessary for him "to consider the necessity of giving a tone to the system in its' out-set, by placing the administration of the laws with the best and wisest of our Citizens" (GW to Pendleton,

28 Sept. 1789). Further, "in appointing persons to office, & more especially in the Judicial Department, my views have been much guided to those Characters who have been conspicuous in their Country; not only from an impression of their services, but upon a consideration that they had been tried, & that a readier confidence would be placed in them by the public than in others, perhaps of equal merit, who had never been proved" (GW to William Fitzhugh, 24 Dec. 1789). Support for the Constitution and the new government was clearly a factor in GW's judicial appointments, as were geographical considerations. Edmund Randolph was his first choice for attorney general and Randolph accepted, though not without considerable vacillation (GW to Madison, 23 Sept. 1789; Randolph to Madison, 19 July 1789 in Rutland, *Madison Papers*, 12:298–300). A number of names were put forward for chief justice, among them John Rutledge of South Carolina, Robert R. Livingston of New York, and Robert Hanson Harrison of Maryland. James Wilson of Pennsylvania applied for the post (see Wilson to GW, 21 April 1789), and Arthur Lee asked to be nominated an associate justice (Lee to GW, 21 May 1789, and GW to Madison, c.8 Sept. 1789). That there was apprehension in some quarters that Alexander Hamilton might be offered the post of chief justice is indicated by a letter from Civis to GW, 1 Sept. 1789, mentioning rumors "that the *Chief* will not be a *native* of america." John Jay may well have had his choice of the State Department or the post of chief justice, for GW wrote Madison on 9 Aug. that he "had some conversation with Mr Jay respecting his views to Office, which I will communicate to you at our first interview." One observer indeed wrote that the "*Keeper of the Tower* is waiting to see which Salary is best, that of Lord Chief Justice or Secretary of State" (Samuel A. Otis to John Langdon, September 1789, in *Letters to John Langdon*, 92–94). Probably GW's final choice lay among Jay, Rutledge, and Wilson, but Jay had the geographical advantage of coming from a state not widely represented at the top of the administration hierarchy. GW evidently made extensive inquiries about the candidates for posts in the judicial system. See, for example, Conversation with Samuel Griffin, 9 July 1789, printed above, and GW to John Rutledge, 29 Sept. 1789). What he apparently failed to ascertain in advance was whether or not individual appointees would accept the post, although he did ask Samuel Griffin to pursue the matter with candidates in Virginia (see Conversation with Samuel Griffin, 9 July 1789). His earlier experience with federal appointments in the revenue service had not prepared him for the number of declinations that he would receive among his appointees to the Judiciary. After considerable vacillation, Robert Hanson Harrison declined his appointment as associate justice on the Supreme Court (see GW to Harrison, 28 Sept. 1789 and note 1) and there were a number of men who refused to accept appointment to the posts of district judge and marshal for various reasons besides political opposition to the new legal system. Thomas Pinckney refused the post of federal judge for the district of South Carolina on the grounds that he had a "numerous family & that my affairs are so situated as to require my own immediate & unremitted exertions" (Pinckney to GW, 22 Oct. 1789). Harrison declined because of poor health. Thomas Johnson turned down the post of

district judge in Maryland, but he accepted an appointment to the Supreme Court in 1791. Edmund Pendleton was not willing to serve as district judge in Virginia. John Marshall refused the appointment of federal attorney for Virginia because he could not reconcile the duties of the office with his practice in the Virginia superior courts (see Marshall to GW, 14 Oct. 1789). Nathaniel Ramsay, in accepting the post of marshal for the district of Maryland, expressed his fears that in Maryland at least, the duties of the district judge and the locations at which he must hold courts would prevent the post being "accepted by any lawyer of abilities and reputation" (Ramsay to GW, 12 Nov. 1789). Even Edmund Randolph had hesitated accepting the attorney generalship until his reservations about the Judiciary might be resolved (Randolph to Madison, 19 July 1789, in Rutland, *Madison Papers*, 12:298–300). The requirement for Supreme Court justices to ride circuit was a principal deterrent to acceptance of a seat on the court. It also was probably GW's reason for not appointing the elderly Edmund Pendleton, one of Virginia's leading jurists, to the court in 1789 (GW to Madison, 23 Sept. 1789), and the prospect of riding circuit made Thomas Johnson hesitate about accepting a post on the court in 1791 (GW to Johnson, 28 Sept. 1789 and notes). By the end of 1789 GW became increasingly reluctant to make judicial appointments "until I can have an assurance—or at least a strong presumption, that the person appointed will accept; for it is to me an unpleasant thing, to have Commissions of such high importance returned, and it will in fact, have a tendency to bring the Government into discredit" (GW to James McHenry, 30 Nov. 1789). In the case of the appointments of Marylanders, GW, after two rejections, requested McHenry to inquire of Alexander Contee Hanson whether he would accept the appointment if it were made. Hanson, already ensconced in the post of chancellor under the state government "did not like the office so well as that of Chancellor, as it would oblige him to attend courts in different parts of the State which would lessen the net income, and as it was in his opinion of less dignity. In short he gave a decided preference to his present station" (McHenry to GW, 10 Dec. 1789).

Other candidates viewed the possibility of appointment to the judicial system with considerably more enthusiasm. Joseph Jones, applying for the post of district judge in Virginia, frankly admitted that the attraction of the post was its salary which would enable him to discharge personal obligations (Jones to GW, c.15 Nov. 1789). Some of John Rutledge's friends had suggested that he might not take a seat on the Supreme Court, but Rutledge accepted with enthusiasm although, as he informed GW, "the future plan of Life which I had formed was that of Ease & Retirement" (Rutledge to GW, 29 Sept. 1789 and note 2). Although criticism of the judicial system continued there appears to have been general satisfaction with the quality of GW's appointments.

From Benjamin Fishbourn

New York City Tavern

May it please your Excellency. Septr 25th 89

I take my departure for Georgia on Monday next; but previous thereto I beg leave to request the favor of your Excellency to signify to me, your approbation of my having sufficiently done away any prejudices, you may have imbibed in consequence of representations having been made against me in the Senate: this request I hope will not prove unreasonable to your Excellency: and the liberty I hope you'l excuse, as I know you ever bear it in remembrence, to do that Justice to all alike, however *unfortunate* his present situation or dignified it may be. this is all I can now ask: that when I return to the Arms of my Family and friends, I may have it to say I have the sanction as well as the good wishes of his Excellency the President of the United States: my Mind however tortured at present it may be, will be much relieved by your Excellencies answer; and I am bold to think I am not undeserving of it.[1] I am with Sentiments of affection, Your Excellencies Most obdt and very humble servant.

Bn Fishbourn

ALS, DNA:PCC, item 78.

For background to this document, see GW to the United States Senate, 6 Aug. 1789, source note; Anthony Wayne to GW, 30 Aug. 1789.

1. On the same day William Jackson replied to Fishbourn on GW's behalf: "In reply to your letter of this date, addressed to the President of the United States I am directed by him to inform you that when he nominated you for Naval Officer of the Port of Savannah he was ignorant of any charge existing against you—and, not having, since that time, had any other exibit of the facts which were alledged in the Senate than what is stated in the certificates which have been published by you, he does not consider himself competent to give any opinion on the subject" (DNA: RG 59, Miscellaneous Letters). Fishbourn had inserted in the New York *Daily Advertiser,* 17 Sept., a certificate dated 27 Aug. from Hugh Lawson, president of the Georgia executive council, and signed by such prominent Georgia residents as Lachlan McIntosh, Nathaniel Pendleton, John Habersham, Matthew McAllister, Anthony Wayne, and James Seagrove, attesting, "in consequence of certain misrepresentations" concerning his character and conduct, to Fishbourn's reputation and to the "general satisfaction" with his conduct of the customs house in Savannah.

Occasional comments on the Senate's first rejection of a presidential nomination continued into the nineteenth century. In 1818 in an editorial on the evolution of procedures in the Senate in Gales and Seaton's *Daily National In-*

telligencer, the editors observed: "There are not many, probably, of the present generation of readers, who remember the fact, that, in the First Session of the first Congress of the United States, President WASHINGTON personally came into the Senate, when that body was engaged on what is called Executive business, and took part in their deliberations. When he attended, he took the Vice President's chair, and the Vice-President took that of the Secretary of the Senate; one or other of the Secretaries occasionally accompanied the President on these visits. The President addressed the Senate on the questions before them, and in many respects exercised a power in respect to their proceedings, which would now be deemed entirely incompatible with their rights and privileges. This practice, however, did not long continue. An occasion soon arose of collision of opinion between the President and the Senate, on some nomination, and he did not afterwards attend, but communicated by message what he desired to lay before them" (*Daily National Intelligencer* [Washington, D.C.], 11 Mar. 1818). According to Stephen Decatur, Jr., there was, among Tobias Lear's papers, an unsigned letter in the writing of Lear's son Benjamin Lincoln Lear which Lear obviously intended to send to the newspaper. "I cannot but suspect some error in the Editorial article in your paper of the 10 [11th] inst. & if there should be, & it can be corrected by the Journals of the Senate, I think such correction due to its importance as an historical annecdote. So far from having any personal knowledge of those times to which it relates, I am, on the contrary, a very young man. I suspect the whole, however, must have arisen from the following circumstances.

"From among the nominations made to the Senate by President Washington, at, I believe, the first Session of Congress, that of the Collector of the Port of Charleston [Savannah], was rejected. The President immediately repaired to the Senate Chambers & entered, to the astonishment of every one. The Vice-President left his chair & offered it to the President, who accepted it & then told the Senate that he had come to ask their reasons for rejecting his nomination of Collector &c. After many minutes of embarrassing silence, Genl. [James] Gunn, rose and said, that as he had been the person who had first objected to the nomination, & had probably been the cause of its rejection, it was perhaps his office to speak on this occasion. That his personal respect for the personal character of Genl. Washington was such that he would inform him of his grounds for recommending this rejection, (and he did so,) but that he would have it distinctly understood to be the sense of the Senate, that no explanation of their motives or proceedings was ever due or would ever be given to any President of the United States. Upon which the President withdrew.

"This annecdote I received from one who enjoyed Genl. Washington's most intimate friendship & to whom the Genl immediately on his return from the Senate Chamber, expressed his very great regret for having gone there" (Decatur, *Private Affairs of George Washington*, 58–59).

No other indication of such a visit to the Senate by GW has been found. No mention of the visit survives in the Senate's journals, and William Maclay, the indefatigable chronicler of the Senate's proceedings, was absent because of illness, although he noted on 16 Aug. that "The President, shewed great want of temper, (as Mr. Z [Izard] said) when One of his Nominations was rejected" (Bowling and Veit, *Diary of William Maclay*, 121).

From John Hall

sir   New York Sepr 25th 1789

As I understand the Judiciary Sistem is nearly concluded I take the liberty to request your attention to an application for the office of Marshall to the District Court of Georgia; any information respecting the confidence which may be reposed in me I beg leave to refer you to the Gentlemen Senators and Representatives from Georgia.[1] I have the Honor to be sir your mo. obt and mo. Hble Sert

John Hall

ALS, DLC:GW.

1. GW had already made the appointments for state marshals on 24 September. See his list of nominations to the Senate on that date. Hall received no appointment.

To Alexander Hamilton

Dear Sir,   [New York] 25th Sepr 1789.

From a great variety of characters who have made a tender of their services for *Suitable Offices*, I have selected the following. If Mr Jay & you will take the further trouble of running them over to see if among them there can be found one, who, under *all circumstances* is more eligable for the Post Office than Col. O.[1]—I shall be obliged to you both for your opinions thereon by Eleven 'Oclock—Another Paper which is enclosed, will shew how the appointments stand to this time.[2] And, that you may have the matter *fully* before you, I shall add that, it is my *present* intention to nominate Mr Jefferson for Secretary of State, and Mr Edmd Randolph as Attorney Genl; though their acceptance is problamatical—especially the latter. Yrs Sincerely

Go: Washington

Mr Gorham	Massachuts
General Cobb	Do
Colo. Osgood	
Colo. Smith	N. York.

Colo. W: White	Do
Mr Lewis Pintard	Do
Mr John R. Livingston	Do
Commodore Nicholson	Do
Mr Blagge	Do
Colo. Giles	Do
Genl Webb	Do
Doctr Cochran	Do
Mr Wm Denning	Do
Mr Wm W. Morris	Do
Captn Thos Randall	Do
Mr Paul R. Randall	Do
Majr North	Do
Mr Hazard Incumbt	Do
Mr Henry Remsen	Do
Genl Moylan	New Jersey
Mr Wm Temple Franklin	Do
Colo. Cummings	Do
Mr Jno. Bayard	
Mr Thos Barclay	Pennsyl.
Mr Chas Pettit	Do
Mr Jas Milligan	Do
Doctr Tilton	Delaware
Colo. Jno. Parke	Do
Mr Broom	Do
Mr Cyrus Griffen	
Mr Arthur Lee	
Mr Richd Harrison	
Mr Jonathan Dayton	
Genl Gist.	
Chancellor Livingston	

ALS, DLC: Hamilton Papers.

1. See Jacob Richardson to GW, 1 Oct. 1789, n.2.

2. This enclosure, "A List of persons holding Offices of a general Nature with the states to which they belong annexed," in Tobias Lear's handwriting, is in DLC: Hamilton Papers.

Letter not found: from Joseph Martin, 25 Sept. 178[9]. In his Memoranda on Indian Affairs, 1789, printed below, GW describes this letter as follows: "Jos. Martin—from Long Island of Holstein Says (in his Letter dated the 25th of Septr 1789) that on the 27th of August an

Express had arrived to him from the Chicasaw Nation with 4 strings of White Beads from Piemingo & other Chiefs of that Nation requesting his advice & assistance in carrying on a War with the Creek Indians—but having no powers to do this he had sent on their talks to the Comrs who were to treat with the Creeks the 15th of Septr. It was unanimously agreed (he says) between the Chicasaws & Choctaws that Piemingo should come in person with four others to lay their grievances before the Presidt of the U. States.

"He states the claim of John Brown to Lands on the Savanna opposite to Augusta—this merits consideration.

"Mentions his own case, by way of exculpation against charges—which he says—were unjustly alledged[1]—and adds that if there should be any commands for him, they may after the 10th of Octr and until the beginning of Feby meet him in Henry County Virginia."[2]

1. For Martin's current difficulties, see George Walton to GW, 11 Mar. 1789, n.1.
2. On 18 Nov. 1789 Tobias Lear wrote Henry Knox transmitting Martin's letter (DLC:GW).

To the United States Senate

Gentlemen of the Senate,

United States
September 25th 1789.

I nominate

James Duane, Judge } for the District
William S. Smith, Marshall } of
Richard Harrison, Attorney } New-York.

David Brearly, Judge, } for the District
Thomas Lowry, Marshall, } of
Richard Stockton, Attorney. } New-Jersey.

and
I likewise nominate
Thomas Jefferson for Secretary of State
Edmund Randolph for Attorney-General
Samuel Osgood for Post Master-General

Go: Washington

LS, DNA: RG 46, First Congress, Records of Executive Proceedings, President's Messages—Executive Nominations; LB, DLC:GW.

From David Humphreys

My dear Genl,　　　　　　　　Rock Landing Septr 26th 1789

Finding an opportunity to Augusta, I could not excuse myself from giving you the progress of our negotiation since my last.[1]

On monday last (that is to say the day after the arrival of Genl Lincoln & myself) a deputation from all the Creeks of the Tuccasee, the Hallowing & the Tellasee Kings, waited upon us, to congratulate us on our arrival, to express in general terms their desire for peace, to smoke the pipe of friendship as a token of it, and to brush our faces with the white wing of reconciliation in sign of their sincere intention to wipe away all past greivances—We gave them friendly assurances in return; they, with the fat King, the Euchee King and two or three other great Chiefs dined with us, & seemed well satisfied—in the afternoon we crossed to the Indian Camp, had an interview with McGillivray, shewed him our full powers, and asked in writing for such Evidence of theirs, as the nature of the case would admit. Much general Talk, expressive of a real desire to establish a permament peace upon equitable terms, took place.

The next day McGillivray dined with us, & although he got very much intoxicated, he seemed to retain his recollection & reason, beyond what I had ever seen in a person, when in the same condition. At this time I became intimate to a certain degree with him & endeavored to extract his real sentiments & feelings, in a conversation alone, confidentially. He declared he was really desirous of a peace, that the local situation of the Creeks required that they should be connected with us rather than with any other People, that, however they had certain advantages in their Treaty with Spain, in respect to a guarantee & Trade, which they ought not in justice to themselves to give up without an equivalent. Upon his desiring to know what were our intentions, especially as he knew from my character & from my having been long in habits of intimacy with Genl Washington that I would tell him what he might depend upon; I assured him upon my honour that our policy with respect to his nation was, indeed, founded upon honesty, magnanimity & mutual advantages. We descended to no particulars, farther than my assuring him of our good opinion of his abilities & desire to attach him, upon principles perfectly consistent with the good of his Nation, to our interest. I concluded by intimating what, in that case, we might possibly consider ourselves at liberty to do for him. Mr Griffin arrived that night.

Wednesday was occupied in arranging the proposed Draught of a Treaty, & drawing up a Talk to be delivered the next day. The other Commissioners desired me to go over the Oconee & communicate these draughts in confidence to McGillivray. I did, and found him dissatisfied with the proposed boundary & some other things. Genl Lincoln had in the morning been in Mc-Gillivray's camp & agreed with him that the Chiefs should receive our propos[it]ions at our Camp: but finding a jealousy prevailed with some of the Indians, lest a design might be formed to circumvent them. On my return we wrote, that if it was more convenient we would make our communications in their Camp. This proposal they acquiesced in very gratefully.

On thursday at 11 O'clock, we were received with more etiquette, than ever I had before witnessed, at the great Ceremony of *Black Drink.*[2] We made our Communications in the Square of the nation; and returned.

Yesterday morning McGillivray, wrote to us, that the Chiefs had been in council untill late the night before; that they objected to some part of our Talks, & principally to that which related to Boundary; that it was however *His* decision, that the matter should rest as it was for the present; and that a kind of Truce should be established, untill they should hear farther from us on the part of the United States. In the mean time he signified that some presents to the Chiefs would be necessary. In answer we wrote him, after recapitulating the substance of his letter, that, as the Cheifs objected to some of the articles proposed by us, we desired to receive from them in writing the only terms upon which they would enter into a Treaty with us; that as we were as well prepared to treat now as we should be at any other time, we did not believe that it was by any means probable that the United States would ever send another Commission to them & that we were not authorised to make any presents whatsoever, unless we should conclude a Treaty of Peace with them—Finding from verbal information, that a capital misconception had happened to the Indian Chiefs, with regard to one of the Rivers marked in the Boundary; the other Commissioners [wanted] me to go over to the Creek Camp, explain the mistake to McGillivray & make the necessary alteration in the Draught. I had a very long private conversation with him, and he appeared for himself to be much better contented than he had hitherto been.[3] The difficulties in regard to Boundaries seemed to be in a great measure overcome, and an apprehension of the ill consequences of their breaking with Spain, together with an earnest solicitude to have a free (unencumbered) Port were now apparently the great obstacles. He was very much agitated—very much embarrassed; and hardly knew what to determine upon. After I left him, he expressed to an Interpreter a belief that a permanent Peace might take place before we parted. How that may be probably this day will decide. In the afternoon yesterday, McGillivray sent over John Galphin, with Galphin's father in Law, the Hallowing King, to acquaint us that all the Towns, except the Cowetas were removed about two Miles back; for the sake of pasture for their Horses. Should they go off without any farther discussions, it will be a clear indication that they prefer a connection with Spain rather than with America; and that they wish for war, rather than for Peace.

I have not leisure to give you a discription of the person & character of McGillivray. His countenance has nothing liberal and open in it—it has however sufficient marks of understanding. In short, he appears to have the good sense of an American, the shrewdness of a Scotchman, & the cunning of an Indian. I think he is so much addicted to debauchery that he will not live four years. He dresses altogether in the Indian fashion, & is rather slovenly than otherwise. His influence is probably as great as we have understood it was. And his services may certainly be very important, if he can be sincerely attached to our Interests—I hope to have hereafter the honor of reporting to you the substance of several confidential discourses which have occurred between him & me. My most affectionate regards to Mrs Washington & the family conclude me with every sentiment of devotion & consideration My dear General Your Most obliged friend & humble Servant

D. Humphreys

The Commissioners have acted perfectly harmoniously in every measure which they have hitherto taken. The Characters of

Genl Lincoln & Mr Griffin have the greatest weight with the Geo. & the Creeks.

ALS, DLC:GW.

For the negotiations of the American commissioners to the southern Indians, see David Humphreys to GW, 21, 27 Sept., 13, 28 Oct. 1789, Alexander Hamilton to GW, 20 Oct. 1789, and Henry Knox to GW, 18 Oct., 21, 27 Nov. 1789. See also GW's Memoranda on Indian Affairs, 1789.

1. See Humphreys to GW, 21 Sept. 1789.

2. Frederick Webb Hodge describes the black drink as "a decoction, so named by British traders from its color, made by boiling leaves of the *Ilex cassine* in water. It was employed by the tribes of the Gulf states and adjacent regions as 'medicine' for ceremonial purification" (*Handbook of the American Indians*, 1:150).

3. Humphreys' interviews with the Creek chief were perhaps not as amiable as the commissioner implied to GW. As McGillivray later reported, "that puppy Humphries" came to his camp "to argue me out of my objections, but he did not succeed, and came over the two following days; and having no communication with Lincoln & Griffin, I concluded that they pitted that Gentleman against me, being fluent of Speech, and a great boaster of his political knowledge, and his assisting at the former Treaty with the Courts of Versailles, Berlin, &a. He shifted his ground, modes of attack in various shapes. The arts of flattery, ambition and intimidation were exhausted in vain. I at last told him that by G—I would not have such a Treaty cram'd down my throat. On his departure I told my Warriors that it was in vain to expect to bring them to do us the justice we wanted; my opinion was that as we came in a body, so we should retreat as peaceably as we came, and not to be laying there wrangling with them, lest bad consequences might ensue: So the next day I removed back to the Okmulgee where I was overtaken by Genl. Pickens, Cols. Few & Sanders, with the Holloing King. We had a long conversation, but I would not by any means consent to return to the Rock Landing, without they would pledge themselves that the Commissioners would consent to treat us as we wanted on equal terms: This they could not do, so I remained obstinate to my purpose and came on" (McGillivray to William Panton, 8 Oct. 1789, 8 May 1790, in Caughey, *McGillivray*, 251–55, 259–63). See also Humphreys to GW, 27 Sept. 1789.

From Beverley Randolph

Sir,   Richmond September 26th 1789.
The inclosed Letter from the Lieutenant of Woodford County containing the latest accounts of the Situation of the Kentucky District I do myself the Honour to forward to you, as

the most probable means of affording relief to the distresses of the Inhabitants of the Western Frontier.[1] I have &c.

Beverley Randolph.

LB, Vi: Executive Letter Books.

1. The letter from Robert Johnson, county lieutenant for Woodford County, has not been found. On 26 Sept. Randolph wrote Johnson that he had "received your Letter without date giving an account of the Depredations lately Committed on the Frontier of your County, which I immediately forwarded to the President of the United States as the only means in my power to relieve the Distresses of the Western Inhabitants. After the Defence of the Frontier had been taken up by the General Government and the Executive were assured that Treaties had been formed with all the Tribes of Indians which from their situation were able to commit Depredations upon that quarter of the Country they could not justify the continuance of the scouts and Rangers at the particular expence of this state" (Vi: Executive Letter Books).

To the United States Senate and House of Representatives

United States,

Gentlemen of the Senate,   September 26th 1789.

Having yesterday received a letter written in this month by the Governor of Rhode Island, at the request in behalf of the General Assembly of that State, addressed to the President, the Senate, and the House of Representatives of the eleven united States of America in Congress assembled, I take the earliest opportunity of laying a copy of it before you.[1]

Go: Washington

LS, DNA: RG 46, First Congress, Records of Legislative Proceedings, President's Messages; copy, DNA: RG 233, First Congress, Records of Legislative Proceedings, Journals; LB, DLC:GW.

1. See Rhode Island Legislature to GW, 10–19 Sept. 1789. GW's message was received in the Senate and the House on 26 September. In both houses the letter and message were directed to lie for consideration (*DHFC*, 1:193–94, 3:237).

From William Bedlow

Sir   Sept. 27th 1789.

If these lines should be improper by being addressed to you, Pardon the freedom, as nothing but the distressed cituation I am put in by being deprived of my Office at this season of the Year could induce me to trouble you with a detail of it.

I suffered largely in my property dureing the War, I came into this City on the Evacuation of the Brittish with the appointment of Postmaster, House rent Convenient for the Office excessive high this with Clerks Sallery. fire and Candle for the office left me not £200 a Year. with it and the small productive part of my Estate I was Satisfied, in hopes that the Office when properly Arranged would be more beneficial—It is now taken from me at a time of Year when I cannot make an Arrangement for Support. To sell part of my property now would be to a great disadvantage.

But above all this, it may leave a Stigma on my Character by persons who do not "feel anothers woe" I can appeal to my Own Breast for my fidelity in the office, and the Merchts and Citizens of this City will do me Justice to say I gave general Satisfaction. Could Mr Osgood have known my peculier cituation, sure I am he could never have tho't of dismissing of me to provide for another, without some Misdemenor of mine. Once more Sir pardon this intrusion from him who ever has, and ever will pray for your Health & Happiness and is with all due respect. Your Excellency's most Obt Humble Servt

William Bedlow

ALS, DNA:PCC, item 78.

William Bedlow (1722–1798) served as a captain and and commissioner of building fortifications in 1775, and as a construction supervisor of obstructions in the Hudson River in 1777. A former sea captain and merchant, Bedlow became postmaster of New York in 1784. He may have retained his post since Samuel Osgood wrote him as late as 23 Feb. 1790 concerning his accounts (DNA: RG 28, Letters Sent By the Postmaster General, 1789–1836).

From David Humphreys

My dear General.   Rock Landing Septr 27th 1789
Since I had the honor of writing to you yesterday, some things have happened, of which I conceive it expedient to give information by this conveyance.

On the evening of the 25th McGillivray omitted to comply with his positive promise to write to us or come over the river, in order to explain the objections of the Chiefs to the Project of the

Treaty which we had proposed to them, and to propose alterations. Instead of removing, as he had intimated by Galphin, two miles back for the sake of pasture; we were informed in the forenoon yesterday that he had set out on his return to the Nation, without even deigning to send us any written or verbal Message.[1] It is true, he permitted an Indian Trader to inform us (of his own motion) of this fact, and that he (McGillivray) would halt for that day, at Commissioners' Creek, fifteen or eighteen miles distant. McGillivray's pretences for this movement homeward (if rightly reported) are of the most frivolous & unjustifiable nature. He is said to pretend to be dissatisfied, that, in a private conversation, I had questioned the Powers of himself & those present to make a Treaty that would be binding upon the whole nation. The fact is far otherwise. When he spoke of the invalidity of some of the Treaties between Georgia and the Creeks, because the latter were not fully represented; I asked him, how it was to be proved that their Nation was fully represented at this time? I lamented that the uncivilised state of the nation would not perhaps admit of the same Evidence to legalize Proceedings which civilised Nations required, and inquired whether the *White Leiutenant* (a very great Chief not present)[2] would agree to whatever should now be done. It is farther said by the Indian Trader abovementioned, that McGillivray pretended I had told him, that, upon making this Treaty with us, he must entirely break with the Spanish government. I told him, on the contrary, that, as far as I could learn from him the nature of his connection with Spain, I did not suppose the proposed Treaty to be incompatible with it: that I would not wish him to do any thing which should in the least injure his good faith: but that, if a connection with us and with Spain was incompatible, it was doubtless in his option to decide which of the two Powers he would be connected with.

These misrepresentations are not the only reprehensible things we have seen in his conduct. He made a false pretext, "that the Indians were so much alarmed for their personal safety that they dared not trust themselves in our Camp and that two Towns were on the point of going home on the same account," in order that we might go over and make our talk in their Camp. And indeed he insists, that though we were formerly, when connected with Britain, styled their father & older brother; yet we are at present truly their younger Brother. The falsehood of the pretext that the Indians were so much alarmed for their safety that they dared not trust themselves in our Camp was clearly evinced yesterday. About 11 O'Clock almost or quite all the principal Chiefs of the Upper & Lower Towns (with a great number of Individuals) came over to shake hands with us, and to assure us in a long talk that they were not at all offended with us; that they desired peace very much; that, though they could not conclude a Peace without McGillivray their beloved man (who was sick), yet they had inculcated upon all their People to abstain from all hostility & plundering, under threats of the severest punishment. In short they seemed to consider a peace as mutually wished for, and, in fact, agreed upon, except in the forms. In answer we gave them assurances that the States entertained the most just & friendly dispositions towards them, and hoped that a Treaty might still be concluded before we seperated finally. We wished them to use their influence with McGillivray that he would return & renew the negotiation. For which purpose we informed them we were sending one more pressing Message to McGillivray by Genl Pickens & Mr Few: who went soon after to see him accordingly. Several of the Kings dined with us & remained untill night, with the greatest possible apparent good humour and indications of a sincere desire for Peace. The White Bird King spoke first in the name of the Whole. The Tellasee King, after dinner, made a long, and, as well as we could understand from an indifferent interpretation, a pathetic Oration to all the Kings, Head Men & People, urging the necessity of being in strict Amity with the Whites, as they prised their existence & every thing dear to them. All were greatly affected & some shed tears. The only great Representative from the Seminolies sent back, after he left us, a confirmation of the same good dispositions by the Interpreter. Upon the whole, I believe that no room for doubt was left in the mind of any one present, that, if a Peace shall not be concluded, the fault will rest with McGillivray alone. Who holds up in his coversations, as it best suits his convenience, that he does every thing himself in national affairs, or that he can do nothing with[out] humouring & consulting the Indians. It is a melancholly consideration to reflect that a whole Nation must sometimes perish for the sins of one man.

I shall defer closing this letter, untill the return of Genl Pickens & Mr Few. While I feel a consciousness that our transactions will stand approved in the eye of reason & justice; I apprehend that we can never depend upon McGillivray, for his firm attachment to the interests of the United States. And yet I believe he regards the interests of the United States just as much as he does the interests of the Creek Nation. If I mistake not his character, his own importance & pecuniary emolument are the objects, which will altogether influence his conduct. It was held out in discourse yesterday by John Galphin, a Creature of McGillivray, that a pressing invitation has just been sent from the Spaniards (accompanied by a vast quantity of Ammunition) for McGillivray to come & treat with them. I fancy he now wavers between Spain & America: for which reason he wishes in all likelihood to postpone the farther negotiation with the latter untill the Spring. It is however questionable whether he has ever had a formal Treaty with, or received a genuine Commission from, the King of Spain. Probably his hopes have been much elevated lately, insomuch as to induce him to believe that he can obtain better terms for himself from the King, than from us.

Genl Pickens & Mr Few are just now returned, and report, that they found McGillivray, not at the distance he was said to be, but on the other side of the Ockmulgee. He would not give the terms on which the Creeks would make Peace, or come back to renew the negotiations on the subject. He objected only to three Articles, being under the protection of the United States, not having a port perfectly free from duties, and the proposed boundary—but his objection seemed to be of the least weight with himself against the last. They fully coincide with me in opinion that he is determined to see, whether he cannot obtain more advantageous terms from Spain than from the United States. The fact is also said by these Gentlemen to be established that a large quantity of Arms & Ammunition has lately arrived in the Creek Nation, with a friendly Talk, from the Governor at Pensacola. McGillivray wrote us a letter in very general terms in which he affected to consider our first Draught of a Treaty, as our ultimatum. This was both contrary to his good sense, & to repeated positive assurances. We shall write to him by an Indian Trader to day very explicitly.[3] and after taking such farther measures to ascertain facts as may be in our power; we shall commence our Journey through North Carolina to New York. Thus the business seems to be terminated for the present, though not according to our wishes. With sentiments of the purest respect I have the honor to be My dear General Your most obliged & Most humble Servt

D. Humphreys

ALS, DLC:GW.

For the negotiations of the American commissioners to the southern Indians, see David Humphreys to GW, 21, 26 Sept. 13, 28 Oct. 1789, Alexander Hamilton to GW, 20 Oct. 1789, and Henry Knox to GW, 18 Oct., 21, 27 Nov. 1789. See also GW's Memoranda on Indian Affairs, 1789.

1. See Humphreys to GW, 26 Sept. 1789, n.3.

2. The White Lieutenant of Okfuskee was a principal chief of the Upper Creek.

3. McGillivray's letter, 27 Sept. 1789, and the commissioners' reply, 28 Sept., are in *DHFC*, 2:229–30.

From John Sullivan

Durham in New Hampshire
much Esteemed Sir   September 27th 1789

Sensible that your Excellencys exalted Station drew with it an Increase of Cares difficulties and ill judged applications I therefore amidst the dealing out of offices & making the necessary appointments have remained Silent untill your Excellencey saw the proper opportunity of reminding me that my Services were not forgotten but being informed this day by Letter from the Honble Judge Livermore that myself and Mr Pickering are both in nomination as District Judge for this State your Excellency will pardon me for putting in my Claim. I have nothing to say against the other Gentleman in nomination we are nearly of the same Standing in the Law Department I have been for a number of years attorney General, and repeatedly solicited to accept the office of chief Justice of our Superior Court & as often refused he is Now Actually appointed to that office but has not given his answer we were both zealous for Establishing the present Constitution but in the revolution he & I differed so much in Sentiment that he would not Act or appear in the American Councils for a number of years—your Excellencey knows where I was and the part I was Acting at that time—if all other things are

equal in your Excellenceys mind perhaps this consideration
would give the preference to my Claim which will ever be Acknowledged with gratitude by your Excellenceys most obedience & very Humble Servant

Jno. Sullivan

P.S. as to my office as President of this State I can no Longer
bear the Expence of it.

ALS, DLC:GW.

   After his stormy career during the Revolution, John Sullivan (1740–1795)
returned to New Hampshire, serving from 1782 to 1786 as attorney general
and in 1786 and 1787 as president of the state, a post to which he was re-
elected in 1789. Both Sullivan and John Pickering were under consideration
for the post of district judge for New Hampshire. Tobias Lear wrote John
Langdon on 24 Sept. that he had "just returned from the Senate where I have
been to give in the President's nominations—a list of which you have enclosed—The Gentlemen from New Hampshire were of opinion that Genl Sullivan would accept the office of District Judge if he should be appointed
thereto—as the sallary annexed to it was larger than that of President of the
State—that it would leave him a very considerable portion of time to attend to
his private affairs—and that it was a permanent provision not depending on
the popular view, & a dignified office. Upon these considerations—the idea of
his not being willing to accept the appointmt was removed, & the President
conceived that he would be a proper man for that office, & accordingly put
him in nomination" (NhHi: Langdon-Elwyn Family Papers). After Sullivan's
death in 1795, John Pickering succeeded him in the post (*Executive Journal*,
1:172).

From Henry Bicker, Jr.

New York September 28th 1789

The Petition of Henry Bicker Jun. of the City of New york Most
Humbly Sheweth

   That in the Year 1775 your Petitioner being well acquainted
with the Use of Arms was called upon to teach the Militia of the
City of Philadelphia—And for this Purpose left his Business in
this City and went to Philadelphia where he instructed the
Citizens in the Manual and other Exercises without Fee or Reward—that some Time in latter End of 1775 your Petitioner
having accomplish'd his Design in the City of Philadelphia, he
went to the State of New Jersey, and there instructed the Militia
of several Counties in the Military Art—That in January 1776

your Petitioner had the Honor of recieving a Lieutenants Commission in the Pensylvania Line, and join'd the Army under your Excellency's Command at the City of New york—That your Petitioner was made a Prisoner of War in the Capture of Fort Washington and remained in Confinement until 1778— That being Exchanged and promoted to the Rank of Captain in the 4th Pensylvania Regiment your Petitioner join'd a Detachment under the Command of General Wayne and marchd to Virginia—That after the Capture of Lord Cornwallis your Petitioner was again orderd to join the Troops under the Command of General St Clair and marched to the State of South Carolina where he remained until the End of the War—Your Petitioner therefore prays that, in Consideration of his early and continued Services, his Impair'd State of Health, from the Heat of the Southern Climates—His reduced Circumstances and want of Means to support a young Family—Your Excellency will relieve his Distresses by appointing him an Inspector of an Invalid Corps or to some other Office that in your Wisdom he may fill with Honor to himself and Service to his Country And as in Duty bound he will ever pray &c.

Henry Bicker Jur

ALS, DLC:GW.

The military career of Henry Bicker, Jr. (c.1749–1820), is substantially as he states in his letter. He received no major appointment from GW, but he is listed in the New York City *Directory* for 1790 as an "inspector," residing at "43, Crown-street." By 1799 Bicker had moved to Philadelphia where he opened a business with his brother Walter (d. 1821). "The brothers Bickers inform the public that they are returned to their old professions of hatters, which they abandoned to defend the liberty of their country" (*Aurora* [Philadelphia], c.24 Jan. 1799, quoted in *Pennsylvania Magazine of History and Biography*, 78 [1954], 90).

Tobias Lear to Clement Biddle

Dear Sir,   New York, September 28th, 1789.

Your much esteemed favors of the 16th[1] & 25th[2] instts are before me. The President's acct contained in the former is right. Mrs Washington will thank you to get for her and send on here, 15 Yards of Padusoy of the enclosed Pattern.[3]

The President wishes to procure a considerable quantity of

Clover seed; I will, therefore, thank you to inform me at what price a quantity can be had with you—and the shortest time in which it can be delivered *with certainty*. I shall make similar inquiries here, and shall finally procure it at the place where it can be had at the lowest price, and del[ivere]d in the shortest time. The *time* is an essential consideration with the President— he suffered greatly last year by not receiving his Clover seed from this place so early as he should have had it by agreement; and he is now determined to get it in the fall at all events.[4]

I congratulate you, my Dear Sir, on your appointment to the Office of Marshal for the District of Pennsylvania. You will, in due time, have official information of it.[5] I am, Dr Sir, with great esteem, Your most Obedt Servt

Tobias Lear.

ALS, PHi: Washington-Biddle Correspondence; ADfS, ViMtV; LB, DLC:GW.

1. See Lear to Biddle, 14 Sept. 1789, n.3.
2. Letter not found.
3. Lear had written Biddle on 21 Sept.: "Mrs Washington is desirous of having a gown of Padusoy, Ducape or Tabby as near the color of the enclosed patterns as can be had—and will thank you to send her patterns from Phila- delphia with the prices" (PHi: Washington-Biddle Correspondence). Biddle sent the silk on 30 Sept. (Lear to Biddle, 2 Oct. 1789).
4. Biddle replied on 5 Oct.: "I have been among the Dealers in Clover seed, but they say are not yet sufficiently informed of the Crop to determine the quantity and price which they can furnish in Certain time to ship this fall but will inform me in about a fortnight" (PHi: Clement Biddle Letter Book, 1789–92). Lear informed Biddle on 17 Nov. that "the Clover seed which I mentioned in a former letter has been procured here @ 10d. per lb." Biddle responded: "I am Glad that you have procured the red Cloverseed as after diligent Enquiry of the Dealers in Town and persons who raise it in the Coun- try I find none Can be depended on before the Close of the Winter & a very little which Comes out has sold at 60/ ℔ Bushel which is much higher than you mention" (Biddle to Lear, 22 Nov. 1789).
5. See Biddle to GW, 19 June 1789 and source note.

To Robert Hanson Harrison

Dear Sir,   New York Sep. 28th 1789.

It would be unnecessary to remark to you, that the adminis- tration of Justice is the strongest cement of good Government, did it not follow as a consequence that the first organization of the federal Judiciary is essential to the happiness of our Country, and to the stability of our political system.

Under this impression it has been the invariable object of my anxious solicitude to select the fittest characters to expound the Laws and dispense justice. To tell you that this sentiment has ruled me in your nomination to a seat on the Supreme Bench of the United States, would be but to repeat opinions with which you are already well acquainted—opinions which meet a just coincidence in the public Mind.

Your friends, and your fellow-citizens, anxious for the respect of the Court to which you are appointed, will be happy to learn your acceptance—and no one among them will be more so than myself.

As soon as the Acts which are necessary accompaniments of these appointments can be got ready, you will receive official notice of the latter.[1] This letter is only to be considered as an early communication of my sentiments on this occasion and as a testimony of the sincere esteem and regard with which I am Dear Sir Your Most Obedt and Affectionate Hble Servt

Go: Washington

ALS, DNA: RG 266, HR 22A-B1, HR–155; DfS, partly in GW's writing, DNA: RG 59, Miscellaneous Letters; LB, DLC:GW.

Robert Hanson Harrison (1745–1790) was born in Charles County, Md., but moved to Virginia before 1765 when he was certified to practice law in Fairfax County. Harrison was active in Patriot circles in Alexandria in the early 1770s and in November 1775 became one of Washington's aides-de-camp with the rank of lieutenant colonel, a post he held until March 1781. After the war Harrison settled in Maryland and was appointed chief judge of Maryland's General Court.

1. Harrison replied to GW's offer of a seat on the court on 27 Oct.: "I received on the 9th Instt your very obliging & interesting Favor of the 28th Ulto—and request you to be assured, that the perusal of it, for the matter and the manner of the communication, filled me with every emotion, which friendship & gratitude could inspire.

"In the first place permit me, My Dear Sir, to apologize for the time, which has elapsed without this acknowledgement. On no occasion of my life have I been under an embarrasment so painful. It is at length with a difficulty almost inconceivable, after revolving every circumstance, & after many days & nights of anxious sollicitude, that I have come to a final determination that I cannot but decline the appointment. On the one hand, a sincere & lively gratitude for the honour conferred by the public, and the transcendent proof of your regard & confidence; an animated love to our Country; an attachment to the Government not yet compleatly organized; a conviction that it is incumbent on every virtuous Citizen to exert his endeavours in rendering it firm, respectable & happy: All these considerations pressed powerfully on my mind, and at times almost irresistibly urged my acceptance. On the other hand, considerations which at first sight may not appear so striking, laudable & weighty, disuaded & restrained me.

"In the most favourable view of the Subject it appeared, that the duties required from a Judge of the Supreme Court would be extremely difficult & burthensome, even to a Man of the most active comprehensive mind; and vigorous frame. I conceived this would be the case, if he should reside at the Seat of Government; and, in any other view of *my* residence I apprehended, that as a Judge sollicitous to discharge my trust, I must hazard, in an eminent degree, the loss of my health, and sacrafice a very large portion of my private and domestic happiness. Should I however, enter on the duties, required by my appointment, I should be constrained to take the more unfavourable residence, from the circumstances of my family." Harrison's younger brother William had recently died, and Harrison had assumed responsibility for his young family. "When I tell you, My dear Sir, in addition to these most interesting considerations, that I feel a distrust of my competency to the arduous & exalted Station, and a full persuasion that my declining it will not be attended with any public detriment—I flatter myself, you will think me at least justified to my own conscience. It is my ardent wish to be justified in your opinion. Be assured that no circumstance of my life ever caused me so much anxiety & doubt. The alternative before me was either to act against the dictates of my own Judgement, to forego the considerations of my domestic happiness, and in a great measure to desert the interests of those, with whom I am connected by the dearest ties; or, in appearance, to slight the calls of my Country—it's proffered honours, and (what infinitely concerns me) the duty I owe to your inestimable disinterested friendship. I entreat you to pardon the detail of private matters" (DNA:PCC, item 59).

Harrison wrote GW a second letter on the same day, acknowledging receipt of the commission, which GW had forwarded on 30 Sept., and again declining the post. Reiterating his reasons for doing so, he stated that "these considerations, Sir, and one more, of still greater weight—a distrust of my competency to the arduous & exalted Station" (DNA: RG 59, Letters of Resignation and Declination). On 14 Nov. James McHenry wrote GW that he had held several conversations with Harrison on the subject of his appointment, "and from what he says I cannot but think he was greatly influenced in returning the commission from an apprehension you might be embarrassed should he have kept it longer for consideration. No one except myself is yet acquainted with what he has done, and he assured me this morning, before leaving town, that he thought he had been premature, and wished to be again in possession of the commission, although he was by no means certain that he would finally be enabled to come to a different determination.

"Well knowing the value of this man his goodness of heart and unalterable attachment to you, I thought it my duty to communicate these circumstances in hopes that it may not yet be too late to place him in a situation for further deliberation. My own opinion is that he will serve in case his brother in law dies, an event which I look upon to be at no great distance from a letter I have seen of Dr Brown's on the subject.

"I hope most sincerely that your health has been improved by your journey. If the secret and public wishes of good men can conduce to this end it will be a long time before you will have any need of the faculty. But you have created a new fountain of blessings. In your nominations and appointments you have had respect to want and wretchedness, where united with worth and capacity, and have thereby drawn upon you more prayers and gratitude than has ever fallen to the lot of any dead or living Sovereign prince or first magistrate whatever" (DLC:GW).

GW answered Harrison's misgivings on 25 Nov.: "I find that one of the reasons, which induced you to decline the appointment, rests on an idea that the Judicial Act will remain unaltered. But in respect to that circumstance, I may suggest to you, that such a change in the system is contemplated, and deemed expedient by many in, as well as out of Congress, as would permit you to pay as much attention to your private affairs as your present station does.

"As the first Court will not sit until the first Monday in Febry, I have thought proper to return your Commission, not for the sake of urging you to accept it contrary to your interest or convenience, but with a view of giving you a farther opportunity of informing yourself of the nature & probability of the change alluded to. This you would be able to do with the less risque of mistake, if you should find it convenient to pass sometime here, when a considerable number of Members of both houses of Congress shall have assembled; and this might be done before it would become indispensable to fill the place offered to you. If, on the other hand, your determination is absolutely fixed, you can, without much trouble, send back the Commission, under cover.

"Knowing as you do the candid part which I wish to act on all occasions; you will I am persuaded, do me the justice to attribute my conduct in this particular instance to the proper motives, when I assure you that I would not have written this letter if I had imagined it would produce any new embarrassment. On the contrary you may rest assured, that I shall be perfectly satisfied with whatever determination may be consonant to your best judgment & most agreeable to yourself" (ALS, DNA: RG 233, HR 22 A-B1, HR–155). GW's comments on the court follow closely an undated paper in John Jay's handwriting, probably presented to the president by the acting secretary of state, headed "Remarks respecting Mr Harrisons objections" (DNA: RG 59, Miscellaneous Letters). Alexander Hamilton also urged Harrison to reconsider: "One of your objections I think will be removed—I mean that which relates to the nature of the establishment. Many concur in opinion that its present form is inconvenient, if not impracticable" (27 Nov. 1789, in Syrett, *Hamilton Papers*, 5:562).

Harrison apparently decided to accept GW's suggestion for a visit to the capital. On 21 Jan. 1790 he wrote the president from Bladensburg, Md.: "I left home on the 14th Instt with a view of making a Journey to New York, and after being several days detained at Alexandria by indisposition came thus far on the way. I now unhappily find myself in such a situation, as not to be able to proceed further. From this unfortunate event and the apprehension that my indisposition may continue, I pray you to consider that I cannot accept the Appointment of an Associate Judge, with which I have been honoured. What I do, My dear Sir, is the result of the most painful and distressing necessity.

"I intreat that you will receive the warmest returns of my gratitude for the distinguished proofs I have had of your flattering and invaluable esteem & confidence" (DNA: RG 233, HR 22 A-B1, HR–155). This was presumably Harrison's final notification to the president of his intentions although a letter from Tobias Lear to Thomas Jefferson, 29 July 1791, enclosing commissions lists Harrison as declining his appointment on 26 Dec. 1789 (DNA: RG 59, Miscellaneous Letters). Harrison died on 2 April 1790 at his home near Port Tobacco in Charles County, Maryland.

From Moses Michael Hays

Sir   Boston Septemr 28th 1789

For The Freedom I use in addressing you, I shall rely on The Friendship of General Knox to offer Such Opology, as will impress on you a favorable reception of this Letter.[1] its Motive is to Solicit the appointment of the Collectorship for the Port of New Port Rhode Island—When That State shall embrace the Feoderal Constitution and appearance Indicate Such measure not to be farr distant; It will not be improper, I presume to Inform your Excellencey, That I am a Native of this Country, Much attacht to its interests & wellfare, a Merchant and resident for many years at Rhode Island, when I should have remained untill this Moment, had it not been possessed by British Forces. When I left it, and Since their departure From thence, The Trade has been so interupted & Much lessned That I Have not as yet, Been induced to return.

I shall Leave my Friends to Say How Farr I merit attention and your Countenance, and will beg Leave to assure Your Excellencey, That any Confidence, placed in me, will Be fully justified, by a Steady Pursuit of rectitude and Integrity, with Profound Respect I am Yr Excellencey's mos. obedient Hble Servant

M. M. Hays

ALS, DLC:GW.

Moses Michael Hays (1739–1805) was trained as a watchmaker. He moved to Newport in 1769 and became a prominent member of the Jewish community there. An active Mason, he was deputy inspector general of the Masonic lodge for North America in 1768. In Newport he founded a shipbuilding

business with Myer Polock (d. 1779) and was involved in banking and the
China trade. In 1782 he moved to Boston and set up an insurance business,
specializing in maritime underwriting (Rosenbloom, *Biographical Dictionary of
Early American Jews*, 59).

1. On 12 Sept. Hays had written Knox, requesting his "recommendation
and Influence for the appointment of Collector at New Port" (MHi: Knox
Papers).

To Thomas Johnson

Dear Sir   New York Septr 28th 1789.
   In assenting to the opinion that the due administration of
Justice is the strongest cement of good Government, you will
also agree with me that the first organization of the Judicial
department is essential to the happiness of our Country, and to
the stability of our political system—hence the selection of the
fittest characters to expound the Laws, and dispense Justice has
been an invariable object of my anxious concern.
   Consulting your domestic inclinations and the state of your
health I yielded on a recent occasion, to the opinions of some of
your friends who thought that you would not be prevailed on
to leave your State to mingle in the administration of public
affairs—But I found it impossible in selecting a character to
preside in the District Court of Maryland, to refuse to, what I
conceive to be, the public wish, and to the conviction of my own
Mind, the necessity of nominating you to that Office—And I
cannot but flatter myself that the same reasons which have led
you to former sacrafices in the public service, will now operate to
induce your acceptance of an appointment so highly interesting
to your Country.[1]
   As soon as the Acts, which are necessary accompaniments of
the appointments can be got ready you will receive official notice
of the latter. This letter is only to be considered as an early
communication of my sentiments on this occasion and as a
testimony of the sincere esteem and regard with which I am
Dear Sir Yr most Obedt & Affecte Servt

                                            Go: Washington

ALS, IaU; DfS, partly in GW's writing, DNA: RG 59, Miscellaneous Letters;
LB, DLC:GW.
   For background to GW's Judiciary appointments, see his letter to the

United States Senate submitting his nominations for judicial posts, 24 Sept. 1789.

1. Johnson declined the judgeship of the federal district court in Maryland although he served as a justice on the Maryland General Court from April 1790 to October 1791. On 14 July 1791 GW offered Johnson the seat on the Supreme Court left vacant by the resignation of John Rutledge. Deterred principally by the demands of riding circuit, Johnson vacillated for several weeks but finally accepted, retaining the post until 1793. See GW to Johnson, 14 July and 7 Aug. 1791, Johnson to GW, 27, 30 July and 13 Aug. 1791.

To Samuel Langdon

Sir,   New York September 28th 1789.

You will readily beleive me when I assure you that the necessary attention to the business in which I have been lately engaged is the sole cause of my not having sooner acknowledged the receipt of your letter of the 8th of July—and made a proper return for your politness in sending me the sermon which accompanyed it.[1] You will now, Sir, please to accept my best thank[s] for this mark of attention, as well as for the friendly expressions contained in your letter.

The man must be bad indeed who can look upon the events of the American Revolution without feeling the warmest gratitude towards the great Author of the Universe whose divine interposition was so frequently manifested in our behalf—And it is my earnest prayer that we may so conduct ourselves as to merit a continuance of those blessings with which we have hitherto been favoured. I am Sir, with great esteem Your most obedt Servt.

Df, DNA: RG 59, Miscellaneous Letters; LB, DLC:GW. The endorsement on the draft notes that it was "sent by Mr Gilman."

1. See Langdon to GW, 8 July 1789, n.1.

To Edmund Pendleton

New York Septr 28th 1789[1]

I write to you, my dear Sir, on a subject which has engaged much of my reflection, and to which I am persuaded I shall obtain your ready and candid attention.

Regarding the due administration of Justice as the corner stone of good government, I have considered the first arrange-

ment of the judicial department as essential to the happiness of
our country, and to the stability of its' political system—Under
this impression it has been an invariable object of anxious solicitude with me to select the fittest characters to expound the laws
and dispense justice.

Concurring in sentiment with some others of your friends
that the functions of the Supreme Bench, which involve the
fatigue of circuit courts, would be too much for the infirm state
of your health, I believed it necessary, to avail our Country of
your abilities and the influence of your example, by nominating
you to the office of Judge of the District-Court of Virginia,
which will not require much greater personal exertion than the
duties of your present station—and I trust the hope, with which
I flatter myself, that I shall have the pleasure to hear of your
acceptance of the appointment, is well founded—indeed I cannot doubt it, when I again consider the necessity of giving a tone
to the system in its' out-set, by placing the administration of the
laws with the best and wisest of our Citizens.[2]

As soon as the Acts, which are necessary accompaniments of
these appointments can be got ready you will receive official
notice of the latter. This letter is only to be considered as an early
communication of my sentiments on this occasion and as a
testimony of the sincere esteem & regard with which I am Dr Sir
Yrs &ca.

G. W——n[3]

DfS, partly in the writing of GW, DNA: RG 59, Miscellaneous Letters; LB,
DLC:GW.

For background to GW's Judiciary appointments, see his letter to the
United States Senate submitting his nominations, 24 Sept. 1789.

1. The dateline is in GW's writing.

2. At this point the following paragraph is deleted: "You will, I hope, attribute my late silence to its true cause, when you recollect that I have not yet
been favored with the annual letter."

3. The last paragraph and the closing are in GW's hand. On 13 Oct. Pendleton replied: "If Motives of a General Nature had been wanting to induce
my Acceptance of the Commission to be the Fœdral Judge of this District, wch
I have had the Honr of recieving, they would have been abundantly Supplied
by reflecting on the happiness of being Selected by you, my Dear & Venerable
Sir, (not only unasked For, but wholly unexpected) to fill an Office in that
branch which you justly deem of great Magnitude, as one of the Pillars on
which the New Fabric of Government must rest; and by your very polite &
friendly prefatory Favr of the 28th past, placing every motive in it's strongest

& most pleasing point of view. The subject commanded my immediate & *close* Attention. *Candid* I could with difficulty be since one side of the question presented prospects Flattering to my Character, and was Aided by lucrative considerations, to me not un-important: the Struggle was great, And like Females who deliberate on certain Occasions, I might have been over come, if a Cough or short-breathing had not come to my Aid, by reminding me of the true State of my Constitution, & producing the reflections & resolution to decline, contained in my Public Letter: After all, the choice was relunctantly made, & would have been more so, but for two reflections, A confidence that my successor will possess superior Abilities, and equal Integrity & Fortitude in the exercise of the Functions of his Office; and that an honest upright State Judge may as effectually serve all the just purposes of the General Government; as one in the Fœdral line; Since it seems to me that the same Rule of decision must govern both in questions respecting Jurisdiction & Constitutional powers, as well as in those relating to Civil rights.

"That I may stand acquited to you, Sir, of being influenced by any private or Other motives than those assigned, permit me to take notice of two, wch are all that Occur As subjects of Suspicion, My want of Ardour in the Fœdral Cause, and that my Ambition was not gratified in the Grade of Appointment. As to the first, My Zeal For the Union of America as involving not only the Peace & happiness, but the very existence of it's Members; and my Warm Attachment to a temperate, but firm energetic Government in the Fœdral Head, as indispensible to the preservation of Union, which have been uniformly manifested in my conduct since the Subject has been Agitated, must fully acquit me. And as to the other—I can truly say, that having resolved to call me into Office, your Usual Sagacity was conspicuous in the choice of it, there being none other in the Government, about accepting which I could have Ballanced a Moment, the higher Offices in the Judiciary, requiring the Circuit duty, being impossible to me.

"May the Goverment prosper and prove a terror to all evil doers, & the protection of virtuous Citizens. May you live long & happy in the office of diffusing it's blessings, and may I never Forfeit your Esteem and regard until I cease to be my Countrey's & My Dear Sir Your mo. devoted, Affecte & Obedt Servt" (DNA: RG 59, Acceptances and Orders for Commisions).

Letter not found: to John J. Pringle, 28 Sept. 1789. On 30 Oct. Pringle wrote to GW: "I have had the pleasure to receive your Excellency's very polite and obliging letter of the 28th last month."

To Edmund Randolph

Dear Sir,   New York Septr 28th 1789.[1]

Impressed with a conviction that the due administration of justice is the firmest pillar of good government, I have considered the first arrangement of the judicial department as essential to the happiness of our country and to the stability of its' political system—hence the selection of the fittest characters to expound the laws, and dispense justice, has been an invariable object of my anxious concern.

I mean not to flatter when I say that considerations like these have ruled in the nomination of the Attorney-General of the United States &, that my private wishes wd be highly gratified by yr accepte of the Office—I regarded the office as requiring those talents to conduct its' important duties, and that disposition to sacrifice to the public good, which I believe you to possess and entertain—in both instances, I doubt not, the event will justify the conclusion—the appointment, I hope, will be accepted, and its' functions, I am assured, will be well performed.

Notwithstanding the prevailing disposition to frugality, the salary of this office appears to have been fixed, at what it is, from a belief that the station would confer pre-eminence on its' Possessor, and procure for him a decided preference of Professional employment.[2]

As soon as the Acts, which are necessary accompaniments of the appointment can be got ready you will receive official notice of the latter—this letter is only to be considered as an early communication of my sentiments on this occasion and as a testimony of the sincere regd and esteem[3] with which I am &ca.

DfS, partly in the writing of GW, DNA: RG 59, Miscellaneous Letters; LB, DLC:GW.

For background to GW's Judiciary appointments, see his letter to the United States Senate submitting his nominations for judicial posts, 24 Sept. 1789.

1. The dateline is in GW's writing. The receiver's copy of this letter was apparently dated 27 September. See Randolph's reply in note 3, below.

2. "An Act for allowing certain Compensation to the Judges of the Supreme and other Courts, and to the Attorney General of the United States" allowed yearly compensation of fifteen hundred dollars to the attorney general (1 *Stat.* 72 [23 Sept. 1789]).

3. The closing is in GW's writing. Randolph replied to GW's letter on 8 Oct.: "Altho' it may be improper to express my thanks to the chief magistrate of the union, for any act of office, yet you will pardon me, I hope, for assuring you, that your very friendly communication of the 27th Ulto is truly cordial to me.

"The appointment is by no means unacceptable for its duties; nor will I say any thing as to salary. My wish therefore to obey your summons will be restrained by the following considerations only: an ignorance whether it will require me to remove from the seat of fœderal government, to attend any court, and a difficulty in arranging my private affairs, early enough for the service of the United States. The former obstacle will, I suppose, be destroyed, or confirmed on the inspection of the judiciary bill—the latter is of a more serious cast. My worthy uncle [Peyton Randolph] left me all, that he ought to have given me; but it was not much better, than a nominal estate; since the money, which I have been obliged to pay for his debts, and those of my father, in which he was bound, took three fourths of the value of that property, in actual cash acquired by my profession. But I have added to this mischief, by two injudicious purchases of land, made after the decline of its price. These are loads around my neck, and are rendered more oppressive, by the partition of my bonds into many hands. Time alone can bring this evil to an end. I pass over other debts, as well as the necessity of putting my plantations, lying in distant counties, (Albemarle and Charlotte) on a proper footing.

"If however the act, when examined, should not, as I suppose it does not, contain any provision, which I cannot get over, I will repair to New-York, as soon as I possibly can. I trust that March may be in time; for then I can carry my whole family. In the mean time, if any professional aid should be demanded by government, I hope that there would be no impropriety in soliciting the aid of some gentleman of the law on the spot, to render it in my behalf.

"But I cannot conceal a desire to remain in the assembly until the end of the ensuing session. I have been employed for more than six weeks, in completing a revision of our laws upon a scale, which alone will please a majority. Their confusion has caused calamities, scarcely to be conjectured. Our statute laws are dispersed thro' six unwieldy volumes, of which ten copies are not to be found, I verily believe, in the state. Our local acts are in eight different volumes—amount to at least 1300, and may be reduced to 350. This work will, I am confident, miscarry, without the support of some man, who has it's success at heart. I can signify my acceptance, without being disqualified, and finish this indispensable business. With your permission therefore I will, should I determine to accept at last, postpone an answer, until you drop me a hint on the subject of delay.

"This letter is written under the affliction of a violent fever, into which I have relapsed, after a perfect cure, as I presumed, about two weeks ago. But knowing, that I write to one, who has always shewn himself regardful of me, beyond my deserts, I shall conclude with repeating to you, my dear sir, that I am yr obliged & affectionate friend" (DLC:GW).

For a more detailed account of Randolph's reservations about accepting a post in the new government, see his letter to James Madison, 19 July 1789, in Rutland, *Madison Papers*, 12:298–300. On 23 Dec. he sent GW a formal reply, stating that he accepted the commission. "I purpose to be present at the supreme court in february. But the peculiar situation of my family and of my private affairs will probably prevent me from fixing my residence in New-York immediately; if the nature of my duties will permit, (as I hope they will) my absence, until my final arrangements can be made" (DNA: RG 59, Acceptances & Orders for Commissions). Randolph arrived in New York around 2 Feb. 1790 (Reardon, *Edmund Randolph*, 191).

To Thomas Hartley

Sir,   New York September 29th 1789

As you are about to return to your own State, you will oblige me by informing the Gentlemen to whom you wrote some time ago—or any others in whom you can place entire confidence that I will give £400 Pennsa currency (to be paid in specie) for twenty mares of the annexed description, delivered at my Seat of Mount Vernon in Virginia (which is only nine miles from Alexandria) and I will allow besides a commission of 5 ℔ cent on the said £400 as compensation for the trouble of purchasing, which two sums I mean to be in full of *all* expences, risk &ca in delivering of them as above.

Description

None of the above mares are to be under *15 hands high* by a proper standard measure—not to exceed *six years old* last spring—and *to be warranted sound*. Bays or Blacks would be preferred, but no colour rejected—They must not be low in flesh, or have marks of abuse about them—being a little rubbed by collars will not be regarded.

If a contract of this sort can be made, The mares must all be taken to Mount Vernon at one time—and duplicate descriptive lists of their colours, brands, and marks, minutely detailed— One of which must be sent to me by the post, when the mares set off for Mount Vernon—the other will accompany them to that place, in order to receive at the foot of it the receipt of my nephew Major George Augt. Washington, who lives at my house, which receipt will entitle the Purchaser, or bearer thereof with your order annexed to the aforesaid sum of £420 which shall be paid at this place at any moment it is presented.

As I have no doubt of getting mares answering this description for 40 or 50 dollars and am assured of this fact by Col. Thos Lowry,[1] I am not inclined to exceed the sum of £420 for the above mentioned 20—and therefore beg the favor of you as soon after your return home as you can make it convenient to let me know if I may depend upon that number in your parts for this price—Should this commission be executed to the entire satisfaction of my Nephew, who will be charged with the examination of the mares, and will be instructed to reject any, and all, that deviate from the above description, it is not only possible, but very probable that I may take 20 more on the same terms, from the same or other persons, being more convenient than any that could be bought in Jersey.[2] I am &ca

G. Washington

LB, DLC:GW.

In the summer of 1789 GW, hoping to purchase "a number of good brood mares to send to Virginia" in order to raise mules by them from his jackasses, opened correspondence on the subject with several individuals in the New York–Pennsylvania–New Jersey area. See GW to Abraham Hunt, 20 July 1789, Hunt's reply, 21 July 1789, and Thomas Hartley to GW, 31 July 1789. Both Hunt and Hartley were encouraging about the possibility of purchasing mares suiting GW's specifications.

1. Conversations with Lowrey during the summer apparently had led GW to believe the mares could be easily acquired in New Jersey. On 1 Oct. 1789 he wrote GW from Alexandria, N.J., that he had purchased a "pair of Bay mares for you, six years old next Spring. full fifteen hands high proportionable and well Built . . . next week I shall send them down by a Carefull hand" (ViMtV).

2. On 6 Oct. Hartley wrote GW from Lancaster, Pa., that consultation with his contacts in Pennsylvania had indicated that mares of the type required by GW could not be purchased in Pennsylvania for less than £25, not counting the additional costs of sending them to Mount Vernon and that he was pessimistic about the chances of purchasing at GW's price in New Jersey (NjMoNP). Hartley's letter arrived while GW was on his New England tour, but on his return he wrote Hartley, 20 Nov., "I was in hopes, from the knowledge I had of what such mares, as I described, are now and then bought for in Virginia—from what Colonel Lowry told me of the price of them in New Jersey—from the season of the year, when Farmers find it convenient to dispose of superfluous mouths, and from the number it was probable I might take (which made it an object) that the price offered by me, in my letter of the 29. of september last, would be sufficient to procure them.

"I have neither seen, heard from, nor written to Colonel Lowry since my return to this city on the above subject, and believing that *better* mares for my purpose, and more convenient, can be had in Lancaster county than in Jersey, I am disposed to give Five hundred pounds, Pennsylvania currency, for Twenty mares, such as are therein described; delivered as there directed. This sum of £500 Pennsa currency I mean to be in full for the purchase and all incidental expences attending the mares. In other respects my letter of the 29 of September, alluded to, is expressive of my desires, and must be referred to in case of a purchase." In a postscript, GW added: "For your information *only*, I will add, that rather than not get the mares I will allow besides the Five hundred Pounds for twenty—Twenty shillings for each for the expence of transportation—but it is *really* too much; and nothing but the expectation of having fine Mares would induce me to exceed the sum proposed in my former letter" (LB, DLC:GW. In the letter book this letter is mistakenly dated 20 Oct.).

GW could not have found Hartley's reply of 2 Dec. encouraging. Although, Hartley stressed, he intended to devote his best efforts to carrying out GW's instructions, "The Mares of the description you wish, are only to be found in the hands of the rich and powerful Farmers, who are under no necessity of parting with them; indeed, next to a good Plantation, they esteem those large breeding Mares most, and they are not to be obtained from the holders of them without the utmost difficulty" (ViMtV). On 7 Dec. Hartley again promised to continue his search, "tho' I must confess my Expectations are not so sanguine as they were" (ViMtV).

Hartley had been working through various business contacts in Pennsylvania in his search for the mares, and in mid-January he gave GW in New York a letter from Paul Zantzinger, 3 Jan. 1790, to Hartley, enclosing a list of animals that had been offered for sale to him and one of his colleagues (DLC:GW; the list is also in DLC:GW). GW wrote Hartley, 16 Jan. 1790, that he had read Zantzinger's letter "and considered, and feel myself under very great obligations to those Gentlemen, and to you, Sir, for the disinterested trouble you have already taken, and are willing to continue to procure for me the number that I want.

"It was not my intention to give this trouble to any one without making compensation, and, for that reason I placed my business upon the restrictive footing of my former letter—But, as these Gentlemen, are so obliging as to undertake this business merely to serve me (for which, through you, I beg to offer my acknowledgements) it would not only be uncivil, but unjust to expect they should incur any expence or run any risque in the prosecution of it on my account—I would therefore leave it to them to act for me as they would for themselves in the purchase of 17 mares which, with the three you conditionally contracted for will complete my object—but I must still require That the average price of the above 17 may not exceed £25 or £26 Pennsylvania currency—That all such as may be under 15 hands (by standard measure) shall not exceed 4 years old next spring—and, in this case, none may be under 14½ hands high. That none may at any rate exceed six years old and be perfectly sound—the loss of an eye, if not proceeding from a mad or restive disposition I should not regard, as the defect will no doubt be considered in the price. That they shall be sent to Mount Vernon, at my expence, under the conduct of a careful man, with a descriptive list not only of the *exact* height and colour but of the minutest marks, natural and accidental, and a duplicate thereof to me—This may be useful on many accounts, and without it, a man not *very* scrupulous might exchange the best of them for others of inferior quality answering a *general* description.

"Receiving them at Mount Vernon any time in the month of February will answer *my* purposes fully, but I should be unwilling to incur the expence of keeping them until that time at the house of the Sellers. It may rest therefore with Colonel Miller and Mr Zantzinger whether they will send the whole to Mount Vernon at one or at two trips as they may be purchased.

"I will lodge in Colo. Biddle's hands £400 subject to the orders of the above Gentlemen, and whatever this may fall short of the purchase shall be paid as soon as it is made known . . . " (LB, DLC:GW).

On 22 Feb. 1790 Hartley informed GW that "eleven Mares from Lancaster and three from Yorke are sent on to Mount Vernon. I enclose you a Duplicate Discriptions &c. and shall do myself the Honor of waiting upon you to Morrow Morning and will shew You some Letters and Papers respecting that Business." Hartley's letter and the lists of the mares and their owners, 15 and 22 Feb. 1790, are in DLC:GW. By 15 Mar. the dealers had sent the last four mares to Virginia (Hartley to GW, 15 Mar. 1790, DLC:GW). "The 6 mares which remain to complete the 20 purchased by Mr Zantzinger arrived here on Friday night last," George Augustine Washington wrote GW on 26 Mar., "a Copy of the discriptive list which accompanied them is enclosed, of these I do not think less favorably than the first sent" (ViMtV). For a description of the mares, see George Augustine Washington's letter to GW, 26 Mar.; see also Zantzinger to George Augustine Washington, 9 and 14 Mar., and Washington to Zantzinger, 20 Mar. (ViMtV) for the transportation of the mares to Mount Vernon. On 10 April 1790 GW wrote Zantzinger and Adam Reigart: "Colonel Hartley has put into my hands the account of the mares, which you have been so obliging as to purchase for me, and I have paid to that Gentleman the balance due upon your account. I have received from my Nephew, Major Washington, information of the safe arrival of all the Mares at Mount Vernon, and he appears to be much pleased with them.

"When I expressed to Colonel Hartley my wish to procure a number of mares for breeding from your quarter, I fully expected to compensate the trouble of the person who might purchase them for me, by commission or otherwise. But, Gentlemen, your declining to accept any thing more than an indemnification for the cost and expence which attended the purchase of them, has added to the obligation which I feel for your having executed the commission in so satisfactory a manner—and I beg you to be assured that I have a proper sense of your politeness on this occasion" (LB, DLC:GW).

See also Lear to Biddle, 17 and 21 Jan. 1790 (PHi: Washington-Biddle Correspondence), and Biddle to Lear, 24 and 28 Jan. 1790 (PHi: Clement Biddle Letter Book, 1789–92).

From Benjamin Palmer

[29 September 1789]

The Petition of Benjamin Palmer Most humbly Sheweth.

That your Petitioner lived on Minefords Island commonly called City Island in the State of New York in the beginning of the War between Great Britain and those States and your Petitioner with all his Family were taken Prisoners by the British who used us very Ill. And then ordered us off my Plantation which I then had on said Island down to New York where I have continued with my Family ever since—The case of their using me so ill was on Account of sending a Letter to General How the Commander of the British Army in Vindication of and setting forth the just Case of the people of this Country had to oppose the King's orders—A copy of said Letter I wish to lay before your Excellency[1] with the proceedings our people made to take away my Lands from me after they had got quiet possession of those States with several other copies of Letters of consequence, which your Petitioner has a great desire that your Excellency will take some suitable time to peruse them. And your Petitioner as in duty Bound will ever pray &c.

Benjn Palmer

LS, NHi: Palmer Papers; ADfS, NHi: Palmer Papers.
  Benjamin Palmer, a locally prominent New York landowner, purchased City Island, a long, narrow strip of land of some 230 acres located in the northerly side of Eastchester Bay, in 1761. In 1756 he had led in the construction of a bridge from the island at Spuyten Devil, in the process running afoul of Col. Thomas Philippse, a local landowner who was deprived of tolls by the bridge's location. In retaliation, Philippse had reputedly "twice caused Palmer to be impressed as a soldier for service in Canada" (Jenkins, *Bronx*, 190, 428).
  1. The enclosure has not been found.

Proclamation on the Treaty of Fort Harmar

[New York, 29 Sept. 1789]
By the President Of the United States of America.
A Proclamation.

Whereas by Virtue of Powers given by the United States in Congress assembled, to Arthur St. Clair, Governor of the Territory Northwest of the Ohio, and Commissioner Plenipotentiary for treating with the Indian Nations in the Northern Department, a Treaty was concluded at Fort-Harmar, on the ninth Day of January last past, by the said Arthur St. Clair, on the Part of the United States, with the Sachems, Chiefs and Warriors of the Wyandot, Delaware, Ottawa, Chippawa, Pattiwatima and Sac Nations.[1]

And whereas I have, by and with the Advice and Consent of the Senate, in due Form ratified the said Treaty,—NOW Therefore, to the End that the same may be observed and performed with good Faith on the Part of the United States, I have ordered the said Treaty to be herewith published; and I do hereby enjoin and require all Officers of the United States, Civil and Military, and all other Citizens and Inhabitants thereof, faithfully to observe and fulfil the same.[2]

Given under my Hand in the City of New-York, this Twenty-ninth Day of September, in the Year of our Lord One Thousand Seven Hundred and Eighty-nine, and in the Thirteenth Year of the Sovereignty and Independence of the United States.

G. Washington.

By Command of the President of }
the United States of America, }
    H. KNOX
    Secretary for the Department of War.

Broadside, DLC: Peter Force Collection, Northwest Territory Miscellany. Another copy of this broadside was sold by Parke Bernet in 1943 (Historical & Literary Autographs Collected by A. C. Meyer).

1. See Arthur St. Clair to GW, 2 May 1789. The text of the two treaties of 9 Jan. 1789, one with the "Wyandot, Delaware, Ottowa, Chippewa, Pattewatima, and Sac Nations" and the other with the Six Nations, are printed in *DHFC*, 2:152–63. The treaties, in the writing of Josiah Harmar and Arthur St. Clair, respectively, are in DNA: RG 11, treaties 15 and 16.

2. The second page of the broadside in the Peter Force Collection begins "GEORGE WASHINGTON, President of the United States of America. To All to Whom These Presents Shall Come, *Greeting*: *Whereas a Treaty between the* United States, *and the* Wyandot, Delaware, Ottawa, Chippewa, Pattawatima, *and* Sac *Nations of* Indians, *was in due Form made and concluded at Fort-Harmar, on the ninth Day of January last past, by* Arthur St. Clair, *Governor of the Territory North-west of the Ohio; who was duly authorized thereto by the said States on their Part, and by the Sachems and Warriors of the said Nations on their Part: Which Treaty is in the Form and Words following*, viz." The text of the treaty follows.

To John Rutledge

Dear Sir,   New York Septr 29th 1789

In requesting your candid attention to a subject, which I deem highly interesting to our Country, I am convinced that I address myself well.

Regarding the due administration of Justice as the strongest cement of good government, I have considered the first organi-

sation of the judicial department as essential to the happiness of
our Citizens, and to the stability of our political system. Under
this impression it has been an invariable object of anxious solicitude with me to select the fittest Characters to expound the laws
and dispense justice.

This sentiment, Sir, has over-ruled, in my mind, the opinions
of some of your friends, when they suggested that you might
not accept an appointment to a seat on the supreme Bench of
the United-States—The hesitation, which those opinions produced, was but momentary, when I reflected on the confidence
which your former services had established in the public mind,
and when I exercised my own belief of your dispositions still
further to sacrifice to the good of your country.

In any event I concluded that I should discharge the duty
which I owe to the Public by[1] nominating to this important office
a Person whom I judged best qualified to execute its' functions—and you will allow me to repeat the wish that I may have
the pleasure to hear of your acceptance[2] of the appointment—
My best respects are offered to Mrs Rutledge and with sentiments of very great esteem and regard I am, Dear Sir, Your Most
Obedient and Affectionate Humble Servant

George Washington

Df, DNA: RG 59, Miscellaneous Letters; LB, DLC:GW.
For background to GW's Judiciary appointments, see his letter to the
United States Senate, 24 Sept. 1789.

1. At this point the words "appointing the person" were written and
crossed out.

2. The remainder of this paragraph and the closing are taken from the
letter-book copy. Rutledge replied on 27 Oct.: "I have had the pleasure of
receiving the Letter, of September 29th, with which you were so kind as to
favour me, & request that you will be pleased to accept my warmest Acknowledgements, for the Opinion you express of my former Conduct, & present
disposition.

"I esteem it highly honourable, to be selected as one of the fittest Characters to fill the Supreme Judicial Department, & associated with Gentlemen of
such Ability & Integrity as those whom you have chosen for that purpose.

"The future plan of Life which I had formed was that of Ease & Retirement: But, on considering the Subject of your Letter, with the Attention
which it merited & excited, I have determined to accept the Trust committed
to me, &, by a faithful Execution of it, contribute my best Endeavour⟨s⟩ to
promote the Stability of our political System, & Happiness of our Country"
(DLC:GW).

To the United States Senate

United States
Gentlemen of the Senate.   September 29th 1789.

I nominate William Carmichael as Charge des affaires from the United States of America to the Court of Spain.

Go: Washington

LS, DNA: RG 46, First Congress, Records of Executive Proceedings, President's Messages—Executive Nominations.

To the United States Senate

United-States
Gentlemen of the Senate,   September 29th 1789.

Agreeably to the act of Congress for adapting the establishment of the Troops in public service to the Constitution of the United States,[1] I nominate the Persons, specified in the enclosed list, to be the commissioned Officers thereof.

This nomination differs from the existing arrangement only in the following cases—to wit.

Lieutenant Erkuries Beatty promoted to a vacant captaincy in the Infantry—Ensign Edward Spear promoted to a vacant Lieutenancy of Artillery—Jacob Melcher, who has been serving as a Volunteer, to be an Ensign, vice Benjamin Lawrence, who was appointed nearly three years past, and has never been mustered, or joined the Troops.

It is to be observed that the order, in which the Captains and Subalterns are named, is not to affect their relative rank, which has been hitherto but imperfectly settled, owing to the perplexity of promotions in the State-quotas conformably to the late confederation.

Go: Washington

LS, in the writing of William Jackson, DNA: RG 46, First Congress, Records of Executive Proceedings, President's Messages—Executive Nominations; LB, DLC:GW.

1. "An Act to recognize and adapt to the Constitution of the United States the establishment of the Troops raised under the Resolves of the United States in Congress assembled, and for other purposes therein mentioned" continued the military establishment provided for in the resolve of the Confederation Congress of 3 Oct. 1787 (*JCC*, 33:602–4). Section 5, for "the purpose of pro-

tecting the inhabitants of the frontiers of the United States from the hostile incursions of the Indians," authorized the president "to call into service from time to time, such part of the militia of the states respectively, as he may judge necessary for the purpose aforesaid" (1 *Stat.* 95–96 [29 Sept. 1789]).

Enclosure
Nominations for the United States Army

United States September 29th 1789.
Officers of the Regiment of Infantry

Leiut. Colo. Commandant Josiah Harmar	And a Brigadier General by brevet, he having been appointed such by a resolve of Congress of the 31st of July 1787[1]

Majors
  John Plasgrave Wyllys
  John F. Hamtramck
Captains
  Jonathan Heart
  David Zeigler
  William McCurdy
  John Mercer
  David Strong
  John Smith
  Joseph Ashton
  Erkuries Beatty.
Lieutenants
  John Armstrong
  John Pratt
  Ebenezer Frothingham
  William Kersey
  Thomas Doyle
  William Peters
  Jacob Kingsbury
  Ebenezer Denny
Ensigns
  Francis Luse
  Cornelius Ryrer Sedam
  Nathan McDowell

Abner Prior
Robert Thompson
Asa Hartshorn
John Jeffers
Jacob Melcher
Surgeon
Richard Allison
Mates
John Elliot
John Scott
John Carmichael
Joshua Sumner
Officers of the battalion Artillery
Major Commandant John Doughty
Captains
Henry Burbeck
William Ferguson
Joseph Savage
James Bradford
Lieutenants
John Pierce
Moses Porter
William Moore
Di[r]ck Schuyler
Mahlon Ford
Matthew Ernest
Edward Spear
Ebenezer Smith Fowle
Surgeon's Mate
Nathaniel Heyward

Go: Washington

DS, in the writing of Tobias Lear, DNA: RG 46, First Congress, Records of Executive Proceedings, President's Messages—Executive Nominations; LB, DLC:GW.

1. *JCC*, 33:440.

To the United States Senate and House of Representatives

United States
Gentlemen of the Senate,   September 29th 1789.

Having been yesterday informed by a joint-Committee of both Houses of Congress, that they had agreed to a Recess to commence this day, and to continue until the first monday of January next, I take the earliest opportunity of acquainting you that, considering how long and laborious this Session has been, and the Reasons, which, I presume, have produced this Resolution, it does not appear to me expedient to recommend any measures to their consideration at present—or now to call your attention, Gentlemen, to any of those matters in my Department, which require your advice and consent, and yet remain to be dispatched.

Go: Washington

LS, DNA: RG 46, First Congress, Records of Legislative Proceedings, President's Messages; copy, DNA: RG 233, First Congress, Records of Legislative Proceedings, Journals; LB, DLC:GW.

To the United States Senate and House of Representatives

United States,
Gentlemen of the Senate.   September 29th 1789.

His Most Christian Majesty, by a letter dated the 7th of June last, addressed to the President and Members of the General Congress of the United States of North America, announces the much lamented death of his Son the Dauphin.[1] The generous conduct of the French Monarch and Nation towards this Country renders every event that may affect his or their prosperity interesting to us, and I shall take care to assure him of the sensibility with which the United States participate in the affliction which a loss so much to be regretted must have occasioned both to him and to them.

Go: Washington

LS, DNA: RG 46, First Congress, Records of Legislative Proceedings, President's Messages; copy, DNA: RG 233, First Congress, Records of Legislative Proceedings, Journals; LB, DLC:GW.

1. For the background to the death of the dauphin, see Louis XVI to GW, 7 June 1789, n.1.

From Hezekiah Welch

Sr   Boston Sept. 29 1789

The Goodness of the Gentman I am Addresing my self to, and the Necessity that I am under Obliges me to make though to you Sr am an onknown Stranger but your Goodness Emboldings me to send a fue Lines to inform you, I bore a Commission in the Continental Sea Service during the whole of the war. I had with most part of the time three son's am now some what Advanced in Age with a Fameley yet to bring up should always be happay to be Employde in some thing to Support them when Peace took Place I had Due to me for wages in the Servis near a Eleven Hundred Dollers which through Necessity I was Obliged to sell for four & Eight Pence in the Pound to Support my Fameley and am now Living upon that Little at Preasent I was in Hopes when I heard General Lincoln was Chosen Corlector for the Port of Boston I should have bin so happay as to have Receive'd some appointment as I was Acquainted with the General at the seige at So. Carolina but could not Obtain it, all though I Applide to the General and Suppose it was to so many Applications that it was not in his Power to do as he could have wish'd, the Vice President knowes me Sr I have Applyde to him before and now make bold to wright again to him hoping I shall find some Friends, Any Recommendations which may be wanting can be furnish'd by my Brother Saml Adams who is Leiut. Govenour of this Common wealth and by a Number of Other Gentlemen if Necessary, Excuse me Sr if I have done wrong or maide my Self to Bold in Persuming to Wright to you but Nesessity Obliges me to do it. and am Sr your most Obedent Servant at Command

Hez. Welch

ALS, DLC:GW.

Hezekiah Welch (1734–1797) was commissioned a lieutenant in the Continental navy in October 1776, served as a lieutenant commanding the ship

Boston in 1778, and later as first lieutenant of the *Alliance*. During the 1790s he served as mate of the Massachusetts revenue cutter.

From Zacharias Sickels

May it Please your Excellency   New York September 1789
    Having laboured hard for some time past in making Interest with such of the Members of both Houses as I was acquainted with to assist me in procuring only a Clerks birth in one of the Offices to be established under the present Government; The Gentlemen to whom I have applied is General Schuyler of the Senate and Mr Egbert Benson and Judge Lawrance of the lower House, they have promised me all their Assistance in procuring a birth for me, but am fearful their application will be too late, their being many watching every chance, therefore have thought proper to address these few lines to his Excellency hoping through his goodness I may not be neglected, but am fearful the attempt is too great knowing his Excellency must have more business of Importance than to trouble himself with this.

    Shortly after the Peace took place I moved to this City to begin some kind of business, was scarcely settled before I was burnt out, and again returned to the Country and stay'd till May last when I moved to this again to try what I could do in the Tobacco Business, but have again failed, being in want of a Capital and too many in the business at present, I am almost tired out with the Promises of my friends assistance in procuring me a birth; want of employ has given rise to my intruding on his Excellencys patience.

    I have a Family to provide for, I have no trade but the Quill being brought up in the Mercantile Line, and sorry I am for it. During the Late War I served in the Northern Department with Colo. Morgan Lewis from May 1777 to June 1781 for which services have received Certificates as compensation at present worth very little, and then not 'till the Year 1786, in July 1781 entered with Colo. Varick on his Excellencys business and continued 'till the close of it, for which service received a handsome compensation should heartily rejoice to be again employed in business of like kind.

I do not mean by the above (nor do I expect it from so great a Character as his Excellency) that his Excellency should interfere in the business by speaking to any of the Gentlemen appointed but to advise me how or in what manner to proceed in procuring for myself what I so much want, and so ardently wish a Clerks birth or any other business that may enable me to live untill a change of times takes place, for never was such times known in this City for Poor people to get a living as the present.

I must again beg his Excellency to pardon me for daring to intrude upon his patience in troubling him with such trifling affairs, (to Public business,) but as trifling as it may appear to me of great importance to succeed, I am in duty bound to Subscribe myself Your Excellency's Most obedient most devoted & most hume servant

Zachs Sickels

If his Excellency should condescend to commit any thing to writing for my conduct and instruction I shall rejoice to call on his Excellency for it.

ALS, DLC:GW.

During the Revolution Zacharias Sickels (died c.1793) served as a store-keeper for the northern department at Albany (Col. Morgan Lewis's lists of employees for the northern department, DNA:PCC, item 173, vol. 1, 105, 269). In the early 1790s he was apparently working as a cooper in New York City ("Letters of Administration," *New-York Historical Society Collections*, 38:359).

From Betty Washington Lewis

My Dear Brother   October 1th 1789
I receiv'd your Letter Sepbr 13th in answer to that of Colo. Balls, George, Bushrod, and Corbin is here at this time I shall indeaver to have Every thing done as you desire[1] you mention in your Letter to me that the Negros was to be divided into five Parts and one fifth part would be mine, Bushrod informes me that I have no Right to any Part,[2] there is with that negro that you have thirteen which divided in to fore Parts thear would be more than fore to your Share, the other things that was her property not mention'd in the will, sutch as was left in the House I wish to hear from you how thear to be dis Posed of, the Docters

bills is more than I expectted, Halls Bill is £45P.—Mortemores £22P.[3] the Debts I think will be upwards of one Hundred Pounds, there is several we have Heard of not brawt in as yet, Colo. Ball thinks the Crop will Pay of the Debts, if that is the Case the Money then ariseing from the Plantation utensils and st[o]ck must be divided, we shall be able to give an Exact accompt of the debts by the next Post, I am Dear Brother With Love to my Sister Washington Robert and the Children Your Affecte Sister

Betty Lewis

ALS, ViMtV.

1. George is probably George Lewis (1757–1821), son of Fielding and Betty Washington Lewis. During the Revolution Lewis had served as a captain of an independent troop of cavalry which was part of GW's personal bodyguard. After the war Lewis and his wife lived near Berryville in what was then Frederick County, Va., but by 1785 apparently had moved to Fredericksburg. For Bushrod Washington, see his letter to GW, 9 Nov. 1788, source note. Bushrod and Corbin Washington (1765–c.1799) were GW's and Betty Lewis's nephews and the sons of John Augustine and Hannah Bushrod Washington.

2. Augustine Washington's will specified that all of his slaves, except those individually devised, be divided among "my Wife and my three sons, Samuel, John and Charles." After Mary Ball Washington's death the surviving slaves and their issue were to go to GW, Samuel, John, and Charles (will, 11 April 1743, DLC:GW). See Memorandum: Division of Slaves, 1762, source note.

3. Doctors Charles Mortimer and Elisha Hall of Fredericksburg had attended Mary Ball Washington in her last illness. See GW to Richard Conway, 6 Mar. 1789, n.2; Burgess Ball to GW, 25 Aug. 1789.

From Jacob Richardson

Sir, Newport Octor 1. 1789.

By Capt. Clarke, who arived here last evening, in 50 days from Nants in France I receiv'd a number of Letters, into the Post Office, one of which was for you Sir, which I enclose, & Send by one of our Packets, which wish safe to your hands, I send it in this way that it may gett to you sooner than by Post, we have but one Post in a Week to N. york, goes from here Tuesdays, and getts to N. york on Saturday following. I am wishing you health and happiness. Your most hume Servt

Jacob Richardson

P.S. I have Just heard that Mr Osgood, is appointed, Post Master General,[1] if you Sir, would be so kind as to request of him my continuance in this small Office, provided he has a good Report of my services in said Office from 1784 to this time, you will do me a particular favour.[2]

ALS, DNA: RG 59, Miscellaneous Letters.

Jacob Richardson (c.1738–1818), longtime postmaster for Newport, was perhaps best known for his dispute in the late 1780s with Gov. John Collins over the payment by Rhode Islanders for postage in depreciated currency. See Polishook, *Rhode Island and the Union,* 175–78; *Columbian Centinel* (Boston), 14 Oct. 1818. Richardson retained his post under the new government. See correspondence with the postmaster general in DNA: RG 28, Letters Sent by the Postmaster General, 1789–1836, passim.

1. Samuel Osgood (1748–1813) of Andover, Mass., had studied for the ministry at Harvard but after graduating in 1770 joined a business firm with his brother. During the Revolution he served as aide-de-camp to Artemas Ward. In 1781 he was elected to Congress and served until 1784; in 1785 he became a member of the Board of Treasury. Although Osgood had not supported the Constitution in the struggle for ratification, GW nevertheless appointed him to succeed Ebenezer Hazard as postmaster general in September 1789. Osgood served until the government moved to Philadelphia in the summer of 1790.

2. Tobias Lear replied to this letter on the president's behalf on 12 Oct., acknowledging Richardson's letter and informing him that "I am directed by him to inform you, in answer to that part of your letter which relates to the Post Office, that he never interferes in the appointment of any Officers whose appointment does not by law come under his immediate cognizance. Mr Osgood must act as he pleases in the appointment of his deputies" (DNA: RG 59, Miscellaneous Letters; LB, DLC:GW). The letter-book copy of Lear's letter was inadvertently addressed to the postmaster at Providence.

Tobias Lear to Clement Biddle

Dear Sir,   New York, October 2d, 1789.

Your favor of the 30th ultimo came to hand last evening accompanied with the Padusoy for Mrs Washington, the bill of which was enclosed.[1]

The President will thank you to get from Mr Bartram a list of the plants & shrubs which he has for sale, with the price affixed to each, and also a note to each of the time proper for transplanting them, as he is desireous of having some sent to Mount Vernon this fall if it is proper.[2]

It is customary for those persons who publish lists of their plants &c. to insert many which they have had, but which have been all disposed of—the President will therefore wish to have a list only of what he actually has in his Gardon. I am, Dear Sir, with very great esteem Your most Obedt St

Tobias Lear.

ALS, PHi: Washington-Biddle Correspondence; ADfS, ViMtV; LB, DLC:GW.

  1. Biddle's letter of 30 Sept. has not been located.
  2. William Bartram (1739–1823) and his brother John Bartram, Jr. (1743–1812), operated a botanical garden on the Schuylkill River about three miles from Philadelphia. GW visited the gardens in 1787 when he was at the Constitutional Convention. At that time he was not particularly overly impressed with the Bartrams' establishment "which, tho' Stored with many curious plts. Shrubs & trees, many of which are exotics was not laid off with much taste, nor was it large" (*Diaries*, 5:166–67). GW was eventually successful in acquiring plants from the Bartrams. One shipment was sent by the firm in March 1792, and as some of the plants failed to survive, a second shipment was sent in November of that year. See Catalog of Plants from John Bartram, March 1792.

Circular to the Governors of the States

Sir,   United States October 2nd 1789.
  In pursuance of the enclosed resolution I have the honor to transmit to your Excellency a copy of the amendments proposed to be added to the Constitution of the United States.[1] I have the honor to be, with due consideration, Your Excellency's most obedient Servant.

Go: Washington

LS, to John Collins, R-AR; LS, to John Hancock, DLC: U.S. Constitution—Amendments to the Constitution; LS, to Samuel Huntington, owned (1989) by the Forbes Magazine Collection, New York; LS, to Samuel Johnston, Nc-Ar: Governor's Papers; LS, to John Langdon, MnMAt; LS, to Thomas Mifflin, PHi: Gratz Collection—Federal Convention; LS, to Charles Pinckney, ScCA: Records of the General Assembly, Governor's Message no. 511; LS, to Beverley Randolph, PHi: Dreer Collection; LS, MdHi.

  1. On 24 Sept., while the amendments to the Constitution were still under consideration by the Senate and House of Representatives, the House resolved that "the President of the United States be requested to transmit to the executives of the several states which have ratified the Constitution, copies of the amendments proposed by Congress to be added thereto; and like copies

to the executives of the states of Rhode-Island and North-Carolina." By 28 Sept. both the House and Senate had agreed to the amendments and the Senate agreed to the House's resolution requesting GW to transmit the amendments to the states (*DHFC*, 3:229, 238).

The enclosure to GW's circular reads:

"Congress of the United States
begun and held at the City of New York on
Wednesday the fourth of March.
one thousand seven hundred and eighty nine."

"The Conventions of a number of the States, having at the time of their adopting the Constitution, expressed a desire, in order to prevent misconstruction or abuse of its powers, that further declaratory and restrictive clauses should be added: And as extending the ground of Public confidence in the Government, will best secure the beneficent ends of its institution;

"Resolved by the Senate and House of Representatives of the United States of America, in Congress assembled, two thirds of both Houses concurring, that the following Articles be proposed to the Legislatures of the several States, as amendments to the Constitution of the United States, all, or any of which Articles, when ratified by three fourths of the said Legislatures, to be valid to all intents and purposes, as part of the said Constitution; Vizt

"Articles in addition to, and amendment of the Constitution of the United States of America, proposed by Congress, and ratified by the Legislatures of the several States, pursuant to the fifth Article of the original Constitution.

"Article the first. After the first enumeration, required by the first Article of the Constitution, there shall be one representation for every thirty thousand, until the number shall amount to one hundred, after which the proportion shall be so regulated by Congress, that there shall be not less than one hundred Representatives, nor less than one representative for every forty thousand persons, until the number of representatives shall amount to two hundred, after which the proportion shall be so regulated by Congress, that there shall not be less than two hundred Representatives, nor more than one Representative for every fifty thousand persons.

"Article the second. No law varying the compensation for the services of the Senators and Representatives, shall take effect, until an election of representatives shall have intervened.

"Article the third. Congress shall make no law respecting an establishment of religion, or prohibiting the free exercise thereof; or abridging the freedom of Speech, or of the Press; or the right of the People peaceably to assemble, and to Petition the Government for a redress of grievances.

"Article the fourth. A well regulated militia, being necessary to the security of a free State, the right of the people to keep and bear Arms shall not be infringed.

"Article the fifth. No soldier shall in time of Peace be quartered in any House, without the consent of the owner, nor in time of War, but in a manner to be prescribed by law.

"Article the sixth. The right of the people to be secure in their persons, houses, papers, and effects, against unreasonable searches and seizures, shall

not be violated and no warrant shall issue, but upon probable cause, supported by oath or affirmation, and particularly describing the place to be
searched, and the persons or things to be seized.

"Article the seventh[.] No person shall be held to answer for a capital, or
otherwise infamous crime, unless on a presentment or indictment of a Grand
Jury, except in cases arising in the land or naval forces, or in the Militia, when
in actual service in time of war or public danger; nor shall any person be
subject for the same offence to be twice put in jeopardy of life or limb, nor
shall be compelled in any criminal case to be a witness against himself, nor be
deprived of life, liberty or property, without due process of law; nor shall
private property be taken for public use, without just compensation.

"Article the eighth[.] In all criminal prosecutions, the accused shall enjoy
the right to a speedy and public trial, by an impartial jury of the State and
district wherein the crime shall have been committed, which district shall have
been previously ascertained by law, and to be informed of the nature and
cause of the accusation, to be confronted with the witnesses against him; to
have compulsory process for obtaining witnesses in his favor, and to have the
assistance of counsel for his defence.

"Article the ninth[.] In suits of Common law, where the value in controversy
shall exceed twenty dollars, the right of trial by jury shall be preserved, and
no fact tried by a jury shall be otherwise re-examined in any court of the
United States, than according to the rules of the common law.

"Article the tenth[.] Excessive bail shall not be required, nor excessive fines
imposed, nor cruel and unusual punishments inflicted.

"Article the eleventh[.] The enumeration in the Constitution of certain
rights, shall not be construed to deny or disparage others retained by the
People.

"Article the Twelfth[.] The powers not delegated to the United States by
the Constitution, nor prohibited by it to the States, are reserved to the States
respectively, or to the people" (photocopy, DLC: U.S. Constitution—Amendments to the Constitution). The document is signed by Frederick Augustus
Muhlenberg as Speaker of the House of Representatives and John Adams as
president of the Senate and attested by John Beckley, clerk of the House of
Representatives, and James Otis, secretary of the Senate. The first two articles
were not finally ratified by the states.

From John Moriarty

Salem [Mass.]
May it please your Excellency—   2d October 1789
I came here from Ireland in the begining of the late war &
Cheerfully Contributed to the Cause of freedom & to maintain
our rights, and amply bore my share of the burthen.
In the year 1782. my losses in trade by Capture and other

Casualties were great; & to Compleat my ruin £32000. of the old Emmission died in my hands, which the Records of the state Treasurer will Verify—Since which, I have been Strugling to Support my family—and *Hope* has kept me from Despair, & Chear'd me with the thought that under the new Government I might have Some appointment of which I was Capable that would make some amends for my losses and afford a Support— I flatter myself that in the appointment officers under the Revenue Law I might have been so happy as to obtain one, I applyed to Some of the members of the Honorable house, who I had earnestly Intreated to Solicit in my behalf, but in this, was disapointed as prior Engagemts & motives of Consanguinity Superceded my Claims to their Intercessions—Some friends Inform me that there Will be many other Offices to fill that my abilities & Services may Intitle me to a place in, & advise me to apply directly to your Excellency.

With these Encouragements I venture to address your Excellency with all due Difference to your Exalted Station—Humbly to Implore your Condescention to notice me thus far as to appoint me to Some Office that may afford me a support.

The Honorable Robert Morris Esquire will give you my Character, & Shew your Excellency in ample manner how Strongly I have been recommended to him by Some respectable Characters in Europe, that may Claim your favourable notice. May God long prosper your Excellency a Savior to this Country in as Eminent and Illustrious a manner as you have been its Defender—is the prayer of your Excellency's Most Obedient Humble Servant

John Moriarty

ALS, DLC:GW.

During the Revolution John Moriarty (d. 1797) had owned at least four Salem-based privateers (Allen, *Massachusetts Privateers*, 132, 201). For more information on his early career, see his letter to GW, 8 Mar. 1784, requesting help in establishing himself in business. At one time he was apparently moderately successful since he owned an impressive house in Salem. William Bentley, pastor of the East Church in Salem, in an entry in his diary for 22 Aug. 1797, describes Moriarty's end: "Last night one John Moriarty, an Irishman, well known for his revels, was upon his late return homewards, & being ill able to find his way, both from the darkness of the night & of his own faculties, tumbled into a well in Ash Street, which was deep but entirely dry, & perished. He was not found until towards night, having been about twelve hours in this condition. Said John has been a remarkable settler of accounts, & very busy in litigious suits at Law, a writer in the Clerk's office & at last a Bookseller. He came from Ireland to the Bay of Fundy, & at the Commencement of the Am. war, to Salem. Purchased an estate . . . & lost it & went through many revolutions in his affairs. . . . The woman who prepared his grave Cloathes, found his pinch of snuff fast between his thumb & finger" (Bentley, *Diaries*, 2:234).

Circular to the Governors of the States

Sir   United States Octr 3d 1789
   I do myself the honor to enclose to your Excellency a Proclamation for a general Thanksgiving which I must request the favor of you to have published and made known in your State in the way and manner that shall be most agreeable to yourself.[1] I have the honor to be your Excellency's most obedient Servant
                                                  Go: Washington

LS, to Thomas Mifflin, CSmH; LS, to John Sullivan, MB; LS, to George Walton, NcD: George Walton Papers; LB, DLC:GW; Df, DNA: RG 59, Miscellaneous Letters. There are minor changes in wording in the letters.

   1. On 25 Sept. Elias Boudinot introduced in the House of Representatives a resolution "That a joint committee of both Houses be directed to wait upon the President of the United States, to request that he would recommend to the people of the United States a day of public thanksgiving and prayer to be observed by acknowledging, with grateful hearts, the many signal favors of Almighty God, especially by affording them an opportunity peaceably to establish a Constitution of government for their safety and happiness." The House was not unanimous in its determination to give thanks. Aedanus Burke of South Carolina objected that he "did not like this mimicking of European customs, where they made a mere mockery of thanksgivings." Thomas Tudor Tucker "thought the House had no business to interfere in a matter which did not concern them. Why should the President direct the people to do what, perhaps, they have no mind to do? They may not be inclined to return thanks for a Constitution until they have experienced that it promotes their safety and happiness. We do not yet know but they may have reason to be dissatisfied with the effects it has already produced; but whether this be so or not, it is a business with which Congress have nothing to do; it is a religious matter, and, as such, is proscribed to us. If a day of thanksgiving must take place, let it be done by the authority of the several States" (*Annals of Congress*, 1:949–50). Citing biblical precedents and resolutions of the Continental Congress, the proponents of a Thanksgiving celebration prevailed, and the House appointed a committee consisting of Elias Boudinot, Roger Sherman, and Peter Silvester to approach GW. The Senate agreed to the resolution on 26 Sept. and appointed William Samuel Johnson and Ralph Izard to the joint committee. On 28 Sept. the Senate committee reported that they had laid the resolu-

tion before the president (*DHFC*, 1:192, 197, 3:232, 238). GW issued the proclamation on 3 Oct., designating a day of prayer and thanksgiving. See his Proclamation, this date.

Whatever reservations may have been held by some public officials, the day was widely celebrated throughout the nation. The Virginia assembly, for example, resolved on 19 Nov. that the chaplain "to this House, be accordingly requested to perform divine service, and to preach a sermon in the Capitol, before the General Assembly, suitable to the importance and solemnity of the occasion, on the said 26th day of November" (*Journal of the House of Delegates*, 1789, 70). Most newspapers printed the proclamation and announced plans for public functions in honor of the day. Many churches celebrated the occasions by soliciting donations for the poor. Tobias Lear wrote to John Rodgers, pastor of the two Presbyterian churches in New York City, on 28 Nov., that "by direction of the President of the United States I have the pleasure to send you twenty five dollars to be applied towards releiving the poor of the Presbyterian Churches.

"A paragraph in the papers mentioned that a contribution would be made for that purpose on Thanksgiving day; as no opportunity offered of doing it at that time, and not knowing into whose hands the money should be lodged which might be given afterwards—The President of the United States has directed me to send it to you, requesting that you will be so good as to put it into the way of answering the charitable purpose for which it is intended" (DNA: RG 59, Miscellaneous Letters).

From James Duane

Sir   New York 3d October 1789.

I want words to express, as I ought, my grateful acknowledgements for the high honor of your communication this day enclosing my Commission as district Judge.[1]

Happy in seeing, thro many difficulties, the first object of my wishes accomplished by the establishment of our national government, I aspired after no personal emoluments or promotion; but was contented to contribute the little in my power to it's prosperity in the public stations I possessed, or in private life. Unexpectedly, and I fear from too partial an estimate of my abilities; ranked among those distinguished Characters on whom you are pleased to rely to give stability and dignity to our national government; I can only promise that if my success shall any wise equal the rectitude of my intentions, and the fervor of my desire to promote the happiness of our Country and the glory of your administration, my appointment will not prove a misfortune.

That you may long continue to preside over our Nation in glory and tranquillity, is the earnest prayer of him who has the honor to be with the utmost respect and most inviolable attachment Sir Your most obedient most obliged and most faithful Servant

Jas Duane

ALS, DNA: RG 59, Miscellaneous Letters; ADfS, NHi: James Duane Papers. There are minor differences in wording between the draft and the ALS.

James Duane (1733–1797), who came from a substantial New York mercantile family, studied law with James Alexander and began his successful legal career with his admission to the bar in 1754. Duane combined his law practice with extensive and profitable ventures in land speculation. During the Revolution he was a member of the Continental Congress, and in the 1780s he served in the New York senate. From 1784 to September 1789 he was mayor of New York City. Duane wrote to GW from New York City on 28 Sept. thanking the president for his appointment (DNA: RG 59, Miscellaneous Letters), although he was not officially notified until he received GW's pro forma letter of appointment, 30 Sept. 1789.

1. No letter from GW to Duane of 3 Oct. has been found, but a photocopy of an LS of GW's pro forma letter of 30 Sept., enclosing Duane's commission, is in NHi: Duane Papers.

Thanksgiving Proclamation

[New York, 3 October 1789]

By the President of the United States of America. a Proclamation.

Whereas it is the duty of all Nations to acknowledge the providence of Almighty God, to obey his will, to be grateful for his benefits, and humbly to implore his protection and favor—and whereas both Houses of Congress have by their joint Committee requested me "to recommend to the People of the United States a day of public thanksgiving and prayer to be observed by acknowledging with grateful hearts the many signal favors of Almighty God especially by affording them an opportunity peaceably to establish a form of government for their safety and happiness."

Now therefore I do recommend and assign Thursday the 26th day of November next to be devoted by the People of these States to the service of that great and glorious Being, who is the beneficent Author of all the good that was, that is, or that will be—That we may then all unite in rendering unto him our sincere and humble thanks—for his kind care and protection of the People of this Country previous to their becoming a Nation—for the signal and manifold mercies, and the favorable interpositions of his Providence which we experienced in the course and conclusion of the late war—for the great degree of tranquillity, union, and plenty, which we have since enjoyed—for the peaceable and rational manner, in which we have been enabled to establish constitutions of government for our safety and happiness, and particularly the national One now lately instituted—for the civil and religious liberty with which we are blessed; and the means we have of acquiring and diffusing useful knowledge; and in general for all the great and various favors which he hath been pleased to confer upon us.

and also that we may then unite in most humbly offering our prayers and supplications to the great Lord and Ruler of Nations and beseech him to pardon our national and other transgressions—to enable us all, whether in public or private stations, to perform our several and relative duties properly and punctually—to render our national government a blessing to all the people, by constantly being a Government of wise, just, and constitutional laws, discreetly and faithfully executed and obeyed—to protect and guide all Sovereigns and Nations (especially such as have shewn kindness unto us) and to bless them with good government, peace, and concord—To promote the knowledge and practice of true religion and virtue, and the encrease of science among them and us—and generally to grant unto all Mankind such a degree of temporal prosperity as he alone knows to be best.

Given under my hand at the City of New-York the third day of October in the year of our Lord 1789.

Go: Washington

DS, CStbKML; DS, DLC:GW; copy, sold by Christie, Manson, & Woods, International, 21 Oct. 1977. The proclamation was also printed as a broadside. Copies of the broadside are at Harvard University, Yale University, and the Pierpont Morgan Library. Other copies are owned (1992) by Marshall B. Coyne, Washington, D.C., and Ralph Geoffrey Newman, Inc., Chicago.

For background to this document, see Circular Letter to the Governors of the States, 3 Oct. 1789, n.1.

From Solomon Bush

No. 7 Boulton Street Piccadilly

May it Please your Excellency   London 4th Octr 1789

I took the liberty to address you some time since, sincerely congratulating your Excellency on your late dignified appointment,[1] which be assured proceeded from the effusions of a Heart fervently thankfull to the great Author of all good for the blessings he has been pleas'd to shower down on my Country— The many respectable Patriots in this Country must give the greatest pleasure to every Man of Virtue, among whom I beg leave to mention Atkinson Bush Esqr. of this City to whose humanity many of my suffering Countrymen were much indebted for numerous Comforts they receivd during rigorous confinement in the inhospitable Prisons of this Kingdom at Mr Bushs request I beg leave to transmit the proceedings and interposition of the City of London during our late Glorious Struggle of which he begs your Excellency's acceptance—as well as a Letter from his son Mr Michael Bush a Gentleman of respectability and one of the Livery of London.[2] With every mark of sincere Respect, I have the honour to subscribe Your Excellency's most Faithfull Obdt Hble Sert

S. Bush

ALS, DNA:PCC, item 78.

1. See Bush to GW, 20 July 1789.

2. Atkinson Bush (c.1735–1811), a well-known London proctor, lived on Great Ormond Street. The letter from Michael Bush, 29 Sept. 1789, requested that GW "permit an obscure Individual, a Native of England but nevertheless a Citizen of the World to join in the general Joy and to gratulate your Excellency on an Event so singularly prosperous & providential—an Event which at the same Time that it chears the Heart of every true American must give Joy to every *true* Englishman; When I reflect on the various Duties you have discharged, of a Patriot, a General and a Statesman with Honour to yourself and Advantage to your Country, it is impossible to convey one's genuine Sentiments of a Character so exalted without Adulation.

"Not only you, Sir, but every real Friend to civil and religious Liberty in every Quarter of the Globe has Reason to thank divine Providence for his very wise and gracious Interposition in Favour of a Country which at one Time seemed to be threatned with the Extirpation of Liberty but which ultimately proves to be the Favourite of Heaven; Had it not been for his abundant Goodness Freedom would have been annihilated and the persecuted and oppressed of future Ages left destitute of an Asylum—an Asylum which must flourish because it was gained by the Resistance of Virtue and Valour to vicious Corruption and despotic Tyranny, a Corruption more wickedly devised or a Tyranny more wantonly and cruelly exerted are not to be discovered in the History of the World . . ." (DNA:PCC, item 78). The enclosure from Atkinson Bush has not been identified.

GW replied to Solomon Bush's letter on 24 Nov., thanking him for his congratulations, for his assistance during the seizure of an American ship, and for forwarding Atkinson Bush's enclosure. "I request you to present my thanks to Mr Bush . . . and accept the same for your trouble in transmitting it" (Df, in writing of Tobias Lear, DNA: RG 59, Miscellaneous Letters).

From William Dawson

May it Please your Excellency   October 5th 1789

You will please to remember that I was manager for Colo. George Mercer on his Estate in Frederick County when the Sam⟨e⟩ was Sold off by your Excellency,[1] and your Excellency may also remember that Mr Jas Mercer was very often Complaing and Scolding, while at Sd Sale, and that one morning I informed your Excellency before Mr Mercer, what a hard year I had had of it, on account of the Overseers knowing they ware agoing off and the Negroes knowing they ware to be Sold, your Excellency acknowledged, you Exspected it had been the Case with me, but Blam'd me for one thing, that was for not haveing the Crop of Tobo all Cleared out & finish'd I acknowledged I ware in that perticular blameable, had there been any Tobo of Consequence unfinished; but Told your Excellency that their was Some ground leaves, which I thought would not pay a person for troble in Steming &c. and that on finishing the Sale that was an overpless of Corn left and Some wheat to finish, the Whole Care then Divolved on me for the Business of Every place, while Mr Mercer was then up, we appointed the first thursday in January following to Settle our accounts, So I pursued the Business of Delivering Corn &c. Mr Snickers I Suppose (as it had been his Practice before as I can Shew by a letter under Mr Mercers hand) wrote to Mr Mercer informing him of bad Conduct in many things of me, on which Mr Mercer wrote me a letter Baring Date 17th Decr 1774.[2] Sent it to Said Snickers, and by him to me, informing me of what he had from your Excellency by Letter, and others, and that your Excellency had named

Capt. Edward Snickers as a fit person for the Supervising and finishing Said Crop of wheat &c.[3] the Said Snickers on Receiving Such Instructions, or authurity, came to the place where I lived Nailed up my Corn house Door and forwarnd me from opening the Same or Concearning with any thing farther I began to remonstrate with him and Shew the hardship I was Under, he Told me if I offered to Concearn or open my Cornhouse Door, that Mr Mercer had ordered him to have a general Court Writ Served on me, this So alarmed me, that I Truly ware in Such A strait, I new not what to do, Considering your Excellency who Mr Mercer wrote had informed him of bad Conduct of me which your Excellency had heard from Severals while at the Sale from which I Conceived your Excellency were against me,[4] Mr Mercer himself then a general Court Lawer and Mr Snickers at that time in great Cr. with Lord Dunmore &c. &c. I thought myself, under the disagreable Nesessety, of giving up my Land &c. I had purchased to my Securitys (as I did not wish to involve those my friends) and remove to a place, to Seek for Bread and get Redress'd. And fully intended to have Brought Suit against Mr Mercer for his Treatment. However the war began with Great Brittan which Prevented, and by a paper Inclosed your Excellency will find I Step'd fauth to defend my Countrys Rights &c.

after the Paper money was funded I wrote to Mr Mercer informing him of my intention of going to the Southern Country and wished to Settle up all my accounts with him and that I would Leave any Dispute to Gentlemen of Carrecter to decide, he Sent me word to come and See him I went. and he asked me what accounts I wanted to Settle at that time of Day, I told him all my Transactions while Manager for his Brother, he Said he would have nothing to do with me, I Emediately Braught Suit against him in the County Court, and he remooved the Same by writ of Accessory, to the General Court, in which affidavit he took to remoove Sd Suit, if I remember Right Said that your Excellency advised to bring Suit against me for Damages A copy of Said affidavit is inclosed for your Excellencys Perusel as I this very Material[5] I hope your Excellency will Excuse me for Trobleing your Excellency with it, the Said Suit was Sent to the district Court Since which his Honour Mr Mercer hath Refere'd the Same Mr Mercer's Plea against my Claim is that of non asumsit & Act of Limitations, Should Mr Mercer pursue this Plea and make it good he will Leave me in great Distress. I am with all Due rispects your Excellencyes Most Obedient Hble Servt

W. Dawson

William Dawson's Questions to Ask his Excellency George Washingto[n] Esquire in writing whos ansr is to be received by the referres, and alow'd as Testimony—warr not, the Middle, the Lower, and the three New Plantations, under good fencing, and Good Crops of wheat Sowed, at Each of Sd plantations.

Did not my Self and Famely, Treat your Excellency and his Honour Mr Mercer with due respects while at the Sale.

Did your Excellency write to Mr Mercer informing of him that Severals had informed your Excellency of my Selling Stock &c. and that your Excellency Disired Mr Mercer to do his Brother Justice, at our Settlement and Sue me for Damages.

Did any Person Inform your Excellency besides Mr Snickers of any Bad Conduct of mine.

How much Tobo Did Said Snickers render to your Excellency as finished by him after he turn'd me off

Did Not the Black people belonging to the Estate of Colo. Mercer all Look well from the greatest to the Least young and old according to their ages.

ALS, ViMtV.

1. For background on GW's involvement in George Mercer's complicated affairs and his role in the sale of Mercer's land in Fauquier, Prince William, Loudoun, and Frederick counties, see Statement concerning George Mercer's Estate, 1 Feb. 1789, source note. William Dawson lived on Mercer's Shenandoah tract in Frederick County (advertisement for sale of Mercer's land in the *Virginia Gazette* [Rind], 30 June 1774). He also acted as one of Mercer's managers, and in the fall of 1789 he was suing James Mercer, as attorney for his deceased brother George Mercer's estate, "for three years Stewardship & the Shares of Crops made on my Brothers plantations in Frederick County for three years previous to the Sale thereof in the year 1774 and for turning him off without Notice at the Sale, greatly to his loss" (Mercer to GW, 15 Oct. 1789). For additional information on Dawson's problems, see James Mercer to GW, 15 Oct. 1789, GW to Mercer, 17 Nov. 1789, and Dawson to GW, 4 Nov. 1789.

2. Edward Snickers (d. 1791) operated an ordinary, sometimes patronized by GW, near Buck Marsh Run in Frederick County. Part of George Mercer's land offered for sale in 1774 lay opposite Snickers' ordinary.

3. No letter from GW to Mercer recommending Snickers has been found.

For an indication that Snickers' own conduct was not above reproach, see a letter from George Mercer's father castigating the conduct of "that scoundrel Snickers," who had been pillaging Mercer land "these several years, under pretence of paying 1000 lb tobo yearly rent which however, he has never yet paid, but by crediting it on a piece of paper" (John Mercer to George Mercer, 28 Jan. 1768, in Mulkearn, *George Mercer Papers*, 213–14).

4. At the time of George Mercer's sale in 1774, GW wrote James Mercer that "I am very thoroughly convinced of Mr Dawson's being a consummate rascal, & intended to have acquainted you with my suspicions, when I wrote to you, in order that you might be upon your guard at a settlement with him." Snickers had reported to GW that Dawson had sold 300 pine trees and a dozen or more horses belonging to Mercer, "one in particular to Benji. Berry for twelve or fourteen pounds, which Barry immediately sold for twenty six" (GW to Mercer, 12 Dec. 1774).

5. The affidavit was returned to Dawson. See GW to Mercer, 17 Nov. 1789.

To John Jay

Sir, United States, October 5th 1789.

It is with singular pleasure that I address you as Chief Justice of the supreme Court of the United States, for which office your Commission is here enclosed.

In nominating you for the important station which you now fill, I not only acted in conformity to my best judgement; but, I trust, I did a grateful thing to the good citizens of these united States: and I have a full confidence that the love which you bear our Country, and a desire to promote general happiness, will not suffer you to hesitate a moment to bring into action the talents, knowledge and integrity which are so necessary to be exercised at the head of that department which must be considered as the Key-Stone of our political fabric.[1] I have the honor to be, with high consideration and sentiments of perfect esteem, Sir, Your most Obedient and most Humble Servant,

Go: Washington

LS, LNHT; LB, DLC:GW; Df, DNA: RG 59, Miscellaneous Letters.

For background to GW's judicial appointments, see his letter sending nominations to the United States Senate, 24 Sept. 1789.

1. Jay replied on 6 Oct.: "When distinguished Descernment & Patriotism unite in selecting men for Stations of Trust and Dignity, they derive Honor not only from their offices, but from the Hand which confers them.

"With a Mind and a Heart impressed with these Reflections, and their correspondent Sensations, I assure you that the Sentiments expressed in your

Letter of Yesterday, and implied by the Commission it enclosed, will never
cease to excite my best Endeavours to fulfill the Duties imposed by the latter,
and as far as may be in my power, to realize the Expectations which your
nominations, especially to important Places, must naturally create" (DNA: RG
59, Miscellaneous Letters).

From John O'Connor

Sir   George Town Potowmack Oct. 5th 1789
   You should not be interrupted by this address if I thought
that any Citizen of America had a heart more sincerely attached
to your person than the unhappy and obscure Individual who
presumes to submit to your perusal his reflections on an important question.
   Tho you are not probably a Stranger to my afflictions in this
land and the weight of Calumny to which I have been compelled
to submit, yet you may be unacquainted with that reverence and
awe, I glory to entertain for thy Character and thy measures—
These are the impressions which have given me confidence to
accompany the enclosed pamphlet with a few lines.
   If moral writers of every age and clime have not been deceived in estimating the turpitude of sin by the malignity of the
intention, I will under the favour of divine providence soon
convince the World that some of my fellow travellers have injured Innocence—It was, and is my determined intention to
publish the History of America—My Circumstances are improving and all my resources point to that Event, previous
to whose accomplishment, I can enjoy no peace nor relish any
satisfaction except what I may receive in contemplating the
prosperity of my Country under thy auspicious Administration.
I have the honor to be Sir with respect your most obliged and
most Devoted Hume Sert

                                                    John O'Connor

ALS, DNA:PCC, item 78.
   John O'Connor, who described himself as an Irish barrister, arrived in Virginia in 1788 and was currently selling subscriptions to a multivolume geographical and topographical history of the Americas (*Maryland Gazette* [An-
napolis], 6 Dec. 1787). In spite of constant assurances to his subscribers that
the history was nearly completed and the first volume in press, inquiries re-
vealed that no part of the work had been delivered to O'Connor's printers in
Philadelphia (*Maryland Journal, and Baltimore Advertiser*, 13 May 1788). GW

was not one of the subscribers, although on 3 Feb. 1788 O'Connor dined with him, probably in an effort to enlist his aid. O'Connor's wife, Eliza Harriot, who had opened an academy for young ladies in Alexandria in 1788, attempted to secure GW's support to open a school in Edenton, North Carolina. See Eliza H. O'Connor to GW, 7 and 18 Oct. 1788, and GW to Eliza H. O'Connor, 17 Oct. 1788. See also *Diaries*, 5:272–73, 409.

From Samuel Osgood

Sir   General Post Office New York October 5th 1789

I do myself the honor to inclose a Copy of an Advertisement which I propose to have published tomorrow, relative to Contracts for the conveyance of the Mail for one year to commence on the first Day of January next, at which time the present Contracts expire.[1]

It is not materially different from the Advertisement ⟨*illegible*⟩ By the ⟨*illegible*⟩ for the ⟨transportation *illegible*⟩ the Post Office, the Post Master General is as he ought to be, made subject to the direction of the President of the United States in performing the duties of his Office and in forming Contracts for the transportation of the Mail.

I shall be extreemly happy to know your pleasure, and will at all times use my utmost indeavours to execute the same with fidelity.

I have appointed for my Assistant Jonathan Burrall, one of the late Commissioners for settling Public Accounts—His past services, as well as his Abilities entitle him in my opinion to a better place and I hope in the new arrangement this Office will be made better.

I propose to send him immediately to the southward in order that he may, on the spot examine into the Character of the Deputies, and to reappoint such as have behaved well and ⟨can⟩ give good security to discharge faithfully the Trust resposed in them—To displace such as have not, and to appoint others in their places.[2]

I have appointed a Deputy Post Master Sebastion Bea⟨*illegible*⟩ Bauman for the City of New-York, and Robert Patton for Philadelphia.

I hope these appointments will meet with your approbation. From Mr Patton who has been several years in the Post Office at

Philadelphia I have acquired nearly all the information I now possess relative to the Post Office business. His conduct in that Office has rendered him universally agreeable to the Citizens of Philadelphia—as will apear from the recommendations in my possession. I have The Honor to be &c.

LB, DNA: RG 28, Letters Sent by the Postmaster General, 1789–1836.

1. The advertisement, dated 5 Oct. 1789 from the general post office in New York, invited proposals for the delivery of mail to major cities in the United States between Portland, Maine, and Savannah, Ga. (*Maryland Journal, and Baltimore Advertiser*, 16 Oct. 1789).

2. For an example of the controversy over Osgood's failure to reappoint incumbents, see Mary Katharine Goddard to GW, 23 Dec. 1789.

To Arthur St. Clair

Sir,	[New York, 6 October 1789]

Congress having by their Act of the 29th of September last empowered me to call forth the Militia of the States respectively, for the protection of the frontiers from the incursions of the hostile Indians, I have thought proper to make this communication to you, together with the instructions herein contained.[1]

It is highly necessary that I should as soon as possible possess full information whether the Wabash and Illinois Indians are most inclined for war or peace—If for the former it is proper that I should be informed of the means which will most probably induce them to peace—If a peace can be established with the said indians on reasonable terms, the interests of the United States dictate that it should be effected as soon as possible.

You will therefore inform the said indians of the dispositions of the general government on this subject, and of their reasonable desire that there should be a cessation of hostilities as a prelude to a treaty—If however notwithstanding your intimations to them, they should continue their hostilities, or meditate any incursions against the frontiers of Virginia and Pennsylvania, or against any of the troops or posts of the United States, and it should appear to you the time of execution would be so near as to forbid your transmitting the information to me, and receiving my further orders thereon, then you are hereby authorised and empowered in my name to call on the Lieutenants of the nearest Counties of Virginia and Pennsylvania for such detachments of Militia as you may judge proper, not exceeding however one thousand from Virginia and five hundred from Pennsylvania.

I have directed Letters to be written to the Executives of Virginia and Pennsylvania, informing them of the before recited Act of Congress,[2] and that I have given you these conditional directions, so that there may not be any obstructions to such measures as shall be necessary to be taken by you for calling forth the militia agreeably to the instructions herein contained.

The said militia to act in conjunction with the federal troops in such operations, offensive or defensive, as you and the Commanding officer of the troops conjointly shall judge necessary for the public service, and the protection of the inhabitants and the posts.

The said Militia while in actual service to be on the Continental establishment of pay and rations—they are to arm and equip themselves, but to be furnished with public ammunition if necessary—and no charge for the pay of said Militia will be valid unless supported by regular musters, made by a field or other Officer of the federal troops to be appointed by the commanding Officer of the troops.

I would have it observed forcibly that a War with the Wabash Indians ought to be avoided by all means consistently with the security of the frontier inhabitants, the security of the troops and the national dignity—In the exercise of the present indiscriminate hostilities, it is extremely difficult if not impossible to say that a war without further measures would be just on the part of the United States.

But if after manifesting clearly to the indians the dispositions of the general government for the preservation of peace, and the extension of a just protection to the said indians, they should continue their incursions, the United States will be constran'd to punish them with severity.

You will also proceed as soon as you can with safety to execute the orders of the late Congress, respecting the inhabitants at St Vincennes and at the Kaskaskies, and the other Villages on the Mississippi—It is a circumstance of some importance that the said inhabitants should as soon as possible possess the lands to which they are entitled by some known and fixed principles.[3]

I have directed a number of copies of the treaty made by you at Fort Harmar with the Wyandots &c: on the 9th of January last to be printed, and forwarded to you, together with the ratification, and my Proclamation enjoining the observance thereof.[4]

As it may be of high importance to obtain a precise and accurate knowledge of the several Waters which empty into the Ohio on the North West—and of those which discharge themselves into the lakes Erie and Michigan; the length of the portages between, and the nature of the ground, an early and pointed attention thereto is earnestly recommended. Given under my hand in the City of New-York, this 6th day of October, in the year of our Lord One thousand seven hundred and eighty nine, and in the thirteenth year of the sovereignty and Independence of the United States.

Copy, DNA: RG 233, First Congress, Records of the Office of the Clerk, Records of Reports from Executive Departments; copy, DNA: RG 46, First Congress, Records of Legislative Proceedings, Reports and Communications Submitted to the Senate; copy, InHi; copy, NHi: Henry O'Reilly Collection.

1. Section 5 of "An Act to recognize and adapt to the Constitution of the United States the establishment of the Troops under the Resolves of the United States in Congress assembled, and for other purposes therein mentioned" (1 *Stat.* 95–96 [29 Sept. 1789]) authorized the president to call out the militia if it became necessary to protect the frontiers from Indian attack. See also St. Clair to GW, 14 Sept. 1789, and GW to the United States Senate and House of Representatives, 16 Sept. 1789.

2. Secretary of War Henry Knox wrote Beverley Randolph, governor of Virginia, on 6 Oct. that he had been "directed by the President of the United States to transmit to your Excellency the enclosed extract of a Law enacted by the Congress on the 29th day of September last—And I am further directed Sir to inform you that the state of intelligence from the frontiers has rendered it expedient for the President of the United States to instruct provisionally the Governor of the Western territory to call forth the Militia of the nearest counties for the protection of the frontier inhabitants from the hostile incursions of the indians, limiting the Militia to be so called forth to the number of one thousand from Virginia and five hundred from Pennsylvania.

"The said Militia while in actual service are to receive the same pay and rations as the troops of the United States provided that no charge for pay be admitted as valid unless the Militia shall be mustered by an officer of the said troops to be appointed by the commanding officer thereof.

"It is expected the Militia will be armed and accoutred at their own expence, but to be furnished with ammunition if necessary by the United States.

"Your Excellency will make such use of this information as you shall judge proper, in order to facilitate such orders as the Governor of the Western territory may find it necessary to issue.

"The President of the United States has also directed me to acknowledge the receipt of the letters you were pleased to transmit to him written by Colonel Robert Johnson of Washington [Woodford] County and dated the 22d of August.

"The Measures directed to be taken by the Governor of the Western territory are intended to prevent a repetition of similar depredations stated by Colonel Johnson—And it is to be expected that they will in a great degree be effectual, in conjunctions with the regular troops, who have lately taken a position in force near the Great Miami" (ViHi).

3. Vincennes, Kaskaskia, and other settlements in what became known as the Illinois country were acquired for Virginia as the result of George Rogers Clark's military activities in the area during the Revolutionary War. After Virginia's acquisition of the area, its inhabitants, mostly French and Canadian, became citizens of the state. When Virginia ceded its western lands to the union, the deed of cession, 1 Mar. 1784, provided that "the French and Canadian inhabitants, and other settlers of the Kaskaskies, St. Vincents, and the neighbouring villages who have professed themselves citizens of Virginia, shall have their possessions and titles confirmed to them, and be protected in the enjoyment of their rights and liberties" (*JCC*, 26:113–16). By the mid–1780s, other settlers from Kentucky and Virginia had moved into the area and joined the original settlers in inundating Congress with petitions to establish government in the area and settle the confused land questions. See, for examples, the petitions of the inhabitants of Post Vincennes, 26 July 1787, 28 Feb. 1788; petitions from the inhabitants of the Illinois country, 27 Aug., 15 Sept. 1787, all in DNA:PCC, item 48; report of committee of Congress on the petition of George Morgan, 20 June 1788, and petition from the French inhabitants of Kaskaskia, Cahokia, Prairie de Rocher, and St. Philip, 27 Aug. 1787, both in Carter, *Territorial Papers, Northwest Territory*, 2:112–15, 68–70. The question of the Illinois settlements was frequently before the Confederation Congress in the late 1780s. One report, by a committee consisting of James Madison, Abraham Clark, and Nathan Dane, stated that the committee found the inhabitants "disposed to submit to Government and good order, and solicitous to receive their laws and protection from the United States, that for want of criminal laws and magistrates among them to administer their exisiting laws and customs they are subjected to very great inconveniences, and many mere land Jobbers are induced to intrude on their lands and disturbe their possessions, wherefore the Committee are clearly of opinion that Congress ought without delay to provide for the administration of Government" (*JCC*, 32:266–69). As the result of the report of another committee on 29 Aug. 1788 Congress resolved that "measures be taken for confirming in their possessions and titles the french & Canadian inhabitants and other settlers at post St. Vincents who on or before the year 1783 had settled there and had professed themselves citizens of the United States or any one of them, and for laying off for them at their own expence the several tracts which they rightfully claim & which may have been allotted to them according to the laws & Usages of the Government under which they have respectfully settled." The

resolution also reserved 400 acres for every head of family (Carter, *Territorial Papers, Northwest Territory*, 2:145–46). When GW took office the matter was still pending.

4. See GW to the United States Senate, 25 May and 17 Sept. 1789.

From Pierre Marmie

Sir   Philadelphia October 7th 1789

Early in the year 1784, the company I was connected with, and in whose behalf I have now the honor of adressing you, made purchase from Messrs Penn, late proprietaries of Pennsilvania, of that part of their mannor of Pittsburgh, which includes Fort Pitt, and the Whole of its appurtenances. our view was to Erect a distillery, and to make use of Such of the buildings, particularly the brick barracks built by the British, as with Some Small alterations, had been judged convenient for the purpose; In consequence whereof, we had the necessary materials transported from this city, early in the fall of the Same year, to forward our undertaking.

By a law of the Commonwealth of Pennsilvania enacted in february 1780, in consequence of a recommendation of congress, all landed property, which the necessities of the war, had induced the officers of congress, to make use of, was directed to be Surrendered by them, to the owners of Such land, as Soon as peace Should take place; but in defiance of said law, under various pretences and in opposition to our repeated remonstrances on this Subject, the possession of the abovementioned property, is at this late day, witheld from us, though perhaps, it will be found of little or no use to the troops of the united States.[1]

As a post of defense, your Excellency who knows the ground, can best determine, whether it is any ways tenable against an Ennemy in force: as a place of communication and of deposit for military Stores, it may perhaps be of Some Service; but I beg leave to observe, that we did never refuse to lett the continent, have the use of Such parts of the fort & Buildings, as might be convenient for the public Service, even upon a very triffling consideration: the right of the Soil is what we contend for, and to be masters of the disposal of the ground for Such purposes as may be most conducive to our advantage.

The injury we have Sustained by this detention, is far beyond Description, but I Shall not trouble your Excellency with this consideration, as we Shall fully enter upon this Subject, before the persons, who will have to pronounce on the damages incurred, and the indemnity we deem ourselves entitled to: I Shall only entreat your Excellency to make Some enquiries on the Subject, and to give Such instructions to the Secretary at war, as being conducive to the public Wellfare, may not be injurious to us as individuals.[2] I am with respect Your Excellency's most Obedient and most humble Servant

P. Marmie

ALS, DNA:PCC, item 78.

Pierre Marmie was a Frenchman reported to have come to America with French forces during the American Revolution. After the war he settled in western Pennsylvania and in 1784 helped found the firm of Turnbull, Marmie, & Co., which eventually included William Turnbull, John Holker, Stephen Bayard, and Isaac Craig. In addition to operating a distillery, the firm engaged heavily in the acquisition and sale of Pittsburgh real estate, including among their possessions the site of Fort Pitt. The partnership dissolved in 1788, and much of the firm's Pittsburgh land was advertised for sale (*Western Pennsylvania Historical Magazine*, 5 [1922], 99–107, 7 [1924], 66, 10 [1927], 206, 14 [1931], 209–10, 42 [1959], 226–39). By the time this letter was written, Marmie, Turnbull, and Holker were involved in the establishment of the Alliance Ironworks, opened in 1790 near the mouth of Jacobs Creek in Fayette County. Successful at first—the furnace produced some of the armament supplied to Anthony Wayne's army in 1794—it later fell on hard times, and according to local legend Marmie, driven insane by his misfortunes, committed suicide by throwing himself into the furnace (*Historic Places*, 81).

1. As early as 1785 Turnbull, Marmie, & Co. petitioned Congress for the return of Fort Pitt to their firm. At that time a committee of Congress recommended that the memorial "cannot be granted, it being necessary under present circumstances that the Post of Fort Pitt should remain in the possession of the troops of the United States" (*JCC*, 28:197). Soon after, however, the firm received a portion of the fort, but United States troops continued to occupy the remainder of the post (Dahlinger, *Fort Pitt*, 57–65; *Pennsylvania Archives*, 1st ser., 10:462, 464, 497). By October 1788 a committee appointed to inquire into the proceedings of the War Department reported that Fort Pitt had only "an officer and a few men to receive the supplies and dispatches forwarded to the Troops by the Secretary at War" (*JCC*, 34:583), and in May 1789 Knox reported that the situation had not altered (Knox to GW, 13 May 1789). The United States government did not evacuate the fort until

May 1792 when a new fort farther up the Allegheny River was established.

2. On 14 Oct. Tobias Lear replied to Marmie's letter: "The President of the
United States has received your letter of the 7th inst—and I am directed by
him to inform you, that he finds your case relative to the land on which Fort
Pitt stands, was laid before the late Congress, and by their order, the Secy of
War reported thereon—Upon his present view of the matter the President of
the United States is not satisfied that there would be a propriety in his taking
any step in the business" (DNA: RG 59, Miscellaneous Letters).

From Burgess Ball and Charles Carter

Dear sir,   8th of October 1789

We have perused your Letter to Mrs Lewis dated the 13th of
September, and shall take pleasure in giving her all the Assistance in our power. We shall in the next paper advertize the
Stocks &c. to be sold abt the 29th Inst., and, in the same Paper
shall request all Persons having Claims against the Estate, to
bring 'em in properly attested, but, we believe we have already
the whole Accots (as we have personally applyed where we
expected there were any) the Amot of which will be, we expect,
abt £100, of which the Doctors Bills are £76.2.11.[1]

The Crops of wheat Corn & Tobo, we are in hopes will pay the
Debts—The Negroes, from what Bushrod says of your Fathers
Will, are to be divided among the Sons only (Mrs Lewis being
excluded) so that we shall want your further directions respecting the division of them.[2] We got Mr Chs Yates, Mr Thos Colson
& Doctor Mortimer to examine & set a Value on the Lotts, as we
expected the sooner they cd be sold,[3] (agreeable to your directions) so much the better, as the Winter is now approaching, &
some Gent. were wanting them, 'tho they wd not oblige them-
selvs to abide by what they shd be valued at—They were valued
at £450 payable in 2 Years with Intt—Mr Carter wanted 'em but
thought the price too high—Majr Day has a Notion of 'em, @
£400 if the Credit can be extended to three Years[4]—They must
be rented or sold as quick as possible or the Houses & Pailing will
go to ruin—We wish your further directions, but, shd a good
offer turn up, we shall embrace it, so as to leave the final desicion
with you.

Mr Mercer we've been with several times, 'tho he has retd but very few days from his Circuit, & he has promis'd us his Oppinion in writing, but the hurry of the Court here has prevented him—He says that nothing on your part is necessary, & that every thg may be done without much trouble or formality. We will however transmit his oppinion the next opporty.

A Frost which fell here last Week it is suppos'd has distroy'd half the Tobo in the state & a great deal of Corn and Fodder. Wishing you every filicity your troublesome Station will admit, and best respects &c. to Mrs Washington We are Dear sir with every Sentiment of Esteem Your mo: obt servts

Chs Carter
B: Ball

LS, in the writing of Burgess Ball, DLC:GW.

1. The notice, signed by Betty Lewis, appears in the *Virginia Herald and Fredericksburg Advertiser*, 15 Oct. 1789. See GW to Betty Lewis, 13 Sept. 1789, n.7.

2. See Betty Lewis to GW, 1 Oct. 1789, n.2.

3. Charles Yates (1728–1809) and Thomas Colson (d. 1805) were Fredericksburg merchants. Ball and Carter are referring to the house and two lots which GW purchased for the use of his mother when she moved to Fredericksburg in 1773.

4. Benjamin Day (1752–1821), a Fredericksburg merchant, had served as an aide to Gen. William Woodford and as an assistant adjutant general of Virginia troops during the Revolution.

From John Dandridge

Sir,   Williamsburg Octr 8th 89
I take this moment to inform you that I have just recorded a Deed of the Land in Gloucester, to you, agreeable to the price offered in your Letter on that subject; to wit £800.[1]

You will be so good as to present my affectionate duty to my Aunt, & inform her that her Friends here are well. I am, Sir, with respectful regard, Yr Obt Sert

J. Dandridge

ALS, ViMtV.

For background to this letter, see Dandridge to GW, 27 Oct. 1788.

1. See GW to Dandridge, 26 Mar. 1789.

From John Macpherson

N. York Ocr 8th 1789

Much Respect'd and Sincerely Esteemed Sir

As I propose seting of for Philadelphia Tomorrow or next day, I did myself the honor to wait upon the Vice President; to take a dutiful leave of him and family.

As Mr John Adams has long honor'd me with sincere friendship; I communicated to him, some Improvements of my Own; in the Art of war, he was pleased to reply he was a perfect Stranger to war, but thought it wou'd be proper I Shou'd wait upon your Exellen'y before I left New york; as you are a judge of those Matters; and the only person in North America that Cou'd direct or permit these Operations.[1]

If your Excellency will be pleased to appoint any hour, when I can have the honor of a few Minuts Conversation with you, Genl Knox to whom I have Communicated part of my Plans; and who is pleased to approve all that I have Communicated to him will wait upon you. I am Sincerely Esteem'd Sir Your faithful Subject and most Hble Servant

John Macpherson

LS, DNA:PCC, item 78.

John Macpherson (1726–1792), a native of Edinburgh, was a successful privateer during the French and Indian War, losing an arm in the course of his maritime activities. After the war Macpherson settled in Philadelphia, where in 1785 he published the city directory. Pursuing an active interest in scientific affairs, he attempted in 1787 to interest Congress in his discovery of "a concise, plain and easily practicable mode of ascertaining the Longitude" (petition to Congress, 17 July 1787, DNA:PCC, item 41; *JCC,* 32:382).

1. Macpherson is probably referring to some aspect of a plan he developed in the late 1780s for the construction of "a Fort, that One thousand Men, can with ease, and safety, defend against all the other men on earth, All the Cannon and Mortars in the World cannot Injure it, It is impossible to Injure it by Mining; nor is it possible to Starve the Garrison" (Macpherson's petition to Congress, undated but read in Congress 29 May 1788, DNA:PCC, item 41).

From James Maury

Liverpool 8 Octr 1789

Having already experienced the obliging Condescension with which your Excellency was pleased to honor the Offer of my

Services on my settling here in the commercial Line,[1] I am emboldened to inform your Excellency that, for two or three years previous to my Departure from Virginia, I had been a Candidate with the late Congress for an Appointment in the consular Department; but these Arrangements never having been fully concluded on.

I now beg Leave most respectfully to continue to your Excellency the same Tender of my Services in Case an office of the Kind shall be deemed necessary for this port,[2] with the Assurance of the Satisfaction I ever shall have in my Endeavors to be useful to the Country from whence I come, and to evince the profound Respect & Veneration with which I have the Honor to be your Excellency's most obedient & most devoted Servant

James Maury

ALS, DLC:GW.

1. See Maury to GW, 3 Dec. 1786, 30 July 1787, and GW to Maury, 24 Feb. 1787.

2. When the consular service was established in June 1790, Maury was appointed United States consul at Liverpool (*DHFC*, 2:75, 77).

From Wakelin Welch & Son

London 8th October 1789

We had the honr of receiving your Excellencys favour of the 16th Augst the two inclos'd Letters therein we forwarded & whenever Messrs Fenwick & Co. draws for the Wine their order shall be punctualy paid.

One Adams here is Suppos'd to be the first optician we have, he purposes to make the Terrestial Globe upon the New & approv'd method, it may take up two Months to Compleat & that will be as early as a Conveyance may offer, for after this Vessell none is expected to Sail before February.[1]

The Bag Sent by the Packet is as yet not Sent up, they come no further than Falmouth, & whether the Capt: is permitted to forward it, without an order from the Post Office we shall make an Enquiry after. We beg leave to Subscribe Ourselves Your Excellys Much Oblig'd & Hume Servts

Wake. Welch & son

LS, DLC:GW.

1. The terrestrial globe was made by Dudley Adams, the son of George Adams, instrument maker to George III. After his father's death in 1773 he joined his brother George Adams the younger (1758–1795) who had succeeded to the elder Adams's optical business as well as to his official post. The firm, established on Fleet Street, became one of Great Britain's leading optical manufacturers. In their letter to GW of 14 Feb. 1790, Wakelin Welch & Son announced they had shipped the terrestrial globe, charging GW £28.19 for the purchase (Ledger B, 302). It now stands in GW's study at Mount Vernon.

From Henry Knox

Sir   War Office October 9th 1789.

I have the honor to submit to your inspection a general return of the Ordnance, Arms, and Military Stores in possession of the United States specifying the places at which they are deposited.

The stores in general were placed in their present situation by the chances or events of the late War—Springfield in Massachusetts and Carlisle in Pennsylvania excepted—At these places buildings were directed by Congress to be erected for the reception of the public Stores[1]—The buildings at Springfield are of wood and of course will soon decay, excepting the Magazine which is of brick well constructed and executed—The buildings at Carlisle are numerous and well constructed being all built of brick and stone—There are but few stores there at present, most of the unserviceable stores having been sold by order of Congress—The buildings were also directed to be sold to the trustees of Dickenson Colledge, but they and the Board of Treasury could not agree respecting the price[2]—Some of the buildings having been damaged by a late hurricane are ordered to be repaired, and I have directed that such of them as are not immediately wanted for the public use be rented to the trustees of the said Colledge to be returned whenever demanded for the public use—From the inland situation of Carlisle it is very equivocal whether it would be wise in the public to make it one of their principal Arsenals—The expence of transportation and retransportation would in a very few years amount to an excessive sum.

The stores contained in the return are highly valuable and

require a constant attention in order to preserve them, particularly the Arms and Powder.

The powder at Springfield and West Point, in which is included the greatest quantity in possession of the public is in good order, great attention having been paid to its preservation.

The Arms at Springfield and those at West Point which have been repaired are in order for immediate use—The arms in Philadelphia require to be cleaned.

The damaged Arms at West Point and in Virginia are generally worthy of repairs.

The stores at the several places are in charge of store keepers, or a Commissary or deputy Commissary of stores, who are allowed annually the sums herein specified.

	Dollars
Providence	
A store keeper	96
Springfield	
A Deputy Commissary	480
An Assistant	180
Fort Harkimer and the Mohawk river	
A Store keeper	172
West Point	
A deputy Commissary	480
Philadelphia	
One Commissary	500
One Assistant	360
French Creek a keeper of the Magazine	60
Carlisle A store keeper	100
New London & Manchester	
A deputy Commissary	480
Charleston South Carolina	
A Store keeper	100
	3008

The public are annually charged with the following sums for the rents of buildings, and the post of West Point—To wit

Philadelphia	752.66⅔
Manchester & New London	350
For the Post of West Point	400
	1502.66⅔

The places at which the stores generally are deposited ought to be considered merely as temporary accomodations. They are improper for the permanent Arsenals of the United States— But as this is an object of great national importance it will require a particular discussion—I shall therefore have the honor Sir of submitting to your consideration some ideas on this subject, and a general plan for the establishment of naval and military Arsenals for the service of the United States. I have the honor to be With the most perfect respect Sir Your Obedient Humble Servant

H. Knox

LS, DLC:GW; LB, DLC:GW.

1. The magazine and laboratory at Carlisle was authorized by the Continental Congress 27 Dec. 1776 (*JCC*, 6:1044). For the resolution, 14 April 1777, establishing a laboratory and magazine at Springfield, see *JCC*, 7:266.

2. By the mid–1780s the public buildings at Carlisle had ceased to be of much importance to the government and were steadily deteriorating. On 16 Jan. 1785 the trustees of the newly founded Dickinson College in Carlisle petitioned Congress to permit them to lease or purchase the buildings for the use of the college (DNA:PCC, item 42, signed by Benjamin Rush). Congress reacted favorably to the petition but delayed action until an examination could be made of the stores at the facility (Burnett, *Letters*, 8:17). A resolution agreeing to allow the college to lease the buildings was presented in Congress, 7 Feb. 1785, but failed to pass (*JCC*, 28:44). Although over the next several years Rush continued to pursue his aim of leasing or purchasing the buildings, the college again failed to acquire the buildings when the Board of Treasury opened bidding on them in 1787 (*JCC*, 33:401). See also report of committee on the memorial of the trustees of Dickinson College, 23 July 1787, DNA:PCC, item 20; Tousey, *Military History of Carlisle and Carlisle Barracks*, 160–63.

To Louis XVI

New York the ninth Day
Great and Beloved Friend and Ally,   of October 1789

By the change which has taken place in the national Government of the United States, the honor of receiving and answering your Majesty's letter of the 7th of June, to "the President and Members of Congress," has devolved upon me.

The painful event communicated in it, could not fail to affect the Sensibility, and excite the Regret of the People of the United States, who have so much Reason to feel an Interest in whatever concerns the Happiness of Your Majesty, your Family and Nation. They very sincerely condole with you on the Occasion, and are sensible how greatly this Misfortune must have been enhanced, by those Qualities in the Dauphin, which promised to have rendered that Prince a blessing, not only to his Family, but to his Nation.

Permit me to assure your Majesty of the unceasing Gratitude and Attachment of the United States, and of our Prayers, that the Almighty will be pleased to keep you, our great and beloved Friend and Ally, under his constant Guidance and Protection.

Go: Washington

Copy, DNA: RG 59, Credences; LB, DLC:GW; copy, DLC: William Short Papers.

For the background to this letter, see Louis XVI to GW, 7 June 1789, and GW to the U.S. Senate and House of Representatives, 29 Sept. 1789.

From Richard Law

New London [Conn.] Oct. 10th 1789. Acknowledges commission as district judge for Connecticut. "A good Judiciary, am sensible, is of the utmost importance, and essential to the well being of every free Government—how far the present Judicial System will answer the Valuable End designed, is perhaps somewhat problematical, and must depend on experiment—much wisdom care & attention has ben, doubtless, employed in the formation & construction of so complicated a Machine, in order to make it answer all the fœderal purposes and yet not to clash or interfere with the State Judiciaries, however as the modes of proceeding are left in some measure undefined, and the Objects are Sarious & complex—much skill, prudence & delicacy will be requisite to preserve harmony & Consistancy in the Execution."

ALS, DNA: RG 59, Acceptances and Orders for Commissions.

Richard Law (1733–1806) graduated from Yale in 1751 and read law with Jared Ingersoll. An active Patriot in the early days of the war, he represented his state in Congress in 1774, 1776, 1777, and 1780–83. From 1773 to 1784 he served as judge of the New London County court and in the latter year was appointed a judge of the Connecticut Superior Court. In 1784, with Roger Sherman, Law published *Acts and Laws of the State of Connecticut, in America,* a codification of Connecticut laws.

From Edward Newenham

Dear Sir   10th october 1789

I would not omit the first opportunity of expressing the *Additional* obligation your Excellency has conferred on me, by introducing me to that Respectable Character Mrs Montgomery; She forwarded your Letter by the post, as she is at Lord Ranelaghs twelve miles from this;[1] Early the Next morning Lady Newenham & I paid our Respects, & had the pleasure of meeting her; Anxious to enjoy her Company we pressed her to return and Spend a few days here; She returned the Visit on the following day & has promised on her return from Visiting her late *Brave soldiers*[2] Relations to favor us with her Company; I introduced her into my American Room, which gave her much Satisfaction, as she saw your Excellencys & the pictures of all the Respectable Characters in America; she remarked with pleasure the picture of One Arnold *reversed* and his *Treason* wrote under it—she viewed the Bust of the Venerable and Great Franklin with Sensible Emotion—we had but a short Time for Conversation, as Lord Ranelagh was in a hurry to attend at the Levee of the Lords Justices—little did I expect to see the widow of that Man, on whose Death I publickly expressed my sentiments of the American War and his Character, by appearing in Parliament in full mourning and attending Levees in the same Dress—at that Period others were afraid to express their feelings, but from that moment, the papers announcing what I did, public Conversation became more free & the merits of the Attack and Defence of Liberty were properly canvassed—It was soon Afterwards that I was Chairman of the *first* meeting that reprobated & Stopped the plan of Sending *all* the Military of this Kingdom to America, & hiring Hessians & Hannovarians from the Carcass Butchers of Germany.

I acquainted the Duke of Leicester Lord Charlemont &c. &c. of Mrs Montgomerys arrival; they immediately wrote me word, *"that they would wait on her, & particularily so, on account of the Great Character that recommends her"* these are the words of *all* the Answers I have got—General Massy with whom General Montgomery was well acquainted at the first Siege of Quebec, has paid his respects to her, the very day I wrote to him; Lady

Newenham will Continue her attention—I sent the Duke of Leicesters & Lord Charlemont letters to her.[3]

Every day brings accounts of the Spirit of Liberty Spreading through Europe—though nothing of that Kind has, as yet, occurred in Sweden, I am inclined to think that if the King is not very Circumspect, the People will renovate the Constitution, & again recall their right of Elections & priviledges—there is much discontent in that Country, & Russia is growing too ponderous & Extensive for the Sovereign of *Petersborough* to Command so distant an Empire.

a Number of the first Men of Character Rank & fortune in this Country have associated under the Name of the Whig Club, & Each Member is pledged under his hand to Support Certain popular Measures; it will, I hope, encrease to a proper degree of Strength & Consequence[4]—Something of that Kind is now wanting for the present Administration is taking longer Strides to Despotism, than ever any former Administration attempted, Even North & Bute never ventured to insult this Country, as our present Vice-roy has presumed to do—he did not think himself very Safe here, therefore he left us & I beleive will not return again—Reports Say that Weymouth (the foe of American Freedom) is to succeed him.[5]

I have the Honor to send your Excellency a few papers, hoping they may not be delayed, as they Contain the truest accounts from France—though it may happen that you have recived them before the arrival of this Letter.

There is a Spirit arizen in the City of Dublin against the unconstitutional & expensive Police, which is an absolute Burthen of £21,000 a year instead of £4600, exclusive of the Ministerial patronage—as it adds 240 Votes to their Interest in the City, & near 100 in this County—their Greatest Efforts will be exerted at the Ensuing Election to Carry one Member for the City & two for this County; in the Latter Case they have got (as they have done for these 21 years) the other two Candidates to Join against *me*—however I *hope* to Succeed—though I never *Spend* in *money*, *Meat*, *Drink* or *Promises* the Value of one *Shilling* on the Contests for 21 years, except the poll Clerks, one Lawyer & advertizements—I never have an Election Dinner—I laid down this Rule on my first Entrance into Public Life & have never altered my plan—nor do I ever solicit any Voter a second Time.

This season has been the wettest, most Stormy & irregular, which has happend here these 15 years—between the blasts, rains & *Lightning* all our fruit was destroyed—our Corn damaged, but we have Still enough for our own Consumption; Hay in greater plenty than has been Known for 7 years—that will prevent the great rize (with *abundance* of Potatoes) of other Articles. With the warmest Sentiments of Respect for your Excellency, and an unalterable attachment to the Liberties of America I remain Dear Sir your most faithfull & most obt Humble Sert

Edward Newenham

Lady Newenham joins in best regards to Mrs Washington.

I should be glad of the Journals of the New Congress—why has Mr Thompson resigned.[6]

ALS, DLC:GW.

1. For GW's letter of introduction for Janet Montgomery, the widow of Revolutionary War general Richard Montgomery, see his letter to Newenham, 29 July 1789. Ranelagh's is probably the Irish seat of Charles Jones, fourth viscount Ranelagh.

2. At the bottom of the page Newenham noted: "This was her own Expression."

3. Newenham is referring to George Townshend, created earl of Leicester in 1784, who had served in North America during the French and Indian War; to Irish statesman James Caulfeild, fourth viscount and first earl of Charlemont (1728–1799); and to Gen. Eyre Massey, later first Baron Clarina (1719–1804), who had served in North America as a major and lieutenant colonel in the 46th Foot and the 27th Inniskillings during the French and Indian War.

4. The Whig Club, consisting mostly of Protestant Whigs, was formed in June 1789 in Dublin for the purpose of preventing parliamentary union with Great Britain and retaining the Constitution of 1782, which had guaranteed a separate parliament to Ireland. Similar clubs soon appeared in Belfast and other Irish towns. Although the clubs sought parliamentary reform, they were committed to retaining the connection with Great Britain. Among the first members were Charlemont, Henry Grattan, and George Ponsonby.

5. George Nugent-Temple, first marquis of Buckingham, resigned as lord lieutenant of Ireland on 30 Sept. 1789 and left Ireland in October. Thomas Thynne, third viscount Weymouth and first marquis of Bath, did not become lord lieutenant of Ireland after Buckingham's resignation; the post went instead to John Fane, tenth earl of Westmoreland, who held it until 1795.

6. For Charles Thomson's failure to secure a post in the new government, see his letter to GW, 23 July 1789, source note.

From Lewis Nicola

Sr   Philada 10th October 1789

Relying on your Excellencies goodness to excuse my trespassing on your time devoted to so important attentions I take the liberty to inform you that the, to me, unfortunate resolve[1] of Congress passed in 1785 not allow any State interest paid by them to publick creditors, having occasioned a general belief that the State of Pensylvania would pay any more to its citizens compelled me to try some other means of supporting my family, to accomplish which I was obliged to sell my certificates at three fourths loss, but miscarrying in my schemes I was reduced to the necessity of accepting an employment degrading to that I had the honour to fill under the United States, and more immediately under your command. This employment is Keeper of the publick Workhouse in this city & one years experience shewing that the income is inadequate to providing a maintenance & enabling me to discharge some pecuniary obligations I am under compels me to look up to your Excellency. I am informed that an officer is to be appointed in each State for the purpose of inspecting & paying the Pensioners, should you not think me disqualified & are not already engaged I entreat your appointing me to that office.

Not to trespass further I shall only request you will present my respects to Mrs Washington & accept from Your Excellencies Most humle and Obedient Servant

                                          Lewis Nicola

ALS, DLC:GW.

Lewis Nicola (1717–1807) was born in France but came to Philadelphia from Dublin around 1766. He soon became active in scientific and military circles in Pennsylvania and in the early days of the Revolution produced several military treatises and military maps. During the war he served as colonel of the Corps of Invalids. For his suggestion for the establishment of a monarchy with GW as king, see William Gordon to GW, 24 Sept. 1788, n.4. Nicola was brevetted brigadier general in 1783 and after the war held a number of positions in Philadelphia. He left the city briefly in the mid–1780s, but by 1788 he had returned and became commandant of the invalid corps. He retained his position as director of the Philadelphia workhouse until 1793. GW did not provide him with federal employment.

1. In MS this word reads "relsove."

From Otho Holland Williams

Dear Sir   Baltimore 10th October 1789.

The appointment of Coll Harrison to the Office of Judge in the supreme Court; and that of Mr Hanson to the Office of Chancellor, in this State;[1] have created vacancies in the Commission of our general Court which, it is expected, will be filled by some of our most antient law Characters, to whom that situation will be most agreeable.

The resignation of Mr Thomas Johnson,[2] which is here spoken of as a matter of certainty, induces me to mention these circumstances: and to embrace the opportunity of introducing to your Notice, Mr Robert Smith, of this town, as a Gentleman eminently Qualified to succeed Mr Johnson in the Office of district Judge.[3] The facility with which recommendations are to be procured by any body, and from, almost, every body, renders that mode of judging of merit little worthy of your confidence; But, Sir, if the most Flattering sentiments in Mr Smiths favor, expressed by the most learned, and respectable, Men in Maryland will justify the liberty I now take, there will be no difficulty in obtaining that Testimony. In the mean time I beg leave to inform you that Mr Robert Smith is the Son of Mr John Smith, Senator in this State: and Brother to Colonel Samuel Smith, who has the honor to be known to you.[4] Mr Smith studied Law five years in the Office of Mr Robert Goldsborough, the elder,[5] with the professed design of qualifing himself as a Councellor and has been, since, six Years in very successful practise in the most considerable Courts of Law and Equity in this state. He is much esteemed as a gentlemen; and, as a Citizen very much respected; particularly by the friends of the present government, in the support of which his exertions have been sensibly felt by its adversaries.

The great object of an established System being secured, Mr Smith, and his brother Coll Smith have been principally instrumental in composing the Political differences, in this town; in consequence of which the late Election here was determined without a contest. These matters, Sir, are mentioned not only to give Some testimony of his abilities, but to evince the Estimation of his Character in the opinion of the public.

As this is a private letter I beg Your permission to add a line on another Subject.

Mrs Carroll prevented my intended visit to Mount Clare, by doing me the honor to call at my House in town. We recapitulated all circumstances respecting the fruit trees: and agreed that it is most eligible, at Present, to send only the small ones. I expect to Ship half a dozen, for Mount Vernon, tomorrow.[6] I am, Dear Sir, Your Most Obedient and Most humble Servant

O. H. Williams

ALS, DLC:GW; ADf, MdHi: Otho H. Williams Papers.

1. For Robert Hanson Harrison's appointment, see GW's letter to him, 28 Sept. 1789. Mr. Hanson is probably Walter Hanson (1712–1794), a prominent Maryland jurist and the uncle of Samuel Hanson of Samuel.

2. See GW to Thomas Johnson, 28 Sept. 1789.

3. For Robert Smith's application for office, see his letter to GW, 5 Sept. 1789. Writing to William Jackson on 10 Oct., Williams submitted "to your perusal the enclosed *private* letter to the President. Its contents will inform you of my Wishes. Bob Smith is related to Mrs Williams, it is very true. But you will not believe that therefore I think him fit to be a Judge. I sincerely believe that he has talents to reflect an honor on the Office[.] You know best how to Seal and deliver my letter to the President, and to your conduct, which I know can influence its fate I commit it" (MdHi: Otho H. Williams Papers). For GW's comments on Smith's application for a post in the Judiciary, see his letter to Williams, 22 Nov., and to James McHenry, 30 Nov. 1789.

4. John Smith (1722–1794) emigrated with his parents from Ireland to Pennsylvania around 1728, where the elder Smith established himself as a merchant in Philadelphia and served in the Pennsylvania assembly. He moved to Baltimore in the late 1750s where he and William Buchanan founded the mercantile firm of Smith & Buchanan. In 1774 he took his sons into the firm, and it operated under the name of John Smith & Sons, during and after the Revolution. Smith's eldest son, Samuel (1752–1839), had served as captain, major, and lieutenant colonel during the Revolution. In 1793 he was elected to the House of Representatives and represented Maryland until 1803 and from 1816 to 1822. From 1822 to 1833 he served in the United States Senate.

5. Robert Goldsborough (1733–1788) of Cambridge, Dorchester County, Md., studied law and was admitted to the bar in London in 1757. After his return to Maryland in 1759 he served on a number of state courts, in the legislature, and as the state's attorney general. In 1788 he attended the Maryland Ratifying Convention.

6. For the background to the shipment of plants from Margaret Tilghman Carroll's greenhouse, see GW's letter to her, 16 Sept. 1789.

From William Allibone

Sir   Philadelphia October 12th 1789

at the request of A number of my fellow citizens I take the liberty of Offering myself A candidate for the appointment of superintendance of the Several Establishments for the security of the navigation in the Bay and River Deleware, that I am thus late in making my application arises from the following causes, it not being well understood that a general apointment of that kind was to be made, and from the act of legislature of this state ceding the same being hastily passed at a time it was not Expected in the latter part of their late session. as well as that they yet Remain under the Imediate care and mannagement of myself. as Master Warden of the port, in pursuance of which duties as well as those of my late profession of A mariner I am led to Believe that I have perfect knowledge of their nature and consequence. as I have not the Honor of being personally known to your Excellency I have accompanied this address with A recomendation put into my hands by some of those Gentlemen who are and Such whose reputation will I hope be of use to me in forming your Opinion,[1] should that be Favourable to my pretentions, it will ever be held in gratefull remembrance by one who has the honor to Subscribe himself your most Obedient and most Humble Servent

Willm Allibone

ALS, DLC:GW.

William Allibone, a Philadelphia merchant and shipmaster, had served from time to time in the city's militia. During the Revolution he served as commissioner for the defense of the Delaware Bay and River and, as he indicates in his letter, was now master warden for the port.

1. The recommendation is now missing. Allibone also wrote to Alexander Hamilton on this day, informing him of his application to the president. "Some of my Friends, on finding I had an Inclination to apply for the appointment of Superintendant of the light house, Beacons Buoys and publick Piers, have put Into my hands A Recommendation . . . addressed to the president. . . . I . . . am at A loss whether to attend at the seat of government in person or not and should consider it as A particular Favour if I could receive Information on that head" (DNA: RG 26, Lighthouse Letters Received, Vol. "A," Pennsylvania and Southern States). In January 1790 Hamilton gave Allibone a temporary appointment as superintendent, made permanent in April (Hamilton to GW, 3 Jan. 1790, Allibone to Hamilton, 29 April 1790, both in Syrett, *Hamilton Papers*, 6:43–49, 398–99).

To Henry Laurens

New York October 12. 1789.
The packet of seeds which accompanies this letter is part of a parcel sent to me by Mr Anderson of St Vincent at the request of Mr Benjamin Vaughan of London, which I do myself the pleasure to distribute agreeably to that Gentleman's intention—subjoining an extract from Mr Anderson's letter for your government in sowing the seed.[1]

They would have been forwarded sooner had not my late indisposition and multiplied avocations since my recovery intervened to prevent it—But as they will arrive in season for sowing next year, and as they did not reach me in time for this, no inconvenience will result from the delay.

G. Washington.

LB, DLC:GW.

The letter-book copy of this document is addressed to Henry Laurens and "Professor Madison," indicating that identical copies were sent to both men. On his release from his wartime imprisonment in the Tower of London, Henry Laurens (1724–1792) spent almost two years in England on official business for the Congress and then returned to South Carolina. He spent the remaining years of his life in retirement at his plantation. Bishop James Madison (1749–1812), president of the College of William and Mary, was at this time teaching in the college and was heavily involved in the reorganization of the Episcopal church in Virginia.

1. For Alexander Anderson, see Anderson's letter to GW, 18 Nov. 1789, source note. Benjamin Vaughan (1751–1835) was the eldest son of GW's friend Samuel Vaughan (see Vaughan to GW, 4 Nov. 1788). The younger Vaughan was educated at Cambridge and Edinburgh and during the Revolution was a strong supporter of the American cause. A protégé of Lord Shelburne, Vaughan acted as Shelburne's agent to the American commissioners during the peace negotiations at Paris in 1783 and became a close friend of Benjamin Franklin. In the mid–1780s Vaughan was a member of Parliament and in 1798 emigrated to the United States. No correspondence from Benjamin Vaughan or Anderson to GW on this subject has been found.

To Betty Washington Lewis

My Dear Sister, New York, Oct. 12th 1789
Your letter of the first of this month came duly to hand.—I believe Bushrod is right with respect to the distribution of the negroes—When I gave my opinion that you were entitled to a

child's part it did not occur to me that my Mother held them under the will of my Father who had made a distribution of them after her death.—If this is the case, and I believe it is, you do not come in for any part of them.[1]

I thought I had desired in my former letter that all personal property not specifically disposed of by the will had better be sold. This is my opinion as it is from the Crops and personal Estate that the Debts must be paid.—The surplus, be it more or less, is divided among her children; and this I presume had better be done in money than in Stock, old furniture or any other troublesome articles which might be inconvenient to remove, but in one or the other of these ways they must be disposed of, as they are not given by the Will.—If there is anything coming to the estate it ought to be collected.—In a word, all the property except Lands and negroes is considered as personal, and after the Debts are discharged is to be equally divided into five parts one of which five you are entitled to.

A sort of epidemical cold has seized every ⟨*illegible*⟩ under it[2]— hitherto I have escaped and propose in two or three days to set out for Boston by way of relaxation from business[3] and re-establishment of my health after the long and tedeous complaint with which I have been afflicted, and from which it is not more than ten days I have been recovered, that is since the incision which was made by the Doctors for this imposthume on my thigh has been cured.

Mrs. Washington joins me in every good wish for you and our other relations in Fredericksburg. And I am My dear Sister Your most affectionate Brother

Go. Washington

Memoirs of the Long Island Historical Society, 4 (1889), lvi-lvii; ALS, *American Book Prices Current*, 22 (1916), 1061.

1. See GW to Betty Lewis, 13 Sept. 1789.
2. GW is referring to a widespread epidemic of respiratory ailments that began in the southern and central states and by the late fall of 1789 was spreading into New England. Because it affected many of the spectators who stood outdoors at various ceremonies during his New England tour, GW was accorded the dubious honor of having the disorder named for him. As Joseph Crocker wrote from Boston to Henry Knox, "I find the Inhabitants in Town universally seized with the same disorder as the Inhabitants of your City have been troubled with, but they call it the President's Cough, supposing they

caught it on the day of the parade when the President entered the Town"
(1 Nov. 1789, MHi: Knox Papers). It was even more commonly referred to as
Washington's influenza. In late October GW himself fell victim to the ailment
(see *Diaries*, 5:477). See also *Pennsylvania Packet, and Daily Advertiser* (Philadelphia), 18 Nov. 1789, and *American Mercury* (Hartford), 9 Nov. 1789.

3. For some time in the fall of 1789 GW had apparently considered a tour
of the New England states "during the recess of Congress to acquire knowledge of the face of the Country the growth and Agriculture there of and the
temper and disposition of the Inhabitants towards the new government" (*Diaries*, 5:452–53). Following his usual practice of consultation he approached his
cabinet and other advisers concerning the propriety of the scheme. James
Madison and Henry Knox approved, and Alexander Hamilton "thought it a
very desirable plan and advised it accordingly." Chief Justice John Jay "highly
approved of it—but observed, a similar visit wd. be expected by those of the
Southern [states]" (ibid., 452, 453, 454, 456).

GW left New York City about nine o'clock on the morning of Thursday, 15
Oct., with a party composed of Tobias Lear, David Humphreys, William Jackson, and a retinue of six servants. Hamilton, Jay, and Knox accompanied the
party some distance from the city (ibid., 460). The trip, a triumph in terms of
support for GW, lasted a month, and before he returned to New York on 13
Nov. GW had visited or passed through nearly sixty towns and hamlets. See
map of the tour, pp. 200–201. For his detailed diary account of the events and
festivities of his journey, see *Diaries*, 5:460–97.

To William McWhir

Sir,   New York, October 12th 1789.
I have received your letter of the 18 ult., and am glad to learn
from it that my Nephews apply with diligence to arithmetic and
english composition—these are two branches in which I have
always thought them deficient—and have ever been pressingly
desirous that they should be made well acquainted with them.[1]

George may be instructed in the french language, but Laurence had better apply himself, for the present, to his arithmetic,
writing and composition.

As you have failed in your endeavors to obtain a mathematical
Instructor, it is not probable that any success would attend
an advertisement in a paper here—however, I will have one
inserted.

I can give no particular opinion respecting the Boy whom you
represent to be an uncommon Genius—but I would willingly
give any reasonable encouragement towards the cultivation of

talents which bid fair to be useful. I am Sir, your most obedient Servant

G. Washington.

LB, DLC:GW.
   1. Letter not found. For background to GW's perennial problems with the young sons of his brother Samuel, see Francis Willis, Jr., to GW, 24 Sept. 1788, source note, Charles Washington to GW, 7 Jan. 1789, Samuel Hanson to GW, 12 Jan. and 19 Feb. 1789, GW to Hanson, 16 Jan. 1789, and GW to George Steptoe Washington, 23 Mar. 1789.

To Joseph Mandrillon

Sir,   New York, October 12th 1789.
   At this late hour I do myself the pleasure to acknowledge the receipt of your letter of the 25. of October 1788—and thank you for the book, which you were so polite as to send to me entitled *"Literary and Political fragments collected in a journey to Berlin."* I am Sir, Your most obedient servant

G. Washington.

LB, DLC:GW.

To John Mason

Sir,   New York, October 12th 1789.
   I have received your letter of the 14th of August together with its enclosures, for which, as well as for the polite offer of your services, I beg you to accept my best thanks.[1]
   On the 16th[2] and 25th of August I wrote to the House of Fenwick, Mason and Co. requesting them to furnish me with a quantity of the best claret, which letters, I presume have got to hand. I am Sir, your most obedient Servant

G. Washington.

P.S. I enclose to you the first of a set of exchange on Messrs Jauge et du Preis which I will thank you to receive for me when it becomes due.[3]
   It was given for money advanced to a Frenchman who was in distress—to pay his passage to France.

LB, DLC:GW.

1. Mason's letter is dated 4 rather than 14 August.

2. For GW's letter to Fenwick, Mason & Company, 16 Aug., see his letter to Wakelin Welch & Son, 16 Aug. 1789, n.2.

3. No record of this transaction has been found.

To Thomas Newton, Jr.

Sir,   New York Octr 12th 1789

A variety of avocations has prevented my giving an earlier acknowledgment to your letter of the 17th of July. I will now thank you, Sir, to furnish me with an Acct of the quantity & cost of the materials which have been placed on Cape Henry by the Commissioners appointed by the Assembly of Virginia, for the purpose of building a Light-house—as you have been so obliging as to offer to do it.[1]

I am sorry that you have not yet recd any of my outstanding debts, but am not without hope that you will be able to collect at least some part of them shortly. this case is hard, and I believe singular. I am, Sir, Your most Obedt Sert

G. Washington

Df, DNA: RG 59, Miscellaneous Letters; LB, DLC:GW.

1. Virginia was in the process of erecting a lighthouse on Cape Henry in the summer and fall of 1789. "An Act for the establishment and support of Lighthouses, Beacons, Buoys, and Public Piers," enacted by Congress into law on 7 Aug. 1789, provided that the federal government would assume responsibility for such construction within the limits of the United States and that the Treasury Department would pay the expenses involved provided that all such installations would be ceded to the United States by the states (1 *Stat.* 53–54). Virginia conveyed jurisdiction over the Cape Henry lighthouse to the United States in November 1789. See "An Act authorising the Governor of this Commonwealth, to convey certain land to the United States, for the purpose of building a light-house" (13 Hening 3–4; *Journals of the Council of State of Virginia*, 5:144–45). The legislature spent considerable time in the fall of 1789 deciding what disposition to make of the large amount of building supplies that had been assembled for the lighthouse. See, for example, *Journal of the House of Delegates*, 1789, 127; *Journal of the House of Delegates*, 1790, 12.

To Henrich Wilmans

Sir,   New York, October 12th 1789.

I have now before me your several favors of the 19th of March, the 12th and 24th of June,[1] and must beg your acceptance of my best thanks for the satisfactory manner in which you have executed the commission that you was so polite as to take upon yourself—I also feel myself obliged by the offer of your future services.[2]

The Gardner who you have been so good as to procure for me arrived here on the 14 of september, and set off a few days after for my seat in Virginia, where he will enter upon his duty,[3] and, from the account which you have given of him, I have no doubt but I shall be pleased with his services—The plants and seeds, which you were so good as to send to me arrived safe, and the Gardner has taken them to Virginia with him.

In your letter of the 12th of June you observed that you were in treaty with a weaver who you expected to engage for me, but as you mentioned nothing more of the matter in your subsequent letter, I presume that you were disappointed in your expectations of engaging him.[4] However, if you should in future have an opportunity of procuring a good linen weaver for me, upon reasonable terms, I shall thank you to do it, and, in that case, it is my wish that he should be sent over in some vessel bound to the Potomac, for the expence of transporting a person from hence to Virginia is no inconsiderable addition to the cost of obtaining him. I am Sir, &ce

G. Washington.

LB, DLC:GW.

1. Letters not found.

2. Henrich Wilmans of Bremen, Germany, had assisted GW in employing a gardener. See John Christian Ehlers to GW, 24 June 1789, source note.

3. For the arrangements made by Tobias Lear for John Christian Ehlers's trip to Mount Vernon, see Lear to John Inskeep, 16 Sept. 1789 (DLC:GW), and Lear to Clement Biddle, 16 Sept. 1789 (PHi: Washington-Biddle Correspondence).

4. See Wilmans to GW, 28 Feb. 1790.

From John Blair

Sir   Williamsburg, Octr 13th 1789.
   The honourable commission which you have been pleased to offer me in the service of the United States came to hand the tenth instt accompanied by your very polite letter, & the laws which have passed relative to the office.[1]
   When I considered the great importance, as well as the arduous nature of the duties, I could not but entertain some fears, that I might find them well adapted neither to my domestic habits, my bodily constitution, nor my mental capacity; in every other respect, the office promises me a very desirable situation, for which I know not how sufficiently to declare my gratitude.
   I have determined to make an experiment, whether I may be able to perform the requisite services, with some degree of satisfaction, in respect both to the Public and my self; and I request permission to assure you, Sir, that if any extrinsic circumstance were necessary to induce my acceptance of the appointment, I could find none so powerful as a wish of the man, who possesses the love & veneration of every American, the respect & admiration of all the world. I have the honour to be, with more deference & esteem than I know how to express, Worthy Sir, Your most obedient & affectionate servant,

                                                      John Blair

ALS, DNA: RG 59, Miscellaneous Letters.
   John Blair (1732–1800) attended the College of William and Mary and studied law at the Middle Temple in London. Before the Revolution he represented the college in the House of Burgesses and served as clerk of the council. In 1776 he became a member of the Virginia privy council, in 1777 one of the judges of the general court, and in 1780 a judge of the high court of chancery. Blair represented Virginia at the Constitutional Convention and was a member of the Virginia Ratifying Convention in 1788, where he supported adoption of the Constitution.
   1. GW's letter to Blair offering him one of the associate judgeships on the Supreme Court has not been found, but it was undoubtedly similar to those sent to the other appointees on the court. See, for example, GW to Robert Hanson Harrison, 28 Sept. 1789, and GW to John Rutledge, 29 Sept. 1789. Blair held his position on the court until 1796.

To D'Estaing

Dear General,   New-York, October 13th 1789
     I have been honored with the receipt of your letter of the 8th
of June enclosing a list of Officers who wish to receive diplomas
from the society of the Cincinnati.
     General Knox will forward to your Excellency, by the Count
de Moustier,[1] who is so obliging as to favor this letter with his
care, Diplomas for the first forty five names on your list[2]—he
has sent to the Commandant of the Squadron, now at Boston,
Diplomas for the Vicomte de Pontever Gien, Marquis de la
Galisoniere, Monsieur de Durand de Braiye, and the Marquis de
Traversay—and he hopes to obtain a sufficiency of Diplomas to
complete your list, which he will transmit to you by the next
Packet for France.[3]
     I am assured that I shall add to your Excellencys satisfaction
by telling you that the political circumstances of the United
States are in so pleasing a train as to promise respectabillity to
their Government, and happiness to our citizens.
     The opposition offered to the reform of our federal Constitu-
tion has in a great measure subsided, and there is every reason
to predict political harmony and individual happiness to the
States and Citizens of confederated America.
     The Revolution, announced by the intelligence from France,
must be interesting to the Nations of the World in general, and
is certainly of the greatest importance to the Country in which it
has happened.
     I am persuaded I express the sentiments of my fellow-
citizens, when I offer an earnest prayer that it may terminate in
the permanent honor and happiness of your Government and
People.[4] with sentiments of respectful Affection and esteem, I
have the honor to be, Dear General Your Most obedient Servant.

Copy, DNA: RG 59, Miscellaneous Letters; LB, DLC:GW.
     1. See GW to Rochambeau, 13 Oct. 1789, n.1.
     2. In his letter of 8 June d'Estaing had submitted two separate lists of ap-
plications for diplomas, one for French army officers who had served in
America and one for French naval officers, who were now admitted to membership in the society. When the Society of the Cincinnati was established in
France membership was at first confined to officers who had served in the
army. See Barras to GW, 23 Jan. 1784, and notes.
     3. In September and October 1789 a squadron of vessels of the French

navy, under the command of Henri-Jean-Baptiste, vicomte de Pontevès-Giens, visited several American ports. Pontevès-Giens, Athanase-Scipion-Barrin, marquis de La Galissonnière, Jean-Baptiste-Alexandre Durand de Braye, and Jean-Baptiste Prévost de Sansac, marquis de Traversay, had all served with the French navy during its American campaigns. Galissonnière was second in command in the squadron. William Eustis, writing Henry Knox in the fall of 1789 on the "danger in giving a diploma to any foreign officer," observed that it was the opinion of Galissonnère, "the other brethren in the fleet, & I believe of all the other officers that the Viscount de Ponteves, commander of the squadron, has been made a member *thro' mistake.* . . . I am persuaded that time & its information will convince you that he was not entitled to become a wearer of the bald eagle" (Eustis to Knox, 13 Nov. 1789, MHi: Knox Papers).

4. D'Estaing replied to this letter on 20 Mar. 1790: "The letter with which you have had the goodness to honor me, dated October 13th, has been transmitted to me by M. le Comte de Moustier, as well as the diplomas with which he was charged. I have transmitted them to the Officers to whom they were destined. Deign to accept, I beseech you, with that indulgent goodness which is your characteristic, the homage of my thanks. Those which Each one of my comrades have charged me to tender to you, vary in expression, but unite in sentiment. Some envy the good fortune of the Squadron which was at Boston—others desire to be so happy as to shew their duty to you; and none fail to signify the satisfaction which they feel in possessing so honorable a title and to transmit it to their families. The Signature of M. George Washington is placed above those of the greatest Sovereigns that ever existed; they shew it with a Kind of religious veneration; for when liberty is rightly understood it becomes the divinity of the human Race—and you, Sir, ought not be surprized that you are the Messiah of it.

"Those Officers who have not received their diplomas express the greatest desire to obtain that benefit—they have charged me to solicit it—deign, I pray you, to speak of it to His Excellency General Knox. All my friends threaten to quarrel with me if they have not also this signature which is superior to all titles. The name of Cæsar among the Romans was considered as the first of all honorable titles—and the Emperors of Germany decorate themselves with it to this day; Cæsar enslaved his Country—you have liberated your's. How much more worthy are you, than he, of this homage! Your fellow-citizens and posterity have decreed that the name of . . . [Washington] shall not be lessened by any qualifications (titles). The United States owe to you, peace & political energy—the two bases of all good Government, which cannot exist & be durable longer than while the executive authority enjoys all its powers within the immutable bounds of liberty. As an American Citizen I partake of this good fortune by my attachment to my new Country, and I take the most lively and sincere interest in the glory which you have procured for it; I do not fear to add, as a French Citizen, that I not only expect the moment in which I can say as much of this country—but that I think and hope it is not far distant" (DSoCi). D'Estaing also wrote a private letter to GW on 20 Mar. 1790 which is printed below.

Tobias Lear to Alexander Hamilton

Sir   United States October 13th 1789

The sum of two thousand five Dollars is necessary to be advanced to take up notes which were given for money advanced for the household of the President of the United States previous to the organization of the Treasury Department.[1]

This sum added to two thousand Dollars which you have already advanced for the purpose of taking up Notes, will compleat the payment of all Monies advanced for the use of the President of the United States previous to your coming into Office—One thousand Dollars will likewise be wanting for the President and a Dft on Boston for five hundred[2]—In my absence Mr Robt Lewis will draw from you such money as may be wanting for the use of the House-hold during the journey of the President. I have the honor to be with perfect respect Sir Yr most Obt Servant

Tobias Lear
S. P. U. States

LB, DLC:GW.

1. From this time on Tobias Lear periodically submitted requests to the Treasury Department for sums of money for expenses to be deducted from the president's yearly compensation of $25,000. The Treasury Department in turn issued warrants for the sums requested. Since GW came to New York in April with very little in the way of personal funds (see GW to Richard Conway, 4, 6 Mar. 1789, and to Mathew Carey, 22 May 1789), it is likely that most bills for household expenses were not settled until the organization of the Treasury Department in September.

2. These funds were intended to cover the expenses of the presidential party on GW's New England tour. An entry in the household accounts made after GW's return to New York indicates that the expenses of the trip totaled £276.9.8½ (CtY: Household Accounts, 21).

From David Humphreys

Seventeen Miles east of Camden [S.C.]

My dear Genl   Octr 13th 1789.

Having been led to believe that this route was the shortest & best, we left Augusta this day week; and having now an opportunity by Charles Town, I write (in conformity to the intimation you was pleased to give) for the purpose of keeping you advised of our progress.

From the Savannah at Augusta to the Congaree at Friday's ferry, a distance of about 80 or 90 Miles, is a continuation of Sandy Roads and Pine Woods. Houses are scarce & accomodations miserable. The Congaree, formed by the junction of the Saluda & Broad River just above *Friday's ferry*, is navigable for Boats with 60 Hogsheads to the *latter*. Two miles from which is the new Town of Columbia, now the Capital of the State, in which they are erecting the largest State House on the Continent, for the General Assembly to occupy next Spring. At Camden Elliot Lee is said to have lost at play Magnolio & a dozen more excellent Horses.[1] Magnolio is now at Santee about 20 Miles below Camden; & might be purchased for two hundred Pounds.

In our Journey we broke, at different times, the Pole & Axtle Tree of the Carriage, which we got repaired at Friday's ferry.

On the 10th we made a Journey of forty miles from the Congaree to the Wateree. At the Head of the Boat Navigation, on the latter, Camden is situated. The two Rivers Congaree & Wateree form the Santee by their conflux, about 20 Miles below Camden. At this place we passed Sunday, visited the grave of De Kalb & obtained some informations relative to the interesting military transactions which happened in & near it. Camden does not contain quite so many Houses as Augusta, but they are larger and better built. The Inhabitants have an elegant Assembly Room, and are entertained with Concerts or Plays every week. We drank Tea at the House of a Colo. Kershaw, who was the very first Settler of Camden; & who is also the founder of three other considerable Towns.[2] He had been extremely useful to Genl Lincoln in the War.

Yesterday we came from Camden to this place by 12 O'Clock. After refreshing our Horses, we set out to make another Stage. In passing from the House on a side-hill, one of the hind Wheels crushed to the ground under us, and every spoke in it was broken. At some places, where we found nothing but pines for 20 miles & not a House in that space, the Catastrophe would have been truly distressing. Here we were fortunate in finding accidentally a House-Joiner from Camden. We collected Tools enough in four or five Miles to begin a new wheel; and I hope the disaster will not retard us more than 24 hours. Although we have very unfavorable accounts of the heaviness of the roads through which we are to pass; I expect we shall reach the borders of North Carolina by a great exertion, tomorrow night.

We have not yet heard any thing from New York Since we left it. The only News Paper which has fallen into our hands was from Charles Town, & contained accounts of violent tumults in France. Curiosity is strongly excited, but I do not imagine we shall learn the farther particulars before our arrival in Virginia—Adieu, my dear General, and be pleased to believe me Your sincerest friend & most devoted Servt

D. Humphreys

ALS, DLC:GW.

For the negotiations of the American commissioners to the southern Indians, see David Humphreys to GW, 21, 26, 27 Sept., 28 Oct. 1789, Alexander Hamilton to GW, 20 Oct. 1789, and Henry Knox to GW, 18 Oct., 21, 27 Nov. 1789. See also GW's Memoranda on Indian Affairs, 1789.

1. In the late fall of 1788 GW had exchanged his prized Arabian horse Magnolio for two tracts of land owned by Henry Lee in Kentucky. For the transaction, see GW's letter to Henry Lee, 30 Nov. 1788, source note. Elliot Lee is probably William Aylett Lee, a son of Thomas Ludwell Lee and a cousin of Henry Lee.

2. This is probably Joseph Kershaw (c.1723–1791), who was a militia captain during the Revolution. In 1791 during GW's southern tour, Kershaw presented the address from the citizens of Camden to GW (*Diaries*, 6:147).

From John Jay

New York 13th October 1789.

Mr Jay has the honor of informing the President of the United States, that yesterday afternoon he received a letter from Sir John Temple[1] in the following words, vizt

"New York 12th of October 1789, Sir. I beg leave to submit in the most respectful manner, the enclosed memorial to the consideration of the Government of the United States. The memorialist informs me he hath in his possession all necessary and proper vouchers and documents to establish fully the facts set fourth in his said memorial. I am with very great respect, Sir, your most obedient and most humble Servant. John Temple."

The memorial mentioned in this letter is herewith enclosed, No. 1.[2]

That considering the informality of the measure, he thought it best to give Sir John an opportunity of reconsidering it, especially too as the propriety of any application to Government on the subject was at least doubtful, he therefore wrote this morning to Sir John as follows.

"New York 13th October 1789. Mr Jay presents his compliments to Sir John Temple and returns herewith enclosed the memorial which accompanied the letter Sir John did him the honor to write yesterday.

Mr Jay takes the liberty of advising Sir John to consult some able and discreet Councellor as to the measures proper to be taken on the occasion; unless the intention of his letter is merely to convey intelligence of the facts stated in the memorial, in which case Mr Jay on its being returned will immediately lay it before the President."

That he has just received from Sir John Temple a letter herewith enclosed, No. 2.[3]

As Sir John requests nothing of Government it does not appear to Mr Jay necessary that the President should at present do any thing on the subject.

Mr Jay would have waited on the President with these papers, but he really finds himself too much indisposed to go out, having just returned from a ride with a severe head ache.

LB, DNA: RG 59, Domestic Letters; LB, DNA: RG 59, Correspondence with the Secretaries of State; LB, DNA: RG 59, Miscellaneous Letters; LB, DLC:GW.

1. Sir John Temple (1732–1798), a Loyalist from Boston, had been British consul general at New York since 1785.

2. The enclosure was a memorial from Thomas Moore Savage, a British sea captain and master of the sloop *Sally* out of Kingston, Jamaica. Savage had sailed from Norfolk on 27 Aug. 1789 bound for Jamaica and carrying British colors, when, off Cape Henry, he was deliberately rammed by the French public ship *L'Active*, nearly destroying the sloop and damaging its cargo. Officers from the French frigate boarded the sloop, demanding its colors and making "use of much abusive and ungenteel Language." Unable to continue its voyage the sloop returned to Norfolk. The French frigate also put into Norfolk, and Savage, conceiving "the Injury done to him and the said Vessel, is against the Laws of Nations, against the Peace established between the Courts of Great Britain & France, and against the Protection due to british Vessels in the Ports,

and within the Jurisdiction of the United States of America," appealed to
Temple for assistance (DNA: RG 59, Miscellaneous Letters).

  3. Enclosure no. 2 is a letter, 13 Oct. 1789, from Temple to Jay, asking the
secretary to lay the matter before the president (DNA: RG 59, Miscellaneous
Letters).

To Thomas Jefferson

Sir,   New York Oct. 13th 1789
  In the selection of characters to fill the important offices of
Government in the United States I was naturally led to contemplate the talents and disposition which I knew you to possess and
entertain for the Service of your Country. And without being
able to consult your inclination, or to derive any knowledge of
your intentions from your letters either to myself or to any other
of your friends, I was determined, as well by motives of private
regard as a conviction of public propriety, to nominate you for
the Department of State, which under its present organization,
involves many of the most interesting objects of the Executive
Authority. But grateful as your acceptance of this Commission
would be to me, I am at the sametime desirous to accomodate to
your wishes, and I have therefore forborne to nominate your
Successor at the Court of Versailles until I should be informed
of your determination.
  Being on the eve of a journey through the Eastern States, with
a view to observe the situation of the Country,[1] and in a hope of
perfectly re-establishing my health, which a series of indisposition has much impaired, I have deemed it proper to make this
communication of your appointment in order that you might
lose no time should it be your [wish][2] to visit Virginia during the
recess of Congress, which will probably be the most convenient
season, both as it may respect your private concerns and the
public service.
  Unwilling as I am to interfere in the direction of your choice
of Assistants, I shall only take the liberty of observing to you
that, from warm recommendations which I have received in
behalf of Roger Alden Esqr., Assistant Secretary to the late
Congress, I have placed all the Papers thereunto belonging
under his care.[3] Th⟨ose⟩ Papers which more properly appertain
to the Office of Foreign-Affairs are under the Superintendance

of Mr Jay, who has been so obliging as to continue his good-offices; and they are in the immediate charge of Mr Remson.[4] With sentiments of very great esteem & regard—I have the honor to be Sir—Your Most Obedt Hble Servt

Go: Washington

I take this occasion to acknowledge the receipt of your several favors of the 4th and 5th Decr of the last—and 10th of May of the present year and to thank you for the communications therein.[5] G.W.

ALS, DLC: Jefferson Papers; LB, DLC:GW; DfS, DNA: RG 59, Miscellaneous Letters.

1. See GW to Betty Lewis, 12 Oct. 1789, n.3.

2. This word is missing from the ALS and has been supplied from the draft.

3. For Alden's recommendation for a public post, see Charles Thomson to GW, 23 July 1789, especially note 1.

4. Henry Remsen, Jr., son of Henry Remsen, a New York merchant, served as under secretary for foreign affairs during the Confederation. Under the new government he became chief clerk of the Department of State.

5. According to the endorsement on this letter, Jefferson received it at Eppington, Va., on 11 Dec. 1789.

To La Rouërie

Dear Sir   New-York Octr 13th 1789

I have been honored with the receipt of your letters of the 5th October 1788[1] and 18th June last—the former I only received a few days ago by Major de Berdt.

In answer to your observations respecting the monies due to your Officers from the United States, I can only express my regret that the political circumstances of the country have not heretofore capacitated a more punctual compliance with its engagements—But as there is a prospect that the finances of America will improve with the progression of its government, I can not but entertain a belief that the cause of the complaint will be removed and Confidence restored to our public Creditors— The measures to effect this desireable purpose must be proportioned to the means we possess: and altho' they may be slow, yet I trust they will be certain in their operation—I shall add to your satisfaction by informing you that the political affairs of the

United States are in so pleasing a train as to promise respectability to our Government and happiness to our Citizens.

The opposition offerd to the reform of our federal Constitution has in a great measure subsided and there is every reason to predict political harmony and individual happiness to the States and Citizens of confederated America.

The Revolution announced by the intelligence from France, must be interesting to the Nations of the World in general, and is certainly of the greatest importance to the Country in which it has happened—I am persuaded I express the sentiments of my fellow Citizens, when I offer an earnest prayer that it may terminate in the permanent honor and happiness of your government and people.

I am much obliged by the flattering and affectionate sentiments expressed in your letters—and I request you to believe that I am with great regard Dear sir your most obedient Servant

Go: Washington

Df, DNA: RG 59, Miscellaneous Letters; LB, DLC:GW. In the letter book this letter was inadvertently addressed to the comte de Rochambeau and the letter to Rochambeau of this date, printed below, was addressed to La Rouërie.

1. Letter not found.

To Gouverneur Morris

Dear Sir,   New York, October 13th 1789.

In my first moments of leisure I acknowledge the receipt of your several favors of the 23 of February, 3 of March and 29 of April.

To thank you for the interesting communications contained in those letters, and for the pains you have taken to procure me a watch,[1] is all, or nearly all I shall attempt in this letter—for I could only repeat things, were I to set about it, which I have reason to believe have been regularly communicated to you in detail, at the periods which gave birth to them.

It may not however be unpleasing to you to hear in one word that the national government is organized, and as far as my information goes, to the satisfaction of all parties—That opposition to it is either no more, or hides its head.

That it is hoped and expected it will take strong root, and that the non acceding States will very soon become members of the union—No doubt is entertained of North Carolina, nor would there be of Rhode Island had not the majority of that People bid adieu, long since to every principle of honor—common sense, and honesty. A material change however has taken place, it is said, at the late election of representatives, and confident assurances are given from that circumstance of better dispositions in their Legislature at its next session, now about to be held.

The revolution which has been effected in France is of so wonderful a nature that the mind can hardly realise the fact—If it ends as our last accounts to the first of August predict that nation will be the most powerful and happy in Europe; but I fear though it has gone triumphantly through the first paroxysm, it is not the last it has to encounter before matters are finally settled.

In a word the revolution is of too great magnitude to be effected in so short a space, and with the loss of so little blood— The mortification of the King, the intrigues of the Queen, and the discontents of the Princes, and the Noblesse will foment divisions, if possible, in the national assembly, and avail themselves of every faux pas in the formation of the constitution if they do not give a more open, active opposition.

To these the licentiousness of the People on one hand and sanguinary punishments on the other will alarm the best disposed friends to the measure, and contribute not a little to the overthrow of their object—Great temperance, firmness, and foresight are necessary in the movements of that Body. To forbear running from one extreme to another is no easy matter, and should this be the case, rocks and shelves not visible at present may wreck the vessel.

This letter is an evidence, though of a trifling sort, that in the commencement of any work one rarely sees the progress or end of it. I declared to you in the beginning that I had little to say. I have got beyond the second page, and find I have a good deal to add; but that no time or paper may be wasted in a useless preface I will come to the point.

Will you then, my good Sir, permit me to ask the favor of you to provide and send to me by the first Ship, bound to this place, or Philadelphia mirrors for a table, with neat and fashionable but not expensive ornaments for them—such as will do credit to your taste—The mirrors will of course be in pieces that they may be adapted to the company, (the size of it I mean) the aggregate length of them may be ten feet—the breadth two feet—The panes may be plated ware, or any thing else more fashionable but not more expensive. If I am defective recur to what you have seen on Mr Robert Morris's table for my ideas *generally*. Whether these things can be had on better terms and in a better style in Paris than in London I will not undertake to decide. I recollect however to have had plated ware from both places, and those from the latter came cheapest—but a single instance is no evidence of a general fact.

Of plated ware may be made I conceive handsome and useful Coolers for wine *at* and *after* dinner. Those I am in need of viz. *eight* double ones (for madeira and claret the wines usually drank at dinner) each of the apertures to be sufficient to contain a pint decanter, with an allowance in the depth of it for ice at bottom so as to raise the neck of the decanter above the cooler— between the apertures a handle is to be placed by which these double coolers may with convenience be removed from one part of the table to another. For the wine *after* dinner *four* quadruple coolers will be necessary each aperture of which to be of the size of a *quart* decanter or quart bottle for four sorts of wine—These decanters or bottles to have ice at bottom, and to be elevated thereby as above—a central handle here also will be wanting— Should my description be defective your imagination is fertile and on this I shall rely. One idea however I must impress you with and that is in whole or part to avoid extravagance. For extravagance would not comport with my own inclination, nor with the example which ought to be set—The reason why I prefer an aperture for *every* decanter or bottle to coolers that would contain two and four is that whether full or empty the bottles will always stand upright and never be at variance with each other.

The letter enclosed with your draught accompanying it will provide the means for payment[2]—The clumsy manner in which Merchants (or rather their Tradesmen) execute commissions, where taste is required, for persons at a distance must be my apology, and the best that can be offered by Dear Sir Your most obedient and affecte humble Servant

G. Washington.

Mrs Washington presents her compliments to you.

P.S. I was in the very act of sealing this letter when yours of the 31st of July from Dieppe was put into my hands—accept my sincere thanks for the important communications contained [in] it, and for the tables which accompanied. I shall add no more now, except that in the morning I commence a tour, though rather late in the season, through the States eastward of this.[3] Adieu, yours

G. Washington

LB, DLC:GW.

1. GW asked Morris to have a watch made for him in France. See his letter to Morris, 28 Nov. 1788, and Morris to GW, 23 Feb. 1789, n.2.

2. GW enclosed in this letter to Morris a letter to Wakelin Welch & Son, stating that he had "requested my friend and acquaintance Gouvr Morris Esqr—now either in London or Paris to procure and send to me by the first conveyance which shall offer to this City or Philadelphia Plated Coolers—Mirrors—and other Ornaments for a Table; and to draw upon you for the amount" (ALS, PWacD, on deposit at PPAmP). He wrote Wakelin Welch & Son again on 1 Mar. 1790, reminding them that he had requested Morris "to provide, and send to me, some plated ware, and other ornaments for a dining table—There are some other matters still wanting to complete them, which, as he is knowing to my ideas in this respect, I have written to him for—The cost will perhaps amount to fifty or sixty guineas, which I pray you to advance him—This sum may exceed what I have in your hands, for I do not know precisely how the account stands between us—but I shall hope, notwithstanding, that Mr Morris will be furnished with the money, as not receiving the things would be a disappointment to me" (LB, DLC:GW). Morris was able to send GW an elaborate arrangement of biscuit figures in January 1790 (see his two letters to GW of 24 Jan.), but he had more difficulty in finding silver plate and the plateaus, or mirrored salvers, and still abide by GW's price requirements. See Morris, *Diary of the French Revolution*, 1:478, 548; 2:56. Morris delivered GW's letter to Wakelin Welch & Sons on 22 April, but on 3 May Welch informed him "that he is not in Cash for Genl Washington to the Amount I have already expended for his Use and does not chuse to advance. He is to pay me the Ballance in his Hands" (ibid., 1:488, 502). GW's purchases eventually amounted to £91 (Ledger B, 302).

3. See GW to Betty Lewis, 12 Oct. 1789, n.3.

To Gouverneur Morris

Sir   New York 13th October 1789

My letter to you, herewith inclosed,[1] will give you the Credence necessary to enable you to do the Business which it com-

mits to your management, and which I am persuaded you will
readily undertake.

Your inquiries will commence by observing, that as the present Constitution of Government and the Courts established in
pursuance of it remove the objections heretofore made to putting the United States in possession of their frontier posts, it is
natural to expect from the assurances of his Majesty and the
national good faith, that no unnecessary delays will take place.[2]
Proceed then to press a speedy performance of the treaty, respecting that object.

Remind them of the article by which it was agreed that negroes belonging to our Citizens should not be carried away; and
of the reasonableness of making compensation for them.[3] Learn
with precision, if possible, what they mean to do on this head.

The commerce between the two Countries you well understand—you are apprized of the sentiments and feelings of the
United States on the present State of it; and you doubtless have
heard that in the late Session of Congress, a very respectable
number of both Houses were inclined to a discrimination of
duties unfavorable to Britain; and that it would have taken place
but for concilitary considerations, and the probability that the
late change in our Government and circumstances would lead to
more satisfactory arrangements.[4]

Request to be informed therefore, whether they contemplate
a treaty of commerce with the United States, and on what
principles or terms in general. In treating this subject, let is be
strongly impressed on your mind, that the privileges of carrying
our productions in our vessels to their Islands, and bringing in
return the productions of those Islands to our own ports and
markets, is regarded here as of the highest importance, and you
will be careful not to countenance any idea of our dispensing
with it in a treaty. Ascertain if possible their views on this point;
for it would not be expedient to commence negociations without
previously having good reasons to expect a satisfactory termination of them.

It may also be well for you to take a proper occasion of
remarking, that their omitting to send a Minister here, when the
United States sent one to London, did not make an agreeable
impression on this Country; and request to know what would be
their future conduct on similar occasions.

It is in my opinion very important that we avoid errors in our system of policy respecting Great Britain, and this can only be done by forming a right judgment of their disposition and views. Hence you will perceive how interesting it is that you obtain the information in question, and that the business be so managed, as that it may receive every advantage which abilities address and delicacy can promise and afford. I am Sir your most obedt humble servant

Go. Washington

LB, DNA: RG 59, Dispatches from U.S. Ministers to France; LB, DNA: RG 46, First Congress, Records of Executive Proceedings, President's Messages—Foreign Relations.

In the fall of 1789 GW considered sending an unofficial envoy to Great Britain to settle outstanding problems between that country and the United States. Among the points of contention were the retention by the British of the western posts on United States territory, the delay in the payment of British creditors by several of the states, and the lack of a commercial treaty between the two powers. Earlier attempts during the Confederation years for similar conversations and for an exchange of ministers had resulted in rebuffs by the British government. If the appointment of the envoy was unofficial, there would be less risk of humiliation for the administration if the British refused to negotiate. On 7 Oct. GW approached John Jay "on the propriety of takg. informal means of ascertaining the views of the British Court with respect to our Western Posts in their possession and to a Commercial treaty" (*Diaries*, 5:454). Jay had just communicated to GW the purport of instructions received by Sir John Temple, the British consul in New York, from the duke of Leeds, British secretary for foreign affairs, that Temple should collect extensive information concerning American trade, duties, commodities, manufactures, emigration, and population (ibid.). Jay approved the idea of dispatching an unofficial envoy to Britain and "mentioned as a fit person for this purpose, a Doctr. [Edward] Bancroft as a man in whom entire confidence might be placed.

"Colo. Hamilton on the same subject highly approved of the Measure but thought Mr. Gouvr. Morris well qualified" (ibid., 454–55). The president approached James Madison on 8 October. Madison "thought if the necessity did not press it would be better to wait the arrival of Mr. Jefferson who might be able to give the information wanted on this head—and with me thought, that if Mr. Gouvr. Morris was employed in this business it would be a commitment for his appointment as Minister if one should be sent to that Court or wanted at Versailles in place of Mr. Jefferson—and Moreover if either of these was his Wish whether his representations might not be made with an eye to it. He thought with Colo. Hamilton, and as Mr. Jay also does, that Mr. Morris is a man of superior talents—but with the latter that his imagination sometimes runs a head of his judgment—that his Manners before he is known—and where known are oftentimes disgusting—and from that, and immoral & loose expressions had created opinions of himself that were not favourable to him and which he did not merit" (ibid., 456). Madison followed what may have been a verbal opinion with a written statement of his views: "On the supposition that the business can be more properly conducted by a private Agent at London, than a public Minister at a third Court, the letter and instructions for the former character appear to be well adapted to the purpose. If any remark were to be made, it would relate merely to the form, which it is conceived would be made rather better by transposing the order of the two main subjects. The fulfilment of the Treaty already made seems to be primary to the enquiries requisite to a subsequent Treaty.

"The reasoning assigned to those who opposed a commercial discrimination, states the views of a part only of that side of the question. A considerable number, both in the Senate & H. of Reps. objected to the measure as defective in energy, rather than as wrong in its principle. In the former, a Committee was appointed, who reported a more energetic plan. And in the latter, leave to bring in a bill, was given to a member who explained his views to be similar. Both of these instances were posterior to the miscarriage of the discrimination first proposed.

"As Mr Jefferson may be daily expected, as it is possible he may bring informations throwing light on the subject under deliberation, and as it is probable use may be made of his own ideas with regard to it, A quere suggests itself, whether the advantage of consulting with him might not justify a delay, unless there be special reasons for expedition" (c.8 Oct. 1789, DLC: James Madison Papers). GW had evidently shown Madison an earlier draft of his letter, since he follows Madison's advice on the transposition of the contents in the final version. He did not however follow his advice on waiting for Jefferson's arrival in the capital.

Morris had been in France since early 1789 engaged, among other business affairs, in settling Robert Morris's tobacco contract with the Farmers General and in negotiating a highly speculative enterprise to purchase the American debt to France. Not only was his presence abroad convenient but, since his appointment was unofficial, it would not have to run the gauntlet in the Senate where there was considerable suspicion of Morris's political principles and personal morality. Morris received GW's instructions on 21 Jan. 1790 and informed the president that he would leave for London "as soon as I possibly can." See Morris to GW, 22 Jan. 1790. The British had at least some advance advice of Morris's mission. In the course of discussions on improving relations between Britain and the United States with George Beckwith, unofficial agent of the British government in New York, Hamilton informed Beckwith on 25 Oct. that "I am not sufficiently Authorized to say so, it is not in my department, but I am inclined to think *a person will soon be sent to England to sound the disposition of Your Court upon* it" (Conversation with George Beckwith, October 1789, in Syrett, *Hamilton Papers*, 5:482–90). The information was forwarded to England on 25 Oct. 1789 (Guy Carleton, Lord Dorchester, to William Wyndham Grenville, 25 Oct. 1789, Public Archives of Canada, Ottawa, Ontario).

1. The enclosure, also dated 13 Oct., reads: "It being important to both Countries, that the Treaty of Peace between Great Britain and the United States, should be observed and performed with perfect and mutual good faith; and that a Treaty of Commerce should be concluded by them on principles of reciprocal advantage to both, I wish to be ascertained of the Sentiments and intentions of the Court of London on these interesting subjects.

"It appears to me most expedient to have these Inquiries made informally, by a private Agent; and understanding that you will soon be in London, I desire you in that capacity, and on the Authority and Credit of this Letter, to converse with his Britannic Majesty's Ministers on these Points—vizt— Whether there be any and what objections to now performing those Articles in the Treaty, which remain to be performed on his Part: and whether they incline to a Treaty of Commerce with the United States on any and what terms.

"This communication ought regularly to be made to you by the Secretary of State, but that Office not being at present filled, my desire of avoiding delays induces me to make it under my own Hand. It is my wish to promote Harmony and mutual satisfaction between the two Countries, it would give me great pleasure to find that the result of your Agency in the business now committed to you, will conduce to that end" (ALS, NNC: Gouverneur Morris Papers).

2. It was generally assumed that the federal courts would deal with any violations of the 1783 treaty with Great Britain in respect to state barriers to the collection of legitimate debts owed to British creditors. British officials had frequently used such lack of compliance with article 4 of the treaty as an excuse for retention of the western posts.

3. Article 7 of the treaty provided that the British army should withdraw from United States territory "with all convenient speed, & without causing any Destruction or carrying away any Negroes, or other Property of the American Inhabitants" (Miller, *Treaties*, 2:99). The dispute between the United States and Britain centered around the slaves that had been manumitted when they fled to British lines and were removed when the British evacuated their forces at the end of the war. The United States contended that such removal was a violation of the treaty while the British held that the slaves' manumission had made them free men.

4. GW is referring to the debates over the impost and tonnage bills in the House of Representatives in the spring and early summer of 1789. Led by James Madison, a considerable faction in the House advocated discriminatory duties against nations not in commercial treaty with the United States; duties on the products of those nations that had signed treaties would be assessed at a lower rate. Both the impost and tonnage bills from the House carried such discriminatory clauses—on distilled spirits and on tonnage—but the clauses were struck down in the Senate, an action reluctantly agreed to by the House.

To Rochambeau

Dear General,   New York, October 13th 1789
I have been honored with the receipt of your letters of the
31st of January and 17th of February last—and I should have
had the pleasure to address you sooner, but a tedious indisposition, and very numerous avocations, since my recovery, have so
entirely engaged my time as to leave me but very little, or no
leisure for the agreeable duties of friendship.

I embrace the obliging offer of His Excellency the Count de
Moustier (who favors my letter with his care)[1] to renew an
intercourse which will ever give me pleasure—and to enhance
your satisfaction by telling you that the political affairs of the
United States are in so pleasing a train as to promise respectability to their government, and happiness to our citizens—The
opposition offered to the reform of our federal constitution has
in a great measure subsided, and there is every reason to predict
political harmony and individual happiness to the States and
citizens of confederated America.

The Revolution, announced by the intelligence from France,
must be interesting to the nations of the world in general, and is
certainly of the greatest importance to the country in which it
has happened—I am persuaded I express the sentiments of my
fellow-citizens, when I offer an earnest prayer that it may terminate in the permanent honor and happiness of your government and people. with sentiments of respectful affection and
esteem I am, Dear General, Your most obedient Servant
                                        G. Washington

Df, DNA: RG 59, Miscellaneous Letters; LB, DLC:GW. The copy in DNA:
RG 59 is mistakenly addressed to La Rouërie.
    1. The comte de Moustier, French minister to the United States, wrote
John Jay on 6 Oct. that he had received permission from his court to "pass
sometime in the Kingdom for the re-establishment of his health and on account of his own private affairs" and asked Jay to arrange a meeting with GW
to take his formal leave of the president. He also asked the acting secretary of
state to inform the president that Louis Guillaume Otto, French chargé d'affaires in the United States, would remain at the French legation (DNA: RG
59, Domestic Letters). On 9 Oct. GW noted in his diary: "Received from the
French Minister, in Person, official notice of his having recd. leave to return to
his Court and intended embarkation—and the orders of his Court to make
the following communication—viz.—That his Majesty was pleased at the Alteration which had taken place in our Government and congratulated this

Country on the choice they had made of a Presidt. He added that *he* should take care to make a favourable representation of the present State of things here to his Master who he doubted not would be much pleased therewith. Hitherto he observed that the Government of this Country had been of so fluctuating a nature no dependence could be placed on its proceedings; whh. caused foreign Nations to be cautious of entering into Treaties &ca. with the United States—But under the present Government there is a head to look up to—and power being put into the hands of its Officers stability will be derived from its doings" (*Diaries*, 5:457). Moustier and the marquise de Bréhan sailed for France on 18 October.

From Beauregard and Bourgeois

[New Orleans, 14 October 1789]
We the underwritten Subjects of his Catholick Majesty residing in New Orleans on the River Missisipi, most respectfully beg leave to address ourselves to your Excellency on a subject in which we find ourselves aggreved and that we are in Duty bound to communicate to you, who are the Father and great Protector of your Country, whose Honor we are persuaded you will not suffer, *even in the smallest degree* to be tarnished with Impunity.

Oliver Pollock acted as Agent for Congress and the State of Virginia in this Town during the early part of the late Revolution which has terminated so happily for the Rights of Mankind and to your immortal Glory. In the Year 1780 he had occasion for Money to support the Demands of the Army of Virginia then acting in the Western parts of that State; and to raise the necessary supply for that purpose, he offered us for Sale Bills of Exchange on France, at this Time we knew Pollocks circumstances to be very low, we always knew his Abilities as a Man of understanding to be mean, and that he being Ambitious, and grasping it was not improbable that he had rather assumed the Character of Agent than that he actually enjoyed it by any Appointment or Authority from Congress or the State of Virginia for indeed we conceived his Capacity inadequate to any office beyond that of a Pensylvania Constable. We therefore refused to purchase his Bills untill he convinced us that he was a regularly appointed Agent. This he delayed not to do, & by producing to us a Letter bearing date the 6th of November 1779 from Govr Jefferson of Virginia and the Board of Trade of that State authorizing & empowering him to draw Bills on the House

of Penet, Dacosta Freres & Co. of Nantz for 65.814 Dollars &
five Ryals; This Letter at once removed our Doubts as to Pollock's appointment, and as to his right of drawing Bills of Exchange as above related, and considering the afore said Letter as
a Caution and Ample Guarantee to us for the due Payments of
the Bills or in the alternate case of their being returned unpaid,
that we should be reimbursed with all Damages which we might
sustain in consequence, conformable to the usage of Merchants
and the Laws of Bills of Exchange we unfortunately bought his
Bills & paid him instantly in Gold & Silver for them.

These Bills we sent to our respective Correspondents in
France to do the needfull for us. we waited 18 Months in painful
suspence for their Fate; at length we received advice that they
were not and would not be accepted this information to us was
alarming and it was rendered still more dreadfull to us by the
news we had from the North that Lord Cornwallis had in the full
carreer of success entered the State of Virginia from the South,
Burnt all the Tobacco, and Ware Houses of that Country and
from all and every appearance of things the War at that time did
not promise a favourable termination for America, at this Period Pollock had neither Fortune, Character, or Credit, His
insignificance, Poverty, and the general dislike of the good
People of this Country towards him readily procured him a
Passport to quit this Country leaving us hopeless, of ever touching a farthing of the Money he received of us for the aforesaid
Bills, but the War took a favourable turn in 1782 and Great Sir
under the Protection of Heaven as you evidently have been
during the great revolution of America, you conquered your
Enemy you conquered the most Puissant Power of Europe, and
in the Year 1783 restored Peace to your grateful Country; Our
hopes then revived, that Virginia ever famed for good faith
would reimburse us the Money we advanced her Servant Pollock, in the moment of her Want.

In 1784 we were informed that Mr Pollock had settled all his
Publick Accompts with the State of Virginia in which he included our Demands with an allowed Damage of 18 ₩ Cent and
an Interest of 6 ₩ Cent ₩ annum. Yet untill the Year 1787 we
heard no more on this Subject, When Daniel Clark, Pollock's
Agent here and they say is concerned with him, did inform us
that he had orders from Mr Pollock to take up our Protested

Bills and to allow us 12½ ℔ Cent damages & 5 ℔ Cent ℔ annum Interest and this in the Paper money of this Country of which 162½ Dollars were only equal to 100 Silver Dollars, we consented to take any Payment he made us having still confidence in the Honor and Justice of Virginia, that on a Representation from us she would reimburse us the difference between what he Pollock paid us and what he Pollock has charged the State with.

As Mr Pollock has settled his account with the State of Virginia in solid Mexican Dollars so we humbly conceive he ought to have settled with us in the same solid money and not in Paper Currency at 62½ ℔ Cent Loss. If Mr Pollock charges Virginia 18 ℔ Ct Damages & 6 ℔ ct ℔ annum Interest on our protested Bills we humbly conceive he as an honest Man, should allow us the same.

We are the fair Creditors and Claimants of the State of Virginia, we ask no more of her than what is honestly our due; She nobly settles with Pollock, and Pollock basely attempts to defraud us, as we believe he has defrauded her, We paid Pollock for his Bills in Gold and Silver, How does he reimburse us at the end of 9 Years? in paper Currency depreciated 62½ p. % under par. To God, the Honor of Virginia, and the Justice of the President of Congress, we submit our Claim with Humility trusting that the unconscionable and avaricious Pollock shall be compelled to pay us, a Sum equal to that which Virginia on the same account and for the same Purpose allows to him.

We humbly take leave to enclose a State of our Accounts from a comparative view of them it may be seen at a Cast of the Eye how much Mr Pollock would wish to rob us of;[1] Individuals may rob States with Impunity but they are seldom allowed to rob each other without being exposed.

We now conclude this Representation with an humble Request that your Excellency will cause Justice to ⟨be⟩ done between us and Mr Pollock; praying the Omnipotent to take you into his holy Keeping & that you may be as successful in governing the United States of America as you have been in the Command of her Armies.

Luis Toutant
Beauregard
Le Bourgeois

LS, DNA: RG 59, Miscellaneous Letters.

This memorial concerns the involved affairs of Irish-born Oliver Pollock
(1737–1823), who had settled in New Orleans around 1768. Pollock spent
some time in Philadelphia before the Revolution developing a network of contacts with commercial firms in the city and acted as New Orleans agent for the
Philadelphia firm of Willing & Morris. In 1778 Congress appointed Pollock
its commercial agent in New Orleans. In the same year Virginia used Pollock's
resources to provision George Rogers Clark's forces in the Illinois country.
Most of the provisions for Clark were contracted for by Pollock, using his own
credit and the modest contributions made by Congress and by the state of
Virginia. The memorial of Luis Toutant Beauregard and S. Bourgeois, New
Orleans merchants, concerned these transactions. Enclosed with the memorial were accounts of each of the merchants and a certificate from Pollock's
agent Daniel Clark. By the end of the war Pollock's claims against Virginia
reached nearly $140,000. According to Pollock, in 1783 the state of Virginia
stopped payment of the bills he had drawn on Penet, d'Acosta, Frères & Cie.
At that time Esteban Miró, governor and intendant of Louisiana, listed the
sum of $4,892 due to Beauregard and $22,519.1 to Bourgeois (Pollock to
Miró, 18 Aug. 1783, and Miró to Pollock, 8 Oct. 1783, in Kinnaird, *Spain in
the Mississippi Valley*, vol. 3, pt. 2:77–78, 87–88). See also *Calendar of Virginia
State Papers*, 5:230–31, 244, 432. A persistent creditor, Beauregard went to
Virginia in 1780 in a vain attempt to secure payment (Boyd, *Jefferson Papers*,
3:320, 482–83).

GW received the merchants' memorial early in 1790, and on 6 Feb. Tobias
Lear sent the document to Edmund Randolph, with the president's request
for the attorney general's opinion "Whether it can be considered as in any
manner relating to the General Government—or to the State o[f] Virginia—
or be viewed as a Mercantile transaction between persons unconnected with
the public" (DNA: RG 59, Miscellaneous Letters). Randolph replied on 7 Feb.
in one of his first opinions as attorney general: "I had the honor of receiving
last night a letter of the 6th instant, from your Secretary, Mr. Lear, inclosing
by your order a representation from Louis Poutant [Toutant] Beauregard and
Le Bourgeois, two different statements of their respective accounts with
Oliver Pollock, and a certificate of Daniel Clark, and requiring my opinion
thereupon.

"From these documents, I understand that in the year 1780, Pollock being
an agent for the western army of Virginia, and authorized by the Governor
and board of trade of that State, to draw bills of exchange on the house of
Penet, Decosta, Freres and company of Nantz, for 65,814 dollars and five
ryals, Beauregard and Cadet Sardet, deceased, bot. three of those bills, and
paid for them instantly in Gold & Silver; that after the expiration of eighteen
months, advice was received of the non-acceptance of the bills thus purchased
from Pollock; that in 1784, Pollock settled his accounts with Virginia in silver
dollars, included in them Beauregard's and Sardet's demand, and obtained
damages at the rate of Eighteen per centum, and an interest of six per centum
per annum; that Bourgeois has married the widow of Sardet; and that in
1787, Clark being Pollock's agent, took up the non-accepted bills which had

been protested at the damages of twelve and a half per centum, and at an
interest of five per centum per annum, and paid the amount estimated on
these principles, in the paper money of New Orleans; and that one hundred
and sixty-two dollars and on[e] half of this paper money, was no more than
equal to one hundred silver dollars.

"Upon these allegations, a request is founded that the President of the
United States *'will cause justice to be done.'* By *Justice* is me[a]nt a compensation
for the difference between the damages of eighteen and twelve and a half per
centum, between six and five per centum per annum, and between silver dollars and the paper dollars of New Orleans.

"To me it appears that these transactions do in no manner fall within the
sphere of the President:

"1st. It is not pretended that the bills in question were drawn by Pollock in
behalf of the United States, or under their license; on the Contrary, he was
treated with as the agent of Virginia, and under the particular powers of the
Governor and board of trade of Virginia—consequently, the debt arising
from the protest of these bills never was a debt of the United States.

"2d. Let it then be allowed for a moment that Virginia is bound to make the
compensation required. The Constitution of the United States extends the
Judicial power to all cases between a state and foreign subjects. Beauregard
& Bourgeois profess allegiance to his Catholic majesty, and therefore have
the courts of the United States open to their claims against Virginia.

"3d. Perhaps, however, the President may sometimes think it advisable to
remonstrate with a state on its conduct towards foreigners; But on this occasion, the truth seems to be that Virginia will always be able to defend herself.
The papers are silent as to many important facts which ought to be ascertained, and which, when ascertained, might probably by their own weight,
support the refusal of Virginia to pay what is claimed; But enough is in my
opinion disclosed for this purpose. It is admitted that Beauregard & Bourgeois consented to accept in the paper money of New Orleans the damages of
12½ per centum, and the interest of five per centum per annum. The course
of business renders it certain that Clark received the protested bills from
Beauregard & Bourgeois, and that they were delivered up to Virginia when
Pollock closed his accounts with her. Virginia then, ignorant of the distant
negotiations betweeen them, and finding Pollock in possession of the bills,
infers with great propriety that the rights of all other claimants were relinquished in favor of Pollock, and adjusts the debt as it is agreed fairly & hon-
orably. Nay, even if Virginia had been apprized at the time of the adjustment,
that Beauregard & Bourgeois had made a bad bargain with Clark, it surely
was not proper for her to undertake to rectify the want of prudence in individuals, who resigned everything when they surrendered the bills. These reasons apply with equal force against any reimbursement for depreciation. But
it may be added with respect to this point, that Clark, altho' he paid paper
money, paid a money which was legitimated by the sovereignty of New
Orleans.

"4. In short, (if a dispute can be said to exist at all) it must lie between
Beauregard & Bourgeois and Pollock. If he had deceived them, the laws of

the United States afford redress. But as the merits of their contest do not
relate to the General Government, I shall not trouble you with any observations upon it" (*Calendar of Virginia State Papers*, 5:109–11). By GW's order,
Lear transmitted a copy of Randolph's opinion to Beauregard and Bourgeois
on 16 Feb. 1790 (DNA: RG 59, Miscellaneous Letters).

In 1790 and 1791 Pollock was in Virginia attempting to settle his account
with the state. See *Calendar of Virginia State Papers*, 5:230–31, 244, 432; *Journals of the Council of State of Virginia*, 5:63, 69, 184, 238, 254–55. His own views
on the Beauregard-Bourgeois appeal to GW appear in a letter to Beverley
Randolph, governor of Virginia, 22 Jan. 1791: "By your Excellency's order at
my request, the clerk of the Honourable the Council has handed me Copy of
a scurrilous paper directed to the President of the United States, signed by
Lewis Toutant Beauregard and S. Le Bourgeois, accompanied by a voluntary
certificate signed by Dan'l Clark, dated New Orleans, 14th October, 1789. I
was honoured at the same time with Copy of the Attorney-General's oppinion
upon those papers, dated New York, 7th Feb'ry, and given by order of the
President.

"This oppinion is so fully pointed to the Purpose, that it leaves but little for
me to say on the subject; therefore I do not mean to trouble your Excellency
with a tedious argument upon a business already so Discussed, that inspiration could hardly throw a new light upon it. There are, however, some points
in view which the authors of those papers maliciously insinuates, lst, that I
never had anything to loose, and of course they never looked to me for the
money; and lastly, that I may have *defrauded* the State as well as them. Respecting those charges I have lst to observe that I carried on an extensive and advantageous commerce for twelve years before the revolution; during which
time I was supply'd with dry-goods from London, negroes from Africa, and
flour from Philad'a to the River Mississippi, (for all which I had no bills protested); and by the Correspondence I had with the principal Commercial
Houses in Philad'a, I became known to the United States, and early in the
revolution I was solicited by them & this state for important supplys which I
then furnished with my own funds, and my own Credit long before I had the
honour to touch Beauregard or Bourgeois' money for the unfortunate bills
upon Pinet, Dacosta & Co.

"Those Gentlemen, say: 'In 1784 we were informed that Mr. Pollock had
settled all his publick accounts with the State of Virginia in which he included
our demands with an allowed damage of 18 p'r cent., & Interest of 6 pr. Ct.
pr. annum. Yet untill the year 1[7]87 we heard no more on the Subject.' They
must have had more than common indulgence in their debtors to remain
three years in silence without making any demand on me, and nine years without making any demand even on the State, which they now say was their
whole Dependance for their money; but I presume they forgot how they commenced suits against me at the Havana & New Orleans. . . . It now only remains to inform your Excellency respecting the paper money busines. In the
years 1787 & 1786, I shiped my attorney (then Mr. Clarke), negroes from
the West Indies & flour from Philad'a to New Orleans, to be there disposed to
the very best advantage to take up those bills, and all others that unfortunately

had my signature hanging over me for the publick service. Mr. Clarke in this transaction received the current money of the country for my property, and, of course paid it away as received.

"It appears also by this Gentleman's certificate that I had gained 1 p'r Ct. Interest & 5½ p'r Ct. damages. Granted he acted as my attorney and did only his duty to make the best bargain he could for me, 'however sorry he or them may be for it now,' for which I paid him 5 p'r Ct. on the sales of my Goods, and 5 p'r Ct. for taking up those bills, but this is out of my own pocket, as I did not act in this instance as agent for the State, or did the State furnish me with funds or Credit to take up those bills, but on the contrary, I risked my own funds and my own credit in the regular line of Commerce, and paid those gentlemen in their own Currency at their own door, and if I have any proffits by the negociation, I presume all men of candour will think me justly entitled to them, but what is most to be lamented that they have got the paper money which was Equal to Gold and Silver at New Orleans when I was there last year, and I am, to this day, not only laying out of my Capital but also out of the Interest of my money.

"I observe Mr. Clark's certificate cloaths Mr. Beauregard with the dignity 'of one of his Majistie's council of Loussiana.' I hope he has got better credentials to produce for it than that flimsy voucher, but if he has such appointment it does him honour, and it is probably from that circumstance of his having acquired a proper knowledge of the Rectitude of that Government, that prevented him from having the audacity to lay such a claim before that Honourable Tribunal, although I was on the spott at New Orleans at the verry time he secretly put it forward to the President of the United States, & by that artifice put it out of my power to bring them to Justice" (*Calendar of Virginia State Papers*, 5:251–54). For an enthusiastic letter of support for Pollock attesting to his zeal in settling his accounts in New Orleans, see Esteban Miró to the governor of Virginia, 27 July 1790, in ibid., 192.

1. The enclosures were a "Statement of Mr Toutant Bourgards accompt with Oliver Pollock as settled by Daniel Clark said Pollock's Agent at New Orleans," a "Statement of Oliver Pollock's accompt with Toutant Bourgard, agreeable to the Settlement which the said Oliver Pollock made with the State of Virginia," a "Statement of Oliver Pollock's account with the Representatives of Cadet Sardet as said Pollock has settled the same with the State of Virginia," and a "Statement of Oliver Pollock's account with the Heirs of Cadet Sardet deceased as Settled with Mr Bourgois who married the widow of said Cadet by Daniel Clark Agent of said Pollock at New Orleans." All of these documents are in DNA: RG 59, Miscellaneous Letters.

To Lafayette

New-York, October 14. 1789

This is the first time I have written to you, my dear Marquis, since I have been in this place—and I have not received a line

from you in the same space of time. This has been a long interval
of silence between two persons whose habits of correspondence
have been so uninterruptedly kept up as ours; but the new and
arduous scenes in which we have both been lately engaged will
afford a mutual excuse.

I wrote to you very fully in my last letters from Mount Vernon; and since that time the gazettes, which I know you receive,
have given a pretty ample detail of our public proceedings—I
therefore take the advantage of the politeness of the Comte de
Moustier, (who is about returning to France)[1] more with a view
of assuring you that you are still remembered by me with affection—than with an intent to convey any political intelligence—I
will only observe, generally, that the prospect is favourable to the
political happiness of this country.

The revolution, which has taken place with you, is of such
magnitude and of so momentous a nature that we hardly yet
dare to form a conjecture about it. We however trust, and
fervently pray that its consequences may prove happy to a nation, in whose fate we have so much cause to be interested and
that its influence may be felt with pleasure by future generations.

Mrs Washington joins me in best wishes to you and your
amiable Partner. I am, my dear Marquis, with very great affection, Yours

G. Washington.

LB, DLC:GW.
    1. See GW to Rochambeau, 13 Oct. 1789, n.1.

From John Marshall

Sir   Richmond October 14th 1789
    Not having been in Richmond when your Excellencys letter
arriv'd, enclosing me a commission as Attorney for the United
States in the Virginia district, I coud not, sooner, acknowlege the
receit of it.[1]

    I thank you sir very sincerely for the honor which I feel is
done me by an appointment flowing from your choice, & I beg
leave to declare that it is with real regret I decline accepting an
office which has to me been render'd highly valuable by the

hand which bestow'd it. Coud a due attention to the duties of the office have consisted with my practice in the superior courts of this state I shoud with great satisfaction have endeavord to discharge them, but the session of the foederal & state courts being at the same time in different places an attendance on the one becomes incompatible with the duties of an Attorney in the other.[2] With every sentiment of respect & real attachment I remain Sir Your most obedt Servt

John Marshall

ALS, PP.

1. GW's letter to John Marshall has not been found, but it was probably similar to other letters written in late September covering appointments in the Judiciary. See, for examples, GW to Thomas Johnson and to Edmund Randolph, both dated 28 Sept. 1789. It is possible the letter was simply the form letter usually covering commissions. See Cullen and Johnson, *Marshall Papers*, 2:41–42.

2. GW replied to Marshall's letter on 23 Nov. 1789: "Upon my return to this place from a tour through the eastern States, I met your letter of the 14th Ultimo, giving me information of your declining the appointment of Attorney for the district of Virginia, and assigning the reasons for so doing.

"Your name was mentioned to me for that Office by Colo. Saml Griffin as a request of your own—to which my feelings assented with peculiar pleasure—and I am sorry that circumstances are such as render your acceptance of the appointment incompatible with your business.

"As some other person must be appointed to fill the Office of Attorney for the district of Virginia it is proper your Commission should be returned to me" (Df, in writing of Tobias Lear, DNA: RG 59, Miscellaneous Letters). Marshall's name appeared on a list Samuel Griffin left with GW in the course of an interview concerning Virginia appointments to the Judiciary. See Conversation with Samuel Griffin, 9 July 1789, printed above.

From James Mercer

Sir   Virginia—Fredericksbg Oct: 15th 1789

I hope the necessity of the Case, will be a sufficient appollogy for my intruding myself on your Excellency, who must be too much engaged in the business belonging to yr important & very high office, to attend to business of a private Nature—I have however purposely delayed this application untill the recess of Congress, hoping that your Excellency may by that event, have the leisure to favour my request.

The Records accompanying this, will shew your Excellency,

that this request is justifyable as far as the Consent of the parties interested requires—and I doubt not, if Leisure permits I shall be favoured with your Excellency's answer previous to the 2d Day of December.

It is however necessary for your Excellency's understanding the points to which your answer is thought to be material to inform you, that I am sued as an attorney of my late Brother Colo. George Mercer by Wm Dawson—for three years Steward-ship & the Shares of Crops made on my Brothers plantations in Frederick County for three years—previous to the Sale thereof in the year 1774 and for turning him off without Notice at the Sale, greatly to his Loss.

The truth is, this Man was the most Stupid & ignorant Man ever entrusted with even the Care of Six Negroes[1]—I never saw him from the time of first employing him but for an hour or so—never had or cou'd get any account from him the whole time—& was allways paying orders to Sherifs—blk Smiths Car-penters Wagoners &ca and the little that was made except the Wheat delivered at your Mill, he applyed to his own use, he sold the Stock at his pleasure, and went so far as to pillage the Lands of pine Timber, tho a very precious Article to the Estate—In one word his Conduct compelled my Brother to sell his Estate, which is now totally gone and now he demands of me out of my own Estate a Debt which if just cou'd have paid out of my Brother's Estate, had he given Notice thereof while there was any Estate left—But on the contrary tho' he promised me in your Excel-lency's presence at the Sale to come & settle with me so soon as the sale shou'd be over, I never saw, nor heard of or from him, from the conclusion of the Sale untill the day I was arrested at his Suit about two years ago, after an interval of thirteen years; by which all persons privy to his bad Conduct, are now either dead, or removed to Kentucky—I trust however that your Ex-cellency may at this day recollect enough to do me justice before Gentlemen—this Suit being now referred to such & got out of the Hands of Overseers, the common Jurors in Virginia.

I have, also to shorten your Excellency's trouble as much as I cou'd drafted a form of what I expect your recollection will enable you to say on this Subject which may be the easier varyed shou'd my expectations exceed your recollection[2]—tho' I think it probable that you may remember the wretched situation of the plantations under his care at the time of the Sale—his stupidity, & allmost idiotism at the Sale, so that he did not even know the Negroes or any thing else & was of no more use than a perfect Stranger[.] It is yet more likely that you may recollect the Trick he meant to put upon us, by directing us a round about Route to Mr Booths where we went to dine on a Sunday[3]— purposely to avoid our seeing the Pine Timber cut on the Right Road which he sold to one Brady who had a saw mill—this I well remember accusing him off before you to convince you that I knew nothing of his flagitiousness, and I hope you recollect this & in particular, that he begged me not to say any thing to him then—and that he promised to come down & settle with me so soon as I shou'd be returned from the Sale.

I have now only to add, that Dawson declines writing your Excellency as was agreed upon, he having nothing to communi- cate; I am therefore compelled to make my application singly[4]—And beseeching your excuse for this trouble I beg leave to assure your Excellency that I am with the highest Re- spect & with constant prayers for your Happiness—Yr Excel- lency's most respectfull—most obedient & very humble Servant

Js Mercer

ALS, DLC:GW.

For background to this letter, see William Dawson to GW, 5 Oct. 1789.

1. See Dawson to GW, 5 Oct. 1789, n.4.

2. The statement Mercer prepared for GW reads: "Mr James Mercer of Fredericksbg—having by Letter requested my answer to certain interogato- ries respecting what I know, in Relation to a Mr William Dawson who was a Steward for Colo. George Mercer on his Estate in Fredk County in the yr 1774—and it appearing by a certified Copy thereof attested by J. Chew Clerk of the District Court holden at Fredericksbg that Mr Dawson hath consented that my Relation of Facts by way of a Letter shall be admitted as Evidence before the Arbitrators whom Mr Mercer & Mr Dawson have chosen to arbi- trate the diffrences subsisting between them—respecting Mr Dawson's Stew- ardship—and ever willing to give any information I may have & which may be thought by those interested to contribute to Justice—I answer as well as my memory will inable me to do as follows—

"I (with Colo. Tayloes & Mason) was appointed an Attorney in fact for Colo. George Mercer then of London & also for a Mr Gravett and a Miss Wroughton his Mortgagees—a part of my authority was to sell the Lands & Slaves, Stocks &ca of Colo. Mercer then being in Fredk County on Shennon- doah River—I accordingly advertized a Sale thereof & attended the same with Mr James Mercer some time in the Month of November 1774 and continued on that Estate about four days—lodging & continuing in the House then oc-

cupyed by Mr Dawson a Steward or Overseer of Colo. Mercer on that Estate—
This was the first time I ever saw Mr Dawson—nor have I seen him since—of
course I can not be acquainted with him—but I then observed to Mr Mercer
that Mr Dawson was incapable of the charge committed to him—I really
never saw plantations in such bad order in my Life and Mr Dawson appeared
so easy or simple that he was of no service in bringing the Slaves or Stocks to
Sale—and that business was much forwarded & eased by the assistance of Mr
James Mercer—I do not know what were the amount of the Crops made
on the Estate that year—but I recollect the Crops of Corn which were sold
were very triffling & not enough to maintain the Plantations had they been
continued.

"I also remember to have seen on my way to Mr Booths where Mr Mercer
& myself were invited to dine during the Sale—several pine Treefresh cut that
Fall so close to the Ground & in such a manner as to attract the Notice of both
of us & on in⟨spection⟩ we found that the Trees grew on Colo. Mercer's Lands,
then to be sold—and Mr D. had cut them or given leave to the owner of some
saw Mill to whom Mr Dawson had sold them so to do—that upon Mr James
Mercers complaining of that transaction as well as other things Mr Dawson
requested Mr Mercer not to say any thing to him then, & Mr Dawson then
promised Mr Mercer that he wou'd come down to him as soon as he Mr Mercer shou'd be returned home & render an Account of all his transactions on
that Es⟨tate.⟩

"I also remember that Mr Dawson then purchased of me as atty of Colo.
Mercer & his mortgagees—a Lot of Land & I believe some Slaves, Stocks, &
plantation Utensils being on the Lot where he resided—for which he like the
other purchasers gave Bond with Security payable to me as attorney without
asking any discount for any Debt as due him from Colo. Mercer, nor did he to
my knowledge say that any thing was due to him for the managing of that
Estate either as Steward or Overseer—but I recollect that all the Corn was
sold without any Claim of his share thereof. This is all I can now recollect
relating to this business" (D, in writing of James Mercer, DLC:GW).

3. GW and Mercer dined with William Booth on Sunday, 28 Nov. 1774.
Booth, an old friend of GW's from Westmoreland County, had recently
moved to Buck Marsh Run in the area of the Mercer land. See *Diaries*, 3:293.

4. GW replied to Mercer's letter on 17 Nov. 1789.

From Thomas Paine

My Dear Sir   London Octr 16th 1789
    I need not tell you how much I rejoice at the prosperous
accounts from America, or how happy I feel that you have
relinquished the temptations of quiet retirement for the busy
scenes of Public Good. Had the opportunity of your coming
once more forward not have offered itself you might have in-
joyed retirement with serenity; but retirement would have lost

its felicity, had it been haunted, as would have been the case, with the impression of having declined, for the sake of ease, a station in which you could be so publicly useful. I am certain you will feel the happier for this sacrifice, because to be perfectly so the mind must justify itself in every thing.

Mr Mappa the Gentleman who will present you this is an exiled Hollander, and, as I am informed, very capital in his line which is that of a letter-founder[1]—I have given him a letter to Dr Franklin, the proper Patron of his Art, and as it is a branch in which improvement is wanted in America, I hope his coming will benifit both the Country and himself.

Mr Jefferson who, I expect, will arrive as soon as this letter, will inform you of my proceedings here—I am constructing a Bridge of one Arch in Partnership with the Walkers[2] of Rother-ham Yorkshire—The Arch is 110 feet Span and five feet high from the Cord line—We began it in July and I expect it in London about the Middle of Novr—In the mean time I am going over to France—A Share in two revolutions is living to some purpose—I shall be exceedingly happy to see a line from you, which if addressed to the Care of Benjn Vaughn Esqr.— Jeffries Square London will find me any where. With every Wish for your happiness and Mrs Washington's—I am—my Dear Sir your most affectiona. obedient Humble Servant

Thomas Paine

Please to remember me among the Circle of my friends.

ALS, DLC:GW.

After the Revolution Thomas Paine (1737–1809) settled on a confiscated Loyalist farm at New Rochelle, N.Y., given to him by the state. He lived there and in Bordentown, N.J., until 1787 when he went to England to promote his new invention, an iron bridge (see Seitz, "Thomas Paine, Bridge Builder," 571–84). For the next two years he divided his time between England and France, proselytizing his ideas on liberty and revolution in both countries.

1. Adam Gerard Mappa (d. 1828), a native of Delft in Holland, after service in the Dutch army turned to typefounding and an active interest in Dutch politics. His involvement with the Patriot party led to his banishment from Delft. After several years spent in France, Mappa sailed for the United States, bringing with him his family and almost the entire apparatus of his foundry. He arrived in New York in December 1789 and set up a typefoundry on Greenwich Street, specializing in producing Dutch and German type. His foundry proved less than successful, and in 1793 he became an agent for the Holland Land Company (Thomas, *History of Printing in America*, 33; Fairchild, *Francis Van Der Kemp*, 140–52; Evans, *Holland Land Company*, 75).

2. Walker is probably used here in the sense of an officer or agent who had charge of a certain section of the river bank.

To the Congregational Ministers of New Haven

Seventeen Miles east of Camden [Conn.]

Gentlemen, October 17th 1789.

The Kind congratulations, contained in your address, claim and receive my grateful and affectionate thanks—respecting, as I do, the favorable opinions of Men distinguished for science and piety, it would be false delicacy to disavow the satisfaction, which I derive from their approbation of my public services, and private conduct.[1]

Regarding that deportment, which consists with true religion, as the best security of temporal peace, and the sure mean of attaining eternal felicity, it will be my earnest endeavor (as far as human fraility can resolve) to inculcate the belief and practice of opinions, which lead to the consummation of those desireable objects.

The tender interest which you have taken in my personal happiness, and the obliging manner in which you express yourselves on the restoration of my health, are so forcibly impressed on my mind as to render language inadequate to the utterance of my feelings.

If it shall please the Great Disposer of events to listen to the pious supplication, which you have preferred in my behalf, I trust that the remainder of my days will evince the gratitude of a heart devoted to the advancement of those objects, which receive the approbation of Heaven, and promote the happiness of our fellow men.

My best prayers are offered to the Throne of Grace for your happiness, and that of the Congregations committed to your care.[2]

Go: Washington

LS, CtY; LB, DLC:GW.

1. After leaving New York on his tour of New England (see GW to Betty Lewis, 12 Oct. 1789, n.3), GW traveled to Stamford, Ct., and, passing through Norwalk, spent the night of 16 Oct. at Fairfield. Leaving Fairfield early on the morning of 17 Oct., he breakfasted in Stratford, visited Milford, and arrived in New Haven "before two Oclock." Along the way he "missed a Committee of

the assembly, who had been appointed to wait upon, and escort me into town" (*Diaries*, 5:464). According to a brief note from John Chester to GW, 17 Oct. 1789, the committee had waited for GW at Woodruff's Tavern, about five miles from New Haven (DLC:GW). The committee had been appointed by the legislature "to prepare an Address and to conduct me when I should leave the City as far as they should judge proper. The address was presented at 7 Oclock and at Nine I received another address from the Congregational Clergy of the place. Between the rect. of the two Addresses I received the Compliment of a Visit from the Govr. Mr [Samuel] Huntington—the Lieutt. Govr. Mr [Oliver] Wolcott and the Mayor Mr. Roger Shurman" (*Diaries*, 5:464). For GW's comments on New Haven, see ibid., 464–66. According to GW's diary account there were "3 Congregational Meeting Houses and a College in which there are at this time about 120 Students under auspices of Doctr. [Ezra] Styles" (ibid., 463–64).

The address from the Congregational ministers, 17 Oct. 1789, was signed by Stiles, James Dana, Jonathan Edwards, Samuel Wales, and Samuel Austin, Jr.: "We presume that we join with the whole collective Body of the Congregational Pastors and Presbyterian Ministers throughout these States in the most heartfelt joy, and the most cordial congratulations of themselves, of their Country, and of Mankind, on your elevation to the head of the combined American Republic. As Ministers of the blessed Jesus, the Prince of Peace, we rejoice and have inexpressible pleasure in the demonstrations you have given of your sincere affection towards that holy religion, which is the glory of Christian States, and will become the glory of the world itself, at that happy period, when Liberty, public right, and the veneration of the most High, who presides in the Universe with the most holy and benevolent sovereignty, shall triumph among all the Nations, Kingdoms, Empires, and Republics on earth.

"We most sincerely rejoice in the kind and gracious Providence of almighty God, who hath been pleased to preserve your life during your late dangerous sickness, and to restore you to such a degree of health as gives us this opportunity to express our joy, and affords us the most pleasing hopes that your health may be firmly established.

"We pray the Lord of Hosts by whose counsel and wisdom you have been carried triumphantly and gloriously thro' the late war, terminating in the establishment of American Liberty, and perhaps in the liberty of all nations, that he would be pleased ever to have you under his holy protection, continue to render you a blessing to Church and State, support you under your arduous cares, and perpetuate that estimation and honor, which you have justly acquired of your country. And may this new rising republic become under your auspices, the most glorious for Population, Perfection of policy, and happy administration that ever appeared on earth. And, may you, Sire, having finished a course of distinguished usefulness, receive the rewards of public virtue in the Kingdom of eternal glory" (DLC:GW).

2. GW left New Haven at 6:00 A.M. on 19 October. Passing through East Haven, he breakfasted at Wallingford. Traveling on through Durham, Middletown, and Weathersfield, the party arrived at Hartford at the end of the day (*Diaries*, 5:467–68).

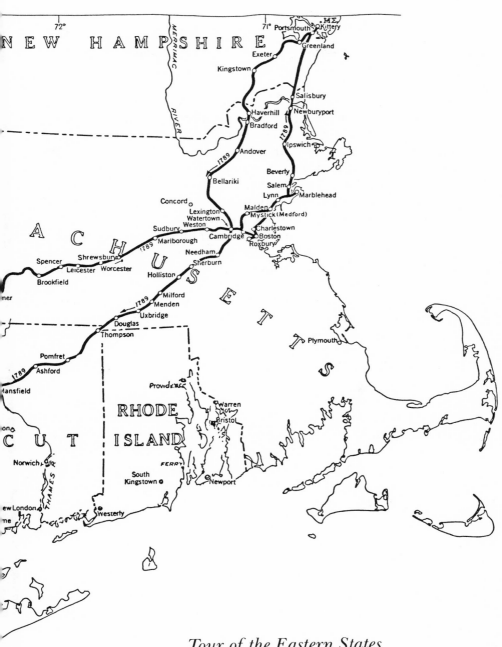

NEW HAMPSHIRE

MERRIMAC RIVER

72°   71° Portsmouth ○ Kittery MΣ
                    Greenland
              Exeter
          Kingstown
                        Salisbury
                        Newburyport
              Haverhill
              Bradford   Ipswich
                  1789
          Andover
      Bellariki   Beverly
                        Salem
  Concord ○   Lynn ○ Marblehead
          Lexington   Malden
          Watertown   Mystick (Medford)
  Sudbury   Weston   Charlestown
  Marlborough Cambridge Boston
          1789   Roxbury
  Spencer Shrewsbury Needham
          Leicester Worcester Sherburn
  Brookfield   Holliston
                      Milford
                1789 Menden
                  Uxbridge
                  Douglas
                  Thompson   Plymouth
  Pomfret
  1789 Ashford
  Mansfield
                Providence
          RHODE   Warren
                        Bristol
          ISLAND
                      FERRY
  Norwich ○
                South
                Kingstown ○   Newport
  New London
                  Westerly

Tour of the Eastern States
15 October—13 November 1789

To the Connecticut Legislature

Gentlemen,   New-Haven October 17th 1789.

Could any acknowledgement, which language might convey, do justice to the feelings excited by your partial approbation of my past services, and your affectionate wishes for my future happiness, I would endeavor to thank you: But, to minds disposed as yours are, it will suffice to observe that your address meets a most grateful reception, and is reciprocated, in all its' wishes, with an unfeigned sincerity.[1]

If the prosperity of our common country has in any degree been promoted by my military exertions, the toils which attended them have been amply rewarded by the approving voice of my fellow-citizens—I was but the humble Agent of favoring Heaven, whose benign interference was so often manifested in our behalf, and to whom the praise of victory alone is due.

In launching again on the ocean of events I have obeyed a summons, to which I can never be insensible—when my country demands the sacrifice, personal ease will always be a secondary consideration.

I cannot forego this opportunity to felicitate the Legislature of Connecticut on the pleasing prospect which an abundant harvest presents to its' citizens—May industry like theirs ever receive its' reward, and may the smile of Heaven crown all endeavors which are prompted by virtue—among which it is justice to estimate your assurance of supporting our equal government.

                                        Go: Washington

LS, Ct: Unbound Manuscripts Collection; LB, DLC:GW.

For background to GW's tour of the eastern states, see his letter to Betty Lewis, 12 Oct. 1789, n.3. See also GW to the Congregational Ministers of New Haven, 17 Oct. 1789.

1. The address from the Connecticut legislature, signed by Samuel Huntington, reads: "Impressed with sentiments which animate the millions of our fellow-citizens, We, the Legislature of the State of Connecticut, cannot on this occasion be silent.

"Your presence recalls to our admiration that assemblage of talents, which with impenetrable secrecy and unvarying decision, under the smiles of divine providence guided to victory and peace the complicated events of the late long and arduous war.

"The scenes of perilous honor through which you conducted the american arms taught your country and mankind to revere you, as the greatest of heroes. Your sacred regard to the rights of freemen and the virtues of humanity inspired the united voice of all America to hail you as the first and worthiest of citizens.

"With grateful veneration we behold the Father of his country, our friend, our fellow-citizen, our supreme magistrate.

"When peace had succeeded to the vicissitudes of war, your ardent desire for retirement was sanctioned by the voice of patriotism, Your country has again solicited your aid; In obedience to her wishes you have sacrificed the felicity of dignified retirement, and have hazarded, on the tempestuous ocean of public life, the rich treasure of your fame. This display of patriot zeal gives you a new right to what you before possessed, the hearts of all your fellow-citizens.

"While we thus express our sentiments, and those of the freemen, whom we represent, we beg liberty to assure you of our zeal to support our public administration.

"May the divine Being who has given you as an Example to the world, ever have you in his holy keeping. May he long preserve you the happiness and the glory of your country. May the assurance that the government, formed under your auspices will bless future generations, rejoice the evening of your life— and may you finally be rewarded with the full glories of immortality" (DLC:GW).

From H. Duplessis

Honored Sir   New Haven [Conn.] 17th October 1789.

Altho it is the Highest of Presumption in Such unworthy object as me to dare to approach your excellency; yet that universal benevolence and Hospitality, which is the Characteristick of your Excellency has made me take the Liberty of troubling your excellency with my present distressed Situation. I have had the Honour of being during Sept. [7] years Professor of the french Language in the College of Maryland which bear your Illustrious name, where I discharged faithfully my Duty as will appear to your Excellency by the Letter, which I have taken the Liberty to inclose, from Dr Wm Smith to Dr Griffith. I was also honoured by General Smallwood with a letter for your excellency, which was handed to you, Honored Sir, by Dr Craig of Alexandria, being prevented by Sickness to wait personnally on your excellency. having fail'd in my expectation of being employed at Alexandria, I went to frederiskburg, where I Spent last winter, having gain'd the esteem and Approbation of the Gentlemen of that Town, as the numerous Testimonies which I have by me Testifys, and have for the Satisfaction of your excellency, taken the Liberty of inclosing a Letter from Gen: Weedon to me written few days before I left that place—Since that Time, please your excellency, I have been the Sport of Adverse fortune, in So much that I have been obliged to dispose of my cloaths for Substenance, & that I am at this moment in custody for the Sum of three pounds lawful money, without any means Whatever of being released, and to continue my Journey to Boston, where I have friends that would better my situation— thus have I Taken the Liberty to intrude on your excellency with a Short detail of my distresses, in full Hopes that your excellency will not think me absolutely unworthy of its Notice, and will charitably take my distressed Situation into your consideration, and will gladden my Heart by being relieved from confinement, and able to pursue my Journey—Accept, Honoured Sir, the wishes and Sincere Prayers which I Shall continue to offer to God for the perservation of your excellency's Life. I have the Honour to be with all possible Respect Your excellency most humble & most obliged Servant

H. Duplessis

P.S. the Bearer is the officer who has me in custody.

LS, DLC:GW.

   None of the enclosures mentioned in this letter have been located.

To Burgess Ball and Charles Carter

Dear Sirs,   Newhaven 18th Oct. 1789.

   Having set out on a tour through the Eastern States, it was at this place your letter of the 8th Instt overtook me.

   Not having my fathers Will to recur to when I wrote to my Sister, nor any recollection of the Devises in it, I supposed she was entitled to a Childs part of the Negros; but if they were otherwise disposed of by that Will (as I believe is the case) she is certainly excluded; and the Sons only, and their representatives, come in. In this manner the division must be made.[1]

   Every thing of personal property, not specifically disposed of by my Mothers Will had better be sold: with the proceeds of which, and the Crops, the Debts must be paid. The surplus if any, must be divided among the heirs.

   Being well convinced that the Gentlemen who were so obliging as to examin and set a value upon my Lots acted from their best judgment, I am perfectly satisfied with their decision; and beg my thanks may be presented to them for the trouble they have had in this business.[2] If they are not already sold, I am willing to allow three instead of two years credit for the payment of the purchase money—Interest being paid. In a word, as I do not want to tenant them, I should be glad to sell them on *any reasonable terms*, as that kind of property, at a distance, is always troublesome and rarely productive.

I did not mean to give Mr Mercer the trouble of stating any formal opinion—all I had in view was to know if the formalities of the Law with respect to Inventorying, appraising, &ca could be dispensed with. If it could, I was sure no other difficulty would arise, as I knew my Mothers dealings were small—and the business consequently easily closed.

I am exceedingly sorry to hear of the loss the Country has sustained from the Frost—The Crops of Corn in this State (Connecticut) along the road I have travelled, are abundantly great. I offer my best thanks to you for your kind services—and my best wishes to my Nieces and your families—and with sincere esteem and regard I am Your most Obedt and Affecte Hble Servt

Go: Washington

ALS, PWacD: Feinstone Collection, on deposit at PPAmP; LB, DLC:GW.
1. See Betty Lewis to GW, 1 Oct. 1789, n.2.
2. See Ball and Carter to GW, 8 Oct. 1789, n.3.

From Henry Knox

Sir   New York 18 October 1789

In obedience to your commands to write to you on all occasions I have the honor to inform you that Mr Kean arrived here yesterday from South Carolina.[1] He brings a report which he received through such a channel as induces him to credit it, That a Mr Clark[2] arrived at Savannah on the 2d of this month from the Rock Landing on the Oconee, and informed that the treaty had abruptly broken up without the Commissioners having been able to effect any thing owing to the excessive demands of McGillivray—That the day the indians went off the Commissioners sent Genl Pickens and Colonel Few after McGillivray with an invitation to return, which he refused with circumstances of insult—And that the conduct of McGillivray and the indians is imputed to the intrigues of the Spania⟨rds⟩. If this report should be well founded we may soon expect to hear by the way of Savannah from the Commissioners. Any thing that may be received shall be immediately transmitted to you.[3]

The Count de Moustiers and the Marchioness de Brehan sailed this day. The Marchioness was exceedingly affected on her embark.[4]

The English packet for September arrived on the 16th— Letters from England state the National Assembly of France to be divided into parties.

I had the pleasure of seeing Mrs Washington at Church to day in perfect health. I have the honor to be with the most perfect respect Sir Your Obedient Servant

H. Knox

ALS, DLC:GW; LB, DLC:GW.

1. John Kean, one of the commissioners to settle state accounts, had just arrived in New York from Charleston in order to attend a meeting of the commissioners scheduled for late October.

2. Mr. Clark is probably William (Billy) Clarke, the son of Elijah Clarke (1733–1799). A native of South Carolina, the elder Clarke moved to Georgia in 1774 where he served as a partisan commander during the Revolution and after the war became known as a leading defender of Georgia's interests in the state's conflict with the Creek. During the 1780s he operated a trading post on the Ogeechee River and in 1793–94 was deeply involved in the filibustering schemes of Edmund Genet, France's minister to the United States. William Clarke, also active in Georgia-Indian relations, was a colonel in Georgia's state forces. The younger Clarke and other Georgia officers had met Alexander McGillivray some eighteen miles from Rock Creek Landing in early October (McGillivray to William Panton, 8 Oct. 1789, in Caughey, *McGillivray of the Creeks*, 251–52).

3. For the negotiations of the American commissioners to the southern Indians, see David Humphreys to GW, 21, 26, 27 Sept., 13, 28 Oct. 1789, Alexander Hamilton to GW, 20 Oct. 1789, and Henry Knox to GW, 21, 27 Nov. 1789.

4. See GW to Rochambeau, 13 Oct. 1789, n.1.

From James Wilson

Sir   [18 October 1789]

Your Commission, appointing me one of the associate Justices of the Supreme Court of the United States, and your very obliging Letter, with which it was accompanied, I have had the Honour of receiving.[1]

Be assured, Sir, that I entertain a just Sense of the delicate and pleasing Manner, in which you describe the Motives and the Objects of your Choice. Permit me to add—I hope I do it with Justice and without Vanity—that you are correct in your Conjecture concerning the Principles, which lead me to an Acceptance of the Commission.

I have taken the Qualification prescribed by the Law; and hold myself in Readiness to perform the Duties of my Office.

I have the Honour to be, with Sentiments of the highest Respect and Esteem.

AL, DNA: RG 59, Miscellaneous Letters; ADf, PU-L.

For background to GW's judicial appointments, see his letter to the United States Senate submitting nominations for judicial posts, 24 Sept. 1789.

1. GW's pro forma letter to Wilson enclosing his commission, 30 Sept., is in PU-L.

From Samuel Coleman

Richmond, 19 Oct. 1789. "If the United States should want an Officer, in any of the departments of Government in this State, who ought, in the execution of his office, to possess abilities, integrity and Application in an uncommon degree; give me leave to recommend to your Notice Colonel Thomas Meriwether, a Gentleman who hath long served this Commonwealth with honour to himself and great benefit to his Country."[1]

ALS, DLC:GW.

Samuel Coleman became assistant clerk to the Council of State of Virginia in December 1786 (*Journals of the Council of State of Virginia*, 4:17). He may be the same Samuel Coleman who served in the 1st Artillery as second lieutenant in October 1777, was promoted to first lieutenant in June 1778, and then taken prisoner by the British and held to the end of the war (Gwathmey, *Historical Register*, 167).

1. Thomas Meriwether served as assistant clerk of the Council of State, with various interruptions, from 1782 until his resignation in June 1789.

From Alexander Hamilton

Sir   New York October 20th 1789.

Agreeably to your desire, I sit down to commit a few lines to the Post.

Nothing worth particular mention has occurred since your Departure; except a report brought by Mr Keane from So. Carolina, that McGilivray the Indian Chief had, after a short conference, left our Commissioners, declaring that what they had suggested was only a repe[ti]tion of the old Storey and inadmissible, or something to this effect.[1] It is added that the lower Creeks appear'd notwithstanding, willing to go into a Treaty, but the upper ones declin'd it—Genl Knox who has particularly conversed with Mr Keane, will doubtless give you a more accurate statement of what he brings[2]—It seems however that he has his intelligence at second or third hand. With the utmost respect I have the honor to be Sir Your Obt and humble Servant

A. Hamilton

P.S. I have just seen a letter from a private gentleman of considerable intelligence now in N: Carolina, who gives an ill picture of the prospect there, respecting the adoption of the Constitution.

LB, DLC:GW.

1. For the negotiations of the United States commissioners to the southern Indians, see David Humphreys to GW, 21, 26, 27 Sept., 13, 28 Oct. 1789, and Henry Knox to GW, 21, 27 Nov. 1789. See also GW's Memoranda on Indian Affairs, 1789.

2. See Henry Knox to GW, 27 Oct. 1789.

To the Officials of Hartford

Gentlemen,   20 October 1789

Grateful for the favorable disposition discovered towards me in your address, I receive your congratulations with pleasure, and I thank your goodness with sincerity.[1]

The indulgent partiality, with which my fellow-citizens are

pleased to regard my public services, is the most acceptable compensation they can receive, and amply rewards them.

While industry gives an assurance of plenty, and respect for the laws maintains the harmony of society, there is every reason to hope for the individual happiness of our citizens, and the dignity of our government in conduct like yours.[2]

G: Washington

LB, DLC:GW.

For background to this document, see GW to Betty Lewis, 12 Oct. 1789, n.3, and GW to the Congregational Ministers of New Haven, 17 Oct. 1789, n.2.

1. The address reads: "The Mayor, Aldermen, and Common-Council of the City of Hartford, beg leave most respectfully to congratulate the President of the United States on his accession to the high office of chief magistrate, and with cordial hearts to welcome his arrival in this City.

"We feel ourselves bound by every tie of duty and patriotism to acknowledge in common with the People of America our gratitude for your signal and disinterested services during the late war, by which the citizens of the United States have been protected in their claims for liberty and independence—that you have been pleased to relinquish the pleasures of retirement to insure, by a wise administration, the continuance of those blessings to the People. Also to profess our sincere attachment to your person—and determination to support the honor and welfare of your government" (DLC:GW).

2. Because of a heavy rain GW did not leave Hartford until after 10:00 A.M. on 21 Oct. and reached Springfield, Mass., by 4:00 P.M., passing through Windsor and Suffield on his way. The party spent the night at Parsons' Tavern in Springfield, which Washington termed "a good House" (*Diaries*, 5:470).

From William Reynolds

Sir   Virginia York 20th October 1789

The vicissitudes of fortune all Men are subject to, and perhaps few have experienc'd the truth of the observation more severely than myself. A small inheritance from my Father, somewhat accumulated from five years close and successfull application to business previous to the War, had encouraged me to look forward with satisfaction. but a series, I may say of almost uninterrupted ill success in trade during the War, in addition to receiving most of my specie debts in paper, hath reduced my funds so low, as to prevent my attempting to retreive those losses by pursuing the same line of business, finding myself at present posses'd of little else except a large family depending on my efforts for their support. under those circumstances I was induced to request our Representative Colo. Griffin to offer my name as a Candidate for yr favour to some appointmt under the Federal Govermt.[1] I rely on your goodness, in construeing this in the light I mean it which is truly to convey to you, the reasons which prevaild on me to ask employment of my Country, and to assure you it did not proceed from a desire of adding to a fortune already easy but purely to aid me in the support of an unfortunate family. I am with the greatest respect, & esteem sir Yr mo. Obedt Servt

Wm Reynolds

ALS, DLC:GW.

In 1768 William Reynolds (d. 1802) was sent to London by his guardians to serve as an apprentice in the London countinghouse of John Norton & Sons. He remained in London until 1771 when he returned to Yorktown, setting up as a merchant in the town. In 1777 he was one of three paymasters for Virginia troops. He later served as an alderman of Yorktown and a member of the town's council (Mason, *John Norton & Sons*, 61–62, 74–75, 518–19). Reynolds did not immediately receive an appointment from GW, but in December 1794 the president named him collector and inspector of the revenue for the port of Yorktown (*Executive Journal*, 1:165).

1. See Conversation with Samuel Griffin, 9 July 1789, and John Page to GW, 14 July 1789, n.1.

From Thomas Smith

Sir   Carlisle [Pa.] 20th October 1789

I had the honour of receiving your Letter of the 23d Ulto with its inclosures, by Mr Scott[1] while I was attending Bedford Court last week, whereupon I sent up by the same Gentleman Directions to the Prothonotary of Fayette County to Issue a writ against John Stephenson without loss of Time, & gave pointed directions to the Sheriff to serve it immediately—I thought this necessary, because Mr Stephenson has sold his Land & is going to Kentucke as soon as possible—indeed he would have gone down before this Tim[e] had he not been detained by some Judgments which I had obtained against him as Executor of Col. Crawford. Mr Whaley, whom perhaps you remember, gave me this information the week before last at Westmoreland Court, &

expressed his fears that you would lose your Debt, or that the widow of the other obligor (who is already nearly ruined by being obliged to purchase Valentine Crawford's Land a second Time) would be obliged to pay it; whereupon I requested Mr Whaley to write to you on the subject, which he accordingly did in the Letter which I herewith inclose[2]—I think it proper still to send it, because although what he read to me related to this subject only, it may contain something else.

Being on my way down from the western Courts when I was honoured with your Letter, it will be some time before I return to them, & therefore I sent your Letter to Mr Cannon by Mr Scott,[3] by whom I also wrote to Mr Cannon on the subject of it, in pointed Terms, if you should much longer have cause of complaint, I shall entertain a different opinion of Mr Cannon from what I have hitherto had: I informed him that should he find it difficult to transmit money to you, he can send it to Carlisle, almost every week from Pittsburg, & I will with much pleasure send it forward without loss of Time; I have the honour to be with the utmost respect Sir your most obedient & very humble Servant

Thomas Smith

ALS, DLC:GW.

For background to this letter, see GW to John Stephenson, 13 Feb. 1784, n.2, and GW to Thomas Smith, 23 Sept. 1789.

1. This is probably Thomas Scott of Washington County, Pa., United States congressman from Pennsylvania. The House of Representatives adjourned on 29 Sept. and it is likely that Scott carried the letter to Smith on his way home.

2. Benjamin Whaley's letter to GW, 9 Oct., reads: "the Demand that you Have against the Estate of Richard Stephenson deceased wherein Colo. Jon Stephenson and Hugh Stephenson give their Bond for the a Mount of your account I Should think it Proper to Inform you that Colo. Jon Stephenson is going down to Kentuckey this faull or earley next Spring & I Should be glad that your demand Should Be Laid in Before Colo. Stephenson gos down the River as the Estate of Colo. Hugh Stephenson is & will Be Liable to pay your demand If it is not Pade in time you gave Me the a Mount of your account when I was @ your House In May 1786 and I also Caulled upon Colo. Stephenson to discharge the account & He Promised that He wood But I Belive He never has as I transact the Business of the Estate of Hugh Stephenson I Should Be glad that the Matter Should Be Settled Before Colo. Jon Stephenson Leaves this Country theirefore If your Honour think it necessary please to Instr[u]ct the Gentlemen How dos your Bussiness In this Country to Re-

cover your Money I am Confident that If Colo. Stephenson finds that the Bond Is in Attorneys Hands that he will pay the Money without a Law Suit it is onley neglect I am satisfied" (DLC:GW).

3. See GW to John Cannon, 24 Sept. 1789.

From John Hancock

Sir,   Boston October 21st 1789

Having received information that you intended to Honor this State with a visit, and wishing personally to shew you every mark of attention which the most sincere friendship can induce. I beg the favor of your making my house the place of your residence while you shall remain in Boston. I could wish that the accommodations were better suited to a Gentleman of your respectability but you may be assured that nothing on my part shall be wanting to render them as agreeable as possible.

As Governor of the Commonwealth I feel it to be my duty to receive your visit with such tokens of respect as may answer the expectations of my Constituents & may in some measure express the high Sentiments of respect they feel towards you. I have therefore issued orders for proper escorts to attend you, & Colo. Hall, Deputy Adjutant General will wait upon you at Worcester, & will inform you of the disposition I have made of the Troops at Cambridge under the command of General Brooks & request that you would be so obliging as to pass that way to the town where you will receive such other tokens of respect from the People as will serve further to evince how gratefully they recollect your exertions for their Liberties & their confidence in you as President of the United States of America. The Gentlemen of the Council will receive you at Cambridge & attend you to town.

I should be obliged to you on the return of this express to let me know when you propose to be in Boston & as near as you can the time of the day. I have the Honor to be, with every Sentiment of Esteem & Respect, Sir, Your most obedt & very hble Servant

John Hancock

ALS, DLC:GW.

For background to this letter, see GW to Betty Lewis, 12 Oct. 1789, n.3, and GW to the Officials of Hartford, 20 Oct. 1789, n.2. Setting out from Springfield at seven o'clock on the morning of 22 Oct., GW and his party stopped briefly for breakfast at Palmer and proceeded to the vicinity of Brookfield where an express arrived bearing Hancock's letter of 21 October. For GW's reply, declining Hancock's invitation, see his letter to the governor, 22 October. See also Hancock's two letters to GW, 23 Oct., and GW to Hancock, 23 October. The party continued on to Spencer where they "lodged at the House of one Jenks who keeps a pretty good Tavern" (*Diaries*, 5:472). On 23 Oct. GW set out early and in Leicester was welcomed by "some Gentlemen of the Town of Worcester on the line between it and the former to escort us. Arrived about 10 Oclock at the House of [ ] where we breakfasted. . . . Here we were received by a handsome Company of Militia Artillery in Uniform who saluted with 13 Guns on our Entry & departure. At this place also we met a Committee from the Town of Boston, and an Aid of Majr. Genl. Brooke [John Brooks] of the Middlesex Militia who had proceeded to this place in order to make some arrangements of Military & other Parade on my way to, and in the Town of, Boston" (*Diaries*, 5:472). Brooks's aide, Joseph Hall, probably brought Brooks's letter of 21 Oct. to GW: "The people of Middlesex participate largely of the joy, with which the prospect of a visit from their beloved President has inspired their brethren in the Capital. As a testimony of this, a military parade has been determined on; & a body of about 800 men, will be under arms at Cambridge on the day of your entering into Boston. The troops will occupy the ground on which the continental army was formed for your reception in the year 1775. Major [Joseph] Hall, one of my Aid de camps, will have the honour, Sir, of waiting on you herewith: He will at the same time acquaint you with the particular arrangements for the day, & with our ardent wishes to be indulged with an oppertunity once more of paying you military respect" (DLC:GW). As GW approached Boston, officials of the town and its surrounding districts scurried to make arrangements. The committee "from the Town of Boston" brought GW a letter from the Boston selectmen, 21 Oct.: "The Town of Boston desirous of Expressing in a Public manner their Joy at being again honored by your presence, and of preventing disorders which might otherwise arise from the eagerness of the Citizens to behold so Illustrious a Character, have Found it necessary to arrange the Citizens in their several Professions for your reseption. The Town will be happy should their intentions meet your approbation, and have directed us, their Committee, to communicate them to you. This Communication will be made by Joseph Barrell, Samuel Breck & William Eustis Esqrs. who are appointed a Committee for that purpose" (DLC:GW). In Boston, as elsewhere, GW's intention of staying only in public lodgings (see GW to Hancock, 22 Oct. 1789) was not widely known, and he received various offers of hospitality from public officials and private individuals. His wartime aide Caleb Gibbs wrote him on 16 Oct. offering GW "my house (in Summer Street) as your Lodgings, This would add greatly to Mrs Gibbs's happiness and my own, and Conferring an honor upon us never to be forgotten. I live in a remarkable pleasant, Central situation and in a very Genteel part of the Town" (NNC). "Fearing there might be a possibility of Miscarriage," he repeated his offer in a letter of 19

Oct. (NNC). Former governor of Massachusetts James Bowdoin wrote on 21 Oct., hoping "for the honour and pleasure of Seeing you at my house; and that among your numerous engagements you will reserve a day for that purpose" (DLC:GW).

To John Hancock

Sir,   Brookfield [Mass.] October 22nd 1789.

A few miles west of this village I met the Express, who delivered me Your Excellency's letter of yesterday. I have been so fortunate as to proceed thus far without any accident to delay my journey—should nothing occur to prevent me, I shall be at Weston to-morrow night—and I purpose taking dinner so early at Watertown on saturday, as to reach Cambridge by half past 2 o'clock. Thence I presume we shall arrive within an hour at Boston. I am highly sensible of the honor intended me: But could my wish prevail I should desire to visit your Metropolis without any parade, or extraordinary ceremony.

From a wish to avoid giving trouble to private families, I determined, on leaving New York, to decline the honor of any invitation to quarters which I might receive while on my journey—and with a view to observe this rule, I had requested a Gentleman to engage lodgings for me during my stay at Boston.

I beg your Excellency to be presuaded of the grateful sense which I entertain of the honor you intended to confer on me— and, I desire to assure you of the respectful regard with which I am Your obliged and obedient Servant.

Df, in writing of William Jackson, DNA: RG 59, Miscellaneous Letters; LB, DLC:GW.

For background to this letter, see GW to Betty Lewis, 12 Oct. 1789, n.3, and John Hancock to GW, 21 Oct., source note.

From Henry Knox

Sir   War office 22 October 1789

Nothing of importance has occurred since the letter I did myself the honor of writing you on the 18th instant. I am anxiously expecting to hear from the southern Commissioners.

Major Wyllis and the other Officers have been detained by business Untill this day.[1] They have taken young White Eyes under their protection.[2] I have the honor to be Sir Your obedient Servant

H. Knox

ALS, DLC:GW; LB, DLC:GW.

1. Maj. John Palsgrave Wyllys (d. 1791) was in command of army forces stationed at Fort Steuben at the Falls of the Ohio. Wyllys left his post at Fort Steuben on 24 May to visit New York. Upon his return to the Ohio country he was apparently ordered to Post Vincennes, but in February 1790 he resumed his old command at Fort Steuben (Joseph Asheton to John Francis Hamtramck, 31 May 1789, and Josiah Harmar to Hamtramck, 20 Feb. 1790, in Thornbrough, *Outpost on the Wabash*, 172–73, 219).

2. For information on George Morgan White Eyes, see his letters to GW, 2 June, 8 July, 8 Aug. 1789, and Elizabeth Thompson to GW, 18 Aug. 1789. By the late 1790s White Eyes was living in what is now Columbiana County, Ohio. In the fall of 1789 he was probably to travel to the Ohio country under Wyllys's protection.

From Thomas Pinckney

Sir   Charleston 22d Octr 1789

I embrace the earliest opportunity of conveying to you my most grateful acknowledgements for the appointment of Judge in the fœderal Court of this District; and at the same time of expressing the extreme regret with which I am constrained to decline this flattering testimony of your approbation.[1]

I am well aware, Sir, that with You no considerations arising from personal inconvenience will, or ought, to justify a Citizen in withholding his Services from his Country; but, Sir, when you are informed that I have a numerous family & that my affairs are so situated as to require my own immediate & unremitted exertions, I trust I shall be exculpated from the censure of a criminal neglect of duty to my Country, and of an undue sense of the honor conferd by the appointment, in declining a favor, the remembrance of which I shall ever cherish with the most grateful sensations. With every sentiment of respectful affection I remain Sir Your much obliged and most obedient Servant

Thomas Pinckney

ALS, DNA: RG 59, Acceptances and Orders for Commissions.

Thomas Pinckney (1750–1828) of South Carolina studied law at the Middle Temple and was admitted to the English bar in 1774. Upon his return to South Carolina he began a law practice that was interrupted by extensive and distinguished military service during the Revolution. Much of his property was destroyed by the British in the course of the war, and upon his return he began a successful legal career in Charleston. In 1787 he was elected governor and served two one-year terms; in 1788 he was president of the South Carolina Ratifying Convention. Undeterred by Pinckney's refusal of the post of district judge, GW appointed him minister to Great Britain in November 1791, and in 1795 he served as envoy extraordinary to Spain, negotiating the treaty that bore his name.

1. GW had written Pinckney a pro forma letter on 30 Sept. offering him the post of United States judge for the district of South Carolina (LS, privately owned).

From John Hancock

Sir   Boston 23d October 1789

Your Letter by the return Express I had the honour to receive at three OClock this morning: it would have given me pleasure had a residence at my house met with your approbation.

I observe you had proposed taking an early dinner at Watertown, and proceed to Cambridge, and from thence to Boston on Saturday afternoon; I beg leave, if it should not interfere with your determination, or prove inconvenient, to request that you would so far vary your former intention, as to arrive in Boston by one OClock; in case this request should meet your approbation I beg the favour that you with the Gentlemen of your suit would honor me with your company at Dinner on Saturday, *en famille*, at any hour that the circumstances of the day will admit.

I shall esteem it an honor if you will favour me with a few Lines by the return express with your determination on the subject. I have the honor to be with every sentiment of Esteem and Respect Sir Your very humble Servant

John Hancock

ALS, DLC:GW.

For background to this letter, see John Hancock to GW, 21 Oct. 1789, source note, and GW to Hancock, 22 Oct. 1789.

To John Hancock

Sir,   Weston [Mass.] October 23d 1789
I have this moment received your Excellen[c]y's polite letter of
today—and have the honor to inform you that in consequence
of suggestions made by the Gentlemen from Boston and the
Depy Adjut. Genl (whom I met at Worcester this morning) that
it would make it more convenient for the troops, many of which
lived at a distance from the place of parade, if I should pass
through Cambridge at an earlier hour than I intended, I
thought it best to alter the time of my arrival at that place, which
I had the pleasure to mention to your Excellency in my letter of
yesterday—and the alteration which I had made I immediately
communicated to you by a letter which the Gentlemen from
Boston were so kind as to take charge of—but lest any accident
should prevent that letter from getting to your hands, I would
here mention that it is my determination to be at Cambridge
tomorrow at 10' o'clock, and from thence proceed to Boston as
soon as circumstances will permit—where it is probable I may
arrive by 12 o'clock, and will do myself the honor to accept your
Excellency's polite invitation of taking an informal dinner with
you. I have the honor to be, Your Excellency's most Obedt Servt[1]
                                                   Go: Washington

Df, in writing of William Jackson, DNA: RG 59, Miscellaneous Letters; LB,
DLC:GW.
For background to this letter, see John Hancock to GW, 21, 23 Oct., and
GW to Hancock, 22 Oct. 1789.
1. Hancock replied to this letter with a note, dated 23 Oct.: "I have just this
moment received your Letter of this morning and would acquaint you that no
change will interfere with the arrangements I have made" (DLC:GW).
On Saturday, 24 Oct., GW "dressed by Seven Oclock, and set out at eight.
At ten we arrived at Cambridge According to appointment; but most of the
Militia having a distance to come were not in line till after eleven; they made
however an excellent appearance with Genl. Brook at their Head" (*Diaries*,
5:473). For the ceremonies taking place during GW's stay in Boston from his
arrival on 24 Oct. until his departure on the morning of 29 Oct., see GW's
diary entries and notes in ibid., 5:473–81.

From Orina

My Friend,   Concord [Mass.] October 23, 1789.
The disposition which the British and other nations have Shown to acknowledge our independence, with the perfect liberty we enjoy, plainly indicate that Sovereign providence has bestowed upon us mental abilities Superior to what are in the possession of any foreigners.

I am an original professor of human law, Social relation and civil policy; and with my most intimate Correspondent have found the principles of this inestimable Science altogether free from any kind of embarrassment both in theory and practice.

By Divine favour, I will the fore-part of next week call at your lodging, and know whether you are disposed for a few minutes conversation with me: and as your feelings Shall then be they will doubtless be gratified. My Friend, Your most affectionate neighbour,

Orina

ALS, DLC:GW. The author of this anonymous letter has not been identified.

From George Cabot

Sir   Beverly [Mass.] October 24th 1789
The public papers having announced "that the President of the United States is on his way to Portsmouth in New Hampshire," it immediately occurred to me that your rout wou'd be thro' *this village*, & that you might find it convenient to stop here & take a little rest: shou'd this prove to be the case, permit me Sir to hope for your acceptance of such accomodations & refreshment as can be furnished in my humble dwelling, where 2 or 3 beds will be at your disposal.

I am fully aware that by indulging this hope I expose myself to the imputation of vanity as well as ambition, & therefore shou'd hardly dare to have my conduct tried by the cool maxims of the head alone, but wou'd rather refer it to the dictates of my heart, where I gratify a sensibility which, in the most affecting concerns of life, I believe to be a sure guide to what is right.[1] I have the honor to be Sir with sentiments of the most profound respect your devoted & most obedient Servant

George Cabot

ALS, DLC:GW; copy, MHi: W. C. Endicott Papers.

1. GW stopped only briefly in Beverly on 30 Oct., visiting the Beverly Cotton Manufactory of which Cabot was one of the founders (*Diaries*, 5:485–86).

From Thomas Fielder

Boston 24th Octr 1789

T. Fielder presents most sincear Respects to his Excellency The President, of the united States of America[.]

Has an uncommunicated Idea on Machinary which he hopes might be of utility to the Country.

If when F. calls on Monday Morng at Eight his Excellency will condescend to appoint when he will honor him with a short interview, it will be esteem'd a very particular favor.[1]

AL, DLC:GW.

1. GW evidently acceded to Thomas Fielder's request for an interview. On 29 Oct. Fielder wrote the president that his "condescendg kindness on Monday last cannot but excite sincerest gratitude In Consequence of it . . . I laid the Model with an explanation before a Capt. Goodwin who judges the principle to be new & calculated to answer the proposed purpose. I hope sir you will excuse my mentiong that havg made a suppos'd improvmt in the Article of American Rum I have taken the liberty of troubling Mr [William] Jackson with a Sample from a Hhd of it in it's original state & one also in it's alterd state in which it appears on Trial to be divested of it's perniceous quality shoud you sir see it right to order an investigation of it, I can render it for the whole of the United States at an advance of Two Pence ⅌ Gallon" (DLC:GW).

The model Fielder exhibited to GW undoubtedly concerned "an apparatus for facilitating navigation" for which he petitioned a loan of money from Congress on 11 April 1792 (*Journal of the House*, 1:574). Richard Wells noted in a letter to William Thornton on 11 May of that year that "another great adventure[r]—the great walking Fielder, has obtained a Patent for a boat to work by—Magic, I suppose, for I do not know any Agency he is to employ more than the Hands on board" (DLC: Peter Force Collection, John Fitch Papers). See also Fielder's advertisements in the *Federal Gazette* (Philadelphia), 21 May and 4 June 1792. Unsuccessful in his attempt to raise money in Congress—the House of Representatives tabled his petition—Fielder again wrote GW, this time from Philadelphia, on 23 Feb. 1792. "Unforseen occurrences intervening have retarded for a long time my attempting to facilitate navigation," Fielder wrote, but he had "now endeavor'd to simplify my Ideas by compleating a Model Draft, & specification, which I conseive will prove to be of general utility." He asked GW to examine the model (DNA: RG 59, Miscellaneous Letters). By August 1793 Fielder was working on a new invention. On 19 Aug., "Having ascertained that my Machine for making Hay &c. is adapted to facilitate (perhaps particularly) the State of Virginia," he wrote GW requesting his aid in the invention "being brought into immediate effect" (DNA: RG 59, Miscellaneous Letters). There is no evidence that GW gave particular support to the invention, but aid in another form was forthcoming. On 29 Aug. Fielder wrote GW that "Your favor of Twenty Dollars on Loan I receive with gratitude. I regreted much that . . . my utmost exertions were not sufficient to be in time to explain to your Excellency how far the utility of my Machine for improving Agriculture extends, the experience of which has only been obtain'd by my accurately observing on its operations, as I understand by Mr Howell that you intend me the Honor of making one for your Estate, if admissable to favor me with an opportunity of being farther explanatory" (DNA: RG 59, Miscellaneous Letters).

From the Massachusetts Legislature

[Boston] Saturday October 24th 1789

The Governor & Council present their respectful compliments to the President of the United States & request the Honor of his company with his suite to Dine on Tuesday next at the Coffee house in State Street at 3 o'Clock P.M.[1]

L, DLC:GW.
For background to this letter, see GW to Betty Lewis, 12 Oct. 1789, n.3, and to John Hancock, 23 Oct. 1789, n.1.

1. On 25 Oct. the dining arrangements were changed, the governor and council informing GW that "for the better accommodation of the Company the place of dining on Tuesday next is altered for Fanieul Hall at three o'Clock P.M. The Company will proceed from the Senate Chamber in the State House" (DLC:GW).

On Saturday, 24 Oct., the wardens of Trinity Church, preparing for the next day's services, wrote GW that "a Seat is appropriated for his Use in said Church, should his Inclinations lead him to attend public Worship there tomorrow or at any other Time" (DLC:GW). On Sunday, 25 Oct., GW attended services held at Trinity Church by the Rev. Samuel Parker in the morning and in the afternoon was present at the Brattle Street Congregational Church, presided over by the Rev. Peter Thacher (*Diaries*, 5:476).

Letter not found: from Thomas Newton, Jr., 24 Oct. 1789. On 23 Nov. GW wrote to Newton: "Your letter of the 24th of October . . . has been duly received."

From Jonathan Titcomb

Newburyport [Mass.] Oct. 24th 1789.

Major General Titcomb presents his profound respects to the President of the United States & would humbly beg to be informed when he intends passing through the County of Essex. The Major General, & the militia of the County wish to be prepared to embrace the opportunity which thus happily presents, to exhibit as far as in their power their veneration for the high and important station & their admiration of the personal character of the President of the United States; Major Hooper who presents this request will wait on the President for an answer as he shall be pleased to appoint.[1]

Sprague transcript, DLC:GW.

For Jonathan Titcomb, see his letter to GW, 19 June 1789. For background to GW's New England tour, see his letter to Betty Lewis, 12 Oct. 1789, n.3.

1. On Saturday, 30 Oct., Titcomb was among the citizens who met GW at the line between Essex and Middlesex counties. GW spent the night of 30 Oct. in Newburyport (*Diaries*, 5:486).

From Jabez Bowen

Sir   Providence [R.I.] Octobr 25 1789

I should have done my self The Honour of paying my Respects to you in person, did not my Duty require my attendance at The General Assembly tomorrow at South Kingston, where The great Question of calling a State Convention to adopt the Federal Constitution will be acted upon. we hope for a favourable Issue, but cannot be free from Fear, lest we may be disappointed Thro The Intrigues of The Enemies of all good Government. if we can agree to Call a Convention all will end well, if not our situation will be truly miserable.[1]

I shall be at Home on Sunday next and shall Think my self highly Honoured if you[r] Excellency will take Providence in your way on your Return, and spend a little time with us.[2] I should hope That your Thus kindly noticing of us will not be of any disadvantage towards Establishing The great Cause That we have been so long engaged in promoting.

Mrs Bowen presents her most Respectfull Compliments and hopes you will favour us with a Visit.[3] with sentiments of the highest Respect and Esteeme, I Remain Your Excellencys, most Obedent and verry Humble Servant

Jabez Bowen

ALS, DLC:GW.

1. The Rhode Island assembly was meeting at South Kingstown. The *United States Chronicle: Political, Commercial, and Historical* (Providence), 29 Oct. 1789, noted in a comment dated 29 Oct. that although it had been widely anticipated that "a Vote recommending a Convention for determing on the new Federal Constitution would at this Session be obtained—but from the Instructions given by a large Number of the Towns, at the Town-Meetings on Monday last Week, there is reason to fear this desirable Event will not take Place at the present Meeting." On Thursday, 29 Oct., the assembly rejected the convention by a vote of 39 to 17 and adjourned until January 1790 (*United States Chronicle*, 5 Nov. 1789).

2. GW did not, of course, visit Rhode Island on his New England tour.

3. Bowen's wife was Sarah Bowen (c.1752–1800).

From Henry Knox

Sir   New-York 25th of October 1789

No further intelligence has been received from Georgia since the arrival of Mr Kean.[1]

This silence, and the powers with which the commissioners were invested to render the treaty advantages to the Creeks generally, and to their cheif particularly are sufficient to arrest the beleif of the report.

The report itself originated perhaps in the apprehension or misrepresentations of some of the White people in Georgia.

No occurrence since my last worthy of being commmunicated to you. I have the honor to be sir with the highest respect Your obedient Servant

H. Knox

ALS, DLC:GW; LB, DLC:GW.

1. See Knox to GW, 18 Oct. 1789.

From Matthew Whiting

Dear Sir,   Snow-Hill 25th October 1789.

The willingness with which you have ever extended your Beneficence to those whose Misfortunes required it, has implanted in the Breast of every Citizen, the most sensible Joy, that you, above every other Person, are possessed with the Means of rendering Assistance to those whose peculiar Situations entitle them to your Favor. It is no less under this Impression, than from that Confidence which, a long and intimate acquaintance with you has given me of your Friendship, that I now solicit your friendly Assistance and Favor, in a Matter, in which, from your high Station, and extensive Correspondence, I have the most flattering Hope it is in your Power to be essentially serviceable. It has been my Misfortune to lose an only Son whose Desire for Travel prompted him to leave this Country at an early Period of Life, and in Times of much Danger, to visit those Countries which were more distant. With this View he sailed from Charles Town in the Year 1779 among a Number of Gentlemen of Distinction, in a Ship destined for France, and of which, there has been no certain Account ever since: From the Length of Time that has elapsed since his Departure, the Perils attending a Sea Voyage, and a Variety of other Circumstances, I have not had the smallest Ground to cherish a Hope, that he is at this Time in Existence. To my small Encouragement, however, several Accounts have lately occured, of his being in the Hands of the Algerines. One was delivered by a Man about twelve Months ago, who made his Escape from the Emperor of Morocco's Dominion, and who said, that he was desired by a Person, by the name of Whiting, at that Time in Slavery in the Sea Port Town of Salee, to inform his Friends, if he should ever escape, that he was in that Situation. Another Account, and which I have enclosed, in Corroboration of what I have before heared, comes from a Man who lately made his Escape from Algiers, and says, that he was personally Acquainted with a Person by the Name of Whiting whilst a Companion in his Misfortunes.[1] These Accounts, altho' rendered improbable by the Circumstance of his Destination when he sailed from Charles Town, are yet possible: and as it is utterly impracticable, from any Intercourse in my Power (except through the Channel of a Friend) to find out whether the Information which I have received be true or not; the only Resource left me is to solicit the Assistance of one, whose Correspondence with foreign Countries affords the most probable Chance of Information. In this Light I have considered you. Permit me, therefore, My Dear Sir, to solicit it as a

Favor which will confer the most lasting Obligation on me, that you will render this Assistance, by conveying a Letter to every Quarter, where you may suppose that there will be a Chance of Information with respect to him. And should your Enquiry be successful, permit me to beg, as a further Favor, that you will also endeavor to negotiate the Terms of his Ransom. Any Part, or the whole of my Fortune, I shall deem an inconsiderable Price for his Freedom, to be delivered at any Time, and at any Place, it shall be appointed. I have the most flattering Ground to hope, that, if in any Person's Power to procure this Intelligence, it is in your's: And as, through your friendly Intercession, it may be practicable (should [he] be in that Situation) to obtain Access to him, I have thought proper to subjoin some Particulars with respect to his Situation before he left this Country, his Birth, his Connections, and Person, by which, the Person who makes the Enquiry, will be enabled to determine with certainty whether it be the same Person or not.[2]

He was Lieutenant in the 3d Virginia Regt commanded by Coll Marshall—after which, he became Aid-de-Camp to Genl Lincoln—His Mother's maiden Name was Hannah Washington who was Sister to Coll Warner Washington—He had 2 Uncles & 3 Aunts—Frances Whiting one of his Uncles intermarried with Betty Kemp of Glo[uce]ster County—His other Uncle's Name was John who never married—Mary Whiting one of his Aunts married Capt. John Waith—Anne Whiting another Aunt, married Coll Humphrey Brooke—and Elizabeth Whiting his other Aunt married John Ariss—He was himself very sensible, a spair Man, with black hair & Eyes, and, if now living, is 34 Years old.

I must beg that you will let this Description accompany the Enquiry; and should any Person be found to answer it—those Doubts which I have had with respect to his Existence will be entirely removed. 'Til I can receive some Information upon whh I can depend, I must forever remain disconsolate; and this, I humbly hope it will be in your Power to procure. Should no other Good result from the Enquiry, I shall at least have the Consolation to think, that every Exertion which the most tender Solicitude of a Parent could invent have been used to restore him to his Country and his Friends. You will be so obliging as to inform me whether this Letter comes to your hands.

With the most fervent Prayers for the Prosperity and Happiness of yourself and Lady, I have the Honor to be with great Esteem, Dear Sir, Your most affectionate, and obt hume Sert

Matthew Whiting.

ALS, DLC:GW.

Matthew Whiting (d. 1810) of Gloucester County, Va., moved about 1770 to Snow Hill on Bull Run in Prince William County. This letter concerns his son Matthew (born c.1755).

1. For information on the American captives in Algiers and earlier attempts by the United States to free them, see Mathew Irwin to GW, 9 July 1789. Whiting's information probably stemmed from a story concocted by a sailor, Archibald Ross, and some of his cohorts to cover an act of piracy committed in the Mediterranean. Ross's account, which involved a fictitious ship, the *Julius Caesar*, out of Philadelphia and supposedly captured by the Algerians around 1785, listed numerous individuals among the crew, now supposedly captives in Algiers, and gave detailed accounts of the conditions of their captivity. Among his descriptions of the captives, Ross noted that "he saw a Captain Henry Whiting, belonging to Virginia, in slavery" (New York *Daily Advertiser*, 24 June 1790). Although Ross's story did not appear in print until mid–1790 some garbled version of it may well have reached Whiting earlier. Upon its publication in New York newspapers, Jefferson immediately launched an investigation. See Boyd, *Jefferson Papers*, 16:562–65. For correspondence relating to the episode, see also DNA: RG 59, Domestic Letters, 4:169–75.

2. GW replied to Whiting's letter on 18 Nov.: "Since my return from the Eastward I receiv'd your letter respecting your Son. Had I receiv'd it sooner, it should have been answerd sooner.

"Upon the receipt of it I immediately made application to the Office of Foreign Affairs, from whence alone any information upon such a subject could be derived—A Copy of the report from that Office you will receive with this—Whatever means of affording assistance in cases like this I may be possessed of, shall be most chearfully exerted, and if the desired end could be attain'd, I should receive great pleasure from it—The only channel thro' which at present, (as I have just above observ'd) any information can be procur'd, is the Office of Foreign Affairs, nor do I know or believe that any other will present itself, unless it be thro' Mr Jefferson the American Minister at the Court of France, whom I daily expect here on his return from thence—But here give me leave to advise you not to cherish too fondly your hopes—I know full well that persons of that description from whom you have accounts of your Son's being in captivity at Algiers, make a practice of fabricating such tales, with a view of getting money from those, to whom, the persons of whom they give such accounts, are related—This has been done in other instances—I well know too that small circumstances will induce and encourage great hopes, where the object of our hopes is the object of our love & strongest affection" (Df, DNA: RG 59, Miscellaneous Letters).

No letter from GW to Jay requesting information on young Whiting has been found; GW's request may well have been verbal. On 16 Nov. Jay sent the president an account of the current status of the Americans held captive by the Algerians: "Mr Jay has the Honor of observing to the President, that on examining the Papers relating to the american Captives at algiers, the names only of the Captains & mates appear to be mentioned. The enclosed Paper states all the facts which in his Judgmt are material to the Inquiry in Question—To render it the more perfect, he has obtained and added the Information of Mr [Paul R.] Randall, who was Secy to Mr [John] Lamb."

The "enclosed paper" reads: "It appears from Papers in this Office that two american Vessels have been taken by the Algerines, vizt.

"The Ship Dauphin of Philadelphia commanded by Richard O'Bryan, which was captured the 30th July 1785, 50 Leagues to the Westward of Lisbon by an Algerine Chebeck, and carried into Algiers the 16th August following. She was bound from St Ubes: And the Schooner Maria of Boston commanded by Isaac Stevens, bound from Boston to Cadiz, which was captured the 25th June 1785 by an Algerine Cruizer of 20 Guns, and carried into Algiers.

"That the Officers and Crews of these two Vessels, including two Passengers, amounted to twenty one Men, of whom three have since died.

"That the Names of the Captains are Richard O'Bryan, Isaac Stevens and Zaccheus Coffin, the last of whom was a Passenger and is dead; and the Names of the Mates are Alexr Forsyth and Andrew Montgomery, one of whom was also a Passenger.

"That only eight of the said Captives were Natives of America.

"That no other american Vessels appear to have been captured by the Algerines; nor any by Tunis nor Tripoli. And that those taken by the Moors have been released.

"Mr Randall who was at Algiers with Mr Lamb, says, that during the time he was there, he dined in company with the american Captains, and had much Conversation with Capt: O'Bryan; that Captain O'Bryan was an Irishman, and he understood from him that all his Crew were foreigners; and that the eight american Captives were Eastern Men. That the three american Captains were at liberty to walk about, the french Consul and afterwards the Spanish Envoy having become answerable for them, that the two Mates were exempted from hard Labour, and that it was only the common Men on whom it was imposed. That if any young Man had been among the common Sailors, who was in any degree superior to them, he would *at least* have met with the same Indulgence as the Mates; that he did not hear of any such person, and does not believe there was" (DNA: RG 59, Miscellaneous Letters).

From Edward Carrington

Sir   Richmond Octo. 26th 1789
    I had the honor a few days ago to receive your Letter of the 30th Ult. enclosing a Commission for the Office of District

Marshal for Virginia, together with sundry Acts upon the Judiciary system.[1] The confidence you are pleased Sir, to repose in me, in confering this Commission, is an evidence of your good opinion exceedingly flattering and gratifying; and the terms in which you have thought proper to communicate it, excite in my mind the highest sensations of gratitude and respect.

Having indeavoured to possess myself of the extent of the duties and degree of responsibility involved in this Office, and also of the probable competency of emoluments to enable the occupant to execute it properly, I perceive that the former are very considerable, and that the latter can only be ascertained from experiment:[2] this experiment I am willing to make, and shall be happy to continue in the appointment, should I find myself enabled to execute it with honor to myself, and advantage to the public.

Being a Member of the State Legislature now in session, it is my wish not to vacate my Seat before the duties of this appointment may require it; this I Conceive will not happen before the period appointed for the sitting of the first District Court on the third tuesday in December, when I shall be ready to accept the office of Marshal, and to quallify according to the terms thereof.[3] I have the Honor to be Sir, with the greatest respect your Most Obt humble Servt

Ed. Carrington

ALS, DNA: RG 59, Acceptances and Orders for Commissions.

1. GW's pro forma letter of appointment, 30 Sept. 1789, to Carrington was sold in 1947. See *American Book-Prices Current*, 53:594.

2. No fixed compensation for marshals appointed under article 27 of the Judiciary Act was specified by law.

3. Carrington's letter of acceptance, 14 Jan. 1790, is in DNA: RG 59, Acceptances and Orders for Commissions. He apparently accepted the post with some reservations. On 25 Oct. he wrote Henry Knox, thanking the secretary of war for his good offices in securing the appointment. "What will be the real Value of the appointment confered upon me is yet to be ascertained from experiment, & my acceptance will be founded upon a determination to resign or hold it, according to the discovery which shall be made, as to the adequacy of compensation to the responsibility of the Office. upon this there are various calculations. . . . The Judiciary system is so defective that it will doubtless undergo much alteration in the next session of Congress" (MHi: Henry Knox Papers).

From John Hancock

Sunday ½ past 12 oClock
[Boston, 26 October 1789]

The Governours Best respects to The President, if at home & at leisure, the Governour will do himself the honour to pay his respects, in half an hour[1]—This would have been done much sooner, had his health in any degree permitted, He now hazards every thing as it respects his health, for the desirable purpose.

L, DLC:GW.

For background to GW's New England tour, see his letter to Betty Lewis, 12 Oct. 1789, n.3.

1. This incident produced a minor contretemps with implications for state and federal relationships. GW had assumed that he as president would receive the first visit from John Hancock representing state authority. As he noted in his diary, "Having engaged yesterday to take an informal dinner with the Govr. to day (but under a full persuasion that he would have waited upon me so soon as I should have arrived) I excused myself upon his not doing it, and informing me thro his Secretary that he was too much indisposed to do it, being resolved to receive the visit" (*Diaries*, 5:475). Hancock's illness was reported to be gout. On Sunday, 25 Oct., according to GW's diary account, "I received a visit from the Govr., who assured me that Indisposition alone had prevented his doing it yesterday, and that he was still indisposed; but as it had been suggested that he expected to *receive* the visit from the President, which he knew was improper, he was resolved at all hazds. to pay his Compliments to day." GW returned Hancock's call the next evening (ibid., 476–77). According to Boston newspapers the governor was not well enough to attend the dinner for GW on the afternoon of 27 Oct. but was present at the ball on Wednesday, 28 Oct. (*Boston Gazette*, 26 Oct., 2 Nov. 1789; *Massachusetts Centinel* [Boston], 28 Oct. 1789). Squabbling between state and local officials had apparently resulted in violations of protocol even before GW entered the town. In response to inquiries from Jared Sparks in the 1830s, Benjamin Russell, one of the members of the committee of arrangements for GW's reception into Boston, reported that the governor had claimed the right of welcoming the illustrious guest into Boston, while representatives of the town insisted that as he was entering the city the formal welcome was their prerogative. The governor, they contended, should have met the president at the boundary of the state. "The President was approaching the town, and they were ready to render civic honors to him. The controversy was without result. Both authorities remained in their carriages, while the aids and marshals were rapidly posting between them. Both contended that the point of etiquette was on their side. The day was unusually cold and murky. The President with his secretary

had been mounted for a considerable time on the *Neck*, waiting to enter the town. He made inquiry of the cause of the delay, and, on receiving information of the *important* difficulty, is said to have expressed impatience. Turning to Major Jackson, his secretary, he asked, 'Is there no other avenue to the town?' And he was in the act of turning his charger, when he was informed, that the controversy was over, and that he would be received by the municipal authorities" (Russell to Sparks, 22 May 1835, in Sparks, *Writings*, 10:491–93). See also Ford, *Writings of Washington*, 11:445.

To John Hancock

> Sunday 1. o'clock Boston October 26th 1789

The President of the United States presents his best respects to the Governor, and has the honor to inform him that he shall be at home 'till 2 o'clock.

The President of the United States need not express the pleasure it will give him to see the Governor—but, at the same time, he most earnestly begs that the Governor will not hazard his health on the occasion.

Copy, DLC:GW.
For background to this document, see John Hancock to GW, 26 Oct. 1789.

From Michael Lacassagne

Sir   Louisville, October 26th 1789. (Rapids of Ohio)

An affair has lately happened on the North West side of the Ohio, within the federal territory, which has, in a very great degree, excited my indignation, and which, in the opinion of all friends to liberty, in this quarter, calls aloud for the interposition of the supreme authority. You need not be informed that the legislature of Virginia granted to the officers and soldiers of the regiment distinguished by the name of the Illinois regiment, 150,000 acres of land, on the North West side of the Ohio, as a compensation for their extraordinary services in the late war;[1] in this grant I possess a very considerable interest, and being anxious, both on my own and the public accounts to encrease the value of land on that side of the river, I have, at great trouble and expence, effected a settlement in the vicinity of *Fort Steuben*, a continental post, a small distance above the rapids, at present commanded by Capt. Joseph Ashton.[2] This settlement, tho' unprotected, and consequently exposed to the incursions and depredations of the Savages, whereby it has actually Suffered, yet, from the encouragement given to settlers, promised, in opposition to every obstruction, a rapid increase. But the prospect, however flattering, from the idea of its being productive of both public and private advantage has been blasted by the imprudent (to say no worse of it) conduct of Capt. Ashton.

One of the settlers owed another a small debt, which he was either unable or unwilling to pay; the creditor having no tribunal to which he could apply for the recovery of his debt, seized in a public manner upon an ax, the property of the debtor, which he declared he would keep as a security until his debt should be satisfied. The debtor applied to Capt. Ashton for redress, who heard his complaint, deputed the complainant a Constable, and ordered him to bring the creditor before him. The complainant being thus cloathed with power, set out on the execution of his new office, and seeing the creditor, who, from a suspicion of the complainant's design in going to the garrison, had followed to know the event. They both appeared before the captain. The charge of having taken the complainants axe was then exhibited against him, and being asked what defence he had to make, he repeated the circumstances respecting the taking of the axe, as before stated, upon which the captain, without any proof of a felonious intention in the defendant, without consulting an officer of the garrison on the occasion; in short, without any thing to justify his judgement, pronounced the defendant guilty of Theft, and sentenced him to receive forty lashes at the public whipping post, which was accordingly executed.

To a man who has any degree of sensibility—To a man who has ever tasted the sweets of liberty—To a Citizen of America, who feels himself secure in the consideration that he cannot be deprived of his liberty, or subject to punishment, but by the laws of his country—such a sentence executed in such a manner, must be worse than death itself. I love liberty—I reverence the laws of my country—but I detest and abhor the lawless hand of tyranny and oppression—To you, Sir, as the founder, the protector of American Liberty, I have ventured in this case to appeal; and tho' this information is by a private individual, who has no other claim to your confidence than what arises from a consciousness of the rectitude of his intentions, I hope it will not, on that account, pass unnoticed, but that an examination into this case may be directed, on which Every thing herein asserted, will by the testimony of men of character be proven incontestibly. I wou'd not be understood to mean, that I wish this enquiry to gratify any personal resentment against Capt. Ashton. No, Sir, I have lived on rather an intimate footing with that gentleman since his residence at the rapids, and never but in one instance similar to the present, have I, or I believe any person, had reason to censure his conduct—He is generally esteemed a good officer, but in the present case, and the one just alluded to, he has certainly acted subversive of those principles established by the American revolution. The public good is my object—I wish it to be universally known, and acknowledged throughout America, that the military must be subordinate to the civil power, and that in no government which boasts the honor and happiness of having you Sir, at its head, shall the military, on any pretence whatever, assume any authority or Jurisdiction in civil affairs—The reverse of this, particularly in the federal territory, must be pregnant with the worst of consequences—a man who Settles on the North West side of the Ohio, must do it under the persuasion, that he is amenable only to the known—the written laws of the government under which he lives—was it otherwise—was he to be subjected to the capricious will of some petty tyrant who may happen to command at some federal post, whose uninformed judgment shou'd be the Standard of distributive justice, the federal territory would continue a wilderness, and the fertility of the soil in vain court the hand of the husbandman.

Nothing, Sir, I assure you, but a sense of the importance of the subject of this address cou'd have induced me to trouble you, and when I reflect (as I often do with pleasure) on the sacred regard you have always manifested to the rights of mankind in general, I flatter myself you will not suffer a citizen of America however obscure, to be unlawfully deprived of the benefit of those blessings which have been obtained at the expence of so much blood and treasure.[3] With great respect, I am Sir Your most obedient & very humble servant

Ml Lacassagne

Copy, MiU-C: Josiah Harmar Papers; copy, WHi: Draper Manuscripts, Harmar Papers.

Michael Lacassagne (d. 1797) immigrated to the United States from France and established a mercantile business in Louisville, Ky., where he also became active in politics. In 1788 he served as a member of the Kentucky convention for statehood and in 1794 was postmaster of Louisville.

1. One of the reservations in Virginia's 1781 cession of lands northwest of the Ohio River to the United States was the grant of 150,000 acres for the officers and men of George Rogers Clark's Illinois regiment. The grant was to be "laid off in one tract . . . in such place on the north west side of the Ohio as the majority of the officers shall choose, and to be afterwards divided among the said officers and soldiers in due proportion according to the laws of Virginia." See 10 Hening 565.

2. Fort Steuben, constructed in 1786 by troops under the command of Capt. John Hamtramck, was on the right bank of the Ohio River opposite Louisville. Capt. Joseph Asheton had served in the Revolution and remained with the United States Army's meager forces after the war, serving until 1792. Asheton was in command at Fort Steuben during the absence of Maj. John Wyllys. See Henry Knox to GW, 22 Oct. 1789, n.1.

3. Upon receiving Lacassagne's letter in December 1789 GW instructed Tobias Lear to request that the secretary of war investigate the matter (Lear to Knox, 17 Dec. 1789, DLC:GW). Knox in turn wrote Josiah Harmar, 19 Dec., directing Harmar to launch an inquiry "& report thereon, & you will also confer with the Governor and take his opinion thereon. If the case be truly stated, Capt. Ashton must have proceeded in an unjustifiable manner, which will require the interposition of Government" (WHi: Draper Manuscripts, Harmar Papers). Ashton had received all of the pertinent correspondence by the end of January 1790 when he wrote Harmar that he had requested Maj. John Doughty to hold a court to inquire into his conduct. "Part of the Evidence has been gone through this morning—the rest is to be finished next Monday. I flatter myself that Michl Lacassagne's mountain will then appear no more than a mole-hill" (Ashton to Harmar, 28 Jan. 1790, WHi: Draper Manuscripts, Harmar Papers). The issue apparently was resolved in Ashton's favor, since he wrote Harmar in August 1790 that "I am under the strongest obligations to you for the very favorable paragraph in your letter to the Secretary at War, respecting *Lacassagns* complt" (Ashton to Harmar, 22 Aug. 1790, WHi: Draper Manuscripts, Harmar Papers).

From Warner Lewis

Virginia, Warner Hall,
Dear Sir,   October 26'th, 1789.

Engaged as you have been for some months past, I apprehended it would be intrusion for me to trouble you with a letter. With a hope that in the recess of Congress you have somewhat more leisure allowed you, I now take the liberty of replying to your favor of May last.

You put a question the most proper that could be imagined to obtain the information you desire of the value of the land that was Bristow's; and if my judgment does not err in returning an answer to your question, you will indeed have almost as good an idea of it as if you had seen it. I will not, as I dare say you will readily believe, Sir, intentionally deceive you, but give it as my opinion, that if Bristow's be worth eight hundred pounds, the like quantity of such land as is about Warner Hall, with no more wood and timber, and equally destitute of improvements, would be worth sixteen hundred.

I received not long since a letter from a Mr John Nicholson, who lives in Gloucester, wherein he makes the following enquiries, which I beg leave to give you in his own words—"What will General Washington take for his land on Back-creek, one half cash, the other half in good bonds, to be assigned and warranted?"

"What will he lease it for, for two lives, the lessees obliging themselves to build a two story wooden house of four rooms, with all necessary out-houses and a barn?"

"What credit will the General sell it for, or will he take good bonds on demand, warranted and assigned?"

As it was not in my power to give mr Nicholson an answer to either of his interrogatories, I have thought it proper to make you acquainted with them, and whatever answer you may be pleased to return me, I will communicate to him.[1]

With the sincerest wishes for your health and happiness, and with the most perfect respect and esteem, I am, Dear Sir, your most obedient, and very humble serv't

Warner Lewis

Copy, ViMtV.

For background to this letter, see John Dandridge to GW, 27 Oct., 6 Dec.
1788, GW to Dandridge, 18 Nov. 1788, 26 Mar. 1789; GW to Warner Lewis,
19 Dec. 1788, 24 May 1789, and Lewis to GW, 1, 11 Mar. 1789.

1. Lewis's letter to GW evidently went astray. On 18 Feb. 1790 he wrote the
president: "At the request of mr Nicholson I take the liberty of inclosing
to you the duplicate of a letter, which I had the honour of writing you by
post some months ago, but which I suspect from some accident or other
did not get to your hands" (ViMtV). For GW's reply, stating the terms on
which he would sell his Gloucester County lands, see his letter to Lewis, 5 Mar.
1790.

From Moses D. Nathans

Boston Orange street October 26th 1789

Providance who has bestowed his Blesing on your Excelence,
full of the Spiret of Wisdom, and meek above all man, on this I
tak the liberty to lieu befor your Excelence a Scheme, which in
my humble opinion me be a great benefit to this Country,[1] but if
this chall not be successful, prey Sir for Gods sake order this
papers to be burnt, that not another chall Know of this freedom,
then I will not be achamed that I hef transgressed against you,
and you, great Jenral, you'r more then man, pordon the bold-
ness of one drooping in Misfortune and tries to seve him and his
famille by a reward of a Project, this is the case of Your Excelence most humble and most Obedient Servt

Moses D. Nathans

ALS, DLC:GW.

This Moses D. Nathans is probably not the prominent Philadelphia and
New York merchant and stockbroker Moses Nathans (Nathan; 1749–1815),
who was also a member of the council of the Congregation Mikreh Israel of
Philadelphia. The 1790 census lists a Moses Nathans living in Boston with one
white male and two white females in his family (*Heads of Families* [Massachu-
setts], 188).

1. Nathans enclosed with his letter "A proposition to the benefit [of] the
Commonwealth," suggesting that it would be advisable to "recall in every state
in the Union, their Public Securities, and in return to be given a Land Obligation at 4 per cent Interest, the said Obligation to be printed and nombert for
year blank, and as many printed orders for six monthly Interest, no obligation
to be less then 50 Dollers, and for the amaunt of two per cent more which the
Auditors is promised, to secur all the nombers of the said Obligations in a

Wheel, and evry Six Monath so mainy nombers to be drean as half the Sum of the said two per Cent amaunt, and to paid in full. this will lessen the Debt, and evry Six monath befor the draing the prize of the Obligations will resse so much that the holders will gain their two per cent taken from them, in Comerce such Obligations will be Equal to Cash, all Nation will buy them. this will bring mony in Cerculation, and no doubt in a shart time the Value will be from 70 to 75 per 100, this Advantage is great. more can be mentiond if I was not affright to be troublesome. I leave it to your Excelence Consideration. but for all Debts less than 50 Dollers a printed Certificate to be given, suppose it his demant will be 51 Dollers. he will recive a Land obligation of 50 Doller and a Certificate for one Doller, 3. his demant will be 99 Dollers will recive a Land Obligation for 50 dollers and a Certificate for 49 Dollers, for such Certificates no Intres to be paid, but the holders to recive their full payments, to begin from the lost sums, the first year all Certificates of one and two Dollers, second the 3 Dollers Certificates and so on till all paid, this will satisfy the Creditors, and the benefit of the Public will be great" (DLC:GW).

To the Citizens of Boston

Gentlemen   [Boston, 27 Oct. 1789]
  The obligations, which your goodness has imposed upon me, demand my grateful acknowledgements—Your esteem does me honor, and your affection communicates the truest pleasure—by endeavoring to deserve, I will indulge the hope of retaining them.[1]
  Over-rating my services, you have ascribed consequences to them, in which it would be injustice to deny a participation to the virtue and firmness of my worthy fellow-citizens of this respectable Town and Commonwealth.
  If the exercise of my military commission has contributed to vindicate the rights of humanity, and to secure the freedom and happiness of my country, the purpose for which it was assumed has been completed, and I am amply rewarded—If, in the prosecution of my civil duties I shall be so fortunate as to meet the wishes of my fellow-citizens, and to promote the advantage of our common interests, I shall not regret the sacrifice which you are pleased to mention in terms so obliging.
  The numerous sensations of heartfelt satisfaction, which a review of past scenes affords to my mind, in a comparison with the present happy hour, are far beyond my powers of utterance to express.

I rejoice with you, my fellow-citizens, in every circumstance that declares your prosperity—and I do so, most cordially, because you have well deserved to be happy.

Your love of liberty—your respect for the laws—your habits of industry—and your practice of the moral and religious obligations, are the strongest claims to national and individual happiness, and they will, I trust, be firmly and lastingly established.

Your wishes for my personal felicity impress a deep and affectionate gratitude, and your prayer to the Almighty Ruler of the universe, in my behalf, calls forth my fervent supplication to that gracious and beneficent Being, for every blessing on your temporal pursuits, and for the perfection of your happiness hereafter.

G: Washington

LB, DLC:GW.

For background to GW's New England tour, see his letter to Betty Lewis, 12 Oct. 1789, n.3.

1. The address to GW from the citizens of Boston reads: "We beg leave to express our happiness in the honor you confer upon us by your visit to this Capital. We are happy in the opportunity of again making our personal acknowledgements to a character, to which, on every principle, we are so deeply indebted.

"Every motive of esteem, duty, and affection have conspired to form in our minds the strongest attachment that the freest people can feel to the most deserving citizen. As men, we have long since considered you, under God, as the great and glorious avenger of the violated rights of humanity—As citizens, we have observed with peculiar satisfaction, that you have invariably respected those liberties, which you have so successfully defended. And as Inhabitants of a great commercial Town, we attribute the security we enjoy to the singular merit and success of those measures, in the progress of the war, which you had the honor to conduct.

"It cannot but afford you the highest pleasure when you compare our present situation with the signal distresses to which we were exposed during the period in which this Town was in the possession of exasperated Enemy. Indignant at the multiplied restraints of hostile domination we sought an assylum among our friends and connections in the country, and cheerfully abandoned our property and possessions in the common cause of America. That we were so soon happily reinstated, may be justly imputed to the wisdom of those arrangements which compelled our Invaders, in their retreat, to adopt a less destructive policy than that which, on other occasions, they so wantonly practised. In every trying vicissitude we have marked the conspicuous, and unaffected piety of your heart, and the wisdom and moderation of your councils.

"We have seen you relinquish the ease and independence of private fortune, to lead in the untried dangers of a war, at the risque of your life and reputation. With pleasure we have viewed you retiring in victory, and exhibiting a new example of patriotic virtue to an admiring World. And we now feel a still higher satisfaction at your having once more sacrificed the sweets of domestic Retirement in obedience to the united voice of your countrymen.

"These, Sir, are the sentiments and reflections which naturally occur on an attentive consideration of your past conduct. To the future we look for those virtues, which adorn the Man, and mark the wise and accomplished Legislator. We anticipate from your discernment the happy union of liberty and law, lenity and vigor, mercy and justice: The enlightened policy of a mind calm amidst the influence of Power, and uncorrupted by the fascinating allurements of Avarice or Ambition.

"With these impressions the preservation of your life through the varied scenes in which you have been engaged demands our grateful acknowledgements to the beneficent Disposer of human events.

"It is one of the first wishes of our hearts that you may be as happy in your present elevated station, as you have been distinguished in your military character, and it is our fervent prayer to the almighty Ruler of the universe that the invisible hand which led the citizens of America through the dangers and calamities of War, may still guard and protect you, as an ornament to human nature, and a blessing to your country" (DLC:GW).

GW noted in his diary that "when the committee from the Town presented their Address it was accompanied with a request (in behalf they said of the Ladies) that I would set to have my Picture taken for the Hall, that others might be copied from it for the use of their respective families" (*Diaries*, 5:478). The selectmen's letter implored GW to sit for his portrait to satisfy Boston's ladies "who are ambitious of transmitting to their Children a perfect likeness of their justly Beloved President at the moment he blessed them with his presence; when his benign countenance made such an impression on their hearts as they wish to recognize in his Portrait, in future. If favored with this Indulgence their intentions are to present it to be placed in Faneiull Hall, as the greatest Honor confered in granting them an opportunity of expressing *their* respect and Esteem for the Man so distinguished by the affections of the People" (DLC:GW). GW informed the group that as "I was engaged to leave town on Thursday [28 Oct.] early, I informed them of the impracticability of my doing this, but that I would have it drawn when I returned to New York, if there was a good Painter there—or by Mr. [John] Trumbull when he should arrive; and would send it to them" (*Diaries*, 5:478). Apparently some preliminary sketches for a portrait were made in Boston by Christian Güllager (1762–1827), and GW gave Güllager a sitting on 3 Nov. in Portsmouth. The resulting Portsmouth bust portrait, probably completed from memory by Güllager, was eventually presented to the Massachusetts Historical Society (Eisen, *Portraits of Washington*, 2:427–28; *Diaries*, 5:490).

On 26 Oct. James Lovell wrote Tobias Lear that the recently appointed Boston port officers wished to take the opportunity of GW's visit to the city to "have a personal Opportunity of thanking Him for his Confidence in their

Appointments—an Opportunity which his and their official Engagements will never probably again admit" (DLC:GW).

From Thomas Bartholomew Bowen

Charleston, South Carolina, October 27th 1789

From the exalted Station to which the unanimous suffrages of your admiring Country have called you, will you, illustrious Sir, in the Chair of Empire, amidst the arduous direction of a multiplicity of important affairs, deign to honor with your recollection an inconsiderable and humble Individual, benignly listen to his simple story, and grant the prayer of his petition?

Having dedicated my prime of life (and I hope not altogether in vain) to the service of the American cause in the late glorious contest, during the whole course of the War, and generally in the main Army under the immediate command of your Excellency, I had the honor to retire with the rank of Major, and the happiness of posessing the esteem of the Officers under, and with whom I served: as a testimony of which, I was, by the whole Pennsylvania line, unanimously chosen their Agent for receiving and delivering to them their Certificates of final settlement; and discharged that trust to their satisfaction and the approbation of the State legislature. I was also chosen by the Cincinnati of that State one of their Delegates to the first general meeting of the Society at which your Excellency in person presided.[1] I have been likewise informed that I had also the honor of being, by the recommendation of General St Clair, on the return of Officers nominated by your Excellency on the proposed peace-establishment in 1783.[2]

Disappointed in the latter expectation and determining to apply myself to Industry for my future subsistance, I sold my Certificates, purchased the materials of a printing Office, and having taken into partnership a brother Officer who had been bred to that business, we in the latter part of 1784 commenced the publication of a Newspaper in this State under the title of "The Columbian Herald," which is dignified, as its greatest merit, with a Head of your Excellency for a device. That partnership has been three years dissolved; and owing to my ignorance of the mechanic part of the printing business, the conducting which became an additional expence consequent thereon, my profits have since scarcely afforded me a decent subsistance.

Conscious of my want of consequence, and sensible of the variety of worthier applications which must have been made to you for Offices under the new Constitution, I had not yet presumed to solicit your auspicious patronage: But as I feel the imbecilities of a premature old age, and labour under the afflictions of ill health and a broken constitution (the consequences of so many years hardships in the field, uncommon even to a military life;) and well knowing, by having been long an obscure observer of your exalted *virtues*, that Benevolence (particularly to the Officers of the late Army) is one of those nearest your heart, I am encouraged to apply for your favor to render the short remainder of my life more probably guarded against the miseries of Age in want.

An appointment to the trust and direction of the Post-office in this City, joined to my business here, would conduce to render this desirable end more easily attainable. If this inferior appointment is not immediately in the gift of your Excellency, a hint of your pleasure signified to the Principal in that department must of course have a decided effect.

For this I humbly implore your benign and powerful influence; beseeching your gracious pardon for whatever inadvertant impropriety may appear in this direct application to the Great Chief Magistrate of the United States, and presuming to commit my fate to his beneficent hands.

My Services, however inconsiderable, have at least entitled me to subscribe myself, Illustrious Sir, Your Excellency's Most devoted and obedient Old Soldier and Servant

Thomas B: Bowen

ALS, DLC:GW.
Thomas Bartholomew Bowen (1742–1804) was born in Ireland. During the American Revolution he served in various Pennsylvania regiments, and in 1784 he was appointed one of two Continental agents for issuing certificates for arrears of pay to the officers of the Pennsylvania line. Bowen settled in Charleston in 1784 and opened a printing business in the city. In the same year he established with John Markland the *Columbian Herald, or the Patriotic*

Courier of North-America. Markland was replaced by new partners in 1786, but Bowen continued as publisher until 1795. Bowen was active in Masonic circles in Philadelphia and Charleston and in various charitable enterprises. He did not receive a federal appointment (*JCC*, 26:341; Harris, *Eleven Gentlemen of Charleston*, 45–47; Brigham, *American Newspapers*, 2:1028–29).

   1. See General Meeting of the Society of the Cincinnati, 4–18 May 1784.

   2. In a letter to the president of Congress, 21 Dec. 1783, GW included Bowen's name among a list of officers "who from various motives are desirous of being arranged on any Peace Establishment that may take place" (DNA:PCC, item 152).

From Richard Cary

Charlestown [Mass.]
Honoured and much Esteemed Sir,   Octor 27 1789
   I am prevented by the Weather (being Unwell) of Personally waiting on You, a Duty, I should have performed with great Pleasure.
   Its to be Regreted, Your Continuance among us, is so short.
   I look back with Gratitude, on Your Goodness, and Condescension, to me, when Your Family, was at Cambridge, and my Friend, the Late Mr Reed, was Your Secretary.
   I Request the Favour of Your Acceptance of the Inclosed, which perhaps may Afford some Satisfaction, on Reading, at Your Leisure.[1]
   I add my best wishes, that You may be long Continued, [to] the care of a Gracious Providence, a Blessing to Mankind, and Enjoy every Felecity this, and a better World, can Afford.
   With Dutifull Regards to Your Good Lady, I Begg Leave to Subscribe, Honoured Sir, Your Obedient Humble Servant
                                                    Richard Cary

ALS, DLC:GW.
   Richard Cary (c.1746–1806), the son of a prosperous Charlestown, Mass., merchant, graduated from Harvard in 1763 and served briefly in the British army before entering his father's mercantile firm. His business affairs took him first to Maine and then to Maryland. He was apparently residing in Chestertown, Md., in 1775 when he traveled north to join GW's troops outside Boston. On 15 Aug. 1775 he was appointed a brigade major and on 21 June 1776 became aide-de-camp to GW with the rank of lieutenant colonel. After he left GW's staff in the early part of the Revolution, he spent the remainder

of the war operating a mercantile trade from St. Croix. He settled in New York City around 1790, declared bankruptcy in 1796, and died in Cooperstown, New York.

1. On 23 Nov. 1789 GW wrote Cary that "When I was in Boston I received your letter of the 27th of October enclosing a pamplet relating to donations which were made by Colo. Alford for civilizing & christianizing the Indians, and for other valuable purposes. My time was so occupied while on my tour to the eastward that it was not in my power to make an acknowledgement for this mark of polite attention 'till my return to this place—and I now beg you to accept it" (Df, in writing of Tobias Lear, DNA: RG 59, Miscellaneous Letters). The enclosure in Cary's letter was an eight-page pamphlet including a letter from Cary, 1 July 1786, to the members of the "Society for propagating the Gospel among the Indians, and others, in North-America," praising the late John Alford for his bequest to continue the society's work. A copy of the pamphlet is in DLC:GW.

To the Society of the Cincinnati of Massachusetts

Gentlemen,   Boston, October 27th 1789
In reciprocating, with gratitude and sincerity, the multiplied, and affecting gratulations of my fellow-citizens of this commonwealth,[1] they will all of them, with justice, allow me to say that none can be dearer to me than the affectionate assurances which you have expressed—dear, indeed, is the occasion, which restores an intercourse with my faithful associates in prosperous and adverse fortune—and inhanced are the triumphs of peace, participated with those, whose virtue and valour so largely contributed to procure them. To that virtue and valour your country has confessed her obligations: Be mine the grateful task to add the testimony of a conviction, which it was my pride to own in the field, and it is now my happiness to acknowledge in the enjoyments of peace and freedom.

Regulating your conduct by those principles, which have heretofore governed your actions as Men, Soldiers, and Citizens, you will repeat the obligations conferred on your country—and you will transmit to posterity an example, which must command their admiration, and obtain their grateful praise.

Long may you continue to enjoy the endearments of fraternal attachment, and the heartfelt happiness of reflecting that you have faithfully done your duty! While I am permitted to possess the consciousness of that worth, which has long bound me to you by every tie of affection and esteem, I will continue to be your sincere and faithful friend.

Go: Washington

LS, owned (1986) by James F. Ruddy; LB, DLC:GW.

1. The address of the Massachusetts Society of the Cincinnati, dated 27 Oct. and signed by William Eustis, vice-president, reads: "Amidst the various gratulations, which your arrival in this metropolis has occasioned, permit us the members of the Cincinnati in this commonwealth, most respectfully to assure you of that ardor of esteem, and affection, which you have so indelibly fixed in our hearts, as our glorious leader in war, and illustrious exemplar in peace.

"After the solemn and endearing farewell on the banks of the Hudson, which our anxiety presaged as final, most peculiarly pleasing is the present unexpected meeting.

"On this occasion we cannot avoid the recollection of the various scenes of toil and danger through which you conducted us.

"And, while we contemplate the trying periods of the war, and the triumphs of peace, we rejoice to behold you, induced by the unanimous voice of your country, entering upon other trials, and other services, alike important, and in some points of view equally hazardous.

"For the completion of the great purposes which a grateful country has assigned you, long, very long, may your invaluable life be preserved! And, as an admiring World, while considering you as a Soldier, have long wanted a comparison, may your virtues and talents, as a Statesman, again leave them without a parallell.

"It is not in words to express an attachment founded like ours. We can only say, that when Soldiers our greatest pride was a promptitude of obedience to your orders, as Citizens, our supreme ambition is to maintain the character of firm supporters of that noble fabric of Federal Government, over which you preside.

"As members of the Society of Cincinnati, it will be our endeavor to cherish those sacred principles of Charity and fraternal attachment, which our institution inculcates. And while our conduct is thus regulated we can never want the patronage of the first of Patriots, and best of Men" (DLC:GW).

From John Coles

Charlestown [Mass.] 27th Octr 1789

Be Pleased Great Father of thy people, to pardon the Presumption of this Address, and behold thy Ser[v]ant, at this time, Surrounded with, (not uncommon to him) but Heart Breaking

Cares, for the fate of things, has Ordered them to Continnue, for Seven Years, and Seven, and almost Seven again, Whereby thy Servants Patience, and fortitude, has Came to a Stand, and he is Ready to fall, beneath the Burthen, of Sum of the Laws of his Country. thy Servant, was Born at Boston, and Brought up, to the Courts and Heraldry Painting, Married a faithfull Partner, at 19 years of Age, & Lost father, and mother, before he was twenty two, was an only Child, and Left to the wide world, with out friends or money. his family Increaseing, he Applyed him Self, to the Strickest Rules, of Industry, & Oconamy, and had not Sickness ben hard a pon him he might Prehaps, have ben Better of, However, haveing an Enterprizeing mind, he has by the Blessing, of Divine Providence, Notwithstanding all human things, Seemed to be against him, Suported his family, in the following Charrecters. Viz. a tradesman, a Labourer, a Soldier,[1] a Seaman, and a Merchant, and is now Surrounded by, (whome Next to his Country he wishes to Live for) 9 Children, from 3 years old upwards, all he Ever had, 3 Boys, and 6 Girls, who together with there Parents Are now, Rejoicing on the arival of the Man, to whom only, they Can, unfold there Sorrows. Now if it may Plese thy Great Mind, to Consider, that thy Servant has by Great pains, and Labour, Paid up fifteene hundred Silver dollars, on Acount of his Losses at Sea, over and above the Loss of all the Vessels he was Conscerned in, and Still thare Remains a Ballance to his Credettors of 500 Dollars. this no Dowt thy Servant Could Pay, in two or three years Time, by Observeing the Same Rules, he has Done in all His former Payments, Viz. Receveing, nor Paying, no Visits. Subsisting on the meanest food, and dressing in the Meanest garb, also Divideing his time in Masonic Order. thus thy Servant has Proceeded, Amidst Discouregments, almost Insurmountable, haveing nearly all his Credettors Pushing at One and the Same time, Serveing Writs, with thair Great Expences, on thy willing, but Unable Servant. and the Payment of One Dett was only Reason for Saying, and why did you not Pay me, by another, and often has thy Servant, ben as it ware Obliged, to hurt his feelings by promasing, on a Poor foundation, to keep him Self from being imprisoned, and Rendered Unable, to Any way Provid for his young, and Helpless family. thus your Servant is the worst of Slaves, in a Country of Freemen, and the Lives & Morals, of thy young Servants, his Children, Exposed by Poverty, Notwithstanding thy Servant has ben invinceable with Respect, to the Common Learning of his Children, which a few Lines, inclosed from his Oldest Son, may Evidence,[2] thy Servant Prays, nither for Power, Riches, nor Honour, but only, if it may Plese, the President, of these United States, in Due time, to Remember the Poor mans Prayer and to use, his influence, with the Congress, when the Bankrupt Act, may Come forth, as that it may be Calculated to Defend, the Helpless, honest, and industrous Man and to Grant him Time, to Labour, for the Payment of his Just Detts, and Seport of his Family. Which if thy Servant Mistakes not, no Laws, with in these States, Defend him in at Present and thy Servant as in Duty bound, Shall Ever Pray.

John Coles

ALS, DLC:GW. This letter is headed "The Poor Man's Prayer."

John Coles (1750–1809) is listed (as John Cole) in the Charlestown entry of the federal census for 1790 as heading a household of five white males and seven white females (*Heads of Families* [Massachusetts], 137). See also death listing in the *Columbian Centinel* (Boston), 20 Sept. 1809.

1. At this point Coles inserted an asterisk for a note that appears at the end of the document: "when a Soldier thy Servant had the Honour to Command the guard who Delivered general Washington at Cambridge, Perhaps the first Prisoners by Sea Viz. Capt. Hunter &c. of the Ordanance Brigd & with 2000 Stand of Arms &c. &c. &c."

2. Enclosed in Coles's letter is a note from Charles Lee Coles "Aged 12 years," also dated 27 Oct. and directed to the president of the United States: "How Oft, Great Sir, has thy Sacred, Name been Sounded in Our Infant Ear, By Our honrd Father, and How Oft, has our Tender Mother taught us, to Love, Honour, and Obey the Name of Washington, and, How Great should be Our gratitude, to the Supreem Ruler of the Universe, For preserveing us through our helpless Years, in war, to behold thy face in peace, and to Lisp forth, the Immortal praise, Of the savour of his Country" (DLC:GW).

From Cadwallader Ford, Jr.

Massachusetts Middlesex County Wilmington

Sr   October the 27th 1789

Duty and gratitude, obliges me to Express the greatest Hapiness in your safe Arival, and the Honor you confer on this Commonwealth and the Inhabitants thereof by your Visit to the

Capital And Other Places.[1] I Think my self happy, and it gives me the greatest pleasure once more to Behold that Character which the King of Kings haith raised up, and Quallyfied for a Leader & Commander of our Armies; And the Avenger of the Violated rights of humanity, and haith Inspired with a wise and Understanding Heart; to Judge this so great a People; and to know what the American Israel ought to doo.

Blessed be God who directed his People to the Choice and Inclined your Heart to relinquish the Ease & Domestick felicity of Private Fortune, to lead Forth our Armies through a Long and Distressing war, and Crowning your Labours with success and Victory; And haith Inclined your Heart once more, to Sacrifice your sweet Retirement, to Accept of the Great and Arduous Trust to which you are now Elected: Let all the Earth Rejoice & shout aloud for Joy; and the People Say, Amen, Amen.

May the Great Universal Parent of all Mankind who hath preserved your Life in Perrills of Dangers, and maintained your Health all your Life Long, Continue to be Gracious, that you may Long Live to Sway the American Scepter in Righteousness, and be a great and Lasting Blessing to this Feoderal Empire, and the People Rejoice under your wise and Judicious Administration, and at some far, Verry far distant Period, may you be received to mantions of Bliss—is the Sincere desire and hearty Prayer of your most Dutifull and Very Humble Servant.

Cadwallader Ford Junr

P:S: Pardon Me Dear General in thus Attempting to Adress you, and beleive me to be sincere, when I tell you I have a son, Baptized by the Name of George Washington; should your Excellency think this poor performance worthy of an Answer, Please to direct to be left at the Post Office in Boston.

ALS, DNA:PCC, item 78.

Cadwallader Ford, Jr. (1743–1804), often referred to as "Captain," was a lifelong resident of Wilmington.

1. See GW to Betty Lewis, 12 Oct. 1789, n.3.

To the President and Fellows of Harvard University

Gentlemen,   Boston October 27th 1789.

Requesting you to accept my sincere thanks for the address with which you have thought proper to honor me, I entreat you to be persuaded of the respectful and affectionate consideration with which I receive it.[1]

Elected by the suffrages of a too partial country to the eminent and arduous station, which I now hold, it is peculiarly flattering to find an approbation of my conduct in the judgment of men, whose reverend characters must sanction the opinions they are pleased to express.

Unacquainted with the expression of sentiments which I do not feel, you will do me justice by believing confidently in my disposition to promote the interests of science and true religion.

It gives me sincere satisfaction to learn the flourishing state of your literary Republic—assured of its' efficiency in the past events of our political system, and of its' further influence on those means which make the best support of good government, I rejoice that the direction of its' measures is lodged with men, whose approved knowledge, integrity, and patriotism give an unquestionable assurance of their success.

That the Muses may long enjoy a tranquil residence within the walls of your University, and that you, Gentlemen, may be happy in contemplating the progress of improvement through the various branches of your important departments, are among the most pleasing of my wishes and expectations.

                                                       Go: Washington

LS, MH-Ar; LB, DLC:GW.

On 26 Oct. Joseph Willard, president of Harvard, wrote GW a brief note inquiring whether "the President has determined upon the time, when the Corporation of the University in Cambridge may have the honor of waiting upon Him, to present their Address, He may have the opportunity of informing Dr Willard by the bearer, who will wait his commands" (DLC:GW). According to GW's diary entry of 27 Oct., the Harvard address, along with several others, was presented before 3:00 P.M. on that day (*Diaries*, 5:477).

1. The address from Harvard, dated 27 Oct. and signed by Joseph Willard, states that "It is with singular pleasure that we, the President and Fellows of Harvard University in Cambridge, embrace the opportunity, which your

most acceptable visit to this part of the country gives us of paying our respects to the first magistrate of the United States.

"It afforded us the highest satisfaction to find this large, and respectable nation unanimous in placing at the head of the new Government the firm and disinterested Patriot—the illustrious and intrepid Soldier, who, during her struggles in the cause of Liberty, braving every difficulty and danger in the field, under the smiles of a kind Providence, led her armies to victory and triumph and finally established her freedom and independence. Nor were we less gratified when we found that the Person, whose military skill and exertions had been so happily succeeded, actuated by the same spirit of Patriotism, did not decline the arduous and toilsome office, but, listening to the voice of his country, left the tranquil scenes of private life to secure those national blessings we were in the utmost danger of losing. We were fully persuaded that the Man who during so great a length of time, and in the most trying circumstances had been accepted by the multitude of his brethren, would in this new station, enjoy their entire confidence and enjoy their highest esteem: nor have we been disappointed.

"Permit us, Sir, to congratulate you on the happy establishment of the Government of the union, on the patriotism and wisdom which have marked its public transactions, and the very general approbation which the People have given to its measures. At the same time, Sir, being fully sensible that you are strongly impressed with the necessity of religion, virtue, and solid learning for supporting freedom and good government, and fixing the happiness of the People upon a firm and permanent basis we beg leave to recommend to your favorable notice the University entrusted to our care, which was early founded for promoting these important Ends. When you took the command of the troops of your country, you saw the university in a state of depression—its members dispersed—its literary treasures removed—and the Muses fled from the din of arms, then heard within its walls. Happily restored in the course of a few months, by your glorious successes, to its former privileges, and to a state of tranquillity, it received its returning members; and our youth have since pursued, without interruption, their literary courses, and fitted themselves for usefulness in Church and State. The public rooms, which you formerly saw empty, are now replenished with the necessary means of improving the human mind in literature and science; and every thing within the walls wears the aspect of Peace, so necessary to the cultivation of the useful arts. While we exert ourselves, in our corporate capacity, to promote the great objects of this Institution, we rest assured of your protection and patronage.

"We wish you, Sir, the aid and support of Heaven while you are discharging the duties of your most important station. May your success, in promoting the best interests of the Nation, be equal to your highest wishes! And after you shall have long rejoiced in the prosperity and glory of your country, may you receive the approbation of him who ruleth among the nations" (DLC:GW).

From Henry Knox

Sir   War Office Tuesday evening 27th October 1789

I have this moment received a letter from Mr Habersham at Savannah dated the 14th instant informing that he had received a letter from the Commissioners dated at Augusta the 5th instant, directing him to engage a passage for Captain Burbecks company to New York, which he had accordingly done with Captain Schemmerhorn who was to sail about the 20th instant.[1]

Mr Habersham adds "You will doubtless hear before you receive this, that they (the Commissioners) were disapointed with respect to a treaty with the Creek Indians."

I have not received any thing from the Commissioners. The Captain who brought the letter says McGillivray was affronted on his being asked whether he had powers to treat. A short time will bring the necessary explanations.[2] I have the honor to be sir with the highest respect Your Obedient humble Servant

H. Knox

ALS, DLC:GW; LB, DLC:GW.

1. John Habersham was collector for the port of Savannah. Capt. Henry Burbeck's company of artillery accompanied the commissioners to Georgia. See GW to the Commissioners to the Southern Indians, 29 Aug. 1789. For the negotiations of the commissioners, see David Humphreys to GW, 21, 26, 27 Sept., 13, 28 Oct. 1789, Alexander Hamilton to GW, 20 Oct. 1789, and Knox to GW, 18 Oct., 21, 27 Nov. 1789. See also GW's Memoranda on Indian Affairs, 1789.

2. On 28 Sept. the commissioners to the southern tribes wrote Knox: "We have the Mortification to inform you that the Parties have separated without forming a Treaty. The Terms which were offered by us at the commencement of the Negotiation were not agreeable to Mr. McGillevray; but neither would he come forward with written objections or propose any Conditions of his own. His verbal Communications were inadmissable upon the Spirit or Words of our Instructions.

"We shall have the honor of stating this Business very fully at a future day" (*DHFC*, 2:230).

Upon their return to New York, the commissioners sent Knox a lengthy account of their negotiations with McGillivray, dated 20 Nov. 1789, and a journal of their trip, dated 17 Nov. 1789 (ibid., 210–40). See also GW's Memoranda on Indian Affairs, 1789.

To the Massachusetts Legislature

Gentlemen,   [27 October 1789]

To communicate the peculiar pleasure which I derive from your affectionate welcome of me to the Commonwealth of Massachusetts, requires a force of expression beyond that which I possess.[1] I am truly grateful for your goodness towards me, and I desire to thank you with the unfeigned sincerity of a feeling heart.

Your obliging remembrance of my military services is among the highest compensations they can receive—and, if rectitude of intention may authorise the hope, the favorable anticipation, which you are pleased to express of my civil administration will not, I trust, be disappointed.

It is your happiness, Gentlemen, to preside in the councils of a Commonwealth, where the pride of independence is well assimilated with the duties of Society—and where the industry of the citizen gives the fullest assurance of public respect and private prosperity. I have observed too, with singular satisfaction, so becoming an attention to the militia of the State as presents the fairest prospect of support to the invaluable objects of national safety and peace. Long may these blessings be continued to the Commonwealth of Massachusetts! and may you, Gentlemen, in your individual capacities, experience every satisfaction, which can result from public honor and private happiness.

G: Washington

LB, DLC:GW.

1. On behalf of the Massachusetts legislature, John Hancock sent the following address, dated 27 Oct., to GW: "We meet you at this time with hearts replete with the warmest affection and esteem to express the high satisfaction we feel in your visit to the Commonwealth of Massachusetts.

"We can never forget the time when in the earliest stage of the war, and the day of *our* greatest calamity we saw you at the head of the army of the United States, commanding troops determined, though then undisciplined, by your wisdom and valor, preventing a sanguinary and well appointed army of our enemies from spreading devastation through our Country, and sooner than we had reason to expect, obliging them to abandon the Capital.

"We have since seen you in your high command, superior to the greatest fatigues and hardships successfully conducting our armies through a long war till our enemies were compelled to submit to terms of peace, and acknowledged that independence which the United States in Congress had before asserted and proclaimed.

"We now have the pleasure of seeing you in a still more exalted station to which you have been elected by the unanimous suffrages of a free, virtuous, and grateful country.

"From that attachment which you manifestly discovered while in your military command to the civil liberties of your country, we do assure ourselves that you will ever retain this great object in your view; and that your administration will be happy and prosperous.

"It is our earnest prayer that the divine benediction may attend you here and hereafter; and we do sincerely wish that you may through this life *continue* to enjoy that greatest of earthly blessings to be accepted by the multitude of your Brethren" (DLC:GW).

From Jacob Milligan

Charleston [S.C.] 27 Oct. 1789. "Mrs Milligan has taken the liberty to Send to Your Ladie a Preasent of A Baskett of the Fillagree Work of her Own Make which She begs Mrs Washington's Acceptence of."

ALS, DLC:GW.

Jacob Milligan was commissioned a third lieutenant on an armed South Carolina naval ship in 1775 and by December 1776 was serving on board a privateer (Clark, *Naval Documents*, 3:136, 7:467). He also served as harbormaster of Charleston and in 1793 as assistant to the federal marshal of South Carolina. His second wife, Mary Milligan, died in 1793.

From John Sullivan

Illustrious Sir   Portsmouth [N.H.] October 27th. 1789

having the happiness to be informed that your Excellencey intends honoring this State with a visit,[1] will you have the goodness to direct one of your aids to inform at what time you expect to leave Newbury, that your excellencey may be met at the Line and escorted to whatever Town you may think proper to honor with your presence; your Excellency may rely that although every Inhabitant of this State ardently wishes to pay you all the respect due to so exalted a Character yet being apprized of your Excellenceys wishes; every possible measure will be taken to prevent your being fatigued with such Acts of parade as will give pain to the great personage to whom they feel themselves so much indebted; & for whose person and virtues they have such a well gounded Love and veneration. I therefore hope that your Excellencey will not deny them the satisfaction of paying to the Deliverer of their Country such marks of respect as may give the Least pain and trouble to the man they delight to honor. I have the honor to be Sir with the highest respect and Esteem your Excellencys most obedient and very humble Servant

Jno. Sullivan

ALS, DLC:GW.

1. John Langdon, U.S. senator from New Hampshire, had also dispatched a messenger to GW on 23 Oct. with a note "asking the favor, that you will accept of my house during your tarry in this town" (DLC:GW).

From Sampson Brown

Sir   Wednesday morning, 8 oClock [28 October 1789]

Permit me with every sentiment of duty and submission to intrude the following lines, nothing doubting they will have a suitable effect upon the Guardian of Columbia, and the particular friend of Wounded Veterans.

From a train of accidents Sir, I have but the necessary written vouchers of my being an Invalid; and the original Officers to procure others from are uncomatable by me at present. which circumstances lays me under the disagreeable apprehension, "that I shall be deprived by that means of the benefit which will be the result of your late Orders for the benefit of the Corps of Invalids;" tho I have sufficient evidences present, Gentlemen of rank and Character, who can avouch for my transferr and Identity.

As I have formerly been employed about your person, I flatter myself you will recognize me at first view; which induces me to presume upon your verbal Orders, for which I most submissively attend your pleasure: and am with every sentiment of unfeigned respect and with my most ardent prayers for your present and future Happiness, Sir Your most Devoted Humble Servant

Sampson Brown

ALS, DLC:GW.

Sampson Brown is listed in the 1790 census as a resident of Boston (*Heads of Families* [Massachusetts], 190).

From David Humphreys

My dear General.   Petersburg [Va.] Octr 28th 1789

I am taking occasion by a water conveyance to inform you, that we are thus far on our way to New York. But my principal object is to mention the political intelligence which we obtained in North Carolina. The prevailing opinion in that State (so far as we could ascertain it from repeated enquiries) is, that the Constitution will be adopted. However, many of those who are opposed to it think otherwise.[1] I believe the information, most to be depended upon was given by Judge Williams of the Supreme Court (then sitting at Halifax) Mr Ireton of the Council, and Colo. Davie, viz., that the State is divided into ten Districts, that the members of seven of them taken collectively are equally divided for and against the adoption of the Constitution, and that the remaining three have a decided majority in favor of it. For example, Edenton District comprehends five Counties, & each County sends five members, who are said to be every one for the adoption. The other two reputed federal Counties are those beyond the Mountains.

I have taken considerable pains to learn how the persons appointed to offices in the several States are considered by their fellow Citizens; & am happy to assure you that the appointments in general have met with almost universal approbation. The selection of Characters to fill the great Departments has afforded entire satisfaction: particularly in the Judiciary. I heard it repeatedly said in Halifax, that the Supreme Court would be the first Court in the world in point of respectability. These things cannot but augur well.

We met your relation Colo. Washington, with his family, on their way to Charles Town.[2]

I will not intrude any longer on your time, than to assure you, that I am with the most unalterable & perfect friendship My dear General Your most obedient & very humble Servt

D. Humphreys

ALS, DLC:GW.

Humphreys was returning from his journey south with Cyrus Griffin and Benjamin Lincoln in an attempt to negotiate with the southern tribes. See David Humphreys to GW, 21, 26, 27 Sept., 13 Oct. 1789, Alexander Hamilton to GW, 20 Oct. 1789, and Henry Knox to GW, 18 Oct., 21, 27 Nov. 1789. See also GW's Memoranda on Indian Affairs, 1789.

1. North Carolina ratified the Constitution in November 1789.

2. William Washington (1752–1810), a cousin of GW, had served with distinction in the southern campaign until his capture at the battle of Eutaw Springs in September 1781. After the war he settled in Charleston, South Carolina.

From the Massachusetts Veterans

Boston October 28th 1789.

The Petition of a Number of Invalids, late belonging to the Massachusetts line, in said Army, Humbly Sheweth,

That although the Honble Congress of the United States have made Provision for the payment of Pensions Granted to Invalids of the said late Army,[1] Yet, the period, at which the payment of the first half Year is to be made, is so far distant, And as they have not Received any Pension money for Upwards of 3 Year past, And as a hard Winter is Approaching, Unless they can receive some present releif, they will Inevitably Suffer.

They therefore Humbly Pray Your Excellency, their late Worthy General, would be pleased to Commiserate their Unhappy Situation, and Grant them some immediate relief; without which they must still Suffer as they have hitherto. And as in duty bound shall ever Pray.

LS, DLC:GW. The petition is signed by Daniel Jennings, Benjamin Goold, William Spooner, Richard Witcom, John Hunewell, and Amarian Use. It was probably presented to GW while he was in Boston. The petition is addressed "To His Excellency George Washington Esqr. President of the United States, and late Commander of the American Army."

1. See "An Act providing for the payment of the Invalid Pensioners of the United States," 1 *Stat.* 95 (29 Sept. 1789). See also the Invalid Pensioners of Pennsylvania to GW, 1789.

To the Inhabitants of Salem

Gentlemen,   Salem [Mass.] October 29th 1789.

Would words express the feelings of my heart, I should have the happiness to demonstrate to my fellow-citizens of Salem, that their affectionate address is received with gratitude, and returned with sincerity.[1]

To your goodness I refer myself for a just construction of thoughts which language will not explain.

Honored by the high, yet hazardous, appointment which my Country has conferred upon me, it will be my best ambition to discharge its' important trusts with fidelity—for the rest I must cast myself upon her candor, and kind indulgence.

Towards you, Gentlemen, permit me to assure you, I entertain every disposition that is due to your virtue—and the promotion of your interests will be among the most grateful of my Employments. From your own industry and enterprize you have every thing to hope that deserving Men, and good citizens can expect.

May your Navigation and commerce flourish—your industry, in all its' applications, be rewarded—your happiness, here, be as perfect as belongs to the lot of humanity—and your eternal felicity be complete!

Go: Washington

LS, NNS; LB, DLC:GW.

GW left Boston about eight o'clock on the morning of 29 Oct., proceeding to Cambridge, "attended by the Vice President, Mr. Bowdoin, and a great number of Gentlemen." From Cambridge he passed through Mystic, Malden, Lynn, and Marblehead on his way to Salem. "At the Bridge, 2 Miles from this Town, we were also met by a Committee—who conducted us by a Brigade of the Militia, & one or two handsome Corps in Uniform, through several of the Streets to the Town or Court House—where an Ode in honor of the President was sung—an address presented to him amidst the acclamations of the People—after which he was conducted to his Lodgings" (*Diaries*, 5:481–83). On 23 Oct. the inhabitants of Salem, "anxious of paying every mark of attention to the President of the United States do by their Committee Messrs John Norris, Joshua Ward, James King, John Saunders Junr, Jona. Waldo John Hathorne & John Derby Junr most respectfully present their Compliments, & earnestly request The Honour of a Visit from him at an Entertainment which they have provided for the Occasion" (DLC:GW). On 29 Oct. the managers of the Salem assembly sent GW an invitation, this date, requesting "the honor of his company at Concert-Hall this eveng" (DLC:GW). In the evening "between

7 and 8 Oclock" GW attended the assembly, "where there were at least an hundred handsome and well dressed Ladies" (*Diaries*, 5:483).

1. The address reads: "The inhabitants of the Town of Salem, upon receiving a Visit from a personage the first Object of their esteem, cannot forbear expressing those Sensations which an Occasion so pleasing must naturally excite. While We view it as an high honour done us, a most obliging mark of Condescension & regard shewn us, in making us this Visit; most readily would We manifest the Satisfaction We feel, in being gratified with an Opportunity, of Seeing the Man, whose Deeds have been So illustrious; & of paying our particular respects to the Character, which not only the people of America, but all the World are agreed to admire, & Celebrate. How great Soever, Sir, We had Conceived our Obligations to be, & how Strong Soever the Motives of attachment we were under to you, for those Military Services, & Atchievements, from which Such essential benefits have been deriv'd; An Addition to those Obligations we are sensible is Now made; & Still further reasons of attachment Are presented, from your Acceptance of that important trust in our Newly instituted government, which was so earnestly, & universally desir'd. That remarkable Spirit of patriotism, of benevolence towards this people, which has been so Conspicuous in your past Conduct, We doubt not has determined you to this Arduous undertaking. Whatever therefore may Contribute to the ease, & happiness of your administration, whatever returns of respect, & dutiful Submission, it becomes a grateful people to make, We wish you to receive, & enjoy.

"Long may you be Continued, diffusing those blessings of freedom, & good government by which our prosperity shall be further promoted. Long may you be indulged a Series of the best Satisfactions, which the honours & enjoyments of this world can Afford & by that Almighty Being, whose agency & Aid you have ever Acknowledged, in those great events you have been improved to Accomplish, with distinguish'd honours, & felicities, May You finally be rewarded" (NNS). The address is signed by Benjamin Goodhue, John Treadwell, Nathan Goodale, John Fisk, and Jacob Ashton.

From the Vermont Legislature

Sir   [Westminister, Vt. 29 October 1789]
  The Governor, Council, and Representatives of the State of Vermont in General Assembly, convened.

  Considering the natural connexion of this State with the United States, and deeply impressed with a sense of your affection for your Country, and the eminent Services you have rendered the United States, by your Wisdom perseverance and fortitude so constantly displayed in the recovery and establishment of their Rights, embrace the earliest opportunity of congratulating you on your Appointment to the exalted station in which the Suffrages of a free people have placed you.

The Citizens of this State, though early and uniformly engaged in the late revolution, have had no voice in forming that Federal System, which not only promisses stability to the Government, but peace and Security to the United States, Yet we should do injustice to their feelings, should we omit to express their warmest Sentiments of friendship to the United States, and their general wish to participate in the benefits of that Government to which from their local situation they chearfully contribute a proportionable part of their property.

Be assured Sir, they feel the sincerest satisfaction in your appointment to the highest Station in the Federal Government, and wish you all that support and Assistance which may be necessary to the discharge of so important a trust, relying on the justice of the Government over which you preside, we presume those Obstacles which hitherto have prevented a Union of this State with the United States, will speedily be removed; and when we contemplate the disinterested principles which have always adorned your Character we cannot doubt your influence to hasten that happy period.

Permit us Sir, to close this address with the most fervent prayers, to Almighty God, for a continuance of his Blessings on your person and Family, and that under your Administration, America may long be continued a free and happy Nation.[1]

L, DNA: RG 59, Miscellaneous Letters.

Since the end of the American Revolution, Vermont, led by Ethan Allen, his brothers Ira and Levi, and their supporters, had pursued accord with the British government more assiduously than connections with the other American states. The Allen faction considered Vermont's ties with the province of Quebec a necessity to the state's economic survival and in the course of the decade secured important trade concessions from the Crown. Ethan Allen and his supporters set up the Republic of Vermont in 1778, but New York and New Hampshire, both engaged in land disputes with Vermont, and some large southern states opposed Vermont's entrance into the Union. Vermont sent no representatives to the Constitutional Convention in 1787 and was not admitted to the Union until 1791. Ethan Allen died in February 1789, but at the time this letter was written Levi Allen was in London negotiating with the British for closer political and economic ties. During the Confederation years, however, a coalition of opponents to the Allen–Thomas Chittenden faction had developed, consisting largely of conservative and nationalist merchants, lawyers, and former Revolutionary War officers, many of whom lived in the Connecticut Valley and in Vermont's southwestern region, within the commercial sphere of the United States. The leaders, most of whom supported the Federalist party after Vermont joined the Union, included Lewis R. Morris of the New York Morris family, Moses Robinson, Jacob Bayley, Isaac Tichenor, and Nathaniel Chipman. Although the Allen–Chittenden faction controlled Vermont politics for more than a decade—Chittenden was elected governor without interruption after 1778—a land scandal involving the group in 1789 so outraged Vermont voters that the control of the executive branch passed to the conservatives with Moses Robinson as governor. This letter to GW was a step in the direction of Vermont's settlement of its disputes with its neighbors and its admission to the Union.

1. At the bottom of this letter the following statement appears: "State of Vermont In General Assembly Westminster Octr 29. 17⟨89.⟩ Resolved that the foregoing Address be presented to his Excellency the President of the United States, by the Agents appointed to attend on Congress, and that the same be sent to the Governor & Council for Concurren⟨ce.⟩ Attest Lewis R. Morris Clerk[.] State of Vermont In Council Westminster October 29th 1789[.] Read & concurred. Attest Joseph Fay Secy." The letter from the Vermont legislature was sent to GW on 9 Feb. 1790 by the commissioners Isaac Tichenor, Stephen R. Bradley, and Elijah Paine (DNA: RG 59, Miscellaneous Letters).

From Catharine Sawbridge Macaulay Graham

Sir   Bracknal Berks [England] Octbr [30] 1789

It is now about a year and a half since I had the honor of receiving a letter from you dated Novbr. 16. 87. I do not pretend to make you any apology for not troubling you with an acknowledgment sooner, tho I rather think it necessary to make one for troubling you in the important station you now fill, with my congratulations on the event, which placed you at the head of the American government. But it is not you Sir, that I consider as benefited by the unanimous election of the Americans; yr philosophic turn of mind would have lead you to the completion of human happiness in a private station; but the Americans in their judicious choice, have I flatter my self, secured to themselves the full and permanent enjoyment of that liberty for which they are indebted to yr persevering valor in the first instance. Yr wisdom and virtue will undoubtedly enable you to check the progress of every opinion inimical to those rights, which, you have so bravely and fortunately asserted; and for which many of yr Country men have paid so dear: and you will be a bright example to future presidents of an integrity rarely to be met with in the first stations of life.

All the friends of freedom on this side the Atlantic are now rejoicing for an event which in all probability has been accelerated by the American revolution. You not only possess yrselves the first of human blessings but you have been the means of raising that spirit in Europe, which I sincerely hope, will in a short time extinguish every remainr of that barbarous servitude under which all the European Nations in a less or a greater degree, have so long been Subject.

The French have justified the nobleness of their original character, and from the immerssions of Luxury and frivolity, have set an example that is Unique in all the histories of human society. A populous nation effecting by the firmness of their union, the Universality of their sentiments; and the energy of their actions; the intire overthrow of a Despotism that had stood the test of ages. We are full of wonder in this part of the world, and cannot conceive how such things should be.

Yr Friend and Eleve the Merquis de la Fayette has acted a part in this revolution which has raised him above his former exploits; because his conduct has been directed to the good of his distressed country men and shews him far above those base and narrow selfishnesses with which particular privileges are so apt to taint the human mind.

I have heard that a Mons: Brissot de Warville has lately become a citizen of America; he is a warm friend to liberty and a man of the first rate abilities. He is a great friend of mine and as I presume he has been presented to yr Excelency; will take the liberty which yr known goodness inspires to beg that you would remember me to him and to assure him of my wishes for his happiness and prosperity.[1]

Mr Graham joins me in best respects to yr self and Mrs Washington. We contemplate with no small pleasure the advantage America will reap from that check to all the luxuries of dress which her example of an elegant simplicity in this article will undoubtedly effect. I am Sir Yr Excellencies Most Obednt And Obliged Humbe Servt

Cath: Macaulay Graham

ALS, DLC:GW.

Catharine Sawbridge Macaulay Graham (1731–1791), with whom GW had carried on a cordial correspondence since her visit to Mount Vernon in June 1785, was prominent in British literary and philanthropic circles. Between 1763 and 1783 she had produced in eight volumes a well-received *History of England from the Accession of James I to That of the Brunswick Line*. See also *Diaries*, 4:148; Richard Henry Lee to GW, 3 May 1785, n.3.

1. See William Duer to GW, 4 Nov. 1788, n.1.

To the Citizens of Newburyport

Gentlemen,   [30 October 1789]

The demonstrations of respect and affection which you are pleased to pay to an individual, whose highest pretension is to rank as your fellow-citizen, are of a nature too distinguished not to claim the warmest return that gratitude can make.[1]

My endeavors to be useful to my country have been no more than the result of conscious duty—Regards like yours would reward services of the highest estimation and sacrifice: Yet it is due to my feelings, that I should tell you those regards are received with esteem, and replied to with sincerity.

In visiting the Town of Newburyport, I have obeyed a favorite inclination, and I am much gratified by the indulgence. In expressing a sincere wish for its prosperity, and the happiness of its inhabitants, I do justice to my own sentiments, and their merit.

G: Washington.

LB, DLC:GW.

Leaving Salem "A Little after 8 Oclock" on the morning of 30 Oct., GW and his party passed through Beverly, stopping to view the Beverly Cotton Manufactory, continued to Ipswich, and arrived in Newburyport about 4 o'clock in the afternoon (*Diaries*, 5:485–86).

1. The address of the citizens of Newburyport reads: "When by the unanimous suffrages of your countrymen, you were called to preside over their public councils, the citizens of the Town of Newbury-Port participated in the general joy that arose from anticipating an administration conducted by the Man, to whose wisdom and valour they owed their liberties.

"Pleasing were their reflections that he, who by the blessing of Heaven, had given them their independence, would again relinquish the felicities of domestic retirement to teach them its just value.

"They have seen you, victorious, leave the field, followed with the applauses of a grateful country, and they now see you entwining the olive with the laurel, and, in peace giving security and happiness to a People, whom, in war, you covered with glory.

"At the present moment they indulge themselves in sentiments of joy, resulting from a principle, perhaps less elevated, but exceedingly dear to their hearts; from a gratification of their affection in beholding personally among them, the friend, the benefactor, and the father of their Country.

"They cannot hope, Sir, to exhibit any peculiar marks of attachment to your person, for could they express their feelings of gratitude, the most ardent and sincere, they would only repeat the sentiments, which are deeply impressed upon the hearts of all their fellow-citizens: But in justice to themselves, they beg leave to assure you, that in no part of the United States are those sentiments of gratitude and affection more cordial and animated than in the Town, which at this time is honored with your presence.

"Long, Sir, may you continue the Ornament, and support of these States, and may the period be late, when you shall be called to receive a reward, adequate to your virtues, which it is not in the power of your country to bestow" (DLC:GW). A note at the bottom of this document, attested by Mr. Hodge, town clerk of Newburyport, indicates that Benjamin Greenleaf, Jonathan Jackson, Edward Wigglesworth, and Micajah Sawyer were appointed a committee to present the address to GW.

From John C. Ogden

Sir   Portsmouth [N.H.] October 30th/89

Overwhelmed as Your Excellency is, by the Invitations and Solicitations of our grateful and virtuous Countrymen, who wish to pay every tribute of veneration, and give every possible proof of their Affection for your Person, and Reverence for the high office, which you have condescended, to accept for the public good; I would spare you the trouble of this, and in silence rejoice at our being favored with your visit to this quarter, and at a distance recognize the man who possesses the Love and Applause of a World.

But, My Family is composed of Madam Wooster the Lady of the late General Wooster, the father of Mrs Ogden.

I have with me also, my own Parent, the Mother of two amiable young men who lost their lives during the late revolution; who with me were Brothers to Mrs Barber, The Relict of your much valued Officer Colol Barber.[1] May I ask your Excellency kindly to condescend, to give us such part of your time while here; as shall be most convenient, and appointed by yourself. Or may I mention, our having your company at tea on Sunday afternoon.

If this is agreable to Your Excellency⟨,⟩ President Sullivan, has promised to attend you to The Parsonage.

Come My Dear Sir, and do me this greatest of favors—and give pleasure to a family bereaved of their most valued friends; and joy to two venerable women, whose fortitude under sufferings, does credit to American Matrons, as well as to human nature. I have the honor and happiness to be, with the greatest respect, Your Excellency's most obedient and most humble servant

John C. Ogden
Rector of Queens Chapel

ALS, DNA:PCC, item 78.

John Cosens (Cousins) Ogden (1751–1800), a 1770 Princeton graduate, lived in New Haven until 1786 when he was ordained a priest in the Episcopal church by Samuel Seabury. From 1786 until his retirement in 1793 upon "his mind becoming deranged," he was rector of St. John's Episcopal Church in Portsmouth (Alexander, *Princeton College*, 136). In 1800 he published *A Excursion into Bethlehem & Nazaraeth, in Pennsylvania in the Year 1799; With a . . . History of the Society of the United Brethren* (Philadelphia, 1800).

GW had left Newburyport shortly after eight o'clock on the morning of 31 Oct. and, reaching the line dividing Massachusetts and New Hampshire, "was recd. by the President of the State of New Hampshire—the Vice-President; some of the Council—Messrs. Langdon & Wingate of the Senate—Colo. Parker Marshall of the State, & many other respectable characters; besides several Troops of well cloathed Horse in handsome Uniforms, and many Officers of the Militia. . . . With this Cavalcade we proceeded and arrived before 3 Oclock at Portsmouth" (*Diaries*, 5:486–87). GW apparently declined Ogden's offer of tea, but on 1 Nov. "Attended by the President of the State (Genl. Sullivan) Mr. Langdon, & the Marshall [John Parker]; I went in the fore Noon to the Episcopal Church under the incumbency of a Mr. Ogden" (ibid., 488).

1. Ogden's mother-in-law was Mary Wooster, the daughter of Thomas Clap, a president of Yale College, and the widow of David Wooster, one of the Continental army's less competent general officers, who was killed in action in 1777. Ogden's sister Anne was the widow of Col. Francis Barber (1751–1783), and his mother was the widow of Moses Ogden.

Letter not found: from Piomingo, 30 Oct. 1789. In a letter to Henry Knox, 18 Nov. 1789, Tobias Lear stated that GW had received a letter "from Piamingo or the Mountain Leader, a Chickasaw Chief, requesting a supply of powder & ball for his Nation—dated Richmond October 30th 1789."[1] In his Memoranda on Indian Affairs, 1789,

printed below, GW describes this letter as follows: "From—Piamingo—Richmond 30th Octr Mentions the long friendship which
has subsisted between the United States & his Nation, the Chicasaws.
the distressed situation it is in for want of Ammunition. His having
set out on a journey for the Seat of Federal Governmt to solicit a
supply—But the delays he had met with and the temporary aid he
had obtained from the State of Virga had determined him to return,
least his people might be distressed—2000 lbs. of powder & Lead
equivalent having been furnished him. The Creek Indians attack his
people as well as ours; but he wishes not to fight with them if they will
make satisfaction & give assurances of good behaviour in future;
however, he requests & entreats that they may be furnished with powder & Ball against the Spring, as then the War must become general
with the Creeks, unless they will listen to reason. *Their* Nation he says
depends upon the U. States—The Choctaws seem friendly, & will be
consulted by him on his return. Refers to Genl Lincoln & the Commrs
whom he saw at Richmond—gives strong assurances that he will hold
me by the right hand of friendship; and requests in strong terms that
I will speedily send a letter to him expressive of what he may depend
upon."

Piomingo or Mountain Leader was a Chickasaw war chief whose friendship
for the United States dated back to the early 1780s when he was instrumental
in negotiating a treaty of friendship between Virginia and the Chickasaw at
French Lick (Nashville). In 1786 he was one of the Chickasaw chiefs who
signed the Treaty of Hopewell with the Confederation government. Although
he was not always pleased with the progress of United States–Chickasaw relations (see his speech to Joseph Martin, 17 Feb. 1787, in Williams, *Lost State of
Franklin*, 142), Piomingo remained friendly to the United States. In the late
winter of 1789 the Washington administration was counting on his support in
establishing the new post at Muscle Shoals. See GW to the Chiefs of the Choctaw Nation, 17 Dec. 1789, source note.

1. DLC:GW.

From John Sullivan

Much respected Sir   Durham [N.H.] October 30th 1789
As your Excellency is about to visit the Metropolis of this
State, and as I have no House in that Town, will your Excel-
lencey have the goodness to indulge me with the honor of your
company with your Suite to a family Dinner at my House in
Durham on Wednesday next—Your Excellencey will please to

excuse my a⟨sking⟩ the favor at so late a Day; and indeed my ⟨*mutilated*⟩ inclination led me to petition for it, on your ⟨*mutilated*⟩ arrival: But it was considered that you wou⟨ld⟩ be much fatigued on Saturday; that on Sunday you did not incline to dine in public; That on monday you might incline to visit The Town Harbor &ca and the Honorable Mr Langdon who Lives in Town informed me that for these Reasons he meant to solicit the honor of your Excellencys company on that Day; On Tuesday the Executive of The State mean to entrat the favor; and wednesday being the first day that I can consisten[t]ly I must beg leave to put in my claim & petition for the gratification the grant of which will exceedingly oblidge him who has the honor to be with the most exalted Esteem and respect your Excellenceys most obedient and devoted Servant

Jno. Sullivan

ALS, DLC:GW.
    GW left Portsmouth early on Wednesday, 4 Nov., and did not accept Sullivan's invitation. He did, however, call on the president on Tuesday, 3 November. For GW's activities during his stay in Portsmouth, see *Diaries*, 5:487–91).

Letter not found: from Edward Rutledge, 31 Oct. 1789. On 23 Nov. GW wrote to Rutledge: "I have been favoured with your letter of the 31st ultimo."

To the Synod of the Dutch Reformed Church in North America

Gentlemen, [October 1789]
    I receive with a grateful heart your pious and affectionate address,[1] and with truth declare to you that no circumstance of my life has affected me more sensibly or produced more pleasing emotions than the friendly congratulations, and strong assurances of support which I have received from my fellow-citizens of all descriptions upon my election to the Presidency of these United States.
    I fear, Gentlemen, your goodness has led you to form too exalted an opinion of my virtues and merits—If such talents as I possess have been called into action by great events, and those

events have terminated happily for our country, the glory should be ascribed to the manifest interposition of an over-ruling Providence. My military services have been abundantly recompensed by the flattering approbation of a grateful people; and, if a faithful discharge of my civil duties can ensure a like reward, I shall feel myself richly compensated for any personal sacrifice I may have made by engaging again in public life.

The Citizens of the United States of America have given as signal a proof of their wisdom and virtue in framing and adopting a constitution of government, without bloodshed or the intervention of force, as they, upon a former occasion, exhibited to the world of their valor, fortitude, and perseverance; and it must be a pleasing circumstance to every friend of good order and social happiness to find that our new government is gaining strength and respectability among the citizens of this country in proportion as it's operations are known, and its effects felt.

You, Gentlemen, act the part of pious Christians and good citizens by your prayers and exertions to preserve that harmony and good will towards men which must be the basis of every political establishment; and I readily join with you that "*while* just government protects all in their religious rights, true religion affords to government its surest support."

I am deeply impressed with your good wishes for my present and future happiness—and I beseech the Almighty to take you and yours under his special care.

G. Washington.

LB, DLC:GW.

1. The address, dated 9 Oct. and signed by eight members of the synod, reads: "The Synod of the reformed Dutch Church in North America embrace the occasion of their annual session, being the first since your appointment to present you their sincere congratulations, and to join in that great and general joy testified by all descriptions of Citizens on your acceptance of the highest office in the Nation.

"We cannot forbear expressing our gratitude to God for preserving your valuable life amidst so many dangers till this time; for inspiring you with a large portion of the martial spirit, and forming you also for the milder and more agreeable arts of government and peace; for endowing you with great virtues and calling them into exercise by great events; for distinguishing you with honors and giving remarkable prudence and moderation—And for making your extraordinary talents the more conspicuous, useful, and durable, by superinducing the noble ornament of humility. Your Country has with one voice attested your excellence by inviting you again to public life, and you have confirmed it's judgement by returning to fresh scenes and toils after you had retired to the shade from the burden and heat of a long day.

"Among the many signal interpositions of divine providence we remark the late important change in the general government—a change neither effected by accident, nor imposed by force, but adopted in the bosom of peace after a free and mature deliberation; and in which a people widely extended and various in their habits are united beyond the most raised expectation. In these respects the United States of America stand single among all the nations of the earth. Other revolutions may have been more dignified and splendid, but none more honorable to human nature, and none so likely to produce such happy effects. This Government being now completely organised, and all its departments filled, we trust that God will give wisdom to its councils, and justice to its administration, and that we shall at length realise those blessings, which animated our hopes through a difficult and ruinous war.

"To our constant prayers for the welfare of our country, and of the whole human race, we shall esteem it our duty and happiness to unite our most earnest endeavors to promote the pure and undefiled religion of Christ; for as this secures eternal felicity to men in a future State, so we are persuaded that good Christians will always be good citizens, and that where righteousness prevails among individuals the Nation will be great and happy. Thus while just government protects all in their religious rights, true religion affords to government its surest support.

"We implore the Lord God to be your Sun and Shield. May your administration be prosperous. May the blessings of millions come upon you, and your name be grateful to all Posterity. Above all, may you finish your course with joy, be numbered among the Redeemed of the Lord, and enter into everlasting rest" (DLC:GW).

To the Society of Quakers

Gentlemen,   [October 1789]
I receive with pleasure your affectionate address, and thank you for the friendly Sentiments & good wishes which you express for the Success of my administration, and for my personal Happiness.[1]
We have Reason to rejoice in the prospect that the present National Government, which by the favor of Divine Providence, was formed by the common Counsels, and peaceably established with the common consent of the People, will prove a blessing to

every denomination of them. To render it such, my best endeavours shall not be wanting.

Government being, among other purposes, instituted to protect the Persons and Consciences of men from oppression, it certainly is the duty of Rulers, not only to abstain from it themselves, but according to their Stations, to prevent it in others.

The liberty enjoyed by the People of these States, of worshipping Almighty God agreable to their Consciences, is not only among the choicest of their *Blessings*, but also of their *Rights*—While men perform their social Duties faithfully, they do all that Society or the State can with propriety demand or expect; and remain responsible only to their Maker for the Religion or modes of faith which they may prefer or profess.

Your principles & conduct are well known to me—and it is doing the People called Quakers no more than Justice to say, that (except their declining to share with others the burthen of the common defence) there is no Denomination among us who are more exemplary and useful Citizens.

I assure you very explicitly that in my opinion the Consciencious scruples of all men should be treated with great delicacy & tenderness, and it is my wish and desire that the Laws may always be as extensively accomodated to them, as a due regard to the Protection and essential Interests of the Nation may Justify, and permit.

Go: Washington

ALS, PHC: Quaker Collection; LB, DLC:GW; copy, Berkshire Record Office, Shire Hall, Reading, England; copy, NHpR: Collection of Naval and Marine Manuscripts. GW headed this address: "The answer of the President of the United States to the Address of the Religious Society called Quakers, from their yearly Meeting for Pennsylvania, New Jersey, Delaware, and the Western parts of Maryland and Virginia."

1. The address of "the Religious Society called Quakers, from their Yearly Meeting for Pennsylvania, New-Jersey, and the western Parts of Virginia and Maryland," held in Philadelphia, 28 Sept.–3 Oct. 1789, reads: "Being met in this our Annual Assembly for the well-ordering the Affairs of our Religious Society, and the Promotion of universal Righteousness, our Minds have been drawn to consider that the Almighty, who ruleth in Heaven and in the Kingdoms of Men having permitted a great Revolution to take place in the Government of this Country, we are fervently concerned that the Rulers of the People may be favered with the Counsel of God, the only sure Means of enabling them to fulfill the important Trust committed to their Charge, and in an

especial manner that Divine Wisdom and Grace vouched from above, may qualify thee to fill up the Duties of the exalted Station, to which thou art appointed.

"We are sensible thou hast obtained great Place in the Esteem and Affe[c]tions of People of all Denominations, over whom thou presidest; and many eminent Talents being committed to thy Trust, we much desire they may be fully devoted to the Lord's Honour and Service, that thus thou mayest be an happy Instrument in his Hand, for the Suppression of Vice, Infidelity and Irreligion, and every Species of Oppression on the Persons and Consciences of Men, so that Righteousness and Peace, which truly exalt a Nation, may prevail throughout the Land as the only solid Foundation that can be laid for the Prosperity and Happiness of this or any Country.

"The free Toleration which the Citizens of these States enjoy in the publick Worship of the Almighty, agreable to the Dictates of their Consciences, we esteem among the holiest of Blessings; and as we desire to be filled with fervent Charity for those who differ from us in Faith and Practice, believing that the general Assembly of Saints is composed of the sincere and upright hearted of all Nations, Kingdoms and People; so we trust we may justly claim it from others, and in a full Persuasion that the Divine Principle we profess, leads into Harmony and Concord, we can take no part in carrying on War on any Occasion, or under any Power, but are bound in Conscience to lead quiet and peaceable Lives in Godliness and Honesty amongst Men, contributing freely our Proportion to the Indigences of the poor and to the necessary Support of civil Government, acknowledging those 'who rule well to be worthy of double Honour,' and if any professing with us, are, or have been ⟨of a con⟩trary Disposition and Conduct, we own them not therein, having never been chargeable from our first Establishment as a Religious Society, with fomenting or countenancing Tumults or Conspiracies or Disrespect to those who are placed in Authority over us.

"We wish not improperly to intrude on thy Time or Patience, nor is it our Practice to offer Adulation to any; but as we are a People whose Principles and Conduct have been misrepresented and traduced, we take the Liberty to assure thee, that we feel our Hearts affectionately drawn towards thee, and those in Authority over us, with Prayers that thy Presidency may, under the Blessing of Heaven, be happy to thyself and to the People; that through the encrease of Morality and true Religion, Divine Providence may condescend to look down upon our Land with a propitious Eye and bless the Inhabitants with a Continuance of Peace, the Dew of Heaven, and the Fatness of the Earth, and enable us gratefully to acknowledge his manifold Mercies. And it is our earnest Concern, that he may be pleased to grant thee every necessary Qualification to fill thy weighty and important Station to his Glory; and that finally, when all terrestial Honours shall fail and pass away, thou and thy respectable Consort may be found worthy to receive a Crown of unfading Righteousness in the Mansions of Peace and Joy for ever" (NHpR). The address is signed by Nicholas Waln, clerk of the assembly.

A second address from the assembly, also signed by Nicholas Waln, was addressed to GW, the Senate, and the House of Representatives: "Firmly believing that unfeigned righteousness in public as well as private stations is the only sure ground of hope for the divine blessing, whence alone rulers can derive true honour, establish sincere confidence in the hearts of the people, and feeling their minds animated with the ennobling principle of universal good-will to men, find a conscious dignity and felicity in the harmony and success attending the exercise of a solid uniform virtue; short of which the warmest pretensions to public spirit, zeal for our country, and the rights of men, are fallacious and illusive.

"Under this persuasion as professors of faith in that ever blessed all perfect Lawgiver, whose injunction remains of undiminished obligation on all who profess to believe in him; 'whatsoever ye would that men should do unto you, do ye even so unto them,' we apprehend ourselves religiously bound to request your serious christian attention to the deeply interesting subject whereon our religious society in their annual assembly in the Tenth month 1783, addressed the then Congress, who, though the christian rectitude of the concern, was by the Delegates generally acknowledged, yet, not being vested with the powers of legislation, they declined promoting any public remedy against the gross national iniquity of trafficking in the persons of fellow-men; but divers of the legislative bodies of the different states on this continent, have since manifested their sense of the public detestation due to the licentious wickedness of the African trade for slaves, and the inhuman tyranny and blood guiltiness inseparable from it; the debasing influence whereof most certainly tends to lay waste the virtue, and of course the happiness of the people.

"Many [of] the enormities abhorrent to common humanity [in] this abominable commerce, are practised in some of these united states; which we judge it not needful to particularize to a body of men chosen as eminently distinguishable for wisdom and extensive information; but we find it indispensably incumbent on us as a religious body, assuredly believing that both the true temporal interest of nations, and eternal well being of individuals depend on doing justly, loving mercy, and walking humbly before God, the creator, preserver, and benefactor of men, thus to attempt to excite your attention to the affecting subject, earnestly desiring that the infinite Father of Spirits may so enrich your minds with his Love and Truth, and so influence your understanding by that pure wisdom which is full of mercy and good fruits, as that a sincere and impartial enquiry may take place, whether it be not an essential part of the duty of your exalted station, to exert upright endeavours to the full extent of your power, to remove every obstruction to public righteousness, which the influence and artifice of particular persons, governed by the narrow mistaken views of self interest has occasioned; and whether notwithstanding such seeming impediment, it be not in reality within your power to exercise Justice and Mercy; which if adhered to, we cannot doubt, must produce the Abolition of the Slave Trade.

"We consider this subject so essentially and extensively important, as to warrant a hope that the liberty we now take will be understood, as it really is, a compliance with a sense of religious duty; and that your christian endeavours to remove reproach from the land, may be efficacious to sweeten the labour and lessen the difficulties incident to the discharge of your important Trust" (DNA: RG 46, First Congress, Petition and Memorials, Resolutions of State Legislatures, and Related Documents).

From the Citizens of Haverhill, Mass.

Haverhill Novr 1st 1789

The Inhabitants of the Town of Haverhill address their most sincere Respects to the President of the United States & assure him, that they should esteem themselves highly honoured in his passing thro' this Town in his Route to New York and of giving them an Opportunity of testifying to him the Respect due to so distinguished a Character.

D, DLC:GW.

For background to GW's tour of the eastern states, see his letter to Betty Lewis, 12 Oct. 1789, n.3.

GW and his party arrived in Haverhill on Wednesday, 4 Nov., about two-thirty in the afternoon and spent the night at Harrod's Tavern. During the day GW visited the Sailcloth Manufactory at Haverhill. "The Inhabitts. of this small Village were well disposed to welcome me to it by every demonstration which could evince their joy" (*Diaries*, 5:491–92).

From Francis Willis, Jr.

gloster [Va.]

May it please your Excellency   Novr 1st 1789

At the request of Colo. Henry I again trouble you on the subject of the Negroes he bought[1]—he apprehends I did not state the situation of the Idiot he bought, as he could wish therefore inclosed you will please to receive his letter to me,[2] & if you will please to honour me with your opinion on the matter I will instantanously proceed agreeable to it I am Sr yr Most Obedt hbl. Sert

Francis Willis Jr.

ALS, DLC:GW.

1. See Willis to GW, 24 Sept. 1788.

2. Willis enclosed a copy of a letter written to him by Col. James Henry on 16 April 1789: "I observe by Mr Whiting's Letter of the 27th of October last, that he had applied to General Washington on the Subject of the doubtful Title of those negroes I purchased from you & Mr Perrin, and that the General was of Opinion my Claim to a deduction, *under the Circumstances of the Sale*, was unjust; but he Suggests that if I still think the bargain a hard one, the negroes may be returned.

"I am very desirous this matter may be finally settled in my day and while you & Mr Perrin are both alive, because I assure my Self that so far as it rests with you, we can discuss the subject in the easiest way.

"If you will ⟨please—⟩ to have recourse to my letter to you in May 1787. Soon after the last Payment made to Mr Dobson, I made three propositions; to return the wench with as many Children in number and Value as I received, and to admit interest to be counted on the purchase money, up to the times of Payment—or, to return the Boy in question, upon your deducting out of the whole purchase money, what I was by our bargain to give for him, notwithstanding I have paid 4 years taxes on him, or lastly, if neither of these propositions should be agreeable, that the Boy should be valued by persons mutually chosen for the purpose, & their Valuation to finish the business.

"But as it seems now to turn out that the Title to these Negroes is vested in General Washington, and his Concurrence, & approbation thereby become necessary, I can only again assure you I am still willing to have it settled in any of these ways which may be preferred.

"If therefore you, Sir, will take the trouble to write again to the General; inform him of the proposals I have made, or inclose him my letter, I cannot but suppose, he will authorize you to put it in a way of final adjustment, by one or other of the methods proper and the sooner this is done, the more agreeable it will be to Sir, Your very humble servt" (DLC:GW).

To the Citizens of Marblehead

Gentlemen,   [2 November 1789]
The reception with which you have been pleased to honor my arrival in Marblehead, and the sentiments of approbation and attachment which you have expressed of my conduct, and to my person, are too flattering and grateful not to be acknowledged with sincere thanks, and answered with unfeigned wishes for your prosperity.[1]

Avoiding to dwell on the diminution of pleasure, which the mention of your impaired circumstances occasions me, I desire to engage your thoughts on the pleasing prospect presented to all our interests, and particularly to our fishery, in the efficiency of our government and the invigorated industry of our citizens.

Protected in the exercise of those means, which the beneficent Parent of mankind has furnished for their sustenance and comfort, the Citizens of America, animated by virtuous enterprize, and actuated by due obedience to the laws and regulations of their government, may expect with confidence, to enjoy every blessing which industry can promise, and national union may ensure.

Your attachment to the Constitution of the United States is worthy of men, who fought and bled for freedom, and who know its value.

Your anxiety for my health, and your prayers for my happiness are replied to with solicitude for your welfare, and an earnest entreaty to the Author of good for your felicity.

G. Washington.

LB, DLC:GW.

For the background to GW's tour of the eastern states, see his letter to Betty Lewis, 12 Oct. 1789, n.3.

GW had stopped briefly in Marblehead, "which is 4 Miles out of the way, but I wanted to see it," on 29 Oct. on his way to Salem. For GW's description of the town and its hospitality, see *Diaries*, 5:483–84.

1. During his stay in Marblehead, the citizens presented GW with the following address, dated 29 Oct.: "Your presence has inspired the inhabitants of the Town of Marblehead with the most unbounded joy: But they cannot express, as they would wish their grateful sense of the honor done them on this occasion.

"The too visible decay and poverty of this Town must be their excuse, that they have not offered to the illustrious character, who now visits them a reception more becoming his dignity, and more expressive of their own veneration.

"The blessings of Independence and a republican Government must ever excite our gratitude and affection to so eminent a Supporter of the public liberty, whose wisdom and valour have so successfully defended the rights of his country. The establishment by the United States of a secure and efficient government gives us the pleasing expectation of the gradual revival of our Fishery and commerce, objects of the industry and principle means of the subsistence of the Inhabitants of this place for above a century previous to the late Revolution.

"In the commencement of the contest with Great Britain, this Town was early in their exertions in the common-cause, and were not discouraged when

they foresaw that reverse of their situation which the war necessarily produced. The return of Peace did not restore to us the former advantages of the
fishery, which hath remained under peculiar discouragements; and we have
yet patiently to expect that attention of the General-Government, which may
remedy these evils, and which the subject may deserve from its extensive importance to the commerce of the United States.

"The present Government of the United States commands our most ready
submission and inviolable attachment and we deem it a peculiar felicity, that
the highest dignity of that Government is so properly vested in you, in whom
all America repose the most entire confidence—in whose administration the
world will admire the example of a Patriot-Ruler.

"Sir, Our anxiety for your health and long life is proportionate to our most
ardent wishes for the prosperity of our country; and we are well assured that
you will ever partake in the happiness of that numerous people over whom
you preside. May the Divine Providence continue to favour your care and
guidance of their most important public affairs, and reward your virtues,
which have shone forth such virtues to Mankind" (DLC:GW). The address is
signed by the selectmen of Marblehead.

To the Citizens of Portsmouth

Gentlemen,   [2 November 1789]
I am sensibly impressed with your friendly welcome to the
Metropolis of New Hampshire, and have a grateful heart for
your kind and flattering congratulations on my election to the
Presidency of these United States.[1]

I fear the fond partiality of my countrymen has too highly
appreciated my past exertions, and formed too sanguine anticipations of my future services—If the former have been successful, much of the success should be ascribed to those who
laboured with me in the common cause—and the glory of the
event, should be given to the great Disposer of events.

If an unremitting attention to the duties of my office, and the
zeal of an honest heart can promote the public-good, my fellow-
citizens may be assured that these will not be wanting in my
present station.

I can claim no particular merit, Gentlemen, for the preservation of your town from the devastation of the enemy. I am
happy if by any event of the war your property has been preserved from that destruction, which fell but too heavily on your
neighbours—and I sincerely condole with you for the loss which
you sustained in navigation and commerce: But I trust that

industry and oeconomy, those fruitful and never failing sources of private and public opulence, will, under our present system of government, restore you to your former flourishing state.

The interest which you take in my personal happiness, and the kind felicitations which you have expressed on the recovery of my health, are peculiarly grateful to me; and I earnestly pray that the great Ruler of the Universe may smile upon your honest exertions here, and reward your welldoings with future happiness.

G. Washington

LB, DLC:GW.

For background to GW's tour of the eastern states, see GW to Betty Lewis, 12 Oct. 1789, n.3, and John C. Ogden to GW, 30 Oct. 1789, source note.

1. The address from the citizens of Portsmouth, 2 Nov. 1789, was signed by John Pickering and reads: "Sensible of the honor done them by this visit from Your Excellency, the Inhabitants of Portsmouth improve this first opportunity of bidding you welcome to New Hampshire: and beg leave to mingle their warmest congratulations with those of their Brethren throughout the Union, upon your election to the high and important office of President of the United States.

"We attempt not to recount the number, variety, and merit, of your important services to our common country—these are already written in indelible characters on the heart of every true American, which the faithful page of history will transmit to generations yet unborn: But to express our gratitude to him, who with a magnanimity peculiar to himself, under the smile of Heaven, defended the rights, and gave birth to the empire of America.

"Permit us to add the grateful sense we entertain of our high obligations to you, Sir, as a Town, for our security from that devastation, which was the fate of many other sea-port Towns in the Union, and would probably have been ours, had not the enemy, by your wise and spirited exertions, been drawn from the capital of a neighbouring State, and compelled to seek an Asylum, for a while, within their own dominions.

"Our happy escape from this calamity, while it demands our devout ascriptions of praise to the Great Ruler of all events, consoles us under the many heavy losses we have sustained in our navigation and commerce during the war—the distressing effects of which we still but too sensibly feel.

"It is with pleasing emotions we recognize the dispensations of divine providence towards the United-States in placing the Deliverer of his country at the head of the General Government by the unanimous suffrages of a free and grateful people, at a crisis when none but the Man who has long enjoyed, and richly merited the confidence of America, and the plaudits of an enlightened world, could be found equal to the arduous task.

"We felicitate you and these States on your speedy recovery from your late sickness, and ardently wish your life may be continued a blessing to yourself, and your country; and that, at some far distant period, full of years and the most benevolent and glorious atchievements, embalmed with the tears of grateful millions, you may be called to inherit an incorruptible crown in the realms of glory" (DLC:GW).

To the Presbyterian Ministers of Massachusetts and New Hampshire

Gentlemen,   [Portsmouth, N.H., 2 November 1789]

The affectionate welcome, which you are pleased to give me to the eastern parts of the union, would leave me without excuse, did I fail to acknowledge the sensibility, which it awakens, and to express the most sincere return that a grateful sense of your goodness can suggest.

To be approved by the praise-worthy is a wish as natural to becoming ambition, as its consequence is flattering to our self-love—I am, indeed, much indebted to the favorable sentiments which you entertain towards me, and it will be my study to deserve them.[1]

The tribute of thanksgiving which you offer to "the gracious Father of lights" for his inspiration of our public-councils with wisdom and firmness to complete the national constitution, is worthy of men, who, devoted to the pious purposes of religion, desire their accomplishment by such means as advance the temporal happiness of their fellow-men—and, here, I am per-suaded, you will permit me to observe that the path of true piety is so plain as to require but little political direction. To this consideration we ought to ascribe the absence of any regulation, respecting religion, from the Magna-Charta of our country.

To the guidance of the ministers of the gospel this important object is, perhaps, more properly committed—It will be your care to instruct the ignorant, and to reclaim the devious—and, in the progress of morality and science, to which our govern-ment will give every furtherance, we may confidently expect the advancement of true religion, and the completion of our happi-ness.

I pray the munificent Rewarder of virtue that your agency in this good work may receive its compensation here and hereafter.

G: Washington

LB, DLC:GW. This letter is addressed to "the Ministers and Ruling Elders delegates to represent the Churches in Massachusetts and New Hampshire, which compose the first Presbytery of the Eastward."

For background to GW's tour of the eastern states, see his letter to Betty Lewis, 12 Oct. 1789, n.3.

1. GW is replying to an address of the Presbytery of the Eastward, dated 28 Oct. 1789: "We the Ministers and ruling Elders delegated to represent the Churches in Massachusetts and New Hampshire which compose the first Presbytery of the eastward, now holding a stated session in this Town, beg leave to approach your presence with genuine feelings of the deepest veneration and highest esteem. We ask the honor of a place among the multitudes of good citizens who are ambitious of expressing the heartfelt satisfaction, with which they bid you welcome to these eastern parts of your government.

"In unison with rejoicing millions, we felicitate our country, and ourselves on your unanimous election to the highest office a nation can bestow—and on your acceptance of the trust with every evidence, which a citizen can give of being actuated thereto by the purest principles of patriotism, of piety and of self-denial.

"Great was the joy of our hearts to see the late tedious and destructive war terminated in a safe and honorable peace—to see the liberty and independence of our country happily secured—to see wise constitutions of civil government peaceably established in the several States—and especially to see a confederation of them all finally agreed on by the general voice. But amid all our joy, we ever contemplated with regret the want of efficiency in the federal government—we ardently wished for a form of national union which should draw the cord of amity more closely around the several States—which should concentrate their separate interests—and reduce the freemen of *America* to *one* great Body—ruled by *One* head, and animated by one Soul.

"And now we devoutly offer our humble tribute of praise and thanksgiving to the all-gracious *Father* of *lights* who has inspired our public Councils with a wisdom and firmness, which have effected that desireable purpose, in so great a measure by the National-Constitution, and who has fixed the eyes of all America on you as the worthiest of its Citizens to be entrusted with the execution of it.

"Whatever any may have supposed wanting in the original plan, we are happy to find so wisely providing in its amendments; and it is with peculiar satisfaction we behold how easily the entire confidence of the People, in the Man who sits at the helm of Government, has eradicated every remaining objection to its form.

"Among these we never considered the want of *a religious test*, that grand engine of persecution in every tyrant's hand: But we should not have been alone in rejoicing to have seen some Explicit acknowledgement of the *only true God and Jesus Christ, whom he hath sent* inserted some where in the *Magna Charta* of our country.

"We are happy to find, however, that this defect has been amply remedied, in the face of all the world, by the piety and devotion, in which your first public act of office was performed—by the religious observance of the Sabbath, and of the public worship of *God*, of which you have set so eminent an example—and by the warm strains of christian and devout affections, which run through your late proclamation, for a general thanksgiving.

"The catholic spirit breathed in all your public acts supports us in the pleasing assurance that no religious establishments—no exclusive privileges tending to elevate one denomination of Christians to the depression of the rest, shall ever be ratified by the signature of the *President* during your administration.

"On the contrary we bless God that your whole deportment bids all denominations confidently to expect to find in you the watchful guardian of their equal liberties—the steady Patron of genuine christianity—and the bright Exemplar of those peculiar virtues, in which its distinguishing doctrines have their proper effect.

"Under the nurturing hand of a Ruler of such virtues, and one so deservedly revered by all ranks, we joyfully indulge the hope that virtue and religion will revive and flourish—that infidelity and the vices ever attendant in its train, will be banished [from] every polite circle; and that rational piety will soon become fashionable there; and from thence be diffused among all other ranks in the community.

"Captivated with the delightful prospect of a national reformation rising out of the influence of your authority and example; we find the fullest encouragement to cherish the hope of it, from the signal deeds of pious and patriotic heroism, which marked the steps of the Father of his country, from the memorable hour of his appearance in Congress, to declare the disinterested views, with which he accepted the command of her armies, to that hour, not less memorable, when, having gloriously acquitted himself in that important trust, and completely accomplished the design of it, he appeared in the same great Assembly again; and resigned his commission into the hands that gave it.

"But glorious as your course has been as a Soldier in arms, defending your country, and the rights of mankind; we exult in the presage that it will be far outshone by the superior lustre of a more glorious career now before you, as the Chief Magistrate of your nation—protecting, by just and merciful laws—and by a wise, firm, and temperate execution of them, enhancing the value of those inestimable rights and privileges, which you have so worthily asserted to it by your sword.

"Permit us then, great Sir, to assure you that whilst it ever shall be our care, in our several places, to inculcate those principles, drawn from the pure fountains of light and truth, in the sacred scriptures, which can best recommend your virtues to their imitation, and which, if generally obeyed, would contribute essentially to render your people happy, and your government prosperous; Our unceasing prayers to the *great Sovereign of all* nations, shall be that your important life, and all your singular talents may be the special care of an indulgent Providence for many years to come; that your administration may be continued to your country, under the peculiar smiles of Heaven, long enough to advance the interests of learning to the zenith—to carry the arts and sciences to their destined perfection—to chace ignorance, bigotry, and immorality off the stage—to restore true virtue, and the religion of *Jesus* to their deserved throne in our land: and to found the liberties of America, both religious and civil, on a basis which no era of futurity shall ever see removed: and, finally, that, when you have thus done—free grace may confer on you, as the reward of all your great labours, the unfading laurels of an everlasting crown" (DLC:GW). The address was signed on behalf of the First Presbytery, by Joseph Prince, moderator.

To the Governor and Legislature of New Hampshire

[Portsmouth, N.H., 3 November 1789]
Allow me, Gentlemen, to assure you that grateful as my heart is for the affectionate regards which my fellow-citizens have manifested towards me, it has at no time been more sensibly impressed with a consciousness of their goodness than on the present occasion.

I am truly thankful for your expressions of attachment to my person, and approbation of my conduct—and I reciprocate your good wishes with unfeigned affection.

In exercising the vigilance and attention, with which you are pleased to compliment my military command, I did no more than what inclination prompted and duty enjoined.

In discharging the duties of my civil appointment, I can sincerely promise that the love of my country will be the ruling influence of my conduct.

The success, which has hitherto attended our united efforts, we owe to the gracious interposition of Heaven, and to that interposition let us gratefully ascribe the praise of victory, and the blessings of peace.

May the State, in whose councils you worthily preside, be happy under your administration, and may you, Gentlemen, partake of the blessings which your endeavors are intended to bestow.

G. Washington.

LB, DLC:GW; copy, DLC:GW.

For background to GW's tour of the eastern states, see his letter to Betty Lewis, 12 Oct. 1789, n.3.

According to GW's diary account "About 2 Oclock I recd. an Address from the Executive of the State of New Hampshire; and in half an hour after dined

with them and a large Company at their Assembly room which is one of the
best I have seen any where in the United States" (*Diaries*, 5:490). The address,
signed by John Sullivan and dated 3 Nov., reads: "Amidst the applause and
gratulations of millions, suffer the Executive of New Hampshire with grateful
hearts to approach you, Sir, and hail you welcome to this northern State—To
a Government, whose metropolis was at an early stage of the late war by your
vigilance and attention saved from destruction. And the whole of which was,
at an after period, rescued from impending ruin by that valour and prudence,
which eventually wrought out the salvation of our common country, and gave
birth to the American empire.

"Deeply impressed with the remembrance of these important events, you
will permit us to say that among the vast multitude of your Admirers, there is
not a People who hold your talents and your virtues in higher veneration than
the Inhabitants of New Hampshire.

"We beg you, Sir, to accept our most cordial thanks for the honor done to
this State by your more than welcome visit at this time. And that you will believe that we shall not cease to unite our most fervent prayers with those of
our american Brethren that you may be continued a lasting blessing to our
nation—and long, very long, be suffered to rule in Peace over those, whom
you have protected and defended in war" (DLC:GW).

From William Dawson

Sir   Westmoreland [County, Va.] Novr 4th 1789
It is humbly represented to your Excellency by William Dawson who in the Year 1774 acted as Manager for Colo. George
Mercers plantations in Frederick County that unable to precure
A settlement or induce the Honourable James Mercer to make
him payment for Such his Services, he was Compell'd to bring
his action for the recovery; to this his Claim, Mr Mercers Plead-
ing the act of Limitations has prevented him from proving the
Justice of his demand in a point of Law.

In this forlorn and oppress'd Situation he was induse'd to
propose and accede to an Arbitration by Consent Sir, your
Answer to the Quaries he has now the Honor of Submitting to
your Excellency, will be Respectfully Receiv'd as Proof.

He Submits to your Excellencys recollections? if the Middle
and Lower Plantations, and the three New Quarters ware not
under good fencing? if there ware not good Crops of wheat
Sown at Each? if the Stock as also the Tools ware not in good
order at the Day of Sale? if your Excellency received any Infor-

mation of his misconduct or mismanagement from any other Person then a certain Mr Edward Snickers of Frederick County? if this Mr Snickers did not Sucseed him as manager after having diprived him and his family of their Bread? if Sir whin you Blamed him for not having finish'd all the Tobo on the Plantations: did he not Convince your Excellency what a most Sevear Laborious and unthankful years Service he had contended against, occasion'd by the overseers and Negroes knowing they ware to leave the Estates at the Exspiration of the Year? if he did not Convince you Sir, that all the Tobacco was finished Excepting Some Ground leaves? what Quantity of Tobacco did Mr Snickers Prize for the E[s]tate after the Sale? if the Negroes did not all appear in Good Condition according to thier ages? if he and his Family, did not Conduct themselves with respect to your self Sir, and Mr Mercer? And if your Excellency advis'd Mr Mercer to Sue him for Damages from Instances that you had discover'd of Either his Misconduct or Mismanagement—He inclose's the affidavit of Mr Mercer for a supersedeas: the Real And imaginary Losses that Gentn attributes to his Misconduct, he Considers to have been Occasioned by the Cruel Aspersions with which a Mr Edward Snickers branded his Character; your Excellency will Pardon a warmth occasion'd by the Recollection of Wantonly Malicious Injuries, as he is firmly Perswaded, that had not this Mr Snickers coveted the Said Earned Livelyhood he then Possess'd, the Honorable Mr Mercer would not have added the Injustice of his Plea to his approbious Reflections, on an Injured character, nor Should your Excellencys Valuable time been encroach'd on by his Narrative of the oppression he has Contended Against himself. He has the Honor of Subscribing Your Excellencys most Obedient Servant

W. Dawson

N.B. your Excellency will please to direct your answer to the Clerk of the District Court of Fredericksburg.

ALS, ViMtV.

For background to this letter, see William Dawson to GW, 5 Oct. 1789, James Mercer to GW, 15 Oct. 1789, and GW to Mercer, 17 Nov. 1789.

From Joseph Willard

Sir,   Cambridge [Mass.] November 7. 1789.
   When you were in the Philosophy Chamber of the University
in this place,[1] you may perhaps remember, that I expressed my
wishes, that your Portrait might, some time or other, adorn that
Room. Since that, Mr Savage, the Bearer of this, who is a
Painter, and is going to New York, has called on me, and of his
own accord, has politely and generously offered to take your
Portrait for the University, if you will be so kind as to sit.[2] As it
would be exceedingly grateful to all the Governors of this literary Society, that the Portrait of the Man we so highly love, esteem
and revere, should be the property of, and be placed within
Harvard College, permit me, Sir, to request the favor of your
sitting for the purpose; which will greatly oblige the whole
Corporation, and particularly him, who has the honor of being,
with sentiments of the highest respect, Sir your most humble
and obedient servant

                                              Joseph Willard

ALS, DLC:GW.
   Joseph Willard (1738–1804) served as president of Harvard from 1781 to
1804.
   1. During his New England tour GW visited Harvard on 29 Oct. 1789 and
was received in the "Philosophy-room of the University" (*Pennsylvania Packet
and Daily Advertiser* [Philadelphia], 13 Nov. 1789). As GW noted in his diary
entry for this day, "I was shewn by Mr. Willard the President the Philosophical
Aparatus and amongst other Popes Orary (a curious piece of Mechanism for
shewing the revolutions of the Sun, Earth and many other of the Planets)—
The library (containing 13,000 volumes) and a Museum" (*Diaries*, 5:481–83).
   2. The painter Edward Savage (1761–1817) began GW's portrait in New
York on 21 December. GW noted that he "Sat from ten to one Oclock for a
Mr. Savage to draw my Portrait for the University of Cambridge in the State
of Massachusetts at the request of the President and Governors of the said
University" (ibid., 509). The portrait "represents Washington in a military
coat, with angular opening between coat collar and lapel. On the latter are two
large buttons. . . . On the left lapel is the badge of the Order of the Cincinnati" (Eisen, *Portraits of Washington*, 2:457, 462–65). GW gave Savage further
sittings on 28 Dec. and 6 Jan. 1790 (*Diaries*, 5:511, 6:2). GW replied to Willard's letter on 23 December.

From Nicholas Eveleigh

New York, 8 November 1789. Acknowledges appointment as comptroller of the treasury. "I consider it, Sir, & the consideration affords me the most heart-felt satisfaction, as an unequivocal proof, that I am view'd by you in a favourable light. to be thought well of by a man, himself not only universally thought well of, but respected & revered, cannot fail of proving to me a source of the highest gratification; but, Sir, it will have another effect; that of stimulating me to a faithful discharge of the duties connected with the office now intrusted to my charge."

ALS, DNA:PCC, item 78.

Nicholas Eveleigh (c.1748–1791) of South Carolina was educated at the University of Edinburgh and returned to Charleston in 1774 to become a planter. During the Revolution he served with South Carolina forces and from April to August 1778 was deputy adjutant general for South Carolina. During the 1780s he was a member of the South Carolina legislature and from 1782 to 1783 represented his state in the Confederation Congress. GW appointed him comptroller of the treasury on 11 Sept. 1789, and he served until his death.

To Samuel Taft

Sir,   Hartford [Conn.], November 8. 1789.

Being informed that you have given my name to one of your Sons, and called another after Mrs Washington's family—and being moreover very much pleased with the modest and innocent looks of your two daughters Patty and Polly I do, for these reasons, send each of these Girls a piece of chintz—and to Patty, who bears the name of Mrs Washington, and who waited more upon us than Polly did, I send five guineas, with which she may buy herself any little ornaments she may want, or she may dispose of them in any other manner more agreeable to herself.[1]

As I do not give these things with a view to have it talked of, or even to its being known, the less there is said about the matter the better you will please me; but that I may be sure the chintz and money have got safe to hand, let Patty, who I daresay is equal to it, write me a line informing me thereof directed to "The President of the United States at New York." I wish you and your family well and am Your humble Servant

G. Washington.

LB, DLC:GW.

Samuel Taft kept a tavern near Uxbridge, Massachusetts. GW and his party stayed in the tavern on the night of 6 Nov. 1789 while on his tour of New England and noted in his diary that although "the people were obliging, the entertainment was not very inviting" (*Diaries*, 5:494).

1. Taft's daughter acknowledged the gift on 28 Dec.: "May it please your Highness Agreeable to your commands, I, with pleasure, inform the President, that, on the 25th inst., I received the very valuble present, by the hand of the Revd Mr Pond of Ashford, you, Sir, were pleased to send me and my Sister, accompanied with a letter from your benevolent hand, of 8th ult.

"The articles mentioned in the letter, viz., two pieces of chintz, containing 30 yds and, five Guineas, came safely to hand, well seeled.

"As it was far beyond my deserving, to receive such a distinguishing mark of your approbation, so it wholly exceeded my expectation.

"And I want words, to express my gratitude to you, Great Sir, for the extraordinary favours & honour, conferred on me and our famaly, both, at this time, and while your Highness was pleased to honour my Papa's house with your presence—I shall endeavour to comply with your desires expressed in the letter—And, as I have great Reason, I shall ever esteem, and Revere the name of him whose noble deeds and Patriotism, has laid a permanet obligation on all the Sons & Daughters of the American Empire ever to adore their unequaled Benefactor.

"And my ardent desires are that the best of heavens blessings may, both in this, and in the future world ever rest on the head of him who stands at the head of our United Empire—My sister joins with me in the unfeigned acknowladgement I've made, likewise hord [honored] Papa and Mama with sincere thanks and duty desirs to be remembred to your Highness, I conclude, resting assured, that it's wholly unnecessary a pologize for the incorrectnss of the a bove to him whose candour will paliate the want of ability and Education, in her, who is unacquainted with epistolary, correspondence, epeciely with one of the first charecters on the Globe" (DLC:GW). The letter is signed by Mercy Taft, with a note appended: "Pray pardon me sir if I mention the mistake in my name you se Sir, it is not Patty."

From John Bondfield

Sir   Bordeaux [France] 12 9bre 1789

The great and Urgent wants of this Nation, occation'd by the faileur of the two last Crops of wheat, creates dreadful Alarms, to this add the low State of the finnances, occation'd by the Great Revolution effecting; for the two last six months few have paid the Usual Tax's, that the Treasury is exhausted, this forces the National Assembly to extraordinary exertions, to avert the ill consiquences that may attend a real want of dayly subsistence of Bread to the Nation.

The 7th Instant a Motion was made in the National Assembly to impower Le Ministre du finnance to make application to the United States of America, for a supply, and from the Crampt state of the Finnances to Ask a reimburssment, and that in Grain in part of the advances due by America to france[.][1] their Arguments.

In Urgent need America applied to france. france granted powerful Assistance simular circumstances creates simular demands The Glorious revolution now greatly advanct calls in a Multiplied Capacity every exertion of Succor from Antient Amitie strengthend by the new Constitution forming on Simular liberal Principles.

A ship sailing to morrow for Philadelphia engages my taking the liberty to transmit you advice of what is here agitating so far as relates to the United States.[2]

In an Assembly held yesterday by the Magistrates of this City being call'd on for my sentiments on the dependance of Supplies I assurd them that every exertion on the part of the United States will be made for the releif of this Nation. with due respect I have the Honor to be Sir Your most Obedient and most Humble Servant

John Bondfield

ALS, DNA:PCC, item 78; LS (duplicate), DNA:PCC, item 78.

John Bondfield operated a mercantile establishment in Quebec at the beginning of the American Revolution. A supporter of the American invasion of Canada, he helped to provision American troops in their retreat following the Canadian campaign. Forced to leave Quebec because of his aid to the American forces, Bondfield settled briefly in Philadelphia but went to France in 1777, establishing a mercantile firm in Bordeaux. For Bondfield's detailed account of his services to the United States during the war, see his letter to Jefferson, 8 Oct. 1790, in Boyd, *Jefferson Papers*, 17:573–80. Bondfield hoped for an appointment to the post of United States consul at Bordeaux when consular appointments were made in 1790, but the post went instead to Joseph Fenwick. See George Mason to GW, 19 June 1789, and notes.

1. By the end of 1789 the United States Revolutionary War debt to France had reached $6,296,296, a sum that included the 10 million livres borrowed in Holland in 1782 and guaranteed by France (see Board of Treasury to GW, 15 June 1789, n.13). At the beginning of 1790 arrearages of interest amounted to $277,777.77. In addition the United States was in arrears to the

amount of $1,388,888.88 for payments on the principal of the debt due in 1787, 1788, and 1789 (Report on Public Credit, 9 Jan. 1790, in Syrett, *Hamilton Papers*, 6:112–13). Whatever differences of opinion existed in the United States concerning the retirement of the domestic debt, there was general agreement that putting the foreign debt in train of payment was a matter of the first priority in order to protect the United States' fiscal reputation abroad. Shortly after his appointment as secretary of the treasury, Hamilton assured France's representatives in the United States that the United States fully intended to honor its commitment although he hoped that France would offer to suspend payments until the United States could put its financial house in order (Moustier to Montmorin, 17 Sept. 1789, Louis G. Otto to Montmorin, 30 Oct. 1789, both in Arch. Aff. Etr., Corr. Pol., Etats-Unis, vol. 34; Hamilton to Lafayette, 6 Oct. 1789, and Hamilton to William Short, 7 Oct. 1789, in Syrett, *Hamilton Papers*, 5:425–26, 429–30). The debates concerning the use of the debt for securing provision for France took place on 5 and 6 Nov., and in Bondfield's duplicate letter the date of Mirabeau's motion is given as 6 Nov. (*Archives Parlementaires*, 9:705–11). Concerning the debates William Short, United States chargé d'affaires in Paris, wrote acting secretary of state John Jay on 7 Nov.: "It was moved two days ago in the National Assembly that His Majesty should be requested to send persons of confidence as Envoys extraordinary to the United States to negotiate the payment of our debt in flour. This motion was made by the Count de Mirabeau in the course of the debate it was said by some of the members that the debt of the United States must be considered as a *bad debt*—the motion was adjourned to some days hence—as I think it probably will pass I have thought it proper to give you this early notice of it." On 19 Nov., however, Short informed Jay that the motion had not been renewed and the plan was not likely to be revived (DLC: William Short Papers).

2. Bondfield enclosed in his letter a broadside of the "Motion de M. Le Comte de Mirabeau, à L'Assemblée Nationale, Ayant pour objet de demander des Blés Aux Etats-Unis de l'Amérique, en payement de ce que ces Etats doivent à la France" (DNA:PCC, item 78).

From Nathaniel Ramsay

S⟨ir⟩   Char[l]es-Town [Md.] Novemr 12th 1789

I have to acknowledge the receipt ⟨of your⟩ letter accompanying a Commission for the office of Marshal for the district of Maryland.[1] I have a most grateful ⟨sense of⟩ the honor you have confered on me by the appointment, and fondly hope that my conduct in transacting the important duties of the Office will so far correspond with my determined resolution as to merit your future approbation.

Mr Johnson ⟨*illegible*⟩ nonacceptance of the office of Judge, has ⟨completely⟩ deranged the Judiciary business,[2] particularly that of the Admiralty and has occasioned a considerable failure of Justice to the disadvantage of the revenue and to the emolument of offenders against the laws. I cannot help expressing my fears that the extent of the duties required of the District Judge, encreased by the ⟨*illegible*⟩ of places at which he must attend to hold his Courts, when comp⟨*mutilated*⟩ary will be an effectual ⟨*mutilated*⟩ing accepted by any lawyer of abilities and reputation.

I must crave your Excellencies forgiveness for presuming to hint that perhaps Mr Paca might be an exception to the foregoing supposition.[3] He is a man of an un⟨*illegible*⟩ fortune, and at present engaged in no business either public or private, he has ever shewn a disposition to be amused and pleased with Judical proceedings, and his Integrity and abilities as a Judge is in high estimation.

He has in an eminent degree possessed the confidence of this State, and whatever he may have lately lost of it by his op⟨position⟩ to the present government, he is now fast regaining by his heart⟨*mutilated*⟩ cheerful acquiescence under it.

I have not conversed with Mr Paca or any of his particular friends on this subject, and therefore have no authority for my opinions, other then my own surmises. Your Excellency will have the goodness to attribute the liberty which I have now taken in submitting to you, these suggestions, to an ardent desire to see the new Government administered with efficiency and reputation.

I have hitherto delayed writing on this subject, from a daily expectation, that the acceptance of the Judge would have put it in my power ⟨*mutilated*⟩quainted your Excellency; that I not only meant to accept of my Commission, but, also, to inform you, that I had actually taken upon me the execution of the Office. I am with the highest respect your Excellencies most d[e]voted Humble servant

Nat: Ramsey

ALS, DNA: RG 59, Miscellaneous Letters.

For background to GW's judiciary appointments, see his letter to the United States Senate submitting nominations for judicial posts, 24 Sept. 1789.

1. GW's letter of appointment to Ramsay has not been found, but it was undoubtedly similar to those sent to other judicial appointees.

2. See GW to Thomas Johnson, 28 Sept. 1789.

3. For William Paca's appointment, see GW to James McHenry, 30 Nov. 1789, especially note 6.

George Washington
by Edward Savage

Oil on canvas, 75.1 × 62.2 cm (30 × 25 in.)
Signed "E. Savage Pinx 1790"

Harvard University Portrait Collection

Provenance: Given by the artist to Harvard University in 1790 in
whose possession it has remained.

Edward Savage (1761–1817) was born in Princeton, Mass., 26 Nov.
1761. Nothing is known of his artistic training in America where he
painted from 1784 until going to London in 1791. After his return to
the United States in 1793, he operated a museum first in Philadelphia, then in New York, and finally in Boston. Savage painted this
portrait as a gift for Harvard University (Willard to Washington, 7
Nov. 1789). In New York, on 21 Dec. 1789, Washington "Sat from ten
to one O'clock for a Mr. Savage to draw my Portrait for the University
of Cambridge in the State of Massachusetts at the request of the President and Governors of the said university," and two days later he
wrote President Willard that Savage was "engaged in taking the portrait." On 28 Dec. he "Set all the forenoon for Mr. Savage," and on 6
Jan. 1790 he noted in his diary that he "Sat from half after 8 oclock
until 10 for the Portrait Painter, Mr. Savage, to finish the Picture of
me." Harvard University thanked Savage on 30 Aug. 1791 for his
"polite and generous attention to the University, in painting a portrait
of the President of the United States, taken by him from life."

Washington is shown wearing his military uniform and the badge
of the Order of the Cincinnati.

George Washington
by Edward Savage

Oil on canvas, 76.2 × 63.5 cm (30 × 25 in.)
Signed "E. Savage Pinx 1790"

Collection of the Adams National Historic Site

Provenance: Painted for John Quincy Adams, this picture has always
hung in the Adams family home in Quincy, Mass., now the property
of the United States Department of the Interior, National Park
Service.

The second life portrait of Washington by Edward Savage was
painted at the request of John Adams, then vice president of the
United States. Washington's diary indicates that on 6 April 1790 he
again "Sat for Mr. Savage at the request of the Vice-President to have
my Portrait drawn for him." This portrait varies from the first portrait in that the badge of the Order of the Society of the Cincinnati
has been omitted. The receipt for the portrait, at the Adams National
Historic Site, reads: "Received N.Y., 17th April, 1790, of the Vice-
President of the U.S., fortysix and 66/100 for a portrait of the Pres. of
the U.S. and his lady. Edward Savage."

George Washington
by Christian Güllager

Oil on canvas, 73.5 × 51 cm (29¾ × 24¹¹⁄₁₆ in.)

Collection of the Massachusetts Historical Society

Provenance: Won in a raffle from the artist by Daniel Sargent, Jr.,
who presented the picture to Dr. Jeremy Belknap. It was listed in
the inventory of Belknap's estate in 1798 as "Portrait of Geo.
Washington (value) $1.50." Inherited by Jeremy Belknap's daughter,
Elizabeth Belknap, upon whose death in 1865 it was left to Edward
Belknap. Upon his death, it was inherited by his daughter Mrs.
Arthur Codman. Given by Mrs. Codman to the Massachusetts
Historical Society in 1921.

(Amandus) Christian Güllager was born in Copenhagen on 1 Mar.
1759. He studied art at the Royal Academy and was awarded the Lille
Solvmedaille in 1780. About 1783 he came to the United States where
he pursued his career in Boston and Philadelphia and worked briefly
in Charleston and New York City. He died in Philadelphia, 12 Nov.
1826. In addition to this painted portrait, Güllager is supposed to
have made a sculpted portrait of George Washington, but the present
whereabouts of that portrait is not verified. A bronze medal with a
profile portrait of George Washington on the obverse has also been
attributed to him (Marvin Sadik, *Christian Güllager, Portrait Painter to
Federal America* [Washington, D.C.: National Portrait Gallery, Smith-
sonian Institution, 1976], 35–41).

According to Dr. Jeremy Belknap's account on 27 Oct. 1789, "while
he [Washington] was in the chapel [in Boston], Güllager, the painter
stole a likeness of him from a Pew behind the pulpit. N.B. Güllager
followed Gen. W. to Portsm where he sat 2½ hours for him to take his
portrait wh he did & obtained a very good likeness—after wh he laid
aside the sketch wh he took in the chapel—wh however was not a bad
one." The "Chapel" sketch is unlocated, as is another replica (ibid.,
74–76).

George Washington
by Madame la Marquise de Bréhan

Watercolor on ivory, grisaille 6.8 × 5.2 cm (2⅝ × 2⅛ in. oval)
Signed "Me La Msse de Bréhan F"

Yale University Art Gallery, The Mabel Brady Garvan Collection

Provenance: Martha Washington to her granddaughter, Martha
Custis Peter, to her daughter, Mrs. John Upshur, to her daughter
Kate Upshur Moorehead (Mrs. F. F. Moorehead) to her son, Upshur
Moorehead, to present owner 1947.

Madame la marquise de Bréhan accompanied comte de Moustier,
French minister plenipotentiary to the United States in 1788. An
amateur artist, Madame de Bréhan spent four days at Mount Vernon
in November 1788 where she first met George Washington. Nearly a
year later, Washington sat for her on 3 Oct. 1789 and wrote in his
diary: "sat about two Oclock for Madame de Brehan to complete a
Miniature profile of me which she had begun from Memory and
which she had made exceedingly like the Original." The miniature,
framed back to back with the marquise's miniature of Nelly Custis,
Mrs. Washington's granddaughter, was taken back to France to be engraved. That the marquise painted several replicas and the picture
was engraved is substantiated by a letter to George Washington from
the comte de Moustier of 11 May 1790. The letter also indicates that
the marquise intended to send the original portrait to Mrs. Washington and make a replica for herself.

From Joseph Jones

Dr Sr   [c.15 November 1789]

After a conflict in my breast for two weeks past, whch I should transgress a rule from which I have in no instance departed, al[t]ho' honoured with several respectable appointments by my Country, I have determined to inform you of my wish to come into the office of district Judge—the emoluments of the appointment with the profitts I could make from my fortune though small would enable me to disc[h]arge in a few years a debt I owe the estate of the late Col. Tayloe for which I am much pressed and to pay which demand I have offered to sell my land in King George County but cannot (such is the depreciation of property) obtain a reasonable price for it or indeed as yet any offer. Necessity I well know is an unfavourable pretence to offices of great trust, but I think I have integrity and resolution sufficient to bear me through any trial I may be exposed to where doing justice shall occasion the embarrassment—the principal difficulty with me was whether I could execute the trust with propriety, and if I do not deceive myself, notwithstanding my having been long out of the business of the Courts, and am as the common phrase is rusty, yet I Fear not being able to put the business in motion and to carry it on in such manner as not to disgrace the appointment—I should not have presumed to come forward while the office was open to Pendleton, Wythe, Blair and E. Randolph, but as they are no longer in the way should you be at liberty to nominate me consistent with the ⟨rules⟩ prescribed to yourself for such important appointm⟨ents⟩ you may rely my best endeavours shall be exerted in the office and that should I find myself unequal to the undertaking I shall as soon as the discovery is made afferd you an oppertunity of introducing a more proper person—let the issue of this application be what it may, you will hear no complaint from but as usual retain the good wishes of Dr Sr aff. & obed. Servt

                                             Jos: Jones[1]

ALS, PWacD: Feinstone Collection, on deposit at PPAmP.

Joseph Jones (1727–1805) of King George County was a prominent Virginia jurist. He served as a delegate to the House of Burgesses before the Revolution, as a member of the Continental Congress during the war, and as a judge of the Virginia General Court from 1778 to 1779 and from 1789 to 1805.

1. On 30 Nov. GW replied to Jones's letter: "Your favor, without date, came to my hands by the last post, but not till after I had decided in favor of Mr Cyrus Griffin, and directed the commission to be made out—This being the case your application for the office of District Judge has not, nor will it be mentioned by me" (LB, DLC:GW). The remainder of GW's letter to Jones dealt with his reasons for appointing Griffin to the post and is printed in Griffin's letter of application to GW, 10 July 1789, source note.

From Pierce Butler

Sir   New York Novbr the 16th 1789
My situation as a senator from Carolina obliges me to trouble You with the perusal of the inclosed letters.[1] As they will speak for themselves I will not intrude further on Your time. I have the honor to be with great respect and attachment Sir, Yr Most Obedt Servant

                                                    P. Butler

ALS, DNA:PCC, item 78.
   1. The enclosures have not been identified.

From Sarah Gardner

Sir.   New-York Monday Novr 16th 1789.
I should pay a very undeserved compliment to the well known goodness of your Excellency's heart, not to flatter myself, that this address will be deemed, in some degree, pardonable. I shall only observe, that it would not obtrude, but that your Excellency was engaged, when I did myself the honor, this morning, of making a personal application to your Excellency. As the patron of the liberal arts, and that of literature in particular, it would be an Author's pride, humbly to sue to your Excellency for countenance, and patronage but in the present instance, a more noble cause kneels at your feet for favor, and protection. The cause of *humanity*. Two helpless innocents (children of the late Mr Ryan comedian)[1] experience at this time every distress that can arise from the necessaries of life being tendered them in a very sparing degree, and ⟨*illegible*⟩ especially, a total want of the benefits of education⟨,⟩ that necessary cultivation, to "teach the

young idea how to shoot," and form and improve the infant mind to such acts as do honor to human nature, and make natives of America (for such they are) social citizens of the world. The great obligations which every inhabitant of this delivered, and flourishing country has to the brave defender of her natural liberty, and the glorious protector of her constitutional rights, stimulate them, for their own honour, to attend to whatever your Excellency shall condescend to approve: and the honor of your Excellency's presence, would insure to these poor orphans, a considerable emolument; which emolument, permit me to assure your Excellency, is to be appropriated solely to defray the expence of schooling, which they greatly stand in need of. It is for *their* benefit alone, and which benefit, would be publickly advertised, but from a point of delicacy, and the uncertainty of success.

Suffer me further to inform your Excellency, that I would not presume to solicit the honor of your Excellency's presence but that the entertainment is wholly of the genteel kind, and calculated entirely for the amusement of persons of fashion; and tho' truly comic, is at the sametime strictly moral. With profound respect, and the most perfect esteem, I have the honor to subscribe myself, Sir, Your Excellency's most devoted and most obedt Servant

Sarah Gardner.

ALS, DLC:GW.

Sarah Gardner had appeared at the Drury Lane Theatre in London in 1763 under the name of Miss Cheney. She was supposed to have trained under David Garrick and Samuel Foote and had acted at the Covent Garden and Haymarket theaters. She is undoubtedly the same Mrs. Gardner who appeared with the Old American Theatre Company in Kingston, Jamaica, in 1778 (Odell, *Annals of the New York Stage*, 1:174). Mrs. Gardner gave an entertainment at the City Tavern in New York City on 17 Nov. 1789 and subsequently appeared with the Old American Company at the John Street Theatre, although she was probably not a member of the company (Seilhamer, *American Theatre*, 298).

1. Dennis Ryan and his wife, actors who were probably of Irish origin, began appearing with the Baltimore theater company in 1782, and in February 1783 Ryan assumed management of the company. After a season in New York in 1783, the company returned to Baltimore, and Ryan remained in charge through the 1783 season (Seilhamer, *American Theatre*, 85, 96, 114). He then apparently found himself in serious financial difficulty and may have considered opening a theater in Richmond. For GW's marginal involvement in his

business affairs, see GW to Alexander Henderson, 20 Dec. 1784, Henderson to GW, 11 Jan. 1785, GW to Bushrod Washington, 22 Jan., 3 April 1785, James Rumsey to GW, 10 Mar., 24 June 1785, and GW to Rumsey, 5 June 1785. Ryan died in Baltimore in 1786. He is occasionally confused with the Ryan who was prompter and actor with the Old American Company in New York during the 1790s.

From Samuel Osgood

Sir General Post Office New York Novr 16th 1789
Agreeably the Advertisement of the 5th Ulto ⟨*illegible*⟩ proposals for Carrying the Mail for the Year 1790.[1] I have received a ⟨*illegible*⟩ as stated in the enclosed Schedule, which I have now the Honor to ⟨lay⟩ before you—The time for receiving proposals expired last saturday.

The following are the persons that appear to me to be entitled the carriage of the Mail:

Joseph Barnard from Portland to Portsmouth.

David Barker from Portsmouth to Boston.

The Stage Drivers have made no proposals for the last mentioned Distance tho' they have had the carriage of the Mail the present year—It is suggested that they intend to make proposals, ⟨but⟩ that they have miscarried—I propose to suspend for a few days Mr Barkers right as he did not make his Proposals in consequence of the Advertisement and they are not so particular as they ought to be.

The Stage Drivers have performed the business with propriety, and Punctuality, and I hope they continue to do the same.

Daniel Salmon and Co. have made the lowest Proposals for carrying the Mail by Stage betwen Boston and New-York.

Inskeep and Cummings between New York & Philadelphia⟨—⟩ their Proposals for carrying the Mail Three times in Summer and Twice in Winter is the lowest—but their Proposal for carrying it fives times a Week through the Year, will in the opinion of all I have conversed with, increase the Revenue of the Post Office, much more than the difference between the two sums. The Public will in my opinion, be best served by adopting this proposal.

Van Horne & Kerlin between Philadelphia and Baltimore—Their proposal for carrying the Mail three times a Week through the year, appears to me to be the most eligible. It is also the lowest.

Gabriel Patterson Van Horne between Baltimore and A[l]exandria.

John Hoomes between Alexandria and Edenton.

Bryan McCabe between Edenton and Washington.

John G. Blount from Washington to Newberne.

A[l]exr McKenzie from Newberne to Wilmington.

From Wilmington to Charlestown no proposals.

Jackson Betts & Co. between Charlestown & Savannah.

Dehart & Kenney from New York to Albany.

James Stought from Philadelphia to Pittsburgh.

Robt Hodgson from Philadelphia to Easton.

Levi Pease has established, and is the proprietor of the Stages between Boston and New York—And it is suggested that the persons who have underbid him, are not of sufficient Ability to Set up a line of Stages—if however it should be found that they are able, and can give good security for the faithful performance of the Contract, they are undoubtedly entitled to it.

Mr Pease informs me that he has been at great trouble and Expense in establishing the Stages I believe it to be true; and further think that he is the only person that will Keep up a good line of Stages and between this and Boston.

D. Salmon is not here himself, nor has any Agent appeared here for him—Under these circumstances I do not think I should be Justified in deciding immediately in his favor notwithstanding the lowness of his proposals. I am Sir &c.

[Samuel Osgood]

LB, DNA: RG 28, Letters Sent by the Postmaster General, 1789–1836.

1. See Samuel Osgood to GW, 5 Oct. 1789, n.1.

Tobias Lear to Clement Biddle

Dear Sir,   New York November 17th 1789

I have to acknowledge the receipt of your favour of the 5th ultimo, in which you mention your having given the memo. contained in my letter of the 2d of october to a nephew of Mr Bartram who would deliver it to his uncle;[1] but I have not since received any information relative to the plants & shrubs, my absence from New York with the President has undoubtedly been the cause of it.

The President will thank you to pay the Honble Robt Morris Livres 32.12.2 being a balance due to Gouvr Morris Esqr. for something which he purchased for the President in France: and also to know from him (R.M.) the amount of some floor-matts and a ps. of blk Sattin brot from India the summer before last in one of Mr Morris's Ships, and pay the same.

You will be so good as to inform me in your next the price of Buck wheat, and if any quantity could be had on short notice in Philadelphia if it should be wanted.[2] The Clover seed which I mentioned in a former letter has been procured here @ 10d. per lb. With very great esteem I am, Dear Sir, Your most Obedient Servant

Tobias Lear.

ALS, PHi: Washington-Biddle Correspondence; ADfS, ViMtV; LB, DLC:GW.

Lear returned to New York with GW from the New England tour on 13 November.

1. Lear wrote this letter on 2 Oct., and the next day he sent Biddle another letter requesting him to forward letters containing commissions for judicial officers to Congressman John Brown of Kentucky (Lear to Biddle, to John Brown, and to the Pittsburgh postmaster, all dated 3 Oct. 1789, DLC:GW). Biddle's reply to Lear on 5 Oct. reads: "On Saturday Evening I received your favour of 2d Inst. and gave the Memorandum for Mr Bartram, who lives in the Country to his Nephew who happened to be at my house and I have requested his answer as speedily as possible" (PHi: Clement Biddle Letter Book, 1789–92).

2. See Lear to Biddle, 21 Dec. 1789, n.2.

From Andrew Dunscomb

Sir,   Beekman Street No. 8 New York Novr 17th 1789

As an Old and faithfull servant of the United States I presume to address you, and to solicit your attention and favor.

The services I have been engaged in, as particularized in the accompanying Paper No. 1 commenced with the Revolution, nor did they cease when Peace was established[1]—thus employed, I have been prevented from obtaining more than a mere living—Attentive to the Duties and fettered by the Scruples of Office, I suffered the certainty of making an Independant living, or at least, of placing my self in easy circumstances to pass by unimproved, by which means I am now left with little other comfort than that peace of mind the result of a well directed conduct in the service of my Country. For all my labours during the War I have received a Certificate from the Registers Office—the value of which is well known.

I beg to refer you Sir, to the Certificates and Letters accompanying, as more proper testimonials of my Conduct than any thing I could say on the subject on these and on your goodness I rest my hopes of an Appointment to an Office suited to my Abilities and adequate to the support of a Family.

I entreat a pardon Sir for the liberty I have taken to make my wish known to you. I have the Honor to be With respect—Esteem and Regard Sir Your most Obt servt

Aw Dunscomb

ALS, DLC:GW.

Andrew Dunscomb (c.1758–1802) of New York served as auditor of army accounts in 1778 and later in the quartermaster department. In 1782 he became Virginia's agent for settling accounts with the Confederation government and from 1784 to 1787 served as assistant commissioner for army accounts in Virginia.

1. Dunscomb's supporting letters and documents are with this letter in his file in DLC:GW. On 8 Jan. 1791 and on 23 April 1794, Dunscomb again wrote GW letters applying, unsuccessfully, for federal appointments (DLC:GW).

Letter not found: from Fenwick, Mason, & Company, 17 Nov. 1789. The dealer's catalog states that this letter deals with matters "regarding the purchase of champagne, claret, etc."

LS, sold by Hanzel Galleries, item 50, 23–24 Sept. 1973.

From Samuel Goodwin

Pownalborough: on Kennebeck river in the
County of Lincoln and State of Masschusets

Sir   November 17th 1789

I Most Humbly beg leave: to lay before your Excellency, that when there was an Expedtion To Quebeck in: 1775: by the way of Kennebeck River, & over the Carrying Places: to Amaguntick Lake or, Pond, &c. and to Choudire river & to the River St Lawrance, & Quebeck I haveing A Plan of the Sea Shore, (from

then Falmouth Now Portland) in Cascobay & as fair as penob-
Scut river; of the Great & most leading river Kennebeck: & the
Carrying Places, to the river St Laurence &c.; your Excellency
was pleased To derict me by Mr Ayers to Copy A plan for the
Then Colonal Bennedick Arnold Esqr. To whome Your Excellency Gave the Command of that Army; I went to work Amead-
itly in Obedience To your Excellency's Command; and did Compleat A large plan: (& also two Small plans, the two Small plans
was by, Said Arnolds order) I Delivered them to Said Arnold on
Thursday the 21st Of Sepetember. the Great Plan I Delivered
at my house: & on the 23d the two Small Plans at Fort western
about 16 miles, above where I Hunt I then haveing; Planing
Paper & Coulering and all things Redy, for Copying Plans; I also
Gave him Said Arnold, A Journal: in June and July: 1761 Containing forty Seven pages in Quarto, from Quebeck by the way
of Chaudiere river and the river dsloop [Du Loup] & the head of
PenobSecut River & Carrying placesses into Moose Lake which
is at the head off the North east branch of Kennebeck river: and
through Said lake and Kennebeck river, To Fort Hallefax
And: then from, Said Fort Hallefax up Said Kennebeck river,
and over the Carrying placesses on the west Side of Said Kennebeck river to the Dead river, So Called, being, the western
branch of Said Kennebeck river, & then up Said Western
Branch; over Carrying Placess To Amaguntick Lake or pond, &
through That Lake to Chadiere river, & down Said River to the
river St Lawrance and then To Quebeck; there is some blanks
left in Said journal; but for what reason I Could Never learn;
every one hath had a Compansation for what they did; except
my self, who had nothing but your Excellencys Letter by Mr
Stephen Moylan, dated at Cambridge the 4th of November A.D.
1775 which is as follows Viztt

Sir   Cambridge 4th of November 1775
    I am Commanded by his Excellency To acknowledge the
Recept of your favour of the 17th of October he is pleased that
you had supplied Colonal Arnold with the plans for his Rout to
Quebeck; if it Should be found Necessary to lay out the road you
mention, his Excellency wont be unmindfull of your offer of
Service for that Purpose: I am Sir Your H: St

                                                Stephen Moylan
                                                S: P: J.

A Copy from the orignal.

Sir I have suffered much by the Late Times if your Excelleny: would be pleased to Think off: and Grant me some favour it Will lay me under Great obligations: as well as Most Dutefull obedients; or other wise as Your Excellency in your Great Wisdom Shall Think Proper: And I as in Duty bound Shall ever Pray

Samuel Goodwin

N.B. I Most Humbly beg your Excellencys Pardon for Giveing you Any Trouble: about my affairs but your publick & universall; Known Goodness and Charity: who hath ben the means under God of Giveing peace & Liberity to Millions: make me attempt it; When your Excellency was at Boston &c: I attempted to wate on you there to Pay my Duty, but money: was not to had To beare my Expences: So Could not have the Honour to pay my Duty to your Excellency and lay my affairs before you: A Person Distressed in the decline of life is heard I enjoy a Good measur of health Blessed be God; I hope your Excelleny will Pardon Every thing amiss & the in correctness of This and I as in Duty bound &c.

Samuel Goodwin

ALS, DNA: RG 59, Miscellaneous Letters.

Samuel Goodwin (1716–1802) was the son of one of the proprietors of the Kennebec Purchase. In the mid–1770s the younger Goodwin served as surveyor for the proprietors. He was also a merchant and innkeeper in Pownalborough (now Dresden, Maine) and was active in local civic affairs. For the background to his Revolutionary War connections with GW and the Canadian campaign, see Goodwin to GW, 17 Oct. 1775, and John Sullivan to GW, 29 Oct. 1775. For Goodwin's interest in having a federal port on the Kennebec River, see his letter to GW, 25 Nov. 1789.

To James Mercer

Sir,   New York Novr 17th 1789.

During my absence on a tour through the Eastern States, your letter of the 15th Ulto, enclosing an Order of the District Court which had been in Session at Fredericksburgh, came to this City. This is the reason why you have not recd an earlier acknowledgment of them; for I did not return until the 13th instt—too late for the Posts of last week.

A bad memory, and no memorandums or Papers to refer to,

added to the Multiplicity of occurrences which have happened to lay claim to my closest attention since the year 1774, have obliterated almost every thing relating to the conversations & conduct of Mr Dawson at the Sale of Colo. Mercers Estate in the month of Novr of that year. All that remains upon my mind respecting his conduct (for my business you will recollect was not with him, but to sell the Estate) is, that the Plantations appeared to me to be in bad condition—and himself too simple, easy and incompetent for the management of them. I have some faint recollection also, that there were suspicions of, or charges against him for, his having disposed of Pine timber. And I think he was under promise to be down soon after the Sale to settle, & render an acct of his Stewardship. But, the most certain thing of all to me, is, that the whole has more the semblance of a dream than reality; for which reason and because I wish to do no injustice to either party, I pray that no stress may be laid upon any thing I have here written, touching this business, further than it is corroborated by the testimony of others. With esteem & regard—I am Sir Yr Most Obedt Hble Servt

Go: Washington

P.S. Mr Dawson has written to me on this subject—his letter dated the 5th of Octr—and propounded questions which my memory does not enable me to answer. The certificate which he enclosed to me, I now return, with a request that it may be handed to him.

G: W——n

ALS, PHi: Dreer Collection; LB, DLC:GW.
For background to this letter, see William Dawson to GW, 5 Oct. 1789.

To Alexander Anderson

Sir,   New York [November] 18 1789[1]
I have been favored with the receipt of your letter of the 14th of may last accompanying a parcel of seeds, which have been disposed of agreeably to the disposition suggested to you by Mr Benjamin Vaughan.[2]
I desire to express my sense of your obliging kindness and to assure you that I shall be happy to aid beneficent intentions on

any other occasion. I am Sir very respectfully your most obedient Servant

G. Washington

LB, DLC:GW.

Alexander Anderson (d. 1811), the English botanist, had been named superintendent of the government's botanical garden on St. Vincent in the Windward Islands, British West Indies, in 1785. In 1791 Anderson led a major botanical expedition to Guiana and received a number of honors for his work in the garden on St. Vincent. He held his post until shortly before his death.

1. The copyist dated the letter 18 Oct. 1789 in GW's letter books. Since the president was on his New England tour in October it is likely the letter was sent in November.

2. Letter not found.

From William Cushing

Sir,   Boston November the 18th 1789.

On Saturday the 24th of October, at Taunton while on the circuit, I had the honor of receiving your letter of the 30th of September last with a commission for the office of an associate Justice of the Supreme court of the united States.[1] Decency & duty would have prompted an earlier answer, but that two of our state courts, at Cambridge & Salem remaining to conclude the business of the year, Judge Sewall, who has been appointed to the office of district Judge,[2] thought with me, that two immediate resignations would have endangered the falling through or a distant adjournment of those courts, to the public inconvenience & the injury of individuals; which, I doubt not, therefore, you will approve as an apology for the delay. You condescend, Sir, to consider the Judicial System as the chief pillar of our national government, and kindly to say, that you have nominated to that department such men as you concieved would give dignity and lustre to our national government. I should be glad if my poor abilities could in any measure give ground for such a hope respecting myself; but I beg leave to say, that my wish has been from the beginning, to have such a national government take place, as should effectually secure the union, the authority, the peace & prosperity of these states. And since you have been pleased to express a desire of my ready acceptance of the office,

I do now, with the greater confidence, but hoping for your candor, of which I shall stand in need, declare my acceptance of it. I must take the liberty to express my regret at being de-preived of the honor of paying my respects to you at Boston, and joining publickly in the universal joy occasioned by your honoring these northern States with a visit; owing to a bad cold joined to the foulness of the weather the monday & Tuesday after your arrival here. Without troubling you, Sir, with my sense of the great things you thought it your duty to do and Suffer for us during the war, I shall only add my hearty wish, that you may long preside over, and thereby continued to ren-der happy, the people of America. I have the honor to be, with the deepest respect, Sir, Your most obedient obliged humble Servant

William Cushing

ALS, DNA: RG 59, Acceptances and Orders for Commissions.

1. GW's pro forma letter enclosing Cushing's commission is in MHi: Rob-ert Treat Paine Papers.

2. David Sewall (1735–1825), a 1755 graduate of Harvard, was appointed a justice of the Massachusetts Supreme Court in 1777, and in 1789 GW named him United States district judge for Massachusetts.

To William Drayton

Sir.   United States Novr 18th 1789
The Office of Judge of the district Court in and for South Carolina District having become vacant; I have appointed you to fill the same, and your Commission therefor is enclosed.

You will observe that the Commission which is now transmit-ted to you is limitted to the end of the next Session of the Senate of the United States. This is rendered necessary by the Constitu-tion of the United States, which authorizes the President of the United States to fill up such vacances as may happen during the recess of the Senate—and appointments so made shall expire at the end of the ensuing Session unless confirmed by the Senate; however there cannot be the smallest doubt but the Senate will readily ratify & confirm this appointment, when your commis-sion in the usual form shall be forwarded to you.

I presume, Sir, it is unnecessary for me to advance any arguments to shew the high importance of the Judicial System to our National Government, and of course the necessity of having respectable & influential Characters placed in the important offices of it. The love which you bear our Country will, I am persuaded, lead you to do every thing in your power to promote its welfare; and upon this principle I flatter myself you will accept the above appointment.[1] I am Sir Yr most Obdt Hble St.

Df, in the writing of Tobias Lear, DNA: RG 59, Miscellaneous Letters; LB, DLC:GW.

For background to GW's judicial appointments, see his letter to the United States Senate submitting nominations for judicial posts, 24 Sept. 1789.

William Drayton (1732–1790) of South Carolina studied law at the Middle Temple in London and was admitted to the English bar in 1755. Upon his return to South Carolina he began a legal career that included service as chief justice of the state, judge of the admiralty court, and associate justice of the state supreme court.

1. Drayton replied to this letter on 12 Dec., accepting the appointment (DNA: RG 59, Acceptances and Orders for Commissioners). GW presented Drayton's name to the Senate on 9 Feb. 1790, and the appointment was confirmed on 10 Feb. (*DHFC*, 2:59, 62). He served as United States federal judge until his death on 18 May 1790.

Tobias Lear to Henry Knox

Sir,   United States. November 18th 1789

I am directed by the President of the United States to transmit to you the enclosed letters which have been received by him, and which come properly under the cognizance of the Secretary of War.

The letters enclosed are as follows, viz.

one from Samuel McDowell, as chairman of a committee of a Convention in Kentuckey, upon Indian Affairs in Kentuckey, and containing a list of sundry tribes of Indians not included in any treaty between the United States and Indian tribes. dated Da[n]ville July 26th 1789.[1]

One from Daniel Smith, relative to the Chickasaw nation and enclosing a list of depredations committed by Indians on the Inhabitants of Cumberland since may last—dated Miro District on Cumberland River in North Carolina Augt 23d 1789.[2]

One signed by a number of respectable Inhabitants of Kentuckey recommendg the Mountain leader a Chickasaw Chief—dated Septr 8th 1789.[3]

One from Jos. Martin relative to the Chickasaw nation &c—lands claimed by John Brown &ca—dated Long Island of Holston Septr 25th 178[9].[4]

one from Piamingo or the Mountain Leader, a Chickasaw Chieef, requesting a supply of powder & ball for his nation—dated Richmond October 30th 1789.[5] I have the Honor to be with perfect respect Sir, Your most Obedient Servant

Tobias Lear
Secretary to the President of the United States.

ADfS, DLC:GW; LB, DLC:GW. It is possible that some of the letters cited in Lear's letter to Knox were not addressed to GW.

1. See the Kentucky Convention to GW, 25 July 1789.

2. Letter not found. GW included an abstract of this letter in his Memoranda on Indian Affairs, 1789, printed below. Daniel Smith (1748–1818) was a resident of Sumner County, N.C. (now in Tennessee), and a prominent surveyor. The North Carolina legislature appointed Smith in 1784 to lay out the town of Nashville. In the late 1780s he was a commissioner for Sumner County, a brigadier general in the Mero District militia, and a member of the North Carolina Ratifying Convention. In June 1790 GW appointed him secretary of the Northwest Territory.

3. Letter not found, but see entry under that date.

4. Letter not found. This letter is dated 25 Sept. 1788. GW included an abstract of it in his Memoranda on Indian Affairs, 1789.

5. Letter not found.

Letter not found: to George Augustine Washington, 19 Nov. 1789. In a letter to GW of 14 Dec. 1789 Washington referred to "Your favor of the 19th."

From James Madison

Dear Sir   Orange [Va.] Novr 20 1789.

It was my purpose to have dropped you a few lines from Philada but I was too much indisposed during my detention there to avail myself of that pleasure. Since my arrival here I have till now been without a fit conveyance to the post office.

You will recollect the contents of a letter shewn you from Mr Innis to Mr Brown.[1] Whilst I was in Philada I was informed by the latter who was detained there as well as myself by indisposition, that he had recd later accounts though not from the same correspondent, that the Spaniards have finally put an entire stop to the trade of our Citizens down the river. The encouragements to such as settle under their own Government are continued.

A day or two after I got to Philada I fell in with Mr Morris. He broke the subject of the residence of Congs, and made observations which betrayed his dislike of the upshot of the business at N. York, and his desire to keep alive the Southern project of an arrangement with Pennsylvania.[2] I reminded him of the conduct of his State, and intimated that the question would probably sleep for some time in consequence of it. His answer implied that Congress must not continue at New York, and that if he should be freed from his Engagements with the E. States by their refusal to take up the bill and pass it as it went to the Senate, he should renounce all confidence in that quarter, and speak seriously to the S. States. I told him they must be spoken to very seriously, after what had passed, if Penna expected them to listen to her, that indeed there was probably an end to further intercourse on the subject. He signified that if he should speak it would be ⟨in earne⟩st, and he believed no one would pretend that his conduct would justify the least distrust of his going throug[h] with his undertakings; adding however that he was determined & accordingly gave me as he had given others notice that he should call up the postponed bill as soon as Congs should be re-assembled. I observed to him that if it were desirable to have the matter revived we could not wish to have it in a form more likely to defeat itself. It was unparliamentary and highly inconvenient, and would therefore be opposed by all candid friends to his object as an improper precedent, as well as by those who were opposed to the object itself. And if he should succeed in the Senate, the irregularity of the proceeding would justify the other House in withholding the signature of its Speaker, so that the bill could never go up to the President. He acknowledged that the bill could not be got thro' unless it had a majority in both houses on its merits. Why then, I asked, not take it up anew? He said he meant to bring the gentlemen who had postponed the bill to the point, acknowledged that he distrusted them, but held his engagements binding on him, until this final experiment should be made on the respect they meant to pay to theirs. I do not think it difficult to augur from this conversation the views which will govern Penna at the next Session. Conversations held by Grayson both with Morris & others in Philada and left by him in a letter to me, coincide with what I have stated.[3] An attempt will first be made to alarm N. York and the Eastern States into the plan postponed, by holding out the Potowmac & Philada as the alternative, and if the attempt should not succeed, the alternative will then be held out to the Southern members. On the other hand N.Y. and the E. States, will enforce their policy of delay, by threatening the S. States as heretofore, with German Town or Trenton or at least Susquehanna, and will no doubt carry the threat into execution if they can, rather than suffer an arrangement to take place between Pena & the S. States.

I hear nothing certain from the Assembly. It is said that an attempt of Mr H. to revive the project of commutables has been defeated, that the amendments have been taken up, and are likely to be put off to the next Session, the present house having been elected prior to the promulgation of them.[4] This reason would have more force, if the amendments did not so much correspond as far as they go with the propositions of the State Convention, which were before the public long before the last Election.[5] At any rate, the Assembly might pass a vote of *approbation* along with the postponement, and Asign the reason of referring the *ratification* to their successors. It is probably that the scruple has arisen with the disaffected party. If it be construed by the public into a latent hope of some contingent opportunity for prosecuting the war agst the Genl Government; I am of opinion the experiment will recoil on the authors of it. As far as I can gather, the great bulk of the late opponents are entirely at rest, and more likely to censure further opposition to the Govt as now Administered than the Government itself. One of the principal leaders of the Baptists lately sent me word that the amendments had entirely satisfied the disaffected of his Sect, and that it would appear in their subsequent conduct.[6]

I ought not to conclude without some apology for so slovenly a letter. I put off writing it till an opportunity should present itself not knowing but something from time to time might turn up that would make it less unworthy of your perusal. And it has

so happened that the oppy barely gives me time for this hasty
scr⟨awl⟩. With the most perfect esteem & affect. attachment I
remain Dear Sir Yr Mot Obedt ⟨servt⟩

Js Madison Jr

ALS, DLC:GW; copy, in Madison's writing, DLC: James Madison Papers.
 1. The letter from Harry Innes to John Brown has not been located.
 2. For the proceedings in Congress over the location of the Federal City, in
which Sen. Robert Morris played a leading role, see Pierre L'Enfant to GW, 11
Sept. 1789.
 3. For Grayson's comments on congressional dissension over the site for
the new Federal City, see his letter to Madison, 7 Oct. 1789, in Rutland, *Madison Papers*, 12:431–32.
 4. For Patrick Henry's unsuccessful attempt in the Virginia house of delegates to make hemp and tobacco commutable for the payment of 1789 taxes,
in addition to payments in specie, see *Journal of the House of Delegates*, 1789, 57.
 5. For the amendments to the Constitution submitted to the states for ratification, see GW's Circular to the Governors of the States, 2 Oct. 1789. Virginia was in the forefront of the states demanding that a bill of rights be added
to the Constitution, and some members of the state ratifying convention had
considered conditional ratification until such amendments were introduced.
As Madison later observed, "In many States the Constn. was adopted under a
tacit compact in favr. of some subsequent provision on this head. In Virga. It
would have been *certainly* rejected, had no assurances been given by its advocates that such provisions would be pursued" (Madison to Richard Peters, 19
Aug. 1789, in Rutland, *Madison Papers*, 12:346–48). The Virginia Ratifying
Convention had formulated twenty articles to constitute a bill of rights, and it
had suggested another twenty additional amendments to the Constitution.
See Robertson, *Debates and Other Proceedings of the Convention of Virginia*, 471–
75, for the text of the twenty articles. Even after ratification, many of the
opponents of the Constitution in Virginia, as well as in other states, advocated
calling a second convention to consider amendments limiting federal powers.
During the debates in Congress over the amendments in the summer of 1789,
senators Richard Henry Lee and William Grayson campaigned vigorously
and unsuccessfully to have all of Virginia's amendments submitted to the
states. Their apologetic letters to the governor and the house of delegates are
printed in note 4 of Edmund Randolph's letter to GW, 26 Nov. 1789. When
the twelve amendments enacted by Congress were finally presented to the
states in October 1789, some Antifederalists in Virginia, as in other states,
opposed them as inadequate. See, for example, Edmund Randolph to GW, 26
Nov., nn.3 and 4, and 6, 11, and 15 Dec. 1789, David Stuart to GW, 3 Dec.,
and Madison to GW, 5 Dec. 1789. Critics of the Constitution continued to
push for prohibitions against standing armies and direct taxes and for protection for paper money already in circulation, and Virginia continued to agitate
for adoption of the amendments promulgated in the state's ratifying convention. The amendments were submitted to the states in October 1789. See
GW's Circular to the Governors of the States, 2 Oct. 1789. When the amend-

ments were introduced in the Virginia general assembly, Patrick Henry led
the opposition. Perhaps the best description of the proceedings concerning
amendments in this session of the house of delegates is found in a letter from
Edward Carrington to Madison, 20 Dec. 1789: "During the session, there has
been much less intemperance than prevailed last year. Mr. H[enry] was disposed to do some antifederal business, but having felt the pulse of the House
on several points and finding that it did not beat with certainty in unison with
his own, he at length took his departure about the middle of the session without pushing any thing to its issue. His first effort was to procure an address of
thanks, or in some other mode the acknowledgements of the House, for the
great vigilance of our senators manifested in their letter upon the subject of
our forlorn prospect in regard to such amendements as will secure our liberties under the Government. Upon this point he made a Speech to the house,
but it not appearing to take well, it was never stirred again. This letter was
considered by some of the most violent of the Anti's as seditious and highly
reprehensible. His next effort was to refer the amendments sent forward by
Congress, to the next session of Assembly, in order that the people might give
their sentiments whether they were satisfactory, alledging that in his opinion
they were not. To this purpose he proposed a resolution, but finding the disposition of the house to be otherwise, he moved that it might lie on the Table,
and went away without ever calling it up again. Somewhat later in the session
the subject of the amendments was taken up—the ten first were, with the
exception of perhaps not more than ten Members, unanimously agreed to—
on the eleventh and twelfth some difficulty arose, from Mr. E. Randolphs ob-
jecting to them as unsatisfactory—after much debate they were rejected in the
Committee of the whole but the report being defered a few days they were
accepted in the House by a pretty good Majority thus the whole were adopted
in the lower house—they went to the senate in one resolution where they
remained long—the resolution at length returned with a proposition to
amend by striking out the 3d. 8th. 11th. & 12, these to be refered to the consideration of the people. To this amendment the lower house disagreed and
requested a conference—the Senate insisted, and assented to the conference,
this was, however, productive of conviction on neither side, the Committee on
the part of the Senate returned with S[tevens] T[homson] Mason at their
head, to their House, which upon his Motion, immediately adhered before
any thing further passed between the two Houses; the delegates could in no
stage have seen cause to recede from their disagreement, but under this in-
temperate and unprecedented Conduct they were left without a choice of any
thing but to adhere also, and thus the whole amendments have fallen. The
sense of the house of delegates was fairly & fully passed on the propriety of
adopting them, and the intemperance manifested in the conduct of the Senate, will doubtless shew the people whether this fate of the amendments, was
produced from a want of merit in them, or in the senate. Through the whole
course of the business in that house there was on the several questions equal
divisions of the members, so, as to leave the decision to the chair. Notwithstanding the unequivocal decision in the house of delegates for adopting the
amendments, yet in the course of the discussion some intemperance was gen-

erated—this led to propositions which in the earlier parts of the session none would have thought of, and it was with difficulty that a proposition for demanding a compliance with the amendments proposed by our convention, so far as they have not been agreed to, by Congress was prevented from passing. This proposition was presented to the house as often as three times, at first it was rejected by a great majority, at the next attempt it was rejected by a less majority, and at the third by the vote of the Speaker. Had Mr. Henry conceived that such would have been the temper in the latter stages of the session, he would not have left us" (Rutland, *Madison Papers,* 12:462–65). For other comments on the journey of the amendments through this session of the Virginia legislature, see Randolph to GW, 22, 26 Nov., 6, 11, and 15 Dec. 1789, and Madison to GW, 5 Dec. 1789.

6. Virginia Baptists were among the most avid supporters of a bill of rights containing clauses guaranteeing not only their right to worship freely but relieving them for the support of an established church. Encouraged by the provisions of the 1776 Virginia Declaration of Rights assuring the free practice of religion, they led the opposition in the early 1780s to a bill in the legislature granting state subsidies to religious education and to the Incorporation Act of 1784 designed to preserve the glebe lands held by the Episcopal church (see Randolph to GW, 22 Nov. 1789, n.6). For a statement of their views, see the church's address to GW, printed in the notes to GW's letter of reply, May 1789.

From George Plater

Dear Sir   Sotterley Novr 20th 1789

Mr Johnson, who was appointed Judge in the federal Court for the State of Maryland, having declined to accept[1]—I hope I shall be excused for taking the Liberty of recommending to your Excellency Mr John Allen Thomas, an old practitioner of Law, & who has frequently served his Country both in the Cabinet & the field[2]—You are not a Stranger to him, & therefore it becomes unnecessary for me to say more than that I am, with the highest Consideration, Yr Excellency's most obt hble Servt

Geo: Plater

ALS, DLC:GW.

For background to GW's Judiciary appointments, see his letter to the United States Senate submitting nominations for judicial posts, 24 Sept. 1789.

1. See GW to Thomas Johnson, 28 Sept. 1789.

2. John Allen (Alleyne) Thomas (1734–c.1797) of Talbot County was a prominent Maryland attorney who had served in the state legislature in the 1770s and 1780s and held several minor judicial appointments in St. Mary's

County. He received no federal appointment. Thomas was also recommended to GW by William Fitzhugh in a letter of 4 Dec. 1789 as "respectable in the profession of the Law, and very deservedly I am persuaded in high Estimation for his Integrity" (DLC:GW).

From Henry Knox

Sir   War Office November 21st 1789
I have the honor to submit to your inspection the report and letter which I have just received from the Commissioners of Indian Affairs for the Southern district.[1] I have the honor to be Sir With the highest respect Your Most Obedient Humble Servant.

H. Knox

LS, DLC:GW; LB, DLC:GW.
1. Knox is undoubtedly referring to the letter of 17 Nov. 1789 to him from Benjamin Lincoln, Cyrus Griffin, and David Humphreys, the United States commissioners to the southern Indians, enclosing their report on their negotiations with the southern tribes. The letter and report are in *DHFC*, 2: 210–36, and *ASP, Indian Affairs*, 1:68–78. Also enclosed may have been the commissioners' letter to Knox of 20 Nov. 1789, reporting on Indian affairs on the southern frontier and recommending measures to deal with Indian problems in the area (*DHFC*, 2:236–40; *ASP, Indian Affairs*, 1:78–79). GW abstracted material from this report in his Memoranda on Indian Affairs, 1789, printed below.

Tobias Lear to Henry Knox

Sir,   United States November 21st 1789
I have the honor to enclose you three letters from the supreme Executive of the State of Virginia upon the subject of Indian Affairs. These letters are addressed to the President of the United States, and have been duly acknowledged by him. As the President of the United States has directed me to transmit to you all letters & papers which have been received by him upon the subject of Indian Affairs, I now transmit the inclosed tho' of a distant date—which are all of the above description that are in my possession.
The enclosed letters are as follows viz.
One dated May ⟨4⟩ 1789, from the Honbl. James Wood a

member of the supreme Executive Council of Virginia, enclosing Letters and papers relative to murders committed by the Indians in Monongahalia County, Virginia, together with the advice of Council thereon.[1]

One dated June ⟨5th⟩ 1789 from His Exy Beverly Randolph—relative to retaining troops in the service of the State of Virginia to protect the frontiers thereof.

One dated June 6th, 1789 from His Excellency Beverly Randolph enclosing a letter from the Lieutenant of the County of Green Briar on the subject of Indian Affairs.[2] I have the Honor to be with perfect Respect, Sir, Your most Obedt Servt

Tobias Lear.
Secretary to the President of the United States.

ADfS, DLC:GW; LB, DLC:GW.
1. Letter not found. This letter was addressed to Beverley Randolph rather than GW. See GW to Randolph, 16 May 1789.
2. Letter not found.

From Charles-Bertin-Gaston Chapuy de Tourville

Calais, France, 21 Nov. 1789. Requests membership in the Society of the Cincinnati for the officers of the régiment d'Auvergne (formerly the régiment de Gatinais).

ALS, in French, DSoCi.
Charles-Bertin-Gaston Chapuy de Tourville (1740–1809) entered the French service in 1755 and by April 1776 had risen to the rank of major in the régiment de Gâtinais. He served with the comte d'Estaing in Rhode Island, was wounded during the siege of Savannah, and participated in the Yorktown campaign. He eventually was accorded membership in the Society of the Cincinnati.

Clement Biddle to Tobias Lear

Phila Sunday November 22d 1789
After the Departure of the last post I recd your favour of 17th Instant handed me by major Jackson. I did not expect the return of the president so early or should have lodged Mr

Bartram's Answer which did not reach me til some time after I wrote to him—I waited on Mr Morris to pay him the 32 £s 12 s. 2 d. Balance due to Governeur Morris Esqr. & for the Black Sattin & Floor Matts—Mr Cottringer[1] is to send me the Account which he Could not then make up but expects to do it tomorrow and I shall be Careful to Call again to discharge it. I am Glad that you have procured the red Cloverseed as after diligent Enquiry of the Dealers in Town and persons who raise it in the Country I find none Can be depended on before the Close of the Winter & a very little which Comes out has sold at 60/ ℔ Bushel which is much higher than you mention.

It has been a favourable year for Buck Wheat and any quantity may be had but I Cannot yet ascertain the price as little has been brought to Market but suppose about 2/ ℔ Bus.

On Friday I was shewn Mr Merediths Note to Mrs Meredith desiring me to procure a Conveyance to Mount Vernon for some red potatoes[2]—two vessels were going off the same Evening for Alexa. which was too late to have the potatoes dug & brought to town but Cap. Carhart is expected shortly from Alexa. & to return immediately,[3] of this or any Earlier Conveyance I shall take Care to inform Mrs Meredith & her Overseer tells me the potatoes shall be ready.

I have Called at the Stage Office a great Number of times to pay the passage of the German Gardner[4] but the proprietor Mr Inskeep tells me he has no Account yet of his Passage & Baggage from the southern Stages, but expects it soon & will Call on me first—I shall thank you to remind me if any other Commands are unexecuted & you may Depend on my Strict Attention to them.

C.B.

LB, PHi: Clement Biddle Letter Book, 1789–92.

1. Garret Cottringer was an associate of Robert Morris.

2. The Merediths are Margaret (Peggy) Cadwalader Meredith, one of five daughters of Dr. Thomas and Hannah Lambert Cadwalader, and her husband Samuel Meredith, the treasurer of the United States, and their seven children. GW frequently visited the Merediths for dinner and tea at their home on Front Street. See, for example, *Diaries*, 3:181, 284, 331; 5:170, 239.

3. Captain Carhart commanded the sloop *Dolphin*, which arrived in Philadelphia on Tuesday, 8 Dec., and sailed back to Virginia on 24 Dec. (*Pennsylvania Packet, and Daily Advertiser* [Philadelphia], 8 Dec. and 24 Dec. 1789).

4. The "German Gardner" was John Christian Ehlers. See his contract with GW, 24 June 1789, and notes. See also Lear to Biddle, 16 Sept. 1789.

From Edmund Randolph

Dear Sir   Richmond November 22. 1789

Immediately upon the receipt of your private communication of my appointment, I wrote to you with a head, very much disordered by a fever.[1] As soon as I recovered, I should have written to you again, had I not heard of your tour to the East. By this time I presume you have returned, & therefore beg leave to inform you, that I shall leave Virginia on the 15th of January for New-York. The reason, why I do not make an official reply to your official favor is stated in my former letter.[2] Should you wish to see me earlier than the day, which I have fixed above, I will endeavour to obey your summons.

In a fortnight the assembly will rise. Mr Henry has quitted, rather in discontent, that the present assembly is not so pliant as the last. He moved before his departure to postpone the consideration of the amendments until the next session. His motion now lies upon the table, to be discussed tomorrow. I think the result will be, to ratify the first ten, and adjourn the remaining two over, on account of their ambiguity.[3]

A motion will also be made tomorrow to publish an inflammatory letter, written by our senators to the assembly.[4] This will be opposed so far, as relates to a publication under legislative sanction. As soon as I can with propriety procure a copy, I will forward it to you. We have reduced the taxes a fourth below the taxes of the last year, and about 25000£ short of our actual demand. Mr Henry pressed a reduction of a third, and declared that he would come even to a half. He also urged commutables; but the payment is to be made in Specie, and warrants equivalent only.[5] For this year the military certificates will probably support their value. But the draught, which will be made from the next assembly, of men, who are friends to public faith, will I fear leave them in an unprotected state.

The plan for a revisal of our la⟨ws⟩ as mentioned in my former letter, has been approved, after a marked malignity shewn to it by our demagogues.

In a day or two we shall be agitated by a question on the sale of the glebes.[6] The partizans of this iniquity wish to keep it off until next year. But it is determined to prepare an antidote for their misrepresentations, by stating the title of the church in a pointed manner. If we find it practicable, we shall draw the assembly to a final decision. I am dear Sir your obliged and affectionate friend & servant

Edm: Randolph.

ALS, DLC:GW.

1. See GW to Randolph, 28 Sept. 1789.
2. For Randolph's letter of 8 Oct., see GW to Randolph, 28 Sept. 1789, n.3.
3. For the actions of the Virginia legislature on amendments to the Constitution, see James Madison to GW, 20 Nov. 1789, n.5.
4. The letter from senators Richard Henry Lee and William Grayson to the Virginia house of delegates is printed in Randolph to GW, 26 Nov. 1789, n.4.
5. See Madison to GW, 20 Nov. 1789, n.4.
6. The issue of the glebe lands of the Episcopal church agitated dissenters in Virginia for some years. The parish lands had been granted by the Crown to the parishes of the established church for the care of the poor, although dissenters charged they were not always used for that purpose. At the October 1789 session of the Virginia general assembly, seven Baptist congregations petitioned the house of delegates that all lands belonging to the church should be sold and "the churches heretofore used by the Episcopalians, may be used in common by all religious societies." On 27 Nov. a committee of the assembly reported that since the subject of the petition "involves in it one of the great rights of the people; and justice, as well as policy, dictate that it ought to be acted on with the greatest deliberation," the remonstrance ought to be referred to the next session of the assembly (*Journal of the House of Delegates*, 1789, 83, 113). The Baptists were finally able to get a vote on selling the glebe lands in November 1790, but it was defeated by a vote of 52 to 89 (*Journal of the House of Delegates*, 1790, 73). The question surfaced from time to time during the 1790s and was not settled until "An Act to repeal certain acts, and to declare the construction of the bill of rights and constitution, concerning religion," passed 24 Jan. 1799, repealed all of the statutes granting privileged status to the Episcopal church. "An Act concerning the glebe lands and churches within this commonwealth," 12 Jan. 1802, reiterated the right of the assembly to authorize the sale of land and property attached to the glebes, subject to certain rights of tenants on the land (Shepherd, *Statutes at Large*, 2:149, 314–16).

From George Savage

Sir   Virginia Northampton Novr 22d 1789

I beg leave to return you my most grateful Acknowledgment for the Commission appointing me Collector of the port of Cherry-Stone. Though The Revenue arising to the Union from the Collectorship of that port as also the profits of office will yield very little, there being few or no Sea Vessels that belong to the County; Yet from it's extent, being upwards of 40 miles long, the number of Inlets & Rivers both on the Sea & bay side, will render it always necessary in my opinion, to keep there an Office to prevent Smugling, and by that means have a tendency to promote the Interest and advantage of the Union.

A Commissioner of Wrecks, I was appointed, upwards of seven years ago, & as that Office will not interfere with the one to which your Excellency has been pleas'd to appoint me, I shou'd be glad, if it is your Excellencys pleasure, to be continued. Mr John Upshur Senr has acted with me as a Commissioner for several years past, and from that Gentleman's integrity, his knowledge of the different inlets, Isles and harbours both on the Sea & Bay side, I cannot helph expressing a Wish that it may please your Excellency, to continue him also. I have the honour to be your Excellency's most Obedt & very hum: Servt

George Savage

ALS, DLC:GW.

George Savage (d. 1824) of Northampton County, Va., a member of an established Eastern Shore family, had served as naval officer and commissioner of wrecks under the state government since 1782. In 1786 GW purchased corn from him for Mount Vernon. See GW to David Stuart, 24 Dec. 1785, and to Savage, 8 Feb. 1786, and Savage to GW, 18 Feb. 1786. Savage resigned as collector at Cherrystone in early 1790 and in October 1791 was appointed sheriff of Northampton County (*Executive Journal*, 1:44; *Journals of the Council of State of Virginia*, 5:328). John Upshur became a commissioner of wrecks in March 1785 (ibid., 3:430).

To Otho Holland Williams

Dear Sir,   New York 22d Nov. 1789.

Upon my return to this City, after making a tour through the Eastern States, I received your favour of the 29th of October enclosing one from Mrs Carroll; and two days ago I received another letter from you, dated the 10th of the same month.

I can no longer refuse the kind and pressing offer of bearing fruit trees from that good Lady—and in the enclosed letter to her, have informed her that when the Season will permit, you will do me the favor of embracing the first favourable oppertunity of forwarding them to Mount Vernon.[1]

From the promising abilities, and good character I have heard of Mr Robt Smith, I entertain a very favourable opinion of his merits; but as, in the person of a judge, the World will look for a character & reputation founded on Service & experience, I cannot conceive that the appointment of so young & inexperienced a Man as Mr Smith would be considered as a judicious choice by the community in general, though it might meet the approbation of those who have had the best opportunities of becoming acquainted with his talents. In such important appointments as the Judiciary, much Confidence is necessary; and this will not be given *fully* to an untried man.[2] With esteem & regard—I am—Dr Sir Yr Most Obedt Servt

⟨Go: Washington⟩

AL⟨S⟩, MdHi: Otho Holland Williams Papers; LB, DLC:GW.

1. For Margaret Carroll's gift to GW of plants from her greenhouse, see GW's letter to her, 16 Sept. 1789.

2. Robert Smith had earlier applied for a judicial appointment (see his letter to GW, 5 Sept. 1789), and Williams had recommended him to GW in his letter of 10 October.

To John Brown Cutting

Sir,   New York Novr 23d, 1789

I have received your letter of the 25th of July enclosing sundry papers respecting the state of public affairs in France, for which mark of attention I request you to accept my best acknowledgements. I am, Sir, Your most Obedt Servt.

Df, in the writing of Tobias Lear, DNA: RG 59, Miscellaneous Letters; LB, DLC:GW.

On this day GW also wrote similar brief letters of acknowledgment to John Skey Eustace for his letters of 24 July and 18 Aug. and to Lucy Paradise for her letter of 12 May. On 24 Nov., using the same form, he acknowledged Richard Claiborne's letters of 10 June and 23 July. Drafts of all of these short acknowledgments, in the writing of Tobias Lear, are in DNA: RG 59, Miscellaneous Letters.

To Thomas Newton, Jr.

Sir,   New York Novr 23d 1789
    Your letter of the 24th of October, containing an estimate of the cost of a Light-house which was to have been erected on Cape Henry—a draft of the same—and an account of materials placed upon the spot for the purpose of building, has been duly received;[1] and I beg you to accept my thanks for your trouble in preparing & forwarding them—I am, Sir, Your most Obedt Servt

                                            Go: Washington

Df, in the writing of Tobias Lear, DNA: RG 59, Miscellaneous Letters; LB, DLC:GW.
    1. Letter not found. On 21 Nov. Tobias Lear wrote Secretary of the Treasury Alexander Hamilton that "I am directed by the President of the United States to enclose and send to you, a letter addressed to him from Thomas Newton, Junr Esquire of Norfolk, dated October 24th 1789, containing an estimate made by Commissioners appointed by the States of Maryland and Virginia of the cost of building a lighthouse on Cape Henry in Virginia— an account of materials which were placed on the spot for that purpose—and likewise a dft of the lighthouse which was to have been erected" (DNA: RG 26, Light House Services Correspondence, Vault Materials). Hamilton acknowledged the letter on the same day, requesting Lear to "inform the President that I shall pay due attention to the information it convey's" (DLC:GW). See also Newton to GW, 17 July 1789, and GW to Newton, 12 Oct. 1789.
    Newton may have written GW a second, private letter on 24 Oct.; a second letter sent by GW to Newton on 23 Nov. acknowledges Newton's letter of "24th ultimo respecting the state of accounts between us, and the outstanding debts due to me, which I make no doubt you will use your best endeavors to recover" (LB, DLC:GW).

To Edward Rutledge

Dear Sir,   New York Novr 23d 1789.
    I have been favoured with your letter of the 31st ultimo,[1] and am very happy to learn that the appointments under the general Government have given so much satisfaction in your part of the Union. Added to the consciousness of having brought forward

such characters only to fill the several offices in the United States, as, from my own knowledge, or the strictest inquiries, I conceived would do justice to the public & honor to themselves, I have the happiness to find, so far as my information extends, that they are highly acceptable to the good people of this Country.

Your brother's acceptance of his appointment has given me much pleasure;[2]—and I should have been glad if Major Pinckney could have found it compatible with his interest to hold the office of District Judge;[3] however, I am persuaded the duties of that office will be ably and faithfully discharged by Mr Drayton whom I have appointed to fill it, in consequence of your warm recommendation of him,[4] and the concurrent testimony given of his abilities and integrity by those Gentlemen who are acquainted with him, & who have spoken to me on the subject.[5] I am, Dear Sir, with sentiments of affection & esteem Your most Obedt Humbe Servt.

Df, in the writing of Tobias Lear, DNA: RG 59, Miscellaneous Letters; LB, DLC:GW.

1. Letter not found.
2. See GW to John Rutledge, 29 Sept. 1789.
3. See Thomas Pinckney to GW, 22 Oct. 1789.
4. No letter from Rutledge recommending Drayton has been found.
5. See GW to William Drayton, 18 Nov. 1789, Pierce Butler to GW, 8 Aug. 1789, and GW to Butler, 10 Aug. 1789.

To Abigail Adams

Tuesday November 24 [1789]

The President of the United States having understood that Mrs Adams intends visiting the Theatre this evening, he presents his Compliments to Mrs Adams, and requests her acceptance of a Ticket for his Box.

The Play begins at 6 o'clock.[1]

L, in the writing of Tobias Lear, owned (1976) by Mrs. Harry Hull, Manchester, Massachusetts.

1. GW's diary entry for this day notes: "Went to the Play in the Evening. Sent Tickets to the following Ladies and Gentlemn. & invited them to Seats in my Box viz.—Mrs. Adams (Lady of the Vice-President) Genl. [Philip] Schuyler & Lady, Mr. [Rufus] King & Lady, Majr. [Pierce] Butler and Lady, Colo.

[Alexander] Hamilton & Lady Mrs. [Catherine] Green—all of whom accepted and came except Mrs. Butler who was indisposed" (*Diaries*, 5:500). The play was a comedy, *The Toy; or a Trip to Hampton Court*, performed by the Old American Company at the John Street Theatre (Ford, *Washington and the Theatre*, 37–38). A New York newspaper observed that "On the appearance of THE PRESIDENT, the audience rose, and received him with the warmest acclamations" (*Gazette of the United States* [New York], 28 Nov. 1789).

From David Sewall

Sir　　　　　　　　　　　　　　　　York 24th November 1789.

the letter and Commission from the President of the United States, with sundry Statutes relating to the Judicial department did not find me, until some time after their date. This was not oweing to any failure in the conveyance by Post, but to my absence from hence on a remote Circuit of the Supreme Judicial Court: this circumstance, it is presumed, will be an apology, for not earlier noticing their reception.

The appointment of Judge of the district Court of Maine was on my part unsolicited and unexpected. I fear Sir, my abilities have by the partiality of some of my acquaintance been overrated. For altho' the Judicial decisions of the highest law Court of Massachusetts, have for a series of years, met the general approbation of its Cytizens and Suitor's: this may be satisfactorily accounted for, from the abilities of the worthy Gentlemen with whom I have had the honour to be connected in that department. In this new appointment the Judge is to stand alone, and unassisted, and in some instances in matters of the greatest magnitude—Such as relate to the life of Man. Some unhappy Persons are now under Confinement within the district upon a charge of Pyracy and Felony on the high Seas; and whose situation will claim an early attention in this Court.[1]

But from the laws of the United States hitherto Enacted, it strikes me, that some other provision is necessary to be made, before a Trial of this nature can with propriety be had: And more specially, in case of Conviction, to have the Judgement carried into Execution. These difficulties I shall take the liberty of stating to some Gentlemen in the legislature, to the end they may be there considered and obviated; rather than arrest your attention from the many other important businesses of the Union.

Permit me now Sir, to thank you for the particular mark of confidence manifested in this appointment. To acquaint you That impressed with an Idea of the necessity of Civil government in the nation, over which in the course of Divine Providence, you are called to Preside. With a considerable degree of diffidence in my own abilities, I have concluded to accept the appointment of Judge of the district Court of Maine and shall in a few days proceed to Portland, about fifty miles, distant to organize the same. Whether my Services in this new department will meet the approbation of my fellow Citizens or the reasonable expection of those who have placed me in the Situation, Time must determine. All I can promise on the occasion, is, that I will endeavour to merit them—by striving to discharge the duties of the office with fidelity and impartiality according to the best of my abilities. I am Sir with the greatest Esteem and respect your most humble Servant

David Sewall

ALS, DNA: RG 59, Miscellaneous Letters.

1. Sewall is probably referring to the application of section 9 of "An Act to establish the Judicial Courts of the United States," which gave original jurisdiction to federal courts in cases pending in the state courts involving seizures on the high seas (1 *Stat.* 76–77 [24 Sept. 1789]). For one of the "unhappy persons" awaiting trial in Maine, see Thomas Bird to GW, 5 June 1790, and notes.

From Samuel Goodwin

Pownalborough, District of Maine, 25 Nov. 1789. Suggests that a lighthouse be established on the island of Seguin, near the entrance of the Kennebec River, and describes the advantages of the location.[1]

ALS, DNA: RG 59, Miscellaneous Letters.

1. Goodwin sent GW a second petition, dated November 1789 and probably enclosed in this letter, stating: "A great many peoples are Very uneasy that there is no Port of entry & Delivery for foriners, on the Great and leading river Kennebeck, which is settled about A 140 miles as the river runs." Kennebec River "is settled up it about 50 or 60 miles; as that runs: & Some Says

more; about 20 thousand Souls on Kenebeck river including both Sides thereof & to the west line of the County of Lincoln; & People a settleing continually . . . & Such a Number of inhabitants Worth notice; and to make every thing as easy for them as for other parts . . . A man Can live as well in the Southern Colony's with two days work in a week as they Can here with 6 days, Work in a week—it is a Cold Climat; and the True Calculation of the Seasons here is 4 months summer—2 months fall; 4 months Winter and two months Spring: & after our Crops is Cut Short: as it was the last Season & Very Short, too & many must Pinch Very heard this Winter; By not haveing Ports of Entry & Delivery on the large River of Kennebeck for foriners—Will Cause Smugling & So deprive the publick of their Just dues . . . if your Excellency Knew the Truth and facts . . . as you are A Star of the first magnitude and Capable & willing to make all happy as fair as human Natur Can be—all eyes are looking to you" (DNA: RG 59, Miscellaneous Letters). Another letter from Goodwin concerning an establishment on the Kennebec River is dated 25 Jan. 1790: "I Most Humly begg leave to Present your Excellency With A Plan Which Please to accept off: it will Give you a General idea: of Kennebeck river and the settlements, and Towns &c; the Sea Shore and other Rivers; in part; from Cape Elizabeth; To Penobscut Rivers mouth; the Sea Shore is from actual Surveys and Kennebeck river, as high up as the Carrying Place, To the first Pond: about A 140 miles from its mouth as the river runs, the Several Surveys, has ben don; by Joseph Heath Esqre Mr Phineas Jones; John North Esqr. and Mr Epheram Jones, Part of the Western branch of Kennebeck river; was Surveyed the Surveyor, was Keld & the Survey Stopt the Rest was taken by Course and imaginary distance; and Moose Lake, was taken from Hunters, som of which was Surveyors, who Gave the form and distance, as Near as they Could, and the Neck of Land, runing into the Said Lake appearing Like A Moose A Drinking; which Gave it the Name of Moose Lake both by Indians and English; the Indians informed me; that when the watter ware up in the, Spring, (they Could Goe from Richmond Fort, which was oppiset swan Island on the West Side of Kennebeck river, about 25 miles from the Sea: they Could Goe in 4 days to Quebeck in a burch Connew). but when the Watters ware down, the uper part of the rivers & Streems Was rocke & Shoal, and Difficelt Passing—the watters when up, Covered the rocks; oh how easy: they distrest the people here I had my Sheer . . . Sir please to Excuse Every thing A Miss— it is Cold weather and Cant be don So well as in Worm weather: we have a Cold Climet and Cold house" (DNA: RG 59, Miscellaneous Letters).

Five thousand dollars was appropriated for the construction of a lighthouse on Seguin in May 1794, after Massachusetts had ceded the necessary land to the federal government (1 *Stat.* 368–69 [19 May 1794]). For the controversy surrounding its construction, see Syrett, *Hamilton Papers*, 17:430, 18:201.

From Elijah Jackson

Sir,   New York November 25th 1789
I hope the Justice of my intensions will excuse the fredom I have taken of Emploreing your Assistance. (For I Solemnly declare in the Name of him whose all searching Eye is Privy to every thing that is Transacted. that it is through Necessity.) I have been somtime Employed in the Study of Physic and my most ardent desire is to gain a Sufficient compotency of Knowledge in the Science in order to render myself Capable of leading a usefull and active life. but to my great and unhappy disappointment, I shall not be able to accomplish my much Desired intension without the assistance of Some Noble and generous hearted Soul. For my finances is Exausted and my Parents reduced by Sickness and other misfortunes, which renders them incapable of assisting me.

Should you O! most Illusterous President. who has proved Yourself to be a friend to Mankind. See it consistent within Yourself to assist your humble Pertitioner, I Shall Esteem it a very great Deed of charity. It will be of the greatest importance to me, as my Present prospect of future Success Depends upon Immediate assistance. I am Sir. Your most Humble Pertitioner.

Elijah Jackson

Sir.
Should it not be to much trouble Please to favaur me with an Answer.

ALS, DNA:PCC, item 78.
No further information on Jackson has been found, and there is no evidence that GW contributed to his education.

Tobias Lear to Henry Knox

Sir,   United States, November 25th 1789
The President of the United States has directed me to return the draft of the letter which you are about to send to the Governor of Georgia and to inform you that it meets his approbations.[1] The President of the United States wishes you to send him the copy of the Instructions given to the Commissioners[2]—

which he will return to you in a few days. I have the Honor to be
with perfect respect Your most Obedt Servt

Tobias Lear
Secy to the Presidt of the U.S.

ADfS, DLC:GW; LB, DLC:GW.

1. Knox's letter to Edward Telfair, recently inaugurated governor of Georgia, has not been identified.

2. See GW to the Commissioners to the Southern Indians, 29 Aug. 1789.

From Edmund Randolph

Dear Sir   Richmond Novr 26. 1789.

Since my last, written about five days ago, the committee of
the whole house have been engaged in the amendments from
congress.[1] Mr Henry's motion, introduced about three weeks
past, for postponing the consideration of them, was negatived
by a great majority.[2] The first ten were easily agreed to. The
eleventh and twelfth were rejected 64 against 58.[3] I confess, that
I see no propriety in adopting the two last. But I trust that the
refusal to ratify will open the road to such an expression of
fœderalism, as will efface the violence of the last year, and the
intemperance of the inclosed letter, printed by the enemies to
the constitution, without authority.[4] However our final measures will depend on our strength, which is not yet ascertained.

I shall set off on the 15th of January, as I took the liberty of
informing you in my last. I am dear sir yr obliged & affectionate
friend

Edm: Randolph.

ALS, DLC:GW.

1. Randolph's "last" was his letter of 22 Nov. to GW.

2. For the Virginia house of delegates' action on the amendments to the
Constitution, see Madison to GW, 20 Nov. 1789, n.5.

3. Twelve amendments to the Constitution were originally submitted to
the states, and two were eventually rejected. One of the rejected amendments
dealt with the rates of apportionment for seats in the House of Representatives, the other with the alteration of congressional salaries. See GW's Circular
to the Governors of the States, 2 Oct. 1789, n.1.

4. Randolph enclosed the broadside printing of two letters from senators
Richard Henry Lee and William Grayson to the governor of Virginia and to
the speaker of the Virginia legislature, both dated 28 Sept. 1789 from New

York. The first letter reads: "We have long waited in anxious expectations, of having it in our power to transmit effectual Amendments to the Constitution of the United States, and it is with grief that we now send forward propositions inadequate to the purpose of real and substantial Amendments, and so far short of the wishes of our Country. By perusing the Journal of the Senate, your Excellency will see, that we did, in vain, bring to view the Amendments proposed by our Convention, and approved by the Legislature. We shall transmit a complete set of the Journals of both Houses of Congress to your address, which with a letter accompanying them, we entreat your Excellency will have the goodness to lay before the Honorable Legislature of the ensuing meeting."

The letter to the speaker of the house of delegates reads: "We have now the honor of enclosing the proposition of Amendments to the Constitution of the United States that has been finally agreed upon by Congress. We can assure you Sir, that nothing on our part has been omitted, to procure the success of those radical amendments proposed by the Convention, and approved by the Legislature of our Country, which as our constituent we shall always deem it our duty with respect and reverence to obey. The Journal of the Senate herewith transmitted, will at once show exact and how unfortunate we have been in this business. It is impossible for us not to see the necessary tendency to consolidated empire in the natural operation of the Constitution, if no further amended than as now proposed; and it is especially impossible for us not to be apprehensive for Civil Liberty, when we know of no influence in the records of history, that show a people ruled in freedom when subject to one undivided Government, and inhabiting a territory so extensive as that of the United States; and when, as it seems to us, the nature of man, and of things join to prevent it. The impracticability in such case, of carrying representation on sufficiently near to the people for procuring their confidence and consequent obedience, compels a resort to fear resulting from great force and executive power in government. Confederated republics, where the Federal Hand is not possessed of absorbing power, may permit the existence of freedom, whilst it preserves union, strength, and safety. Such amendments therefore as may secure against the annihilation of the state governments we devoutly wish to see adopted.

"If a persevering application to Congress from the states that have desired such amendments, should fail of its object, we are disposed to think, reasoning from causes to effects, that unless a dangerous apathy should invade the public mind, it will not be many years before a constitutional number of Legislatures will be found to *demand* Convention for the purpose.

"We have sent a complete set of the Journals of each House of Congress, and through the appointed channel will be transmitted the Acts that have passed this session, in those will be seen the nature and extent of the judiciary, the estimated expences of the government, and the means so far adopted for defraying the latter." In the broadside both letters are printed in italics. The letters were presented to the Virginia house of delegates on 19 Oct. (*Journal of the House of Delegates*, 1789, 3).

From James Boyd

Boston Novr 27. 1789.
To the President the Senate and House of Representatives of the United States of America in Congress assembled.

The Petition of James Boyd of Boston in the County of Suffolk and Commonwealth of Massachusetts Esquire, Humbly sheweth[1]—

That your Petitioner was possessed from the Year 1767 till the Beginning of our Contest with Great Britain of very large Property in Lands situated on the Eastern Bank of the River Schoodick, granted him by the British Government of Nova-Scotia, and that during said Period he introduced many Families on the same Lands at his own Charge, and expended much Property in getting the same under considerable Improvement and Cultivation; But feeling himself attached to the Cause of America, he took such an active Part in their Favour, that the resentment of the British Subjects in that Province compelled him to leave the Country, and flee to the Protection of the United States; & that in Consequence thereof he has suffered Poverty and Distress from that Day to the present Time, that the said Lands which your Petitioner held, are on the western Side of the River St Croix, and within the Dominions of the United States, but unjustly now held in Possession by British Subjects—That the Facts aforesaid and your Petitioner's Situation have been particularly set forth to Congress by the Legislature of this Commonwealth, in a Letter of Instruction to their Delegates in the Year 1786, signed and transmitted by the then Governor Bowdoin, and which is now on the Files of Congress, accompanied wth a Number of Letters from Governor Bowdoin, the present Governor Hancock, and others upon the Subject, to which your Excellency and Honours will please to be refered:[2] that your Petitioner by his thus quitting the British and joining the American Interest has been subjected to peculiar Hardships and Difficulties, which with a large Family he has with great Anxiety sustained: But confiding in the Power and Disposition of the present Congress of the United States to do him compleat Justice, he requests them to put him in Possession of his Lands aforesaid now held by British Subjects, tho' on this Side the Line between the two Dominions, or otherwise recompence your

Petitioner who has lost the whole of his Property and Means of procuring a comfortable Subsistence in Consequence of his Attachment as aforesaid.

Your Petitioner begs Leave to add that he is possessed of Papers, and that John Mitchel Esqr. of the State of Newhampshire (now an old Man about 76 Years of Age)[3] is also possessed of Papers, that may be useful in determining the real Situation of the River St Croix, entended by the late Treaty of Peace to be the dividing Line between the Dominions of the United States & Great Britain, as will appear by a Plan taken in the Year 1764 by the said Mitchel, and another taken by the Surveyor General of Nova Scotia the Year following, and now in the Possession of your Petitioner, who, As in Duty bound will ever pray &c.[4]

James Boyd

DS, DNA: RG 59, Miscellaneous Letters.

James Boyd (c.1736–1798) came to America from Scotland around 1760 to act as agent for his brother in the sale of goods. He eventually settled at Passamaquoddy, Maine. His original scheme for supplying settlers in the area of Schoodic Falls and Outer Island failed, but in 1767 he received a grant of 1,000 acres in the area of Passamaquoddy Bay. Supporting the Patriot cause, he apparently left Maine at the beginning of the Revolution. He is listed in the 1790 census as living in Boston and heading a family consisting of two males over sixteen years old, one under sixteen, and two females (*Heads of Families* [Massachusetts], 187; *Columbian Centinel* [Boston], 6 Oct. 1798; Murchie, *Saint Croix*, 131–32, 138).

1. The heading to this document is partially printed.

2. The British and American negotiators at the Treaty of Paris in 1783 had used Dr. John Mitchell's 1755 map to determine which of the two large streams that flow into Passamaquoddy Bay formed the boundary between the United States and Canada. The fact that Mitchell's map designated the eastern stream as the St. Croix placed the boundary at that river, a point that remained in dispute between the United States and Great Britain until a mixed commission appointed under the terms of the Jay Treaty defined the boundary in 1798 as the western stream, known locally as the Schoodic.

3. Boyd is referring to John Mitchell (c.1713–1801), son of John Mitchell, one of the pioneer settlers at Londonderry, N.H. The younger Mitchell came with his father from northern Ireland around 1719. In his early youth he was apprenticed to a carpenter but soon turned to surveying and land speculation in the area of Belfast, Maine. Because of his interest in mapmaking, the details of his career are occasionally confused with the activities of Dr. John Mitchell (1711–1768), creator of the map used at the peace negotiations in 1783. See, for example, Williamson, *History of Belfast*, 1:63. Mitchell remained in Belfast until 1779, when the British occupied the town. He went to New Hampshire and did not return to Belfast after the war although he retained much of his

property. In 1789 he may have been living with one of his ten children in Chester, New Hampshire.

4. A copy of this letter was sent to the Senate on 9 Feb. 1790. See GW to the United States Senate, 9 Feb. 1790, enclosure.

From Joseph Buckminster

Sire   Portsmouth [N.H.] November 27: 1789
I should not have presumed to intrude upon a moment of your time, filled as I know it must be with a variety of the most important cares, were it ⟨not⟩ to execute a request made when you were at Portsmouth, To present in the name of Lady Pepperell, Relict of Sr William Pepperell the inclosed discourse.[1] Though the connections of her Ladyship have been such as would lead us to suppose that she would have entered into the views and prejudices of the British administration, yet she has invariably been friendly to the american revolution, and wished to give some token of her high esteem and respect for one, who had been so highly honored of God, in effecting it. Her ill health and infirmities forbad her soliciting the honor of a visit when you landed at Kittery, near her mansion: But she wishes you to recieve the inclosed, as a token of her respect, presented by one who begs leave to subscribe himself, with the most fervent prayers for your Prosperity and happiness Your most Obdnt Humble Servt

Joseph Buckminster

ALS, DLC:GW.
    Joseph Buckminster (1751–1812) was educated for the ministry at Yale, graduating in 1770 and then remaining at Yale for some years of additional study and as a tutor. In 1779 he became pastor of the North Church in Portsmouth. Buckminster delivered the sermon at a service attended by GW while he was in Portsmouth in November 1789 (*Diaries*, 5:488). The sermon was published as a *Discourse, Delivered at Portsmouth New Hampshire, November 1st, 1789. On Occasion of the President of the United States Honoring that Capital with a Visit. By Joseph Buckminster, A.M. Pastor of the First Church in Portsmouth* (Portsmouth, 1789). Buckminster's sermon received mixed reviews, one New England clergyman commenting that "The text selected for the occasion was a passage from the twenty fourth Psalm: 'Lift up your heads,' &c. Some thought the selection a great mistake; and some even viewed it as a kind of idolatrous homage to the great man" (Daniel Dana to William B. Sprague, 22 June 1848, in Sprague, *Annals of the American Pulpit*, 2:118–19). An observer commented

that he was informed the president was pleased with his visit to Portsmouth but "if any thing was disgusting to him it was what was said on Sunday, when he was at worship (but this is under the rose at present). Mr Buckminsters sermon or address will be published . . . you may Judge for your Self how far it was Deifying him—Considering he was present" (Jeremiah Libbey to Andrew Belknap, 6 Nov. 1789, MHi: Belknap Papers).

1. Lady Pepperell (d. 1789), the widow of Sir William Pepperell (1696–1759), colonial merchant and soldier, was Mary Hirst Pepperell of Massachusetts, the granddaughter of Samuel Sewell. Lady Pepperell had remained in Kittery, Maine, after her husband's death. The enclosure was a *Sermon Occasioned by the Death of the Honourable Sir William Pepperell, Bart. Lieutenant-General in His Majesty's Service, &c. Who Died at His Seat in Kittery, July 6th, 1759, Aged 63. Preached the Next Lord's-Day after His Funeral. By Benjamin Stevens, A. M. Pastor of the First Church in Kittery* (Boston, 1759). The sermon, dealing in part with the relationship of earthly rulers to God, was in GW's library at the time of his death (Griffin, *Boston Athenæum Collection*, 193–94). In his reply, 23 Dec., GW asked Buckminster to convey his thanks "to the Revd Author with my approbation of the Doctrine therein inculcated."

From Henry Knox

Sir,   War Office November 27th 1789.

I have the honor to submit to you a letter from Brigadier General Harmar dated the 19th of October with several enclosures shewing the State of affairs on the Western Frontiers.[1] I have the honor to be Sir, with the highest respect, your most obedient humble servant

H. Knox

ALS, DLC:GW; LB, DLC:GW.

1. Josiah Harmar (1753–1813) was appointed in 1784 to command the United States Army on the frontier. With his meager force—700 men were authorized for the postwar army but Harmar was rarely able to bring the troops up to complement—he proceeded to establish a chain of forts on the Ohio, and by 1789 construction had reached the Wabash River with the establishment of Fort Knox at Vincennes. Virtually all of the posts were undermanned, poorly provisioned, and vulnerable to Indian attack. They were also powerless to prevent or control the expeditions from Kentucky sent out to avenge the attacks on that region by the Indian tribes north of the Ohio River, expeditions often joined by unruly inhabitants of the settlements that had grown up around the forts. Harmar had a few veteran officers in his command upon whom he particularly relied. These included John Francis Hamtramck (1756–1803), a Canadian who had seen military service with a New York regiment during the Revolution and was now in command at Fort

Knox—a post he held for some six years—and Capt. John Doughty, who in the winter of 1789 was engaged in the construction of Fort Washington on the Ohio at present-day Cincinnati.

The enclosure was Harmar's letter of 19 Oct., written from Fort Harmar, stating that "The Ohio river for this Sometime past has been so Exceeding low that it has been almost next to an impossibility Either to ascend or descend it, but it appears now to be taking a gradual rise.

"The Enclosed Extracts of Maj. Hamtramck's letters, dated the 29th of July, the 14th & 17th of August, will show the state of affairs in that quarter. I understand that another Expedition has gone forward from Kentucky against the Wabash Indians, the result of which has not yet come to my knowledge. Will you be pleased to give me particular and Explicit directions how to act with the inhabitants of Kentucky? Perhaps they may be secretly authorized to form these Expeditions. It certainly places Major Hamtramck in a most disagreeable situation; & when Head Quarters are properly fixed opposite Licking River, frequent applications will most assuredly be made to me, or at least hints for the few Federal troops to countenance and aid them in their operations; if we do not, numberless censures will be cast upon us.

"By the last accounts from Licking, our works were going on rapidly. Major Doughty writes me he was confined to his bed very ill with the ague & fever; I am hourly Expecting his return.

"The presence of the Governor is very much wanted. You will please observe by the Enclosed copy of a letter from the County Lieutenant of Harrison, in Virginia, to the Governor (the original of which I made free to open, & have in my possession until his arrival) the murders that have been committed by the Savages near Clarksburg" (extract, WHi: Draper Manuscripts, Harmar Papers).

The letters from Hamtramck to Harmar, written from Fort Knox and presumably enclosed in Knox's letter to GW, are in MiU-C: Harmar Papers, and printed in Thornbrough, *Outpost on the Wabash*, 178–85, 187. The letter from the county lieutenant of Harrison County, which Knox may also have enclosed, has not been located.

From Winthrop Sargent

Sir

Marietta, Territory of the United States
North West of the River Ohio Novr 27th 1789

I conceive it incumbent on me to acquaint your Excellency with the Death of Saml H. Parsons Esqr. one of the Judges of this territory.[1]

He had been to view some Salt Springs on a Branch of the big Beaver & on the Morng of the 17th Inst: Embarked on Board a Canoe, with one Man only, to descend that River—Before noon on the same Day, the Boat, in a very shattered Condition, with sundry Articles of Baggage known to have been the Property of the Judge, were observed floating by a military Post or Station at the Falls of Beaver (four Miles from the Ohio) & the Officer commanding immediately detached a Party in Search of the Bodies—but without Success. Upon the Eveg of the same Day a Soldier, who was with the deceased at the Time of his embarkation, arrived at the Post, being charged with his Horses & a Message to the Officer that he would dine with him at 12 oClock on the same Day—the 17th.

Upon the 18th and 19th the Bodies were sought after, but in vain—and we have no Intelligence since.[2]

As this melancholy Occasion has given me the Opportunity of introducing myself to your Excellency, devoid of the painful Consciousness of Intrusion I will trespass so far as to express my grateful Satisfaction in the fair Prospects of our Country under the present Constitution & your Excellency's Administration. with every Sentiment of Respect I have the Honour to be your Excellency's most obedient & most devoted Servant

Winthrop Sargent

P.S. The Governour is expected every Moment to arrive at this Place on his Way down the River—as the waters, which have been very low, will now permit his Passage.[3]

This Tour will give me an Opportunity of visiting a Country in which your Excellency, if I am not misinformed, has formerly been conversant[4]—If there should be at this Time, or hereafter, any Services which I can render you—or if your Excellency should be desirous of any Species of Information within my Ability to acquire, it will be highly gratifying to me to devote my attention thereto—for it will add very much to my Happiness to contribute to your Excellency's Pleasures.

W. Sargent

ALS, DNA:PCC, item 78.

Winthrop Sargent (1753–1820) of Gloucester, Mass., graduated from Harvard in 1771 and served in the Continental army during the American Revolution. In 1787 he was named secretary of the Ohio Company and in October of the same year was appointed by Congress secretary of the newly created Territory Northwest of the River Ohio. Because Gov. Arthur St. Clair was so often absent from his post in the territory, Sargent frequently acted as governor, although his intellectual interests and strong Federalist politics did not contribute to his local popularity. In 1798 he became governor of the new Mississippi Territory.

1. In August 1789 GW reappointed Parsons as one of the Northwest Territory's three judges, a post he had held under the Confederation government. See GW to Madison, 9 Aug. 1789, n.2.

2. In his diary Sargent was less circumspect in his comments on Parsons's death. "This Day we receive the Intelligence of Judge Parsons' Death in a Letter from Mr McDowell stationed at the Falls of Beaver. He was drowned in attempting to come down that River (& perhaps near the Falls) in a Canoe with one Man. His Family have suffered a severe Loss, for tho' in years & thereby impaired in his Capacities, he still retained the Ability to have rendered them important Services; that his Death may be amply compensated to this Territory is fully my Opinion & that we may be made the happier in almost any Successor; for such has been the Conduct of the Judge while in Office here that he must have lost the Confidence of honest discerning Men— but he is no more and therefore I will endeavour to draw a veil over the numerous Mementoes of his bad Habits—Alive, I was the Enemy of his *low Cunning*, and Practices which I conceived dishonourable" (Sargent's MS diary, entry for 25 Nov. 1789, MHi: Sargent Papers).

3. St. Clair left New York early in November and arrived at Marietta on 12 Dec. (Sargent's diary, entry for 24 Dec., MHi: Sargent Papers).

4. Sargent is referring to GW's trip down the Ohio in 1770. See *Diaries*, 2:277–326.

From Thomasin Gordon

[New York, 28 November 1789]

Worthy Sir,   No. 4 Crown Street

The Very distressd and Melancholy Situation I am in at this time occasions my taking a Liberty with your Excellency, which otherwise woud Be unpardonable. I am Sir Confind to My bed, with A Violent fever, in a Strange City, far Remov'd from Every friend and Connection, and have not one Shilling to Support myself, or to buy a morsel of Bread for my fatherless Child, for those two days past. I have therefore app[l]y'd to your Excellency Begging your kind assistance with a few dollars To Save me from Starving. as I Realy have not the Common necessaries of life. the Publick Is Indebted to My late husband Colo. John White of Georgia. but I Cannot Get a Settlement of his Accts till Congress Sits again. for Gods Sake Worthy Sir afford Me a little Assistance. And Reap the Reward in a better World than this, Colo. Alexander hamilton Can make you acquainted With my Character and wretched Situation—with Respect I am Worthy

Sir Your Excellencys most obedie[n]t and very distresd humble Sert

Thomasin Gordon

ALS, ViMtV.

Thomasin Gordon was undoubtedly in New York to pursue her late husband's claim with Congress. On 22 Aug. 1789 she presented her petition "praying that the accounts of her late husband, Colonel John White . . . deceased, may be liquidated in such manner that his child may receive in common, the benefits which have been granted to the heirs of other officers deceased." On 21 Sept. the petition was referred to a committee on claims and on 25 Sept. was listed among those referred to the secretary of the treasury to report on at the next session of Congress. Hamilton never reported on the petition, and on 5 Jan. 1795 he enclosed Thomasin Gordon's name in an alphabetical list of ninety-nine individuals who had submitted petitions on which he had not reported (*DHFC*, 3:165, 219, 233, 256; Syrett, *Hamilton Papers*, 18:13; *Petitions, Memorials and Other Documents Submitted for the Consideration of Congress*, 70). The list was enclosed with Hamilton's report to the House of Representatives, 5 Jan. 1795, DNA: RG 233, Reports of the Secretary of the Treasury, 1784–95, vol. 4. John White's claim was settled under the terms of "An Act providing for the settlement of the Claims of Persons under particular circumstances barred by the limitations heretofore established," passed 27 Mar. 1792. A certificate for $3,150 was issued on 1 April 1793 and one for $3,553.57 on 4 June 1793 (1 *Stat.* 245; *ASP, Claims*, 392, 394).

Thomasin Gordon's situation deteriorated after her letter of November to GW. In a letter that is undated but endorsed December 1789 she wrote: "your Excellency w⟨ill⟩ no doubt Pardon the Liberty I have taken in ⟨reque⟩sting Your Charitable Assis⟨tance⟩ To a person Suffering under the Greatest distress In a Loathsome prison—In an Unjust Cruel Manner. By the daughter of My deceased Hus⟨band⟩ Colonel John White, who has Imprisoned Me To Give an account of his property which Woud not pay his debts. as an Inventory Which is in Georgia in the hands of the Register of Probate will fully Shew—Now Sir as I am an Intire Stranger in this City I am not able to Give Security till I Can Send to Georgia to have the Business Explaind I am doom'd to Suffer in this Place both With hunger and Cold. I have not a bed to Lay on nor a Blankett to Cover with nor a Stick of Wood Neither have I a Shilling to Buy my daughter *Kitty White* nor myself a morsel of Bread—I hope your Excellencys Humane, and Charitable heart will Be open to the Cries of a poor distressd woman Who is Suffering in a Cold prison and afford Me Some Relief—and Reap your Reward in A Better world—your Excellency I hope will Pardon this Intrusion and Impute it to absolute distress and Poverty. and must beg your Excellency Will Intercede ⟨*mutilated*⟩ those whom providence has Bless'd with ⟨*mutilated*⟩ to open their Ears to My distress and help me" (ViMtV). It is uncertain whether or not GW came to her aid with a contribution. There are frequent entries in GW's ledger of household accounts for sums given to "a poor woman," to "a poor man," for "a load of wood for a poor

Widow," "cash given to an Indian," and recipients are rarely identified by name. See entries under "Contingent Expenses" in the Household Accounts, CtY, for examples.

Tobias Lear to Alexander Hamilton

Sir,   United States Novr 28th 1789

The President of the U. States being very desirous that the several Accts of those Articles which were furnished by directions of Saml Osgood & William Duer Esqr in pursuance of a resolution of both houses of Congress of the 15th of April 1789 and deposited in the house provided for the President of the United States, for his use, should be settled & paid.[1] He has, therefore, directed me to inform you that it is his wish that the money appropriated to that purpose might be applied thereto as soon as may be; and that you should employ a competent person to examine & settle said Accounts, and previous to their being paid that the person so employed should compare the accounts rendered in, with the articles actually in the house to prevent any abuse. I have the honor to be with perfect respect Sir Your most Obt Servant

Tobias Lear

LB, DLC:GW.

1. For the action of Congress in arranging for the repair and furnishing of the Osgood house in preparation for GW's occupancy, see GW to James Madison, 30 Mar. 1789, n.2. GW's concern for following proper procedures in the matter may have been prompted by the considerable criticism in the spring of 1789 concerning the cost of the renovation and the furnishings for the presidential mansion. The decoration of the house had been fairly elaborate as the niece of Walter Franklin, the original owner of the Osgood house, indicates: "Previous to his [GW's] coming, Uncle Walter's house on Cherry St. was taken for him, and every room furnished in the most elegant manner. Aunt Osgood and Lady Kitty Duer had the whole management of it. I went the morning before the General's arrival to take a look about. The best of furniture in every room, and the greatest quantity of plate and china I ever saw. The whole of the first and second story is papered & the floors covered with the richest king of Turkey and ⟨illegible⟩ carpet. The house did honor to my aunt & Lady Kitty, they spared no pains nor expense on it. Thou must know that Uncle Osgood & Duer were appointed to procure a house and furnish it, accordingly they pitched on their wives as being likely to do it better" (Sarah Robinson to Kitty F. Wistar, 30 April 1789, MSaE: Benjamin Pickman Papers).

Among the register's papers at the National Archives is a list of items furnished the presidential household, with the names of the merchants from whom they were purchased (DNA: RG 53, Records of the Register's Office, vol. 138). Another account of "Sundries bot on account of G.W.," 20 Nov. 1789–96, is in CtY: Washington Family Papers. The lists contain items purchased both in New York and in Philadelphia after the capital moved to that city. They also may include items that were provided by Congress for the Osgood house at the beginning of GW's presidency. Although it is uncertain when and for what purpose these lists were drawn up, it is likely they were prepared as part of GW's final accounting of his office, and they will be printed under the date of March 1797 when he left office. See also "Abstract of Accounts of sundry persons for Goods furnished and repairs done to the House occupied ⟨by the⟩ President of the United States," 29 Dec. 1789 (NHi: Samuel Osgood Papers).

From David Ross

Virginia Richmond 28th Novr 1789.
The Petition of David Ross of the State of Virginia
Humbly Sheweth,
That your Petitioner, being proprieter of certain Salt Springs in the Western Country, at the place known by the name of the Great-Bone Lick[1] is solicited by many of the most respectable inhabitants of Kentucky to establish salt-works at the said springs—That your petitioner would willingly comply with the pressing desire of the people but the situation is at present so much exposed to the depredations of the Indians as to render it too hazardous and expensive for an individual without the assistance of a guard from the public for a short time.[2]
Your Petitioner is well informed that the establishment of salt works at the Great Bone Lick, would not only ensure a plentiful supply of salt so essentially necessary to the inhabitants; but that a guard could perhaps be no where more advantageously placed for the protection of a very valuable part of that Country, and would certainly encourage the settlement of the adjacent lands; so that the public aid would not be long required—From these considerations—your Petitioner presumes to pray, that you may be pleased to grant such public aid as may be necessary, for the protection of the Salt-Works, to be erected at the Great Bone Lick, in the district of Kentucky—and your Petitioner as in duty bound shall ever pray.[3]
David Ross.

LB, DLC:GW; copy, DLC:GW.

David Ross (c.1736–1817) of Petersburg, Va., was a proprietor of an iron mine at Petersburg and owned large plantations in Bedford and Goochland counties. In 1781 Gov. Thomas Jefferson appointed him commercial agent for the state, a post he held until May 1782. In 1786 he represented Virginia at the Annapolis Convention. By the mid–1780s Ross was the absentee owner of 211,417 acres of land in Kentucky (*Journals of the Council of State of Virginia*, 2:184, 278, 3:70, 97; Burnett, *Letters*, 8:390; Watlington, *Partisan Spirit*, 95).

1. The Great or Big Bone Licks were salt licks or springs located in Boone County, Ky., on either side of Big Bone Creek which emptied into the Ohio River about twenty miles below the Falls of the Ohio at Louisville.

2. A petition on the saltworks, addressed to the president of the United States and signed by Charles Scott, Henry Pawlin, Mathew Walton, John Miller, John Hawkins, Charles Smith, Jr., Samuel Taylor, B. Thruston, and Notley Conn, was sent to GW from Richmond on 28 Nov.:

"The memorial of divers persons inhabitants of and
delegates from the district of Kentucky
"Humbly Sheweth—
"That the establishment of salt works, at the place called the great bone Lick, would be of public utility in the district of Kentucky, and the new settlements making on the other side of the Ohio—and is most anxiously desired by the people in general of that Country.

"That the situation is at present too dangerous for an individual to attempt to settle without some assistance—That a guard will for some time be necessary, and that from the particular situation of the place, a small post established there would serve in a great measure to cover and secure a considerable part of the settled Country, whilst it afforded protection to the Salt works.

"Your memorialists also beg leave to represent, that the people of that country, convinced of the propriety of the measure here recommended, will chearfully grant the necessary protection, whenever called under legal authority" (DLC:GW).

3. On 9 Feb. 1790 GW submitted this letter and the petition to Henry Knox with a request for his opinion (Tobias Lear to Knox, 9 Feb. 1790, DLC:GW).

From John Trumbull

Sir   New York 29th Novr 1789.

Had not the subject been accidentally introduc'd in the conversation with which you was pleas'd to honor me this Evening, I should never have thought of mentioning that any application from me bore a part in procurring to Mr Jefferson the civilities wch He receiv'd from the Custom House in England.[1]

But since it has been mention'd you will pardon my enclosing copies of the Letters which I wrote on the occasion to Mr Pitt & which I hope will not meet your disapprobation. I am with all possible Respect sir Your Obligd & Humble servant

Jno. Trumbull

ALS, DLC:GW.

John Trumbull (1756–1843) was the youngest son of Gov. Jonathan Trumbull of Connecticut and the brother of GW's wartime aide Jonathan Trumbull, Jr. John Trumbull also served GW as an aide-de-camp but after a short and somewhat unsuccessful stint moved to active military service and, in the intervals between assignments, continued to study painting. In 1780 he was able, in spite of the war, to make arrangements to study painting with Benjamin West in London. In late 1780 he was briefly imprisoned in London on suspicion of treason. After his release he remained in London, with short interruptions, continuing his work with West and producing a series of paintings dealing with the events of the American Revolution. In 1787 and 1788 he spent some time in Paris, painting French officers associated with the American Revolution. During this time he usually stayed with Jefferson, and shortly before returning to the United States, Jefferson offered Trumbull the post of secretary of legation in Paris (Jefferson to Trumbull, 21 May 1789, in Boyd, *Jefferson Papers*, 15:143–44). In the summer of 1789 Trumbull spent some time in England, making preparations for his passage to America. He arrived in New York City on 26 Nov. (Trumbull, *Autobiography*, 163).

1. Shortly before he sailed from England, Trumbull made extensive arrangements for Jefferson's voyage to the United States. For his good offices in Jefferson's behalf, see Boyd, *Jefferson Papers*, 15:515–17. Trumbull enclosed in his letter to GW a copy of his letter to William Pitt, 24 Sept. 1789, requesting "that orders may be sent down to the Custom House at Cowes, to suffer the Baggage of Mr Jefferson to pass from the Packet in which He will arrive from France on board the Ship in which He will embark for America, without being search'd or open'd," and a second letter, 10 Oct. 1789, thanking Pitt for having "the goodness to comply with the request" (DLC:GW). See also Boyd, *Jefferson Papers*, 15:517–18.

Clement Biddle to Tobias Lear

Tobias Lear   New York November 30. 1789

Since my last I have made further Enquiry Concerning the Buckwheat,[1] and find that altho' the Crops round Town, which I had observed were favourable that they were not equally so further in the Country and a person who purchased two or three hundred bushels within a few Days past for Shipping was obliged to pay 3/ for it. from the best Information, it may be procured @ 2/6 to 2/9 —but will require a little time, and I think, could be had to most advantage during the Winter & Could be Certainly had so as to ship by the first of March for if it is not an Article usually brought to Market in quantity & if suddenly pushed for just at the Close of the River, might not be had under 3/ but it Can be had with Certainty.

Last weeks post brought me a Letter from Major Washington and I have this Day Answd him[2] as above & in Case any Should be ordered have requested to Know what to put it in.

Inclosed is Mr Morris's Acct (except for the Matts which he Could not at present find cost of) amount £9.0.10 & the Stage Keeper account £5.⟨6⟩.0 both wch are Charged to the President.

C.B.

LB, PHi: Clement Biddle Letter Book, 1789–92.

   1. For background to this letter, see Lear to Biddle, 21 Dec. 1789.

   2. Biddle was referring to a letter he received from George Augustine Washington, dated 10 Nov., and his reply, dated 30 Nov. (PHi: Washington-Biddle Correspondence).

To John Jay

[New York] Monday November 30th 1789

The President of the United States presents his best Compliments to the Chief Justice of the United States and his Lady, and encloses them Tickets for the Theatre this evening.

As this is the last night the President proposes visiting the theatre for the season, he cannot deny himself the gratification of requesting the company of the Chief Justice and his Lady— altho' he begs at the same time that they will consider this invitation in such a point of view as not to feel themselves embarrassed, in the smallest degree, upon the occasion, if they have any reluctance to visiting the theatre; for the President presents the tickets as to his friends who will act as is most agreeable to their feelings, knowing thereby that they will meet the wishes of the person who invites them.[1]

L, in the writing of Tobias Lear, NNC: John Jay Papers.

   1. The Old American Company gave a benefit performance on 30 Nov. of "Cymon and Sylvia, Or, Love and Magic," an "Opera, or, Dramatic Romance," at the John Street Theatre (Ford, *Washington and the Theatre*, 40–43). On the same day Jay replied: "The Ch. Justice of the U.S. & Mrs Jay esteem themselves honored & obliged by the Presidts Invitation wh. they accept with Plea-

sure and by his delicate attention to there Embarrassmt wh. he had Reason to think probable, but wh. ceased with all Questions between govt & the theatre" (NNC: Jay Papers). GW was undoubtedly concerned with Jay's reaction to the opposition to the theater in New York City and elsewhere during the mid–1780s. In 1778 Congress had recommended to the states that many public entertainments, among them the theater, should be suppressed as "productive of idleness, dissipation, and a general depravity of principles and manners" (*JCC*, 12:1001, 1118). A number of theatrical companies left the country in search of employment elsewhere. In August 1785 the Old American Company returned to New York City and opened the John Street Theatre without a proper license, provoking tirades in local newspapers against the theater as a "species of luxury and folly" and statements of dismay from official sources that "while so great a Part of this City still lies in Ruins and many of the Citizens continue to be pressed with the Distresses brought on them in consequence of the late War, there is a loud Call to Industry and Œconomy: And it would in a peculiar Manner be unjustifyable in this Corporation to countenance enticing and expensive Amusements. That among these a Play House however regulated must be numbered, while under no Restraint it may prove a fruitful Sourse of Dissipation Immorality and Vice" (*New-York Packet*, 26 Dec. 1785; *Minutes of the Common Council of the City of New York*, 1:178–79). In 1786 a memorial signed by many of New York's leading citizens castigating the theater as one of the "Evils which threaten our City and State" was drawn up for presentation to the legislature (NN: Emmett Collection, item 11167). By mid–1786, however, the Old American Company and the John Street Theatre were firmly established and its productions there well attended.

To Thomas Jefferson

Dear Sir,   New York Novr 30th 1789.

You will perceive by the enclosed letter (which was left for you at the Office of Foreign Affairs when I made a journey to the Eastern States) the motives on which I acted with regard to yourself, and the occasion of my explaining them at that early period.[1]

Having now reason to hope—from Mr Trumbulls report—that you will be arrived at Norfolk before this time[2] (on which event I would most cordially congratulate you) and having a safe conveyance by Mr Griffin,[3] I forward your Commission to Virginia; with a request to be made acquainted with your sentiments as soon as you shall find it convenient to communicate them to me. With sentiments of very great esteem & regard I am—Dear Sir Your Most Obedt Hble Servt

Go: Washington

ALS, DLC: Thomas Jefferson Papers; Df, DNA: RG 59, Miscellaneous Letters; LB, DLC:GW; copy, ViU. Both the draft and the letter-book copy are dated 28 November.

1. See GW to Jefferson, 13 Oct. 1789.
2. See John Trumbull to GW, 29 Nov. 1789.
3. Probably Samuel Griffin, United States congressman from Virginia, who would have been returning home after the adjournment of Congress.

To James McHenry

(Confidential)

Dear Sir, New York Novr 30th 1789.

I have received your letter of the 14th instt—and in consequence of the suggestions contained therein, added to other considerations which occurred to me, I have thought it best to return Judge Harrison his Commission, and I sincerely hope that upon a further consideration of the Subject he may be induced to revoke his former determination & accept the appointmt.[1]

Mr Johnston has likewise declined his appointment of District Judge[2]—and I have no information of Mr Potts, the Attorney, or Col⟨onel⟩ Ramsay the Marshall, having accepted their Commissions.[3] Thus circumstanced with respect to Maryland, I am unwilling to make a new appointment of Judge for that District until I can have an assurance—or at least a strong presumption, that the person appointed will accept; for it is to me an unpleasant thing, to have Commissions of such high importance returned, and it will in fact, have a tendency to bring the Government into discredit.

Mr Hanson is the person whom I now have it in contemplation to bring forward as District Judge of Maryland, and shall do so, provided I can obtain an assurance that such an appointment would be acceptable to him: But as I cannot take any direct measures to draw from him a sentiment on this head, I must request, my dear Sir, that you will be so good as to get for me, if you can, such information upon the subject as will enable me to act with confidence in it, and convey the same to me as soon as possible. I shall leave to your prudence and discretion the mode of gaining this knowledge. It is a delicate matter, and will not bear any thing like a direct application, if there is the least cause to apprehend a refusal.

I have observed in the papers that Mr Hanson has been appointed Chancellor of the State since the death of Mr Rogers. What the emoluments of this Office are—or its tenure—I know not, therefore can form no opinion how far *it* may operate in this matter.[4]

Mr Johnsons resignation came to hand too late to admit of a new appointment, and information to be given of it, before the time fixed by the Act for holding the first District Court in Maryland;[5] however, if this had not been the case, I should hardly have hazarded a new appointment, for the reasons before mentioned, until I had good grounds to believe it would be accepted.

Should it be found that the Office of District Judge would *not* be acceptable to Mr Hanson—Mr Paca has been mentioned for that appointment; and although his sentiments have not been altogether in favor of the general Government—and a little adverse on the score of Paper Emissions &ca—I do not know but his appointment on some other accounts might be a proper thing. However, this will come more fully under consideration if Mr Hanson should not wish to be brought forward—and in that case, I will thank you to give me information relative to Mr Paca.[6]

Mr Gusts Scott, and Mr Robert Smith of Baltimore have also been mentioned for the Office;[7] but the age, and inexperience of the latter is, in my opinion, an insuperable objection. For however good the qualifications or promising the talents of Mr Smith may be, it will be expected that the important Offices of the general Government—more especially those of the Judges—should be filled by men who have been tried and proved.

I thank you, my good Sir, for your kind wishes for my health & happiness—and reciprocate them with sincerity. With very great regard I am—Dear Sir Your Affecte & Obedient Servt

Go: Washington

ALS, CSmH; Df, partly in the writing of GW, DNA: RG 59, Miscellaneous Letters; LB, DLC:GW.

1. See GW to Robert Hanson Harrison, 28 Sept. 1789, n.1.

2. See GW to Thomas Johnson, 28 Sept. 1789.

3. Both Nathaniel Ramsay and Richard Potts accepted their appointments.

4. Alexander Contee Hanson (1749–1806) was educated at the College of Philadelphia and admitted to the practice of law in Maryland in 1773. He served briefly in 1776 as assistant secretary to GW. Hanson served as a judge on the Maryland General Court from 1776 to 1789. Early in December McHenry approached Hanson on GW's behalf. As he reported to the president on 10 Dec., he held a conversation with Hanson that morning. "After some time we spoke of the vacancy of district judge. I remarked that notwithstanding his late appointment of Chancelor was very honorable, and at this moment more lucrative than district judge, yet as the salary of the latter was less subject to caprice, than a salary dependent on our assembly, it was in that point of view a more desirable office independent of its dignity as a part of the federal judiciary. I then wished that an exchange could take place, and said, as I knew he was highly esteemed by the President I beleived a suggestion on the head would affect it. Being in habits of friendship with him, I added, tell me sincerely and freely, 'whether if I should take the liberty to mention the thing to you, he would consent to serve.' This brought the matter to a point. He did not like the office so well as that of Chancellor, as it would oblige him to attend courts in different parts of the State which would lessen the net income, and as it was in his opinion of less dignity. In short he gave a decided preference to his present station. I am very sorry; for he is a man of an excellent understanding and of unimpeached integrity" (DLC:GW).

5. Article 3 of the Judiciary Act specified the first meeting of the Maryland district would be held at Baltimore on the first Tuesday in December 1789 (1 *Stat.* 74).

6. William Paca (1740–1799) was educated at the College of Philadelphia, receiving an M.A. degree in 1759, studied law in Annapolis, and was admitted to practice in Maryland in 1761. He later continued his legal studies at the Inner Temple in London. Before the Revolution he served in the Maryland legislature and was active in Patriot circles as the war approached. He was a member of the Continental Congress from 1775 to 1779. In 1778 he was appointed chief judge of the Maryland General Court and in 1782 was elected governor of Maryland, serving until 1785. Although his support of the Constitution was somewhat lukewarm, he voted for its adoption in the Maryland Ratifying Convention in 1788. In his letter to GW of 10 Dec., McHenry reported that after he discussed the appointment for federal district judge with Hanson, he "saw Mr Paca and had a long conversation with him. He had in view an office in our State judiciary which we are talking about creating; but prefers the appointment in question. I do not detail our conversation; but I have every reason to say, that he will make every exertion in his power to execute the trust in the most unexceptionable and satisfactory manner. I beleive also that the appointment will be highly gratifying to him, and I think may have political good consequences. He will carry a degree of respectability and legal dignity into the office which the other persons you mentioned cannot. On the whole, as Mr Johnson and Mr Hanson will not serve, I am disposed to think that Mr Paca's appointment will be generally acceptable"

(DLC:GW). See also Nathaniel Ramsay to GW, 12 Nov. 1789. Reassured on the probability of Paca's acceptance of the post, GW wrote to him on 24 Dec. offering him the position and enclosing his commission. "You will observe that the Commission which is now transmitted to you is limitted to the end of the next Session of the Senate of the United States. This is rendered necessary by the Constitution, which authorizes the President of the United States to fill up such vacancies as may happen during the recess of the Senate—and appointments so made shall expire at the end of the ensuing Session unless confirmed by the Senate. However, there cannot be the smallest doubt but the Senate will readily ratify and confirm this appointment, when your Commission in the usual form shall be forwarded to you" (copy, DNA: RG 59, Miscellaneous Letters). Paca's appointment was confirmed by the Senate on 10 Feb. 1790 (*DHFC*, 2:61).

7. For Gustavus Scott's application for office, see GW to Scott, 21 Mar. 1789. Scott's name appeared on at least two lists for Maryland appointments. See Otho H. Williams to GW, 5 July 1789, n.2, and Conversation with Samuel Griffin, 9 July 1789, n.2. Robert Smith applied for a post in the Judiciary in a letter to GW of 5 Sept. 1789. For GW's views on Smith's appointment, see his letter to Otho H. Williams, 22 Nov. 1789.

From the Citizens of Mero District, North Carolina

State of North Carolina Miro District
30th Novemr 1789

His Excellency the President, and the Honorable the Congress of the United States.

We the underwritten in behalf of ourselves and others, Inhabitants of the State and District afforesaid, situated on Cumberland River, beg leave to lay before Your Honorable and much esteemed body a true State of the numerous, Singular hardships, dangers and disadvantages, attending a Settlement which (tho of little Significance in its present State) will, we trust in a short period become a valuable member of the United Community.

This Country previous to the late glorious revolution, was purchased, together with that known by the name of Kentucky by Richard Henderson and his associates from whose encouragement many of your petitioners removed and Settled with their families at a place then well known by the name of the French lick, now the Town of Nashville, at the risque of their lives and properties in the heart of a Country Surrounded by

Savages, with a flattering prospect of being the means of encreasing population and cultivation, of this truely rich and valuable country.[1] These pleasing prospects were however for a
short period obscured by the War carried on with our late
mother Country (an Epoch that we look back to with the greater
pleasure as it has been the happy Cause of our present state of
Independance) at the conclusion of which the State Seized and
appropriated that part of the Said Country, where the whole of
your Petitioners live, to the purposes of rewarding our brave
defenders, many of whom have Since removed to and Settled
here under a confidence, in that Community's afording them a
protection against their Savage Neighbours, whose lives, Liberties and properties they had at the risque of their own So
Gallantly defended: In this situation, we continued at this place
Subject to all the hardships and inconvenances naturally attending the Settling a wild uncultivated Country, with the additional
disadvantage of constant depredations from our Savage Neighbours, who have afforded us little, or no respite, for about ten
Years, from all the terrifying calamities of a Savage War, until
the Year 1786, when at the constant pressing Solicitations of the
Inhabitants the General Assembly of the State Summoned so
much humanity as to afford their distressed Supplicants a small
Batallion Consisting of two hundred men properly officered,
for two Years at the expiration whereof they were disbanded
and Your Petitioners left as before without any other dependance than their own strength and determined resolution to
support their little growing Settlement⟨.⟩ those fiew troops,
however advantagious to the Settlement were far from being
able to remove all the disadvantages the Settlers laboured under
on account of the ennemy or preventing many valuable Citizens
from being killed at their habitations on the frontiers and Since
the expiration of their time, the list has been dailey encreasing
So that the number killed Since the first day of January 1788
(from an exact Register that has been kept) Amount to 54
Persons who have been barbarously murdered while at their
domestic employment without the most distant prospect of any
further assistance from the legislative body of the State than
overtures to the Indians for a Treaty of peace and amity which
we have the most alarming reasons to believe from the accounts

received in this place of the Indignities offered by McGilvray to the Commissioners delegated by your Honorable Body to treat with the Creek Nation will never avail us any thing untill an army is Sent into the heart of their Country Sufficient to extirpate their whole Savage race.

We do with the utmost Candour acknowledge that as Members of the State of North carolina we have not at present the least pretence for making this address and prayer to Your Honorable Body: But in full confidence the Convention that is now sitting will adopt the Federal Constitution,[2] we are encouraged to hope that Your Honorable Body will take our Situation into your most Serious consideration, and afford us Such protection and Support, as You in your wisdom may deem Sufficient to prevent the future depredations of our merciless and Savage Enemies—and Your Petitioners, will, as in duty bound, ever pray &c.

Copy, DLC:GW; LB, DLC:GW. This petition is signed by James Robertson, lieutenant colonel commandant of Davidson County, and Isaac Bledsoe, lieutenant colonel commandant of Summer County. A note at the bottom of the letter states that the "commanding officer of the District (General Daniel Smith) is now absent at the General assembly of this State, which is the reason his name is not to the foregoing petition."

The Mero (Miro) District in western North Carolina included settlements extending about eighty-five miles along the Cumberland River. The area is now in Tennessee.

1. Richard Henderson & Company was organized in August 1774 by Richard Henderson and Nathaniel Hart, who negotiated an agreement with the Cherokee for all the land south of the Ohio River between the mouth of the Great Kanawha and Tennessee rivers. The firm was reorganized in January 1775 as the Transylvania Company with additional members and in March signed new agreements with the Cherokee accepting the Kentucky River instead of the Kanawha as the northern and eastern boundaries and the area of the Cumberland River rather than the Tennessee as the southern and western boundaries. For a detailed account of the settlement of the area, its difficulties with Indian raids, and the separatist movement arising on the Cumberland, see Abernethy, *Western Lands and the American Revolution*, 124–25, 228, 338–43.

2. The North Carolina Ratifying Convention convened at Hillsboro on 21 July 1789 and adjourned on 4 August. Word had evidently not reached the Mero District that the state had formally ratified the Constitution on 21 Nov. 1789.

To Edmund Randolph

Dear Sir,   New York Novr 30th 1789.

Your letter of the 8th of October gave me pleasure, as I not only entertain hopes, but shall fully expect from the contents of it, to see you in the Office of Attorney General when the purposes mentioned by you for the delay are answered.[1]

I shall now mention some matters to you in confidence. Mr Pendleton declining to accept the appointment of District Judge has embarrassed me—& this embarrassment was not a little encreased by the lateness of the period at which (being on a tour through the Eastern States) I came to the knowledge of it.[2] When I was about to make the nominations in the Judiciary, for the Union, the character & abilities of Mr Wythe did not escape me & I accordingly consulted such Gentlemen from the State of Virginia (then in this City) as I thought most likely to have some knowledge of his Inclinations. There opinion was, that as he had lately been appointed sole Chancellor (an Office to which by inclination he was led) and engaged in other avocations which engrossed his attentions and appeared to afford him pleasure he would not exchange the former for a federal appointment. However, Since these appointments have been announced, I have heard that it has been the wonder of some, in Virginia, that Mr Wythe should have been *overlooked*. The cause (if the epithet applies) I have assigned. and if there was reason to apprehend a refusal in the first instance the Non-acceptance of Colo. Pendleton would be no inducement to him to come forward in the second. To consult him, through the medium of a friend, there was not time, as the 3d Tuesday in Decr is the day appointed for holding the District Court in the District of Virga—and to hazard a second refusal I was, on many accts, unwilling to do. Under these circumstances I have by the Power of the Constitution, appointed Mr Cyrus Griffin during the recess of the Senate. My reasons for this appointment in preference to any other except Mr Wythe are because he has (as I am informed) been regularly bred to the law—has been in the Court of Appeals— Has been discontinued of the Council in Virginia (contrary to the expectation of his friends here at the time, who thought that his temporary appointment as a Negociator with the Southern Indians would not bring him under the disqualifying law of

Virginia) and thereby throw him entirely out of employment—and because I had it in my power to ascertain with precision his acceptance.[3] I shall say nothing of his being a Man of amiable character & of competent abilities, because in these respects some of the present Judges in that State may be his equals—but to what I have said, may be added, he has *no* employment now and *needs* the emolument of one as much as any of them.

I will not conceal from you, that two motives have induced me to give this explanation. The first, if a favourable opportunity should present itself is, that Mr Wythe may, in a delicate manner, be informed of the principles by which I was governed in this business—the second that my inducements to appoint Mr Griffin may not (if the propriety of it should be questioned) be altogether unknown.[4] For Having in every appointment endeavoured, as far as my own knowledge of character⟨s⟩ has extended, or information could be obtained, to select the fittest and most acceptable Persons; & having reason to believe that the appointments which have been made heretofore have given very general satisfaction it would give me pain if Mr Wythe or any of his friends should conceive that he has been passed by from improper motives.[5] I have prejudices against none[6]—nor partialities which shall biass me in favor of any one. If I err then, my errors will be of the head and not of the heart of—My Dear Sir, Your Most Obedient and Affectionate Humble Servant

George Washington

ADf (incomplete), DNA: RG 59, Miscellaneous Letters; LB, DLC:GW.

1. For Randolph's reply to GW's offer of the post of attorney general, see GW to Randolph, 28 Sept. 1789, n.3.

2. See GW to Edmund Pendleton, 28 Sept. 1789. n.3. See also GW to James Madison, 23 Sept. 1789.

3. See GW to Pendleton, 28 Sept. 1789.

4. See Cyrus Griffin to GW, 10 July 1789, source note.

5. For Randolph's reply to GW's request concerning George Wythe, see his letters to the president, 15 and 23 Dec. 1789.

6. The draft ends at this point. The remainder of the text is taken from the letter-book copy.

From Corbin Washington

Walnut Farm [Westmoreland County, Va.]
Novr 30. 1789

My dear Uncle

   Some time late in September la⟨st I⟩ received a letter from Mr John Marshall informing me that the Suit of the Hites & ⟨Greens⟩ against me for a part of my land in Berkley was set for trial in the succeeding Octr, and, unless I could procure for him sundry papers &c., with which he had not been furnished, he could not maintain the Suit.[1] Upon examination, I found that the papers required were not in my possession, neither did I know where to apply for them. In the height of this dilemma, I had the pleasure of seeing Mr Charles Lee, who informed me, that, in consequence of a conversation he had had with you some time ago, he inclined to believe that you could either inform me where to obtain the necessary papers, or give me some useful instructions respecting the business—if it is in your power to do either, you will much oblige me (Sir) by answering this letter as soon as you conveniently can. I enclose you a copy of Mr Marshall's letter ⟨to m⟩e, which will serve to shew what papers and other proof he wants to secure me.[2] Could you, without ⟨m⟩uch inconvenience to yourself, contrive, a letter on this subject to my brother in alexandria, come by the fifteenth of Decr it will meet with me there on my way to Berkley, and will possibly save me much fatigue & expence. The subject on which I now address you, is of such consequence to me, that I hope it will in some degree justify the liberty I take in calling your attention a few moments from matters of a public nature. Mrs Washington joins me in sincere love to Aunt Washington, and wishing health & happiness to you both.[3] I am Dr Uncle Your Affectionate & Sincere Nephew

Corbin Washington

ALS, NjMoNP.
   Corbin Washington (1765–c.1799) was the youngest son of GW's brother John and Hannah Washington. He was married to Hannah Lee, the daughter of Richard Henry Lee.
   1. Washington's legal difficulties concerned a tract of 850 acres of land on Bullskin Run in Berkeley County, Virginia. The land originally had been sold by Jost Hite to Patrick Matthews and later was claimed by Corbin's father John Washington, either through purchase or as part of his inheritance from his brother Lawrence. Because of the controversial legal entanglements sur-

rounding the case of *Hite v. Fairfax*, still pending in the courts, Washington had not been able to secure a clear title to the tract. John Marshall had acted for the elder Washington in a petition submitted to the High Court of Chancery in November 1786 requesting verification of his title to the land (Cullen and Johnson, *Marshall Papers*, 1:192).

2. Marshall's letter to Corbin Washington, 23 Aug. 1789, concerning the "chasm in the Title" that marred conveyances from various owners of the tract, is in ViMtV. See also Cullen and Johnson, *Marshall Papers*, 2:37–38.

3. GW replied to Washington's letter on 16 Dec.: "Your letter of the 30th Ulto only came to hand last night. To reply to it, therefore by the time requested by you, is impossible. But was it practicable, I can recollect nothing respecting the title of your Lands in Berkeley that would, I conceive, be essent[ial]ly serviceable to you in your dispute with the Hites. Nor is there any papers in my possession, that I recollect, which can throw any light on the matter. It is presumable that the title papers of the Lands in dispute were in your Fathers possession—and that, if the Conveyances to your Uncle Lawrence (from the Proprietors Office, & from individuals) were well drawn, you would there find a proper derivation of the Title. This is the source from whence you have obtained the Land, and the best channel of information that I can suggest to you to ascertain the title to it—Most of the Lands possessed by your father in Berkeley County, being unpatented at the time my Brother Lawrence bought them, were conveyed to him by Deeds from the Lord Proprietor—& to those files you must have recourse—It is possible however the Deeds might be granted to the persons of whom my brother bought the Land, in that case the transfers will be found among the Records of *Frederick* County Court, as they were made *long* before the division of that County took place. Mr James McCormick, & Messrs John Smith & Robt Worthington, if living, are the most likely persons to apply to for oral information—also Abraham Haynes—these being, all of them, persons who were intimately acquainted with all the Lands in that part of the Country; The several claimants of them; And their Alienations. Confident I am that there is no *authentic* document relative to your Land among my Papers at Mount Vernon—but as I surveyed most of the Lands about Bullskin, it is *possible*, tho' not at all *probable*, some minutes may be found or rough draughts had of these lands among my Papers which might lead to some discovery more important; and, if any exist, they are to be found in my Study, among my Land Papers in small parchment covered Books tied together; or in a broad untied bundle of loose & old Plats of Surveys in the Pidgeon holes which are labelled Land Papers. If the spot on which your house stands at the head of the Marsh, is involved in this dispute, you may, probably, derive useful information from Colo. (or Genl) Bull, and the purchasers from the Stephensons; all of whose Lands was originally one tract, and purchased, if my memory serves me, from Hite; consequently must be under one and the same predicament.

"Having suggested every thing that occurs to me on the subject, I have only to wish that no exertions of your own may be wanted to secure Lands which are of *infinite* more value to you than those ⟨you⟩ have chosen for your residence; and where your *essential* interest *loudly* called upon you to establish

yourself. Where, as it is the last time, probably, I shall ever express any sentiment to you upon the occasion, I will venture to predict you might (by living
thereon) have improved your fortune considerably, but without it, will find it
a source of trouble, vexation & loss. So wide an odds is there between having
your business conducted under your own eyes, and those of a manager at a
distance; who, if he possesses skill, honesty & Industry, will extort half the profits for his share—If lazy or dishonest, will make nothing, or apply the whole.
Your Aunt joins me in best wishes for you" (ALS, anonymous donor). On the
same day GW sent this letter, unsealed, to Corbin's brother, Bushrod Washington, "that you may aid it with your own opinion and advice or by searching
among my Papers as directed for any thing that may be serviceable" (ALS,
NHi: George and Martha Washington Papers). On 18 Dec. Corbin Washington sent GW a second letter, containing virtually the same information as that
contained in his letter of 30 Nov., "lest my first letter should not have reached
your hands" (PWacD: Feinstone Collection, on deposit PPAmP).

Two decrees of the High Court of Chancery settled Washington's problem:
the first, 5 Aug. 1790, confirmed his title, pending payment of the purchase
price. This decision was appealed to the High Court of Appeals where the
Court of Chancery's decree was reversed. On 19 Mar. 1792 a revised decree
was issued by the High Court of Chancery (Cullen and Johnson, *Marshall Papers*, 1:192).

Letter not found: to George Augustine Washington, 30 Nov. 1789. In a
letter to GW of 14 Dec. Washington referred to "Your Letter of the
30th Ulto."

From Joseph Ogle

                                    Delaware State Newcastle County
Dear Sir   white Clay Creek hund. No. W. [November 1789]
    I am in the Greatest Distress as per N. 1[1] from Principles of, I
know not what, but to make A Pray of My Fidelety & patriotism,
for the heat of the Enemys, Progress through the Jersey A
Number of the fineest Men we have now was then not to be
found, though at that time I Sacreficed Every thing that was
near & Dear to a Man of feeling & thought I gave up, &
proceeded on till I Seen the Close of the war & then Retired
after, laying out all the money that I had & runing in debt for A
Considirable sum To Support the postes, Near my districk, &
my own Service, & am now to be Devourd by a few who took the
advantage of the Only few who Stood forth to Defend the whole
all I want is that the Certificates in my Name might not be Sold
Till the interest might be paid which is far Inadquait to my

bodyly distress But in General am willing to be Sattisfied With it
Sir I hope youll Pardon me (for Presuming to write to you who
are the head) Whom am & has been a Sincere friend to the
United States as far as my Knowledge led you[r] Hume Sert

Joseph Ogle

ALS, DNA:PCC, item 78.

Joseph Ogle was a member of a prominent New Jersey family. An ancestor,
John Ogle, in New Jersey as early as 1667, settled on land near Christiana
Creek in New Castle County and eventually purchased large tracts of land
elsewhere in the county. In 1804 Joseph Ogle is still listed in county assess-
ments as owning land in White Clay Creek Hundred (Scharf, *History of Delaware*, 933, 935).

1. No enclosures to this letter have been found.

To John Jay

[New York] December 1st 1789

The President of the United States hath read with attention
the Papers herewith returned, relating to our Affairs in Morocco: and as far as he can form an opinion without knowing the
contents of Guiseppe Chiappe's Letters of the 25th of April &
18th of July 1789[1]—no translation thereof being sent—approves the Draft of the Letters to the Emperor and Guiseppe &
Francisco Chiappe;[2] and wishes, as the case seems to require it,
that they may be forwarded by the first good conveyances that
offers.[3]

ADf, DNA: RG 59, Miscellaneous Letters; LB, DLC:GW.

For an account of the services of the Chiappe brothers to the United States,
see Giuseppe Chiappe to GW, 18 July 1789, source note.

1. For Chiappe's letter of 25 April 1789, see his letter to GW, 18 July 1789,
n.1.

2. See GW to Sidi Mohammed, 1 Dec. 1789.

3. GW returned drafts of two letters, one from Jay to Francisco Chiappe,
"Agent of the United States at Morocco," and another to Giuseppe Chiappe,
"Agent of the United States at Mogador," both dated 1 Dec. 1789. The two
letters described the formation of the new government and informed the
brothers of GW's election. Jay wrote Francisco Chiappe that the "President
has been informed how well you and your Brothers deserve of the United
States; and I am persuaded that due Attention will be paid to your and their
Services.

"I have now the Honor of transmitting to you a Letter from the President
to his Imperial Majesty, with a Copy of it for your Information: I also enclose

a Letter for your Brother Guiseppe, which I request the Favor of you to forward to him" (DNA: RG 59, Foreign Letters of the Continental Congress and the Department of State). The letter to Giuseppe Chiappe contained much of the same information: "Your Letters of 25th April and 18th July which were addressed to the President of Congress, arrived after the new Government had taken place; they were therefore delivered to the President of the United States, who possesses Powers and Prerogatives in many Respects similar to those which are enjoyed by the King of England. . . . I am directed by the President . . . to assure you that nothing shall be wanting so to arrange and conduct all Affairs between our two Countries, as may be perfectly satisfactory to his Imperial Majesty" (DNA: RG 59, Foreign Letters of the Continental Congress and the Department of State).

To Sidi Mohammed

[New York, 1 December 1789]

Since the Date of the Letter, which the late Congress, by their President, addressed to your Imperial Majesty, the United States of America have thought proper to change their Government, and to institute a new one, agreeable to the Constitution, of which I have the Honor of, herewith, enclosing a Copy. The Time necessarily employed in this arduous Task, and the Derangements occasioned by so great, though peaceable a Revolution, will apologize, and account for your Majesty's not having received those regular Advices, and Marks of Attention, from the United States, which the Friendship and Magnanimity of your Conduct, towards them, afforded Reason to expect.

The United States, having unanimously appointed me to the supreme executive Authority, in this Nation, your Majesty's Letter of the 17th August 1788, which, by Reason of the Dissolution of the late Government, remained unanswered, has been delivered to me.[1] I have also received the Letters which your Imperial Majesty has been so kind as to write, in Favor of the United States, to the Bashaws of Tunis and Tripoli,[2] and I present to you the sincere acknowledgments, and Thanks of the United States, for this important Mark of your Friendship for them.

We greatly regret that the hostile Disposition of those Regencies, towards this Nation, who have never injured them, is not to be removed, on Terms in our Power to comply with. Within our Territories there are no Mines, either of Gold, or Silver, and this young Nation, just recovering from the Waste and Desolation of a long War, have not, as yet, had Time to acquire Riches by Agriculture and Commerce. But our Soil is bountiful, and our People industrious; and we have Reason to flatter ourselves, that we shall gradually become useful to our Friends.

The Encouragement which your Majesty has been pleased, generously, to give to our Commerce with your Dominions; the Punctuality with which you have caused the Treaty with us to be observed, and the just and generous Measures taken, in the Case of Captain Proctor, made a deep Impression on the United States, and confirm their Respect for, and Attachment to your Imperial Majesty.[3]

It gives me Pleasure to have this Opportunity of assuring your Majesty that, while I remain at the Head of this Nation, I shall not cease to promote every Measure that may conduce to the Friendship and Harmony, which so happily subsist between your Empire and them, and shall esteem myself happy in every Occasion of convincing your Majesty of the high Sense (which in common with the whole Nation) I entertain of the Magnanimity, Wisdom, and Benevolence of your Majesty.

In the Course of the approaching Winter, the national Legislature (which is called by the former Name of Congress) will assemble, and I shall take Care that Nothing be omitted that may be necessary to cause the Correspondence, between our Countries, to be maintained and conducted in a Manner agreeable to your Majesty, and satisfactory to all the Parties concerned in it.

May the Almighty bless your Imperial Majesty, our great and magnanimous Friend, with his constant Guidance and Protection. Written at the City of New York the first Day of December 1789.

Go: Washington

DS, owned (1992) by the Forbes Magazine Collection, New York, New York; Df, NNC; LB, DLC:GW; copy, DNA: RG 59, Ceremonial Letters. Credences. This letter is addressed "To our great and magnanimous Friend, His imperial majesty, the Emperor of Morocco."

Sidi Mohammed (d. 1790) came to the throne of Morocco around 1757. One of the most enlightened of Morocco's eighteenth-century rulers, he was concerned with expanding his country's commerce with other nations. Less successful were his attempts to mitigate Morocco's draconian system of justice. As early as the 1770s Sidi Mohammed had made friendly overtures to the United States although he was discouraged by the failure of the Continental

Congress to respond. By 1786, however, he had signed a liberal treaty of friendship with the United States.

1. DNA: PCC, item 88.
2. Copies of both of these letters were included in Sidi Mohammed's letter to Congress of 17 Aug. 1788. The letter to the Bey of Tunis has not been found, but an Italian translation of the letter to the Basha of Tripoli is in DNA:PCC, item 88.
3. For the case of Captain Proctor, see Giuseppe Chiappe's letter of 18 July 1789, printed above.

From John Habersham

Sir,   Savannah, December 2d, 1789.

The letter which you will herewith receive I beleive respects the appointment of a Collector of the Customs for the Port and District of Brunswick, which is now vacant by the resignation of Mr Handley.[1] Mr Hillary informs me he has applied for it; if he should meet with your approbation, I have no doubt but he will discharge his duty properly, being I beleive a Man of integrity and sufficient ability. I have the honor to be, with due respect, Sir, Your most obedient, humble, Servant

John Habersham
Collector of the Customs at Savannah

ALS, DLC:GW.

John Habersham (1754–1799) served in the Georgia Continental line during the American Revolution, was captured at the fall of Savannah, and ended the war as a major. After the war he returned to manage the plantation left to him by his father, served in the Georgia assembly and in 1785 in the Continental Congress, and strongly supported ratification of the Constitution by his state. In August 1789 GW appointed him collector of the customs at Savannah (Coleman, *Georgia Biography*, 1:379–80).

1. George Handley (1752–1793) was appointed collector of the customs at Brunswick, Ga., in August 1789. He resigned early in 1790 and was replaced in February 1790 by Christopher Hillary (1735–1796), a planter from Glynn County, Ga. (ibid., 387; *DHFC*, 2:23, 59, 492).

From David Stuart

Dear Sir,   3rd Decr 1789 Abingn.

I should have done myself the pleasure of writing to you immediately on my return home, and giving you an account of the progress of the law business I am unfortunately engaged in, for the estate;[1] but understanding you had set out on a tour to the Northward, I thought it best not to interrupt a journey undertaken for health, with a detail, which could not suffer from a short delay—I hope you have returned much benefited by it.

From your knowledge of Alexander, you will not I dare say be surprized, in hearing that my negociation with him, (for which I obtained your approbation) has been fruitless[2]—As he made me the offer in presence of Coll Simms I expected he would have felt some tie on himself to comply[3]—Instead of this he now demands one thousand pounds beyond the appraisement by three indifferent persons—I understand he was much flattered by his Lawyer and encouraged even to expect 48,000 at the expiration of the term—I have had the suit again put off, to try if I cannot obtain better terms—If I should not be able to succeed, I shall in the Spring dismiss it; it being the opinion of my Lawyers, that it will be best to act on the defensive and allow Alexander to sue at the expiration of the term. I informed you sometime ago, that I had been at Stantoun, to attend the trial of the suits against M'Clennegan & Meux, for fourteen negroes sold by Posey to Meux.[4] From the information I obtained, by being accidentally present at the trial of a suit, which M'Clennegan had brought against Meux for a title to the negroes it has been fortunate for the estate that my suits against them were not tried; as it was fully proved in the suit between these two gentlemen, that Mr Custis was Security for Posey to Meux, for the sum of thirteen hundred pounds, or negroes to that amount—Meux had assigned this bond to M'Clennegan, for lands in Augusta, who recieved in discharge of it the fourteeen negroes, which gave rise to the suit brought by Mr Dandridge, and revived by me—As I had no doubt of recovering the negroes, my astonishment was very great, at this discovery, for I had never before heard, that Mr Custis had been Security to Posey, for the land he bought of Meux—Considering therefore, that Posey was worth nothing, and that Mr Custis's estate would be liable for the above sum with interest; if I recovered the negroes which had been recieved in discharge of it; and that it would take near three times that number now, from the reduced value of that species of property, to pay it off; I thought it most advantageous to give

my engagement to dismiss the suits, and get the bond in my
possession—I confess, this circumstance has discouraged me
much, with respect to other suits, as there is no telling from the
confidence reposed in Posey, what he had not a right to do—
The suit against Coll Basset was not tried—He is much alarmed
I understand, and perhaps that is my best foundation for
hopes—Mr Claiborne has informed me, that he shall institute
his suit immediately, for the land in King William[.][5] I was in
hopes that the opinion of Mr Randolph and Innis would have
prevented him—He however informs me, that the opinions of
men equal to them, are in his favor—The great uncertainty of
law makes it I think rather alarming.

During the time of my continuance in Richd on the above
business, the Session of our Assembly commenced—A very
extraordinary letter from our Senators in Congress, complaining of the inefficacy of the proposed amendments, and expressive of their fears, that the State governments would be annihilated; with a strong hint of the insufficiency of one government
for so extensive a country, was recieved and read[6]—I was happy
in hearing much indignation expressed at it, by many who were
strong Antifederalists, and had voted against the constitution in
the Convention—It was generally attributed to an aim at popularity. My belief is, that it was meant by Mr R. H. Lee to serve his
Brother, who is a Candidate for a Judge's seat in this State and
will no doubt assume the merit with his party, of having been
neglected on account of his principles[7]—Grayson's short draft
would be a sufficient motive with him to affix his signature to
it—The letter was evidently in Mr Lees hand—Mr Henry appears to me by no means content—But if the people continue as
much satisfyed, as they at present appear to be, he will be soon
alone in his sentiments—He however tried to feel the pulse of
the House with respect to the Constitution, in two or three
instances, and recieved at length I understood, a very spirited
reply from Coll Lee—By a late letter from Coll Lee, I am
informed that a bill is introduced making Congress a considerable offer, to fix their permanent residence on the Potomac—
Maryland is called on to join in a similar act—In general their
appears to be much satisfaction at the appointments some ⟨few⟩
seem to think, that more Antifœderalists might have been appointed—But the unsollicited appointment of Mr Nelson is

spoke of by all and appears to be highly flattering to this denomination in particular. They consider it as a proof that political
principles have not been alone your guide—I am just informed
that Mr Jones[8] and Roane Henry's son in law[9] are appointed our
judges: So that Mr Henry has still the command of the loaves &
fishes—As Mr Roane is not more than twenty-five, with but little
experience as a Lawyer, it appears to me to be an extraordinary
instance of Henrys influence—The merchants of Alexandria
had yesterday a meeting with the Merchants of Ge[orge]town,
on the subject of the permanent seat of residence. The result of
it, was the appointment of a joint Committee to correspond with
the towns to the Eastward, and give them, the most flaming
accounts they can, of the Potomac; and the greater benefits they
will derive, from it's being fixed there, than on the Susquehana
or the Delaware—As I am one of the Committee, I have my
fears that those sagacious people will laugh at us for our great
pains in teaching them their true interests. I am Dr Sir with
great respect Your affece Servt

Dd Stuart

ALS, DLC:GW.

1. See Stuart to GW, 12 Sept. 1789.

2. For Stuart's involved negotiations with Robert Alexander on behalf of
the Custis estate, see Stuart to GW, 14 July 1789, n.7 and 12 Sept. 1789.

3. For an identification of Charles Simms, see Battaile Muse to GW, 21
Mar. 1789, n.1.

4. John Price Posey (d. 1788), the son of GW's old friend and fox-hunting
companion Capt. John Posey, was a close friend of John Parke Custis and for
a time managed Custis's New Kent County property. There were numerous
questions about the quality of his stewardship. Posey was convicted of arson in
the burning of the New Kent County courthouse in 1788 and hanged. Meux
is probably Thomas Meux (1737–c.1791) of New Kent County, who also
owned land in Hanover and Gloucester counties. For Stuart's earlier comments on John Parke Custis's involvement with John Price Posey, see his letter
to GW, 12 Sept. 1789.

5. See Stuart to GW, 14 July 1789, n.6.

6. For the letters to the executive and legislature of Virginia from senators
Richard Henry Lee and William Grayson, 28 Sept. 1789, see Edmund Randolph to GW, 26 Nov. 1789, n.4.

7. In the months after the formation of the new government Arthur Lee
had become an avid office seeker. For his unsuccessful attempt to secure a seat
on the Supreme Court, see his letter to GW, 21 May 1789, and GW to Madison, c.8 Sept. 1789. For Richard Henry Lee's attempt to aid his brother's quest

for employment, see Lee to Patrick Henry, 27 Sept. 1789, in Ballagh, *Letters of Richard Henry Lee*, 2:504–7.

8. For an identification of Joseph Jones, see Jones to GW, 15 Nov. 1789. Jones was reappointed to the General Court in November 1789.

9. Spencer Roane (1762–1822) of Essex County, Va., married Patrick Henry's daughter Anne in 1786. Roane served as senator in the Virginia legislature and as a member of the council of state. From 1789 to 1794 he was a judge on the General Court.

Tobias Lear to William Duer

Sir   New York December 4th 1789.

The President of the United States will keep the Carriage provided for his use previous to his arrival in New-York—and as it will be considered upon the same footing with other articles furnished at that time and for that purpose[1]—Mr Manley will therefore bring in his Accot accordingly.[2] I am sir, with great respect Your most Obt Servt

Tobias Lear
Secy to the president U.S.

LB, DLC:GW.

1. See Tobias Lear to Alexander Hamilton, 28 Nov. 1789, printed above.
2. Robert Manley was a coachmaker on Dye's Street, New York City.

From Joseph Mandrillon

Great man!   Amsterdam 4th Decr 1789

The kind indulgence which you have deigned to give my productions, is a benefit which expands my soul with a joy which can only be equalled by the sentiment of acknowledgement & gratitude; and to express which, one must possess that elevation—that sublimity of idea which nature has but rarely given to man—and which has been so happily bestowed upon you for the benefit of your country, & for the edification of those who are friends to virtue & liberty.

My friend Mr Cazenove, carrys to your Excellency a copy of my *Patriotic wishes* towards France.[1] After having essayed my zeal in favour of the *regeneration of America,* I ought equally to manifest my patriotic devotion towards France—my Count[r]y.[2]

I observe by the letter of the 12th of October last with which your Excellency has honored me—that my transmissions to America have been retarded; I hope, however to be more fortunate at this time, and that this little work will get quickly to your Excellency, and will be honored with your attention. I have the honor to be, my General, with the most perfect veneration Yr Excellencys most Hble & Obedt Servt[3]

Jos. Mandrillon

P.S. I have but one desire—but one Ambition capable of filling my soul with unalterable felicity—this is the Glory of possessing Your Excellency's portrait. Ah! Great man deign to be interested in my favour & fulfil my expectation.

Translation, DNA:PCC, item 78; ALS, in French, DNA:PCC, item 78. The text is taken from a translation prepared for GW.

1. In a letter of 15 June 1789 Mandrillon had already entrusted another book to the care of Theophile Cazenove, who was preparing to go to the United States as an agent for the Dutch land speculators who in 1792 formed the Holland Land Company. See Mandrillon to GW, 15 June 1789, n.2. Cazenove's departure was evidently delayed since he did not reach the United States until March 1790. The book Mandrillon was enclosing was his *Voeux Patriotiques*, a second edition of which was published in Amsterdam in 1789.

2. Mandrillon is referring to *Le Voyageur Américain, ou Observations sur l'Etat Actuel, la Culture, Commerce des Colonies Britanniques en Amérique. . . .* (Amsterdam, 1782).

3. The French version of this letter reads: "La précieuse indulgence que vous daignez accorder à mes productions est un bienfait qui répand dans mon ame une joie que le Sentiment de la réconnoissance peut Seul apprécier: et pour l'exprimer, il faudroit posseder cette élévation, cette Sublimité d'idée génie que la nature n'accorde que bien rarement aux hommes, et dont elle vous a Si heureusement doué pour le bonheur de votre patrie et l'édification de tous les peuples amis de la vertu et de la liberté.

"Mon ami, Mr Cazenove, porte à Votre Excellence un exemplaire de mes *Voeux Patriotiques* envers la France. Après avoir essayé mon zéle en faveur de la *régènération Américaine*, je devois manifester également mon dévouement patriotique envers la France, ma patrie.

"Je vois par la lettre dont Votre Excellence m'a honoré le 12 Octobr dernier que mes envois en Amérique éprouvent de grands retards; j'espere cependant être cette fois plus heureux et que ce petit ouvrage parviendra promptement à Votre Excellence, et que vous l'honorerez de votre attention. J'ai l'honneur d'être, Mon Général avec la vènération la plus parfaite de Votre Excellence Le trés humble & trés obéissant Serviteur." The postscript reads: "Je n'ai plus qu'un Seul desir, qu'une Seule ambition capable de remplir mon ame d'une félicité inaltérable: Ce Seroit le gloire de posseder le portrait de Votre Excellence. Ah! Grand-Homme, Daignez vous intéresser en ma faveur, et remplir mon attente."

From the North Carolina Ratifying Convention

Fayette Ville, State of North Carolina

Sir,   4th of December 1789.

By order of the Convention of the People of this State, I have the honor to transmit to you the Ratification and adoption of the Constitution of the United States by the said Convention in behalf of the People.[1] With sentiments of the highest consideration and Respect, I have the honor to be, Sir, Your most faithful and Obedient Servant

Samuel Johnston
President of the Convention.

Copy, in writing of Tobias Lear, DNA: RG 46, First Congress, Records of Legislative Proceedings, President's Messages; copy, DNA: RG 233, First Congress, Records of Legislative Proceedings, Journals; LB, DLC:GW.

1. North Carolina ratified the Constitution on 21 Nov. 1789. GW submitted this letter, together with the North Carolina instrument of ratification, to Congress on 11 Jan. 1790 (*DHFC*, 3:258–59). The enclosure was a copy of the "Adoption and Ratification of the Constitution of the United States by the State of North Carolina," 21 Nov. 1789 (DLC:GW).

From Christian Febiger

Sir   Phila. Decembr 5th 1789.

Pardon this Intrusion and believe me, when I solemnly aver, that I have no other Motive, than a real Inclination to promote by every means in my power the Prosperity of our dear Country. At the Time, when we first attempted the manufactury of Cotton in this City, I was one, who paid much Attention to it, I usd every Endeavour to obtain Information on a Subject then little understood, This drew me into a Correspondence with various people, among others with Thomas Diggs Esqr. of Virginia[1] then in Ireland, from whom I have receivd a Number of intelligent Letters, among others the one inclosd.[2] Permitt me Sir to introduce the Bearer of both Mr Thomas McCabe junr of Belfast, he has been here about a Week and much with me, he appears to be a young Man of Probity and well vers'd in his Bussiness, he has won my Friendship, which prompts me to sollicit in his Behalf your Excellencys Patronage & Protection.[3]

He has a great Desire to bring his Family to this Country, he will more fully explain his Intentions & Motives to your Excellency; if your Excellency will condescend to inform me through Mr McCabe, whether & through what Channel a Loan of the Brass Model mentiond by Mr Diggs could be obtaind, it would lay me under singular Obligations.[4]

I further beg Leave respectfully to inform your Excellency, that I had lately the honor of being appointed Treasurer of this State, if in that Capacity or as an Individual, I can render any Information or other Service to Your Excellency or my Country; none will more chearfully do it than he, who has the honor to be with every Sentiment, which the sincerest Veneration & Respect can dictate Your Excellencys Most obedient and most humble Servt

Christian Febiger

ALS, DNA:PCC, item 78.

For an identification of Christian Febiger, see his letter to GW applying for a post in the customs, 6 May 1789.

1. Under "Virginia" the word "Maryland" appears in a different hand.

2. For Thomas Digges's controversial Revolutionary War career, see *Diaries*, 6:333. Finding himself in serious financial difficulty at the end of the war, Digges went from London to Dublin where he soon became heavily involved in the investigation of Irish textile manufacture and the exportation of Irish indentured servants and, in defiance of official policy, encouraged the immigration of artisans skilled in the making of textiles to the United States. For an appraisal of Digges's activities in this field, see Boyd, *Jefferson Papers*, 20:315–22. See also Parsons, "The Mysterious Mr. Digges." The enclosure has not been located.

3. Thomas McCabe, Jr., is probably a son of Thomas McCabe of Belfast, Ireland. The elder Thomas McCabe was originally a London watchmaker who in 1777 formed a partnership with Robert and Henry Joy and John McCracken to operate a mill on Francis Street in Belfast. The mill employed some ninety workers, many of them children from the poorhouse, and received substantial government assistance. By 1789 McCabe was associated with William Pearce, an artisan from Manchester, in the invention and development of textile machinery. In 1791 Pearce went to the United States in the hope of securing an American patent on his newly invented loom (Elias, *Letters of Thomas Attwood Digges*, 423–29, 432–34; Digges to GW, 12 Nov. 1791).

4. Febiger may be referring to models of one of Pearce's inventions, perhaps the one later described by Digges as an invention "for Spining Flax thread (which I saw in a small brass miniature model that convincd me of the principle)" (Elias, *Letters of Thomas Attwood Digges*, 426).

William Jackson responded to Febiger for GW on 11 Dec.: "The President of the United States directs me to acknowledge the receipt of your letter, with the enclosure, which is returned, by Mr McCabe. He is not possessed of such information on the subject of Mr McCabes enquiry, as would enable him to offer any opinion thereon—and, altho' he is much disposed to promote every undertaking that promises advantage to our country, yet, in this particular case, he thinks that a better judgment may be formed from the sentiments to be collected among the Gentlemen, who conduct the Cotton-Manufactory in Philadelphia, than from anything that could be offered on the subject by an individual, unacquainted with its operations, and incompetent, from other causes, to a decision respecting it.

"Mr McCabes knowledge of the business, his opinions on its probable progress in your City which being the wealthiest and most populous, is the best theatre of observation, combined with the advantages of your acquaintance, are sources of intelligence on this subject far superior to any that the warmest zeal, otherwise unassisted, could furnish—The President, in a conversation with Mr McCabe, learns that he is not anxious to see the model, mentioned in Mr Diggs's letter, as more recent inventions and improvements have, in some measure, superseded its utility; He desires me to make his acknowledgments for the polite offer you are pleased to make of your services" (DLC:GW).

From Fenwick, Mason, & Company to GW

Bordeaux [France] 5 December 1789. The dealer's catalog description of this document notes that it deals with GW's order for wine which included twenty-six bottles of claret and twelve dozen "vins de grave.[1] We have taken much pains to procure this Wine and are well persuaded it is the best to be had. But we fear it (the claret particularly) may not be found fit for drinking immediately though it is old pure & of one of the first growths since it has just been bottled. Since the best wine is always bought in cask we beg leave to recommend to you to order always somewhat in advance that it may lie six or eight Months in bottle to ripen." The catalog description notes that the firm informed GW that "no good Champagne wine is to be had but through a friend in Rheims they have secured a case of two dozen bottles which they are taking the liberty to send him."

L, sold by Walter R. Benjamin Autographs, item M–754, catalog no. 867.

1. GW had ordered wine from the Bordeaux firm of Fenwick, Mason, & Company as recently as August 1789. See his letter to Wakelin Welch & Son, 16 Aug. 1789, n.1.

From Harry Innes

sir, Kentucky Danville Decr 5th 1789
I have the hono'r to acknowledge the receipt of your very polite Letter of the 30th of September with the several papers therein inclosed, permit me sir to return my most grateful thanks for the attention paid & the hono'r confered on me by the supreme Executive of the United States.[1]

The Office of Judge is of the first Magnitude, and when I reflect on its importance & my own imbecility it is with diffidence that I accept it, my situation being different from that of any other Judge in the Union; because great will be the business that will come before the Fœderal Court in this District, relative to Landed Property founded on the Laws of this State, which from their ambiguity, & want of certainty, will require certain principles to be established, as rules of decission & which are to be done without the aid of Precedent or a Coadjutor.

Impressed with a due sense of the importance of the Trust I can but accept the Commission with fear & trembling; however, my most active exertions shall be caled forth to support me under it—should I err—I hope & trust it will be imputed to the common frailties of Mankind, for I have the broad Basis of Opinion to Combat. I have the honor to be with great respect & esteem your mo. ob. servt

Harry Innes

ALS, DNA: RG 59, Nominations, Acceptances and Orders for Commissions.
For background to GW's judicial appointments, see his letter to the United States Senate submitting nominations for the Judiciary, 24 Sept. 1789.
1. GW's pro forma letter to Innes offering him the post of district judge for Kentucky, at this time still part of Virginia, is in KyLoF.

From William McNamara

Sir, [5 December 1789]
I would have conformed to my promise of troubling you no more, were I not actuated by the sincerest regret for having undesignedly offended your Excellancy, by my last letter.[1] I was far from imagining, when I wrote it, that it would have been taken as an insult: tho its being wrote in the anguish of disap-

pointment, arrayed it in attire, which it was never intended it
should ware; even then, it was far remote from my thoughts to
use the smallest insolence to your Excellancy, as the letter was
intended, at most, but as a remonstrance. I am not so irration-
al as to be the least displeased with your Excellancy for not granting my reques[t], when unacompanied by recommendations
that seem indispensably necessary; but which are so far removed
from my attainment, that before I could possibly receive them,
the indigence of my circumstances would constrain me to seek
some other mains of support, distant from hear; and were I to
receive them, they could not insure me success; nor do I wish,
for my private interest, the inovation of a custom that might be
very ingerous to the public good. I suppose that I have appered
so insignificant to your Excellancy, that you are very cairless
about my esteem or aversion; and tho you'l neither see me, nor
ever hear of me after this, yet I could not perfectly quiet my
mind, untill I ask your forgiveness, and recall the words that
have offended you. To commit an unjust action would be more
pain-ful to me than poverty: and it would be a piece of injustice
that admits of no apology, to censure that unblemished character, that has deservedly gained the admiration of every people
and country, as far as the American history is known; and that
you deserve nothing but respect and esteem from all men, the
annals of the world, and the personal knowledge of multitudes,
can sufficiently avince. I ever had the utmost respect, admiration, and reverance, for them illustrious virtues you possess; for
thirteen years disinterested, and unremitted endeavours to benefit mankind, which the almight[y] has blessed with success; and
for that mild, an[d] gentle disposition, which is a greate ornament to you, than the station you possess (and that you deserve
no other from me, or any other person, is an incontestable
truth) and tho I have not the honour to be known to you, yet it
would pain me for you to imagin, I thought otherwise.

I hope your excellancy will do me the justice to think, my
present declerations sincere, since they proceed from no motives of interest, nor expectation of favour, as I never intend to
enter your abode, nor ever to adress you any more.

Forgive, great Sir, what you are pleased to term insolence, and
believe me, no person alive can have a truer respect, or more
real esteem, for them excellant qualifications, of which the illus-

trious Washington is possessed, than, Your Excellancies most obediant, humble servant

William McNamara

ALS, DNA:PCC, item 78.
No information on William McNamara or his differences with GW has been found.
1. Letter not found.

From James Madison

Dear Sir   Orange [Va.] Decr 5. 1789.

Since my last I have been furnished with the inclosed copy of the letter from the Senators of this State to its Legislature.[1] It is well calculated to keep alive the disaffection to the Government, and is accordingly applied to that use by the violent partizans. I understand the letter was written by the first subscriber of it, as indeed is pretty evident from the stile and strain of it. The other *it is said*, subscribed it with reluctance. I am less surprized that this should have been the case, than that he should have subscribed at all.

My last information from Richmond is contained in the following extract from a letter of the 28th Novr from an intelligent member of the H. of Delegates.[2] "The revenue bill which proposes a reduction of the public taxes one fourth below the last year's amount is with the Senate. Whilst this business was before the H. of Delegates a proposition was made to receive Tobacco & Hemp as commutables, which was negatived; the House determining still to confine the collection to specie and specie warrants.[3] Two or three petitions have been presented which asked a general suspension of Executions for twelve months; they were read, but denied a reference. The Assembly have passed an Act for altering the time of choosing Representatives to Congress, which is now fixed to be on the third Monday in September, suspending the powers of the Representative until the Feby after his election. This change was made to suit the time of the annual meeting of Congress. The fate of the Amendments proposed by Congress to the Genl Government is still in suspense. In a Com[mitte]e of the whole House the first ten were acceded to with little opposition; for on a question taken on each separately, there was scarcely a dissenting voice. On the two last a debate of some length took place, which ended in rejection.[4] Mr E. Randolph who advocated all the others stood in this contest in the front of opposition. His principal objection was pointed agst the word "*retained*" in the eleventh proposed amendment, and his argument if I understood it was applied in this manner—that as the rights declared in the first ten of the proposed amendments were not all that a free people would require the exercise of, and that as there was no criterion by which it could be determined whether any other particular right was retained or not, it would be more safe and more consistent with the spirit of the 1st & 17th amendts proposed by Virginia that this reservation agst constructive power, should operate rather as a provision agst extending the powers of Congs by their own authority, than a protection to rights reducible to no definitive certainty.[5] But others, among whom I am one, see not the force of the distinction; for by preventing an extension of power in that body from which danger is apprehended, safety will be ensured, if its powers be not too extensive already, & so by protecting the rights of the people & of the States, an improper extension of power will be prevented & safety made equally certain. If the House should agree to the Resolution for rejecting the two last I am of opinion that it will bring the whole into hazard again, as some who have been decided friends to the ten first think it would be unwise to adopt them without the 11 & 12th. Whatever may be the fate of the amendments submitted by Congress, it is probable that an application for further amendments will be made by this Assembly, for the opposition to the federal Constitution is in my opinion reduced to a single point, the power of direct taxation—those who wish the change are desirous of repeating the application, whilst those who wish it not are indifferent on the subject, supposing that Congs will not propose a change which would take from them a power so necessary for the accomplishment of those objects which are confided to their care. Messrs Joseph Jones & Spencer Roane are appointed Judges of the Genl Court to fill the vacancies occasioned by the death of Mr Cary & the removal of Mr Mercer to the Court of appeals."[6]

The difficulty started agst the amendments is really unlucky, and the more to be regretted as it springs from a friend to the

Constitution. It is a still greater cause of regret, if the distinction be, as it appears to me, altogether fanciful. If a line can be drawn between the powers granted and the rights retained, it would seem to be the same thing, whether the latter be secured, by declaring that they shall not be abridged, or that the former shall not be extended. If no line can be drawn, a declaration in either form would amount to nothing. If the distinction were just it does not seem to be of sufficient importance to justify the risk of losing the amendts of furnishing a handle to the disaffected, and of arming N.C. with a pretext, if she be disposed, to prolong her exile from the Union. With every sentiment of respect & attachment I am Dr Sir Yr Obedt & hble servt

Js Madison Jr

ALS, DLC:GW; copy, in Madison's writing, DLC: Madison Papers.

1. Madison's "last" was his letter to GW of 20 Nov. 1789. For the letter from Richard Henry Lee and William Grayson to the Virginia legislature, see Edmund Randolph to GW, 26 Nov. 1789, n.3.

2. The letter to Madison was from Col. Hardin Burnley of Hanover County and Richmond. See Rutland, *Madison Papers*, 12:455–57.

3. See Madison to GW, 20 Nov. 1789, n.4.

4. For the action of the Virginia general assembly on the amendments to the Constitution, see Madison to GW, 20 Nov. 1789, n.5.

5. The seventeenth amendment suggested in the Virginia Ratifying Convention reads: "That those clauses which declare that congress shall not exercise certain powers, be not interpreted in any manner whatsoever, to extend the powers of congress; but that they be construed either as making exceptions to the specified powers where this shall be the case, or otherwise, as inserted merely for greater caution" (Robertson, *Debates and Other Proceedings of the Convention of Virginia*, 475).

6. Richard Cary (c.1739–1789), of Warwick County, served on the General Court from December 1788 until his recent death. James Mercer was appointed to the reorganized Court of Appeals in November 1789 (*Journals of the Council of State of Virginia*, 5:136) and served until his death in 1793.

From William Shepard

Sir   Newbern N. Carolina 5th Decer 1789
    The State of North Carolina having ratified the Federal Constitution, I beg leave to Offer myself to your Excellency as a Candidate for the Naval Office of this Port.
    When the Senators proceed to Congress I shall forward Testimonials of my Character, and Abilities to perform the Duties of

the Office. In the Interim I have the Honor to be with great Respect Your Excellencies Most Humble Servant

William Shepard

ALS, DLC:GW.

In July 1790 Shepard again wrote to GW, this time from New York City, requesting the post of loan officer for North Carolina, representing himself as "a person qualified to discharge the duties of such an Office. I am a Native and citizen of that State, am well acquainted wth Accounts and am possessed of property sufficient to enable me to give good Security for the faithful performance of the trust." For his references he named, among others, Samuel Johnston, Benjamin Hawkins, and Hugh Williamson, all of North Carolina (Shepard to GW, 29 July 1790, DLC:GW). Shepard was not successful in his application for either office.

Farm Reports

[Mount Vernon, 6–12 December 1789]
A Meteorological Account of the Weather
Kept at Mount Vernon 1789

Decr

6th	Murcury in the Morng	48	SWt	Clear	Noon	50		Clear	Night	55 NEt	Clear
					NEt						
7th	Morning	56	SWt	Clear	Noon	58		Cloudy	Night	60 SWt	Cloudy
					SW						
8th	Morning	56	SWt	Cloudy	Noon	59		Cloudy	Night	62 SWt	Cloudy
					SWt						
9th	Morning	44	NW	Clear	Noon	45		Clear	Night	45 NW	Cloudy
					NW						
10th	Morning	41	NW	Clear	Noon	42		Clear	Night	44 NW	Clear
					NW						
11th	Morning	44	NEt	Cloudy	Noon	45		Rain	Night	46 NW	Cloudy
					NEt						
12th	Morning	41	NW	Clear	Noon	41		Clear	Night	41 NW	Clear
					NW						

12th Decr

		Days
Dr.	Dogue Run Plantn for the work of 7 Men & 11 Women Amtg ℔week to	108
Cr.	By breaking up ground in No. 1	4
	By breaking up a p[iec]e of low ground next to the Tumbling dam joining No. 7	12
	By breaking up ground at River plantn in No. 5	8
	By hauling Corn	6
	By gathering ditto	18
	By Husking ditto	42
	By Sickness Lucy in Child bed 6 days, Brunswick 6, Matt 6 days	18
	Total	108

Sent to the Mill 60 Bushels of Oats to grind, 16 Bushels of Corn, 3 Barrels Soft ditto for the hogs, Recd from ditto 3½ Bushels B. Meal and 5½ ditto Ship stuff; Sent to Mansn House 30 Bushels Oats, Used by the Horses 10 Bushels of ditto, fed to the Hogs 3 Barrels soft Corn. *Stock* 56 head Cattle, 92 Old Sheep, 35 Lambs, 8 working Horses, 16 Calves from Mansn House.

		Days
Dr.	Ferry & Frenches Plantn for the work of 7 Men 16 Women and 3 Boys Amtg ℔ week to	156
Cr.	By breaking up ground in No. 2	42
	By hauling Corn	10
	By ditto wood at the Mansn House	2
	By gathering Husking and lofting Corn	72
	By Spinning	6
	By Lucy Confined to the House on acct of her Swell'd legg, & sowing	6
	By Sickness, Cupid 6 days, Lucy 6, Daphney 6 days	18
	Total	156

Recd from the Mill 11½ Bushels B. Meal, Sent to ditto 9¼ Bushels Corn, Sent to Mansn House 4¾ Bushels black Eyed pease, 4¾ Bushs. red ditto and 3 pecks small round ditto, *Stock* 81 head Cattle, 88 old Sheep, 28 Lambs, 15 Working Horses, 2 ditto Mules, 2 ditto Spring Mules Ferriages 20/.

		Days
Dr.	Muddy Hole Plantn for the work of 3 men & 10 women Amtg ℔ week to	78
Cr.	By breaking up ground in No. 6	24
	By hauling Corn and Housing ditto	2
	By hauling Corn at Dogue Run	4
	By gathering Corn	19
	By rip[in]g a House for the Overseer	17
	By grubing in No. 6	6
By Sickness Sacky 6 days		6
	Total	78

Increase 7 Cows Sent from Mansn House, Sent to the Mill 5 Bushels Corn Recd from ditto 11 Bushels bran and Oats Mixed for horse feed and 5½ Bushels B. Meal, Measured this week 7 Barrels Sound Corn 9 ditto of Nubbings, 2 ditto of Soft ditto—Stock 29 head Cattle 20 old Sheep 4 Lambs, 9 Working Horses.

		Days
Dr.	River Plantn for the work of 7 Men 17 women 3 Boys and 1 girl Amtg ℔ week to	162
Cr.	By breaking up ground in No. 5	34
	By hauling Corn; and at Mill 1 day	22
	By dressing Flax	12
	By Striping Tobo	15
	By threshing Oats	18
	By gathering and Husking Corn	55
	By Sickness Essex 6 days	6
	Total	162

Decrease 1 Sheep Sent to the Mill 11½ Bushels Corn 10½ Bushl. Oats fed to the Horses this week 21 Bushels Oats, 1½ to D. Run Horses Stock 91 head Cattle, 129 Old Sheep, 53 Lambs, 14 Working Horses.

		Days
Dr.	Mansn House for the work of 14 Men 9 Boys & 6 Girls Amtg ⅌ week to	174
Cr.	By waggon hauling Hay	4
	By hauling wood for the House, lime kiln, and at Mill	2
	By 1 Cart hauling wood and water	6
	By 1 ditto hauling lime and Sand to the green House	6
	By Cuting wood	6
	By diging post holes and puting up post and rail fence	64
	By baking bread 3 days, tending dairy 2 ditto	5
	By Cuting and Clearing the New road by the Mill	2
	By Cuting Stuff for rails	2
	By loading the waggon with Hay 2 days going to Alexa. with flower 1 Do	3
	By Stoped by rain 6 days, Seting lime kiln 2 ditto	8
	By tending the brick layers	24
	By feeding beeves and Stowing away Hay	6
	By beating out timothy Seed and Stowing away Hay	6
	By Carrying Shells to lime kiln 6 days, Sifting lime 6 days	12
	By Making Baskets	6
	By tending Stock and heaping up Manure	6
	By tending Jacks and going of errands	6
	Total	174

Decrease 7 Cows Sent to Muddy Hole Recd from the Mill 27 Bushels B. Meal Stock 17 head Cattle, 38 Old Sheep, 3 wethers, 18 Lambs, 5 last spring Mules 1 ditto 2 Years Old, 4 ditto spring ditto, 3 ditto Spring Colts, 2 ditto Spring Jennies, 3 ditto Old ditto, 3 ditto Jacks, 1 ditto spring ditto.

		Days
Dr.	ditchers for the work of 5 Men Amtg ⅌ week to	30
Cr.	By ditching finished 28½ roods	20
	By Mortising posts and lost on Acct of rain	2½
	By Sickness, Charles, 4 days, Botswain 3 ditto Robin ½ ditto	7½
		30

		Days
Dr.	Joinners & Carpenters for the work of 4 Men Amtg ⅌ week to	24
Cr.	By Thos Mohony About the green House window Shetters	4
	By Isaac engaged about ditto	6
	By James & Sambo Sawing 8 pieces for the green House & 8 laths 16 feet long	2
	By James Confined to the House having fallen from the saw pit & wounded himself	5
	By Sickness Thos Mohony 2 days	2
	By rounding Shingles	1
	By hewing 10 Stocks 16 feet long 10 Inches deep	4
	Total	24

Mill Grist	Dr.	Wht	Corn	Rye	Oats
Rem[ainin]g in the Mill		890½	14½	2¼	
To toll this week		9½	14		

To Dogue Run plantn	15½	60			
To River plantn		11½	11		
To Muddy Hole Plantn	5				
To Ferry & Frenches Plantn		9			
	900				
		53¼			6
Remg in the Mill	900				

Contra	Cr.	Ship			
		B. Ml	st[uff]	Brn	Hoy	Oats
By D. Run plantn		3½	5½	4	3
By R. Plantn		4¾	4½		
By Muddy Hole Plant.		5½	4	3	
By F. & Frenches Pltn		11½			
By Mansn House		27			1
By Miller & Coopers		1			
		53¼	10	8	1	6

Dr. Coopers for the work of 3 Men Amtg ℔ week to — Days 18

By Cuting hoop poles Cr.	5½
By triming pales	1½
By going to Alexa. with flower	7½
By puting the flower on board of the boat	3½
Total	18

D, in the writing of George Augustine Washington, DLC:GW.

This report and other similar accounts were sent by George Augustine Washington and GW's later managers on a weekly basis during GW's absences from Mount Vernon. During the presidential years GW clearly read the reports carefully and used them in preparing his detailed instructions to his managers on the administration of his plantations during the absences. In comparison to their numbers, relatively few of these reports have survived. See also editorial note to Farm Reports, 26 Nov. 1785–30 Dec. 1786.

From Edmund Randolph

Dear Sir   Richmond decr 6. 1789.
When I had the honor of writing to you last, the amendments had, I believe, been under consideration in a committee of the

whole, and ten were adopted, and the two last rejected.[1] Upon
the report being made to the house, and without a debate of any
consequence, the whole twelve were ratified. They are now with
the senate, who were yesterday employed about them. That
body will attempt to postpone them; for a majority is unfriendly
to the government. But an effort will be made against this
destructive measure.

In the house of delegates, it was yesterday moved to declare
the remainder of the amendments, proposed by our convention, essential to the rights and liberties of the people. An
amendment was offered, saying, that in pursuance of the will of
the people, as expressed by our convention, the general assembly ought to urge congress to a *reconsideration* of them. The
amendment was carried by the speaker, giving a casting vote.[2]
This shews the strength of the parties, and that in the house of
delegates the antifœderal force has diminished much since the
last year. A representation is to be prepared, and the inclosed
speaks the temper, which we wish to exhibit in it. Whether we
shall succeed in our attempt to carry such a remonstrance
through, is with me very doubtful. It will be pushed; because it
seems to discountenance any future importunities for amendments; which in my opinion is *now* a very important point. I
should have been sanguine in my belief of carrying the representation thro' in its present form, if the friends would have
joined the enemies of the constitution, in suspending the ratification of the eleventh amendment; which is exceptionable to
me, in giving a handle to say, that congress have endeavoured to
administer an opiate, by an alteration, which is merely plausible.

The twelfth amendment does not appear to me to have a ⟨very
real⟩ effect, unless it be to excite a dispute between the United
States and every particular state, as to what is *delegated*.[3] It ac-
cords pretty nearly with what our convention proposed but
being once adopted, it may produce new matter for the cavils of
the designing. I am dear Sir yr obliged and affectionate friend
and serv⟨t⟩

Edm: Randolph

P.S. I shall do myself the honor of replying to your official letter
as soon as the assembly rises.

ALS, DLC:GW.

1. See Randolph to GW, 26 Nov. 1789.

2. Randolph enclosed a copy of the assembly's statement, "The General Assembly of Virginia having taken into consideration the articles proposed in amendment of the Constitution have ratified the first &c.

"These subjects naturally turn our attention, to the remaining proposals of Virginia for amendments. The respect which we entertain for the Convention by which they were recommended, impels us to call upon Congress to reconsider them. At the present Day we prefer this mode to a Convention.

"In the tendor of amendments to the Constitution, to which we are one only of many parties, we cannot expect that the individual wishes or judgment of one state should prevent that Decision which seems best for the whole. We desire the reconsideration as suited to the greatness of the Questions; feeling an assurance that when time shall have shewn the Constitution in all its properties, whether good or bad, the same love of our common Country, which first prompted us to unite, will lead us to embrace the improvement which Experience shall suggest" (DLC:GW).

3. For the twelve amendments submitted to the states, see GW's Circular to the Governors of the States, 2 Oct. 1789, n.1.

William Jackson to Clement Biddle

Dear Sir,   New York, December 7th 1789.

The letter for Mr Holker, which encloses one for the Person, applying to be Steward of the Household, is, by the Presidents desire, committed to your care for conveyance.

Be so good as to give it an early transmission.

I shall take the liberty to write to you on my own account within a few days.

The President and Mrs Washington are in perfect good health. I am, very respectfully, Dear Sir, Your most obedient Servant

W. Jackson.

LB, PHi: Washington-Biddle Correspondence.

The letter mentioned has not been found. In December GW began seeking a replacement for Samuel "Black Sam" Fraunces, who entered his employment in May as household steward and chef at $25 per month. Fraunces, landlord of the Queen's Head (Fraunces' Tavern) on Broad Street, from which GW bid farewell to his officers in 1783, had been rewarded by Congress and the state of New York for his help in alleviating the suffering of American prisoners during the Revolution. Ever present and "resplendently dressed in wig and small-clothes," Fraunces especially prided himself on ensuring proper decorum at the presidential table by making certain the meals were always "bountiful and elegant." Ignoring GW's frequent remonstrances against extravagance, Fraunces is quoted as having said, "Well, he may discharge me, he may kill me if he will, but while he is President of the United States, and I have the honor to be his Steward, his establishment shall be supplied with the very best of everything that the whole country can afford." Although not popular with underservants, Fraunces earned GW's approval, and the president gave him a bonus when he quit in February 1790 to help his wife run their tavern (Decatur, *Private Affairs of George Washington*, 15, 19, 51, 116). Fraunces was replaced by John Hyde, who in the fall of 1790 accompanied the president to Philadelphia. To GW's chagrin, his new steward actually spent more money than his predecessor to feed roughly the same number of people. Hyde evidently exercised less control over the other servants. He suddenly gave one month's notice in March 1791 and in 1793 became the proprietor of the Tontine Coffee House at the corner of Water and Wall streets in New York, which was a center for Republican sympathizers with the French Revolution. Fraunces returned to the presidential household in Philadelphia in November 1791 and remained with the family until GW's term of office expired in 1797 (ibid., 116).

Letter not found: from Fenwick, Mason, & Company, 7 Dec. 1789. The dealer's catalog description of this document states that it concerns "the purchase of champagne, claret, etc." [1]

Sold by Hanzel Galleries, September 1973, item no. 50.
    1. See Fenwick, Mason, & Company to GW, 5 Dec. 1789. The manuscript dealer may have misread the date on this document.

From George Washington

Honr'd Sir   Tarboh North Carolina December 8th 1789
    Since the adoption of the Constitution in this State, I have undertaken though with a trembling heart to ask your intrest in appointing me an Officer in the Naval department of this State, for my maintainance, though I must seriously acknowledge to you that I little deserve it, But I must inform your honnor that I am at this Period voi'd both of Fortune & friends, which induce's me to implore your most gracious Benevolence, when I reflect on your extensive Humanity I flatter myself with a feeble hope of acquireing your Paternal attention, there are four Ports in this State, Edentown Washington Bath & Wilmington & should your unden'yable Humanity grant me a Commission, I would rather chuse the latter should it meet with your approbation,

Complying with my request will ever be reflected on by your distres'd Petitioner

Geo. Washington

ALS, CSmH.

No information on this George Washington has been found, and there is no indication he received any federal appointment.

From Elijah Hunter

Dear Sr   Mountpleasant Decbr 9th 1789
I have Been for Some time Past in Greate Contemplation whether I Should Trouble your Excellensy with a Line by way of Remembrance, Respecting Some of the Transactions of the Late war or Not, Which I hope you will Not Take amis, if you Should Not Think it worthy your Notice to answer.

I must also Beg leave to appologise For Languge and Stile To address Such a Character in Life as yourself, For I am Not a Profit Nor a Profits Son Neither was I Brot up at the Feet of Gomalea,[1] But through Divine assistance I Shall be able to Lay Before you Matters of Fact which I Shall only appeal to your Self For the Truth of.

In the First Place In the winter 1779 when your Excellensy had your Quarters at the Rarritan in Newjersy you may Remember I Came to you with a Letter from Genl McDogal—Informing you that Governor Tryon had Sent a Packet of Letters to me and others to be Distributed and one to myself Insinuating with me to alter my Sentaments and Promising me the Protection of Govermt and its Emoluments in Case of my Being discoverd in Giving them Inteligence These Letters with a Letter From Genl McDogal of my Character you had Before you as I was then a Total Stranger to you.[2]

I was also Sent by you to Philadelphia To Congress Mr John Jay Being then Presedent who I was well acquainted with, and you Requested me to Call on you In my Return which I Did.

you then Sr Requested me to Countenance a Corespondance with the British,[3] I then Made Some appoligy that I was unequal to Such a Task and the Resque was Greate, and that I must Become an obnoctious Character on Both Sides, which I Daily Experience to be True, Instances of which if opertunity offerd

Could Site you to—But your Excellensy usd Some Forcable
arguments to Excite me To undertake by assuring me the Protection of the States and in Case of our obtaining Independasy
that Such Persons who Stood forth at Such a Cretical Moment
would Not be Forgot by them, and that it Might be of More
Servise than Five hundred men in the Field at my own Expence—and that I had Taken an active Part In my Countries
Cause, and that it Become Every Man to Take Such a Part for
Gaining our Independansy as Providenc Pointed out, upon thes
Conditions, with Nearly the Same from the Then Presedent of
Congress I Concluded on the Business and your Excellensy
Gave me the Statement of the army and wrote by me to Genl
McDogal[4] and also you may Remember that you made an appol-
ogy to me that it would be attended with Considerable Expence
out of Pocket But the Funds were Low and that you Could Not
Furnish with Cash for that Purpose, Neither have I Recd any
During the war, Except Two half Joes, I Re[ceive]d from you at a
Time at Newinsor when I Brot up Four Men By your Express
Request to be as Pilots on the Sound which Cost I was to and Did
Give them for their Expensis. But if Independansy was obtaind
that No Doubt I Should be amply Rewarded I upon these
Conditions with I Trust a Zeal for the Cause I went on with
Chearfulness and Kep up a Continual Correspondance with
them which Soon Became So General That it Took up all my
Time To Ride To Head Quarters and So to Meet those who were
Imployed Between the Lines This was Kep up More or Less to
the End of the war. Now Sr as to the advantages arising from this
Inteligence I must Leave to yourself But This I have To Give me
Some Satisfaction I have Recd from your Excellensy From west-
point a Letter wherein you Returnd me your Thanks for the
Information Re[ceive]d by yourself & the Different officers of
Ports and also I have a Satificut From you upon your Departure
from Newyork Left with genl McDogal To Secure my Character
and Recommend me to whom it might Consern Such Like ones
I have from Different officers.[5]

But Sr as to the Intelegence which was Given by me I will Site
To Two Instanses Paticulor as No Doubt your Memory may Fail
and as I Conseave it was Important I Shall only mention them
Two one of which when the Enemy Came up the North River
and Took Verplanks Point and Stony Point with an Intent on

West Point and to Make an attack on Connecticut at the Same Time In order to Draw our Troops from the Highlands and also another Instance when Majr Talmage was attacked—at Poundridge which I Gave Talmage Possitive Information Two Days before it happend and the Time when Exactly as I Dont Doubt you will Remember by the Letters which Passed Between you and Talmage about the Matter the other Instance the Information was Given to Genl McDogal Pointedly and the Enemies Design which at First he Could Not Beleave But in a Few Hours Provd the Fact which he has alwaeys acknowledged with the Greatest Gratitude the Many other Instanses would be To Tedious to Mention Genl McDogal a Few Days Before his Death To Two Persons of Character who he Supposd might be of Servise to me in a Future Day Told them that the States were under Greate obligation to Capt. Hunter and was Sorry that he Could Not Se that Full Satisfaction was Made him But it was out of his Power to Do more and Requested as I understand that Those men might Mention this from him In Case it Might Be Nessesary.

But Sr Sometime Previous to this Genl McDogal Through his Influance as a Temporary Releaf obtain from the Treasurer of this State about Eight Hundred Pounds in Satificuts which was at about 3/6 Pounds and that as I was a Capt. Malitia and So was Considerd as Being in Servise and the Reason why this was Done was Because I Did Not Chose to apply to Congress as that must be In Such a Publick Manner that my Situation must be Laid open to the World and which has been the Reason why I have Never Made application Since and in Peticulor Since the New Goverment has Taken Place—as all Debates are Made Publick.

But Sr when I Consider the Justness of my Claim and the Character of the administrator of Goverment and that it is him who I must appeal to as a Living witness of the Truth of these Things, Gives me Courage to Lay the Matter Before you and also another Motive when I Consider that Many Persons who Now Reseave Large Sallar⟨ies⟩ from Goverment who have Never Resqued Life Nor Property In the Servise of the Country and are Now Injoying the Liberties and Emoluments of it, which I as a Siteson am obliged to Pay my Dues and Taxes to Defray the Expence and What I have Recd has Not amounted to half of my

Pock⟨et⟩ Expence I have Sr a Family To take Care of which is Near and Dear to me as Perhaps to any other man, Therefore in Duty to them as well as the Justness of my Cause I Cannot Rest the Matter in Silence any Longer.

I Cannot with Justise omit Mentioning Two Persons who were also Imployed in the Same Servise under my Deretion and your order and approbation who have Not Re[ceive]d one Cop[pe]r and Both Now in Low Surcumstance one of which was a Man of Some Property and Good Character who has Been undone by the war and has Long been Confind in Goal But through my assistance I have Got him out and For Further Peticulors on Many Different Subjects I Shall omit at Pres⟨ent⟩ and Now Dear Sr if what I have Mentioned Should be by you thot worthy your attention Should be Glad if you Could Let me Know whether it would be agreeable For me to Call on you For Further advise on the Matter and That a Line Left With Malankton Smith of Newyork who I Expect will be the Bearer of this or to Samuel Frankling & Co. who will Forward it to me by my Sloop who will Return from Newyork on Friday Next.

Now Dear Sr I Shall Leavve the Matter to your wise Consideration Praying that you may be Led in to all Truth and the God of the universe may bestow on you all that grace wisdom and understanding that you Need For to Direct you in the Greate Important Trust Reposed in you For without that you Cant Do anything, acseptable to him and that you may Finish your Course with Joy and at Last Receave a Crown of Glory Laid up In heven for those who Love the Lord Jesus Christ and his appering which God Grant may be the Happy Lot and Portion of us all for Christ Sake which is the Sinseare Desire of your Humbe Sert[6]

Elijah Hunter

ALS, DNA:PCC, item 78.

Elijah Hunter of Bedford, Westchester County, N.Y., served as a lieutenant and captain in the 4th New York Regiment in 1775 and early 1776 and transferred to the 2d New York in November 1776. He apparently declined the appointment to the 2d New York and retired from the army. According to a statement made by Hunter in 1783 he was approached early in 1779 by Sir Henry Clinton, "Requesting me to Change my Sentiments and assist the British in giving them Information Respecting the army and State of affairs in the Country" (Hunter to GW, 11 Mar. 1783). At that point he approached Alexander McDougall and John Jay, president of Congress at the time, offering his services to the United States as a double agent, claiming he had access to such prominent British officers as Clinton, his aide John André, and Frederick Haldimand (Hunter to GW, 21 May 1779). Both McDougall and Jay passed the information along to GW, Jay stating that he had known Hunter for many years and found him "an honest Man, and firmly attached to the american Cause." In late March GW met with Hunter and somewhat reluctantly approved his proposal to spy for the Americans. Although he had some reservations about the use of Hunter as an agent, his suspicions probably pertained less to Hunter personally than to his views of double agents in general, since he felt "Their situation in a manner obliges them to trim a good deal in order to keep well with both sides; and the less they have it in their power to do us mischief, the better; especially if we consider that the enemy can purchase their fidelity at a higher price than we can" (McDougall to GW, 21 Mar. 1779, Jay to GW, 28 Mar. 1779, GW to McDougall, 25 Mar. 1779). Operating under the code name "H. E.," Hunter apparently delivered relatively extensive information on British plans and movements to his superiors during the war (GW to Hunter, 12 Aug. 1779; Hunter to GW, 11 Mar. 1783).

1. Rabban Gamaliel Ha-Zaken (the elder), the first president of the Sanhedrin in Jerusalem, taught the apostle Paul, who is quoted in the New Testament in the book of Acts 22:3 as saying, "I am a Jew, born at Tarsus in Cilicia, but brought up in this city at the feet of Gamaliel, educated according to the strict manner of the law of our fathers, being zealous for God as you all are this day."

2. See McDougall to GW, 21 Mar. 1779, with enclosures.

3. See GW to McDougall, 25 Mar. 1779.

4. See GW to Hunter, 12 Aug. 1779.

5. See GW to Hunter, 12 Aug. 1779. By March 1783 Hunter was planning to return to his farm in Bedford and approached GW for a certificate attesting to his services during the war (Hunter to GW, 11 Mar. 1783). GW's reply stated that "the Recommendations given in your favor by Mr Jay then President of Congress & Major General McDougall were such as induced me to repose great confidence in you, and to my own knowledge, after being employed in the manner abovementioned you obtained such intelligence, either by yourself or your Correspondents, of various things which passed within the British Lines, as was of considerable consequence to us" (GW to Hunter, 11 June 1783). There is also a draft of another certificate concerning Hunter's services, dated 1 Dec. 1783, in DLC:GW.

6. On 24 Feb. 1790 Hunter again wrote to GW: "you May Remember that Not Long Since I wrote your Excellensy and Stated Some Peticular Facts Respecting Some Transactions of the Late war and as I was Informed by the Person who Deliverd it that your Excellensy had forgot Me and that if it was True that I Should of applied at an Early Period which will appear that I Did if you Take Notise of what I wrote. you also Mentioned to the Person that you had Given Genl McDogal Cash to Settle with those in that Servise which I Never Recd one Farthing of Nor any to My Knowledge which ware Imployed at my Request which were Two who I mentioned In my Letter one of which has Never had any Thing But has Spent his Property and Resqued his Life.

"I Now Transmit to your Excellensy a Number of Papers For your Perusal and an accompt of what the State has Done on My Behalf and that was Done Not as an Adequate Compensation But a Temporary Releaf.

"Now Dear Sr I think that if you upon Examination of these Papers Should Find that I have Done the Servise therein Mentioned with the Greate Expence which I have Been at for upwards of Four year Both in Victicalling and Sending Expresses and Going myself Both to Head Quarters and with Flags to Newyork and the Danger I Put myself in and that I Do ⟨affirm⟩ by the advise and Desire of your Excellensy, at the Rarraton in Newjersy I Never Should of undertaken the Business Now Sir I must appeal to yourself—whether any Man would Resque his Life and Fortune upon Such unsertain Ground and at Such a Cretical Period and at the Close of Such a Contraversy and Git about £832 Satificuts when all my Expenses was in hard Cash. I Shall Now Leave the whole Matter to your wise Consideration. . . . You will Dr Sr Excuse me if I Should Say that it is the Greatest Grief to me when I Understood that you had Forgot there Being Such a Man, as me, it is Clearly acknowledged by Genl McDogal that Trough my Information the Posts in the Highlands were Preservd and many other Important Informations I Could Refer you to and Even from your own Letters one wherein you are Pleasd to Mention your Thanks. . . . Now Sr in my Two Letters I have In Breef Stated the Facts and must Now Leave the whole to your wise Consideration" (DNA: RG 59, Miscellaneous Letters).

On 25 Feb. GW replied: "I have received your letter of yesterday with its enclosures, which are herewith returned. The Gentleman who delivered my message to you, which you say was given in answer to your former letter, mistook the purport of it. It was not your person, or character I had forgotten, but the transactions in detail to which you alluded.

"It is not possible for me, with any degree of propriety, to tread back ground I passed over seven years ago, when no application has been made to me in all that time; and when my accounts with the public closed with the resignation of my Commission—especially too, as it appears by the papers handed to me, that you have been paid, agreeable to your own charge, for the services you are *now* desireous of bringing again to view. To obtain which appears to have been the design of the certificates adduced. The effect of which, to the best of my recollection, was the kind of reward you seemed, at that time, to have had in contemplation.

"As you were employed principally by, or through, Genl McDougall, who, I well remember, had two hundred Guineas put into his hands, with which to pay those who were used as secret Agents, I always supposed (if more than recommending you to the State of New York, which seemed to be your great if not only object, was expected) that this money or a part thereof would be applied.

"From this view of the matter you will readily see that I cannot take any other steps in it than what have been already effected" (copy, DNA: RG 59, Miscellaneous Letters).

No indication has been found that Hunter either applied for or was

granted any further compensation under the new government although one
of his Revolutionary War accounts for commissary expenditures was settled in
1792. See DNA: RG 217, Records of the General Accounting Office, Miscellaneous Treasury Accounts, account no. 2671.

To John Jay

Wednesday December 9th 1789

The President of the United States presents to the *Chief Justice*
of the United States a volume of the laws passed in the first
Session of the Congress of the United States, and requests his
acceptance of the same.[1]

LB, DLC:GW; copy, DNA: RG 59, Miscellaneous Letters.

A note at the bottom of the letter-book copy indicates that "the same card
accompanied a Volume sent to the Secretary of the Treasury—The Secretary
of State—The Secretary of War and each of the Associate Justices."

1. The volume was probably *Acts Passed at a Congress of the United States of
America, Begun and Held at the City of New-York, on Wednesday the Fourth of March,
in the Year M,DCC,LXXXIX. And of the Independence of the United States, the Thirteenth* . . . , the first edition of the federal statutes, published in New York in
1789 by Francis Childs and John Swaine, official printers to the United States.
Jay replied on the same day: "The Chief Justice of the U.S. has recieved, and
presents his respectful acknowledgements to the President of the United
States for the elegant Edition of the Laws passed in the first Session of Congress, with which the President condescended to honor him this morning"
(DNA:PCC, item 78).

William Jackson to ——

Sir,

December 9th 1789.

The President of the United States having occasion for Mitchell's map,[1] which hangs in one of the offices of Congress, and is
supposed to be in your care, requests that you will be so good as
to send it by the Servant, who delivers this note. I am Sir, Your
obedient Servant

W. Jackson.

ALS, DNA: RG 59, Miscellaneous Letters.

This letter is unaddressed, but may have been directed to Roger Alden,
former assistant secretary to the Confederation Congress who had been
appointed by GW to a clerkship in the State Department. All of the earlier

papers of Congress had been placed in his care. See GW to Thomas Jefferson, 13 Oct. 1789, Charles Thomson to GW, 23 July 1789.

1. See James Boyd to GW, 27 Nov. 1789, n.2.

Letter not found: from Robert Morris, 9 Dec. 1789. On 14 Dec. GW wrote to Morris: "I have been favored with the receipt of your letter of the 9th instant."

From Samuel Osgood

Sir   General Post Office New York December 9th 1789

As the meeting of the Congress of the United States is near at hand, it becomes my Duty to state the situation of the Post Office, in order that if any defects shall be found in the present System, the Supreme Executive may make such representation of the same, as the importance of the business may require.

I have employed as much of my time, as could be spared from the necessary and current Transactions of the Office, in exa[m]ining into the nature of the Business, and the Defects of the System.[1] And beg leave to submit the following observations for Consideration.

If the views of the Legislature should be to raise Revenue from the Post Office, in order to aid and support the General Government, the Defects of the present regulations of the Post Office are many, and may easily be pointed out.

If their should be no view of raising a permanant and sure Revenue, yet for the purpose of establishing more confidence, and security in the Post Office Department, in the minds of those that may be interested in it, many alterations will be found essentially necessary.

These alterations cannot all be pointed out by men, from mature consideration; for I find the business is more extensive and various, than I had expected; and that it will require some Months Practice and Experience, to obtain adequate & Just Ideas of it.

The two following articles, upon the present regulation, operate very powerfully against the Revenue.

Any person may receive carry and deliver inland Letters and Dispatches; and is subject to no Penalty, if it is done without hire or reward.

All Masters of Ships and Vessels, and passengers in them, may bring letters to the United States, and are not obliged to carry them to a Post Office, nor are they subjected to a penalty, if the Letters are brought without hire or reward.

The subsequent alterations may be found necessary for greater security in the Post Office, whether Revenue be, or be not an object.

A more acurate and particular description of Offences and frauds, that may be committed by any person employed in any way or manner whatever in the Department; and penalties proportioned to the Injuries that may happen from the committing such Offences, or being guilty of such frauds.

In this way then will be brought into View, such Offences as may be committed by the Postmaster General, and those employed in his Office.

The Deputy Postmasters and such as they employ.

The Contractors for carrying the Mail, and their Agents and Servants.

Many Offences may be pointed out, that probably never have been committed in the United States; but the Opportunity to commit them is great, and the injury may be irreparable, as property to a very great amount is frequently conveyed by the Mail. It therefore appears to me, that it would only be exercising a due Degree of caution and prudence, to guard against them by defining the Crimes, and affixing to them such penalties as would be most likely to deter from, and prevent the actual committing of them—If afterwards they should be committed, the injured person would have the satisfaction of knowing that the Laws of the Country extended to him as much Protection and Security, as he can reasonably expect.

It is not necessary to detail all the Crimes and frauds that may be committed in the Post Office Department; If the Legislature should proceed to a new arrangment of it, they will readily occur in an examination into the nature of the business.

The Duties of the Postmaster General at present seem to be as follows—To keep an Office at the place where Congress may hold their sessions—To obey such orders and Instructions as he may from time to time receive from the President of the United States—To appoint Deputy Postmasters, and instruct them in their Duty in conformity to the Acts of Congress. To receive and examine their Accounts and Vouchers, and draw out of their, Hands Quarterly, the Balances due the United States: To render to the Treasury annually an Account of the Receipts and expenditures for examination, and Allowance; and to pay over the Surplus Monies—To provide by Contract, and otherwise, when Contracts cannot be made, for carrying the Mail; and to pay the necessary expences thereof—To establish and open new Post Offices, and new Post Roads, whenever and wherever they may be found necessary. And in general, to superintend the Department, and to be accountable for it, in the various duties assigned to it, except the carrying of the Mail.

On any Breach of Oath the Postmaster General one[2] due conviction, forfeits to the United States one thousand Dollars.

It is further Ordered, how often he shall cause the Mail to be carried Weekly; and that he shall advertise for proposals for carrying the Mail.

On the accountability of the Postmaster General, I beg leave to observe, that no man can, however great his Industry,[3] however Sagacious and cautious he may be in his appointments, without subjecting himself to a certain loss, be answerable for the conduct of his Deputies. The calculation of loss being certain in case of Responsibility, if he has not a salary sufficient to compensate such Loss, he must transact the business and keep the Accounts in a manner that the Treasury shall not be able to Charge him with any more Money than he chooses to be Charged with; which has in fact been the case, I believe ever since the Revolution. Or he may hold the Office untill he shall find he cannot preserve his Reputation and Credit, and then if he is an honest man he will resign.

The number of times that the mail shall be carried weekly; the advertising for Proposals for carrying the Mail; and the establishing new Post Offices, and new Post Roads, appear to me to be matters, that should remain in the Discretion of the supreme Executive. Very great Embarrassments ensue, when business is pointed out in detail, and there is no Power at hand that can alter that detail, however necesary the alteration may be.

Suitable Penalties should be required of the Postmaster General, in case he neglects or refuses to render true and Just Accounts of the Receipts and expenditures, & to pay over the

Moneys to the Treasury, that may be over and above the annual expenditures, at such periods, as may be required of him.

In some regulations of foreign Post Offices, that I have attended to, it does not appear that the Postmaster General has an Office separate from one, in which common and ordinary business is done—There may be some reasons given why it should be so: The minutiae of the common business, is important— Those who are most likely to be immediately acquainted with any irregularities, are they who have the receiving and Delivering of the Mail—When the Postmaster General keeps a separate Office many of these irregularities escape his notice—or never come to his knowledge.

But these remarks would apply more forcibly if there were in the United States, one City of so much consequence, as to have nine Tenths of all the business Center in it. As this is not the case; many Irregularities may take place, and the Postmaster General whether in an Office or not, when the mail is received and delivered will never be acquainted with them.

I found the General Post Office not blended with one, in which common and ordinary business is done; and it remains in the same situation.

Let the regulations of the Post Office be calculated in the best possible manner to draw business into it, yet the Revenue will be greater or less in proportion to the rates of Postage—The rates at present have reference to two kinds of Letters—Inland Letters, and Letters that pass and repass by Sea. According to what I am informed is the true instruction of the Ordinance of Congress that imposes the Rates; every single Ship Letter, bro't to a post Office ought to be charged, in the first instance, with 24/90 of a Dollar, and if it is forwarded by land, the usual rates of travelling Letters, ought to be added to the same. But in the manner the business has been transacted, these Letters have been a burthen and expence to the General Post Office.

Letters may come from beyond Sea to the United States, in their own Packets, when established, in foreign Packets, and in private Ships or Vessels: So far as I have been able to find out the regulations of other Nations; the rates of Postage are the same, or nearly so, on Ship Letters, let them come in any of the before mentioned ways. The British Postmaster General is subject to a heavy Penalty if he sends any letters in Ships not navigated according to Law.

The Letters that come to the United States by Sea, are very numerous; and may be made a source of considerable Revenue, under Proper Regulation.

With respect to inland Letters, the Prohibition against receiving and carrying them will be of little consequence unless it extends to all persons, who may receive and carry Letters, with or without hire and reward; and proper penalties be annexed to enforce a due observance of it. Some few exceptions may be necessary, where Masters of Vessels carry letters respecting the Merchandize under their immediate care; Letters sent by Friends, or special Messengers, or by common known Carriers if their be such in the United States.

Regulations may probably be found necessary respecting Bye or Way letters: embezzlling or destroying Letters, on which the Postage has been paid. Detaining or opening letters—secreting, embezling, destroying and stealing any valuable papers out of any letters. Against the Carrier of the Mail, in case they neglect or desert it, or loiter on the road. To oblige Ferrymen to set the Mail across in all possible cases, in a given time.

To recover small Debts due to, and from the Postmaster in a summary way.

These are some of the principals that may be found necessary to be introduced into the Regulations of the Post Office, and no doubt many others may suggest themselves to the wisdom of the Legislature.

The Privilege of Franking Letters is claimed, in some instances, where it is supposed the present regulations do not extend it. In doubtful cases I have taken the advice of Council; and have conducted agreeably thereto. It will be found necessary to make alterations with respect to franking Letters.

The Secretary of the Treasury having lately requested my Opinion, as to what might probably be the Surplus Revenue in the Post Office Department upon its present establishment, or any one that might be substituted in the place thereof, I take the liberty of enclosing my answer to him, which contains all that I can say respecting the same, until I shall have better Documents for forming estimates.[4] I have The Honor to be &c.

LB, DNA: RG 28, Letters Sent by the Postmaster General, 1789–1836.

Samuel Osgood (1748–1813) of Andover, Mass., had studied for the ministry at Harvard but after graduating in 1770 joined a business firm with his brother. During the Revolution he served as aide-de-camp to Artemas Ward. In 1781 he was elected to Congress and served until 1784. In 1785 he became a member of the Board of Treasury. Although Osgood had not supported the Constitution in the struggle for ratification, GW nevertheless appointed him to succeed Ebenezer Hazard as postmaster general in September 1789. Osgood served until the government moved to Philadelphia in the summer of 1790.

1. For an account of the post office's problems experienced by Osgood's predecessor, see GW to Ebenezer Hazard, 17 July 1789, n.1.

2. In MS this word reads "one."

3. In MS this word reads "Indrustry."

4. Hamilton requested Osgood's opinion, possibly in a letter of 16 Nov. 1789 which has not been found. Osgood's reply on 28 Nov. 1789 describes in detail many of the fiscal operations of the Post Office Department. Tobias Lear forwarded this document to Hamilton on 16 Jan. 1790 (DLC:GW). For an expanded report made by Osgood to Hamilton, 20 Jan. 1790, which incorporates much of the information as in this letter to GW, see Syrett, *Hamilton Papers*, 6:195–204. Hamilton submitted this letter to the House of Representatives on 22 Jan. 1790 (*DHFC*, 3:270).

From Samuel Powel

Dear Sir   Philadelphia December 9. 1789
   In my answer to the Enquiries made by Major Jackson, when last in this City, respecting the Hessian Fly, I recollect that I informed him that this destructive Insect had disappeared from this State. That answer, I then believed, from all the Information I was then possessed of, that I was fully warranted in giving—but, upon a Conversation[1] that I had last Night with a very intelligent Farmer, I find it necessary to inform you that this Insect still abounds in Pennsylvania.[2]

   The Purport of the Information given by this Gentleman, is, that the Wheat is, at this Time much infested by the Hessian Fly in his Neighborhood in Bucks County; but that those Farmers who have sown the Yellow-bearded Wheat, are not under Apprehensions of a Failure of their Crops at the ensuing Harvest from it's Ravages, as this Species of Wheat has been found from Experience, in Pennsylvania as well as in some other of the

States, to be more capable of resisting its Devastations than any other.

I am sorry to find that Facts are such as to oblige me to contradict the Answer and Information I have given to Major Jackson on this Subject—The Love of Truth, however, will not permit me to withold from communicating this Intelligence, by the first Opportunity after I received it[.] I sincerely hope it may arrive in Time to prevent any Error that might have arisen from my Information to Major Jackson.

Be pleased to accept the best Thanks of the Society for promoting Agriculture for your obliging Care of Mr Young's Tenth Volume. If you should have written to Mr Young on the Subject of the Hessian Fly, I shall take it as a particular Favor if you will be so good as to inform me of it, that I may have it in my Power, immediately, to inform him of the true State of Facts, & how far I have contributed to this Error.[3]

Mrs Powel requests Leave to offer her best Compliments to Mrs Washington, yourself, and all the good Family. I have the Honor to be, with real Respect & Regard Your most obedt humble Servt

Samuel Powel

ALS, DLC:GW.

1. In MS this word reads "Conservation."

2. For the Hessian fly, see Arthur Young to GW, 19 May 1789, n.2.

3. Powel is referring to volume 10 of Young's *Annals of Agriculture*, published in London in 1788. Young wrote to GW on the ravages of the Hessian fly in his letter of 19 May 1789, but GW had not written to Young on the matter. See his reply to Powel, 15 Dec. 1789.

Clement Biddle to Tobias Lear

Philadelphia 10th December 1789

Since my last of the 30th Ulto I have had an Opportunity of further Enquiry Concerning Buckwheat and find that it cannot easily be had before the Close of Winter but can be Certainly procured during the winter about the prices mentioned in my last letter. Capt. Carhart is arrived from Alexandria and tells me he shall return immediately to potowmack if he can procure a Freight and in that Case will sail about the 20th of this Month[1]—

I shall take care to inform Mrs Meredith in time to ship the Potatoes if the Vessel goes for Alexandria.[2]

C.B.

LB, PHi: Clement Biddle Letter Book, 1789–92.

1. On 24 Dec. Lear notified Biddle that "Capt. Carhart could not procure a freight for Alexandria before the Close of the River which is daily expected therefore Could not sent the potatoes & no Opportunity will offer before February or early in March when I expect there will be one or more without doubt" (PHi: Clement Biddle Letter Book).

2. On 14 Dec. George Augustine Washington informed GW that "the Apricot Potatoes you expected to be sent from Maj. Meredith have not come to hand." On 23 Feb. 1790, with a vessel about to depart for Alexandria, Biddle wrote Lear "am I to Call on Mr Meredith for the seed Potatoes for this Conveyance" (PHi: Clement Biddle Letter Book). Lear failed to reply and Biddle again wrote on 6 Mar.: "I was much in Doubt about Calling for the Potatoes from Mrs Meredith and wrote to you the 23d ulto to have your Directions but receiving no Answer I concluded I had but Omit it but if they are to go I expect another vessel will sail for Potowmack in about a fourtnight tho' the time is not yet certain" (PHi: Clement Biddle Letter Book). Lear responded on 10 Mar. that "a delay may be favourable, as we have had weather lately which might have injured them if they had been sent by Captain Ellwood— but by the next Vessel you will be so obliging as to have them sent" (PHi: Washington-Biddle Correspondence). Biddle informed Lear on 27 April that "By the Sloop Polly Capt. Ellwood I have forwarded to Major Washington at Mount Vernon forty Bushels of Seed Potatoes recd from Mrs Meredith" (PHi: Clement Biddle Letter Book). See also Biddle to Lear, 22 Nov. 1789.

Letter not found: to Samuel Hanson, 10 Dec. 1789. On the same day Hanson wrote to GW: "Your favour of this date is just received."

From Samuel Hanson of Samuel

Sir   Alexandria, 10th Decr, 1789.

Your favour of this date is just received.[1]

I am sincerely distressed at having given you one moment's uneasiness, and truly repent the occasion of it. I am ashamed at having subjected you to the trouble of so full & particular a Communication of your sentiments upon a subject, which I had as little right, as intention, to explore. In apology, I can only say that I had not the most remote wish, or expectation, of obtaining any promise in my favour. This I knew to be as impossible as it was improper. The object of my Address was to discover whether there were any circumstances respecting my character which would induce you either, in a private Capacity, to with-hold your testimony in it's support, or, in a publick one, deter-mine you to suppress my Suit, as inadmissible. It is true I was conscious that, if there had ever been any imputation upon me, either as a Man or a Citizen, it had never come to my Knowl-edge. I knew, too, that, with regard to charges of this kind, the Party interested is not usually kept long in ignorance. But the case was possible. I was anxious, therefore, to discover whether my Character appeared as irreproachable in your Eyes as it did in my own, and as, I trusted, it was in reality. Peculiarly situated with respect to the School, I found that, if there was no pros-pect of Success from my application, it was important to me to know it.[2] I was, therefore, desirous of Knowing whether You had determined *against* me; without any design of discovering whether I might reckon upon your patronage and Support. Merely to know that you had not determined to reject my Suit, could not, I conceived, be construed into a promise of Encour-agement[.] Between the State of not being absolutely rejected, and that of certain Success, there appeared to me so vast a difference, that, from the former in favour of the latter, no conclusion, or even Argument, could be drawn. But I am, *now* Sir, sensible the distinction was improper, and am extremely sorry it was attempted to be made.

Begging you to excuse this, *last*, trouble upon the Subject, I remain, with perfect respect & Esteem, Sir your much obliged & most obedient Servant

S. Hanson of Saml

ALS, DLC:GW.

1. Letter not found.

2. Samuel Hanson wrote almost a year before GW assumed the presidency seeking a public appointment from him. See Hanson to GW, 7 Jan. 1789. In particular he desired a position in the Alexandria collector's office. In August 1789 GW gave him the post of surveyor, noting that "poor Hanson" was "wor-thy of something better if with propriety it could be given him" (GW to Rich-ard Henry Lee, 2 Aug. 1789). Hanson may have approached GW on the sub-ject of a further appointment, or his queries may have concerned some matter connected with the Alexandria Academy of which he was a trustee.

To the New Jersey Legislature

Gentlemen,   [New York, c. 10 Dec. 1789]

In replying to the flattering and affectionate address, with which you are pleased to honor me, I confess a want of expression to convey the grateful sentiments which it inspires[1]—You will do justice to those sentiments by believing that they are founded in sincere regard and respectful esteem.

The opportunities which were afforded me, in the trying vicissitudes of our arduous struggle, to remark the generous spirit which animated the exertions of your citizens, have impressed a remembrance of their worth, which no length of time or change of circumstance can efface. To the gallantry and firmness of their efforts in the field, they have added the wisdom and liberality of distinguished patriotism in council—appreciating, with judicious discernment, the blessings of that independence, which their efforts contributed to establish, they were unanimously agreed to secure and perpetuate them by adopting a Constitution, which promises equal and efficient protection to the privileges of confederated America.

The assurance now given by your honorable Body, to support the federal system, is a renewed proof of the estimation in which it is held, and a happy indication of the beneficial effects already experienced, and hereafter expected to flow, from its operations—As such it is to me peculiarly grateful, and must be so to every citizen of the Union, whose wish is private prosperity and public honor—Allow me, Gentlemen, to assure you of every endeavor on my part, to promote these desirable objects.

In making my acknowledgements for the favorable opinions you express of my military conduct, as it reflected the observance of civil-rights, it is justice to assign great merit to the temper of those citizens, whose estates were more immediately the scene of warfare—Their personal services were rendered without constraint, and the derangement of their affairs submitted to without dissatisfaction—It was the triumph of patriotism over personal consideration, and our present enjoyment of peace and freedom reward the sacrifice.

Imploring a continuance of these enjoyments to our country, and individual happiness to the citizens, who procured them,

I offer up a sincere prayer for you, Gentlemen, and your constituents.

Go: Washington

LS, MHi: William Livingston Papers; LB, DLC:GW.

1. The address of the New Jersey legislature, dated 30 Nov.–1 Dec. 1789, reads: "The legislature of New Jersey, altho' fully sensible of the trouble and interruption occasioned by the numerous addresses of congratulation on your acceptance of the highest office in the commonwealth, would neither forgive themselves, nor expect the pardon of their constituents, should they neglect, in this their first meeting after the organisation of the federal Government, to express their joy on seeing you at the head of the United States.

"New Jersey having been the central Theatre of the late war, and the scene of some of the most important military operations, which distinguished the american armies, and added new honors to their illustrious Commander; we are peculiarly induced to commemorate those brilliant exploits, which while they immortalised your name, afforded peace and security to the Inhabitants of the State.

"Adulation, Sir, we are as much indisposed to offer as you can be disinclined to receive: But while we add our voice to that of the world in celebrating your military achievements we cannot refrain from acknowledging the attention, which you have always paid to the laws of the State, and your inflexible perseverance, amidst all the dire necessities of war, in preferring the rights of the Citizen to the convenience of the Soldier: Thus while equal to the most renowned warriors as a Hero, you have proved yourself superior to them as a Citizen.

"As New Jersey was early, and unanimous in adopting the constitution, under which you rule; as every voice called you forth to the office of Chief-Magistrate, and every Person looks up to *it* and *you*, for protection, prosperity, and good government; we may, we trust, assure you that the Citizens of this State will, to the utmost of their abilities, ever strengthen and support you in the discharge of your high and momentous trust.

"We have reason to adore the divine Providence in raising up for us a Leader and Ruler so perfectly suited to our situation and circumstances; and sincerely believe that great and important as your services have been, you will not derive more honor therefrom, than from your humility, and self-denial in modestly ascribing all, as you constantly have done, to the power and wisdom of the most high.

"We earnestly pray that the same kind providence, which hath conducted you with so much honor to yourself, and such unspeakable felicity to the Public, may long continue you a blessing to the United States in your present important office; and at last crown you with that palm of victory, which is promised to those, who by divine assistance, shall finally prove to be more than conquerors" (DLC:GW).

A draft of this letter, in the writing of William Livingston, with somewhat different wording and dated 7 Dec. 1789, is in the Archives Section, Division of Archives and Records, New Jersey Department of State.

From Edmund Randolph

Dear Sir   Richmond Decr 11. 1789.

The senate rejected the third, eighth, eleventh and twelfth amendments. The delegates disagreed to that rejection; and yesterday was spent in a conference between the two houses. I am informed, that the senate are determined to receive the 1st 2d 4th 5th 6th 7th 9th and 10th amendments only.[1] This will probably oblige the delegates to give the rest up for the present. But the responsibility for this conduct will, I hope, be thrown upon the senate.

We shall rise on Saturday, when I shall return home, and prepare for New-York. I am dear Sir yr obliged friend and Servant

Edm: Randolph.

ALS, DLC:GW.

1. For action by the Virginia legislature on the amendments to the Constitution, see James Madison to GW, 20 Nov. 1789, n.5. For the text of the twelve amendments submitted by Congress to the states, see GW's Circular to the Governors of the States, 2 Oct. 1789, n.1.

Letter not found: from James Vaughan, 11 Dec. 1789. In a letter to GW, 15 Oct. 1791, Vaughan stated he sent a letter to GW "the 11th Decr 1789."

From Hopley Yeaton

Sir   Portsmouth New Hampshire December 11th 1789.

Permit an inferior Officer in rank, tho' not inferior in Affection for you in your high Sphere, or for my Country's welfare, amidst the great concerns of a happy Continent, who have called you, by their united voice to your present important Station, to lay before you my humble Memorial, vizt

That I was in the earliest Stage of the late arduous Contest, on[1] the side of my Country;

That I had the Honour to serve as first Lieutenant on Board the Continental Frigate the Deane. That I continued in the Continental Navy in a rank not inferior to that of Lieutenant to the Close of the War, with as much zeal, and I hope as much honor, as will permit me to lay claim to some notice, but give me leave to appeal from myself to those who are well acquainted with my Character on this subject and pleace to Remember that I say nothing of the great pecuniary losses I have sustained, and the Sacrifice of domestic pleasures I have cheerfully made for my country's cause; Whenever therefore, there shall be in your gift, Sir, such Offices in this State, or any other in the Union, for which you shall think I am equal and in which I may deserve from that public to which I have devoted the cream of my life, your united Goodness and Justice will not forget.[2] Sir your dutifull and most devoted Humble Servant

Hopley Yeaton

ALS, DLC:GW.

Hopley Yeaton of Portsmouth, N.H., was a member of the Portsmouth Sons of Liberty before the American Revolution and during the war had extensive experience as an officer on board vessels of the American navy. Returning to Portsmouth after the war, he served as coxswain for the vessel taking GW on a tour of the Portsmouth harbor during the president's visit to the state in November 1789.

1. In MS this word reads "or."

2. When construction began in late 1790 on the cutters authorized for the revenue service by the Collection Act of 1790, Alexander Hamilton recommended Yeaton for command of the New Hampshire revenue cutter *Scammell*. GW appointed him in October (Hamilton to GW, 29 Sept. 1790, and GW to Hamilton, 6 Oct. 1790).

From Philip Dalby

Sir,   Winchester [Va.] 12 Decembr 1789

Presuming upon Favors I have already receiv'd from you, I take the Freedom now to address you, wishing to draw your Attention towards me, if any Opportunity should offer of an Appointment to a small office, appertaining to the Federal Court or otherwise in this part of the World; I am at present but little engag'd in Business (my mercantile Concerns not having answered my Expectations) it wou'd therefore be in my power to attend fully to any post you might [be] pleased to think me adequate to;[1] which would be ever gratefuly acknowledgd by Sir, Your most obligd humble Servant

Philip Dalby

ALS, DLC:GW.

1. Dalby received no federal appointment.

From the Representatives of Ohio, Monongahela, Harrison, and Randolph Counties, Virginia

Richmond 12th Decemr 1789.
From the Representativ[e]s of the frontier counties of Virginia to the President of the United States.

In addition to the address of the General Assembly, on Indian Affairs,[1] We, the Representatives of the counties of Ohio, Monongahalia, Harrison & Randolph, are constrained to take the Liberty of stating to you the defenceless situation of those counties, in order that you may be able to direct such measures, as may be necessary for their defence; as we have every reason to expect that the indians will break in upon our settlements as soon as the weather will permit them in the spring.[2] First from the no[r]thern boundary line where it crosses the Ohio River, at the mouth of the Little Beaver Creek, down the said river to the mouth of Big Sandy Creek, distant about three hundred miles, we lay open to the ravages of the indians, who may attack our settlements in any quarter they may chuse, it may here be supposed that the troops stationed at Muskingum would check their progress in this business; but experience hath taught us, that they are of very little use, for we find that the indians cross the River Ohio, both above and below that garrison undiscovered either on their way to our country, or returning to their own, and indeed such will always be our fate until more effectual measures are adopted for our defence; it may be further supposed that General Sin Clair can grant all the relief that is necessary for our safety; in answer to which we beg leave to observe that although we have the highest opinion of that gentleman's integrity and goodness, but from his necessary calls to visit the different posts on the Ohio River, even as low down as the rapids; we fear it will be out of his power to render us the necessary aid; besides, it is impracticable for us to find him in the hour of distress. We further beg leave to suggest that whilst our operations were confined to a defensive plan only, we have ever found the greatest degree of safety to our country arising from keeping out scouts and rangers on our frontiers; indeed it was owing to that plan, and that only, that large tracts of our country have not, long ere now, been depopulated. These Scouts and rangers were composed of our own militia on whom our people could with confidence depend, as they are well acquainted with our woods, and with the paths the Indians use to come in upon our settlements. Whilst we were thus covered, we lived in perfect security, but as soon as they were withdrawn last spring we immediately felt the effects of indian cruelty, for from the month of April last to the month of October, at which time we left home, there were killed and captivated twenty persons, a considerable number of horse and other property carried off, and several houses burnt in our country. All military regulations being submitted to you, we therefore beg leave to suggest our wishes, that you would continue to us, the aforesaid mode of defence, should you approve of it, or direct to such other measures as you in your wisdom may think more advisable, to be continued in our country until it may be thought necessary to carry on offensive war into the enemy's country as to bring about a lasting peace. Suffer us further to assure you, that we, on the behalf of our bleeding country look up to you, and to you only, for that assistance that our necessities require; and shall conclude with praying that the great Parent of the universe may conduct you under the eye of his special providence, enabling you to fill that exalted station to which he hath called you, as well for the good of your fellow citizens as also for the happiness of mankind, so far as they come within the bounds of your administration. We have the honor to be with very great regard and esteem, your excellency's most obedient servants.

Copy, DNA: RG 46, First Congress, Records of Legislative Proceedings, Reports, and Communications Submitted to the Senate. This document is signed by John P. Duval, William MacMahan, and Archibald Woods of Ohio County, William McClurry and Thomas Pindall of Monongalia County, John Prunty and George Jackson of Harrison County, and Jonathan Parsons and Cornelius Bogard of Randolph County.

1. See Address from the Virginia Legislature on Indian Affairs, 30 Oct. 1789.

2. On 1 June 1789 Gov. Beverley Randolph had informed the county lieutenants of the District of Kentucky, Monongalia, Ohio, Randolph, Harrison, and Washington counties that "the enclosed extract of a letter from the President of the United States rendering it unnecessary that this State should any longer at her own particular charge, support the troops called into service for the defence of the Western frontier you will immediately discharge all the Scouts and Rangers employed in your County. In case of any future incursions of the indians, you will give as early information of them as possible to

the officer commanding the nearest continental post on the Ohio. I have communicated to the President, the instructions now sent you, and have no doubt, but effectual measures will be taken to protect all the frontier inhabitants" (DLC:GW). The enclosure was GW's letter to Randolph, 16 May 1789. Randolph's letter to GW informing him of the withdrawal of state forces from the frontier counties is dated 1 June. Both letters are printed above.

From John Walker

Sir,   Wilmington North Carolina December 13th 1789

I had the honor to be appointed Naval Officer for Port Brunswick in this State by joint ballot of both houses of our Legislature in the year 1782—and have continued in that office untill this time, by the laws of this State it is held during good behaviour—This State has lately ratified the federal Constitution by which I learn that my Office is vacated, and that it is to be filled by your Excellencys appointment.

I am informed that an application is to be made by Mr Callender of this place supported by the petition of many respectable Citizens for his advancement to this Office[1]—Against Mr Callenders merit I have not a word to offer—nor against the Gentlemen whose names are subscribed to his petition, I have however been told that a report prevailed and gained credit with many of those Gentlemen that I had resigned which implied a voluntary going out of Office, which was certainly not true and so far those Gentlemen were deceived, and in order to convince me that they were so, most of those very Gentlemen subscribed the enclosed certificate subsequent to their petition in favour of Mr Callender.[2]

Mr Callender has served in the American Army with reputation during the late war, I also had the honor to serve under your Excellencys command and had once the good fortune to be Known to you but cannot now flatter myself that I retain a place in your recollection—To your Excellencys judgement this will appear of little moment as to the subject on which I trouble you, but I rely on your humanity to excuse me if I betray some vanity in recalling to mind the honor I have enjoyed in being known to your Excellency.

I am not conscious that I have neglected any Duty or committed any ill practice in the Office I have held—I am sure no

complaint has been made that I know of—which the aforemen-
tioned certificate will demonstrate—I am therefore only
removed by this States having entered into the New federal
Government—We have rejoiced at being reunited to the other
States under the New federal Constitution, I trust your Excellency will not make the event painfull to any one.

I beg pardon for the trouble I have given your Excellency—
and beg leave to subscribe myself with th⟨e⟩ greatest respect and
submission, Your Excellencys, Most obedt & Most humbe Servt

Jno. Walker

ALS, DLC:GW; ALS (duplicate), DLC:GW. According to the address sheets
on these letters, one was sent from North Carolina by ship, the other by post.

John Walker (1755–1841) was born in Virginia but moved with his father
to North Carolina. The younger Walker served as a lieutenant and captain
during the Revolution. In February 1790 GW reappointed him to his old
place as collector of the customs at Wilmington (*DHFC*, 2:57, 60).

1. Thomas Callender (d. 1828) was a Wilmington merchant who had
served as a lieutenant and captain during the war. In February 1790 he was
appointed surveyor at Wilmington.

2. The enclosure was a statement signed by seventy-eight citizens of Wilmington attesting that Walker "has always conducted himself as Naval Officer
for Port Brunswick with propriety and perfectly as a Man of Business and can
alledge no reason why he should be removed from that Office" (DLC:GW). At
the end of the enclosure Walker noted: "The Original I have forwarded to
your Excellency by Post—presuming it to be the safest mode of conveyance—
This being a true copy I transmit it to you by water."

To Robert Morris

Dear Sir,   New York Decemr 14th 1789.
I have been favored with the receipt of your letter of the 9th
instant[1]—In reply to the object of its enclosure, I can only
observe that Mr Hamilton is a Gentleman of whom I am inclined
to think well, and to believe qualified for the office he solicits:
But the rule, which I have prescribed to myself, being intended
to preserve a freedom of choice in all nominations, forbids any
engagement whatever until the nomination is made.[2]

I beg you to accept my best thanks for the obliging offer which
you made, through Major Jackson, of accommodating me with a
Steward—and I regret that circumstances do not permit me to
prove to you my belief of it's sincerity: But the multiplied duties

of the station would, I apprehend, be too fatiguing for a Person as far advanced as Constance—and Anthony's youth would disqualify him from obtaining the necessary authority over the other Servants, all of whom are so much his seniors.

I am very sensible of your goodness in agreeing to promote my convenience at the expence of your own, and I am not less grateful than if the intention had been fulfilled.

Be pleased to present Mrs Washington's, and my compliments to Mrs Morris—and believe me, with great regard, Dear Sir, Your most obedient Servant

G.W.

Copy, in the writing of David Humphreys, DNA: RG 59, Miscellaneous Letters; LB, DLC:GW.

1. Letter not found.
2. The enclosure was undoubtedly a letter of 17 Oct. 1789 from John Hamilton of Edenton, N.C., to Robert Morris, seeking a post in the federal Judiciary: "Mr Iredell of this Place I understand has made application thro. Doctr Hugh Williamson for the office of Judge and a Major Clement Hall for that of Marshall. I beg you will excuse my importunity but as others have made such early application I am advised by my Friends to request of you (if consistent with your feelings and Situation) to make as early a Recommendation to the President in my favor as possible for the attorneys Place, more particularly as there is a moral certainty of this States adopting the Constitution, on the third Monday of next Month. I shall do myself the Pleasure of writing you whenever that happy event takes place" (DLC:GW). For Hamilton's application to GW, see his letter of 8 Feb. 1790. When GW made the North Carolina appointments in February 1790, the position of United States attorney for the state went to William H. Hill of Wilmington rather than to Hamilton who received no federal appointment.

From Charles Pinckney

Dear Sir, Charleston [S.C.] December 14 1789

Your avocations have been so numerous & important since your entrance into office that I have not troubled you with but one letter which was to recommend Mr Hall,[1] & to very sincerely congratulate you upon your appointment to the supreme magistracy. I am well convinced that to increase the number of your correspondents unnecessarily is to do you a serious injury, for I should suppose with official communications—with proper & improper applications for favours—& the oppressive correspondence of numbers, who with very little information or pleasure to you write merely for the purpose of boasting the honour of your correspondence—with such I have always considered you as so overwhelm'd that I have hitherto forborne to write you although motives of respect as well as information ought frequently to have induced me.

Upon the present occasion I feel myself in some measure obliged from the situation which I hold to state to you my sentiments on the critical situation of our neighbouring State & eventually the frontiers of this—To predict with some degree of *certainty* what may be the consequence of things remaining in the state they are & no treaty *formed* with the Creeks & southern Indians, permit me to trespass for a moment upon your time by observing—that however I confess it is conjectural, yet there appears to me to be good grounds for supposing that the situation of our foreign concerns is totally changed with respect to Spain—Upon the conclusion of the peace I believe it was the intention of that court to have entered into a treaty of amity & commerce with us—to have been our friends & to have done every thing in their power to have promoted the intercourse— but they mistook the means—for instead of forming a treaty upon those terms which would have insured a reciprocity of Benefits, they thought the best way to remove every future ground of difference—to prevent our becoming dangerous neighbours—& to keep us at a distance was to propose the surrender of a right as degrading to the honour as it would have been ultimately injurious to the interests of the Union[2]—I happened to be in Congress at the time the proposal was brought forward through the then Secretary Mr Jay—having more leisure or having more maturely considered the offer, I was requested by the opponents to prepare an answer to the reasons which Mr Jay offered in support of Mr Gardoqui's proposal— this I did, & being afterwards desired by many of the southern members to furnish them with copies, I had a few printed which were confidentially delivered to some of my friends, for their information upon a subject which at that time very much engaged the attention of the public[3]—I have the honour to inclose you one of the few copies I have left—I do so in order that I may not only more clearly illustrate the observations I am about to make but also that in case another attempt should be made to conclude this treaty you may be informed of the reasons which at that time induced an Opposition—as the Business of treaties must ever be of a secret nature you will no doubt consider the communication as it is intended entirely confidential.

The Court of Spain being defeated in this measure have appeared to me to entirely change their ground—The original & I believe the only reason of Spain's anxiety to conclude a treaty with us was to secure her American Continental possessions from being at any time the object of invasion or insult from the southern or more probably the western inhabitants of the Union—they have ever dreaded the settlement of the western territory & looked forward to the time when it would become necessary for its inhabitants to use the Mississipi, as a period very likely to produce those uneasinesses which would perhaps end in the invasion of their dominions—Had they at first proposed[4] a solid & reciprocally beneficial treaty it would have prevented or at least postponed for a number of years any danger of this sort—but having as I have already observed wrongly concieved the means of effecting it & being foiled in their first attempt they have now changed their ground—They are endeavouring by every exertion in their power to attach not only the southern Indians but as many as they possibly can of the inhabitants of the Western territory closely to their interest—they have compleatly succeeded with some of the most powerful nations of the southern Indians. hence the difficulty of treating with them—& I am sorry to find from accounts which appear to me to be tolerably authentic that they have diverted a considerable number of the inhabitants of some of the States & tempted them to become settlers within their borders—thus situated it seems to me as beyond a doubt that they are the spring of all the present disturbances with the Creeks & that they are cherishing a spirit of discontent & disaffection in them & the western inhabitants to the Government of the Union—By means of their intrigues Georgia has been for some years in a lamentable state of depredation & distress—although they have hitherto forborne to commit hostilities on the citizens of this State, yet the inhabitants of the frontiers are in an uneasy & disagreable situation—they all look up to the Union for the establishment of that solid & permanent treaty which can alone secure to them the peaceable enjoyment of their possessions.

Not having been officially informed of the reasons of the late commissions miscarrying, I am unable to form any judgements of the motives which occasioned it—as I am confident a general Indian War would not only be attended with great inconvenience to Georgia & our frontiers, but with a very considerable expenditure of Blood & Treasure to the Union, I have made it a point to acquire from the most respectable authority on their borders & elsewhere such information as is the most to be depended upon—not to detain you with a circumstantial account of the means used to obtain it, or a detail of their relations, the result is—that however anxious the Spanish Court are to foment & continue the existing animosities, yet there is a disposition in the Indians upon just & proper principles to again become the friends & probably the allies of the Union—In this temper they now are, & I am convinced that detaching Mr McGillivray from his Spanish connexions & confirming him the friend and perhaps the useful agent of the United States is not a difficult or improbable measure. To you Sir I have been repeatedly requested to suggest these opinions—from the weight & influence of your character & situation much is very properly expected—as the organ therefore of a growing & important territory, whose future population & consequence depend upon the friendship & intercourse of their Indian neighbours, I intreat the early & earnest attention of the general Government, to whom with great propriety the sole management of India[n] affairs is now committed—I am the more anxious on this point because on the renewal of hostilities in June last the Executive of Georgia in virtue of the Union made a formal requisition on me for the aid of this State—fortunately a truce was concluded before it was necessary to interfere—When I consider the number & force of the hostile indian tribes—how formidably their number might be increased should the same intrigues induce the Choctaws to join them—how much the power of the Indian nations must be increased by the arrangement of their affairs being in the hands of such a man as Mr McGillivray—& how amply they are assisted by the Spanish Court, not only in stores & money but even in the aid of disciplinarians to introduce as much order as Indians are capable of recieving—when I add to these the little that is to be obtained by a war & the distresses & expences it must occasion, you will pardon I am sure the anxiety

I am under to have a permanent & solid peace—no State arrangement—no truce—no partial compromise will be sufficient, They must be taught to revere the justice of the Union & look up to it as the sole means of giving to them a lasting treaty & the secure possession of their real rights.

So much for Business of a public nature permit me now to thank you for the many marks of regard I recieved while with you in 1787—particularly in furnishing me with introductory Letters to your friends in Europe had I pursued the route I at that time intended[5]—although I have hitherto been prevented by marrying & being requested by my friends to accept the Government I have by no means given it up altogether—My term of office will expire in a twelvemonth—when if nothing prevents I shall endeavour to execute my former plan—I am strengthened in this Idea by the wish of my Wife to revisit that part of the World—she is the daughter of Mr Laurens & sister to your former aid de Camp our deceased & much lamented friend Colonel John Laurens[6]—from the age of seven to fourteen she was educated in France & until she came to this Country remained in England—so that her accurate knowledge of the french language & acquaintance with their customs will be extremely useful should curiosity or Business make it necessary for me to go there or to any of the neighbouring States of Europe—From your late tour we are flattered with the hope of your one day visiting this country—whenever you so far honour us I am sure that every thing in our power will be done to render your Visit pleasing and agreable to you. I am with the sincerest Respect & Esteem much obliged Dear Sir Yours truly

Charles Pinckney.

LS, DLC:GW. Occasionally a few words have been inserted in the body of this letter in a different hand, possibly Pinckney's.

1. See George Abbott Hall to GW, 31 Mar. 1789, n.1. Charles Pinckney (1757–1824) practiced law in Charleston before the Revolution and served as a lieutenant in a Charleston militia regiment during the war. Captured by the British at Savannah, he remained a prisoner until 1781. Pinckney represented South Carolina in the Confederation Congress from 1784 to 1787. A leading member of the Constitutional Convention, he also campaigned vigorously for ratification in his state. In January 1789 he was elected governor of South Carolina. At the time this letter was written he was still a Federalist although he was soon to become a leading Republican critic of Federalist policies.

2. Pinckney is referring to the Jay-Gardoqui negotiations. See Madison to GW, 26 Sept. 1788, n.1.

3. Pinckney's speech was made in Congress on 16 Aug. 1786 in response to an address on the Spanish negotiations made by John Jay on 3 Aug. 1786 (see *JCC*, 31:467–84). Pinckney's address was published as *Mr. Charles Pinckney's Speech, in Answer to Mr. Jay, Secretary for Foreign Affairs, on the Question of a Treaty with Spain, Delivered in Congress, August 16, 1786* (New York, 1786).

4. In MS this word, inserted above the line, reads "oposed."

5. Pinckney is referring to his association with GW at the Constitutional Convention in Philadelphia in the summer of 1787. On 16 Sept. 1787 GW wrote letters of introduction for Pinckney to the comte de Rochambeau, the marquis de Lafayette, and the marquis de Chastellux. Letter-book copies of these letters are in DLC:GW.

6. In April 1788 Pinckney married Mary Eleanor Laurens (d. 1794), the twelfth child of Henry Laurens of South Carolina.

To Beverley Randolph

Sir,   New York December 14th 1789.

I was surprized to find, by your Excellency's letter of the 1st instant,[1] with which I have been favoured, that my dispatches of the 3d of October did not reach you until the last day of November; and, in consequence thereof, I have inquired of the Post-Master in this City to know if they were detained in his Office. He informs me they were not—and, as a proof of it, he refers to the stamp on the face of the letters, which will shew the day of the⟨ir⟩ leaving his Office. And I will thank you, for your own, and my satisfaction, to examine the same.

The detention of these letters is a matter of some importance not only as it respects them, but as to the general regulation of the Post-Office; and I wish exceedingly to know where they were detained, and whether it was owing to the inattention of any Post Master through whose hands they must have passed—or to a worse cause. An investigation and discovery of this matter may prevent future offences of the like nature. You will therefore oblige me, Sir, and render a service to the public, by using your endeavours to know the cause of their detention.[2] I have the honor to be, Your Excellency's most Obedient Servant

Go: Washington

LS, CSmH; Df, DNA: RG 59, Miscellaneous Letters; LB, DLC:GW.

1. Randolph's letter of 1 Dec. was a routine acknowledgment of the receipt

of GW's Thanksgiving Day proclamation and of copies of a number of laws passed by Congress (Vi: Executive Letter Book).

2. On 28 Dec. Randolph replied that "upon examining the cover of your letter of the 3d of October I find stamp'd on it Octr 5th so there can have been no negligence in the Post Master at New York. The time which has elapsed since the receipt of those Dispatches will perhaps render it difficult for me to ascertain the cause of their Detention. You may however be assured Sir, that I shall make every enquiry, which I conceive will lead to a Discovery" (DNA: RG 59, Miscellaneous Letters). Randolph wrote to GW on 1 Jan. 1790 with additional information: "Since my last of the 28th of December, I called upon mr Augustine Davis, Post master at this place, and inquired of him the cause of the Detention of your Dispatches of the 3d of October. He informed me, that about the time which I received them, there came to his office from Savannah, two letters from you directed to me; On the cover of one of which was written in a fair hand, 'These letters have been sent to Savannah by mistake.' I asked him whether there was any check established, by which he could ascertain the particular office, at which this mistake had happened, he answered, that no other entry was made in his Books of free Letters, than their number and the time of their receipt" (DNA: RG 59, Miscellaneous Letters).

From George Augustine Washington

Honor'd Uncle   Mount Vernon Decr 14th 1789.

Such was the disorderd state of my head at the time I last wrote You, that I had scarcely the power of accomplishing the few lines I did—the loss of blood and some medicine since seems to have greatly relieved me of the distressing giddiness, but not so much the pain in my head, which is now accompanied with a weakness and inflamation in my eyes—these complaints I had serious apprehensions would unavoidably lessen, or perhaps put a stop to application to business of any kind had it continued as severe as it had done for a fortnight before but hope as my disposition prompts me to persue the good example I have had set me since I lived with you, that I shall not be deprived the power of endeavouring to improve from it by a steady exertion to imitate it—I have now Your favor of the 19th before me to reply to such parts as I did not observe in the last report. Your Letter of the 30th Ulto has also come to hand[1]—In persuing the modern plan of Farming the rotine of Crops You determin'd on I doubt not must be the most eligable from the great attention you bestowed on the subject, discontinuing the Crop of Sundries except in a small degree and substituting

Buckwheat I have some time thought would be an improvement but my incompetent judgment would not suffer me to offer an opinion when approved by your superior skill—the cultivation of the different things comprehended under the head of Sundries appear'd more complex and laborious than any profit which has been derived from it would repay—You speak of Cultivating Pumpkins with Corn I do not concieve that any additional labor will acrue but after the vines begin to spread that an inconvenience and delay will arise in plowing in very rich ground they are certainly a very great increase but they must be fed away very early or they are lost for no method I fear will be found to preserve them—I tried the mode you directed of slicing and drying them but it did not appear to lengthen their preservation—The ground under the new Post and Rail fence at the Mansion house is not sufficiently rich to lay down in grass in the Spring and I am inclined to think that a summer fallow with what manure we can bestow upon it will prepare it better for wheat in the Fall as by puting any crop in it in spring it may tend to diminish its strength—The Apricot Potatoes you expected to be sent from Majr Meredith have not come to hand— The roof and shed of the Mansion house Barn contained all the Tobacco made here except 3 or 4 hundredweight which Fairfax says will make 2 hoggsheads. he computes the whole crop at 13 hoggsheads 3 at the Ferry 3 at D: Run 2 at Muddy hole and 3 at R: Plantn. Fairfax says that a sufficiency of posts (had not some of them proved too small), with those at Manleys were got before you left home to reach the Mill, but you directed those at Manleys to remain for extending the fence through from the Mill to the Ferry, but not rails enough, and many of those in puting them up proved to small to use for an outer fence but will answer well for others, they have now got within abt 40 or 50 pannels of the willow pond with the Fence—I am as attentive as it is in my power to expedeting your business and endeavoring to make others do it—Fairfax does not to my knowledge absent himself or suffer idleness or I should not keep it a secret from you—immediately after finishing the post and rail fence to the mill and running a temporary fence across the Creek to join the fence on the opposite side which will give security to the fields within—(Frenches wheat field particularly.) by putg up a gate at the Mill it will prevent the intrusion of the Neighbours stock about it, and shall then begin to prepare Posts and rails for enclosing N.E. at Muddy hole, and in running the post and rail on the marsh, I designed to do it in the manner you had directed, and where it was necessary to leave the marsh in running a proper course, to make the fence without a Ditch, as it would only add one rail and two mortis's as the ground will be generally broken and a Ditch subject to be soon distroyed—the makg of a lane will add much trouble I have therefore thought that a gate might be made secure and as it is not a very publick road no objection if you have none can be made by others—I shall write to Colo. Syme[2] requesting he will attend and prove the Deed you mention and in case of his refusal (which I do not apprehend) shall take proper steps to have it done—the tax which has acrued thereon shall be paid. I did not apply to Colo. Mercer For Corn but extended my enquiries beyond this Neighbourhood. I applied to Doctr Stuart who had been below and he would not dispose of it there for less than 12/—and from other enquiries I found that Corn was likely to be high in consequence of the Frost and great exportation of old Corn this fall, in Alexandria—for two months past old Corn has not sold for less than 15/—I advertised offering 10/. for Corn deliverd at the Mill and that I would recieve it in small quantities but found there was no prospect of geting any I engaged the other day with Mr Wilson of Alexa.[3] for 150 Bls of good sound shelled Corn deliverd in the Mill Creek in the month of March a 11/—which has been thought by every one to be a very advantageous contract—I hope this quantity will be sufficient tho the horse feed is very low in consequence of being obliged to use almost the whole of the Rye for the People—we have not finished measuring Corn but think we shall make 600 Bls sound Corn which will be sufficient for the People and 150 or 200 Barrels will I hope be sufficient for other purposes—I have enclosed a Letter I recd from Colo. Biddle a few days ago in answer to one I had writen him respectg Buckwheat[4]—I am inclined to think tho he apprehends it may be high that it will perhaps be as certain and as reasonable getg it from Philadelphia—Your determination I would wish as soon as you can—Mr Thompson said he thought there would be no doubt of getg the quantity but that it could not be deliverd for less than 3/ at Alexandria[5]—When I began this it was my intention to have replied particuarly to your

Letters and wrote respecting some other matters but find myself pressed for time as by the new arrangement the Stage leaves Alexandria at 3 oClock therefore the letters must be in the Post I believe by 2 oClock—Fanny joins me in love and best wishes to You my Aunt & Children—and respects to the Gentlemen of our acquaintance. I am Honor'd Uncle Your truely affectionate Nephew

Geo: A. Washington

ALS, DLC:GW.

1. Neither of these letters has been found.

2. Probably Charles Simms who practiced law in Alexandria and served in the Virginia assembly in 1785–86, 1792, and 1796 as a delegate from Fairfax County.

3. For William Wilson, see Thomas Montgomerie to GW, 24 Oct. 1788, n.2.

4. George Augustine Washington wrote to Clement Biddle in Philadelphia on 10 Nov. 1789 informing him that he needed to purchase about four hundred bushels of buckwheat for the president (PHi: Washington-Biddle Correspondence). Biddle's letter has not been found.

5. Mr. Thompson may be William Thompson, a Colchester, Va., merchant.

From Jabez Bowen

Sir   Providence [R.I.] Decembr 15. 1789

In my Letter that I addressed to your Excellency in Boston I informed you that I should attend the General Assembly, where the Question would be determined wheather we should Call a Convention, or not.[1] altho' we found a small Majority, whose private sentiments were for the motion, yet so many of them were bound by Instructions from their Constituents to vote against it that the motion was lost by a Majority of 22.

The Assembly now stands Adjorned to the second Monday in January then to meet in this Town.

We have just heard of the Adoption of the Constitution by North: Carolina, on which I hartily Congratulate your Excellency, more especially as the Majority is so verry large. This Event will have some weight with the oposition with us, but I am afraid not sufficient to Insure a Convention.

The Towns of Newport Providence Bristol &c. with the whole Mercantile interest in the other Towns in the State are Federal.

while The Farmers in general are against it. Their oposition arises principally from Their being much in Debt, from the Insinuations of wicked and designing Men, That they will loose their Liberty by adopting it; That The Sallerys of the National Officers are so verry high That it will take the whole of the Money Collected by The Impost to pay Them. That The Intrest & principle of The General Debt must be raised by Dry Taxation on Real Estates &c. We have Exerted our utmost abilities to Convince Them of the Errors that they have Imbibed by hearing to The *old Tories* and *Desperate Debtors*. but all in vain, what further Sir is to be done? if we knew what our Duty was, we are willing to do it. Tho' I have no Idea that The Antis will or can be induced to come in without the arm of Power is Exerted and That They shall be taught that The principles that they hoald and Disseminate among the Citizens of The Neighbouring States as well as This is inconsistent, and not propper to be professed by any person or persons that Live on the Teritorys of the United States. their wish is to overturn the whole Federal Government rather Than This State should submitt to it.

If we faile in getting a Convention at the next Meeting of the General Assembly will Congress *protect* us if we seperate from the State Government: and appoint us Officers to Collect The Revennue, if this should be Thot well of and should be put in practice but in part I have no doubt but it will bring the Country part of the Community to their sinses soon—and that one Town and another will be a Dropping off so that The oposition will be done away. be pleased Sir to give me an answer to this proposition as soon as Convenient. wishing for a Continuance of your Health I Remain Sir with sentiments of the highest Esteeme Your Obedient Humble Servant.

Jabez Bowen

This will be deliverd by Major J. S. Dexter who is a Member of our Genl Assembly and to whom I Refer your Excellency for further particulars.[2]
(Private)

ALS, DNA:PCC, item 78.
    1. See Bowen to GW, 25 Oct. 1789.
    2. John S. Dexter, a justice of the peace in Cumberland, R.I., served in the Revolution, ending the war as a major. As a member of the Rhode Island

Ratifying Convention in 1790 he supported ratification of the Constitution by
the state, and in 1791 GW appointed him supervisor of the revenue for the
district of Rhode Island.

From Thomas Jefferson

Sir   Chesterfeild [Va.] Dec. 15. 1789.
    I have received at this place the honour of your letters of Oct.
13 and Nov. 30 and am truly flattered by your nomination of me
to the very dignified office of Secretary of state: for which
permit me here to return you my humble thanks. Could any
circumstance seduce me to overlook the disproportion between
it's duties & my talents it would be the encouragement of your
choice. but when I contemplate the extent of that office, embracing as it does the principal mass of domestic administration,
together with the foreign, I cannot be insensible of my inequal-
ity to it: and I should enter on it with gloomy forebodings from
the criticisms & censures of a public just indeed in their intentions, but sometimes misinformed & misled, & always too respectable to be neglected. I cannot but foresee the possibility
that this may end disagreeably for one, who, having no motive to
public service but the public satisfaction, would certainly retire
the moment that satisfaction should appear to languish. on the
other hand I feel a degree of familiarity with the duties of my
present office, as far at least as I am capable of understanding it's
duties. the ground I have already passed over enables me to see
my way into that which is before me. the change of government
too, taking place in the country where it is exercised, seems to
open a possibility of procuring from the new rulers some new
advantages in commerce which may be agreeable to our countrymen. so that as far as my fears, my hopes, or my inclination
might enter into this question, I confess they would not lead me
to prefer a change. but it is not for an individual to chuse his
post. you are to marshal us as may best be for the public good:
and it is only in the case of it's being indifferent to you that I
would avail myself of the option you have so kindly offered in
your letter. if you think it better to transfer me to another post,
my inclination must be no obstacle: nor shall it be, if there is any
desire to suppress the office I now hold, or to reduce it's grade.

in either of these cases, be so good only as to signify to me by another line your ultimate wish, & I shall conform to it cordially. if it should be to remain at New York, my chief comfort will be to work under your eye, my only shelter the authority of your name, & the wisdom of measures to be dictated by you, & implicitly executed by me. whatever you may be pleased to decide, I do not see that the matters which have called me hither will permit me to shorten the stay I originally asked; that is to say, to set out on my journey Northward till the month of March. as early as possible in that month I shall have the honor of paying my respects to you in New York. in the mean time I have that of tendering you the homage of those sentiments of respectful attachment with which I am Sir Your most obedient & most humble servant

Th: Jefferson

ALS, DLC:GW; ALS, letterpress copy, DLC: Jefferson Papers.

From Charles Morrell

15 Decemr 1789

Pardon me a straing boy for troubling your Excellency on so extrordnor an ocasion, I am the s[on] of James Morell an offcer in the Ammerecan army under Excellencys emedeat Command, but by the war is reduced to poverty unable to help him selfe or me, bound me to a Traid my master beate me severely my father applyd to a Court of justice who releaved me I have acquired as mutch of the traid as will Enable me to carey on the business—Could but prevail on the noble generous mind to aid me a little with Cash to purchess Tools with, Mr John jay hes lent me Three Pounds four shillings untill may nixt Mr John Franklin promisesed to answer as mutch, Could I but prevail on your Excellencys jenerous mind to do me the like favour four Pounds will set m[e] to work and Enable me to assis my father with his large famely help my selfe return the money by may or June with Every degree of thanks I am your Excellencys Most obedeant & verey Humble Sert

Charles Morrell

I wait at your Excellencys dore.

ALS, DLC:GW.

No additional information on Morrell and his problems has been found. GW evidently sent a message to Morrell since on 21 Dec. he wrote GW that "agreeable to your Excellencys desier I waited on Mr Jay but for several days could not have Excess to him in the end he appeared not to be Satisfyed that I had troubled your Excellency on such an ocasion and would not give me a certificate of the money that he him selfe had advansed what to do on the ocasion is more then I can tell I am a burthen to my Parents who are pore insted of assisting them I have got a grait part of my Tools but what way to pay for the remender is more then I can find out" (DLC:GW). There is no evidence that GW made a contribution to Morrell. Young Morrell's father may have been Joseph Morrill (Morell) of New York, who served as a sergeant in the 4th New York from December 1776 to January 1778 when he was promoted to ensign. He transferred to the 1st New York in 1781 and served until June 1783. In September 1782 he was serving under GW's command at Verplanck Point, N.Y. (General Orders, 15 Sept. 1782).

To Samuel Powel

Dear Sir,   New York Decr 15th 1789

I am sorry to find from your favor of the 9th, that you have had cause to recall the report made to Majr Jackson relative to the Hessian-fly. I have not written to Mr Young yet on this subject; perhaps it may be sometime before I shall. In my late tour through the Eastern States I was informed (particularly in Connecticut) that this destructive Insect had also appeared in their fields of Wheat. What an error it is, and how much to be regretted; that the Farmers do not confine themselves to the Yellow-bearded Wheat, if, from experience, it is found capable of resisting the ravages of this, otherwise, all conquering foe.

Mrs Washington and myself are very much obliged by Mrs Powells kind remembrance of us, and offer our best respects and sincerest good wishes in return to her, & yourself. I have the honor to be—Dear Sir Your Most Obedt Servt

Go: Washington

ALS, ViMtV.

From Edmund Randolph

My dear Sir   Richmond decr 15. 1789.
     Your friendly favor of the 30th Ultimo is this moment delivered to me. My three last letters since the 8th of october have, I hope, been received, and will satisfy you of my having determined to proceed to New York about the 15th of next month.[1]
     You may be assured, that Mr Wythe neither wished nor expected to be the successor of Mr Pendleton.[2] I will candidly tell you the reason, upon which this assurance is founded. In the month of July it was intimated to me in a letter from Colo. Griffin, that it was his desire to know, whether Mr Wythe would enter into fœderal employment. The intimation seemed to arise from a purpose to say something to you concerning him. I therefore took an indirect opportunity of communicating Colo. Griffin's request to Mr Wythe; whose answer was, that he could not make a reply in the then state of the application, and even if it were made in a stile, which permitted him to declare himself, he should say, that he was too old and too happy in his present situation to be induced to a change. It is true, that the office of the district-judge would not have compelled him to travel much beyond Richmond; but he sits in a kind of legal monarchy, which to him is the highest possible gratification. We shall however enter into some general discourse, that will lead to a discovery of his true sensations; tho' I am confident, that he felt as much pleasure at the idea of being thought of, as an actual appointment would have afforded.
     Mr Griffin opened the court to-day. He was inclined at first to enter upon duty in the county-court-house. But Colo. Carrington and myself remonstrated with him on the necessity of doing this very publickly, and in the court-room of the capitol. To this remonstrance he yielded. The truth is, that every body is highly pleased, that Mr Griffin is put into the mode of getting a livelihood; and they have an earnest hope, that he will conduct himself in the situation, which requires great prudence, circumspection, and indeed talents.
     The senate, as I mentioned in my last, rejected the 3d, 8th, 11th & 12th amendments, and adopted the rest. It has been thought best by the most zealous friends to the constitution to

let the whole of them rest. I have submitted to their opinion; not choosing to rely upon my own judgment in so momentous an affair. The ground of their opinion is a resolution to throw the odium of rejection on the senate. I am my dear sir your obliged friend and affte servant.

Edm: Randolph.

ALS, DLC:GW.
    1. See Randolph to GW, 8 Oct., 22 and 26 Nov. 1789.
    2. For GW's comments concerning George Wythe, see his letter to Randolph, 30 Nov. 1789. For background to his judicial appointments, see his letter to the United States Senate, 24 Sept. 1789, n.1.

To the Chiefs of the Choctaw Nation

Brothers.   [New York, 17 December 1789]
    I have sent Major Doughty one of our Warriors, in order to convince you that the United States well remember the treaty they made with your Nation four years ago at Hopewell on the Keowee—guard and protect him and show him the places at which trading posts shall be established in order to furnish you with goods; and when the said posts shall be established, support them to the utmost of your power.
    Be attentive to what he shall say in the name of the United States for he will speak only truth.
    Regard the United States as your firm and best support—Keep bright the chain[1] of friendship between the Chickasaws and your nation—reject the advice of bad men who may attempt to poison your minds with suspicions against the United States. Given under my hand and Seal, at the City of New York this seventeenth day of December One thousand, seven hundred and Eighty nine.

Go: Washington
By Command of the President of the United States.
H. Knox
Secretary for the department of War

LS, Archivo General de Indias, Papeles de Cuba; copy, Archivo General de Indias, Papeles de Cuba. This document was addresed to "Yockonahoma great medal Chief of Soonacoha, Yockehoopoie leading Chief of Bugtoogolo, Mingohoopie leading Chief of Haskoogua, Tobocah great medal chief of Congaltoo, Pooshemastubie Gorget Captain of Sonwyazo, and all the other

Medal Chiefs, Gorget Captains, and Warriors of the Choctaw Nation." The document was given into the care of Maj. John Doughty (d. 1826), one of the small postwar army's few career officers. Doughty rose from captain lieutenant to major during the Revolution and remained in the service after the war. During the fall and early winter of 1789 he was engaged in the construction of Fort Washington at Cincinnati and was in command of troops at the fort. The failure of the mission of David Humphreys, Benjamin Lincoln, and Cyrus Griffin to the Creek (see Henry Knox to GW, 4 Jan. 1790, source note) indicated to GW and Knox that new measures must be taken to protect the frontier in case of a major Indian war in the South. One aspect of their policy was the construction of a fort at Muscle Shoals on the Tennessee River "provided the same can be effected with the entire approbation and support of the Chickasaws and Choctaws which there is reason to beleive may be obtained— and the President of the United States has directed that Major Doughty be sent to those tribes to ascertain their sentiments—If the post be established with an adequate force it will enable us either to intimidate the Creeks or to strike them with success" (Knox to Arthur St. Clair, 19 Dec. 1789, in Carter, *Territorial Papers, Northwest Territory*, 1:224–26). Knox sent virtually the same information to Doughty's commander, Josiah Harmar, requesting Harmar to "detach Major Doughty on this business with all possible expedition. Furnish him with Every facility Either by Land or by water, and assist him with one or two intelligent officers, and Such guards as shall be necessary—direct that he be furnished with 20 barrels of powder & a good proportionable quantity of lead." Harmar also was directed to furnish Doughty with money, blankets, and horses, and, if needed, boats for the expedition (Knox to Harmar, 19 Dec. 1789, WHi: Draper Collection, Harmar Papers). Doughty reached the mouth of the Tennessee River on 28 Feb. 1790 and continued some two hundred and twenty miles up the river when he was attacked by a party of Indians from various tribes including Cherokee and Shawnee. Out of Doughty's party of an ensign and fifteen men, six were killed and five seriously wounded. With the group decimated, Doughty retreated to the Spanish post of Ance à la Graisse at New Madrid until aid could be sent from the Northwest Territory (Doughty to John Wyllys, 25 Mar. 1790, in Smith, *St. Clair Papers*, 2:134). Doughty's report to Henry Knox on the expedition, 17 April 1790, advising against an attempt to fortify Muscle Shoals without the consent of the Cherokee and Choctaw, is in MiU-C: Josiah Harmar Papers. For a printed text, see Colton Storm, "Up the Tennessee in 1790: The Report of Major John Doughty to the Secretary of War," in *Eastern Tennessee Historical Society's Publications*, 17 (1945), 119–32. For another account of the attack on Doughty, see Capt. Joseph Ashton to Harmar, 19 April 1790, WHi: Draper Collection, Harmar Papers. On 17 Dec. Knox submitted for GW's approval a "draft of the instructions to Major Doughty, and drafts of Messages to the Chickasaws and Choctaws" (DLC:GW). Doughty's instructions have not been found, nor has the message to the Chickasaw. According to Doughty's report to Knox, Piomingo, a Chickasaw chief long friendly to the United States, had agreed to carry GW's message to his nation and to the Choctaw.

1. In MS this word reads "clain."

To Alexander Hamilton

Sir   United States Decr 17th 1789

As I am uncertain of the condition & even the Office in which the papers containing accounts of our disbursments for subsistence of British prisoners remain; and as it is not improbable that some negotiations may (whenever our Union under the General Government shall be completed) take place between the United States & Great Britain, in which an accurate understanding of those Accots will become necessary—I have therefore thot proper to suggest the expediency of having some immediate attention paid to them.

Notwithstanding, on as fair a statement of Expenditures as could now be made, much property must undoubtedly be lost by the United States for want of Vouchers and by reason of the negligence with which the business was conducted on our part; yet I was always impressed with an idea, that, under all these disadvantageous circumstances, a very considerable balance would still be found in our favor—My present wish is, to have the subject so far investigated, as that we might not commit ourselves, by bringing forward Accounts, which had better continue dormant. Shou'd there be no danger of that Kind, it would then be desirable to have the business placed in a state, which might enable us to speak from a general knowledge of facts, and in a proper tone; in case a demand of the American posts held by the King of Great Britain should draw pecuniary subjects into discussion. I believe Lists of property carried away by the British, at the time when they evacuated the posts they had occupied during the late War, are lodged in the Office of Foreign Affairs. I am sir with great esteem Your most Obt Servant

G. Washington

LB, DLC:GW.

George Augustine Washington to John Francis Mercer

Dear Sir   Mount Vernon Decr 17th 1789.

Your Favor which was dated shortly after I parted with you at Fredericksburg met with some delay in getting to me—The

President has been informed of the contents and in reply says, as an act of Providence has interposed to render a complyance with your promise impracticable he must have further patience[1]—He has also been consulted as you desired to know if wheat would be received in payment—Clean & sound wheat will be taken at his Mill and the Alexandria *Cash* price allow'd for it—The Crop of Corn made here this year will be inadequate to the demands will therefore be glad to be inform'd on the rect of this if you will have any to dispose of and on what terms you will engage to deliver it here, or have it taken from your landing— Mrs Washington joins me in best respects to Mrs Mercer. I am Dear Sir Your most Obt Sevt.

Geo. A. Washington

ALS, ViMtV.

For background to GW's difficulties in collecting the sums due to him from the estate of John Mercer, see his letter to James Mercer, 18 Mar. 1789, n.1. See also GW to John Francis Mercer, 5 April 1789, to James Mercer, 5 April 1789.

1. No correspondence around this time between GW and George Augustine Washington concerning payments from the Mercers has been found.

Tobias Lear to Alexander Hamilton

Sir   United States Decr 18th 1789.

I am directed by the President of the United States to send you the enclosed letter from General Hazen dated Decr 16th— and likewise a memorial from the same person of the 12th inst: together with the Copy of a letter written by the Presidents command in answer to the enclosed Memorial.[1] I have the honor to be with perfect consideration Sir Your most Obedt Servt

Tobias Lear.
Secy to the President U.S.

LB, DLC:GW.

1. None of these documents has been found. Since Moses Hazen was in the process of presenting a claim on behalf of himself and Andrew Lee for Revolutionary War services, the memorial may have concerned this matter. See *DHFC*, 3:346, 349.

From Beverley Randolph

Sir,   Richmond December 18th 1789.

I do myself the honour to inclose you an act of the General Assembly authorizing the Governor of this Commonwealth to convey certain land to the United States in Congress assembled for the purpose of building a light House.[1]

The State had some years ago placed upon the shore at Cape Henry nearly a sufficient quantity of materials to compleat such a light House as was at that time thought convenient, which have been in the course of time covered by sand. Measures are taking to extricate them from this situation and to place them in a more safe one.[2]

If the United States shall accept the cession now offered and will purchase the abovementioned materials the Executive will be ready to dispose of them as soon as their value can be ascertained. I have &c.

                                        Beverley Randolph

LB, Vi: Executive Letter Book.

1. See GW to Thomas Newton, Jr., 12 Oct. 1789, n.1.

2. For GW's concern about the material at the construction site for the Cape Henry lighthouse, see Thomas Newton, Jr., to GW, 17 July, and 24 Oct. 1789, GW to Newton, 12 Oct. and 23 Nov. 1789.

From John Paul Jones

Sir,   Amsterdam December 20. 1789.

I avail myself of the departure of the Philadelphia Packet Captain Earle, to transmit to your Excellency a Letter I received for you on leaving Russia in August last, from my Friend the Count de Segur Minister of France at St Petersburg.[1] That Gentleman and myself have frequently conversed on subjects that regard America, and the most pleasing reflection of all has been the happy establishment of the new Constitution, and that you are so deservedly placed at the Head of the Government by the Unanimous Voice of America. Your Name alone, Sir, has established in Europe a confidence that was for some time before entirely wanting in American concerns, and I am assured that the happy effects of your Administration are still more sensibly felt throughout the United-States. This is more Glorious for you than all the Laurels that your Sword so nobly won in support of the Rights of Human Nature! In War your Fame is immortal as the Hero of Liberty! In Peace you are her Patron & the firmest supporter of her rights! Your greatest Admirers, and even your best Friends, have now but one Wish left for you—That you may long enjoy Health and your present Happiness!

I send by this occasion to Mr C. Thomson & to Mr J. Adams Sundry documents, from the Count de Segur, on my Subject.[2] I presume that those Peices will be communicated to your Excellency. They explain, in some degree, my Reasons for leaving Russia, and the Danger to which I was exposed by the dark Intrigues and mean Subterfuges of Asiatic Jealousy and Malice.

Mr Jefferson can inform you respecting my Mission to the Court of Denmark.[3] I was received and treated there with mark'd Politeness, and, if the *fine Words* I received are true, the Business will soon be settled. I own however that I should have stronger Hopes, if America had created a respectable Marine; for that argument would give weight to every transaction with Europe.

I acquited myself of the Commission with which you honored me when last in America, by delivering your Letters with my own Hand at Paris to the persons to whom they were addressed.[4] I am, Sir, with great respect, esteem, and Attachement Your Excellency's most devoted and most humble Servant

Paul Jones

N.B. In case your Excellency should have any Orders to send me, I think it my duty to subjoin my Address—*Under cover* "To Messieurs N. and J. Van-Staphorst & Hubbard Amsterdam."

ALS, DLC:GW.

1. See the comte de Ségur to GW, 24 Aug. 1789.
2. These documents have not been identified.
3. The Confederation Congress on 1 Nov. 1783 recommended Jones to the United States minister plenipotentiary in Paris as an agent "to solicit under the direction of the said minister" payments owed by European courts for prizes taken by the officers and crews under Jones's command during the war (*JCC*, 25:787–88). Jefferson, during his tenure as minister, had considerable contact with Jones, and Jones was moderately successful in France in the collection of funds. When he went to Denmark in March 1788 to petition for sums due to his command from the Danish court he found the ministry unwilling to negotiate, although King Christian granted Jones a pension of 1,500

crowns for his respect of ships bearing the Danish flag during the war, a payment Jones was later unable to collect.

4. See GW to Jones, 22 July 1787.

Tobias Lear to Clement Biddle

Dear Sir,   New York, December 21st 1789
    I have to acknowledge your three favors of the 22d & 30th of
Novr and 10th of Decr—all of which have been duly laid before
the President,[1] who now directs me to request that you will be so
good as to inform me in your next, at what price per bushel 350
bushels of Buckwht could be delivered at Alexandria if sent in
bags, includg the cost of the Buckwheat—the bags—commission
on purchasing—freight and every incidental charge; and what
would be the cost per bushl if sent in *Barrels* including every
expense as above. He wishes this particular calculation to determine whether he shall procure it from Philadelphia or from the
back Counties in Virginia—and requests this information to be
given, if it can be obtained, in the course of this week, that he
may, in his letter of next week to Major Washington, direct him
to procure it from the back Country or wait its arrival from
Philadelphia. From your last letter it is not probable the Buckwheat could be got in time to send (if it should be ordered)
before the Rivers close, therefore, the calculation, I suppose,
must be made with an idea of its being forwarded as early in the
spring as possible.[2]
    Mrs Washington will be much obliged to you to get from Mr
Reinagle, who taught Miss Custis music last summer, such music
as he thinks proper for her to progress with through the winter—and pay him for the same, which you will be good enough
to forward to New York.[3]
    Present my best Respts to Mrs Biddle—and tell her I will
present her compliments to Mrs Lear on the first day of my
marriage whenever that may be[4]—and I thank you, my dear Sir,
for your kind congratulations which shall be reserved for the
proper occasion.[5] I am, with very sincere esteem Dr Sir, Yr most
Obedt Sert

                                                Tobias Lear.

December 1789

423

ALS, PHi: Washington-Biddle Correspondence; copy, in Lear's handwriting, ViMtV; LB, DLC:GW.

1. All of these letters are in PHi: Clement Biddle Letter Book, 1789–92.

2. On 17 Nov. Lear first inquired of Biddle about buckwheat for GW. In his letter of 22 Nov. Biddle responded: "It has been a favourable year for Buckwheat and any quantity may be had but I Cannot yet ascertain the price as little has been brought to Market but suppose about 2/ ℔ Bus[hel]." His letters to Lear of 30 Nov. and 10 Dec. contained further reports on his attempt to secure buckwheat. George Augustine Washington wrote Biddle on 10 Dec. that the "very short crop of Buckwheat" would create for GW a need of four hundred bushels, which he hoped to procure from "50 or 60 Miles above Alexandria where the culture of this grain is much attended to." On 24 Dec. Biddle sent Lear an "Estimate of the Cost of 100 bushels of Buckwheat which I have extended at 2/6 as Mr Abraham Hunt of Trenton, & some others were of Opinion it probably may be had during the Winter at that price but perhaps may Cost 2/9 which may be Considered in the Estimate and on the other hand the bags charged in the Estimate being of Good Homespun tow Linen may be supposed nearly worth the first Cost for use on a farm and the Barrels including additional freight as they do not stow to such advantage as Bags will be near ⅔ the Cost of the Bags & the Cost nearly ⟨sunk⟩ unless they Can be applied to some use as in such Case we purchase flour Barrels which have been in use" (PHi: Clement Biddle Letter Book).

3. Alexander Reinagle (1756–1809) of Philadelphia was an accomplished composer and performer. Of Austrian descent, he emigrated from England to the United States in 1786 and soon became one of Philadelphia's leading musicians. Reinagle apparently spent some time in New York in the summer or fall of 1789, and GW arranged for Nelly Custis to take lessons on the pianoforte from him (Britt, *Nothing More Agreeable*, 30, 31). In his letter to Lear of 24 Dec. Biddle wrote that "I send herewith by Post the Bundle of Music for Miss Custis procured from Mr Reinagle he intends to send one or more pieces by a future Conveyance" (PHi: Clement Biddle Letter Book).

4. On 18 April 1790 Lear married Mary Long (c.1770–1793) of Lear's native city, Portsmouth, New Hampshire. Upon their return from Portsmouth several weeks after the wedding, the young couple were invited to make their home with the Washingtons. Mrs. Lear, known as Polly, eventually relieved Mrs. Washington of many social chores (Decatur, *Private Affairs of George Washington*, 128–29). She died of yellow fever in Philadelphia during the epidemic in the summer of 1793.

5. On 6 Jan. 1790 Lear wrote Biddle that "I have now before me your much esteemed favor of the 24th Ulto which came duly to hand, together with the music furnished by Mr. Renaigle. The President thanks you for your information relative to the Buckwheat—and requests that you will procure for him two Hundred bushels to be sent to Mount Vernon by the last of Feby or certainly early in March, in good bags marked G.W." (PHi: Washington-Biddle Correspondence).

From Diego de Gardoqui

Bilbao [Spain]

Most Excellent Sir.   21. of December of 1789.

Sir. I avail myself of the first Oppertunity with pleasure to communicate to your Excelly that I happily arrived at this Port the 13th of the last month after a severe Voyage, and not less perilous.[1]

The Surprises thereof, which, together with my Complaints, made me sufficiently to suffer, they brought on a painful disorder which has kept me suffering till the present Time, when already almost restored, I propose proceeding to the Court.

There, as well as in all places, I have no doubt that your Exy will do me the justice of believing that my sincere good wishes for the prosperity of the United States can never fail, nor the personal recognition of the many Honors which I have received from All in general, and very particularly from your Excellency.

In this Sentiment I beg your Excellency will be pleas'd to command my best Services, firmly persuaded that I shall receive the greatest Satisfaction in being employ'd in your Service[.] I can repeat the high Esteem, and perfect good will where with I entreat the Most High, to replenish your Excellency and the United States with the greatest Felicity.

May Our Lord preserve your Excellency's Life many Years.[2] Most Excellent Sir. Your Exys most Obedt Assured Servt

Diego de Gardoqui

L, translation, DNA:PCC, item 97; LS, in Spanish, DNA:PCC, item 97. The text is taken from a translation made by Isaac Pinto and probably prepared for GW.

1. Diego de Gardoqui, Spain's *encargado de negocios* in the United States since 1785, sailed for Spain in October 1789. See his letter to GW, 24 July 1789.

2. A note at the bottom of the translation reads: "Duplicates original of Captain Albidar in Alexandria." The original version of Gardoqui's letter reads: "Mui Señor mio: Me aprovecho con gusto de la primera oportunidad para participar a V.E. que el 13 del mes ultimo llegué con felicidad a este Puerto despues de un viaje bien cruel, y no menos arriesgado.

"Los sobresaltos de él, que, junto con mis achaques, me hicieron sufrir bastante, produxeron una penosa enfermedad que me ha tenido padeciendo hasta el dia, enque ya quasi restablecido, propongo continuar a la Corte.

"Alli, como en todas partes, no dudo me hará V.E. la justicia de crér que jamas podrán fallir mis sinceros deseos por la prosperidad de los Estados Un-idos, ni el reconocimiento personal â las muchas honras que he merecido de todos en general, y mui particularmente de V.E.

"En esta inteligencia pido a V.E. se sirva exercitar mi obediencia, firme-mente persuadido de que me caberá siempre la maior complacencia, si em-pleandome en su obsequio, puedo reiterar el alto aprecio, y fina voluntad con que pido al Altisimo llene a V.E. y los Estados Unidos de las maiores felici-dades."

Gardoqui also included a second, more personal, letter of the same date to GW. The translation reads: "Permit me to add what few lines my health suf-fers me of my own hand in order to repeat my sincere thanks for all your Civilities, & to offer my most respectfull Complements to your worthy Lady with my best wishes for the happyness & prosperity of both & your lovely grand children & Famely.

"My Son joyns with me in the same good wish, & offers his respects to you & your Lady, & I beg leave to add my Complements to the three Gentn your good Aids & to Colo. Humphries.

"I propose to set out for Madrid in very few days, where I shall be sincerely happy to receive your commands. In the mean time I wish you the Comple-ments of the Season & many prosperous New Years & remain with the highest respect Sir Your most obt hble servt" (DLC:GW).

To Joseph Buckminster

Sir   New York December 23d, 1789
Your letter of the 27th of November and the discourse which it enclosed have been duly received.

I consider the sermon on the death of Sir William Pepperell which you were so good as to send me by desire of Lady Pepper-ell his Relict, as a mark of attention from her which required my particular acknowledgments; and I am sorry that the death of that Lady which I see is announced in the public papers pre-vents my thanks being returned to her for her respect & good wishes[1]—You, Sir will please to accept them for your goodness in forwarding the discourse and my request, that they may be added to the Revd Authr with my approbation of the Doctrine therein inculcated. Your most Obedt Servt.

Df, DNA: RG 59, Miscellaneous Letters; LB, DLC:GW.
1. See Buckminster to GW, 27 Nov. 1789, n.1. Lady Pepperell died at Kit-tery, Maine, on 25 Nov. (*Massachusetts Centinel* [Boston], 5 Dec. 1789).

From Mary Katherine Goddard

Baltimore, Decemr 23d 1789.

The Representation of Mary Katherine Goddard, Humbly sheweth—That She hath kept the Post Office at Baltimore for upwards of fourteen years; but with what degree of Satisfaction to all those concerned, She begs leave to refer to the number & respectability of the Persons who have publickly addressed the Post Master General & his Assistant, on the Subject of her late removal from Office; And as Mr Osgood has not yet favoured between two and three hundred of the principal Merchants & Inhabitants of Baltimore with an answer to their last application, transmitted to him by Post on the 19th Day of November ultimo,[1] nor with any Answer to sundry private Letters, accompanying the transcript of a like application, made to Mr Burrell when at Baltimore: She therefore, at the instance of the Gentlemen thus pleased to interest themselves on her behalf, lays before your Excellency, Superintendant of that department, as briefly as possible, the nature & circumstances, of what is conceived to be an extraordinary Act of oppression towards her.

That upon the dissolution of the old Government, when from the non importation Agreement and other causes incident to the Revolution, the Revenue of the Post-Office was inadequate to its disbursements, She accepted of the same, and at her own risque, advanced hard money to defray the Charges of Post Riders for many years, when they were not to be procured on any other terms; and that during this period, the whole of her Labour & Industry in establishing the Office was necessarily unrewarded; the Emoluments of which being by no means equal to the then high Rent of an Office, or to the Attention required both to receive & forward the Mails, as will evidently appear ⟨by⟩ the Schedule, here unto annexed,[2] and therefore, whoever thus established & continued the Office, at ⟨the⟩ gloomy period when it was worth no Person's Acceptance, ought surely to be thought worthy of it, when it became more valuable. And as it had been universally understood, that no Person would be removed from Office, under the present Government, unless manifest misconduct appeared, and as no such Charge could possibly be made against her, with the least colour of Justice, She was happy in the Idea of being secured both in her

Office, and the Protection of all those who wished well to the prosperity of the Post Office, & the new Government in general.

That She has sustained many heavy losses, well known to the Gentlemen of Baltimore, which swallowed up the Fruits of her Industry, without even extricating her from embarrassment to this day, although her Accounts with the Post Office were always considered, as amongst the most punctual & regular of any upon the Continent; notwithstanding which She has been discharged from her Office, without any imputation of the least fault, and without any previous official notice: The first intimation on that head being an Order from Mr Burrell,[3] whilst at Baltimore, to deliver up the Office to the Bearer of his Note; and altho' he had been there several days, yet he did not think proper to indulge her with a personal Interview, thus far treating her in the Stile of an unfriendly delinquent, unworthy of common Civility, as well as common Justice. And although Mr White, who succeeded her, might doubtless have been meritorious in the different Offices he sustained, yet, She humbly conceives, he was not more deserving of public notice & protection in his Station, than She has uniformly been in hers: It must therefore become a matter of serious Importance & of peculiar distress to her, if Government can find no means of rewarding this Gentleman's Services, but at the Expence of all that She had to rely on, for her future dependence & subsistence.

That it has been alledged as a Plea for her removal, that the Deputy Post Master of Baltimore will hereafter be obliged to ride & regulate the Offices to the Southward but that She conceives, with great deference to the Post Master General, ⟨mutilated⟩ impracticable, & morally impossible; because the business of the Baltimore Office will require his constant Attendance, & he alone could give satisfaction to the people, if therefore the duties of the Assistant, Mr Burrells' Office are to be performed by any other than himself, surely it cannot well be attempted by those who are fully occupied with their own; and as two Persons must be employed, according to this new Plan, She apprehends, that She is more adequate to give Instructions to the Riding Post Master, *how to act* than any other Person possibly could, heretofore unexperienced in such business.

She, therefore, most humbly hopes from your Excellency's Philanthropy and wonted Humanity, You will take her Situation into Consideration; and as the Grievance complained of, has happened whilst the Post Office Department was put under your auspicious Protection, by a Resolve of Congress,[4] that Your Excellency will be graciously pleased to order, that She may be restored to her former Office, and as in duty bound, She will ever pray &c.

Mary K: Goddard

ALS, DNA:PCC, item 78.

Mary Katherine Goddard (1738–1816) was born in Connecticut and was the sister of the well-known printer and newspaper publisher William Goddard (1740–1817). The Goddards were the children of Dr. Giles Goddard of New London, Conn., and his wife Sarah Goddard (d. 1770), the daughter of Ludowick Updike of Rhode Island. After her husband's death, Sarah aided her son in his Providence, R.I., printing business and for about two years, after his departure for Philadelphia, managed his printing house and newspaper—the *Providence Gazette*. After William Goddard went to Philadelphia in the mid–1760s, she established her own firm, Sarah Goddard & Company, which included her daughter. In 1768 Sarah and Mary Katherine Goddard moved to Philadelphia to aid William Goddard who was now publishing the *Pennsylvania Chronicle*. Sarah died in 1770, and William Goddard moved to Baltimore in 1773, accompanied by his sister. While her brother was involved in other business and political pursuits, including publication of the *Maryland Journal*, Mary Katherine Goddard managed his printing house, and for over eight years—from 1775 to 1784—the *Maryland Journal* appeared under her name. During most of this time she also ran the Baltimore post office and kept this position when her brother resumed publication of the *Journal* in 1784. When Samuel Osgood took charge of the post office in September 1789 he appointed John White of Baltimore to replace Goddard.

On 6 Jan. 1790 GW replied to Goddard's complaint: "In reply to your memorial of the 23rd of December, which has been recieved, I can only observe, that I have uniformly avoided interfering with any appointments which do not require my official agency; and the Resolutions and Ordinances establishing the Post Office under the former Congress, and which have been recognized by the present Government, giving power to the Postmaster General to appoint his own Deputies, and making him accountable for their conduct, is an insuperable objection to my taking any part in this matter.

"I have directed your memorial to be laid before the Post Master General who will take such measures thereon as his judgment may direct" (copy, DNA: RG 59, Miscellaneous Letters).

1. The petition from the citizens of Baltimore to Postmaster General Samuel Osgood has not been located, but Osgood's somewhat unsatisfactory reply, 7 Jan. 1790, gave no reason for Goddard's dismissal beyond his statement that "the Postmaster General is by the Ordinance of Congress made accountable for the Conduct of his Deputies—The Responsibility is a Matter of very serious Consequence to him—In all such Cases, there seems to be a peculiar Pro-

priety in permitting the Officer to exercise his own Judgement freely. From mature Consideration, I am fully convinced that I shall be more benefitted from the Services of Mr White than I could be from those of Mrs Goddard" (DNA: RG 28, Letters Sent by the Postmaster General, 1789–1836). Goddard continued the pursuit of her post even though Osgood ostensibly encountered some difficulty in settling her accounts (Osgood to Goddard, 9 June 1790, DNA: RG 28, Letters Sent by the Postmaster General, 1789–1836). In the spring of 1790 Goddard unsuccessfully pressed her plea for reinstatement and for payment of a claim against the United States in both the Senate and House of Representatives (*DHFC*, 1:243, 3:415). For the remainder of her life she operated a bookstore in Baltimore.

2. The enclosure to this letter, "A Schedule of the Monies received in quarterly Payments, at the Baltimore Post Office, from January 1776 to April 17⟨8⟩1, inclusive, agreeably to the Baltimore Scale of Depreciation," is in DNA:PCC, item 78, 10:619.

3. Jonathan Burrall, assistant postmaster general.

4. "An Act for the temporary establishment of the Post-Office" placed the postmaster general and the operation of the department under the direct supervision of the president (1 *Stat.* 70 [22 Sept. 1789]).

To Samuel Huntington

Sir,   New York December 23d 1789

I have been favored with your Excellency's letter of the 19th Ultio—recommending General Sage to supply the place of Mr Miller as Surveyor of the Port of Middletown in the State of Connecticut, provided the latter should resign his Office.[1]

I have also received a letter from Genl Sage applying for the appointment, if the office should become vacant. But having had no intimation from Mr Miller of his intention to resign, I cannot at present, with propriety, take any further notice of the application in behalf of General Sage than to acknowledge the receipt of it. I am, with very great regard Your Excellency's Most Obedient Servant

Go: Washington

LS, IPB; Df, DNA: RG 59, Miscellaneous Letters; LB, DLC:GW.

1. For Comfort Sage's application for office and Samuel Huntington's letter of support, see Sage to GW, 31 July 1789. See also GW to Sage, 18 Aug. 1789.

From Edmund Randolph

Dear sir   Richmond decr 23. 1789

I returned from the assembly the day before yesterday. Since my last nothing material has occurred in either house; except that the bill is passed, authorizing restitution to be made of Abingdon to Mr Alexander, if you shall approve.[1]

I found a fortunate moment for a conversation with Mr Wythe. He repeated what I wrote to you in answer to your favor of the 30th Ulto.[2] Indeed he declared himself happy in believing, that he held a place in your esteem; and that he was confident, you had looked towards him with every partiality, which he could wish. Nay without going into the detail of our discourse, I am convinced from his own mouth, that the knowledge of his present situation is considered by him, as the only reason of a seat on the bench, not being tendered to him.

I shall have the pleasure of seeing you so soon, that I shall now only add, that I always am Dear sir yr obliged friend & serv.

                                        Edm: Randolph

ALS, DLC:GW.

1. For background to the Custis-Alexander controversy concerning Abingdon, see David Stuart to GW, 14 July 1789, n.7.

2. See Randolph to GW, 15 Dec. 1789.

From James Read

Sir   Wilmington North Carolina Decr 23rd 1789

The Politeness with which you were always pleased to treat me in the Army, when I had occasion to wait on you, imboldens me to take the liberty of addressing you at present, and soliciting a continuance in the Office that I now hold, which is Collector of Port Brunswick; the General Assembly of this State appointed me to the Office in eightyfour (the first time that Duties were laid since the Revolution) and to continue Collector of the Continental Impost when the rest of the State adopted the measure, recommended by the late ⟨mutilated⟩ I have continued in the Office since that time, and beg ⟨mutilated⟩ to refer to a Certificate from the Treasurer (enclosed) ⟨mutilated⟩ the punctuality of my Settlements.

I served as an Officer in the Army from the Year seventyfive to the end of the War, and after the Defeat of General Gates, when there were no Continental Troops belonging to this State, I offered my Service to the Assembly who gave me the Command of a Regiment of Militia, with which I joined General Greene, and had the Honor of presenting that worthy and respectable Officer's aprobation of my Conduct, to the General Assembly, on my return from the Campaign. I hope Sir you will not think that I mean any thing more by this than that I have been a faithful Servant to the Public. I am Sir with the greatest Respect your obedient and very humble Servant

James Read

ALS, DLC:GW.

James Read (d. 1803) of Wilmington, N.C., rose from ensign to the rank of lieutenant colonel in the North Carolina militia during the American Revolution. GW appointed him collector of the customs for the port of Wilmington in February 1790 and in March 1791 expanded his duties to include the inspectorship of North Carolina survey no. 1. He held the collectorship until he was removed by John Adams in the fall of 1797, apparently under some suspicion of dereliction of duty (*DHFC*, 2:57; John Steele to James Read, 2 July 1798, in Wagstaff, *Steele Papers*, 1:157–58).

William Jackson to George Turner

Dear Sir,   New-York. December 23rd 1789.
The communication which I now make to you though painful, is friendly, and has no other object ⟨*mutilated*⟩ your interest.

I suggested to you, when in Philadelphia that your delay, in repairing to the western-terri⟨tory⟩ would as certainly excite the President's displeasure as I was convinced it would his disappointment.[1] Accustomed to punctuality himself, he expects to see it in others—especially in the discharge of those trusts which involve the most interesting concerns of the ⟨*mutilated*⟩.

You must excuse the freedom and force of this expression—it is the language of truth uttering sentiments of friendship—and better far it should be thus conveyed than take the form of an official communication.

The President of the United States was told, yesterday, that you were still in Philada, and he is, indeed, much dissatisfied at the circumstance.

Let me request you to do away his dissatisfaction by setting out immediately for the place of your official residence, where I wish you to reap a large harvest of honorable fame and private happiness. Being very sincerely Your friend

W. Jackson.

ALS (retained copy), DNA: RG 59, Miscellaneous Letters.

1. For Turner's appointment as judge for the Northwest Territory, see his letter of application to GW, 18 Aug. 1789, and GW's letter to James Madison, c.8 Sept. 1789. Turner's continued absence from his post was a perennial problem in GW's administration. See *JPP*, 69, 88, 89, 110, 112–13, 136.

To Joseph Willard

Sir,   New York Decr 23d, 1789

Your letter of the 7th Ultimo was handed to me a few days since by Mr Savage, who is now engaged in taking the Portrait which you, & the Governors of the Seminary over which you preside, have expressed a desire for, that it may be placed in the Philosophy chamber of your University.

I am induced, Sir, to comply with this request from a wish that I have to gratify, so far as with propriety may be done, every reasonable desire of the patrons & promoters of Science—And at the same time I feel myself flattered by the polite manner in which I am requested to give this proof of my sincere regard & good wishes for the prosperity of the University of Cambridge. I am, Sir with great esteem, Your most Obedt Servt.

Df, DNA: RG 59, Miscellaneous Letters; LB, DLC:GW.

To William Fitzhugh

Dear Sir,   New York, Decr 24th 1789

I have to acknowledge the receipt of your letter of the 4th inst. which announced to us the disagreeable intelligence of Mrs Plater's death—Mrs Washington and myself sincerely condole with you, your Lady and the other friends of Mrs Plater upon this melancholy event.

Mr Johnson has, as you supposed, declined the appointment of Judge to the District of Maryland, and I have lately appointed Mr Paca to fill that office. Mr Thomas whom you recommend for that place undoubtedly possesses all those qualifications which you have ascribed to him[1]—and so far as my own knowledge of that Gentleman extends, he is justly entitled to the reputation which he sustains. But in appointing persons to office, & more especially in the Judicial Department, my views have been much guided to those Characters who have been conspicuous in their Country; not only from an impression of their services, but upon a consideration that they had been tried, & that a readier confidence would be placed in them by the public than in others, perhaps of equal merit, who had never been proved. Upon this principle Mr Paca certainly stands prior to Mr Thomas altho' the latter may possess in as high a degree every qualification requisite in a Judge. With very sincere regard I am, Dear Sir, Your most Obedt Servt.

Df, DNA: RG 59, Miscellaneous Letters; LB, DLC:GW.

1. Fitzhugh's letter of 4 Dec. was in support of John Allen (Alleyne) Thomas for the post of federal judge in Maryland. See George Plater to GW, 20 Nov. 1789, n.2. In his 4 Dec. letter Fitzhugh had also informed GW that the "Death of Mrs Plater Mrs Fitzhugh's only Daughter has occasiond great Distress in our Family." Elizabeth Rousby Plater, the daughter of Ann Frisby Rousby Fitzhugh, William Fitzhugh's second wife, was married to George Plater.

From Benjamin Lincoln

My dear General   Boston Decr 24 1789

Docr Oliphant was during the war at the head of the medical department at the southward[1]—He always supported the character as master of his profession a Gentleman of arangment, of Justice, œconomy & industry—He is among those unhappy men who have suffered by the late war and has seen better days If there should be an opening for him again in the public line I have no doubt but he would honour to any appointment he should receive. I have the honour of being My de[a]r General with the most perfect esteem your most obedient servant

B. Lincoln.

ALS, DLC:GW.

1. David Oliphant (1720–1805), a physician, planter, and politician of Charleston and St. George Dorchester Parish, S.C., was born in Scotland and emigrated to South Carolina after serving as a surgeon at the Battle of Cullo-

den in 1746. Oliphant was a member of the state's legislative council when Congress appointed him director general of the hospitals in the southern department in 1776. He was captured at Charleston and after his exchange served as hospital director under Nathanael Greene and later as deputy director of the medical department of the southern army. After the war he was a member of the South Carolina legislature and practiced medicine, moving to Newport, R.I., in the mid–1780s where he opened a medical practice. Oliphant did not receive a federal appointment.

Tobias Lear to John Henry Livingston

Sir,   New York Decr 24th 1789

The President of the United States observing in the Public Papers that a sermon was to be delivered at the Dutch Church in this City for the benefit of a charity school belonging thereto,[1] and not having an opportunity of contributing toward it at that time, he has now directed me to send you the enclosed sum of ten Dollars to be applied to that purpose. With very great respect I am Sir Yr most Obedt Servt

Tobias Lear
S.P.U.S.

ALS (retained copy), DNA: RG 59, Miscellaneous Letters; LB, DLC:GW.

John Henry Livingston (1746–1825) was the grandson of Robert Livingston, first lord of Livingston Manor. Livingston had studied and was ordained in Holland as a minister in the Dutch Reformed church. A Patriot during the Revolution he left his post in New York City, returning in 1783 and becoming pastor of the Dutch Reformed church in the city. In 1810 he became president of Queen's College (now Rutgers).

1. The Charity School began in 1633 as an outreach of the oldest church in New York City, the Collegiate Reformed Protestant Dutch Church, founded in 1628. A schoolhouse on Garden Street was built in 1748 opposite the church and rebuilt in 1773. Several denominations in the city supported the school, which suspended operation during the Revolution and reopened under the tutelage of Peter Van Steenburgh, master from 1773 to 1791. The school's thirty scholars depended entirely upon charitable contributions for clothing and tuition (Smith, *New York City in 1789*, 125, 135). On Saturday, 12 Dec. 1789, the *New-York Packet* published a notice that a charity sermon would be delivered in the Dutch language the next day at the Dutch Church, and in English the following Sunday at the North Church, to raise money for the thirty scholars then attending the school.

From Alexander Martin

Sir,　　　　North Carolina—Fayetteville December 24th 1789
I do myself the honour to inclose your Excellency herewith a copy of an Act of the General Assembly of this State passed at their last Session at this place, "for the purpose of ceding to the United States of America certain western Lands therein described," which your Excellency will please to lay before the honorable the Congress of the United States at their next Session.[1] I have the Honour to be with the highest respect Your Excellency's most obedient humble Servant[2]

Alex: Martin

Copy, DNA: RG 46, First Congress, Records of Legislative Proceedings, President's Messages; LB, Nc-Ar: Governor's Letter Book, Alexander Martin.

Alexander Martin (1740–1807) graduated from Queen's College (Rutgers) in 1756, moved to North Carolina, and soon became active in politics as a supporter of the Patriot cause. After a somewhat checkered military career—he was court-martialed but acquitted for cowardice at the battle of Germantown—he served in the North Carolina legislature and briefly in the Continental Congress. Martin was elected governor in 1782, 1783, 1784, and again in 1789, serving until 1792.

1. See *N.C. State Records*, 21:697, 25:4–6.
2. GW submitted Martin's enclosure to the State Department on 2 Feb. 1790 (Tobias Lear to Roger Alden, 2 Feb. 1790, DNA: RG 59, Miscellaneous Letters).

From "An Old Soldier"

Great Sr　　Commonwealth of Massachusetts—Decr 25th 1789
I hope it is a moment of leasure if this luckely should fall into your hands—urgent necessity induces me thus humbly to approach your Excellancy—I will not Sr long divert your attention from your arduous employment—but beg leave to observe—that on the first alarm of war I entered the Service of my Country being a minute Man in the then Massachusetts State—and having a fervant zeal to see the Conclusion I engaged from term to term till the first time of Inlisting for the War—which I unfortunately complyed with and had not the advantage of large Bounties as others afterwards had—and being a miner my Master had my wages till the last engagement—when the money began to depreciate—& our nec[e]ssaties so urgent that it pro-

cured but scanty release—hoping and expecting every Campaign to be the last—and not ambitious for office obtain none
took my tour as sentinal at all times and on all occations—cold &
hot—wet & Dry—and being with the infantry was almost continually on the loins of the Enemy—I always loved—and had
the love of my officers—obey'd every order punctually and
considered your Excellencies as sacred—The promises of my
officers—the incoragments in Genl orders—and the Resolves of
the State and Congress induced me to hope and depend on an
aduquate reward for my long toyl—hazard—& sufferings—
when peace should be restored to our country again; but—
alass! how aghast was I when with all my prudance—and many
times suffering pinching need to preserve and save my earn-
ings—& 250 Dollars in final settlements was my only Subsidy.
    And when I reflect on the many—many dark & dangerous
Nights I walked my Post all attentive—the much fatigue naked-
ness—and hunger I have indured—the many hazards I have
run for my country—first on Bunkers-hill—at Perls Point—at
white plains—the fatigueing but glorious action at Trenton &
Princeton—the malancoly retreat from Ty—the Victory at
Bemises-heights—the Battle at Monmouth & the Concluding
seage of Yorktown—and that Eight Years of my prime was
gon—had lost my trade—was unacquainted with husbandry—
had formd the Connection of matremony in a very respectable
family—had Two babes by a most agreable companion—her
father impatent for my return to releave him of the long burden
of my Wife & children—and I—unfortunate Man had no where
to put them nor any provisions made for them—where said I is
my dear General whome I ever hoped would have it in his power
to see us righted—my officers have forsaken me—Congress
dont pay me—my country dont thank nor pitty me! I offered
my Securities for sail they would fetch only 2s./10d. on the
pound—and I resolved if they was ever made good I would have
the benefit of them if I worked my fingers to the bone for
bread—but too close application soon redused my health—and
to keep from goal for the doctors bill my securities are redused
to Two hundred Dollars—Seven Long Years have elapsed and
no releaf till my patiance is nearly gon with my constitution by
unremited strugles at day labour to pay Taxes and bearly support my family which now is Eight in number—six children

untaught through poverty—and by a rearage of rent my land-lord thretens the remainder of my securities @ 5s./2d. on the £ unless a spedy prospect of the Interest being paid saves them to me—Is there or is there not, my dearest of Generals any ground of hope—I ketch at every incouragement—and recolect in the Generals last and farewell orders to the Armies of the United States he observed that "the officers & soldiers may expect considerable assistance in recommencing their civil occupations, from the sums due to them from the public which must and will most inevitably be paid"[1]—also in the Genls presenting his thanks to the several classes of the Army he says—"And to the non commissioned officers and *Soldiers* for their extreordinary patience in suffering, as well as their invincible fortitude in action; to the various branches of the Army the General takes this last and solemn opertunity of profesing his inviolable at-tachment and friendship"—then observes "he wishes more then bare profession were in his power, that he was really able to be useful to them in future life."

Now I trust heaven has put it in his power—And when the new Constitution took place (which was pro⟨*illegible*⟩ of in the above Quoted genl orders) my heart leaped with Joy—but not more than when I was advertized of the great-good Man put at the head of it—and felt confidant of releaf—but how was I affected when I found the old creaditer was neglected and the revenew whittled up among the multiplicity of officers and offices of the new government—may they not with propriety wate for a part of their inormus Sallerys as well as the poor Soldier for his seven Years Interest on his heard earnd pett-ance—one Years neglect more and all my expectations are blasted—my Securities must go to keep me out of goal and my family from Starving—what oppression! what crualty! such a severe Strugle to save my country—and their promised rewards arested from me—through their neglect and my necessity for almost nothing—and I exposed in some future day to pay my proportion of the whole sum to the menopalizer—Dear sr help for all other help but that of Heaven faileth—The demand by Taxes—by my Landlord—by my Family and my infermities bares me down my courage is nearly exosted and I reduced to invy those who—not only bled with me but died in their Coun-tries service and are now mouldring in the dust.

But most worthy Sr—fully confidant of the rectitud of your mind—and your sincere wish to releave all in destress, and especially the deserving—And to distribute Justice to all men; and in perticular to the injuerd—I earnestly implore Heaven to Send all needed aid to the all attentive Preasidents exertians to contribute to all equally the rewards of their Country, according to their deserving—then may I depend on the small pittance due to your Excellancies most devoted & obedeant humbe Servt

An Old *Soldier*

AL, DNA:PCC, item 78.

The "Old Soldier" has not been identified.

1. This and the following quotations are taken from GW's Farewell Orders to the Armies of the United States, 2 Nov. 1783.

From John Ely

SayBrook 25th Decembr 1789

Permitt me Mr President to wish You & your Lady the Compliments of the Season.

And also be Pleased to Permitt me to Inclose you a Coppy of a Letter I wrote you in 1780 and also one to the President of Congress of a Similar Nature, Together with a Petition to Congress,[1] Those Letters Anticipated Events which have since Taken Place, as will appear by my Petition to Congress—I take this Method to Prevent Trouble to the President as I cannot Expect him to Pay Attention to Matters of an Individual Subject, when Great National Matters Calls for his Attention; Yet should I be so Fortunate as to Attract a Moments Reflection on my Conduct & Sufferings while in Captivity it might give a Favorable turn to an Unfortunate man, my Petition was Prefered to the Old Congress about 4 Years Past on which a Committe was appointed, which Committe who consisted of Doctr Johnson Mr Phiny & Mr Henry made a Favourable Report. Leaveing a Blank for the Sum Found Due in which Situation, it now Lies, I Intend to wait on Congress in February Next for a Desition—I Flatter my self if aught in my Carrector Deserves your Notice and that of Congress I shall have Justice Done me. Permitt Further to add that as it is the Opinion of the Mercantile & Tradeing Part of this State that you will Ultimately Think Propper to Establish a Navil

Office at the Port of SayBrook; should that be the Case and I so Fortunate as to have the appointment I should Esteem my self Happy and should keep a good Lookout²—I am with Every Sentiment of Respect to the President—his most Obedt and Very Hume Servt

John Ely

ALS, DNA:PCC, item 78.

John Ely of Connecticut served as a captain with the 6th Connecticut Regiment from May to December 1775 and as colonel of a Connecticut militia regiment in 1777. He was taken prisoner on Long Island in December 1777 and not exchanged until December 1780.

1. Ely's letter to GW may be one of 26 Oct. 1780, complaining of the personal misfortunes resulting from his captivity (DLC:GW). The copy of the petition to the Confederation Congress enclosed in Ely's 1789 letter is undated and deals with his extended captivity and its economic consequences to him (DNA:PCC, item 78).

2. On 9 Jan. 1790 GW wrote Ely that "Upon considering the state in which your application to Congress rested at the conclusion of the former Government, and your intention of renewing it under the present; it occurs to me that it would not be proper for me to express any opinion on the merits of your individual case. In general I may say, without impropriety, that I am not ignorant of your service in your Country's cause; and that it is always my wish that justice should take place" (NCoxHi). On 24 Feb. 1790 Ely's petition, "praying to be compensated for losses or injuries sustained, or for services rendered during the late war," was submitted to the House of Representatives and referred to the secretary of war. Knox reported on 8 Mar., and on 10 Mar. the House ordered a bill to be brought in. The bill was rejected on 5 April, but a second bill "to allow compensation to John Ely, for his attendance as a physician and surgeon on the prisoners of the United States" passed (*DHFC*, 3:305, 306, 319, 325, 356, 374, 392, 394). The matter was not, however, finally settled until 1833 when Congress passed "An Act for the relief of the heirs of Colonel John Ely, deceased," compensating Ely's estate to the amount of $60 per month for his services, travel, and expenses from 9 Dec. 1777 to 25 Dec. 1780 (6 *Stat.* 543 [2 Mar. 1833]).

Indenture with William Gray

[Fairfax County, Va., 25 December 1789]

This Indenture of a Lease made this twenty-fifth day of December Anno Domini one thousand seven hundred and eighty nine by & between George A: Washington, for and in behalf of George Washington Esq. as his true and Lawful Attorney, on the one part and William Gray on the other part, both of the County of Fairfax and Commonwealth of Virginia, Witnesseth that the said George A: Washington for and in consideration of the Rents and covenants, herein after mention'd to be paid and performed on the part of the said William Gray—doth lease and to farm let, unto the said William Gray for the term of one year from the above mentiond date—A certain tract or parcel of Land belonging to the said George Washington Esq. of Mount Vernon, laying in said County of Fairfax and occupied last year by said Gray & John Robinson and being part of a tract formerly known by the name of the Chappel Land.[1]

For and in Consideration of the above being done on the part of sd George A. Washington the said William Gray doth agree to pay unto the sd George A: Washington the full and just sum of ten pounds Virginia Currency in Specie, or the amount thereof in Wheat deliverd into the Mill of George Washington Esq. of Mount Vernon at the market price provided the wheat is deliverd on or before the expiration of the Lease—Said William Gray doth also promise and agree that he will work no greater number of hands on said Land than he did last year, which consisted of himself, his Children & one Negroe—that he will not clear up any more of said Land than what is now cleared— that he will cut no timber off said Land more than is absolutely necessary for repairing the fences of sd Land and that the laps of such Trees shall be made use of for fuel—that he will sell or remove no wood or Timber from the Land—that he will make no more Tobacco than will be made use of in Chewing and smoaking in his own family—that he will make no waste of any kind on said Land—and lastly that he will at the expiration of the year peacibly & quietly give up & quit said premises unless the parties should agree to continue a lease for a longer term.

In testimony of all these things, and for the true and faithful performance of them, the parties have hereunto interchangeably set their hands and seals, the day and year first written. Done in presence of—

Geo: A. Washington
William Gray

DS, DLC:GW. This lease was negotiated in behalf of GW by George Augustine Washington, as manager of Mount Vernon in GW's absence.

William Gray also was GW's weaver (see Ledger B, 263, 303, 331). GW later had reason to complain about his relationship with Gray. In May 1793 he instructed his Mount Vernon manager Anthony Whitting that "Grey should be told that if he does not Weave it [wool] as fast as it is carried to him, that he shall not only loose my custom, but, must look out for some other tenement; because this, and not the Rent, was the inducement for placing him there. However, speaking of the Rent, let me enquire whether he pays it regularly or not?" (GW to Whitting, 19 May 1793). See also GW to Whitting, 2 June 1793, and to William Pearce, 15 and 29 Mar. 1795.

1. The Chapel land was part of a 700-acre tract in the area of Dogue Run granted to William Travers in 1678. After several unsuccesful attempts, GW acquired the land in 1772 from its then owners, Charles and Ann Brown West. See George William Fairfax to GW, 16 Nov. 1765, and GW to Charles West, 6 June 1769.

From Charles Thomson

Sir,   Harriton [Pa.] Decr 25. 1789

At the time I made my resignation, I took the liberty of recommending to your notice John Fisher, who had served as a clerk in the office for several years and whom I then considered not only as sober attentive and diligent, but as *faithful*.[1] To my astonishment and indignation I find by a letter which I received last evening that I entertained an opinion of him which he by no means deserved, I therefore think it my duty as speedily as possible not only to recal my recommendation, but to transmit you a copy of the letter I received with the papers which accompanied it, that you may, if you will deign to take the trouble see the man in his true colours.[2] To give a clearer view of the state of facts, I beg leave to mention, that formerly every individual in the several offices under Congress had an account opened in the books of the treasury, carried in his own account to the board and received his own Money—That Mr Morris, during his administration, fixed the stated quarterly payments and directed the accounts of each individual in the several departments to be included in one account and paid by one warrant drawn on the treasurer, that as I was always averse to have public money pass through my hands, especially when the payments at the treasury began not to be punctual and when the paper money of the states was substituted in the place of specie, I desired Mr Alden, the deputy Secretary,[3] to make up the quarterly account, carry it to the treasury board, receive the Money and pay it as he received it. In doing this it seems Mr Alden for some time past entrusted Fisher to carry some of the money to individuals but that instead of paying he emblezzled part of it. I would not have troubled you with this disagreeable subject, had I not from motives of humanity been led to recommend the man to your notice.[4]

Be pleased to accept, from my retirement, the compliments of the season and my congratulations on the accession of North Carolina to the Union. I now consider the revolution complete, and now it is accomplished I cannot without a mixture of wonder, joy and gratitude to the Supreme disposer of events, reflect on what easy terms compared to what it has cost others in similar circumstances, we have obtained a rank among the nations of the earth, and with what tranquilitty a reform has been made in our constitution & government, which bids fair to transmit the blessings of freedom, independence & happiness to future generations.

Mrs Thomson desires with me to be remembered to Mrs Washington. With the greatest & most sincere esteem & respect I am Sir Your most obedient and Most humble Servt

Chas Thomson

ALS, DNA:PCC, item 49.

1. See Thomson to GW, 23 July 1789.
2. See enclosure.
3. See Thomson to GW, 23 July 1789, n.1.
4. GW replied to Thomson's letter on 10 Jan. 1790: "I thank you for the information which you have given respecting the person whom you had recommended to me for notice. His conduct has been such as justly to exclude him from any place of confidence or trust; and it appears, from the copies of his letters which you have transmitted to me, that he is severely punished by his own reflections.

"I return, with sincerity, the compliments of the season to yourself & Mrs Thomson, in which I am joined by Mrs Washington; and I heartily rejoice with you in the accession of North Carolina to the Government of the Union" (Df, in the writing of Tobias Lear, DNA: RG 59, Miscellaneous Letters).

Enclosure
Roger Alden to Charles Thomson

Dear Sir   Newyork Novr 30. 1789

I have been induced by desire of Mr Fisher to suspend writing to you until this time respecting some transactions in which he is materially concerned. It is a duty which I owe to you to declare the truth. As I never could practise duplicity to serve myself I never will be guilty of it to oblige another.

On the first of this month he asked my permission to be absent 8 or ten days to collect some money due to him at Claverack [N.Y.]. I readily granted his request. A few days after he left town I was informed that he was very much involved and the report was that he had absconded to avoid the payment of his debts. The day that he had promised to return, his wife informed me of his distress & added that he had heard of the reports. She requested me to advise him what was best to be done. I pitied him and wishing to relieve him wrote the letter N1 addressed as I thought to an honest, tho' unfortunate man, and directed her to ascertain the amount of his debts that his friends might be the better able to advise & assist him.[1] Three days after this she told me it was impossible to ascertain the sum—that the manner of incurring his debts doubly encreased her own distress—that he had contracted an unjustifiable acquaintance with a family in town whose interest and happiness he had preferred to his own—that he had retained money which he had received from the public & had expended it for their support. This alarmed me. The same day I examined the files in the Register's office where I had directed the accounts & receipts to be preserved together. But many were missing. I called upon some of the gentlemen whose names she had mentioned, from their information and his papers I found there remained due to

DoctorProvost	£ 50. 0.0
Doctor Rodgers	22.10.0
Berry & Rogers	27.19.6
Mr McLean	17. 1.6
Mr Hodge	9.10.0
Mr Greenleaf	4.13.4
Mr Morton	12. 0.0
	£143.14.4

He had told these gentlemen that the money was not received, but the accounts would be paid when the new treasury department was compleated. This prevented farther enquiries, and having told me that the receipts were lodged with the accounts I never suspected his honesty or veracity.

Having ascertained these facts I was preparing to communicate them to you when I received his letter N2.[2] Agreeably to his request I went to see him at a room his wife had taken in Broadstreet in his absence, being obliged to leave the house in which they had lived. It was such a scene of poverty and distress that I found no object for my resentment. I did not even enquire the causes of his conduct. On examining the paper, he mentioned I found they contained his accounts against the family which he had supported and a list of his debts amounting to £130 exclusive of the above sum. He proposed to surrender all he possessed which is a mere trifle, and was desirous of being continued in the office. To the latter I could not assent. I told him he must make no calculation upon that, and it was unnecessary for me to say more, his own mind could best suggest the reasons which determined me. I was not disposed to encrease the distress of a man whose misery seemed compleat. I rather wished to lessen it and encouraged his wife to summon her resolution by hoping that her husband would become a more industrious man & a better christian after his trials.

I called the next day with Dr Tillary one of his creditors. He advised him to write to his creditors & recommended the taking a lodging house and to begin the world anew. This has been done. Some seem disposed to treat him with lenity and to grant him his liberty for two years. To what they will eventually agree is uncertain.

It is about a year since he has used his discretion in paying the money entrusted to him and such has been his management that his conduct has been unsuspected by me. In Septr last he informed me that a man to whom he was endebted for rent hearing that he was to go with the southern commissioners as he had applied for a place had sued him, and asked me if I would not accept an order for the wages due to him. I replied that I could not—that I would not make myself responsible to any man for the payment of money which it was uncertain I should receive. After painting his troubles and the damage it would be to his reputation he obtained my consent to retain it to my hands and to pay it in the manner expressed in my letter N5.[3] The lawyer gave up his note & took me for security & now demands payment.

His wages from Oct. 1 to the middle of Novr & the debts due

from the family he has supported amounting to above £100 are all the funds he can calculate upon. He is now confined in his house and lies at the mercy of those whose confidence he has betrayed & whose property he has abused. His letters shew the present state of his mind and his countenance discovers all the marks of corroding remorse and aggravated guilt.[4] Had he been imprudent only, a sense of my own faults and failings would dictate some plea for the exercise of charity, but knowing the facts I cannot offer a single word to extenuate his crimes or to avert his punishment. If justice could be satisfied with sufferings the poor fellow has in some degree cancelled his debts.

In this situation what is to be done & how am I to proceed? To whom must the public creditors apply for justice? Here my trouble commences. Some of the accounts are presented for payment. I want your advice & can take no measures until I am honored with your instructions.

Doct. Rogers desired me to enclose the letter he recd.[5] He can say nothing for him, but with me supposes that from a state of facts you will be best able to judge of the man and of his conduct. I don't know what view the unhappy man had in applying to him unless he considered it as a favorable opportunity to shew his contrition and repentence.

Please to make my respects to Mrs Thomson & be assured that to promote your happiness will always give the greatest pleasure to your sincere friend & humble Servt

R. Alden

Copy, DNA:PCC, item 49.

1. Alden's letter to Fisher, 8 Nov. 1789, stated that while Fisher was absent from his post "several gentlemen have called upon me to know when you are to return & to justify their enquiries they have mentioned the cause of them. I have answered them that you left town with my knowledge and that I expected you in the course of 10 days. The general report is that you have absconded to avoid the payment of your debts. Your future conduct will determine whether this is founded in fact. Mrs Fisher with all the affection of a tender wife informed me this morning of your unhappiness and the share which she felt of it convinced me that she merits your love and affection. She desired me to advise you how to proceed. Not knowing the amount of your debts or the causes which have produced your present embarassment I am unable to determine what is best. It appears to me to be the best policy to come immediately to town & by your presence contradict the report not by endeavouring to prove yourself innocent but to convince the world that you are not guilty. With honesty and frankness tell your creditors your situation. The

worst that can be done is to deprive yourself of your liberty for a while. They will be more disposed to treat you with lenity if you offer yourself voluntarily than if you should be arrested after appearing to avoid or defraud them. If you remain out of town you will be constantly encreasing your debts. You must determine to meet your fate & summon all your fortitude to bear it. Time, patience, self denial good management & perseverance will overcome every difficulty that can befal *an honest man.* I shall be always ready to advise you" (DNA:PCC, item 49).

2. Fisher's letter, 15 Nov., informed Alden that Fisher "arrived in the city last evening, should have been here aggreeable to promise, but being apprized of a rumour that I had absconded, which circumstances seem to warrant, I continued in the country, wrote to town by a friend but recd no answer. I was perplexed and knew not what to do, and being confined to my bed four or five days prevented my setting out until yesterday morning. On my arrival at Elizabeth town the tavern keeper handed me your letter of the 8th inst. enclosing one from Doctr [James] Tillary. Had I been so fortunate as to have recd them sooner, nothing would have prevented my return. For I can most assuredly say I never had an idea of going away. You are now acquainted with what I have long and ardently wished, but never had the resolution to communicate—Would to heaven I had & in time craved mercy. But I fear my sin is too great for forgiveness; but as long as there is life there is hope, and with advice and assistance I think I shall be able to pay all the public money I have so unworthily expended & hope to beg day & grace of my creditors and by those virtues you recommend pay every shilling & convince the world that however villainously I have acted, by my future conduct and deportment, that I have seen my error & sincerely repented of it. I have not words to express my feelings—suffice it to say that I abhor myself in dust and ashes. I wish to see you, but no felon ever dreaded the sight of the executioner at his appointed hour more than I do you whom I could once behold with pleasure and confidence. The fault is mine. I am guilty. I am the villain. I cannot ask you to receive me in your office with propriety—but if you could after ⟨securing⟩ you I should by that means ⟨impliedly⟩ retain your confidence & be able to face my creditors with a better grace—but I am resolved to meet my fate whatever it may be. If convenient I should wish to see you to day" (DNA:PCC, item 49).

3. Alden enclosed an unaddressed statement, dated 2 Sept., stating: "There will be due in October next to Mr John Fisher for services in the office of the late secy of Congress £45 which money will pass through my hands, and if it will be the means of preventing him trouble and a sufficient inducement to you to delay urging your demands upon him at present I will retain £22.10 in my hands when recd & it shall only be paid to his order in your favour" (DNA:PCC, item 49).

4. Alden enclosed several additional letters he had received from Fisher concerning his situation. On 22 Nov. Fisher wrote: "To reflect and consider what I once was and now am in your estimation and likewise in the estimation of that good man Mr Thomson, I am driven to distraction and I sincerely and

truly abhor myself. I cannot nor do I pretend to offer any excuse for my wretched conduct—I have done it and what can I say? Nothing but that I am guilty, guilty, before God and Man. I have no desire nor indeed could I continue in the land of the living if it was not, by a future conduct of good behaviour to endeavour to retrieve in some measure if possible that good name I have forfeited & likewise by tenderness & affection convince the best of women that she has not altogether misplaced her affections. Perhaps flattery that bane to mankind and a too easy disposition may have tended to my destruction. I am confident I do not possess a vicious heart. I have often shuddered at the bare thought of my conduct, after I had committed the crime— to relieve others in distress is a christian virtue, but then to do this at the expence of reputation & with the property of another or others is highly & truly reprehensible. I confess I have a feeling heart for anothers distress and perhaps too easy taken in by the artful and designing especially the female part of the creation—not, I can with solemnity declare with the least view or intention of any criminal correspondence—this is a truth, however I may not be believed. . . . I can only say that I have seen and sorely feel the effects of a guilty conscience and let the consequence be what it may, I am determined to live & act as becomes an honest & upright man" (DNA:PCC, item 49). Another letter of 25 Nov. asked Alden to "be so kind as to suspend writing to Mr Thomson till wednesday's post. A friend of mine thinks it best to endeavour to get doctor Rogers to write also to accompany your letter and will undertake to speak to the doctor on the subject—but as it is saturday, somewhat out of season to trouble him on such business, he wishes to defer it till monday. He thinks that the doctrs letter in conjunction with yours may have a good effect with Mr Thomson" (DNA:PCC, item 49).

5. Fisher's abject letter of 30 Nov. to Dr. John Rodgers, pastor of the Presbyterian church in New York, reads: "Probably if you knew from whom this letter came before you opened it, it would not be read—Such has been my conduct for some time past by shamefully abusing the confidence reposed in me, that *you* Sir as my friend protector and patron must feel indignation rise in your breast whenever you hear my name whispered. I mean not to offer, were it possible, the shadow of an excuse for my behaviour—Had I the abilities of the ablest writers, both ancient & modern, I should fall far short—No, Sir, I address you as a wretched being who is truly sensible of his unhappy situation & abhors himself and repents in dust and ashes—mercy is one of the great attributes of the *Divine Being* and we are told he delighteth to forgive when implored in a proper temper and manner, but I dare not presume, a wretched being as I am, to call on his Holy name—May I implore *your mercy* as one of his *Ambassadors* as well as *one* who I have grossly offended. I should have no wish to be continued in existence if it were not to convince, if possible, by a well regulated conduct, that I am not that wretch *in grain* that my behaviour would justify my friends in supposing me. What I could at present say would have no weight—Actions speak louder than the best chosen words— Were I to be called in the most solemn manner to give an account of my behaviour for eighteen months past, I could not, nor even the principle that led

me to it . . . . I am well aware of your feelings on this occasion & dare not look you in the face much less ask a favour; but as I am not capable of writing that venerable and good man Mr Thomson, will you condescend so far as to write to him and let your letter accompany Major Alden's which will go by Wednesday's mail—I do not expect you to say any thing in my favour but wish you to give your own opinion—this much I can with solemnity assert that I acted not from any vicious principle—perhaps the guilt is the same—But bad as I am I must continue in the land of the living until called by that *glorious & just being* whom I have from my beginning offended, and in his awful presence give an account of my transactions in life—Might I have *one* chance more to endeavour to retrieve in some measure what I have lost.

"Believe me Sir I never had an idea that the stings of a guilty conscience was so poignant—My distress in Mind is more than I can bear, but I am convinced not half so severe as I deserve—Unhappily I am not the only person distressed by my conduct—*a loving, tender* and *virtuous wife* shares and that severely in my distresses—this to a person who thinks as *I now do* is enough to drive him to distraction—My heart is full & ready to burst with grief" (DNA:PCC, item 49).

From Burgess Ball

Dear sir,   Travellers Rest [Va.] 26th of Decr 89.

I fear you will think we have been very dilatary respecting the Settlement of the Old Ladys Affairs &c., as it has been a long time since we have given you any Information of them.[1] For my part I have been so embarrass'd for some time by being Security for Majr Willis, that I cd scarcely think of any thg else. The Negroes are at length divided, but all the things of the Old Ladys are not yet quite dispos'd of, as there were many wch cd not (with propriety) be sent to Vandue, and Mrs Lewis sells them off to Private Purchacers—We concluded to divide the Negroes into four parts by wch it ⟨m⟩eans you have a Fellow call'd Dundee in ⟨ad⟩dition to the one you had before—None of the Families are parted, which is a happy Circumstance, but, those whose Husbands or Wives did not belong to the Estate, were obliged to part with such, of Course. Your two Fellows here (George & Dundee) I shall give a Pass to, as soon as the Hollidays are over, to go to Mount Vernon. Mrs Lewis will transmit you an Accot of the Division &c. in a few days.

We have endeavour'd to dispose of your Lotts to sundry Gent. who inclin'd to purchace but the Valuation is, by every Body, (even those who valued 'em) thought to be too high; therefore, least the Houses &c. shd be injur'd this Winter, we have recommended it to Mr Carter to move immediately into them, especially, as he wishes himself to be a Purchacer, & I expect will give as much as any person[2]—He will, I believe give £350 payable in three Years with int. and I do not know any Person who will give so much—If he does not purchace, he will at any time move out for any Person who may. Any Security you shd require he will give. Fanny joins in best Wishes for you & yours & I am with the highest Esteem Dr sir, yr mo. Obt Servt

B. Ball

ALS, DLC:GW.

1. This letter concerns the settlement of Mary Ball Washington's estate. For background, see Burgess Ball to GW, 25 Aug. 1789, GW to Betty Lewis, 13 Sept. 1789, Betty Lewis to GW, 1 Oct. 1789, Burgess Ball and Charles Carter to GW, 8 Oct. 1789, and GW to Ball and Carter, 18 Oct. 1789.

2. See Betty Lewis to GW, 13 Sept. 1789, n.9.

From Perez Morton

Sir   Boston Decbr 26th 1789

If, as the Commerce of the United States is every day extending, & their Intercourse with the East Indias rapidly growing into an established Trade, The Wisdom of the Supreme Executive should suggest the Necessity of appointing Consuls in that Quarter of the Globe, permit me to solicit the favor of an appointment of that kind for the Hither India in behalf of a Brother, Joseph Morton, Merchant at Fort St George, on the Coromandel Coast.[1]

He is twenty five Years of Age; he left this Country early in the Year 1787, and has been established at Madrass in the mercantile Line about two Years. Educated in the habits of Œconomy, he is prudent & discreet beyond his period of Life; and for his Integrity, Capacity and Patriotism I can chearfully pledge myself. least however both the Candidate and the Solicitor may be personally unknown to you, I beg leave to refer you to Genl Lincoln's Letter accompanying this, whose Enquiries respecting the Qualifications & Character of the Candidate have been such, as have induced him to support his Pretensions in the manner he has—I flatter myself, should no other present, who in your Judgement would better serve the Interests of the United States, you will honor him with your Nomination & Support; which will confer an Obligation on him, who has The Honor to subscribe himself, with every Sentiment of Respect your most Obedient and very hu. Servt[2]

Perez Morton

ALS, DLC:GW.

Perez Morton (1751–1837) was born in Plymouth, Mass., but was taken to Boston by his father Joseph Morton who took over operation of the White Horse Tavern on what is now Washington Street. The younger Morton graduated from Harvard in 1771, read law with Josiah Quincy, and was admitted to the Suffolk bar in 1774. From 1775 to 1776 he served as deputy secretary of the commonwealth under Samuel Adams. During the war he held several state offices and acted as aide-de-camp to John Hancock during the Rhode Island campaign. In 1779 he returned to the practice of law and was appointed attorney for Suffolk County. Around 1812 he became attorney general for Massachusetts, a post he held for some twenty years.

1. Joseph Morton (1764–1843) remained in business in Madras for some years but was back in Boston by 1804 (*Records Relating to the Early History of Boston: Boston Marriages*, 206).

2. GW also received a letter of recommendation for the younger Morton from Benjamin Lincoln: "I am informed that Mr Joseph Morton, a native of this town, is now settled at Madrass in the mercantile Line. He is mentioned to me by many of whom I have sought his character, as a gentleman of abilities, integrity, industry and of a fair reputation. Should there be a consul appointed at the port of Madrass and if among the various candidates, which may be placed upon the list, the pretensions of Mr Morton should be equal to any and your mind should ballance between him and an other permit me to assume such an interest for him as shall cause the ballance to preponderate in his favor. This request is dictated by no other motive than a wish to throw before your Excellency the character of a deserving young gentleman who I think would do honour to the appointment should he receive it" (26 Dec. 1789, DLC:GW).

From Poellnitz

Sir   New York 26th Decbr 1789.

The countenance Your Exellency has been pleas'd to give, to my feeble efforts in agriculture, has encouraged the promulgation of this Essay, the manuscript of which, I send to your Exellencys perusal, before I giv' it to the printer, from whom I expect the alteration, of the to a foreigner unavoidable faults of ortography.[1]

Permit' me Sir to decorate this pamphlet with a great Title, by writing on the head "This Essay is respectfully inscribed &.&.&. to your Exellency; this will make more impression on the minds, then all the Arguments contained in the Essay, as it conveys the Idea, that what may be Useful in it, has received your Exellency's gracious Sanction. I am respectfully your Exellencys, most humble, and devoted, Servant.

F. C. H. B. Poellnitz

The quantity the Mill can thrash in an hour, is left in blanco, 'til I receive Your Exellency's Order, for the Experiment.

ALS, DLC:GW.

Friedrich Charles Hans Bruno, Baron von Poellnitz (d. 1801), a native of Poland, lived on a 21-acre farm near Murray Hill on Manhattan. Poellnitz carried on various agricultural experiments on his farm and corresponded with GW on agricultural matters. See Poellnitz to GW, 20 Mar. 1790, 28 July 1795, and GW to Poellnitz, 29 Dec. 1789, 23 Mar. 1790. Sometime before 1795 Poellnitz sold his farm and moved to South Carolina, settling on a plantation on the Great Pee Dee River near Georgetown (Janvier, *In Old New York*, 123–24; *South Carolina Historical Magazine*, 32 [1931], 198; *Pennsylvania Magazine of History and Biography*, 20 [1896], 44).

1. This is undoubtedly an early version of Poellnitz's *Essay on Agriculture*, printed in New York in 1790 by Francis Childs and John Swaine. GW replied on 29 Dec.: "I have received your letter of the 26th; and given such attention to the Manuscript which accompanied it, as my obligations to public duties would permit. I shall always be happy to see experiments in agricultural machines, which can be brought into general use. Of those in your possession I was not able to form a decided judgment, except in the instance of the Horse-Hoe; of the utility of that instrument I was fully convinced. I propose to take some farther occasion of seeing the manner in which the threshing machines operates, when you shall let me know it is in readiness for the purpose" (copy, DNA: RG 59, Miscellaneous Letters). In January 1790 GW visited Poellnitz's farm to observe the operation of one of his threshing machines. See *Diaries*, 6:12.

To Jabez Bowen

Sir   New York Decr 27th 1789.

The letters with which you have been pleased to favor me, dated in Octr and the 15th of the present month came duly to hand, and are entitled to my thanks for the communications contained in them.

As it is possible the conduct of Rhode Island (if persevered in) may involve questions in Congress which will call for my official decisions, it is not fit that I should express more than a wish—in reply to your letter—than that the Legislature at the coming Session would consider *well* before it again rejects the proposition for calling a Convention to decide on their accession to or rejection of the present government.[1] The adoption of it by No. Carolina has left them *entirely* alone. I am much obliged to you for your good wishes, and with esteem & regard I am—Sir Yr Most Obedt Hble Servt

G. W——n

ADfS (facsimile), NN: Emmet Collection; LB, DLC:GW.
   1. See Bowen to GW, 25 Oct. 1789, n.1, and 15 Dec. 1789.

From Christopher and George Champlin

Sir   Newport Decemb. 27th 1789
   The Inclosed came under cover to us which we have the honour of Transmiting to your Excellency.

Mr Hans Rudolph Saaby the subscriber is a merchant of Copenhagen and the acting person in the House of Nicholas Ryburg Esqr. & Co. of that City.[1]

We conceive it a duty incumbent upon us, (not only as Freinds to the Union) but in Justice to the Character of Mr Saaby; to inform your Excllency, that from a Commercial conection of five years Standing, we have found him a Gentleman of information, punctuality, and Probaty. and that the House of Nicholas Ryburg Esqr. & Co. is reputed the most oppulent in Copenhagan; and from thier extensive conections, have it in thier power to render services to the Commerce of this country.

If a Foreigner is admissable to the office of *Consul General.* We have the honour to be with the greatest respect Your Excellencys Most obedient, and most humble servants

Chrisr Champlin
Geo: Champlin

LS, DLC:GW.
Christopher and George Champlin were Newport merchants.
1. For Saabye's application for office, see his letter to GW, 5 Aug. 1789.

From George Clendenin

Richmond, 27th Decemr 1789.
The indians have in the county of Kenawa committed many hostilities; some of which I beg leave to enumerate. They killed a man near point pleasant; took a young man a negrofellow prisoners have shot at others, who made their escape, and have taken between twenty and thirty head of horses, together with other outrages to the manifest injury & distress of the inhabitants.

If protection is not immediately given, I am sure the greater part of our frontiers will be compelled to leave their homes, and either live in forts, or move into the strong settled parts of the neighbouring counties, which I conceive would do great public injury, as well as distress in a great degree the inhabitants, that are thus exposed, who are situated in a part of the country not only to become respectable but very useful.

Excerpt, DNA: RG 46, First Congress, Records of Legislative Proceedings, Reports, and Communications Submitted to the Senate; excerpt, DNA: RG 233, First Congress, Records of Legislative Proceedings, Reports, and Communications Submitted to the House.
By the president's command, David Humphreys sent Clendenin's letter to Henry Knox "to be placed among other Papers on the same subject." Knox included the above excerpt from the letter in his report to Congress on hostilities with the northwestern tribes, 8 Dec. 1790 (Humphreys to Knox, 8 Jan. 1790, DLC:GW; *ASP, Indian Affairs*, 1:85).

From Bushrod Washington

Dear Uncle   Alexandria. Decr 27th 1789.
I Recieved a Letter from my Brother a few days past, enclosing one to you on the same subject with his first, requesting me to forward it, unless I had recieved an answer to his other, which he was apprehensive had miscarryed. I put his second into the Post office and a few days afterwards had the pleasure to recieve

your favour of the 16th Inst. I have mentioned this circumstance in order to account for my Brother's having troubled you with two Letters on that subject. I expect to see him at this place in a few days on his way to Berkly where he is going with a design of collecting such Documents & such parole information as may be necessary for his defence. I shall accompany him in order to give him any Assistance in my power. I hope that the hints contained in your Letter will ⟨*mutilated*⟩ to obtain still further information on that subject. It is certain that he must lose his Land unless he can succeed in collecting the Evidence of which he is in search. I am convinced that those necessary pieces of Testimony exist somewhere tho they may not be discovered, as Colo. Greene informed me in the Year 1787 that my Brothers Title under the Hites was so incontestable that the Suit would be dismissed.

I must here make an apology to you for having so long neglected to answer your very affect. & proper Letter recd some time ago in answer to one on the subject of a foederal appointment.[1] It came to hand a few days before the long Fall Session of Courts took place from which I returned to this place the latter end of October: immediately after that I recd a severe hurt to my right Hand, which prevented me from writing until a few days ago, and even now it is so stiff that I can scarcely make my self to be understood.

whilst I thank you for the good wishes expressed in your Letter, and of which I could never entertain a doubt after the many proofs You have given me of them, permit me to approve and admire the principles upon which you had founded your choice. In Justice to myself I must assure you, that had I supposed that you were to make the nomination, I should never have hinted to you my wishes on that, or any similar subject, well knowing your character, & sensible of the indelicacy of such an application. But I was informed that the nomination & appointment of those inferior officer's were vested in the Judges of the Several Courts agr⟨eeable⟩ to that article of the Constitution which permits this to be done.

You say nothing about my Aunts Health or your own, & I therefore hope the best. Nancy Joins me in Love together with the usual congratulations of the Season—Believe me to be Dr

Uncle with the sincerest wishes for your health & Happiness
Your Affectionate Nephew

Bushd Washington

ALS, ViMtV.

For background to this letter and the documents mentioned in it, see Corbin Washington to GW, 30 Nov. 1789.

1. See GW to Bushrod Washington, 27 July 1789.

From Thomas Harwood

Sir.   Annapolis Decemr 28th 1789.

Having served as Continental Loan Officer in the State of
Maryland, during the Revolution to this present time, and occasionally receiver of the Money appropriated by this State to
Congress, and presuming that under the present Government,
in the Arrangement of the Business of the United States such an
Office or one similar to it may be necessary; and flattering
myself with having the Approbation of Congress and those
under whom I acted in the Business of that Office, beg leave to
Solicit your favor and attention; and a certainty of doing the best
in my Power may be depended on in the Duties of that, or any
other Office that I may be thought Worthy of.

My Brother Mr Benjamin Harwood who has done Business
with me during the time of my being in Office,[1] and who acted
under Mr Morris, while he was Financier, as the Continental
Receiver is at present in no Office, he is well Qualified for any
Business, and should he succeed to an Appointment, I am sure
he would give entire satisfaction; for information respecting my
Brother and myself, I beg leave to refer you to Mr Morris, the
late Board of Treasury and the Senators and Delegates from this
State, who have a perfect knowledge of us. With Sentiments of
the Highest Esteem, I am Sir Your most Obedient and very
Humble Servant

Tho. Harwood

ALS, DLC:GW.

Thomas Harwood (1743–1804) was a wealthy and influential Annapolis
merchant. Appointed treasurer for Maryland's Western Shore by the Maryland legislature in 1775, he held the post until 1804. He served under Robert

Morris and the Board of Treasury as Maryland commissioner of loans from 1777 and was reappointed under the new government in 1790 (*DHFC*, 2:89).

1. Benjamin Harwood, also an Annapolis merchant, was appointed receiver of Continental taxes in June 1780. He succeeded his brother as commissioner of loans for Maryland in December 1792 (*Executive Journal*, 1:126).

Letter not found: to Samuel Huntington, 28 Dec. 1789. In a letter to GW of 2 Jan. 1790, Huntington referred to "your letter of the 28th Ulto."

It is possible that Huntington misread the date of GW's letter to him of 23 Dec. 1789 as 28 December.

Letter not found: to George Augustine Washington, 28 Dec. 1789. In a letter to GW of 15 Jan. 1790 George Augustine Washington refers to GW's letter of "28th Ulto."

From John Daves

Sir: New Bern [N.C.] 29th December 1789.

North Carolina having adopted the new Constitution I presume that Officers are soon to be appointed in the several Ports of this State; In the Year 1784 I was favored by the General Assembly with the appointment of Collector for Port Beaufort to which New Bern belongs—the inclosed Certificates will shew in what manner I have acquitted myself in the discharge of that Office, and if Sir you will have the Goodness to appoint me to the same Office under the new Government, I hope that my future Conduct will not give you any reason to complain.

Having a Wife and some small children, neither the Remains of the pay that I was able to save when the Army was disbanded, nor the profits of the Office I now hold, make it convenient for me to give personal attendance at New York, this circumstance, however, I am persuaded, will have no effect on your deliberations. I have the Honor to be Sir Your most obedient and respectful Servant

John Daves

ALS, DLC:GW.

John Daves (1748–1804), a native of Mecklenburg County, Va., moved to North Carolina before the Revolution and served as an ensign, lieutenant, and captain with North Carolina forces during the war, receiving nearly forty thousand acres of land in Tennessee for his services. He was reappointed collector at New Bern in 1790 (*DHFC*, 2:57, 60, 527).

To the Georgia Legislature

Gentlemen,   [December 1789]
The congratulations presented to me by the different branches of the Legislature of the State of Georgia, upon my having been elected with unanimity to the Presidency of the United States, affect my mind with the most pleasing sensations, and demand my best acknowledgements.[1]

From the observation that "in the great concerns of mankind, success has not always been attendant on the performance of duty, and that, where it has, the sanction of public approbation has frequently been with held" I am naturally led to reflect on the unlimited gratitude which we owe, as a nation, to the supreme Arbiter of human events for his interposition in our favor—as well as on the singular obligations which are due from me as an individual, for the indulgent sentiments which my fellow-citizens have always had the goodness to entertain of my conduct.

Raised, as I am, to the head of a Government pervading so vast a territory—and possessing, as I flatter myself I do, the confidence of the people in regard to my dispositions—I assure you, Gentlemen, that nothing could be more consonant to my wishes than to be favored with such facts and opinions respecting the condition of the States as may appear proper and necessary—for I am duly sensible that many errors which would result from want of information may be obviated by timely and just representations.

I am not ignorant how much the local situation of your State exposed its inhabitants to suffer the distresses of the late war in a severe manner; nor how manfully they exerted themselves in the common cause during the struggle which established our independence. Wasted as your country was at the return of peace, and exposed as your frontiers have since been to the ravages of the Indians; I cannot but flatter myself that you will ere long realise the blessings which were to be expected from your natural resources, and find a compensation for your sufferings in the benefits of an efficient general government.

It will not be expected I presume, on this occasion, that I should enter into the merits of the delicate subject to which you allude. It may be sufficient to say, that, while I regret extremely the failure of the late negociation for peace with the Creek-Indians:[2] I am satisfied that the explanations which have been received through authentic channels will be of eminent service. I am also convinced that nothing will be wanting on your part to concur in the accomplishment of a pacification: and I still hope that under the influence of the general Government that desireable object may be effected—with respect to this subject in general, as well as to the other calamity which you mention as resulting from your being the south frontier of the union, I request you will be persuaded that I shall make such use of the powers vested in me by the constitution as may appear to me best calculated to promote the public good.

I am much pleased, Gentlemen, with the frankness which you have manifested in regard to myself—and return you my hearty thanks for the good wishes you have expressed for my health and happiness, with a sincere prayer that the same blessings may be extended to you and your constituents.

G: Washington

LB, DLC:GW.

1. The address from the Georgia legislature, dated at Augusta, 22 Dec. 1789, and signed by Nathan Brownson, president of the Senate, and Seaborn Jones, Speaker of the House of Representatives, reads: "The federal constitution being adopted it became the wish of the People of this State that you should be elevated to the Presidency of the Union; and the two branches of the Legislature take the first occasion of offering to your acceptance their congratulations on the unanimity of your election.

"In the great concerns of mankind success has not always been attendant on the performance of duty; and where it has, the sanction of public approbation has frequently been withheld; but it was reserved for you, in the midst of the most arduous difficulties, not only to be successful, but to have been so with universal applause.

"Raised by your virtues and services to the head of a government pervading so many independent states, the general confidence is in favor of your justice; and, while the history of Nations informs that the errors of Rulers have often proceeded from the want of information, we shall not hesitate to lay before you such facts and opinion respecting this State, as may appear to us to be incumbent or necessary—In doing this, it shall be our aim to unite plainness with respect, and integrity with truth.

"Sir, In the course of the war which established our independence, our citizens made proportionate exertions with those of any part of the whole, and in point of property, they suffered the most: the peace found the country a waste; with many natural advantages we flattered ourselves with a speedy recovery; when we were attacked by the Indians.

"On this subject we wish to be delicate; much has been already said—we have asserted, and it has been contradicted; removed at a distance from the centre our actions have been liable to misrepresentation; but we trust that by this time, they are better explained—in the meantime while our population has been checked and our agriculture diminished—the blood of our citizens has been spilled, our public resources greatly exhausted; and our frontiers still open to fresh ravages. The failure of the late negociations for a peace with the Creek nation and the circumstances which attended the same, are the best evidence of the necessity of our measures, and a proof of the late hostile dispositions of these People: but under the influence of the government and power of the Union, it is to be hoped and expected that a different conduct will on their part prevail: on our part, nothing shall be wanting to promote so desireable an establishment.

"Another circumstance of additional calamity attendant on our being the south frontier of the Union, is the facility of our black people crossing the Spanish line, from whence we have never been able to reclaim them. This has already been productive of much injury to private persons, and if not speedily restrained, may grow into an evil of national magnitude.

"We take this occasion of bringing this business into view, with a perfect reliance, that you will cause such discussions to be made, as shall be necessary to bring about a remedy.

"We request you will accept our cordial wishes for your health and happiness, and that you may long continue to enjoy that confidence, which has been so eminently placed in you by the people of the United States" (DLC:GW).

2. For the attempt of the American commissioners to the southern Indians to make peace with the Creek, see David Humphreys to GW, 21, 26, 27 Sept., 13, 28 Oct. 1789, Alexander Hamilton to GW, 20 Oct. 1789, and Henry Knox to GW, 18, 27 Oct., 21 Nov. 1789. See also GW's Memoranda on Indian Affairs, 1789.

Farm Reports
Statement of Crops for 1789

First Statement of the Crops in 1789

[1789]

		acs.	Acs.	Har-[veste]d
Corn	375 Acres 1 Plowing in the fall of 1788	375		
	Listing the field in March abt 1/4 of the above work	94		
	Opening the furrows in April 1/3 of the last wk	31		
	Breaking up the balks,[1] in May, 3/4 of the whole	281		
	Plowing Do in June			
	do do	281		

	Ditto in July				
	do do		281	1343	
	Three times harrowed				
	do do 281				843
Rye	375 Acres once plowed for seeding in Septr			281	
	once harrowed at do do				281
Buck Wheat	375 Acrs. 1 Plowing in Autumn after Rye comes off		375		
	1 Ditto in April		375	750	
	3 harrowgs once before & twice after sowing				1125
Wheat	375 Acres Plowing in B: Wheat in June		375		
	Ditto seeding the ground with Wheat in Augt		375	750	
	One harrowg after Sowing				375
Sundries	375 Acres One plowing in fall 1788		375		
	75 of Do in Pease Plowed into 3 ft ridges in April		75		
	Checquered abt ¼ of the above work Apl		19		
	234 do in B[uck] Wht for a crop				
	Plowed in April		234		
	Ditto in July 1st		234		
	3 times harrowed 1st July				702
	8 do Scarcity[2] Plowed in March		8		
	Ditto May		8		
	Ditto July		8		
	8 do Pumpions Plowed in March		8		
	Ditto May		8		
	Ditto July		8		
	20 do Flax Plowed in March		20		
	Ditto April		20		
	Three times harrowed			1025	60
Barley	375 Acres 1st Plowing Jany or Feby		375		
	2d Ditto Feby or March		375	750	
	Three times harrowed				1125
				4899	4511
	Of the above work				
Betwn the 1st of Oct. & Christmas—Corn amounts to			375		
	B: Wheat do		375		
	Sundries do		375	1125	
In Jany & Feby	Barley 1st plowing			375	
Feby & Mar.	Ditto 2 Ditto			375	1125
March	Listg for Corn as above		94		
	Plowing first time for Root of Scar[ci]ty		8		
	Do Do for Flax		20		
	for Pumpions[3]		8	130	
April 2d	Plowing for flax		20		60
	Ditto Pease grd into 3 feet Ridges		75		
	Ditto checquered		19		
	Opening Corn Lists for Plantg		31		
	Buck Wheat for Manure		375	520	1125

May	Ditto for Seed	234		
	Pumpkins 2d Plowg 8 Scar[cit]y do 8	[16]		
	Breaking Balks betwn Corn	281	531	281
June	Plowing Corn 2d time	281		281
	Ditto B: Wheat for Manure	375	656	
July	B: Wheat for Seed	234		702
	3d Plowing of Corn	281		281
	3d Do of Scar[cit]y 8 3d do Pumkns 8	16	531	
Augt	Wheat		375	375
Sept.	Rye		281	281
			4899	4511

Dr.					Cr.			
for					By			
375	bushl Rye for sd @	3/	£ 61. 5.0	5625	bushl Corn	@	3/	£ 843. 0.0
375	do B. Wht do	2/	37.10.0	5625	do Rye		3/	843. 0.0
375	do Wheat do	5/	93.15.0	5625	do Potats.		1/	281. 5.0
750	do Barley do	3/6	131.15.0	4500	do Barley		3/6	937.10.
Sundries—viz.—				Sundries viz.				
75	Bl Pease seed	4/	15. 0.0	1404	bushl B. Wht		2/	140. 8.
234	do B. Wht	2/	28. 8.0	375	do Pease		4/	75.
30	do Flax	3/6	5. 5.0	100	do Flax Seed	3/6		17.10.
3750	lbs. Clover Sd	8d.	125.	Dressed flax				
3120	Bls Corn for			Buck Wheat 375 acs. Manure				
	Neg[roe]s	3/	468.					3924. 3.
2750	do Rye for Hors.	3/	412.10.0	375	acs. Clover	@	20/	375.
100	do of Salt	2/6	12.10.					4299. 3.
330	Gallons Rum	2/	33.10.0	100	M̶ Tobo Hills 20 Hhds			
							£7/10	150.
750	Bls Pots. seed	1/	37.10.0	15	M: Hole			
			1461.18.0	20	D. Run			
				30	Frchs & Ferry			
				35	River			
				100	Total			

2d Statement of Crops for 1789

Corn	375 acres	Same in all respects as No. 1	1343	843
Buck Wheat	375 Acres	One Plowing in Aprl	375	
		2d Ditto last of June	375	750
		Three harrowings		1125
Wheat	375 Acres	One Plowg after the Buck W: is cut	375	
		Two harrowings		750
Sundries	375 Acres	the same as No. 1	1025	762
Barley	375 Acres	Do Do	750	1125
			4243	4605

Of the above Work

Fall	One plowing for Corn 1788	375	
	One Do for Sunds. Do	375	

Jan. & Feby	1st Plowing for Barley	375		
Feb. & March	2d Do for Do	375	750	1125
March	Listing for Corn	94		
	Plowg 1st time for Root of Scarcity	8		
	Ditto for Flax	20		
	Ditto for Pumpions	8	130	
April	2d Plowing for Flax	20		6-
	Ditto Pease grd into 3 feet Ridges	75		
	Ditto checquered	19		
	Openg Corn lists	31		
	1st Pl[owing] of Buck Wheat for a Crop	375	520	
May	1st P[lowing] of Buck Wheat among the Sundries	234		
	Pumpns 2d Plowg 8 acs.			
	Scary 2 Plowg 8 do	16		
	Plowing balks between Corn 1st time	281	531	285
June	Plowing Corn 2d time	281		281
	2d Do of B. Wht Do	375	656	1125
July	Do Do Do Do	234		702
	Corn 3d time	281		281
	3d Plowg of Scarcity 8 Do of Pumpns 8	16	531	
Augt	Plowing for Wheat		375	780
			4243	4905

	Dr.				Cr.		
for				By			
375	Bushl of B. Wht seed	@ 2/	£ 37.10.0	5625 bushls of Corn	@ 3/	£ 843. 0.0	
				5625 do Potat[oe]s	1/	281. 5.0	
375	do Seed Wheat	5/	93.15.0	Buck Wht Plowd in for Mane		nothing	
375	Sundries viz.			3750 bushl Wheat	5/	937.10.0	
75	Bls Pease	4/	15. 0.0	Sundries 375 bls Pease	4/	75. 0.0	
234	do B. Wht	2/	23. 8.0	1404 bls B. Wh.	2/	140. 8.0	
30	do Flax Seed	3/6	5. 5.0	Ba[r]ley 4500 bls	3/6	787. 0.0	
750	Bushl Barley	3/6	131. 5.0	Flax 100 bls	3/6	17.10.0	
3750	lbs. of Clovr Seed	@ 8d.	125. 0.0	dressed flax		3181.13.	
3120	Bushls of Corn			375 Acs. Clovr @ 20/		375.	
	Neg[roe]s	3/	468. 0.0	375 do do do		375.	
2750	do Rye	3/	412.10.0			3931.13.	
100	do of Salt	2/6	12.10.0				
330	Gals. of Rum	2/	33. 0.0				
750	Bushl Pot[atoe]s for seed	1/	37.10.0				
			1396.13.0				

3d Statement of Crops for 1789

Corn	375 Acs. the same as No. 1 & 2			1343	843
Barley	375 acs. Do Do			750	1125

B: Wheat	375 acs. plowed in fall in March & Apl	1125	1125
Wheat	375 acs. Plowed in June to covr B. Wht		
	& Sown in Aug.	750	375
		4008	4468

Of the above Work

Fall	One plowing for Corn 1788	375		
	One do for B. Wht Do	375	750	
Jan: & Feby	1st Plowing for Barley	375		
Feb. & Mar.	2d Do for do	375	750	112
March	Listing for Corn	94		
	2 Plowing for Buck Wheat	375		
	1 Ditto for Flax	20	489	
April	2d Do for Do	20		6
	3d Do for B: Wheat	375		75
	Opening Corn lists	31	426	
May	Breaking up the Balks betwn Corn		281	28
June	2d Plowing of Corn	281		28
	Plowing in Buck Wheat	375	656	
July	Plowing Corn the 3d time	281		
	Plowing for Wheat—on Buck Wheat	375	656	75
		4008	352	

Dr.   Cr.

for   By

750	Bls Barley seed	3/6	£ 131.15.0	5625	bushl of Corn	@ 3/	£ 843. 0.0	
375	do B. Wht	2/	37.10.0	5625	do Potats.	1/	281. 5.	
375	do Wheat	5/	93.15.0	4500	do Barley	3/6	787.	
3750	lbs. Clover Seed	8d.	125. 0.0	3750	do Wheat	5/	937.10.	
30	Bushls flax Seed		5. 5.0	B. Wheat Manure		nothing		
3120	do Corn for			Flax 100 Bls		3/6	17.10.	
	Neg[roes]	3/	468. 0.0					
							2866. 5.0	
2750	do Rye for Horses		412.10.0	Clover 375 Acs.		@ 20/	375.	
100	do of Salt	2/6	12.10.	Do Do Do			375.	
330	gals. of Rum	2/	33.10.	Do Do Do			375.	
750	bushls of Pots.						3991. 5.	
	seed	1/	37.10.					
			1357. 5.0					

Fourth Statement of the Crops 1789

			Acres	
			Plow—Har[veste]d	
Wheat	375	Acrs. on a Clover lay. one Plowing	375	750
Sundries	375	Do pr No. 1	1025	762
Corn	375	Do fall plowing saved—remains then	968	843
B. Wheat	375	Do Plowed in April & June	750	750
Barley	375	Do in Jany and Feby—perhaps—March	750	750
			3868	3855

	Dr.						Cr.			

For

						By				
375	Bushls Seed Wht	5/ @	£ 93.15.0		3750	Bls of Wheat	@ 5/		£ 937.10.0
75	Do Seed Pease	4/	15. 0.0		375	do Pease	@ 4/		75.
234	Do B: Wht	2/	23. 8.		100	do flax Seed	3/6		17.10.
30	Do Flax Seed	3/6	5. 5.			flax lbs. @			
375	Do B: Wheat	2/	37.10.		2250	do B: Wheat	2/		225. 0.0
750	Do Barley	3/6	131. 5.		4500	do Barley	3/6		787. 0.0
3120	Bl Corn for Negros	3/.	468.		5625	do Corn	3/		843. 0.0
2750	Bl Rye for 55 Wk				5625	do Irish Pots.	1/		281. 5
		3/	412.10.0						3166. 5.
100	Bls Salt	2/6	12.10.		375	Acrs. Clovr	@ 20/		375. 0.
330	Gallns Rum	2/	33.		375	Do Do	Do		375.
			£1232. 3.0						3916. 5.
750	Bls Irish Pots. seed	1/	37.10.0						
3750	lbs. of Clovr seed	@ 8d.	125.						
			1394.13.0						

a Fifth Statement

	Dr.						Cr.			

for

						By				
375	Bls of B. Wht for Mane		£ 37.10.0		5625	bushls Corn	@ 3/		£ 843.
125	do do for a Crop		12.10.0		5625	do of Pots.	1/		281. 5.
125	do of Rye do @ 3/		18.15.0		1875	do of Rye	3/		281. 5.
125	do Pease do 4/		25. 0.0		625	do Pease	4/		125.
375	do Wheat 5/		93.15.0		3750	do Wheat	5/		937.10.
750	do Barley 3/6		131.15.0		4500	do Barley	4/		787.
3750	lbs. Clovr Seed @ 8d.		125. 0.0		750	do B: Wht	2/		112.10.
3120	Bls Corn for Neg[roe]s	3/	468.						3367.10.
2750	do Rye for Hos.	3/	412.10.0		375	Acres in Clor	20/		375.
100	do Salt	2/6	12.10.0		375	Do Do	do		375.
330	Gallns Rum	2/	33.10.0						4117.10.
750	Bls Poto Seed	1/	37.10.						
			1408. 5.						

Work for Hooes at the Plantn about 55 exclusive of Plown.

				days
Corn	375 Acs	to plant wch will require abt		12
		replant	ditto	6
		Hoeing	ditto 1st time	12.
		Ditto	Ditto 2d time	12
Pease	75 acs	hilled		6
		Wed 1st time		5

		Do 2 do	5
		Do 3 do	5
Tobaco	36 Acs	Hilled—large & well 4 feet distance	5
		Plantd in May	2
		replanted Do	1
		Weeding Do in June	4
		Ditto do July	4.
		Ditto Do Augt	4
		Ditto the Beds at sundry times	4
		Warming & Succouring Do	5.
Scarcity	8 acs	Planting	1
		Weeding &ca 3 difft times	3
Pumpions	8 acs	Hilling	1
		Weeding 3 different times	3.
			100

AD, DLC:GW.

For background to this document, see Farm Reports, 6–12 Dec. 1789, source note.

1. A balk is a ridge or strip of ground left unplowed as a boundary between two furrows.

2. Root of scarcity (*Beta vulgaris* or mangel-wurzel) is a coarse beet grown primarily as cattle fodder. For additional information on GW's cultivation of this plant, see *Diaries*, 5:298.

3. A pumpion (pompion) is a large melon or pumpkin.

From Alexander Hamilton

[1789–1795]

Mr Hamilton will with pleasure execute the command of the President by the time appointed and have the honor of waiting upon him.

AL, CtY.

From the Invalid Pensioners of Pennsylvania

[1789]

The Petition of The Subscribers, pensioners According to Act of Congress of 7th June 1785[1] in consequence of wounds and disabilities incurred in the service of the United States during the late war with Great Britain, Most respectfully sheweth,

That your Petitioners have found that the legislature of the

Union at their last session have made a temporary continuation for one year of the pension they had hitherto received from the State of Penna as aforesd and that they have with great propriety left with your ⟨Excely⟩ the mode in which they are to receive it.[2] Your Petitioners represent that many of them, nay all of them are in the greatest distress and want occasioned by the late stoppage of their payments, that many of them are maimed so as to be unable to go any great distance for relief. Your Petitioners therefore beg leave to intreat your Excellency to direct that the benefits aforesaid may be speedily extended to them and that it may be paid to them the State of Pennsylvania where they now are and your petitioners as in duty bound will every *pray*.[3]

LS, DNA:PCC, item 78. This letter was signed by fifty-four Pennsylvania veterans. Many of them signed by mark.

1. The resolution of the Confederation Congress of 7 June 1785 specified the procedures by which the states "make provision for Officers, soldiers or seamen, who have been disabled in the service of the United States." See *JCC*, 28:435–37.

2. "An Act providing for the payment of the Invalid Pensioners of the United States" provided that invalid pensions "granted and paid by the states respectively" should be "continued and paid by the United States, from the fourth day of March last, for the space of one year, under such regulations as the President of the United States may direct" (1 *Stat.* 95 [29 Sept. 1789]).

3. In January 1790 GW appointed agents for each state to manage the payment of invalid pensions and turned the administration of the matter over to Secretary of the Treasury Alexander Hamilton. See Hamilton to Jedediah Huntington, 30 Jan. 1790, and to John Haywood, 2 Feb. 1790, in Syrett, *Hamilton Papers*, 6:232–33, 240–41. Sharp Delany, collector of the customs at Philadelphia, was appointed agent for Pennsylvania. In July 1790 the arrangements were continued for another year (1 *Stat.* 129–30 [16 July 1790]). A more permanent arrangement was made for invalid pensioners in 1792. Section 2 of "An Act to provide for the settlement of the Claims of Widows and Orphans barred by the limitations heretofore established, and to regulate the Claims to Invalid Pensions" provided that any disabled officer, soldier, or seaman should be placed on the pension list of the United States for life or during the continuation of his disability. Arrangements were also made for existing arrears of pensions (1 *Stat.* 243–45 [23 Mar. 1792]).

To John Jay

Sunday morng [1789–1797]

The President of the United States presents his Compliments to Mr Jay, and informs him that the Harness of the President's

Carriage was so much injured in coming from Jersey that he will not be able to use it today. If Mr Jay should propose going to Church this Morng the President would be obliged to him for a Seat in his Carriage.

L, in the writing of David Humphreys, NNC.

From Michael McDonnell

Sir   Wednesday morning. [1789]
Permit one of the lowest of the people to approach you with every sentiment of Gratitude and Respect which has been, or can be expressed by any individual, or collective Body in the Union. Likewise to intrude upon your patience with a request, which if inconsistent with your inclination to admit, must rely on your well-known candour to pardon the impertinent intrusion.

I am a person Sir of a tolerable English education, and use a pen in the Character you are perusing, (the same Character in which you were frequently addressed by Brigadier General Nixon in the year 1779 and 80) I never possessed an Interest, but thro a variety of misfortunes, and particularly from a variety of maladies, which attended my own person, from June 1784 to April 1787, (during all which time I could not earn a Shilling) myself and small family are reduced to as much poverty as persons can well suffer: and the beforementioned sickness has so much impaired my formerly robust Constitution, that I cannot gain a subsistence by Labour; my only dependence is my Pen, which procures me (but) a scanty subsistence in temporary Schools. During an interval of fifteen Months, in which time Roxbury has been erecting a New Grammar School I have been employed there as a private Teacher, but that being now completed, I have again lost my Bread for no other reason but my Ignorance of the Learned Languages: I can bring from the most respectable Characters that employed me in that Town, such recommendations as I trust will be satisfactory to any gentleman.

I wish for no more than a decent permanent support for myself and little family; but unhappily I have no connexions or acquaintance of sufficient consequences to introduce me into any permanent Business that may offer; so that I am in the same situation with the poor Man at the pool of Bethsaida.

Under these circumstances I am emboldened to look up to yourself, as the real friend of such as struggle for an honest subsistence thro' the difficulties of Life; and if my pen or figures, both which I can use with accuracy and dispatch can be service-able to yourself, or any of the Gentlemen of your Houshold, I am ready to attend your Commands at any time or place: as my family is at present small, my expectations shall ever be circum-scribed by your own Generosity, and my attention to Business shall be unremitted by night or Day.

Waiting with the utmost deferrence and submission for what you may please to communicate upon the subject, I beg leave to conclude with every sentiment of the most profound respect, Sir, Your ever Obedient and Devoted Humble Servant

Michael McDonnell

ALS, DLC:GW.

No further information on McDonnell has been found. It is possible that this is the Michael McDonald who as a lieutenant in the British army, deserted to the American forces and was appointed a lieutenant in the Continental army in March 1777. McDonald served until January 1781 as a private soldier to prevent recognition, and part of his service was in Col. Thomas Nixon's 6th Massachusetts Regiment (Heitman, *Historical Register*, 276).

Washington's Memoranda on Indian Affairs

[1789]

Extracted from the Report of the Proceedings of the Commissioners, appointed to Treat with the Southern Indians.[1]

Cherokees

In a talk sent by Bennet Bellew[2] & Nohtowaky on the 13th of Septr from Savannah, the Cherokees were informed by the Commissioners, that the peculiar circumstances of No. Caro-lina, with respect to the Union, prevented a full communication of Sentiments at that time; but that the Government of the United States were not unmindful of the terms agreed to by the Treaty of Hopewell,[3] & would take every wise measure to carry it into effect; and to convince them of their disposition to be friendly and to do them Justice, as soon as the difficulties which at present existed were removed. They Approved of the truce entered into on the 16th of June, and that by this truce a Treaty had been stipulated to be held as soon as possible—Exhorting them to be strictly attentive to the observance thereof, which they confirm; and had enjoined on the frontier Inhabitants of No. Carolina to abide by.

Chickasaws—and—Choctaws[4]

Were informed at the same time—of the strong friendship of the United States. and of the hope that the Peace which had been made with them at Hopewell on the Keowee on the 10th of Jany 1786 will last forever. Of the recovering & growing State of the U. States since the War—of their New form of Government—and increase of population. Of their friendly dispositions towards the red men, & determination to do them Justice—approvg of their conduct since the treaty of Hopewell & hopg that they are satisfied with ours. Expect the same open and friendly part will always be observed—assurg them that their interests will always be near our hearts—and that in conformity to the 8th article of the Treaty with them, the United States will, as soon as the circumstances may conveniently admit, take measures for extending more fully to them the benefits and comforts arising from a well regulated, & mutually advantas trade.[5]

Treaty—with the—Creeks[6]

The 2d Article proposes the following boundary—viz.— "from where the former line strikes the River Savannah, thence up the said River to a place on the most Northern branch of the same, commonly called the Keowee, where a No. East line to be drawn from the Top of the Occunna Mountain shall intersect, thence along the said line in a South West direction to Tugaloe River, thence to the top of the Currahee Mountain, thence to the head of the most Southern branch of the Oconee River (that is to say the River Apalachy) including all the Water⟨s⟩ of the same, thence down the said River to the confluence of the Okmulgy, thence on a So. Wt direction to the most Southern part of the River Saint Mary, thence down the said River to the old Line."

By the 3d article the Remaining Territory of the Creek Nation was to be solemnly guaranteed to them by the Union—and secured by a line of Posts if necessary.

Article 4th requires that all the Towns & Tribes of this Nation within the limits of the United States; shall acknowledge themselves to be under the protection of them and no other Sovereign whosoever—also that they will not treat with any State, or with Individuals of any State.

Article 5th authorises the Creeks to punish any Settlers on the Guaranteed Lands as they will be put out of the protection of the United States.

Article 6th—Stipulates a free trade between the United States & the Creek Nation—and gives to the latter a secure Post at Brands bluff on the Altamaha, or any other place—and if necessary to protect it by a Company of regular Soldiers. The number of arms, & quantity of Ammunition to be limited to their actual wants.

Article 7th—respects the regulation of the Trade and prevention of abuses.

Article 8th compels the surrender of any Indian who shall commit a Robbery or Murder, or other Capitol offence, on any Citizen of the U. States; that he or they may be punished according to the Laws of the said States in like manner; as a Citizen thereof would be.

Article 9th Provides for the punishment of a Citizen of the United States, who shall be guilty of like Crimes against an Indian—⟨this⟩ is to be by the Laws of the United States—and in the presence of some of the Creeks, if any will attend.

Article 10th No punishment to be inflicted on the innocent under the idea of retaliation.

Article 11th Property to be restored—and all Prisoners to be set at liberty.

Article 12th Notice of any hostile Intentions of any tribe, or person whosoever, against the Peace, Trade and interest of the United States, is to be given.

Article 13th All animosities for past grievances shall henceforth cease, and the contracting Parties will carry the foregoing treaty into full effect.

The first article of this *proposed* treaty only declared that there should be perpetual Peace between the Citizen⟨s⟩ of the United States, and all the Towns, Tribes and Individuals of the Upper and lower Creeks.

Objections by the Creeks[7]

That they are not entirely satisfied with all parts of the talk particularly with the proposed boundary as marked out. and that it was McGillivray's decision to let the matter stand as it was, for the present, The Chiefs should take care to prevent ev[er]y act of hostility or depredation on the part of the Warriors during the Winter, and until they heard farther from the Commissioners on the part of the United States.

From this resolution, there was no departure on the part of McGillivray, but the Kings & Chief men in a speech made by the White Bird repeated the assurances of their endeavors to preserve Peace: & that if their people do not observe these orders, they shall be siezed and sent down to the Whites.

McGillivray in his last communication—dated Ockmulgee 27th Sep. 1789[8]—says that, in full & free conversation, which he had had with Colo. Humphreys he had signified his expectations "that ample & full justice should be given in restoring to the Indians the Incroachments complained of, in which the Oconee Lands were included"—but finding "that there was no such intention & that a restitution of territory hunting grds was not to be the basis of a Treaty of Peace between the two Nations, he had resolved to return home, referring the matter in full Peace till next Spring[9]—We (the Creeks) sincerely desire a Peace, but cannot sacrafice much to obtain it."

McGillivray is called upon in a letter from the Commrs dated Septr 28th to attend in person, or by his Agent, or Agents, at Augusta the enquiry into the validity of former treaties[10]—Is promised a safe-guard—and called upon in decided terms to prevent all Acts of hostilities against the Settlement of Cumberland River where Murders & Robberies have been committed by them tho' they can have no pretence for doing it.

State of Georgia

The Governor of it, in answer to a request of the Comrs; among other information given, says "that the Lands between the Mountains and the old Ogeeche line, North of the Oconee, were ever equally claimed by the Cherokees and Creeks; and that by a Convention had before the Revolution, the Lands comprehended within the limits afterwards called the ceded Lands, & now Wilkes County, were ceded, at the same time, by the heads of the two Nations—That at the close of the War, these Nations were respectively called upon to make satisfaction for their alternate attacks during the progress of it—That both, having avowed their claim to the Lands in question, agreed to, and signed Treaties of relinquishment the first, that is the Cherokees in the Spring and the latter in autumn of the year 1783.[”][11]

General Pickens

Was sent from Augusta with a second talk to the Cherokees exhorting them to be cautious in listening to bad men—and informing them of the promises of the Creeks to conduct themselves peaceably.[12]

Commissioners

are decidedly of opinion that the failure of the Treaty at this time with the Creek Nation can be attributed only to their principal chief Mr McGillivray.[13] 1st From the repeated declaration of the Kings-head men & warriors of their wishes to establish a permanent Peace. 2d from the proposed boundary being offered to the Great Council of the Nation only as the Basis of amicable Negotiation. 3d from the deception & precipitate retreat of McGillivray without stating his objections to the draught of a treaty either verbally or in writing. 4th From enquiries & his own declarations, that without obtaining a full equivalent for the Sacrafice he would not renounce the close connexion which he has formed with the Spanish government in the hour of distress—a connexion honourable & lucrative to himself, and advantageous to the Crk Nation.

5th From his frequent Intimations that no Treaty could be formed unless a free & exclusive Port should be granted to him upon the Altamaha or the River St Mary. And 6th from the most positive refusal to acknowledge the Creek Nation to be within the limits, or under the Protection of the United States, although in express contradiction to a former letter written by him on the 5th of Septr 1785 to General Pickens.

The Commissioners are moreover of Opinion that the Treaties of Augusta, Shoulderbone & Galphinston are valid, having been made in as formal & full a manner as Treaties with uncivilized people usually are made and that the disputed lands were fairly purchased from the lower Creeks to whom of right they did belong as their hunting ground & for which a valuable consideration was given &

Report[14]

That as Mr McGillivray and all the Chiefs &ca of the Creek Nation have given strong assurances in their talks, and by writing that no farther Hostilities or depredations shall be committed on the part of their Nation (—none of Mr Gillivrays writings promise this longer than till the Spring)—and as the Govr of Georgia will issue a Proclamation enjoining the like on the People of that State—That all animosities with the Creek Nation should henceforth cease. That some person should be dispatched to the said Nation with the ultimate draught of a Treaty to establish perpetual Peace & Amity. That when such a draught of a Treaty shall be properly executed by the leading men of the Nation, all the presents intended for the Indians, and now in the State of Georgia should be distributed among them. That if the Indians shall refuse to execute such draught of a treaty. They humbly submit That the Arms of the Union should be called forth for the Protection of the People of Georgia, in the Peaceable & Just possession of their Lands; and in case the Creeks shall commit further Hostilities & depredations upon the Citizens of the United States that the Creek Nation ought to be deemed the Enemies of the U. States & punished accordingly.

Defensive Measures[15]

A Line of Six posts ought to be established on the Frontiers of Georgia, and two at least to guard the Settlements upon the Cumberland River—The Posts to consist of one compleat Company of each, to be covered by works of sufficient strength to resist any sudden impressions of the Indians, and to serve as places of deposit if Magazines should hereafter be formed. To them also the exposed Inhabitants might, in cases of alarm resort. And it would shew how far this kind of Protection wd be adequate.

Stations in Georgia

Should be. one of the navigable Waters of St Mary. One at Beards bluff upon the Ultamaha. One at the Junction of the Oconee & Okmulgee. One at the Rock landing. One at the Middle trading path. And one at the upper Trading path. The two latter at such positions as will be found the most convenient to protect the Frontiers.

Offensive—Plan

If this becomes necessary they recommmend, in that case, the most vigorous and effectual operations by carrying the arms of the Union into the very heart of the Creek Country—The forces necessary on this occasion should consist of Five Regiments of Infantry 700 Men to each Regiment: One Regiment of Cavalry of 500 Men—and a Corps of Artillery of 250 Men—the whole 4250. Two Regiments of Infantry be inlisted from the State of Georgia, So. & North Carolina—The Cavalry from the States of Virginia & Maryland, and the remainder of the forces from the other States indiscriminately.

General Rendezvous

From their best Intelligence, and from observation they think that Augusta ought to be the place. The Military and Quarter Masters Stores might be transported thither from Savannah by water in 15 days—A full supply of waggons can be obtained at no great distance from thence, and upon the Road towards the Ogichee which might bring with them a load of Corn or flour each.

Routs

From Augusta to the Creek Nation is a good one, little more than 200 miles to their first Towns, and about 300 miles to their western Settlements—Two other Routs present themselves; From Beards bluff to Flint River—distance about 150 Miles—and from Flint River to the Cowetas 70 more—From Bryants trading House on Saint Mary's River to the Cowetas is nearly the same as from Beards-bluff.

Navigation

Is good from the Ocean to Beards-Bluff and to Bryants Trading house from either of them a tolerable good waggon Road may be had into the Creek Nation; Yet both of these Routs, particularly while the Boats shall be going up the River St Mary's or the Altamaha would be attended with considerable embarrassment & Danger to the Troops from the Enemy; and the difficulties and long distance for the Waggons to reach Beards Bluff or Bryants Trading House would be almost insurmountable.

Communications

The Waters of the Mobile are Navigable for large Boats, the one branch 270 Miles from the Ocean, to the hiccory settlement where Mr McGillevray resides; and the Western branches about 320 Miles into the Choctaw & Chicasaw Countries & within 50 Miles of the great bent of the Tennesee. The Waters of the Apalachicola, particularly the Flint River & Catahuhee, and the

Waters of the Ultamaha particularly the Rivers Oconee & Okmulgee are navigable for Boats some hundred miles. From the Northern navigable Streams of these Rivers to the Southern navigable Waters of the Tennesee, there are no established Portages, but the Country is level; good Roads might easily be made, & the greatest distances not more than one hundd miles.

Nature of the Country

The Country of the lower Creeks and Siminolies is Level, Sandy & Piney; the Country of the upper Creeks much broken, with a good Soil and growth; farther to the Westward and even to the Missisipi the lands are rich & rather low & Marshy, abounding with good streams of water & excellent Timber, such as the Oak, hiccory, Bucks eye, Elm & large Gum &ca &ca.

Numbers of the Indian Nations

In the Creek Nation the Number of Warriors are estimated at 4,500—Armed pretty generally with good Rifles—get their Ammunition in presents from the Spaniards. The lower Creeks & Siminolies are about equal to the upper Creeks—the number of Siminolies less than that of the lower Creeks. Old men, women & Children are about 4 times the number of the Warriors. About 80 Towns in the whole, of very different magnitudes; about 45 of which are in the upper Country. The mother Towns have the principal direction in their National Affairs, that is to say, the War Towns in War—& the White Towns (wch have never been stained with blood and are towns of refuge) in peace—The Cherokee Warriors are *supposed* to amount to about 600—The Chicasaws to about 700—And the Choctaws to about 3000 and the old men women & Children in the Proportion abovementioned—The Cherokees & Chicasaws cultivate the ground more than other Indians & possess cattle proportionally in greater numbers—The Choctaws hunt only, are a brave & hardy people in the woods, but indolent to a great degree in the Woods—The Creeks are in a great Measure Hunters; however they cultivate some Indian Corn & Potatoes, possess Cattle & horses & a few Slaves & lately in some instances have introduced the Plow.

Influencial Characters

Mr Alexr McGillivray (a half breed) is the most influencial of all the Creeks—among the upper Creeks the White Lieutenant has the ascendency, and in some respects is considered as the rival of McGillivray. The Mad Dog is next in authority. Among the lower Creeks the Hallowing King & the Cussitah King (the former commandg the War Towns, & the latter the white towns) the Tellessee King, the White bird King, the Tal King, The King of the Siminolies and the King of the Euchees are among the first.

Government

A kind of qualified Monarchy—In the Towns are head men who are respected & have authority in Peace & War—In Districts they have Kings as Chiefs and Warriors—the former have the Influence in time of Peace, and the latter in time of War—Upon all important occasions they meet in great Council and deliberate with freedom, particularly once a year, at the ceremony of the *first fruit*, called the *Busking* when they punish great Delinquents, regulate internal policy, and form plans for hunting or War the ensuing year.

Hunting

Of late years they are not rigidly confined to particular Districts for hunting, but are permitted to go in small parties throughout the whole Nation—yet pretty generally they find it convenient to keep within their respective divisions.

Furs & Skins

Bever, Otter, Mink, Fox, Squirrel & some others—Deer and other Skins—amounting annually to somewhat more than £10,000 Sterling—They are principally sold to the Indian Traders *in* the Nation and exported through the Spanish Settlements. The amount of the European Goods annually consumed is about £12,000 Sterling furnished principally by the House of which McGillivray is a Partner. These are the Exports & Imports of the Creek Nation.

Ginsang

Abounds in the Creek Country; but is not yet gathered in any considerable quantity.

Connexion with the Spaniards

Arises, it is supposed, principally in paying less duties upon Indian Goods imported than the Spaniards themselves pay—By a guarantee of their (the Creeks) Country—and by Military distinctions and presents to Mr McGillivray & other considerable Chiefs—yet it is not believed that they are warmly attached to the Spaniards & would break with them if better terms were offered by the United States.

Recommendation

To preserve the attachment of the several Indian Nations bordering on the U. States, it appears expedient that some adequate means of supplying them with Goods & Ammunition at moderate prices should immediately be adopted and some uniform Plan of granting permits to those who may be employed in the Indian Commerce should be established by the Supreme Authority of the U. States—This would be a part of the duty imposed upon the Superintendant, Agent or Commissary of Indian Affairs in the Southern Department. The fees of office for Granting such permits ought to be moderate, & might be applied towards the payment of Salary. An expedient of this sort is highly necessary to prevent persons of bad character from defraudg the Indns—from making still more unfavourable impressions upon the inimical Tribes—and from Alienating the affections of the friendly Tribes from the United States. This Superintendant by going through the Indian Towns of all the differ[en]t Nations would be able to collect such information as might be extremely useful in forming definite Plans of Trade with those People and in case of War with the Creek Nation—of solid advantages in bringing the Choctaws and Chicasaws to co-operate with the Arms of the U. States.

Accounts

Of the expences of the Commissioners are lodged with the Secretary of the Treasury—The Books No. 1 & 2 deposited in the War Office contain Invoices of all the Articles delivered to the Commissioners for the proposed Treaty, and will acct for the whole of them, by ascertaining the articles which were necessarily expended—and those which now remain in the State of Georgia.

Messrs Pickens and Osborne were called upon to know what was become of certain Goods which were left by the Commissioners after the Treaty of Hopewell in 1786—and for an acct of the Expenditure of monies or goods which may have been recd by them of the States of South Carolina and Georgia. The latter they complied with—but, knew of no Goods left at Hopewell.[16]

All Papers relative to the Mission of the Commrs are lodged in the War Office.

Extracts of Letters from Sundry persons
residing in Kentucky. and other parts
of the Westn Country
Saml McDowell—Chairmn of a Comee
29th July 1789[17]

Writes by order of a Committee which was appointed by the Convention, then sitting to fix, or to decide upon the propriety of forming a New & Seperate State. which Comee was to lay before the Convention at its next meeting what they had done in the matter.

Complains, that in consequence of the dismission of the Scouts by the Govr of Virginia, agreeably to the desire of the President of the United States; their Frontiers were much exposed. that from the extent of them, & the Stations of the Federal Troops, no means can be used for the safety of the People & their property.

That before the Govr of the Western Territory & the Commander of the Federal Troops can be called upon, Murders & robberies are not only committed, but the perpetrators of them beyond the reach of interception or chastisement—whereas if Scouts were kept up they would give timely notice of the danger either to prevent it, or to recover the Prisoners and property that is taken off.

Without such Scouts he thinks the Frontiers of Kentucky will be deprived of security—break up—and the people reduced to the most distressing situation.

Assures, that the Militia of Kentucky from their hardiness alertness & bravery are able to render essential Service to the Inhabitants of the District if they are employed in its defence.

Declares that from the present Stations of the Federal Trps it is absolutely impossible for them (if their numbers were adequate) to render them any service whatever.

Sends a list of the Killed wounded & Prisoners between the 1st of May & date of his letter (29th July)[18]—amounting in the County of Jefferson to 13 killed 5 Wounded & 6 taken prisoners. above 20 horses taken. County of Nelson—2 killed, 2 Wounded & abt 20 horses taken—County of Lincoln—2 killed 2 Wounded abt 25 hs taken Madison County 1 Wounded & a number of horses taken—Bourbon County 2 Wounded & abt 15 horses stolen. Mason County 2 killed & 41 horses stolen.

Woodford County 1 killed and several horses stolen. In all 20 killed—12 Wounded—& 6 Prisoners—121 horses enumerated besides many not ascertd.

Adds that, there is the greatest reason to believe that the Creek Indians did very considerable Mischief in the County of Lincoln in the month of June last.

Encloses a list of Indians Tribes not included in the late Treaty. viz.—No. Wt of Kentucky—Shawanees, Twitchtwees or Picts, Piankeshaws, Kickapoos, Kaskaskies, Wiogtenons, Waweogtenons, Motuckons, Masquaques & a banditti from several Nations now living on the heads of Sandusky, Scioto, & the Miamees of Lake Erie & Ohio.

To the Southward of Kentucky are—The Creeks, Chickamagas & all other Tribes of the Cherokees—Choctaws & Chicasaws.

Danl Smith—Miro District on Cumberland
River—North Carolina.
23d Augt 1789[19]

Introduces Piemingo (or Mountain Leader) the principal War Chief of the Chicasaw Nation. gives his character, & that of his Nation as being friendly to the United States. Mentions the circumstance of Colo. Clarkes beginning a settlement on the Missisipi River just below the Mouth of Ohio in the Chicasaw Country, by order of the State of Virginia, in the year 1780, without consulting these People—the hostile conduct of them in consequence, compelled an abandonment of it. Cumberland Settlement began the year before—much annoyed by the Creeks, Cherokees & a small tribe of the Delawares then living on the Tenesee. In the year 1782 the Chicasaws made a Treaty with ⟨Genl⟩ Donaldson & Genl Martin, Commrs from the State, and kept it faithfully ever since—Have been ill treated by the Creeks & Cherokees for not joining with them to commit hostilities against the White People ⟨this⟩ & the neglect with which they have been treated by us has occasioned *some* of their Chiefs to waver in their attachment—The Mountain Leader, however, has always been steady in his friendship towards us[20]—He, from some late ill treatment which his Nation has recd from the Creeks, meditates in conjunction with the Choctaws, a War with them; & therefore applies for Ammunition, reminding the States of the Treaty of Hopewell by an article of which a Store was to be established on the Tenesee & a regular Trade promoted—Without these supplies, the Chicasaws & Choctaws may be over-run & forced to join the Creeks—Recommends one Fry, the Chicasaw Interpreter, but not from any knowledge he has of the Mans person or character but because he is the only one in the Cumberland settlemt (where he has not been long) who has any tolerable knowledge of the Chicasaw Language. Thinks there is the highest probability that No. Carolina will adopt the Constitution—& that the Bill called the Cession Bill will be revived, by which the western Territory of that State will be ceded to the U. States[21]—In either case he hopes for better protection having been neglected by No. Carolina they look up now to the Genl Government & hope not to look in vain—Sends a list of the Injuries ⟨sus⟩tain⟨ed⟩ by the Inhabitants of Cumberland River from the 1st of May until the 20th of August. amounting to 25 killed and 8 wounded & the number of Horses taken considerable.

Smith from his Writing is sensible.

George Muter, Saml McDowell, Caleb Wallace,
Harry Innes, George Nicholas, Christophr Greenup,
Benja. Sebastian, James Brown, William McDowell,
Thos Barber & Wm Kennedy[22]

Recommend Piemingo or Mountain Leader as a Chief of the Chicasaws applying for supplies of Ammunition for the use of his Nation; who from its friendly conduct towards the People of the United States, are at enmity with, and expect an attack from the Creeks. The Chicasaws they say are at present unconnected with both Spaniards & English, & have no chance ⟨*illegible*⟩ supplies from either, without becoming dependent on the Spaniards, or joining the Creeks, and thence forward more than probably enemies to the U. States. They add, that they are daily suffering from the Incursions of the Creeks; and have every reason to expect that they will be continued—that they have further reason to believe, if the Chicasaws can obtain a supply of Amn, they will cut out work for the former at home—and submit whether this will not be the most effectual, as well as the cheapest mode of retaliating—They are decidedly of opinion that some change should take place in the manner of conducting Indian Affairs in the Western Country.

Jos. Martin—from Long Island of Holstein

Says (in his Letter dated the 25th of Septr 1789)[23] that on the 27th of August an Express had arrived to him from the Chicasaw Nation with 4 strings of White Beads from Piemingo & other Chiefs of that nation requesting his advice & assistance in carrying on a War with the Creek Indians—but having no powers to do this he had sent on their talks to the Comrs who were to treat with the Creeks the 15th of Septr—It was unanimously agreed (he says) between the Chicasaws & Choctaws that Piemingo should come in person with four others to lay their grievances before the Presidt of the U. States.

He states the claim of John Brown to Lands on the Savannah opposite to Augusta—this merits consideration.

Mentions his own case, by way of exculpation against charges—which he says—were unjustly alledged[24]—and adds that if there should be any commands for him, they may after the 10th of Octr and until the beginning of Feby meet him in Henry County Virginia.

From—Piamingo—Richmond 30th Octr[25]

Mentions the long friendship which has subsisted between the United States & his Nation, the Chicasaws. the distressed Situation it is in for want of Ammunition. His having set out on a journey for the Seat of Federal Governmt to solicit a supply— But the delays he had met with and the temporary aid he had obtained from the State of Virga had determined him to return, least his people might be distressed—2000 lbs. of powder & Lead equivalent having been furnished him. The Creek Indians attack his people as well as ours; but he wishes not to fight with them if they will make satisfaction & give assurances of good behaviour in future; however, he requests & entreats that they may be furnished with powder & Ball against the Spring, as then the War must become general with the Creeks, unless they will listen to reason. *Their* Nation he says depends upon the U. States—The Choctaws seem friendly, & will be consulted by him on his return. Refers to Genl Lincoln & the Commrs whom he saw at Richmond—gives strong assurances that he will hold me by the right hand of friendship; and requests in strong terms that I will speedily send a letter to him expressive of what he may depend upon.

Papers from Genl Harmer
From the General himself—dated 19th Oct. 1789.[26]

The River Ohio has been very low, but is gradually rising. Understands that another Expedition *has* gone forward from Kentucky against the Wabash Indians—the result had not come to his knowledge.[27] Wishes for explicit & particular directions how to Act with the inhabitants of Kentucky. These expeditions, he adds, places Majr Hamtramck in a disagreeable situation—expects when headquarters is fixed opposite to Licking River that frequent applications will be made to him for the few federal he has to countenance and aid them in their operations, and that censure will fall on him if they are refused. By his last Accts from Licking their works were going on rapidly—The presence of the Governor much wanted.

Lieutt Armstrongs Report to Majr Hamtramck
11th June 1789[28]

Embarked from the Rapids of Ohio May 30th with 1 Ensign 1 Cadet and 43 Non Comd Officers & privates—Entered the Wabash on the evening of the 3d (June)—on the 4th & 5th Saw tracts of Indians as he was ascending that River—On the 5th he was joined by a detachment from the Garrison under Majr Hamtramck—on the 6th saw at the grand chain where Indians had been in Ambush—On the 9th (between Coffee Island & the White River) destroyed several Perouges & Bark Canoes & routed two parties of Indians—from appearances at this place the enemy was in force—buried a Soldr who was coming to him express & has been killed by the Indians—On the 11th Joined the Detachment of villagers under Majr Hamtramck not far from Fort Knox. He met no unexpected difficulties in his passage up the River (Wabash)—Thinks the mode of supplying the Garrison under the Majr with Provisions, had better be done altogether by Soldiers—assigns reasons for it—and conceives that the passage from the Ohio may be performed in seven days when undertaken by Soldiers but is no⟨w⟩ done in dble that time by the usual mode.

From Majr Hamtramck at Fort Knox
Post Vincennes—29th July 1789
to General Harmer[29]

Encloses Armstrongs Report—Had sent to the Wabash Indians to cease hostilities—a number of them in consequence had come to him from the Weeya—spoke with a submission rare to be met with among Indians—made a thousand protestations of repentance—& assurances that all parties at War should be called in—and that if their young men refused to live peaceably with us, that they, the Seniors would leave them & come under the protection of the U. States—Supposes their poverty obliges them to make friends with us. Gives his reasons for leaving the Fort & going to meet Lieutt Armstrong—The term for which the Magistrates of Post Vincennes were to serve expired last April—wants directions on this head from the Govr of the Western Territory who had been expected at that Post in June or July. Gives an Acct of the latest advices from New Orleans—copied from Mr Peyroux (who is the Commandant of St Genevieve)[30] and extracted from the Governor General of Louisiana's communications to the Commandants of the Posts on the Missisipi.[31]

The King (of Spain) Permits the Inhabitants of the United States (Vagabonds excepted) to settle on the Lands claimed by him—Will allow them to continue in their religion but not to exercise it in public—all Churches therefore are to be Catholic & served by Priests from Ireland. All effects brought by Emigrants will be free from all taxes of Entrance—The Inhabitants of Fort Pitt, Post Vincennes, Kentucky, Cumberland Kaskaskias, Cahokia and other settlements of the U. States will have liberty to send their productions to New Orleans upon paying a duty of 15 pr Ct. He thinks this duty will be a great obstruction to Morgans Settlemt.[32] In a P.S. to his letter he says, he is this momt informed that the People of Kentucky are going on an Expedition agt the Wabash Indians[33]—That he has recd fresh assurances from the Weeya Indians of their friendly dispositions and as a proof of it, had sent in one Deserter & promised to apprehend and send in another a Corporal—That a number of Indians were coming to the Village but that the Expedition from Kentucky will undo every thing—Mortifying it is he add⟨s⟩, to see the Authority of the United States so much insulted.

Majr Hamtramck to Genl Harmer

14th Augt 1789[34]

The Expedition from Kentucky, alluded to in the above Letter, consisted he says of 220 men who have gone near the Weeya, killed 12 Indians, and all this great Campaign performed in 16 days. Calls it a provocative, being well persuaded that they will pay for it, & perhaps the village of Vincennes some Americans of which were with the Kentuckians—If those people are to be taken notice of he (Hamtramck) is ready to execute the orders—again repeating his mortification at Seeing the authority of the Union so much disregarded. The other Deserter (a Corporal) has been brot to him by the Weeya Indians—Many people were gone and about going to the Spanish side from the Illinois in consequence of a Resolve of Congress respecting Negroes who, as it was reported (particularly by Mr Morgan) were free—this he had contradicted[35]—If the Governor or Judges does not go into these parts this year most of the people will go to the Spanish side—They are very sickly at the Post of Vincennes—A Mr Jones[36] writes him from Kaskaskies that strict orders are arrived at St Louis from New Orleans to prevent all Trade or Correspondence between them & Michilimakinac and the Eastern parts of the Missisipi on pain of having their whole property confiscated—but *he* does not give it as certain.

From the same—to the same
17th August 1789[37]

A man who was taken prisoners by the Indians had Just arrived at Post Vincennes from Detroit and reports that the British were about to build a Fort on their side of the River—that 500 Canadians were expected from Canada to build it, and that the Courts of Justice were no more held on our side of the River—One Mr Yourd writes from Detroit that 50 Artificers were arrived from Canada to build & repair the vessels, that a number of Sea Officers & men had also arrived. The Shawanese who are on the other side of the Missisipi might be brot to our side—Mr Vigo can tell how that is.[38]

Ensign McDowell—to—Genl Harmer
Falls of Beaver 3d Octr 1789[39]

When he set out he intended going as far as the Lake, but did not—returned from Mahoning—From the information (but this he ought to have obtained himself) of Majr Finley which agrees with Indian Accts he thinks thier is no useful navigation in Beaver Creek.[40] Many Indians have past by the Falls of Beaver for Fort Pitt the month past—& many Delawares & some Taways are Encamped & Hunting on that Creek. Has not been able to get any aid from Detroit that can be depended on.

His 2d Letter of the same date[41]

Waiting for a guide, he was prevented setting out in a Canoe from the Falls of Beaver till the Water was too low to go in one— The Rapids or Falls of Beaver are about 3 Miles long—the Channel exceeding full of Rocks—in some places scarcely any water to be seen above them—several smaller rapids above them—the general depth of water in these places is about eight inches until he passed Shenango branch (which is about 12 Ms above this—afterwards about 4 Inches—The banks are high— the Soil Sandy, & in most places Stoney—the distance from this (Falls of Beaver) to Mahony by water is about 70 or 75 Miles— From Mahony to standing stone on a branch of Cayahoga is about 18 or 20 Miles—from thence to old Town 12 Miles & Country midling level but in places swampy—Boats have been brought up near to said Town in high Water but at no other time—There are a number of small rapids in this stream (Cayahoga)—these with a quantity of fallen trees which lye in the Channel obstructs the navigation very much—these obstructions continue until within 7 or 8 Miles of the Lake—The distance from old Town to the Lake by water is about 60 Miles and half that distance by Land—The Banks are not high, the Country midling level and a number of small Glades along the River. He cannot say how far these waters may be navigable at particular seasons—but the Beaver has not had water sufficient for a loaded Canoe one mile from the mouth these 4 weeks.

From the Cty Lieutt of Harrison
to the Govr of the Westn Territy
4th October 1789[42]

Supposes from the Accts he has seen & recd that he is empowered to take under his protection sundry Counties to the Westward & is to be applied to in cases of hostilities & danger— applies for Instructions—Informs that on the 19th of Septr a party of Indians killed 4 persons & captivated 4 others (the family of a certain Willm Johnson) within 9 miles of Clarkesburgh—on the 22 killed Jno. Mauks's wife and two of his Children—about the same time they burnt several Houses and stole a number of Horses from the said County—refers to Captn Carpenter for particulars. Assures him that the people of that County are much alarmed. Is of opinion that unless something more than Treaties are made it will be difficult to prevent an evacuation—He has ordered out 6 Scouts, and has had a few rangers employed—these are now discharged but the Scouts are continued—wishes orders for their continuance until the winter sets in severe. with an addition of two more Scouts & assurance of pay—Virga he says has always allowed 5/. pr day & he thinks they cannot be obtained for less. thinks not less than *eight* Scouts can cover that part of the County—about *Six* for Randolph County this Fall.

Morgans—Genl Directions for
laying out & setling his Lands
in the Spanish Territory[43]

His Meridional lines are to be 5 Miles apart—and his East and West lines two miles apart. the latter are to run from the River Missisipi to the River St Francis—The first Meridional line shall be run from the middle range (or E. & W. line) at [   ] Miles from the bank of the Missisipi—the 2d five more westerly & so on. All lines or ranges shall be strongly marked. Before any line shall be run every Instrument shall be compared with & rectified to a standard—so in like manner shall the Chains be—and the Surveyors shall note—in short—every thing, over & near to which the lines shall pass—make drawings of every Beast, Bird, Fish insect &ca—describe all Trees plants &ca not common in Pensylvania—for neglect of these things, or any of them, will be dismissed. Each Surveyor to have his choice of any tract of Land in either of the ranges he shall run, after Colo. Israel Shrieve had made choice, of a District not exceeding 40 square miles[44]— After Colo. Shrieve shall have declared his option in writing to the Secretary or his Deputy, & the Surveyors present have made theirs, Mr Peter Light is to make his choice of 40 square Miles for himself & Associates.[45] Colo. Shrieve &ca is to have one City & 1 out Lot gratis for each Farm paying only one for each Patent—The Surveyors may take up one or more Tracts of 40 square Miles for themselves & their associates & they will have them in the order they apply. The application for any tract of Land shall be To Col. George Morgan—96 Mexican Dollars is to be paid for each Sqr mile on receiving a Patent for each Farm— Surveyers shall be entitled to sell the Farms to any persons and at any price and shall moreover be entitled to one City & 1 out lot gratis for each farm they so engage payg 1 Dollar for each patent[.] Any Hunter, Chain Carrier, Marker, Horse master or other attendant on the Surveyors shall be entitled to a single tract of Land in the order they give in their names, that is to say, the first applier shall have the preference in any Range he assists in running provided the same is not pre-engaged as above mentd—Next to these, all persons going down in his employment either labourers or Artificers shall have one Farm each— The first 600 persons applying for City & Out-lots, who shall build and reside thereon one whole year, or place a family who shall so reside shall have one City lot of half an Acre and one out lot of 5 acres gratis paying only 1 Dollar for each Patent. All the other City & Out Lots will be reserved for Sale—40 Lots of half an Acre each will be reserved for Public uses—two Lots of 12 Acres each laid out and reserved for ever—viz.—one for the King, and 1 for the Public Walks—to be ornamented &ca under the direction of the Chief Magistrate of the City for the time being—There shall be a reserve of one acre at each angle of Intersection of public Roads or highways throughout the whole territory according to the plan laid down for settlement of the Country by which means no farm house can be more than two miles from one of these reserves which are made for ever for the following uses—viz.—the No. Et angle for the use of a School— the No. Wt angle for a Church—the So. Wt angle for the use of the Poor of the District—and the So. Et for the use of the King—In laying out the City all the Streets shall be at right angles & 4 rods wide including the foot paths which shall be 15 feet wide & shall be raised 12 or 15 Inches above the road—all the Squares shall be of the same dimensions if possible—viz.— extending from Et to Wt 80 rods—& from No. to So. 12 perches; so that each square shall contain Six acres, which shall be subdivided by Meridional lines into 12 lots—The middle Street shall be a continuation of the middle range or road, extending from the Missisipi River & shall be called King Street or middle Street—The space between the Eastmost square and the River shall be at least 100 feet at any place from the present bank of the River, to be kept open for ever for the security of health, & the pleasure of the Inhabitants. The Streets to be numbered from Kings Street as follow—viz.—those to the Northward of Kings Street running East & West—first No. Street, 2d No. Street & so on reckoning from Kings Street— those to the Southward of Kings Street running as above first

So. Street, 2d South Street & ca reckoning as above from King Street—& those running No. & So. shall be distinguished by the names of first River Street, 2d River Street & so on reckoning the space between the Eastmost Squares & the River as first or front River Street—The lots of each square shall be numbered from the above space fronting the River—the East most lot of each square being No. 1 and so on to the West most lot of the whole City. The lots No. 1 on each Side of Kings Street are given for ever to the Citizens as market places. The two lots No. 13 on each side of Kings Street are given for ever to the Citizens— viz.—that on the So. side for a Roman Catholic School—and that on the No. side for a Roman Catholic Church. the lots No. 13 in the 5th No. Street are given for ever to the Citizens—that on the So. Side for an Episcopal School—and that on the No. Side for an Episcopal Church—The two lots No. 13 in the 5th South Street are given for ever to the Citizens—that on the So. Side for a Presbyterian School and that on the No. side for a Presbyterian Church—The two lots No. 13 in the 10th No. Street are given forever to the Citizens—that on the So. side for a German Lutheran School and that on the No. side for a German Lutheran Church—The two lots No. 13 in the 15th No. Street are given for ever to the Citizens—that on the So. Side for a German Calvanist School—& that on the No. Side for a German Calvanist Church—In like manner the two lots No. 13 in every 5th No. Street througout the City shall be reserved and given for Churches & Schools to be governed by such religious denominations as shall settle in New Madrid on their respective plans. All these are to be part of the 40 given as mentioned before. Every landing upon the River opposite to the City shall be equally free for all persons—regulated, however, by the Police—No trees in any Street of the City, nor in any Road throughout the Country shall be injured or cut down but under the direction of the Majestrate of the Police or an Officer of his appointment. The banks of the Missisipi throughout the Territory including a space of 4 rods in breadth shall be a high way & kept open for ever as such—The Trees growing threon shall not be injured nor cut down but in manner aforesaid. No white-man who professes himself a Hunter shall be permitted to reside in this Territory—or one who shall make a practice of killing game without bring the meat to his own family—to New Madrid—or to some other Market—This regulation is intended for the preservation of the game—and for the benefit of the Neighbouring Indians—No person is to be concerned in a contraband Trade on any Acct. Every person having permission to settle in this Territory may be allowed to bring with him his family, Servants, Slaves and effects of every kind—but not to export any part thereof deemed contraband (—care will be taken to define what is contraband—) to any other part of his Majestys Dominions—Every Navigable River througout the Territory shall be deemed a highway and no obstruction shall be placed therein for the emolument of any person whatsoever.

Troops in the Western Territory.

1st October 1789.

Fort Harmer	Non Commissd & Privs.		130
Miame	Do	Do	177
Falls of Ohio	Do	Do	65
Post Vincennes	Do	Do	89
			461
Artillery—difft places		viz.	
Miame		67	
Vincennes		65	132
Total Infantry & Artillery			593

From Arthur Campbell Esquire to
the Secretary at War—25th Oct. 1789[46]

The last accts from the Southward indicate hostile intentions in the Creeks. His present design is to let the President of the U. States know that if war is the alternative that on a short notice a Regiment of choice Men raised in the Holstein Valley (a part of the Western Waters) will be ready to obey his orders in reducing the Refractory Southern Tribes—It is a favourable opportunity to fight our Indian enemies with their own Weapons—gaining the confidence of Piemingo will be a great point gained—Has just heared that two men & a woman are killed within the limits of Carolina—adjoing the State of Virga.

From the same—to—the same
14th Novemr 1789[47]

Since McGillivrays return from the Treaty he has sent agents to the several adjoining Indian Nations—those to the Cherokees affect much Secresy; but he has understood from a friendly

Indian Woman that the purport of the Mission is to form a Confederacy, to attack the white People early next Spring. He has an intelligent Corrispondent in the Indian Country who will watch their motions & endeavor to pry into their Councils and should any thing important occur it shall be forwarded by the first safe conveyance.

AD, DLC:GW.

1. For the appointment of Benjamin Lincoln, Cyrus Griffin, and David Humphreys commissioners to the southern tribes, see GW's instructions to the commissioners, 29 Aug. 1789, source note. For the negotiations of the commissioners during their trip south in September and October, see David Humphreys to GW, 21, 26, 27 Sept., 13, 28 Oct. 1789, Alexander Hamilton to GW, 20 Oct. 1789, and Henry Knox to GW, 18 Oct., 21, 27 Nov. 1789. On 17 Nov. after their return from their southern journey, the commissioners submitted a lengthy account in the form of a journal of their negotiations with the southern tribes. The report was sent to GW by Henry Knox on 21 November. The abstracts of the material through the commissioners' opinion on the treaties of Augusta, Shoulderbone, and Galphinton on p.473 were made by GW from this report. For the complete text of the report, see *DHFC*, 2:210–36; *ASP, Indian Affairs*, 1:68–78.

2. For the text of this talk, see *DHFC*, 2:213–14. For Bennet Ballew, see the Cherokee Nation to GW, 19 May 1789, n.3.

3. See the Cherokee Chiefs to GW, 19 May 1789, n.1.

4. The text of this speech is printed in *DHFC*, 2:214–15.

5. Article 8 of the Treaty of Hopewell provided: "It is understood that the punishment of the innocent under the idea of retaliation, is unjust, and shall not be practiced on either side, except where there is a manifest violation of this treaty; and then it shall be preceded first by a demand of justice, and if refused, then by a declaration of hostilities" (Kappler, *Indian Treaties*, 2:10).

6. On 24 Sept. at a meeting on the Oconee River with the Creek emissaries including Alexander McGillivray, the commissioners presented the assembled chiefs with a draft treaty between the United States and the tribes. For the text of the draft treaty, see *DHFC*, 2:223–25.

7. This statement, delivered to the commissioners on 25 Sept., was signed by McGillivray (ibid., 225–26).

8. For the text of this letter, see ibid., 229.

9. McGillivray also stated that "many of the Principals having gone hunting, nothing farther can now be done. I am very unwell and cannot return."

10. For the text, see ibid., 229–30. GW quoted only part of this letter. The commissioners had prefaced their request for McGillivray's return with the following: "We are extremely sorry that you would neither give us your objections to our Propositions for forming a Treaty; nor propose such terms as would be acceptable to the Creek Nation, if acceded to by us. Col. Humphreys asserts, that he neither told or intimated to you, that we had offered any Articles in our project of a Treaty, as an Ultimatum. All our Proceedings evince

the same thing. You could not avoid having understood from our Letter of the 25th (which you received previous to your departure from the Oconee, and which you have not yet answered) that we were desirous of receiving the Terms upon which you & the Chiefs of the Creek Nation would enter into a Treaty with us. You will also be pleased to recollect, that we expressed at the same time an earnest hope and expectation that they would not separate without giving us this satisfaction.

"These Overtures on our part clearly indicated that we were disposed to make a Peace, upon any Conditions, not incompatible with the Dignity & Justice of the United States. Our last Letter to you of the 26th. explained our Ideas & wishes, if possible, still more unequivocally; and informed you, that if you should depart without our having an opportunity of enquiring into the validity of former Treaties, and fully discussing the whole Business, it could not be considered in any other point of light than a refusal to establish Peace upon any terms whatever. Your not having done this, leaves it only in our Power to return and report a state of Facts to the Supreme Executive of the United States. To obtain still farther information, we shall remain until Monday of next week, at Augusta."

11. The commissioners wrote George Walton, governor of Georgia, on 2 Oct. 1789, informing him that they had not been successful in securing a treaty of peace with the Creek. On 3 Oct. they wrote again asking the governor for information concerning the circumstances under which the treaties of Augusta, Galphinton, and Shoulderbone had been negotiated (*DHFC*, 2:231–32). The governor's reply is in ibid., 232–33.

12. Andrew Pickens, a frequent negotiator with the southern tribes, was sent by the commissioners with a message to the Cherokee. For the message, see ibid., 234.

13. These statements come from the commissioners' journal (ibid., 235).

14. The following statements are from the commissioners' journal (ibid., 235–36).

15. This material, as far as the words "in the State of Georgia" on p. 477, is taken from the commissioners' letter to Henry Knox 20 Nov. 1789 (ibid., 236–40).

16. The commissioners' letter to Andrew Pickens and Henry Osborne was dated 26 Sept. 1789. Pickens and Osborne's reply is also dated 26 Sept. (ibid., 240–41).

17. This letter, addressed to GW and signed by Samuel McDowell, president of the eighth Kentucky Convention, on behalf of the convention, is incorrectly dated by GW in the Memoranda. See the Kentucky Convention to GW, 25 July 1789, printed above.

18. This list is in DNA:PCC, item 78, vol. 16, p. 592, and is printed in *ASP, Indian Affairs*, 1:85.

19. The letter from Smith has not been found, but it was transmitted by Tobias Lear to Henry Knox, 19 Nov. 1789. See Lear's letter printed above.

20. The Mountain Leader was also called Piomingo. See Piomingo to GW, 30 Oct. 1789.

21. See *N.C. State Records*, 21:697; 25:4–6.

22. This letter has not been found. It was probably the letter, dated 8 Sept. from "a number of respectable Inhabitants of Kentuckey recommendg the Mountain leader a Chickasaw Chief," that was forwarded to Henry Knox by Tobias Lear on 18 Nov. 1789.

23. Letter not found.

24. For Joseph Martin's difficulties with the Indians and the complaints of the governor of Georgia against him, see George Walton to GW, 11 Mar. 1789, GW to Walton, 29 May 1789, and Bennet Ballew to GW, 22 Aug. 1789.

25. Letter not found.

26. The complete text of this letter may be found in Harmar to Knox, 19 Oct. 1789, WHi: Draper Collection, Josiah Harmar Papers.

27. This is probably the expedition that left Clarksville on 3 Aug., under the command of Maj. John Hardin, to attack the towns of those Wabash tribes that had been devastating Kentucky during the summer of 1789. As early as April John Francis Hamtramck had written Josiah Harmar that "all the Wabash Indians (except those that are out hunting) have gone to war in Kentucky." Hamtramck quoted a Wea chief as saying: "We have killed white men, we have stold their horses, we are now going to steal their cows, and after that we will go and get their women to milk them" (11 April 1789, in Thornbrough, *Outpost on the Wabash*, 166). The August expedition from Kentucky was one day's march from the Wea town when on 9 Aug. they fell in with a party of Shawnee. In the resulting confusion the Kentuckians "only kill'd three men, a boy, three squaws & a child & took two children prisoner; the remainder got off unhurt, and took with them eight or ten of the Kentuckians best horses. Two of the militia were badly wounded and Major Harden returned on the 15th without attempting any thing farther" (Joseph Asheton to Harmar, 26 Aug. 1789, ibid., 182).

28. This letter is printed in ibid., 173–75. Lt. John Armstrong was in charge of a small expedition taking supplies to Fort Knox. A more detailed account of this expedition is in Armstrong to Hamtramck, 11 June 1789, ibid., 173–75.

29. MiU-C: Josiah Harmar Papers, printed in ibid., 178–83.

30. Henri Peyroux de la Coudrenière, a native of France, came to Louisiana with the Acadians as an interpreter and in August 1787 was appointed commandant of St. Geneviève on the Mississippi below St. Louis. He visited the United States in 1793 and in the late 1790s was appointed commandant at New Madrid (Nasatir, *Before Lewis and Clark*, 2:598).

31. This information came from a copy in the possession of Henri Peyroux. According to the extracts of "the latest advice from the governor general of Louisiana to the commandants of the posts on the Mississippy—

"'the king has permited to the inhabitants living on the American side to settle themselfs in this province (vagabonds excepted). Those who will accept of this offer will have liberty to continue in their religion but they will not have the privilage of exercising it in public, therefore all churches shall be Catholick and served by priest from Irland. What ever emigrants may bring with them of commoditys or other effects to them appertaining will be free from all taxes of entrance.

"'The inhabitans of Fort Pitt, Post Vincennes, of Kentuckey, of Comberland, at Kaskaskias, Caokia, and of other settlements, altho' not settled on the territory of Spain will have liberty to send all their commoditys and productions to New Orleans by paying only 15 pr cent of entrance'" (Thornbrough, *Outpost on the Wabash*, 180–81).

32. For George Morgan's settlement at New Madrid, see James Madison to GW, 26 Mar. 1789, source note.

33. See note 27.

34. MiU-C: Josiah Harmar Papers, printed in Thornbrough, *Outpost on the Wabash*, 183–85.

35. Hamtramck stated: "Some people from the Illinois had wrote me conserning it, but I was perfectly ignerant of the matter which induced me to write to Mr. B[arthélemi] Tardeveau at the Falls, and who informs me that he had wrote me last Decemb[er] from New York and to the people of the Illinois on this affair . . . that the resolve of Congress respecting the slavery of this country was not intended to extend to the Nigros of the old French inhabitans, which intelligence I had immediatly published and will communicate to the Illinois as soon as possible." Tardiveau, a French trader from Kentucky and an agent for the Illinois settlers, had written several times to Congress reporting the apprehensions of the French inhabitants that the Ordinance of 1787 prohibiting slavery in the Northwest Territory would force them to move into Spanish territory. See, for example, his letter of 17 Sept. 1788, DNA:PCC, item 48.

36. John Rice Jones (1759–1824), a native of Wales, was educated at Oxford and trained in the law in London. He came to the United States in 1784, settling first in Philadelphia and going west in 1786. From 1789 to 1801 he lived in Kaskaskia and then moved to Vincennes, later becoming attorney general of the Indiana Territory.

37. MiU-C: Josiah Harmar Papers, printed in Thornbrough, *Outpost on the Wabash*, 183.

38. Francis Vigo was an Indian trader based at Vincennes and was usually considered a friend to the United States.

39. A copy of Nathan McDowell's letter to Harmar is in WHi: Draper Collection, Harmar Papers. McDowell, from Pennsylvania, had been appointed to an infantry regiment in September 1789. He resigned from the army in September 1790.

40. Maj. John Finley operated, in partnership with David Duncan, a store at the Falls of the Ohio. He often acted as a contractor for the army.

41. A copy of this letter is in WHi: Draper Collection, Harmar Papers.

42. An excerpt from Benjamin Wilson's letter to Arthur St. Clair is enclosed in Knox's letter to Congress of 8 Dec. 1790 (*DHFC*, 5:1313–14).

43. A copy of "General Directions," George Morgan's detailed plan for laying out the settlement at New Madrid, is in DLC: "Missouri," New Madrid, 1788–89.

44. Israel Shreve (d. 1799) of New Jersey served as lieutenant colonel of the 2d New Jersey Regiment from October 1775 until November 1776 when he was appointed colonel. He resigned in 1782. GW was generally unim-

pressed with Shreve's military ability, noting when he was considered for promotion in December 1780 that "here I drop the curtain" concerning Shreve's qualifications (GW to John Sullivan, 17 Dec. 1780).

45. This may be the Peter Light who was the son of John and Catherine Light who came to Clermont County, Ohio, from Kentucky in 1791. Peter Light settled on Clover Creek in Clermont County, where by 1806 he was justice of the peace under the territorial and state governments and county surveyor. Alternatively, he may be the Peter Light who lived in Berkeley County, Va., during the Revolution and had seven persons in his household in 1782 (Naugle, *Virginia Tax Payers, 1782-87*, 76.

46. Arthur Campbell's letter to Knox has not been found.

47. This letter has not been found.

Memoranda on Thomas Jefferson's Letters

[1789]

Mr Jefferson —27th Augt 1789

Information from our Bankers in Holland that they had money in hand sufft to answer the demands for the Foreign Officers & Captives:[1] and moreover that the residue of the Bonds of the last loan were engaged.

The Sum necessary for the first is

60,393ƀ—17s.—10d. a year—and 26,000ƀ was sent him to complete the business of the Medals. The officers was paid up to the first of the year 1789.

Desires an order may be sent to the Bankers in Holland to furnish, & Mr Grand to pay the arrearages which may be due on the first of Jan. 1790.

The Bankers give it as their opinion that our credit is much advanced on the Exchange of Amsterdam that we may probably execute any money arrangements we may have occasion for on that side of the Water.

280,000ƀ remitted Mr Jefferson by our Bankers in Holland—viz.—Wilhelm & Jan Willinck N. and J. Van Staphorst & Hubbard.

The organization, and operation, these Gentlemen Bankers say of the New Government, has given great strength & stability to our Credit and causes it to be considered as the most certain & solid effects circulating among them.

They propose transfering the French debt here, due from the United States to the Court of Versailles and this without delay.

The Schooner Polly of Salem, Joseph Proctor Master, was siezed by two Moorish Cruizers, on a pretence of not knowing what colours she was under, and carried into Mogadore—The measure was disapproved by the Moorish Monarch who ordered the Vessel to be restored and compensation to be made.[2]

Augt 30th[3]

He mentions, Mr Neckers Loan for 80 Millions was subscribing to fast.

That a Mr Brossier (an unsuccessfuly Trader) applies for the Consulship at Havre—Mr Nathl Cutting of Massachusetts has settled at the place.[4]

Mr Vernes of L'Orient has left that place--And Mr Appleton is no longer at Rouen.[5]

D, in GW's handwriting, DLC:GW.

This letter was written by Thomas Jefferson to John Jay, 27 Aug. 1789 (Boyd, *Jefferson Papers*, 16:356–61).

1. For the debt owed by the United States to French officers who served in the American Revolution, see La Radiere to GW, 26 April 1789, n.1. For the American captives held by the Algerians, see Mathew Irwin to GW, 9 July 1789, source note.

2. For the capture of the schooner *Polly*, Joseph Proctor, master, see Giuseppe Chiappe to GW, 18 July 1789. See also GW to Sidi Mohammed, 1 Dec. 1789.

3. The material from this point to the end of the memoranda is taken from a letter from Jefferson to Jay, 30 Aug. 1789 (Boyd, *Jefferson Papers*, 15:373–74).

4. See James I. Brossier to Jefferson, 10 Feb. 1789, and Jefferson to Brossier, 11 Feb. 1789, ibid., 14:532, 537–38.

5. For Jacob Vernes's application for the consulship in Bordeaux, see his letter to Jefferson, 3 Nov. 1789, ibid., 15:538–43.

From Pierre Penet

to his excellency general Washington   [c.1789][1]

the Subscriber parthener of Emanuel Pliarne decea'd in the year 1777 in crosing Potomock River, then charged of publick affairs, hath the honor to represent to your excellency, that he was in St Eustache in the year 1775 at the arrival of an american Vessel dispatch'd by the governer Coock of providence in the state of Rodeland, wishing to procure munitions of war the inhabitants of that island having refused, to satisfy his demand then the Subscriber offered to the capin of the said Vessel to go the cap francois where he procure him fire arms, powder &ca the Subscriber also Emanuel pliarne his parthener have with generosity supplyed the said Vessel with all the munitions of war without any interest that the satisfaction to Shew their Earnest desire to promote the americain cause they embarked in the Said Vessel to go to Providence, few days after their arrival in November 1775 they were at cambridge to have the honor to See his excellency general Washigon and offered him their Service to Supply the americains with all munitions of war and furnitures wanting for their army, knowing all the importance of our Proposition the general advised Pliarne also the Subscriber to go instantly to Philadelphia and that he will inform the honorable congres of our propositions.

the 28 January 1776 a contract was made between the committee Secret of the honorable congress, the Subscriber and his partherner, for a considerable furniture of munitions of war and other articles necessary for the use of the army and by the Said contract, it is Said in case that the Subscriber and his Parthener Would Succeed in the negociation committed to their care, they Should participate to the future favour of the united States of america.

the subscriber embarked on board of the concorde at Philadelphia for france in March 1776 emanuel Pliarne was resident in this City, When the Subscriber arrived in france he go to Versailles obtained an audience of the Minister, and has been so succesful in his negociation that he is the first frenchman that hath procured useful correspondance between french and america, he give information to his parthener that all the produce and americains Vessel Should be received in the port of Nantes from whence the Subscriber was oblidge to send several Vessel to the Congress the first Were the Hancoke & Adam Capin Smith the Mary elizabetha, loaded with munitions of war, clothing and furniture for the troupes.

in December 1776 his excellency D. B. Francklin delivered letters directed for the subscriber from the Secret committee of the honorable congress he Stay Sometime with him, and I want with him at Paris, after having supply him with Money also the americain frigatte the represaille [*Reprisal*] in which his excellency came to Nantes, the Subscriber continued to do all the advance[2] to all Americain Vessel directed to him by the united states or By the Board of War of Boston the President of which in his letter give acknowledgement that by receiving his invoice of 7000 firearms in due time, they have very much contributed to the glorious Journey of Saratoka. it is with the Same Zeale and fidelity that he hath completed all the order he received during the war as far as his faculty and credit Shoud permit Since 1775 till the peace took place.

the Subscriber wishing to be employed in the americain service asked to your excellency a Brevet of aide de camp which has been granted to him in the year 1776 by the honorable Congress, the importance of the orders successively comitted to his care in Europe for the supplement of the armys in which he has been constantly employed during the War, is the only motive that prevented him to return and to be employed in the americain army. all his familly Wishing for his return in Europe particularly his Brother in law Knight of the order of St Louis and employed in the Royal Corps of artillery in which I have been employed myself before to come in america, in going to his country he wished to have Some mark of distinction to prouve to his nation that he hath fulfil with honor Zeal and fidelity the mission in which he hath been concerned. these be considered the Subscriber beseech your excellency to have him Received as a member of the order of St Cincinnati with permission to make use of the priviliges accorded to the order, in So doing you shall do Justice and the Subscrirer shall for ever pray for your excellency.

(his excelancy the President of the united states of america) it is with respect that I beg your excellency to examine the memoirs of my services here annexed, and I beseech you to be favourable to my demand, if you are So good to protect them, I got no doubt that I shall suceed to obtain the favour that my Zeal and attachment for the americain Cause deserve, having ever been ready to discharge my duty with honour in the mission in which I have been employed for the Service of the united States. in granting my request I Shall have an eternal acknowlegment of your gratitude. I am with Respect the Most obedt humble servant of your excellency.[3]

Df, PHi: Society Collection.

This letter is unsigned, but it clearly was written by Pierre Penet who at the beginning of the American Revolution was a young Alsatian merchant in business at Nantes. He formed a partnership in 1775 with Emmanuel de Pliarne (Plairne, Plaisne) to supply the Continental army with arms and munitions, originally through Gov. Nicholas Cooke of Rhode Island. For the firm's early negotiations with GW, see Cooke to GW, 11 Dec. 1775, GW to John Hancock, 14 Dec. 1775 (second letter), and Pliarne to GW, c.11 Jan. 1776. In October 1776, at Penet's request, GW brevetted the young Frenchman an aide-de-camp without pay (GW to Hancock, 7 Oct. 1776 [first letter]). Penet soon returned to France, and for much of the remainder of the war he dealt with the American commissioners in Paris and occasionally directly with Congress for the delivery of arms for the continent and for individual states. By the end of 1782, however, he was, Benjamin Franklin observed, "broke and absconded" (Franklin to Robert Morris, 14 Dec. 1782, DNA:PCC, item 137). In 1783 Penet returned to America and by the end of the year was purchasing land in upstate New York. By 1787 he had become an influential trader and land speculator among the Oneida Indians, setting up headquarters at Oneida Castle and claiming he had been sent to the tribes by the king of France and the marquis de Lafayette. In the course of the next year he acquired from the Oneida the promise of a grant of land for his services. The grant, 10 miles square or 100 square miles, was guaranteed in the Treaty of Fort Stanwix in 1788 between New York and the Oneida, with Penet free to choose where to locate the grant. See Hough, *Proceedings of the Commissioners of Indian Affairs*, 1:241–47. Penet chose a tract north of Oneida Lake near the St. Lawrence River, in what later became Jefferson County, New York. For the location of Penet's Square, see the "Map of the State of New York Showing the Location of the Original Land Grants Patents and Purchases," inserted at the end of vol. 5 of Flick, *History of the State of New York*. The record of Penet's later movements is vague. He apparently lost the confidence of the Oneida who complained about his activities to Gov. George Clinton. In September 1789 Clinton informed the tribe that "Mr. Penet is only to be considered among you as an adventuring Merchant, pursuing his own private Interest. He holds no Office, nor does he sustain any public Character in this Country; he attempts to deceive you, therefore, when he says he is sent by the King of France and the Marquis Dela Fayette to transact Business with you" (Clinton to the Oneida, 12 Sept. 1789, in Hough, *Proceedings of the Commissioners of Indian Affairs*, 2:350). By late 1789 Penet apparently had disposed of his interest in the square and left the Oneida country although he still was expected to return. Around 1790 he settled in Saint Domingue where he became a sucessful shipowner and merchant and continued to dabble in land speculation in northern New York. He reportedly was lost at sea around 1812. For additional information on Penet, see Thomas F. Powell, *Penet's Square: An Episode in the Early History of Northern New York* (Lakemont, N.Y., 1976); Thomas J. Schaeper, "Pierre Penet: French Adventurer in the American Revolution," *Daughters of the American Revolution Magazine*, 85 (1983), 854–56; Hough, *Pro-*

ceedings of the Commissioners of Indian Affairs, passim. No indication has been found that he was admitted to membership in the Society of the Cincinnati.

1. This letter has been dated 1789 on the basis of Penet's addressing GW as the president of the United States.

2. Penet wrote "advance money," deleted "money" but failed to cross out "advance." He then wrote "do all the" followed by "to all" above the line.

3. The signature "John f. Paroche" appears at the bottom of the page on the manuscript. John Francis Paroche was a trader for Penet at Oneida Castle.

From Alexander White

[1789]

General Edward Stevens—solicits an appointment in the Customs particularly the District of Norfolk He is a Gentleman in high repute in his Country both as a Citizen and a Soldier.[1]

Col: Will. Heth—has I expect explained to your Excellency his particular Views—I have known him from his Infancy. There is not a man in whom I would more readily confide for the discharge of any Office he may undertake—As a Soldier he is probably better known to Your Excellency than to me, though his early exertions may have escaped your notice or your Memory—I know him to be an excellent Accountant, an affectionate and dutiful Son to his indigent Parents notwithstanding his circumstances are narrow and he has a young Wife and an increasing Family.[2]

Col: Gustavus Wallace is desirous of a Collectors Place—particularly that of Rappohannock—I have but a very general acquaintance with him He was an Officer in the Army, from that circumstance, and from what I know of his Connections I presume he is not unknown to Your Excellency.[3]

Hudson Muse, is desirous of the same Office He is an entire Stranger to me—but has been long in that Office, and is recommended by Gentlemen on whom I can depend, as a faithful diligent able man in his office, and a good Citizen.[4]

Col: Christian Febiger—has explained to Your Excellency his particular Views—I knew him well early in the War. he was much esteemed among us at that time, and I understand has supported a good character both as a Soldier and a Citizen ever since.[5]

Elias Langham—is desirous of being appointed a Commissary of Military Stores—He married a young Lady in my Neighbourhood, and lived there sometime, I believe his character is good—and I find he has given satisfaction in his present Office at the Point of Fork.[6]

Frederick Phile—solicits the Appointment of Naval Officer of the Port of Philadelphia He has been twelve years in that Office, and brings ample Testimonials of his faithful discharge of the Duties of his Office, and of his general Good Character—I am not personally acquainted with him.[7]

Joseph Shallcross—solicits the Appointment of Collector of the Customs at Wilmington. He is also a Stranger to me, but from the character given him by those on whom I can rely—I have no doubt of his fitness for the Office, and of his general good character.[8]

ALS, DLC:GW. This letter is undated, but was probably written in the summer of 1789.

1. Edward Stevens (1745–1820), who had served in the Virginia legislature since 1779, was in search of public employment in the summer of 1789. See Conversation with Samuel Griffin, 9 July 1789. He also was recommended to GW by John Page, 14 July 1789.

2. For William Heth's application for office, see his letter to GW, 23 April 1789.

3. Gustavus Brown Wallace had applied for the Rappahannock collector's post on 28 Mar. 1789. See his letter of that date to GW. The position went to Hudson Muse rather than Wallace.

4. For Muse's application for office, see his letter to GW, 20 Mar. 1789.

5. Christian Febiger applied to GW for "some Appointment in the Custom house Department" in a letter of 6 May 1789.

6. In 1786 Elias Langham was appointed by the Virginia council of state as commissary of military stores and stationed at Point of Fork. He retained his post under the state at least as late as October 1791. In May 1791 he also was appointed justice of the peace for Fluvanna County (*Journals of the Council of State of Virginia*, 4:10, 5:289,316).

7. For Frederick Phile's application for office, see his letter to GW, 7 Mar. 1789.

8. George Gilpin applied for a post for Joseph Shallcross on 28 Mar. 1789. See his letter to GW of that date.

From Nathaniel Keais

Sir   Washington No. Carolina Jany 1st 1790
   the Subject of this Letter is to Inform your Excellency that I
now hold the Office of Collector of the Impost for the Port of
Bath—by an Appointment from this State.

   (Should there be no Weighty Reasons Offered to you Against
it) I shall Esteem it as a Perticular Favour to be Reinstated in that
Office under Congress. I am with the Greatest Respect Your
Excellencys Obt Servant

                                             Nathn. Keais

ALS, DLC:GW.

   Nathaniel Keais (1740–1795) served as a captain in the 2d North Carolina
Regiment from 1775 to 1778, as a member of the North Carolina general
assembly in 1777, and as a justice for Beaufort County from 1784 to 1786.
From 1784 to 1790 he was state collector of customs at Bath. As a member of
the North Carolina Ratifying Convention, Keais voted for ratification of the
Constitution. When GW made his appointments for port officers for North
Carolina on 9 Feb. 1790, Keais was named collector for Washington (*DHFC*,
2:58). Keais was recommended by Hugh Williamson in his letter to GW of 5
Feb. 1790.

From John Tanner

His Excellency George Washington Esqr.
President of the United States in Congress
Assembled,   January 1, 1790.[1]
   The humble petition of John Tanner humbly Sheweth,

   That your petitioner having been brought up to the sea from
his Youth in this City (except during the late Contest) in pretty
midling Circumstances & Credet.

   That your petitioner, during the late Contest, was taken a
prisoner by the British 4 times, and lost his all twice, Imprisoned, Abused by his Relations in this City.

   That the above Relations, being left Executors by the Parents
of your Petitioner, to an Estate of £300 pr Annum or more,
during the whole of the late Contest, one or both of the aforesaid Executors, received the Rents & Profits of said Estate, and
Appropriated said Rents & Profits wholly to his or their own
particular uses & benefits.

That your petitioner, immediately on peace taking place—moved to this City from FishKills with his Family, Comme[n]c'd a Suit in Chancery, against said Executors, but on your petitioner's failing in Cash the suit was Stayed, and the Costs to be paid out of the Sales of said real Estate £120.

That your petitioner at same time made a purchase of a Grist Mill and small farm in New Jersey, paid £250 down the Repairs £75—when the above Suit, failing, was under the disagreeable Necessity, of giving up said farm & Grist Mill, on the payments becoming due, with the Loss, of the aforesaid two Sums, of £320, in Gold & Silver.

That your petitioner, through the above losses and many other Misfortunes, during the late Contest, was Reduced to the Utmost Extremity, and almost to Despair, thro' the want of business, for the maintenance of your petitioners family of 6 small Children, & Wife.

That your petitioner, having Strugled & Strove (since the above losses and othe[r] Misfortunes) to recover by going to Sea, but all in vain, thro' the low ebb, our foreign Trade is Reduc'd to at present, and no Demand or Encouragemt, for Seamen, so that your Petitioner, is now Reduc'd to the most Extream Necessity, with a family in want of every, (even the Smallest) Necessaries of Life.

Your petitioner therefore most humbly prays, that your Excellency, will lend a kind Ear, and with a helping hand, Use your influence in behalf of, my Disstress, Consider Dear Sir, consider, what must be the feelings of a Parent (Reduc'd from a comfortable living, to the most Abject state of Want, thro' Misfortunes) when his Children asks for bread, & tis not in his power to give, To you Sr to you I look up, (as a Child to its Parent) for Assistance it is to you Sr I make my application, for your interposition, in my behalf, tis in your power Sr to save an Unfortunate family from the Savage Jaws of hunger, by your power Sr you are Enabled (in a great measure) to grant me either the whole or part of my request, which is only for a small part of business in Public Service, as Guager, Tide waiter, Measurer, a writer or under Clerk, in some public Office, or some kind of Office or business in Call as Doorkeeper, Messenger &ce.

God grant, your Excellency, may Enjoy all the Happiness in this World, that human nature can Attain, and a Crown of immortal Glory in the Next, for which Petitioner, as in Duty bound, shall ever pray.

L, DNA: RG 59, Miscellaneous Letters.

This is probably the John Tanner (1741–1794) who served as a private in a New York unit during the Revolution and was discharged "Ruptured and worn out" in 1782 (DNA:PCC, item 60, p.71). Since his letter indicates some naval experience, he also may be the John Tanner (Turner) who was appointed first mate of the New York revenue cutter *Vigilant*, 23 July 1793 (*JPP*, 205, 206).

1. The dateline appears to be in the same writing as the endorsement.

From Joseph Willard

Sir,   Cambridge [Mass.] Janry 1. 1790

When I had the honor of paying my respects to you, at the University in this place, I took the liberty of mentioning the utility of the Medical Institution, established in it, and at the same time, the disadvantage under which it has labored, from the first, for want of an Infirmary connected with it. As the time and other circumstances would admit but of few words upon the subject, you were so condescending and obliging, as to suggest my writing to you, and precisely stating the wishes of the Government of this Society, respecting a Hospital, and manifested your readiness to do every thing for the Institution, which you might be able, with propriety. Agreeably to this permission, I would take the opportunity of offering a few things upon the subject.

The Medical Institution in this University, for teaching the healing Art systematically by Professors, is the only one in the New England States, and has existed for seven years. The Professors are—one for anatomy and surgery—one for the theory and practice of physic—and one for chemistry and materia medica, who give lectures in their several branches to medical students, both to such as belong to the University, and such as come from abroad. The Professors have, for very small pecuniary inducements, since the establishment of the Institution performed the duties assigned them, greatly to the satisfaction of the Public and to the advancement of regular practice in physic. Their lectures have been attended by students in physic from the neighboring States, but their labors cannot be attended with so great advantage to this most important Art, as they might be, were there an Hospital to which they might introduce their medical pupils, where they would frequently see curious cases in medicine and surgery, as well as the common daily administrations of the Professors, among the Invalids, and the theories of those Gentlemen would be explained, elucidated and confirmed, by lectures at the bed side, and actual practice.

Several years ago, a plan was proposed by the Corporation of the University and the medical Professors, to the General Court of this Commonwealth, for establishing a marine Hospital; and a Committee of the Court was appointed to examine into the usefulness of the measure, and they were so well satisfied of it's utility, that they reported a Bill for the purpose. The present happy system of General Government being prepared, soon after, induced a delay of the Institution, in hopes that one of a similar nature would take place for the Continent, in this Commonwealth, and upon more liberal and extensive principles, than it would be in the power of the State to adopt; and the Bill remains upon the files of the Senate, without being acted upon.

Having seen, the last fall, in the debates of the House of Representatives of the General Government, a motion for establishing marine Hospitals, on the sea coast in the United States, I could not but hope, if they should be established, that as they would subserve the purposes of humanity, by the shelter they would afford to individuals, so they might be made extensively to promote the interests of medical knowlege, by being connected with public medical Institutions.[1] I have communicated my ideas to Gentlemen who have the care and Government of this University, and they all wish, if a marine Hospital should be established in this neighborhood, it might be made beneficial to our medical Institution. What we have therefore to request, Sir, is that the Hospital which may be in this part of the Country, may be fixed in such a situation upon Charles River, that it may be easy of access from the University, and that the Gentlemen, who at present teach the medical branches in it, may have the charge of it, which might be the means of greatly promoting the knowlege of medicine, and of course, saving the lives of many valuable Citizens of the Community. Should there be an impropriety in appointing the three Professors, if some one of them could have the direction of such an Hospital, it would answer the general purposes.

I by no means wish, Sir, to be importunate upon this subject; and I rest fully assured, that your wisdom will direct to that which shall be for the best.[2] I have the honor of being, with sentiments of the highest defference and respect, Sir, your most humble and obedient servant

Joseph Willard.

ALS, DNA: RG 59, Miscellaneous Letters.

Joseph Willard (1738–1804) graduated from Harvard in 1765, where he taught for several years before becoming a minister in Haverhill and Beverly, Massachusetts. During the American Revolution he supported the Patriot cause. Frequently mentioned as a candidate for the presidency of Harvard, he succeeded to the post in 1781 to face the problems of an institution devastated by the war. In the succeeding years his achievements in acquiring both academic and financial support for the college were remarkable. Willard retained the presidency until 1804. While on his New England tour GW visited "the college at Cambridge" on 29 Oct., and Willard conducted him on a tour of the institution (*Diaries*, 5:481–83).

1. On 20 July 1789 the House of Representatives appointed a committee to bring in a bill "providing for the establishment of hospitals for sick and disabled seamen, and for the regulation of harbours." The committee brought in the bill on 27 Aug., and the next day the House voted to commit it to a committee of the whole House on 15 September. On 16 Sept. the bill was postponed to the next session of Congress (*DHFC*, 3:115, 171, 172, 210). Marine hospitals were not actually authorized by Congress until section 5 of "An Act for the relief of sick and disabled Seamen," passed 16 July 1798, authorized the president to establish them and made provision for their support (1 *Stat.* 606).

2. GW replied to Willard's letter on 24 Jan., informing him that "as no determination has yet been taken with respect to the erection of Hospitals for the reception of sick and disabled Seamen, the object to which your request relates is not before me."

"At present I can only repeat the assurances, formerly given, that every thing in my power will be done, consistent with propriety, to promote the wishes of your learned Body on this subject. You will allow me, at the same time, to observe that it might be well to make their wishes on this head known to the Gentlemen, who are in Congress, from the State of Massachusetts" (Df, DNA: RG 59, Miscellaneous Letters).

To the South Carolina Society of the Cincinnati

Gentlemen,   New-York, January 2nd 1790.

From a conviction that the dispositions of the Society of the Cincinnati, established in the State of South Carolina are peculiarly friendly to me, I cannot receive their congratulations on the occasion, which gave birth to their address, without emotions of peculiar satisfaction.[1]

The interest that my fellow-citizens so kindly took in the happiness which they saw me enjoy in my retirement after the war, is rather to be attributed to their great partiality in my favor than to any singular title I had to their gratitude and affection.

Notwithstanding I was conscious that my abilities had been too highly appreciated, yet I felt, that, whatever they were, my Country had a just claim upon me, whenever the exercise of them should be deemed conducive to its welfare. With such feelings I could not refuse to obey that voice which I had always been accustomed to respect, nor hesitate to forego a resolution which I had formed of passing the remainder of my days in retirement. And so far am I from having reason to respect the decided measure I took in the crisis of organising a new general government, that I ought rather perhaps to felicitate myself upon having met the wishes and experienced the assistance of a patriotic and enlightened People, in my arduous undertakings.

Always satisfied that I should be supported in the administration of my office by the friends of good government in general; I counted upon the favorable sentiment and conduct of the Officers of the late army in particular—nor has my expectation been deceived. As they were formerly distinguished by their eminent fortitude and patriotism in their military service, during the most trying occasions; so are the same men, now mingled in the mass of citizens, conspicuous for a disinterested love of order, and a jealous attention to the preservation of the rights of mankind. Nor is it conceivable that any Members of the community should be more worthy of the enjoyments of liberty, or more zealous to perpetuate its duration, than those who have so nobly and so successfully defended its standard in the new World.

I sincerely thank you, Gentlemen, for your expression of

attachment to my person; and wish for my happiness and honor. On my part I only dare to engage it shall be my incessant study that you may happily experience, and long enjoy the fruits of a government, which has for its basis, the good of the American People.

Go. Washington

LB, DLC:GW.

1. The address from the South Carolina Society of the Cincinnati, dated 19 Nov. 1789, at Charleston, reads: "Possessed of every feeling that can act on grateful hearts, the Society of the Cincinnati, established in the State of South Carolina, beg leave to congratulate you on the happy occasion which has once again placed you in the situation of rendering general good to their country.

"Retired from the busy scenes of life to reap the rewards of your virtuous acts, and to enjoy the glory you had already obtained—Your fellow-citizens viewed you with exulting happiness—They saw in you the Patriot-Hero, the Friend, and Saviour of their Country! and, with hearts filled with gratitude and affection, they invoked the omniscient Disposer of human events to render that retirement happy!

"The Period however arrived when the abilities of the virtuous Patriot were again to be called forth to assume a public character.

"A general political Government was formed by which the happiness of the Country, for whose liberty you had fought, was to be established. To preside at the head of this new-Government—to establish it with permanency—the People sought in the great Washington the virtues on which they could rely with safety, and from which they might expect to receive every benefit without alloy—They had experienced his abilities, they had experienced his integrity, and his inviolable love for his country—Nor did they seek in vain. The same noble spirit which actuated you in the beginning of our late contest with Great Britain now operated. You received and obeyed the summons—and, although you should make a sacrifice, yet you nobly determined. It was the voice of your Country, and in whose service every inferior consideration of ease and retirement must give place.

"As Citizens, Sir, we congratulate you on this additional proof of your country's confidence. As Soldiers who partook with you in many of the dangers and hardships which attended the general Army under your Command—We beg leave to express our warmest attachment to your Person, and sincerest wish for your happiness and honor—and that we may, under your rule, supported by your amiable virtues, happily experience and long enjoy the fruits of a government, which has for its basis, the Good of the People of America" (DLC:GW).

From Matthew Clarkson

Sir   Philadelphia Jan. 2d 1790.

Having formerly acted under your immediate Command as a principal in the department of auditor of accounts to the army; I had the honor to become personally known to you; those services I hope were approved. I still wish to be useful to our common country.

From the late proceedings of Congress I have been induced to suppose that that honorable body will shortly determine where their permanent residence shall be fixed, and that the appointment of Commissioners for the locating and establishing thereof will be committed to you.[1] The object of this address Sir! is to make a tender of my services in that employment.

Convinced that the nomination or appointment to offices which you are pleased to make, have suitable qualifications, personal merit and former services for their objects; uninfluenced by the solicitations of friends, I cheerfully rest my application upon that issue as the most honorable.

Should I be so happy Sir! as to meet your aprobation I will endeavor to do justice to your appointment.

With every sentiment of reverence and esteem for your public and private charactor, I have the honor to be with the greatest truth Sir Your most obedient and most humb. servt

Matth. Clarkson

ALS, DLC:GW.

Matthew Clarkson (1733–1800) of Philadelphia served as a quartermaster with Philadelphia forces in 1775 and from 1775 to 1776 as auditor of accounts for the Continental army. From 1777 to 1778 he was an agent to receive subscriptions to Continental loans. In 1779 he was appointed a marshal for the Continental Admiralty Court. In April 1792 Clarkson was elected mayor of Philadelphia, a post he held until 1796.

1. The seat of government bill had been postponed until the second session of the First Congress. See Pierre L'Enfant to GW, 11 Sept. 1789, n.1.

From Samuel Huntington

Sir,   Norwich [Conn.] Jany 2d 1790.

I am honoured with your letter of the 28th Ulto.[1] Sensible that You must be wearied with Solicitations for appointments to

Offices, it is with reluctance that I now take the liberty to mention Dudley Woodbridge jun. Esq: as a suitable character to supply the vacancy lately made by the decease of Genl Parsons in the supreme Court in the western Territory.[2] Mr Woodbridge sustains an amiable & virtuous Character: Having receivd the honours of Yale College with good reputation, he applied to the study of the Law, & made good proficiency under my care and inspection for a number of years & was introduced to the practice of the Law with encouraging circumstances & persevered therein for some time until unfortunately an inveterate Phthisic distressed him in his Exercises as a public Speaker to such a degree as threatened a disolution of his Constitution, & obliged him not without Reluctance to abandon his hopeful prospects in that Profession; he hath since been unsuccessful in trade: having a growing family & his Connections being respectable & influential Characters in this State, he could not endure the prospect of retiring from business in [the] prime of life, with his rising family & amiable partner unprovided for in future; but hath taken the Resolution to settle himself & family, at Marietta where they now dwell. I beleive his character & abilities such as will give satisfaction to the public & do honour to the Office should he be appointed to fill the vacancy I have mentioned, & from the character he sustains with the advantages of his education, more especially his knowledge in jurisprudence he may reasonably expect employment in some learned profession where he may render essential service to mankind, & receive some consolation under his peculiar misfortunes. With the most perfect Esteem and Respect I have the honour to be Your Obedient humble Servant

Saml Huntington

ALS, DLC:GW.

1. No letter from GW to Huntington of 28 Dec. has been found. Huntington may have meant to refer to GW's letter of 23 December.

2. For the circumstances surrounding the death of Samuel Holden Parsons, see Winthrop Sargent to GW, 27 Nov. 1789. Dudley Woodbridge, Jr. (1747–1823), was a native of Stonington, Conn., who moved to Norwich around 1770 and opened a store. During and after the Revolution he held a number of minor posts in the town in addition to running his business. In 1789 Woodbridge moved to Marietta in the Northwest Territory. More information on his background was supplied to GW by Benjamin Huntington in a letter to the president of 23 Mar. 1790, recommending Woodbridge for a

judgeship in the Northwest Territory: "I have been personally acquainted with Mr Woodbridge for more than twenty Years and know his Character is good—He is the Son of Dr Dudley Woodbridge a Reputable and wealthy Gentleman in Connecticut his Wife is of one of the best Families in the State & a Niece of Governor Griswold.

"Honorable Connections are indeed no Qualifications for an Office when not Accompanied with Personal or Professional Accomplishments—Mr Woodbridge had a liberal Education, After which he Studied Law under the Tuition of Governor Huntington he was admitted and Practised as a Lawyer in the highest Courts in the State about five or six Years with Honor and Reputation untill the War at which Time he went into Trade—He took a Decided part with his Country in the Dispute with Great Britain and was a very Useful Man in the Politics and Provisions of his Country—He is about forty Years of Age and I make no doubt of his being an Important man in the Western Territory" (DLC:GW). When the vacancy left by Parsons' death was filled by GW in March 1790, Rufus Putnam, not Woodbridge, received the appointment (*DHFC*, 2:66).

From La Rouërie

Sir   la Rouerie [France] January 2d 90

Was I only acquainted with your high character and the eminent post where it has placed you, as in your most natural position, without Being at the same time incouraged in the respectuous liberty which your goodness inspire, I would restrain the satisfactions of my heart on your account, to the possession of the highest sentiments he is capable of entertaining for the man who the world knows is a compound of the highest virtues, and not indulge myself so often in the warmest desire which, after that of your happiness animate me; that of repeating you how dear your Excellency is to armand; how much it pains me to be so far off, while in the rank of your most sincere admirers; while ever since I quitted you, I am troubled with the desire to go and see you. I have indeed, an opportunity to satisfy my self on that head, But I can only trust it with a letter, and my person, my inactive and perhaps very useless, person, must make a longer stay at home. in the midst of the storm I am too well situated in the affections and regards of the people round me, and indeed, in thoses of the state of Britany, for me to run the risk By such a long Journey as that over to america, to create suspicions on my deeds or principles, more particularly at the moment, where such dissatisfaction may arise, as will require the activity of all friends to humanity.

I do not know indeed what to relate to you of the transactions which rascality, madness, avarice, and that super powerfull love for disorder, which seems to be liberty to the eyes of insurecting slavery, have performed since I had the honour to write to your Excellency By Capt. Bert[1]—you have surely received the most Essentials News; But although your natural perspicacity and your acquired knowledge of men & nations will, not withstand- ing the distance, draw the most Just Consequences from all our sublime havock; I wish for your own recreation, you were for a month an Eye witness; your Excellency would at first rush in anger against rascality—Blush to see so little common sense among things who pretend to have with all nations a common father above; then, sir, you would give a smile of pity, order your ship to put all her sails, and return to your happy country.

our constitution's makers, dispute, slander, fight & kick each other most unmercifully; they reproach each other with being entirely destitute of the parts necessary to the frame of legisla- tors or even administrators; on that point the wise and attentive part of the nation agree pretty well with them; but when once in a Body, they pretend to be the only politick corps in the world on which the almighty has Bestowed the power of making good laws. to hear many of them, your country has not known what she was about, you do not plainly understand the word liberty; you have not snapt at the throat of that goddess like we have done; you love her with her eyes intirely open; we are resolved to have her intirely Blind—you have fought Bravely, most greatly—we have murdered most cowardly, we have stolen & we remain firm in the resolution to steal most admirably; you have understood liberty, the power of every individual to do as he please, provided his doings do not hurt the laws made for the safety and happiness of all the citizens—we have, on this side of the water, understood liberty, the power of every individual to do as he please, provided he do not hurt the laws made, or oppose the laws to Be made, in favor of disorder, crimes & anarchy throughout the empire, but at the same time, he is permitted to do, if he can, worse than the law prescribe—you Believe in god, in the respect due to virtues—we neither Believe

in god or have any respect for virtue—all your laws, obedience
to them, emulation to perfect them, fraternal love betwixt States
and individuals, unity of sentiments, heavenly indulgence for
mistakes, do surely give you now a predominant character
among the nations of the world, and in a short succession of
times, will make you the most flourishing one, and attract over
to you every friend to humanity, if not possibly in person at least
in wishes and hearts—But, Sir, we are an other sort of people,
and despise any ⟨modelation⟩ from abroad; for many years to
come, we shall have no laws, or, which is worse, we shall pay no
attention to them—we have a great emulation & amazing powers to do Bad, we do what we possibly can to destroy our peace,
fortune and happiness at home, and of course, our strength to
repel the foreign invaders of our fields; I do not say of our
kingdom, of our empire, of our government; for there is no
more kingdom, empire, in france; as to government, as the one
we seems to wish for is a mere anarchical one, I believe no body
Besides us can like it, and therefore we shall be left at liberty to
keap it as long as we please. it is true, we have the consolation to
foresee that it can not last longer than the end of the world.

your Excellency may well suppose, from the situation which
for many years past we have been in; from the conduct &
principles of thoses who were appointed to bring the radical
Balsam and everythings to rights—from the coleric temper, the
inconstancy, the want of unanimous or well understood will and
plan of the people at large—from the rapacity, egotisme of their
leaders—from that puffed importance which they Bring in
trifles, as for example to recommand to the respects of the
nation, the extraordinary Bravery, military parts & probity of
fifty of their militia heroes, for having manifested at the utmost
thoses qualifications in their succesful attack on the Garret of a
poor curate of village and to have carried off his grain, while he
in his kitchen philosophis'd on the occasion, and endeavoured
with the assistance of his old maid, to find the meaning of some
passage of the Bible; that when great circumstances offer, he
may mix something of it in his embarassed speech to his parish-
ioner—from that horrid importance and dignity, as for example on the side of the chiefs of the murderers in paris, which
they Bring in the most shamefull & criminal doings—from the
influence of the money's men; who after having lived for many

century, on the purest Blood of the people, acquire yet at this Epoche, a new force to be with more succès their Butchers & rulers, through the analogy which their purse filled up with the fruits of their crimes, have with the inclinations & character of our present, still much Better than it had with our past, state's men—from the favour & protection granted to all the paper's money makers, as the caisse décompte &c.—from the Bills of anticipation, which are orders on the revenue to come, nay, often, and it is now the case, on an imaginary revenue, and are nothing else But paper's money; for when the revenue come, new anticipations are created & allways increased as to the sum; the revenu appropriated to pay the anticipation is spent to other objects when necessity require it; and I never knew such a Beggar, or such a thief, as the Nécéssity of government in our country; she is allways at your door, and has a change of so many faces, shapes, voices & words, that poor people, who know perfectly well their own nécéssity, never can know that of government; I mean, never can distinguish her from what is no Nécéssity—New Bills under new dénominations are succéssively added to the first, and by and By with the help of our loans, which are still paper's money, we are come to have nothing else but paper's money—I call that, in such a Country as this, a perfect state of Bankruptcy—from all thoses, I say, and this is hardly the half of the Basis for Juging right, your Excellency may suppose that the Bulk of the nation is & will grow more and more disatisfyed; that she will first try her power not to obey the laws, then refuse openly to acknowledge the laws, then rise her thoughts & wills to anger & activity, and Be, as it is now the case in many places, adverse to the establishment of any laws, which the ignorant & improvident part of the people should not frame themselves—a civil war appears to me as well near as possible; a général war in Europe, I think unavoidable: we might perhaps foresee the time it shall Begin, as to the end, I believe there are few political physiognomes that can determine.

ah, my dear général, the man ever dear to all sensible and good men; it is not thus that you & your country have conquered liberty; your sword in the hand of equity and honour established the principle; your virtues and thoses of america found, determined and fixed all at once the blessed limits wherein there is a full enjoyment of liberty for honest men, and enough to hinder people of an other cast, from seeking their satisfaction in disorders and crimes.

we have received some month ago four years interest from congress, & we have hopes to be pay'd exactly—I am persuaded we owe this Justice to the attention of your Excellency, Be so good, sir, as to accept of our most cordial & respectfull homages of gratitude[2]—I take the liberty to request my lady washington to accept thoses of my respect. I have the honour to be with that sentiment sir your Excellency's the most obdt hble servants

armand

ALS, DLC:GW; copy, NNC.

For an identification of Charles Armand-Tuffin, marquis de La Rouërie, see his letter to GW, 18 June 1789, source note.

1. Claudius de Bert de Majan carried La Rouërie's letter of 18 June to GW. For an identification of Bert, see note 1 of that letter.

2. La Rouërie is referring to payments on the debt due to French officers who had served in the American Revolution. See La Radiere to GW, 26 April 1789, n.1.

From Winthrop Sargent

Losanteville [Territory N.W. of River Ohio]
Sir   2d Jany 1790

I do myself the Honour to transmit your Excellency the Proceedings of the Governour in his Executive Department from July last, and since his Return to the Territory.[1]

By the Ordinance for the Government of this Country such Communications should have been made to the Secretary of Congress, but a late Resolution has induced me to suppose (though it has not expressed it) that all Official Communications, from me, as well as the Governour, should be addressed to your Excellency.[2]

If I have erred in this Opinion, I request your Excellency would put me right.

Mr Charles Thompson Secretary to Congress furnished me with the Journals, to Novr 1787—If it is proper that they be continued to me, I must take the liberty of asking your Excellency's Order to that Purpose.

The Governour arrived here this Morng & will probably be detained by public Business until the 4th when he expects to take his Departure for Kaskaskias. With the greatest Respect I have the Honour to be your Excellency's most obedient & most devoted Servant

Winthrop Sargent

ALS, DNA: RG 59, Territorial Papers, Territory Northwest of the River Ohio; copy, DNA: RG 59, Territorial Papers, Territory Northwest of the River Ohio.

1. The enclosure was the "Proceedings of the Governor," from 16 to 30 Dec. 1789, an account of the appointments made by Arthur St. Clair for that period, a proclamation concerning a ferry across the Ohio at Wheeling, Va. (now W.Va.), and a statement by St. Clair that "the Governour has observed with some Regret that little Attention is paid to Militia Duties—Though the Settlement is at present in a State of Safety, there is a faithless People on the Frontier, & a People who may be led to Acts of Hostility without any Provocation from the Inhabitants of the Territory—Self Preservation therefore dictates that they be prepared—the Advantages will result to the People themselves and the Penalties of the Law will be avoided" (DNA: RG 59, Territorial Papers, Territory Northwest of the River Ohio). The enclosures are in CD-ROM:GW.

2. Section 1 of "An Act to provide for the Government of the Territory North-west of the river Ohio" provided that when "any information is to be given, or communication made by the governor of the said territory to the United States in Congress assembled, or to any of their officers, it shall be the duty of the said governor to give such information and to make such communication to the President of the United States" (1 *Stat.* 52–53 [7 Aug. 1789]).

From Samuel Shaw

Sir,   Boston, 2d January 1790.

On the 26 January 1786, the then Congress of the United States did me the honor to appoint me their Consul at Canton in China, where I resided till the 20 January 1789, at which time I embarked on my return to America. Being about to go again to that Country, I do myself the honor, Sir, to request, if it be not incompatible with any present public arrangement, that I may be favored with the same appointment, and a new commission, under our present happy government. Though neither salary nor perquisites were annexed to the office, yet the respect to be derived from such a mark of the confidence and esteem of the United States renders it to me, who have experienced the good effect of it, an object truly desirable. I have the honor to be most respectfully, Sir, Your most obedient and very humble servant

S. Shaw

ALS, DLC:GW.

Samuel Shaw (1754–1794) of Boston, served during much of the Revolution as an aide-de-camp to Henry Knox with the rank of major. In 1784 a group of Boston merchants appointed Shaw supercargo on the *Empress of China*, the first American vessel to sail to Canton. Upon his return he served briefly under Knox in the War Department, and in 1786 the Confederation Congress made him the first American consul to China. Shaw served in China for three years, and when consular posts under the new government were filled by GW in February 1790, Shaw was reappointed and returned to China. He died of a liver disease at sea in 1794 while on a return voyage to the United States.

Farm Reports

[Mount Vernon, 3–9 January 1790]
Meteorlogical Account of the Weather
Kept at Mount Vernon 1790

Jany[1]

3	Morning 47 SWt Clear	Noon 54 SWt Clear	Night 57 SWt Clear
4	Morning 49 SWt Clear	Noon 58 SWt Clear	Night 58 SWt Clear
5	Morning 44 NEt Rain	Noon 46 NEt Cloudy	Night 48 NW Clear
6	Morning 36 SEt Clear	Noon 40 SEt Clear	Night 42 SEt Cloudy
7	Morning 37 SWt Cloudy	Noon 41 SWt Clear	Night 46 SWt Clear
8	Morning 39 SWt Cloudy	Noon 42 SWt Cloudy	Night 49 SWt Clear
9	Morning 37 NW Clear	Noon 40 NW Cloudy	Night 41 NW Clear

January 9th

		days
Dr.	Dogue Run Plantn for the work of 7 Men & 11 Women Amountg per week to	108
Cr.	By plowing at the River plantn	4
	By hauling Straw to Cover a farm pen & to make litter	6
	By Making a farm pen	65
	By Clearing and Grubing on the side of the Swamp below ⟨*illegible*⟩ House	9
	By Cuting rails & Trunnels for a Trunnel fence	10
	By Striping Tobo	10
	By Sickness Brunswick	4
	Total	108

Sent to the Mill 11 Bushels Corn Recd from ditto 9 Bushels B. Meal Sent to the Mansn House 6 Barrels Sound Corn, 56 head Cattle 89 Old Sheep, 35 Lambs, & 8 working Horses.

		days
Dr.	Muddy Hole Plantn for the work of 4 Men & 10 Women Amtg per week to	84
Cr.	By breaking up ground in No. 6	22
	By hauling rails and going to Mill	1
	By Clearing and Grubing in no. 6	45
	By Striping Tobo	4
	By Sickness Gabrel & Molly	12
		84

Sent to the Mill 10 Bushels wheat and 6 ditto of Corn Recd from ditto 6¼ Bushels B. meal 2 ditto Oats, 2 ditto Bran Stock 45 head Cattle 15 Old Sheep, 4 Lambs & 9 working Horses.

		Days
Dr.	River Plantn for the work of 7 Men 17 Women 3 Boys & 1 Girl Amounting per week to	162
Cr.	By breaking up ground in no. 7	15
	By hauling Mud on N. 5 and rails to no. 2	20
	By going to Mill with wheat	4
	By Cuting & Mauling rails 16 days Geting Posts 6 ditto	22
	By dressing flax	10
	By Cuting Straw & Grinding axes 3 days Shelling Corn 6 do	9
	By Taking in and threshing wheat	70
	By Sickness Cornelia 6 days Natt 3, & Agness 3 days	12
	Total	162

Decrease 2 wethers—Sent to the Mill 52 Bushels wheat 19 ditto of Rye, Recd from ditto 9½ Bushels Corn meal, 45 Bushels Choped Rye and Bran Mixed, & 5 Bushls Oat Meal—Stock 86 Head Cattle 126 Old Sheep, 53 Lambs, & 14 working Horses.

		Days
Dr.	Ferry & Frenches for the work of 7 Men 16 women & 3 Boys Amtg per week to	156
Cr.	By breaking up ground in no. 2	7
	By ditto ditto in No. 5	16
	By hauling Shingles to the barn, Flax to Mansn House & to the Ferry and at Mill	12
	By preparing for Mauling Rails	2
	By Leveling the dirt around the barn wall	13
	By planting Honey Locust	4
	By threshing & Cleaning wheat	24
	By Carrying Shingles in the barn Celler	6
	By Cuting rail timber & Mauling	22
	By Shelling Corn 4 days dressing Flax 8 ditto	12
	By Grubing in No. 2	3
	By Striping Tobo 11 days Grubing in no. 6 12 ditto	23
	By Spinning & Sewing	12
	Total	156

Decreas 2 Sheep died from Eating Ivey—Sent to the Mill 16 Bushels Corn 14½ ditto of wheat Recd from ditto 11½ ditto Corn meal—Stock 80 head Cattle 88 Old Sheep, 28 Lambs, 15 working Horses, 2 ditto Mules 2 ditto Spring ditto Fernages 24/.

		Days
Dr.	Mansn House for the work of 14 men 8 Boys & 6 Girls Amtg per week to	168
Cr.	By waggon Hauling rails to post and rail fence Hay, wood and at Mill	6
	By 2 Carts hauling wood Sand, & Gravel	12
	By working at Muddy Hole Plantn	18
	By Mauling and Sawing rail Stuff	10
	By Killing Hogs & Striping Tobo	14½
	By diging Holes and puting up post and Rail fence	45½
	By Tenentg rails	5
	By Cuting wood for Mansn House	7
	By Cuting Rail Stuff	3½

By Loading waggon with Hay   1
By hauling with the Muddy Hole Cart for the post & rail fence   2
By tending Knowles[2]   13
By feeding beeves & beating Homeny   6
By burning the Ends of the posts   ⟨illegible⟩
By Currying leather   6
By tending Stock 6 days Making Baskets 3 ditto   9
By Sickness Tom Davis 6 Days Scomburg 3 ditto[3]   9
                                                              Total   168

Recd from the Ferry Plantn 6 Hogs Wt 596—from the River pln 1 ditto Wt 75—Total 671 out of the same was delivered to Isaac 50 Wt to Will 50 ditto—Recd from the Mill 25 Bushels B. Meal 7 Ditto of Oats & 13 ditto of Bran—Stock 17 head Cattle, 32 Old Sheep, 18 Lambs, 5 last Spring Mules, 1 ditto 2 Years Old, 4 ditto Spring ditto, 3 ditto Spring Colts, 2 ditto Spring Jennies, 2 ditto Old ditto, 3 ditto Jacks, 1 ditto Spring ditto

	days
Dr. Ditchers for the work of 5 Men Amtg per week to	30
Cr. By ditching finished 25½ roods	12½
By Sawing & hewing Rails	9½
By hewing posts at Manleys on Acct of Rain	2
By Sickness Pascall	6
Total	30

	days
Dr. Joiners & Carpenters for the work of 4 men Amtg per week to	24
Cr. By Thomas Mohony[4] puting the plates of the barn Shed walls puting up Joists & Posts	4½
By handling 2 Handsaws	1½
By James & Sambo engaged in ditto	10
By Making a Gutter & putg it on the Shed Stable to prevent the water from Injuring the wall	2
By Carrying wheel Stuff from the Top of the Hill to the Houn Kennel for Isaac	1
By Isaac Making a New wheel Barrow and a New wheel to another & assisting about removg the Lemmon & Orange trees to the Green House and finished a New Cart wheel for D. R. Plantn	6
Total	24

Mill Grist	Dr.	Wht	Corn	Rye	Oats
Remg in the Mill		913	19	10½	22
To Toll this week		1½	10		
To R. Plantn		52	11½	18½	
To D. Run Plantn					
To Muddy Hole Plantn		9¾	6		
To Ferry & Frenches		15¼	17		
		991½	63½	29	22

Contra	Cr.	B. Ml	Rye	Ots	Bran
By River plantn		9¾	30		15
By D. Run Plantn		9			
By Muddy Hole Plan.		6¼		2	2
By F. & Frenches		11½			
By Mansn House		25		7	13

By Coopers & Miller	1			
By John Knowles	2½			
	65	30	9	30

		Days
Dr.	Coopers for the work of 2 Men Amtg per week to	12
Cr.	By Making Tobo Hogheads & Flower Casks	11
	By geting the Large boat round in the Mill Creek	1
	Total	12

D, in the writing of George Augustine Washington, DLC:GW.

This report and other similar accounts were sent by George Augustine Washington and GW's later managers on a regular basis during GW's absences from Mount Vernon. See Farm Report, 6–12 Dec. 1789, source note.

For information on many of the slaves mentioned in the farm reports, see particularly the list of GW's slaves "at Mount Vernon and the plantations around it" in *Diaries*, 4:277–83. Slaves were often shifted temporarily from one farm to another. For the location of the various Mount Vernon plantations, see GW to John Fairfax, 1 Jan. 1789, notes.

1. At the beginning of this document George Augustine Washington wrote the following entries and then deleted them:

"1 Morning 46 SW Clear Noon 50 Sw Clear Night 53 SW Clear

"2 Morning 42 Net Clear Noon 51 Set Clear Night 54 SEt Clear."

2. For John Knowles, see GW to George Augustine Washington, 31 Mar. 1789, n.5.

3. Tom Davis was a dower slave attached to the Mount Vernon home house. Davis worked primarily as a bricklayer and stonemason, although he also occasionally did painting and carpentry. Scomburg is probably Schomberg, the slave listed in GW's 1786 slave list as "past labour" (*Diaries*, 4:277).

4. On 1 Aug. 1786 GW made an agreement to pay Thomas Mahony for his services as a house carpenter and joiner "and (when not employed in either of these) in other jobs which he may be set about; and will during the said term, behave himself quietly, soberly, and orderly in the family, persuing the business about which he may be employed with diligence and fidelity." On 15 April 1788 a similar agreement was signed giving Mahony £24 a year and certain perquisites for his services. Both indentures are in DLC:GW and on CD-ROM:GW. Apparently Mahony's behavior, at least in the realm of behaving soberly, left something to be desired. For an account of a drinking spree with GW's overseer Thomas Green, himself no model of sobriety, see Green's letter to GW, 15 May 1788.

Letter not found: from David Forman, 3 Jan. 1790. On 21 Jan. GW wrote Forman "acknowledging the receipt of your letters of the 3rd and 18th instant."[1]

1. See also David Humphreys to John Jay, 8 Jan. 1790, and Tobias Lear to Jay, 20 Jan. 1790.

From Alexander Hamilton

[3 January 1790]

The Secretary of the Treasury having, in consequence of the Act for the Establishment and support of Light-houses,[1] directed his Enquiries to that object begs leave most respectfully to submit the result to

The President of the United States of America.

New Hampshire.

In this State is only one Light house situated on a point of land on the Island of New-Castle, three miles from Portsmouth, without the walls of the Fort which commands the entrance of Piscatqua river. It is under the Superintendance of a Commisary who is Captain of the Fort;[2] and is at present in good repair.

The annual expence of maintaining it, is estimated at   Dollars   217.20.

Massachusetts.

In this State are six Light-houses at the following places vizt
    Boston
    Cape-Ann
    Plymouth
    Plumb Island
    Nantucket
    Portland

The whole expence attending the support of these Establishments including the Officers Salaries, is estimated at
                                  Dollars   5736.

The Officers appointed for their management are,
    At Boston, Captain Thomas Knox with an annual
        Salary of   Dollars   400
    At Cape Ann Mr Samuel Houston with Ditto   400
    At Plymouth the widow of the late General Thomas[3]
        with Ditto   233.50.
    At Plumb-Island Mr [   ] Lowell[4] with Ditto   220.
    At Nantucket, Mr Paul Pinkham with Ditto   250.
    At Portland, the building not being perfectly

completed no person is yet appointed to
superintend it.

Exclusive of the above there is an officer stiled a Commisary who
has the charge of supplying the whole.

This Office is now filled by Mr [   ] Devens,[5] but what allowance he has for executing it, the Secretary has not yet ascertained.

When the building at Portland is completed, the expence of
maintaining it, and the allowance of the Commissary superintending the whole, will probably make the total amount of the
Light-house Establishment in the State of Massachusetts about

Dollars   6000 per annum.

Connecticut.

In this State there is only one Light house which is situated at the
port of New London; it is built of stone, and has lately been
repaired: In the month of May last the General Assembly ordered some Buoys to be fixed in the harbour for the safety of
the navigation, but nothing has been yet done in consequence
of the Act.

The annual expence of this Establishment is estimated at

Dollars   450

At New Haven there is a pier in the harbor which is private
property, & a Buoy at the entrance, two other buoys are judged
necessary for the safety of the navigation.

New York.

At New York there is a Light-house and was lately a Beacon at
Sandy hook, the annual expence of which (exclusive of an allowance to the Wardens of the port) is about

Dollars   1500

The number of the Wardens is four, who have (besides other
Duties incident to their Office) the charge of supplying and
superintending this Establishment. They have each an allowance of one Dollar and an half pr day, when employed in visiting
the works, exclusive of their provisions &c. The Master Warden
is Mr Thomas Randall. The Beacon has been recently blown
down and will require to be replaced; which can be done at an
inconsiderable expence.

In New Jersey.

There is no Light-house, nor any establishment of that nature.

In Pennsylvania.

There is a Light house at Cape Henlopen, and several Buoys, Beacons and Piers for the security of the navigation on the Bay & river Delaware. The annual expence of these establishments which have been under the care of a Board of Wardens of the Port of Philadelphia, is estimated by the present Master Warden at, Dollars 4133. This Office is now filled by Capt. William Allibone.

In Delaware.

There is no Light-house nor other establishment of this nature, those on the Bay & river Delaware answering for that state.

In Maryland & Virginia

There are at present no Light houses, nor any Beacons, Buoys &ca for the security of Vessels navigating the Bay of Chesapeak. I[n] consequence of certain Acts of the Legislatures of these States, stiled the compact Laws, considerable Sums have been collected heretofore, by a Tax upon Tonage, for raising a fund for the purpose of building Light-houses &c. at Cape Henry. The Commissioners appointed by the two States for superintending this work, expended on it previous to the War, in collecting materials &c., at between 7 and £8000 Virginia Currency but it is presumed that no considerable Benefit can be now derived from this Expenditure[6]—The present expence for erecting this Lighthouse &c. (as estimated by one of the Commissioners appointed on the part of the State of Virginia) is comput'd at

Dollars 34.076.66.

The annual Expence of maintaining it would probably not exceed

Dollars 2.000

In South Carolina.

There is one Light-house and the necessary Buoys and Beacons, for the security of the navigation into that harbour—The Lighthouse is in good Condition, but the Buoys and Beacons want repair—The annual expence attending this establishment is computed at

Dollars 1.457.

The officer having charge of them at present is Mr Thomas Hollingsby, who is recommended by the Commissioners of Pilotage for that harbour as a person perfectly qualified for the business;[7] his present salary is Dollars 257.14.

Georgia.

No information has been received from that State on this subject, although the same enquiries have been made there, as in other States.

To this statement of the substance of the information, which he has received respecting the several Establishments in question, The Secretary begs leave to add that most of the persons who have been singly charged with the care of any of them, have been recommended as proper to be continued, & that no objection has been made to any; And that in the two instances in which that care has been commited to Boards (as in the Cases of Pennsylvania and New York) the principals of those Boards are well recommended.

It appears to the Secretary, that it will be expedient to conform to the plan, which exists in Massachusetts, and to substitute Individuals to Boards, where the business has been committed to them; and he thinks it probable that a reappointment of the persons who have been heretofore employed, will be most likely to produce an eligible choice, and to give satisfaction; and also that the allowances heretofore made (as far as they apply) will be a good standard for those to be established. As however it is the intention of the Legislature, that the expenditures for these establishments, should be made by Contract, which from the nature of the objects must generally be conducted on the spot, it seems advisable for this and other reasons, which will occur, that in the distant States, there should be some other persons than the immediate Superintendants of the Light-house connected with them in the business.

As a temporary arrangement for this purpose, the Secretary wou'd propose that the particular Superintendants in the several States, except Pennsylvania and New York, should be put under the direction of the Collectors of the principal ports.

In New Hampshire of the Collector of Portsmouth
In Massachusetts of the Collector of Boston
In Connecticut of the Collector of New London
In South Carolina of the Collector of Charleston
Georgia is omitted from the want of information

Pennsylvania & New York are excepted, because their contiguity to the Seat of Government will place the particular Superintendants sufficiently under the Eye of the Secretary of the Treasury.

Pursuant to the foregoing Ideas the Secretary sub-[mits] the following nomination.

At Boston Capt. Thomas Knox with a Salary of

Dollars	400. pr An.
At Cape Ann—Mr Samuel Houston with do of	400
At Plymouth, the widow of the late Genl Thomas with do of	240.
At Plumb-Island Mr [ ] Lowell with Do of	220
At Nantucket Mr Paul Pinkham with Do of	250
At New London (a person to be nominated by Genl Huntington)[8] with Do of	100
At New York Mr Thos Randall with ditto of	400
At Philadelphia Mr William Allibone with do of	500.
At Charleston, South Carolina, Mr Thomas Hollingsby with Ditto of	260

No account having been received at the Treasury of the Completion of the Light-house erecting at Portland in Massachusetts, the Secretary has not included it in the present nomination; he has also omitted the Port of New Haven in Connecticut, as the piers & Buoys in that harbor, appear to be private property, not that of the State.

In the States of Virginia & Maryland it appears from what is above stated in this report, that there are no establishments in those states, altho' materials have formerly been collected for building a Light-House at Cape Henry. As the Act of the seventh of August last relative to the support of Light-houses &c. renders it necessary to obtain a cession of a proper place near the entrance of the chesapeak previous to the erection of a Light-house in that Quarter, the Secretary submits it to the consideration of the President, whether it would not be advisable to determine on the place best adapted for such an Establishment, in order that an application may be made to the supreme Executive of the State, under whose jurisdiction the same may be, for a cession of the same.[9]

It will be observed, that the secretary has not mentioned a

person for taking charge of the Light-house at New Hampshire—The present Commissary (as before stated) is Capt. of the Fort, near to whose Walls the Light-house is situated, The Collector of the port of Portsmouth is of opinion that the care of it should be entrusted to the Captain of the Fort, but has said nothing as to the qualifications of Mr Clap for this office; or of the Allowance made to him on this account by the State; the Secretary therefore submits the propriety of deferring any appointment for this place, 'till further enquiry is made on these points, to which immediate attention will be paid.

With respect to the Duties of the General Superintendants, as the act contemplates the maintaining, supporting and erecting the Establishments to be by Contract, the Secretary is of opinion, that in all Cases where the nature of the service or supply will possibly admit of the same being so done, with advantage to the public, the Superintendants should be authorised to enter into Contract for the same, subject to the ratification of the Secretary of the Treasury, with the approbation of the President; and where the same cannot be so done, that the General Superintendants shall direct the execution of the necessary business at as low a rate as possible.

This line the Secretary is induced to suggest, as he finds on an Investigation of the different Objects of Expenditure accrueing under these establishments, that Cases will sometimes occur (especially in the repair of works and replacing Buoys &c.) where it will not be possible to Establish any principles of calculation for doing the same by Contract, in which case the party contracting (should such be found) would either demand an extravagant allowance for securing him against the possibility of risque, or endeavour to avoid the same by exectuting his Contract in an inefficient manner. All which is humbly submitted

Alexander Hamilton
Secretary of the Treasury

LB, DLC:GW.

This document is undated in GW's letter book. It is located between letters dated 28 Dec. 1789 and 3 Jan. 1790. In his letter to Hamilton of 4 Jan. GW stated: "I feel myself very much obliged by what you sent me yesterday."

1. See "An Act for the establishment and support of Lighthouses, Beacons, Buoys, and Public Piers" (1 *Stat.* 53–54 [7 Aug. 1789]).

2. The lighthouse keeper was Supply Clap. He was removed from his position in June 1790 (Hamilton to Joseph Whipple, 1 June 1790, DNA: RG 56, Letters to Collectors at Small Ports, Set G).

3. In March 1790 Hamilton asked the opinion of Benjamin Lincoln, collector of customs at Boston, about Hannah Thomas (c.1730–1819), widow of Maj. Gen. John Thomas, noting that she was currently superintendent of the lighthouse at Plymouth, "but whether this has been nominal or real is not known, nor how far public considerations may cooperate with personal ones to recommend a continuance of the arrangements." Lincoln replied 19 Mar. that Mrs. Thomas was indeed considered as the effectual lighthouse keeper. On 6 April, however, he recommended John Thomas, Jr., to succeed to the post since, Lincoln contended, he probably would have been appointed instead of his mother if he had not been a minor at the time of her appointment. On 8 May GW appointed Thomas to superintend the Plymouth light (Syrett, *Hamilton Papers*, 6:297–98, 307, 355, 406, 475).

4. Abner Lowell.

5. Richard Devens.

6. For GW's inquiries concerning the construction of the lighthouse at Cape Henry, see Thomas Newton, Jr., to GW, 17 July 1789, GW to Newton, 12 Oct., 23 Nov. 1789, and Beverley Randolph to GW, 18 Dec. 1789.

7. For later problems concerning Hollingsby and his removal from office, see Hamilton to GW, 26 June 1790, and Tobias Lear to Hamilton, 29 June 1790.

8. Jedediah Huntington.

9. See GW to Thomas Newton, Jr., 12 Oct. 1789, n.1.

From Samuel Meredith

Treasury of the United States

Sir　　　　　　　　　　　　[New York] January 3d 1790

My Accots having lain a considerable time in the Offices for settlement, & being now passed, permit me to lay a Copy of them before you.[1] I have the honor to be with the most perfect respect sir Your most humble Servt

Saml Meredith
Treasr of the U. States

LB, DLC:GW.

It is possible that Tobias Lear misdated this letter in making the letter-book copy. Documents were copied into some of GW's letter books as much as several years after they were written. An identical letter, dated 3 Jan. 1791, was sent by Meredith to Frederick Augustus Muhlenburg, Speaker of the House of Representatives, enclosing Meredith's accounts for 1 July to 30 Sept. 1790 (*DHFC*, 3:791).

1. Copies of Meredith's accounts are not now among the Washington Papers. If the letter is properly dated 1790, the enclosure was undoubtedly the same statement of accounts "of the receipts and expenditures of the public money, from the time of his [Meredith's] appointment, until the thirty-first of December last" that was submitted to the House of Representatives and the Senate on 29 Jan. 1790 (*DHFC*, 1:231, 3:279). A copy of the account is in DNA: RG 233, Accounts of the Treasurer of the United States, vol. 1, and is printed in *DHFC*, 3:599–613. Meredith's 1791 acounts are printed in ibid., 791–811.

To Alexander Hamilton

Dear Sir, [New York] Monday Morng 4th Jany [1790][1]
I feel myself very much obliged by what you sent me yesterday.[2] The letter from Governor Johnston I return—much pleased to find so authentic an Acct of the adoption by No. Carolina of the Constitution.[3] Yrs sincerely & affectly

Go: Washington

ALS, DLC: Alexander Hamilton Papers.
1. GW mistakenly dated this letter 1789.
2. Presumably GW is referring to Hamilton's report on lighthouses, 3 Jan. 1790.
3. The letter from Samuel Johnston, governor of North Carolina, has not been identified.

William Jackson to John Jay

Sir, United States [New York] January 4th 1790
The letter, which accompanies this, addressed to the Vice-President of the United States by Judge Sewall, with its enclosure, having been submitted to the President of the United States, he directs me to transmit them to you, as the objects to which they refer are immediately within the department of the supreme Judiciary, and will, in the first instance, come most properly before you.[1] The President of the United States likewise directs me to inform you that Judge Sewall has hinted at the subject of the enclosed papers in a letter to him, of which, if it is thought necessary, a transcript may be had. I have the honor to be, most respectfully, Sir, Your obedient Servant

W. Jackson

ALS, DNA: RG 59, Miscellaneous Letters; LB, DLC:GW.
  1. This letter has not been identified.

From Christian Charles de Klauman

Richmond [Va.] Janr. the 4 1790
  Your Excellency will pardon the liberty of this address, tho'
the author of it has not the honor of being personally known to
you. My wish is, thro your favor, to be appointed to some
employment whereby I may make a decent living, and my pretensions are these.
  I left the Danish service in the year 1777, and arrived in
Virginia that Fall with an intention of joining your army, but the
Enemy being in the Bay and a passage to the North difficult, I
accepted a Captains Commission in Colo. Marshalls regiment of
Artillery. In the same year I was by Govr Henry appointed to the
duty of Inspector Genr. over the military stores and artillery of
the state of Virginia upon the resignation of Colo. de la Loyaute.
In the year 1779 the Govr and Council recommended me to the
assembly for that post, but the assembly discontinued the Office,
and appointed a board of war, the members of which were to do
this duty in rotation. The same assembly passed a law for raising
two Battallions of Infantry, to one of which they appointed me a
Major, with order to proceed immediately to New Castle in
Virginia and there to remain untill the recruits should be collected. By this means I lost my Commission in the artillery, and
the State not being able to raise men for the two Battallions, the
assembly at their next meeting discontinued them, whereby I
was altogether thrown out of the State line, and deprived of all
the advantages of half pay &c. which were promised me at my
entering into the service.[1] Continuing in the State, I served
during the difrent Invasions with a command in the militia, and
had the honor of serving under your Excellency at the Siege of
york as an Aid to the marquis de St Simon.[2]
  I have lodged with Colo. Bland my Commission and Resignation in the Danish army,[3] as also my recommendations and
Certificates of Service signed by Genr. Weedon & Genr. Mulen-
burg, Baron ⟨de⟩ Steuben, Marquis de la Fayette, and Marquis
de St Simon, which will prove to your Excellency the truth of the

above related circumstances. I have the honor to be with the greatest esteem your Excellencies Most obedient humble Servant

C: C: de Klauman

ALS, DLC:GW.

1. For Klauman's difficulties with the state of Virginia concerning his rank, see the Board of War to Thomas Jefferson, 14 Dec. 1779, and Jefferson to the Board of War, 18 Dec. 1779, in Boyd, *Jefferson Papers*, 3:221, 229–30. From 1778 to 1779 Klauman was commissary of military stores at Point of Fork, Va., and then was assigned to a position under the Board of War.

2. Claude-Anne Rouvroy, marquis de Saint-Simon-Montbléru (1743–1819), served at Yorktown as commander of the 3,000 land troops which the comte de Grasse had transported from the West Indies to serve in the campaign against Cornwallis.

3. Theodorick Bland (1742–1790) was a United States congressman from Virginia.

From Henry Knox

Sir   War Office [New York] January 4th 1790

I humbly beg leave to submit to your consideration a general statement of the Indian Department, and of the South Western frontiers, the same being intimately blended together.

The invitation of the United States to the Creek Nation of Indians, to treat of peace on terms of mutual advantage has not been accepted[1]—The report of the Commissioners A will fully show the precarious state of this business.[2]

The assurances given by some of the Chiefs of the peaceable intentions ⟨of the Creek Nation, are too uncertain in their nature, even if sincere, for the United States to rely upon.

The case seems to require an adequate provisional arrangement, which, on the commission of any further depredations by the Creeks, should be called into activity—After the solemn offer of peace which has been made, and refused, it is incumbent on the United States to be in a situation to punish all unprovoked aggressions.

In case the conduct of the Creeks should Render coercion indispensibly necessary, policy requires that it should be under taken with a force adequate to the speedy accomplishment of the object.

An Army of sufficient strength should be raised to march

into) their country and destroy their Towns, unless they should submit to an equitable peace.

The Warriors of the Creeks have been stated at various numbers from four to six thousand, and are said to be generally well armed, and furnished with ammunition.

To march into the Country of the Upper and Lower Creeks so as to be superior to all opposition would require an Army to be raised of five thousand men—This number after making the necessary deductions for sickness—establishment of posts of communication—and convoys of provision, would probably be reduced to three thousand five hundred effectives.

The troops to be employed on this service ought to be enlisted for the occasion, subject however to be sooner discharged if necessary.

I have formed an Estimate of the expence of such an Army which is hereunto annexed marked No: 1, on the supposition that the pay of the non-commissioned officers[3] and privates may be reduced to the sums therein specified.

But in either event of peace or War with the Creeks the establishment of a line of military posts on the south western frontier appears to be highly requisite. No peace with the Indians can be preserved unless by a military force—The lawless whites as well as Indians will be deterred from the commission of murders when they shall be convinced that punishment will immediately follow detection.

The situation of the Cherokee Nation looking up to the United States for protection in consequence of the treaty of Hopewell, demands attention.[4]

Although existing circumstances may require that the boundaries stated in the said treaty should be more accomodated to the inhabitants who cannot be removed—Yet the other general principles thereof ought to be preserved, and particularly the stipulated protection of the United States—This cannot be afforded but by troops—The friendship of the Chickasaws and Choctaws cannot be cultivated, and the trade stipulated by treaty cannot be extended to them but by means of the protection of troops.

The present military arrangement of the United States consists of one Battalion of Artillery of two hundred and forty non-commissioned and privates, and one regiment of Infantry of five hundred and sixty non commissioned and privates—This force for the following objects is utterly inadequate—To prevent the usurpation of the lands of the United States—To facilitate the surveying and selling of the same, for the purpose of reducing the public debt—and for the protection of the frontiers from Georgia to Lake Erie—If it should be decided to erect a line of posts of that extent, and to leave small guards for the public Arsenals the following establishment would be required.

A Battalion of Artillery of two hundred and forty non commissioned officers and privates—And two Regiments of Infantry of seven hundred non commissioned officers and privates each—the total of the Artillery and Infantry amounting to sixteen hundred and forty non commissioned and privates.

The Estimate hereunto annexed marked No: 2. will exhibit the annual expence of such an establishment[5]—It is to be observed that the Estimate is formed on the principle, that the present pay of the non-commissioned officers and privates may be considerably reduced—But the pay of a Lieutenant Colonel Commandant is enlarged from fifty to seventy five dollars per month—and the pay of the Major Commandant of Artillery to fifty dollars per month—This occasions an encrease for the Lieutenant Colonels and Major Commandant of sixty dollars per month—when the duty and expence of a Commanding Officer of a regiment or battalion be considered, it is presumed, that the proposed additional pay in these instances will promote the oeconomy and good of the service.

Although the proposed reduction of the pay cannot effect the existing stipulations to the troops now in service yet as they are liable to be discharged at any period it is highly probable that in preference thereto, they would accept the reduced pay.

The several representations herewith submitted marked B of the depredations committed by the Indians on the people along the south of the Ohio, and upon Cumberland river, show the exposed situation of those settlements[6]—It seems the posts North West of the Ohio do not afford the necessary protection, and the people claim the employment of their own militia at the expence of the United States—A similar arrangement having been in operation until the organization of the General Government, at the expence of Virginia.

If it shall be decided to afford the protection requested, the propriety of employing the militia of the country for that purpose may be doubted—The oeconomy of disciplined troops is always superior to militia while their efficacy is at least equal— Hence if troops are employed within the district of Kentucky as patroles or otherwise, they ought to be detachments from the regular troops of the United States under the orders of the Commanding Officer on the Ohio—About four companies acting as patroles or scouts would afford all the satisfaction to the settlements which could be derived from defensive measures— but it is only from offensive measures that full security could be obtained.

The various tribes seated on the Wabash river, extending up to the Miami Village, and the several branches of that river, are the indians from whom the settlements of Kentuckey principally receive injury.

But these depredations although perhaps effected with impunity as to the actual perpetrators, are not so to the Indians generally, for the whites frequently make incursions into the Wabash country north west of the Ohio, and it is probable that indiscriminate revenge is wreaked on all bearing the name of Indians—Hence a difficulty arises on the part of the United States, which requires a serious consideration.

That the people of Kentuckey are entitled to be defended, there can be no doubt—But as there seems to have been such a prevalence of hostilities as to render it uncertain who are right, or who wrong—The principles of justice which ought to dictate the conduct of every nation seems to forbid the idea of attempting to extirpate the Wabash indians until it shall appear that they cannot be brought to treat on reasonable terms—If after a treaty should be effected with them, it should be violated, or after an invitation to a treaty which should be refused, and followed by hostilities, the United States will clearly have the right to inflict that degree of punishment which may be necessary to deter the Indians from any future unprovoked aggressions.

If this statement be just it would follow that the Governor of the Western territory should be instructed to attempt to effect a general treaty with the said Wabash tribes on terms of mutual advantage—If they should refuse, and continue, or suffer a continuance from any of their neighbouring tribes of the depredations upon the district of Kentuckey, the Arms of the Union ought to be exerted to chastise them.

The statement hereunto annexed No: 3. will show the application of the sum appropriated during the last session of Congress to indian treaties, and indian expences—The sum remaining unexpended might be applied to a treaty with the Wabash Indians.[7]

Provisions must be furnished the indians during the treaty— Whether any presents shall be added thereto will depend on the decision of Congress—It seems to have been the custom of barbarous nations in all ages to expect and receive presents from those more civilized—and the custom seems confirmed by modern Europe with respect to Morocco, Algiers, Tunis and Tripoli.

The practise of the British Government and its colonies of giving presents to the indians of North America is well known— They seem to have been convinced that it was the cheapest and most effectual mode of managing the Indians—The idea of fear, or purchasing a peace is not to be admitted in the cases above stated—But the conduct appears to have been dictated by wise policy—a comparative view of the expences of an hostile or conciliatory system towards the indians will evince the infinite oeconomy of the latter over the former.

The question then on the point of presents must be simply this—Is the situation of the United States such, with respect to the neighbouring European Colonies, as to render it good policy at this time to annihilate the indian customs and expectations of receiving presents, and thereby disgusting them in such a manner, as to induce them to connect themselves more closely with the said Colonies?

If it should be decided to the contrary, the Estimate of the Governor of the Western Territory for the object of the Wabash indians No: 4 would show the sum required, from which however must be deducted the balance remaining from the appropriation of the last year.[8]

Although the information is not sufficiently accurate whereon to form a decided opinion of the number of indian Warriors within the limits of the United States, yet the evidence seems sufficient to warrant the supposition that they amount nearly to twenty thousand—If to this number we should add for every

Warrior three old men women and children, the total number would be eighty thousand.

Since the United States became a nation, their conduct, and some of the States towards the indians seems to have resulted from the impulses of the moment—Until the treaty effected at Fort Harmar in January 1789, it seemed a prevailing opinion, that the treaty of peace with Great Britain instead of the preemption only, actually invested the United States with the absolute right of the indian Territory—and in pursuance of this idea treaties were made, and boundaries alloted to the indians—But by the directions of Congress of 2d of July 1788 to the Governor of the Western territory to extinguish the indian claims to lands they had ceded to the United States, and to obtain regular conveyances of the same it would appear, that they conceded the indian right to the soil.[9]

The various opinions which exist on the proper mode of treating the indians, require that some system should be established on the subject.

That the Indians possess the natural rights of man, and that they ought not wantonly to be divested thereof cannot be well denied.

Were these rights ascertained, and declared by law—were it enacted that the indians possess the right to all their territory which they have not fairly conveyed, and that they should not be divested thereof, but in consequence of open treaties, made under the authority of the United States, the foundation of peace and justice would be laid.

The individual States claiming or possessing the right of preemption to territory inhabited by indians, would not be materially injured by such a declarative law, the exercise of their right would be restrained only, when it should interfere with the general interests—Should any State having the right of preemption desire to purchase territory, which the indians should be willing to relinquish, it would have to request the General Government to direct a treaty for that purpose, at the expence however of the individual State requesting the same.

But as indian Wars almost invariably arise in consequence of disputes relative to boundaries, or trade, and as the right of declaring War, making treaties, and regulating commerce, are vested in the United States it is highly proper they should have the sole direction of all measures for the consequences of which they are responsible. I have the honor to be Sir, With the highest respect Your Most Obedient Humble Servant.

H. Knox
secretary for the department of War

DS, DNA: RG 233, First Congress, Records of Legislative Proceedings, Reports and Communications Submitted to the House; copy, DNA: RG 46, First Congress, Records of Legislative Proceedings, President's Messages.

1. For the negotiations of the American commissioners sent to negotiate a treaty with the Creek, see David Humphreys to GW, 21, 26, 27 Sept., 13, 28 Oct. 1789, Alexander Hamilton to GW, 20 Oct. 1789, and Henry Knox to GW, 18 Oct., 21 Nov. 1789. See also GW's Memoranda on Indian Affairs, 1789. With his letter to GW, Knox enclosed a copy of the commissioners' report, marked A, consisting of a journal kept by the commissioners of their correspondence concerning their mission. It is printed in *DHFC*, 2:210–41, and in *ASP, Indian Affairs*, 1:68–78. Another copy was submitted to GW by Knox on 21 Nov. 1789.

2. See note 1. GW submitted the commissioners' journal to Congress with his letter of 12 Jan. 1790.

3. Enclosure no. 1 was "An Estimate of the Expences of an Army for one Year including the General Staff, Field and Company Officers, and five Thousand and forty non Commissioned Officers and privates" (DNA: RG 46, First Congress, Records of Legislative Proceedings, President's Messages). It is printed in *ASP, Indian Affairs*, 1:61–63.

4. For the Treaty of Hopewell, see the Cherokee Chiefs to GW, 19 May 1789, n.1.

5. Enclosure no. 2 was "An estimate of the annual expence of a Corps to consist of two Regiments of Infantry of Ten Companies each and one Battalion of Artillery of four companies, each company to be composed of 4 Sergeants 4 Corporals 2 Musicians and 60 privates Amounting in the whole to 1680 non Commissioned Officers and Privates" (DNA: RG 46, First Congress, Records of Legislative Proceedings, President's Messages). It is printed in *ASP, Indian Affairs*, 1:63–64.

6. Enclosure B has not been identified.

7. Enclosure no. 3 was a "Statement of 20,000 Dollars appropriated by Congress on the 20th August 1789 for the expence of negotiations with the Indian tribes" (DNA: RG 46, First Congress, Records of Legislative Proceedings, President's Messages). It is printed in *ASP, Indian Affairs*, 1:64.

8. Enclosure no. 4 was an "Estimate of the expence with which a treaty with the Indians of the Wabash and Miami rivers would probably be attended—Their numbers are supposed to be from twelve to fifteen hundred men" (DNA: RG 46, First Congress, Records of Legislative Proceedings, President's Messages). It is printed in *ASP, Indian Affairs*, 1:64.

9. The Confederation Congress's "Additional Instructions to Governor St. Clair," 2 July 1788, noted that an additional sum of $20,000 had been appropriated to secure a permanent peace with the northwestern tribes by obtain-

ing a boundary advantageous to the United States. Indian land claims were to be extinguished by purchase "in case it can be done on terms beneficial to the Union" (*Territorial Papers, Northwest Territory*, 2:117–18). The $20,000 authorized by Congress was in addition to the $14,000 already appropriated for negotiating Indian treaties with tribes in the northern department, "the whole of the said twenty thousand dollars together with six thousand dollars of the said fourteen thousand dollars to be applied solely to the purpose of extinguishing Indian claims to the lands they have already ceded to the United States by obtaining regular conveyances for the same" (*JCC*, 34:285).

From James Madison

Dear Sir   George Town [Md.] Jany 4 1790
   After being detained 8 or 10 days beyond the intended commencement of my Journey, by the critical illness of my mother,[1] I am now subjected to a further delay by an attack on my own health. A slight complaint in my bowels which I first felt on the day of my arrival here (friday last) very suddenly took the form of a pretty severe dysentery. With the aid of Doctr Stuart who has been good eno' to see me every day, I have I hope nearly subdued the malignity of the disease, and got into a course of recovery. I find myself however much weakened by the joint operation of the malady & the medicine, and shall be under the necessity not only of remaining here a few days longer, but of travelling afterwards with some circumspection.
   You will probably have seen by the papers that the contest in the Assembly on the subject of the amendments ended in the loss of them. The House of Delegates got over the objections to the 11 & 12, but the Senate revived them with the addition of the 3 & 8 articles, and by a vote of adherence prevented a ratification.[2] On some accounts this event is no doubt to be regretted. But it will do no injury to the Genl Government. On the contrary it will have the effect with many of turning their distrust towards their own Legislature. The miscarriage of the 3d art: particularly, will have this effect.
   A few days before I was allowed to set out for N. York, I took a ride to Monticello. The answer of Mr Jefferson to the notification of his appointment will no doubt have explained the state of his mind on that subject.[3] I was sorry to find him so little biased in favor of the domestic service allotted to him, but was glad that his difficulties seemed to result cheifly from what I take to be an

erroneous view of the kind and quantity of business annexed to that which constituted the foreign department. He apprehends that it will far exceed the latter which has of itself no terrors to him. On the other hand It was supposed, & I beleive truly that the domestic part will be very trifling, and for that reason improper to be made a distinct department. After all if the whole business can be executed by any one man, Mr Jefferson must be equal to it; if not he will be relieved by a necessary division of it. All whom I have heard speak on the subject are remarkably solicitous for his acceptance, and I flatter myself that they will not in the final event be disappointed.

In case I should be detained here much longer than I calculate, and any thing should occur, I may trouble you with a few lines further. With every sentiment of respect and attachment I am Dear Sir, Your's truly.

Js Madison Jr

ALS, DLC:GW; copy, DLC: James Madison Papers.

1. Madison's mother, Nelly Conway Madison (1732–1801) was frequently in ill health but lived until the beginning of the nineteenth century.

2. For the action of the Virginia house of delegates on the amendments to the Constitution, see Edmund Randolph to GW, 26 Nov. 1789, and Madison to GW, 28 Nov. 1789, n.5.

3. See Thomas Jefferson to GW, 15 Dec. 1789.

To the United States Senate and House of Representatives

Sir, United-States [New York] January 4th 1790

Whenever there shall be a sufficient number of the two Houses of Congress assembled to proceed to business, I request to be informed of it. And also at what time and place it will be convenient for Congress that I should meet them, in order to make some oral communications at the commencement of their session.[1] I have the honor to be, Sir, Your most humble servant

Go: Washington

LS, DNA: RG 46, First Congress, Records of Legislative Proceedings, President's Messages; LB, DLC:GW.

1. On 7 Jan. the House of Representatives received a message from the Senate that a committee had been appointed "to wait on the President of the United States, and inform him, that a quorum of both Houses of Congress

had assembled, and are ready to receive any communications that he may be pleased to make." On the same day the House appointed Nicholas Gilman, Fisher Ames, and Joshua Seney as a committee to join Caleb Strong and Ralph Izard, the Senate committee, in informing the president of the existence of a quorum (*DHFC*, 1:214, 3:251). The committee reported on the same day that "the President was pleased to say, he would attend, to make his communication to both Houses of Congress, to-morrow morning, at eleven o'clock" (ibid., 3:251).

Tobias Lear to Alexander Hamilton

Sir, United States [New York] January 5th, 1790.
By direction of the President of the United States, I have the honor herewith to transmit to you a letter from the Governor of Virginia, dated December 18th, 1789,[1] enclosing an Act (which is likewise sent you) of the general Assembly of that Commonwealth, passed Novr 13th 1789, to convey to the United States in Congress assembled certain Land for the purpose of building a Light House on Cape Henry. I have the honor to be, with perfect respect, Sir, Your most Obedt Hble Servt

Tobias Lear.
Secretary to the President
of the United States.

ALS, DNA: RG 26, Lighthouse Services Correspondence; LB, DLC:GW.
1. See also Thomas Newton to GW, 17 July and 24 Oct. 1789, GW to Newton, 12 Oct. and 23 Nov. 1789.

To Sarah Bomford

Madam, New York, January 6th 1790.
In answer to your letter of the 23rd of August last,[1] which came to my hands but a few days ago, I must observe that, from the year 1775. to the close of the war with great Britain, my public duties totally precluded me from attending to any kind of private business whatever, and from the latter period to the time of my entering again into public life, I was occasionally so much engaged in correspondencies, and other matters consequent on the station which I had held, that, with the greatest industry I could not find time to pay that attention to my *own* private affairs which they required.

Under these circumstances I had it not in my power to attend particularly to the affairs of Mrs Savage, and, of course, have not that knowledge of the situation of them that Mr Fairfax has, to whom I have transmitted your letter with a request, and not doubting, that he will give it the attention which it deserves, and which the situation of Mrs Savage's affairs will admit of [2]—And I must request that in future you will correspond with him upon this business. I am Madam, Your most obedient Servant

G. Washington.

LB, DLC:GW.

This letter concerns the affairs of the late Margaret Savage, the widow of the Rev. Charles Green, who had married Dr. William Savage of Dumfries. For GW's long and frustrating involvement in the affairs of Mrs. Savage, see particularly *Diaries*, 2:181–82, 2:228, 3:81; GW and George William Fairfax to William Savage, 25 April 1767, GW to Margaret Savage, 28 June 1768, to William Ellzey, 3 Oct. 1769, and to Bryan Fairfax, 6 April 1789, n.3. See also the enclosure to GW to Peter Tenor, 8 Nov. 1786, GW to Newburgh Burroughs, 20 Aug. 1797, George Deneale to GW, 18 April 1798, GW to Deneale, 22 April 1798, and Henry Lee and Daniel Payne to GW, 24 April 1767. For Mrs. Bomford, see GW to Bryan Fairfax, 6 April 1789, n.3.

1. Letter not found.

2. GW wrote Bryan Fairfax concerning Mrs. Bomford's letter on 6 Jan.: "I received the enclosed Letter a few days since from Mrs Bomford, upon the subject of a legacy which was left her by the late Mrs Savage—and likewise requesting payment may be made to her for the diet, lodging &ca of that unfortunate woman for upwards of four years.

"In my answer to the above letter I have informed Mrs Bomford that circumstances have put it out of my power to pay particular attention to the affairs of Mrs Savage—and that I should transmit her letter to you, not doubting but you would give it that attention which it deserved—You will, therefore, my dear Sir, be good enough to give Mrs Bomford such an answer to her letter, as from your Knowledge of the situation of Mrs Savage's affairs you may be enabled to do—and permit me to add, if this business could be brought to a close it would be a most desirable thing.

"You will please to make my best compliments acceptable to Mrs Fairfax and your family, in which I am joined by Mrs Washington—and I assure you we are not a little pleased to hear that you are about to establish yourselves in the neighbourhood of Mount Vernon promising ourselves a new source of pleasure from that circumstance whenever we are permitted to return home" (LB, DLC:GW).

From James Coor

Sir, New Bern [N.C.] January 7th 1790.

The state of North Carolina having Acceeded to the General Government of the United States I am told it becomes my duty to Acquaint You that I have acted at this place as a Naval Officer for port Beauford in this state for many years.

And also to mention that If agreeable to Your Excellency and the Authority which may have such Appointments I should wish to be Continued as Naval Officer for port Beauford which Comprehends the town of New Bern where almost all the trade of the port is transacted. I have the Honour to be Your Excellencys Most Obedt Servt

James Coor

ALS, DLC:GW.

James Coor (c.1737–c.1800), an architect, was probably a native of England. After his arrival in America he settled at first on the Eastern Shore of Maryland and then moved to New Bern, N.C., where he served as architect for a number of residential and public buildings and held a series of local offices. Coor was a member of the colonial legislature for three terms 1773–75, served on the New Bern council of safety and on the provincial council, and frequently represented Craven County in the state legislature. As his letter indicates, he also held the office of naval officer for Beaufort under the state government. Coor wrote GW again on 25 Jan. 1790, this time requesting an appointment as surveyor for Beaufort, "in case You should not think proper to Continue a Naval Officer at this place" (DLC:GW). When GW made the North Carolina customs appointments in February 1790, Coor received neither post.

From John Christopher Kunze

Sir Chatham street [New York] N. 24. January the 7. 1790.

Supposing, that many abuse Your Condescension by taking up Your previous Time in Conferences of an indifferent Nature, I was not bold enough, to intrude myself into Your Presence, without knowing first Your Pleasure, and wishing nevertheless to lay something before You, that appears to me at least to be not incompatible with Your other high Employments, I take this Method, to communicate it.

A Year ago I recieved a Letter, directed to my Father in Law,

Mr Muhlenberg, who was then dead already, from one Mr Anton Theodore Brown,[1] in which he acquainted him, that being convinced of the fundamental Errors of that Church, in which he had been a minister for a Number of Years, the Church of Rome, and not finding any Rest in his Soul at the Attempts to counteract the Dictates of his Conscience and Reason, he begged his Advice and adjoining a Testimony from a Lutheran Congregation in Canada, he wished to be approved and confirm'd by him as a Minister of the Lutheran Church. As the Person, to whom the Letter was intended, was not among the living and as no Investigation could be made without Mr Browns personal Attendance, I took no further Notice of this Matter, mistrusting besides the Sincerity of the Motives a little.

This Gentleman is now in this City and hath by his Testimonials, Conversation, preaching in my Church and Marks of Self denial removed all my Doubts concerning him. Last Sunday he renounced before my Congregation his former Errors and was taken into the Communion of the Lutheran Church.

His Employment in Canada was preaching among the Indians he being a Missionary to them, and for some Years Superior for Six Indian Missions, and understands therefore the Language of the Northern Indians. At present he recieves a little Support from my Vestry and from the german Society in this Town, till I can find an Opportunity, to recommand him to a german Lutheran Congregation in the State.

Yesterday I recieved a Letter from him, which I take the liberty to inclose with an annexed Translation.[2] In a Conversation which I had afterwards with him I could not but judge his Zeal for the Indians commandable, and though I am entirely ignorant of the Practicability of his Proposals, yet I thought it my Duty to lay the Matter before the President of the United States, as we have the Happiness, to be govern'd by a Man, who with the Hero unites the Christian and the Friend of Mankind. Our Government, I know dos' not interfere in Matters of Religion, but to give a small Salary to an Indian Preacher, might perhaps, as Mr Brown imagines, be consider'd in a political Light. At all Events, I think, the President will perhaps deem this truly pious man not unworthy of a kind and condescending Attention, and pardon the Freedom of the Person, who introduced him to His Notice. I am with profound Deference and Respect Sir Your most devoted Servant

John Christopher Kunze
Lutheran Minister in the City of New York

ALS, DNA: RG 59, Miscellaneous Letters.

John Christopher Kunze (1744–1807), a Lutheran clergyman, was pastor of Christ Church in New York City. A native of Saxony, Kunze was educated at the University of Leipzig and in 1770 immigrated to Philadelphia to become coadjutor to Henry Melchior Mühlenberg. He married Mühlenberg's daughter Margaretta Henrietta in 1771. In 1784 he moved to New York City to become pastor of Christ Church, soon becoming popular in New York social circles and widely known as one of the country's leading scholars and linguists.

1. Anton Theodore Braun (Brown; d. 1814) was born in Treves, Germany. After his ordination as a Catholic priest, Braun was sent to North America where he preached for some years to the Canadian Indians in the area of Frontenac and Dundas, Ontario, eventually overseeing six Indian missions. After his conversion to Lutheranism, Braun served at Schoharie Parish from 1790 to 1793, as pastor at Albany from 1794 to 1797, and again at Schoharie from 1798 to 1800. From 1800 to 1814 he was stationed at Troytown, Guilderland, and New Brunswick, New York.

Braun's letter to Kunze, dated at New York, 4 Jan. 1790, described his views on missionary activity to the Indians and advocated the establishment of an Indian mission on the United States–Canadian border. "Many Indians would by the Establishment of such a Mission be united into one Body, their Trade would be ours, and in Case of a War, they could be Serviceable or at least be kept quiet" (DNA: RG 59, Miscellaneous Letters). Braun's letter appears in its entirety in CD-ROM:GW.

2. GW replied to Kunze's letter on 12 Jan.: "The subject of your letter of the 4th [7th] instant enclosing one of the same date from Mr Brown to you, appears to be of a nature requiring the operation of legislative power rather than any agency of mine at present. For however desirous I might be to promote the wishes of Mr Brown, either from a view to benefit the public by attaching those Indians which he mentions to the United States—or to advance their temporal or spiritual good by his services among them, I could not with propriety give encouragement to his plan without the previous interference of the Legislature of the Union.

"I can, therefore, only observe, that the opinion of those Gentlemen in Congress with whom you may be acquainted will enable you to judge of the proper means by which this business might be forwarded" (LB, DLC:GW).

David Humphreys to John Jay

Sir United States [New York] Janry 8th 1790
I am commanded by the President of the United States of America to send to you some Papers which have just come to him, and which are of a nature highly interesting to the Community. His object is to avail himself of your opinion, relative to the measures which should be adopted in consequence of this Communication. I have the honor to be with perfect respect &c.
D. Humphreys

N.B. the above letter was from Genl Forman—giving an acct of the detection of forgeries on the State Notes of New York—& enclosing several of the Counterfiet Certificates.[1]

ALS, DNA: RG 59, Miscellaneous Letters; LB, DLC:GW.
1. The letter from David Forman has not been found.

To the United States Senate and House of Representatives

United States [New York] January 8th 1790
Fellow Citizens of the Senate, and House of Representatives.

I embrace with great satisfaction the opportunity, which now presents itself, of congratulating you on the present favourable prospects of our public affairs. The recent accession of the important State of North Carolina to the Constitution of the United States (of which official information has been recieved)—the rising credit and respectability of our Country—the general and increasing good will towards the Government of the Union—and the concord, peace and plenty, with which we are blessed, are circumstances, auspicious, in an eminent degree to our national prosperity.

In resuming your consultations for the general good, you cannot but derive encouragement from the reflection, that the measures of the last Session have been as satisfactory to your Constituents, as the novelty and difficulty of the work allowed you to hope. Still further to realize their expectations, and to secure the blessings which a Gracious Providence has placed within our reach, will in the course of the present important

Session, call for the cool and deliberate exertion of your patriotism, firmness and wisdom.

Among the many interesting objects, which will engage your attention, that of providing for the common defence will merit particular regard. To be prepared for war is one of the most effectual means of preserving peace.

A free people ought not only to be armed but disciplined; to which end a Uniform and well digested plan is requisite: And their safety and interest require that they should promote such manufactories, as tend to render them independent on others, for essential, particularly for military supplies.

The proper establishment of the Troops which may be deemed indispensible, will be entitled to mature consideration. In the arrangements which may be made respecting it, it will be of importance to conciliate the comfortable support of the Officers and Soldiers with a due regard to œconomy.

There was reason to hope, that the pacific measures adopted with regard to certain hostile tribes of Indians would have relieved the inhabitants of our Southern and Western frontiers from their depredations. But you will percieve, from the information contained in the papers, which I shall direct to be laid before you (comprehending a communication from the Commonwealth of Virginia) that we ought to be prepared to afford protection to those parts of the Union; and, if necessary, to punish aggressors.

The interests of the United States require, that our intercourse with other nations should be facilitated by such provisions as will enable me to fulfil my duty in that respect, in the manner, which circumstances may render most conducive to the public good: And to this end, that the compensations to be made to the persons, who may be employed, should, according to the nature of their appointments, be defined by law; and a competent fund designated for defraying the expenses incident to the conduct of foreign affairs.

Various considerations also render it expedient, that the terms on which foreigners may be admitted to the rights of Citizens, should be speedily ascertained by a uniform rule of naturalization.

Uniformity in the Currency, Weights and Measures of the

United States is an object of great importance, and will, I am persuaded, be duly attended to.

The advancement of Agriculture, commerce and Manufactures, by all proper means, will not, I trust, need recommendation. But I cannot forbear intimating to you the expediency of giving effectual encouragement as well to the introduction of new and useful inventions from abroad, as to the exertions of skill and genius in producing them at home; and of facilitating the intercourse between the distant parts of our Country by a due attention to the Post-Office and Post Roads.

Nor am I less pursuaded, that you will agree with me in opinion, that there is nothing, which can better deserve your patrionage, than the promotion of Science and Literature. Knowledge is in every Country the surest basis of public happiness. In one, in which the measures of Government recieve their impression so immediately from the sense of the Community as in our's, it is proportionably essential. To the security of a free Constitution it contributes in various ways: By convincing those, who are entrusted with the public administration, that every valuable end of Government is best answered by the enlightened confidence of the people: And by teaching the people themselves to know and to value their own rights; to discern and provide against invasions of them; to distinguish between oppression and the necessary exercise of lawful authority; between burthens proceeding from a disregard to their convenience and those resulting from the inevitable exigencies of Society; to discriminate the spirit of liberty from that of licentiousness, cherishing the first, avoiding the last, and uniting a speedy, but temperate vigilence against encroachments, with an inviolable respect to the laws.

Whether this desirable object will be best promoted by affording aids to Seminaries of Learning already established—by the institution of a national University—or by any other expedients, will be well worthy of a place in the deliberations of the Legislature.

Gentlemen of the House of Representatives.

I saw with peculiar pleasure, at the close of the last Session, the resolution entered into by you expressive of your opinion,

that an adequate provision for the support of the public Credit
is a matter of high importance to the national honor and prosperity. In this sentiment, I entirely concur. And to a perfect
confidence in your best endeavours to divise such a provision, as
will be truly consistent with the end, I add an equal reliance on
the chearful co-operation of the othe[r] branch of the Legislature. It would be superfluous to specify inducements to a measure in which the character and permanent interests of the
United States are so obviously and so deeply concerned; and
which has recieved so explicit a sanction from your declaration.

Gentlemen of the Senate and House of Representatives.

I have directed the proper Officers to lay before you respectively such papers and estimates as regard the affairs particularly recommended to your consideration, and necessary to
convey to you that information of the state of the Union, which
it is my duty to afford.

The welfare of our Country is the great object to which our
cares and efforts ought to be directed. And I shall derive great
satisfaction from a co-operation with you, in the pleasing
though arduous task of ensuring to our fellow Citizens the
blessings, which they have a right to expect, from a free, efficient
and equal Government.

Go: Washington

DS, DNA: RG 46, First Congress, Records of Legislative Proceedings, President's Messages; copy, DNA: RG 233, First Congress, Records of Legislative
Proceedings, Journals.

GW delivered his first State of the Union address in the Senate chambers
on 8 January. The *Virginia Herald and Fredericksburg Advertiser*, 21 Jan. 1790,
noted that GW "was dressed in a crow coloured suit of clothes, of American
manufacture. . . . This elegant fabric was from the manufactory in Hartford."
According to Sen. William Maclay's account "The President was dressed in a
second Mourning, and . . . read his speech well. the senate headed by their
President were on his right The House of Representatives . . . with their
Speaker were on his left his [official] Family with the Heads of Departments
attended. the business was soon over and the Senate were left alone" (Bowling
and Veit, *Diary of William Maclay*, 179–80). GW's speech was widely printed in
the newspapers. See, for example, the New York *Daily Advertiser*, 9 Jan. 1790,
the *Virginia Herald and Fredericksburg Advertiser*, 21 Jan. 1790, the *Connecticut
Courant* (Hartford), 14 Jan. 1790, and the *New-York Daily Gazette*, 9 Jan. 1790.
After the president's departure the Senate appointed a committee, consisting
of Rufus King, Ralph Izard, and William Paterson, to prepare a reply. The

committee reported on Monday, 11 Jan., and the following address was adopted in reply to GW's speech: "We the Senate of the United States, return you our thanks for your speech delivered to both Houses of Congress. The accession of the State of North-Carolina to the Constitution of the United States, gives us much pleasure; and we offer you our congratulations on that event, which at the same time adds strength to our Union, and affords a proof that the more the Constitution has been considered, the more the goodness of it has appeared.—The information which we have received that the measures of the last session have been as satisfactory to our Constituents as we had reason to expect from the difficulty of the work in which we were engaged, will afford us much consolation, and encouragement in resuming our deliberations in the present session for the public good; and every exertion on our part shall be made to realize, and secure to our Country those blessings which a gracious Providence has placed within her reach.—We are persuaded that one of the most effectual means of preserving Peace, is to be prepared for War; and our attention shall be directed to the objects of common defence, and to the adoption of such plans as shall appear the most likely to prevent our dependence on other Countries for essential supplies.—In the arrangements to be made respecting the establishment of such Troops as may be deemed indispensable, we shall with pleasure provide for the comfortable support of the officers, and soldiers, with a due regard to economy.—We regret that the pacific measures adopted by Government with regard to certain hostile tribes of Indians, have not been attended with the beneficial effects toward the inhabitants of our Southern and Western frontiers, which we had reason to hope; and we shall chearfully co-operate in providing the most effectual means for their protection; and if necesssary, for the punishment of aggressors.—The uniformity of the currency, and of weights and measures, the introduction of new, and useful inventions from abroad, and the exertions of skill, and genius in producing them at home, the facilitating the communication between the distant parts of our country by means of the Post-Office, and Post Roads, a provision for the support of the department of foreign affairs, and a uniform rule of naturalization, by which Foreigners may be admitted to the rights of Citizens, are objects which shall receive such early attention as their respective importance requires.—Literature and Science are essential to the preservation of a free Constitution: The measures of Government should therefore be calculated to strengthen the confidence that is due to that important truth.—Agriculture, Commerce and Manufactures forming the basis of the wealth, and strength of our confederated Republic, must be the frequent subject of our deliberation; and shall be advanced by all proper means in our power.—Public credit being an object of great importance, we shall chearfully co-operate in all proper measures for its support.—Proper attention shall be given to such papers and estimates as you may be pleased to lay before us.—Our cares and efforts shall be directed to the welfare of our Country; and we have the most perfect dependence upon your co-operating with us on all occasions in such measures as will insure to our fellow citizens, the blessings which they have a right to expect from a free, efficient, and equal government" (*DHFC*, 1:219–20).

On 9 Jan. the House of Representatives appointed a committee of William Loughton Smith, George Clymer, and John Laurance to prepare an answer to GW's address, and on 12 Jan. a committee of the whole approved the following reply: "The Representatives of the people of the United States, have taken into consideration your Speech to both Houses of Congress at the opening of the present session.

"We reciprocate your congratulations on the accession of the State of North Carolina, an event, which, while it is a testimony of increasing good will towards the Government of the Union, cannot fail to give additional dignity and strength to the American Republic, already rising in the estimation of the world in national character and respectability.

"The information that our measures of the last Session have not proved dis-satisfactory to our Constituents, affords us much encouragement at this juncture when we are resuming the arduous task of legislating for so extensive an empire.

"Nothing can be more gratifying to the Representatives of a free people, than the reflection that their labours are rewarded by the approbation of their fellow citizens: Under this impression, we shall make every exertion to realize their expectations, and to secure to them those blessings, which Providence has placed within their reach. Still prompted by the same desire to promote their interests which then actuated us, we shall in the present Session diligently and anxiously pursue those measures, which shall appear to us conducive to that end.

"We concur with you in the sentiment that Agriculture, commerce and manufactures are entitled to legislative protection; and that the promotion of Science and literature will contribute to the security of a free government: in the progress of our deliberations, we shall not lose sight of objects so worthy of our regard.

"The various and weighty matters which you have judged necessary to recommend to our attention, appear to us essential to the tranquility and welfare of the Union, and claim our early and most serious consideration. We shall proceed without delay to bestow on them that calm discussion which their importance requires.

"We regret that the pacific arrangements pursued with regard to certain hostile tribes of Indians, have not been attended with that success which we had reason to expect from them. We shall not hesitate to concur in such further measures, as may best obviate any ill effects which might be apprehended from the failure of those negotiations.

"Your approbation of the vote of this House, at the last Session, respecting the provision for the public Creditors, is very acceptable to us: the proper mode of carrying that resolution into effect, being a subject in which the future character and happiness of these States are so deeply involved, will be among the first to deserve our attention.

"The prosperity of the United States is the primary object of all our deliberations, and we cherish the reflection, that every measure, which we may adopt for its advancement, will not only receive your chearful concurrence, but will at the same time, derive from your co-operation, additional efficacy in ensuring to our fellow-citizens, the blessings of a free, efficient and equal government" (DLC:GW).

From William Temple Franklin

(Private)

Sir,   Philadelphia Jany 9th 1790

I know not whether I am acting improperly, in thus addressing you, but if I am, I beg your Excellency will not impute it to any want of Respect for your exalted Character, or elevated Situation. Thinking as Shakespeare expresses it, that "*There is a Tide in the Affairs of Men, Which taken at the Flood, leads on to Fortune*" has induced me to trouble your Excellency on this occasion: for I consider the improving the present Moment, as important to the Success of my future Voyage through Life.

You well know Sir, the Claims I have both on my own Account, and that of my venerable Grandfather's, on the Justice, as well as the Favor of the United States, and that it is to your Excellency alone that I look up to for both.[1] If I have been rightly informed, it is your Wish to forward my Views in the Line of Foreign Affairs: should this be the Case, an Opportunity will probably soon offer of doing it to the utmost of my Ambition. By Mr Jefferson's accepting his late honorable Appointment, a Vacancy will ensue at the Court of France. This Appointment, of all others, would be the most satisfactory to me, as well as to my Grandfather, who has long been desirous of seeing me employed in the Line to which he brought me up, and to which I have sacrificed every other Pursuit in Life. He would consider it likewise, in some Measure, as an Approbation of his Services in Europe, for which, tho' acknowledg'd to be great, he never has yet receiv'd either Reward or even Thanks. I am the more solicitous of this Appointment, as I have had it in view since my first being employ'd in the Diplomatic Line, and from my long Residence at the Court of France, my Knowledge of the French Language, the Duties of a Plenipotentiary, and the Business that has hitherto been transacted between this Country and that; added to my personal Acquaintance with most of the distinguish'd Characters there, & the Reputation of my Grandfather, I am tempted to believe that I should in that situation, be a Credit to my Country as well as to my Employers. This has also been the Opinion of my Friends both here and in France. Permit me as applicable to this Subject, to enclose an Extract of a Letter from Mr Gouvernour Morris, wrote soon after his Arrival at Paris, in which he takes notice of the deep Impression my Grandfather has made in that Country, and the Utility that would probably result from my being employ'd there.[2]

Thus, Sir, I have taken the Liberty of suggesting my Wishes, relative to a particular Appointment, to which it may be said I have some Claim; but at the same time permit me to add, that I shall be perfectly satisfied with whatever your Excellency may determine on this Subject, and not less grateful should it please you to employ me differently. But having endeavor'd to qualify myself to serve my Country, either at home or abroad, in the Line of Foreign Affairs, I thought my Pretensions in this Line better founded; as well that I might be more useful; few of our Countrymen having attended much to this very important Part of Public-Affairs. When in France, from an Idea, that possibly I might hereafter be concerned here in the Management of Foreign Affairs, or that it might be of Service to those who were; I collected & committed to writing, all the Information I could get, relative to the Duties of a Secretary of State for the foreign Department, as well as the particular Arrangements to be made in his Office, with regard to secrecy; regularity, and Dispatch of Business. This System I will with Pleasure communicate to your Excellency should you be inclined to peruse it.

I cannot conclude without apologizing for having thus intruded on your Time with my Personal Concerns; but I have been imbolden'd to it by the Friendship that has long subsisted between your Excellency and my Grandfather, and the Kindness you have on all occasions shewn me. Another Inducement I have had, and which I need not conceal from your Excellency, is; that being now arrived to *the senatorial Age* (30) I am anxious to be settled in Life, or at least to know what Course I ought to pursue; having hitherto avoided every Engagement however honorable or advantageous that might the least interfere with my favorite Object. My Grandfather, who is sensible that he cannot long resist the effect of Time and a cruel Malady,[3] grows also more & more anxious to see me provided for; and your Excellency will easily conceive the Satisfaction it would give him, to find that his Views in bringing me up to Public Life, have not been unsuccessful, and that the Gratitude of his Country, for his Endeavors to serve it, extends to his Descendant.

That your Excellency may long live, and enjoy the Affections of a grateful People for your eminent Services; and that our Country will, at least in your Instance, be an exception to the Obloquy generally incident to Republics, is the Prayer, of Sir, Your Excellency's, most obedient & devoted humble Servant

W. T. Franklin.

P.S. It is possible that from the Nature of this Letter your Excellency may not think it proper to answer it in Writing, but would prefer conferring with me on the Subject: if so, be pleas'd to mention it to Mr Morris, who will apprise me of it, and I will immediately do myself the honor of waiting upon you.

ALS, DLC:GW.

1. For William Temple Franklin's earlier application for office, see his letter to GW, 20 April 1789.

2. The enclosure was an extract of a letter to Benjamin Franklin from Gouverneur Morris, 23 Feb. 1789: "The Eagerness of Inquiry into everything which relates to your Health or Situation, shews better than any Expressions of Esteem can do it, the deep Impression you have made in this Country. Many have asked me whether you did not intend to return, forgetting (in the Remembrance of what is past) your present Situation, the many Leagues of Ocean which separate America from Europe, and in the Desire to repossess their Friend, they forget also, that you are an American. While on this Chapter, I cannot but regret that my Friend Mr Temple Franklin, is not in a Public Situation here, for certainly his perfect Knowledge of the Manners and the Ton of Society could not but be useful, and I know there are many who would be glad to meet him again in my Situation" (DLC:GW).

3. For Benjamin Franklin's illness, see his letter to GW, 16 Sept. 1789, n.1.

To Catharine Sawbridge Macaulay Graham

Madam,   New York Jany 9th 1790

Your obliging letter, dated in October last, has been received; and, as I do not know when I shall have more Leisure than at present to throw together a few observations in return for yours, I take up my Pen to do it by this early occasion.

In the first place, I thank you for your congratulatory sentiments on the event which has placed me at the head of the American Government; as well as for the indulgent partiality, which it is to be feared however, may have warped your judgment too much in my favor. But you do me no more than Justice, in supposing that, if I had been permitted to indulge my first & fondest wish, I should have remained in a private Station. Although, neither the present age or Posterity may possibly give me full credit for the feelings which I have experienced on this subject; yet I have a consciousness, that nothing short of an absolute conviction of duty could ever have brought me upon the scenes of public life again. The establishment of our new Government seemed to be the last great experiment, for promoting human happiness, by reasonable compact, in civil Society. It was to be, in the first instance, in a considerable degree, a government of accomodation as well as a government of Laws. Much was to be done by *prudence*, much by *conciliation*, much by *firmness*. Few, who are not philosophical Spectators, can realise the difficult and delicate part which a man in my situation had to act. All see, and most admire, the glare which hovers round the external trappings of elevated Office. To me, there is nothing in it, beyond the lustre which may be reflected from its connection with a power of promoting human felicity. In our progress towards political happiness my station is new; and, if I may use the expression, I walk on untrodden ground. There is scarcely any action, whose motives may not be subject to a double interpretation. There is scarcely any part of my conduct wch may not hereafter be drawn into precedent. Under such a view of the duties inherent to my arduous office, I could not but feel a diffidence in myself on the one hand; and an anxiety for the Community that every new arrangement should be made in the best possible manner on the other. If after all my humble but faithful endeavours to advance the felicity of my Country & Mankind; I may endulge a hope that my labours have not been altogether without success, it will be the only real compensation I can receive in the closing Scenes of life.

On the actual situation of this Country, under its new Government, I will, in the next place, make a few remarks. That the Government, though not absolutely perfect, is one of the best in the World, I have little doubt. I always believed that an unequivocally free & equal Representation of the People in the Legislature; together with an efficient & responsable Executive were the great Pillars on which the preservation of American Freedom must depend. It was indeed next to a Miracle that there should have been so much unanimity, in points of such importance, among such a number of Citizens, so widely scattered and so different in their habits in many respects, as the Americans were. Nor are the growing unanimity and encreasing good will of the Citizens to the Government less remarkable than favorable circumstances. So far as we have gone with the new Government (and it is completely organized and in operation) we have had greater reason than the most sanguine could expect to be satisfied with its success. Perhaps a number of accidental circumstances have concurred with the real effects of the Government to make the People uncommonly well pleased with their situation and prospects. The harvests of Wheat have been remarkably good—the demand for that article from abroad is great —the encrease of Commerce is visible in every Port—and the number of new Manufactures introduced in one year is astonishing. I have lately made a tour through the Eastern States. I found the Country, in a great degree, recovered from the ravages of War—the Towns flourishing—& the People delighted with a government instituted by themselves & for their own good. The same facts I have also reason to believe, from good authority, exist in the Southern States.

By what I have just observed, I think you will be persuaded that the ill-boding Politicians, who prognosticated that America would never enjoy any fruits from her Independence & that She would be obliged to have recourse to a foreign Power for protection, have at least been mistaken. I shall sincerely rejoice to see that the American Revolution has been productive of happy consequences on both sides of the Atlantic. The renovation of the French Constitution is indeed one of the most wonderful events in the history of Mankind: and the agency of the Marquis de la Fayette in a high degree honorable to his character. My greatest fear has been, that the Nation would not be sufficiently cool & moderate in making arrangements for the security of that liberty, of which it seems to be fully possessed.

Mr Warville, the French Gentleman you mention, has been in America & at Mount Vernon; but has returned, sometime since to France.

Mrs Washington is well and desires her Compliments may be presented to you. We wish the happiness of your fire side; as we also long to enjoy that of our own at Mount Vernon. Our wishes, you know, were limited; and I think that our plans of living will now be deemed reasonable by the considerate part of our species. Her wishes coincide with my own as to simplicity of dress, and every thing which can tend to support propriety of character without partaking of the follies of luxury and ostentation. I am with great regard Madam. Your Most Obedient and Most Humble Servant

Go: Washington

ALS, Leicester City Museum and Art Gallery, Leicester, Great Britain; LB, DLC:GW.

From Joseph Mandrillon

Amsterdam 9 [January] 1790.

I have the honour of sending to your Excellency a Copy of my letter to the National Assembly[1]—it is a part of my patriotic wishes to which I pray your Excellency to add it after the preface—Mr Cazenove who has saild from London for America, is charged to offer a copy of my wishes to your Excellency,[2] and I pray you to accept them with the same indulgence and the same goodness with which you honor me. I am with the most profound respect Your very humble and very obedt[3]

Jh Mandrillon

ALS, DNA: RG 59, Miscellaneous Letters. The text of this letter is taken from a contemporary translation made for GW.

1. The enclosure has not been identified.
2. Mandrillon had informed GW as early as June 1789 that Theophile Cazenove was carrying a letter and a book from him to the president. See Mandrillon to GW, 15 June 1789. Cazenove arrived in the United States in March 1790, and Franco Petrus Van Berckel, the Dutch minister to the United States, informed GW that Cazenove was carrying letters for him, "which he wished to deliver with his own hands and requesting to know when he might be presented for that purpose. It was thought, before this should be done, it might be proper to know whether they were of a public nature, and whether he was acting in a public character. If so, then to let them come to me through the Secretary of State—if not, then for him to send them, that the purport might be known before he was introduced, which might be at the next Levee when he might be received & treated agreeably to the consequence he might appear to derive from the testimonial of the letters. It being conceived that etiquette of this sort is essential with all foreigners to give respect to the Chief Majes-

trate and the dignity of the Government, which would be lessened if every person who could procure a letter of introduction should be presented otherwise than at Levee hours in a formal manner" (*Diaries*, 6:49).

3. The original version of this letter reads: "J'ai l'honneur d'envoyer à Votre Excellence un Exemplaire de ma *Lettre* à l'*Assemblée Nationale*, elle fait partie de mes *Voeux Patriotiques*, aux quels je prie Votre Excellence de l'ajouter après l'*Avant-Propos*. Mr Cazenove qui a du faire voile de Londres pour l'Amérique S'est chargé d'offrir un Exemplaire [de] mes *Voeux* à Votre Excellence, et je la prie de les accueillir avec la même indulgence et la même bonté dont elle m'honore."

From Francis Adrian Van der Kemp

Sir!   Kingston [N.Y.] 9 Jan. 1790.

The offer of your Excellency's Services to the Patriots and friends to the rights of mankind, with which I was honoured by Your Excellency's favourable letter of 28 May 1788, encouraged me to recommend to your Excellency's attention Mr S. T. G. Mappa, a Gentleman of a distinguished character amongst the Patriots.[1] Upon the advice of respectable men in Europe the advice of his Excellency Jefferson he brought with him a curious letter fondery—wanting to this moment in America, at the value of more than 3000 £ currency. It wil be a blessing for every branch of literature, and every liberal improvements, if that Gentleman meets any encouragement in his undertaking; which can not fail if he is happy enough to be patronised by your Excellency.

Your Excellency wil pardon the trouble, which I occasion unwillingly, daring not neglect Such as fair opportunity of recommending a worthy Subject to Your Excellency's benevolence and assuring that I am with Sentiments of the highest esteem and respect Sir! your most obedient and Humble Servant

Fr. Adr. Vanderkemp

ALS, DLC:GW.

1. Van der Kemp is referring to the printer Adam Gerard Mappa who arrived in New York in December 1789. See Thomas Paine to GW, 16 Oct. 1789, n.1.

From Thomas Hickling

St Michaels Jany 10th 1790.
To His Excellency George Washington Esquire President of the
United States of America, The memorial of Thomas Hickling of
the Island of Saint Michaels one of the Azores or Western
Islands Merchant, Humbly Sheweth,

That your memorialist is a native of Boston in the Massachusetts Bay, but hath resided for several Years past in the Island of
St Michaels aforesaid, That upon the acknowledgement of the
Independence of the united States by her Majesty the Queen of
Portugal, your memorialist being the only Subject of the said
States residing in the said Islands, applied to the Chief Judge of
her faithfull Majesty to be appointed Consul for the protection
of the American Trade to the western Islands aforesaid who was
pleased, by virtue of the powers vested in him by his Court, to
nominate your memorialist to act in that Capacity untill the
pleasure of the United States could be known.[1]

Your memorialist begs leave further to represent that he hath
acted in that Character for several years past, during which time
he flatters himself that he has conducted so as to give general
satisfaction, but your memorialist hath not yet received a Commission from the United States and is advised that an application therefor must be made to your Excellency.

When your Excellency takes into consideration the encreasing commerce between the United States & the western Islands,
& Your memorialist doubts not your Excellency will judge it for
the trading Interest of the States over which you preside to
establish a Consul at Saint Michaels. And as your memorialist is
a natural born subject of America to whose interest he hath ever
been attached, & is well versed in the Portuguese language and
in their laws & Customs so far as they respect trade, he humbly
takes the liberty of requesting your Excellency to do him the
honor to nominate him to the Office of Consul—for the Islands
aforesaid.[2] And your memorialist will ever pray &ca

Thomas Hickling

ALS, DLC:GW.

1. Enclosed in Thomas Hickling's letter was an undated petition to Portuguese authorities requesting that he be named United States consul on St.

Michael and a commission from John Da Costa, chief judge of the island, making the appointment.

2. Hickling was still a candidate for the post at St. Michael when the administration considered consular appointments in June 1790. On his list of candidates for various consular posts Thomas Jefferson noted that "Thomas Hickling of Boston, asks the consulship of the Azores or Western islands. He sets forth that he has resided several years at St. Michael's, is well versed in the Portuguese language and in their laws and customs respecting trade: that on the acknolegement of our independence, he, being the only American residing in those islands, was appointed by the Chief judge Consul for the protection of our commerce to the Western islands in which he has acted since 1783. Mr. [Robert] Yates of New York sais that Hickling is a respectable man of property, and that he has long corresponded with him.

"Qu. if this appointment might not as well be left in it's present state till some good native can be found who will settle at Angra which is central to all the islands? It's connection with Brazil gives it advantage over any other position in these islands" (Boyd, *Jefferson Papers*, 17:251). In August 1790 John Street was appointed vice-consul for the Azores (*DHFC*, 2:88).

From Edmund Randolph

Sir   Philadelphia January 10. 1790.

I do myself the honor of informing you, that the plan for opening a contract with the woollen manufacturer, appears, as far as I am able to judge, to be proper in itself, and likely to be approved by the legislature of Virginia.

But I must confess, that I have paid more attention to the propriety of the President, undertaking a correspondence with the British Artist. I am told and believe, that it is a felony to export the machines, which he probably contemplates to bring with him. Permit me therefore to submit to your consideration, whether the continuance of your agency in this affair may not be somewhat objectionable? The project has been announced to Virginia; and the executive of that state can easily transact this business for themselves. I have the honor, sir, to be, with the highest respect, your mo. ob. serv.

Edm: Randolph.

ALS, DNA: RG 59, Miscellaneous Letters.

For the background to this letter, see Thomas Howells to GW, 14 July 1789, and the source note to that document.

To Noah Webster

Sir,   New York January 10th 1790.

The Book, entitled Dissertations on the English Language, which you was so polite as to send me on the 11th of December, has reached my hands:[1] And your acceptance of my best thanks for this mark of attention will oblige, Sir, Your most Obedt Servt.

L[S], NN: Washington Collection; copy, DNA: RG 59, Miscellaneous Letters; LB, DLC:GW.

1. Webster's *Dissertations on the English Language: with Notes, by Way of Appendix, an Essay on a Reformed Mode of Spelling, with Dr. Franklin's Arguments on that Subject* was published by Isaiah Thomas in Boston in 1789.

From Moustier

Sir,   Paris, January 11th 1790.

Although my absence from the United States denies me the honor of conferring with the President, I dare to flatter myself that I shall be permitted to recall his remembrance of me and to request the continuance of his goodness as well in quality of his dignity, as, in what I desire still more, his personal regard.

Having left America penetrated with sentiments of the truest veneration, of attachment, and gratitude for your person, Sir, I have not ceased to prove and to profess them on all occasions—I have also often enjoyed the satisfaction to render homage to the wisdom of the government of the United States, and to cite it as nearly serving us for a prototype. It was at least to be desired that we had been guided by the same principles; but I know not by what fatality we have found ourselves carried beyond the bounds at which it was desireable to have fixed—I hope that we shall reiterate our steps without being forced to do so—because in that case it might happen that the impulsion which should carry us back, would occasion too much retrograde. I am sorry to say it; but it appears to me too true that we are in want of Leaders enlightened, clearsighted, and, above all, formed by experience—Had not this been the case, we should not have fallen into the error of presenting to the People more advantages, and more independence than comports with the civil estate—That chimera of perfection, which belongs not to man, has seduced many heads among us. I love to believe that error has had more influence in occasioning the faults which have been committed than malice—although it is not to be dissembled that the number of evil-intentioned, that is to say of people who attempt every thing to satisfy their personal views, is always too great in human societies. There exists unfortunately in our nation a mobility, which seems peculiar to it, and which, badly directed, leads to more bad than good actions, which is an extreme desire to be distinguished and to make a figure— Vanity, without doubt, turns more heads in France than elsewhere—indeed we are arrived at a very critical situation—which is equally capable of exciting fear and supporting hope.

I have not neglected, notwithstanding present circumstances, to lay before my Court the solid advantages offered by the present form of government of the United States, as an additional motive for uniting more closely the ties which bind the two nations, and to multiply their relations to each other—This truth has been felt, but I should not be surprised that in a moment when there is the liveliest agitation in the internal affairs, the attention to external matters should be sometime neglected.

I shall not cease to give the most active attention to whatever may interest the United States, and I trust that my perseverance will supply the defect of other means. I should have been very desirous to procure a decision upon an object which I was specially charged to treat. but I have been obliged to content my self to stop that, which I regard as an error, and wait the adoption of what may be most convenient.[1] I believe firmly that nothing will be decided on which may be disagreeable to Congress. You will be informed of whatever is done.

Madame de Brehan charges me to recall her to your remembrance, Sir, and to Mrs Washington to whom I take the liberty of offering my respectful homage.

My Sister regrets much to be absent from America, where She was becoming more and more pleased, which makes me hope that She will again accompany me. I have the honor to be, with respect, Sir, your most humble & most obedt Servt.[2]

ALS, DLC:GW; translation, DLC:GW. The text is taken from a contemporary translation made for GW.

1. In October 1789 Secretary of the Treasury Alexander Hamilton had held several conversations with Moustier concerning the payments due on the

Revolutionary War debt owed by the United States to France. It was generally accepted by the new government that provision would be made by the United States as soon as possible to begin to retire the debt, but in the meantime Hamilton pointed out that it "would be a valuable accomodation to the government of this country, if the Court of France should think fit to suspend the payment of the instalments of the principal due, and to become due, for five or six years from this period on the condition of effectual arrangements for the punctual discharge of the interest which has accrued, and shall accrue." The secretary hoped that the arrangement might be made as a "voluntary and unsolicited offer" on the part of France (Hamilton to William Short, 7 Oct. 1789, in Syrett, *Hamilton Papers*, 5:429–30). For Hamilton's negotiations with Moustier, see ibid., 428–29.

2. The original French version of this document reads: "Quoique mon absence des Etats Unis me prive de l'honneur d'avoir des rapports avec Monsieur Le President, j'ose me flatter qu'il me sera permis de me rapeller à son souvenir et de reclamer la continuation de ses bontés et en la qualité de sa dignité et, ce que je desire encore davantage, en sa qualité personnelle. Etant parti de l'Amerique penetré des sentimens les plus vrais de veneration, d'attachement et de reconnoissance pour votre personne, Monsieur, je n'ai cessé de les eprouver et de les professer en toute occasion. J'ai joui aussi souvent de la satisfaction de rendre homage à la sagesse du Gouvernement des Etats Unis et de le citer comme pouvant nous servir à peu près de prototype. Il seroit à desirer du moins que nous fussions guidés par les mêmes principes, mais je ne sais pas quelle fatalité nous nous trouvons emportés au delà du but auquel il etoit desirable de pouvoir se fixer. J'espere que nous reviendrons sur nos pas sans y etre poussés involontairement, puisqu'alors il pourroit arriver que l'impulsion qui nous remaneroit en arriere, nous fit beaucoup trop retrogrades. Je suis faché de le dire mais il me paroit qu'il n'est que trop vrai que nous manquons de chefs eclairés, prevoyans, et surtout formés par l'experience. Ils n'auroient pas sans celà donné dans l'erreur de faire envisager au peuple plus d'avantages et surtout plus d'independance que l'etat civil ne le comporte. Cette chimere de perfection qui n'apartient point aux hommes a seduit parmi nous beaucoup de tetes. J'aime à croire que l'erreur a plus influé sur les fautes commises que la malice, quoiqu'on ne puisse pas se dissimuler que le nombre des malintentionés, c'est à dire des gens portés à tout tenter pour satisfaire des vues personelles, ne soit toujours trop grand dans les Societés humaines. Il existe malheureusement dans notre nation un mobile qui lui semble particulier et qui mal dirigé porte à beaucoup plus de mauvaises actions que de bonnes, qui est l'envie extrême d'etre distingué et de jouer un role. La vanité tourne sans contredire plus de têtes en France qu'ailleurs. Enfin nous sommes parvenus à une situation très critique. Elle peut egalement exciter la crainte et soutenir l'esperance.

"Je n'ai point negligé, malgré les circonstances, de presenter à ma Cour les avantages solides qu'offre aujourdhui la forme du Gouvernement des Etats Unis, comme un nouveau motif de reserrer les liens qui unissent nos deux Nations et de multiplier les rapports qu'elles ont eû entre elles. Cette verité a été sentie, mais je ne serois point surpris que dans un moment où l'agitation est la plus vive au dedans, l'attention sur les affaires du dehors ne fut quelquefois detournée. Je ne cesserai de donner la suite la plus active à tout qui pourra interesser les Etats Unis et j'espere que ma perseverance supléera au defaut de plusieurs autres moyens. J'aurois bien des procurer une decision sur un objet que je m'etois chargé specialement de traiter, mais j'ai été obligé de me contenter d'arreter dabord, ce que je regarde comme une erreur, en attendant qu'on adopte ce qui seroit plus convenable. Je crois fermement qu'on ne se decidera à rien qui peut etre desagreable au Congrès. Vous en serez, Monsieur, informé d'ailleurs.

"Mde de Brehan me charge de la rapeller à votre Souvenir, Monsieur, et à celui de Madame Washington à qui je prends la liberté d'offrir mes respectueux homages. Ma Soeur regrette beaucoup d'etre absente de l'Amerique où Elle se plaisoit effectivement de plus en plus. Celà me donne l'espoir qu'elle voudra bien m'y accompagner de nouveau."

To Charles Pinckney

Private.
Dear Sir,   New York, January 11th 1790.

Altho' it is not in my power to enter so fully as I could wish into an investigation of the interesting subjects discussed in your letter of the 14th of last month; yet I would not deny myself the satisfaction of acknowledging the receipt of it, and of expressing my obligations for the sentiments which your Excellency has been pleased to suggest.

A new Monarch having acceded to the Throne of Spain, it remains to be ascertained how far his Court may insist upon those exclusive claims to the navigation of the Mississippi, which have hitherto prevented the conclusion of a Treaty between the United States and that Nation. Mr Gardoqui went to Spain some time ago: nor have we received any thing official from thence since his departure. A private Gentleman, (a man of good intelligence) lately returned from Spain to America, mentions a report was believed when he sailed, that the Americans of the United States had formed a successful expedition against the spanish territories in their neighbourhood; and that the report had occasioned great sensations in the Kingdom. Whatever may be the future policy of that nation, I am disposed to become as well acquainted with the merits of the subjects which have been agitated between them and us since the war, as my other duties and avocations will admit. For this reason in particular, I thank your Excellency for your confidential communication.

As to the subject of Indian affairs I can only say in general, that your sentiments on the expediency of entering into Treaties with those Nations, upon just terms, perfectly co-incide with my own. From the official report of the late Commissioners for treating with the Creeks &c. it seems almost certain, that the connection of Mr McGillivray with Spain was the principle cause for preventing the conclusion of the proposed Treaty.[1] Their report (which is this day to be delivered by the Secretary at War to the Senate) will indicate fully the progress and issue of that business. And the Executive will probably be possessed of such documents as may be usefull in taking ulterior measures. For my own part, I am entirely persuaded that the present general Government will endeavor to lay the foundation for its proceedings in national justice, faith and honor. But should the Government, after having attempted in vain every reasonable pacific measure, be obliged to have recourse to arms for the defence of its Citizens; I am also of opinion, that sound policy and good œconomy will point to a prompt and decisive effort, rather than to defensive, and lingering operations.

Should your Excellency, after the expiration of your Office, prosecute your proposed voyage to France, you will find, I presume, most extraordinary events have taken place in that Kingdom. Altho' all their political arrangements are not yet settled; I hope they will be happily, before the period to which you allude.

My late tour through the eastern States has been of salutary consequence in confirming my health. I have likewise had an opportunity of seeing how far the Country is recovered from the ravages of war, and how well the Inhabitants are disposed to support the General Government. Not being master of my own time, or accustomed to make personal engagements which from contingency might become impracticable I can only say in regard to the last paragraph of your letter, that nothing would give me greater pleasure than to have it in my power to visit all the Southern States. With sentiments of the highest respect I am, Dear Sir, Your Most Obedient and Very Humble Servant.

George Washington.

LB, DLC:GW; LB, DNA: RG 59, Miscellaneous Letters.

1. For the negotiations of the American commissioners to the southern Indians, see David Humphreys to GW, 21, 26, 27 Sept., 13, 28 Oct. 1789, Alexander Hamilton to GW, 20 Oct. 1789, and Henry Knox to GW, 18 Oct., 21, 27 Nov. 1789. See also GW's Memoranda on Indian Affairs, 1789, which contains a précis of the commissioners report on their mission.

From Beverley Randolph

Sir,   Richmond [Va.] January 11th 1790

Immediately on the receipt of your letter Covering a proposal for establishing a Woollen Manufactory in this state I laid it before the General Assembly taking care not to communicate the name or residence of the person from whom the proposal Came.[1] I have now the honour to inclose you the Resolutions of the Senate and House of Delegates on that Subject. I am, with the highest respect your Obedient servant

Beverley Randolph

LS, DNA: RG 59, Miscellaneous Letters; LB, Vi: Executive Letter Books.

For background to this letter, see Thomas Howells to GW, 14 July 1789, and Edmund Randolph to GW, 10 Jan. 1790.

1. The enclosure, a copy of a resolution of the Virginia house of delegates dated 17 Dec. 1789, reads: "Mr Edmund Randolph reported from the Committee, to whom was referred a letter from the Governor, with its inclosures, respecting the Establishment of a woollen Manufactory, that the Committee had according to Order had the same under their Consideration, & had agreed upon a Report, and come to several Resolutions thereupon, which he read in his Place and afterwards delivered in at the Clerks Table, where the same were again twice read, amended, and agreed to by the House as followeth.

"Your Committee esteem the patriotic Communication of the president of the United States, as presenting an Opportunity which the actual Circumstances of this Commonwealth forbid to be neglected; By these actual Circumstances your Committee mean, an absolute necessity arising from the Nature of the property in Virginia to endeavour to make the coarse cloathing at least; the intervals which the Hands employed in Agriculture occasionally find; and the Ability of the young and old who are disqualified for the severe Toils of the Field to be useful in manufactures.

"How far Schemes of this Kind ought to be extended, your Committee undertakes not to decide; but they conceive that the Establishment of a Woollen Manufactory highly deserves the public encouragement.

"It seems to be an indispensable Condition of such a Work, that the raising of Wool should be encouraged if possible by Legislative provisions, but those which have occurred to your Committee, from the practice of those Countries where population is thick and there are proper ranges for large flocks, do not appear applicable to this Commonwealth; nothing therefore remains in the power of the General Assembly, but to exhort the several farmers and Planters, to pay strict Attention to the increase of Sheep.

"Your Committee collect from the Communication aforesaid, that machines, which facilitate the manufacture of Woollens are probably attainable: Until the Truth of this Opinion be ascertained, or the plan projected shall be examined your Committee are unable to say what Stipulations ought to be made on the part of the Commonwealth.

"In Consideration of the premises your Committee have come to the following Resolutions thereupon.

"Resolved that it be earnestly recommended to the Good people of this Commonwealth, to attend to the raising of Wool by every possible Means, and to enter into associations for the forming of Rules to be observed & for other purposes adapted to this End.

"Resolved that the Executive open a correspondence with the president of the United States on the foregoing Subject, and that it be lawful for them to bind this Commonwealth in the Sum of ⟨one⟩ thousand pounds, and the further Sum of five hundred pounds per Annum for three years for the prosecution of a Woollen Manufactory on such Terms as they shall approve.

"Resolved that the Executive be requested also to correspond with the president of the United States concerning the lands required from this Commonwealth and to report their proceedings in the Premises to the next Session of Assembly.

"Ordered that Mr Edmund Randolph do carry the Resolutions to the Senate & desire their Concurrence" (DNA: RG 59, Miscellaneous Letters). See also *Virginia House of Delegates Journal*, October 1789 sess., 114, 134.

Letter not found: from Edward Rutledge, 11 Jan. 1790. The dealer's catalog quotation from this letter reads: ". . . I have lately recd. Letter from some of my Friends in Congress which gives me Reason to hope that the time is not far distant when we shall have the Happiness of seeing you in this State: and as there is no Citizen in this Country who feels a stronger affection to you than I do or wd. been more rejoiced at your coming I hope you will permit me to request that you wd. make my House your Head Quarters whilst you remain in this City.— I know there are many persons who would prize the Honor which I seek as justly as they ought but the great never failing Regard that I have cherished towards you from the first moments of my political Life, thro' all the Chances of and the Turns of Fortune gives me I shd hope at least an equal if not a superior Claim to you & entitles me to lodge under my own Roof the President in the Friend. As another Inducement I must assure you my dear Sir that we have not one Public House in the whole State which is fit for your Reception, & that to be accomodated with even a moderate Degree of Convenience you must receive it in a private House if therefore you will not take up your Residence in mine, I must provide you with one from some of my particular Friends who may be in the Country."

ALS, *The Frederick S. Peck Collection of American Historical Autographs* (Philadelphia, 1947), 27–28. The documents in this collection were sold at auction by Samuel T. Freeman & Co., 17 Mar. 1947.

To the United States Senate

United States [New York]
Gentlemen of the Senate   January 11th 1790.
I have directed Mr Lear, my private Secretary, to lay before you a copy of the adoption and ratification of the Constitution of the United States by the State of North Carolina, together with the copy of a letter from His Excellency Samuel Johnson President of the Convention of said State to the President of the United States.[1]
The Originals of the papers which are herewith transmitted to you will be lodged in the Office of the Secretary of State.[2]
Go: Washington

LS, DNA: RG 46, First Congress, Records of Legislative Proceedings, President's Messages; LB, DLC:GW; copy, DNA: RG 233, First Congress, Records of Legislative Proceedings, Journals.

1. See the North Carolina Ratifying Convention to GW, 4 Dec. 1789. GW's letter was read in the Senate on 11 January. See *DHFC*, 1:218–19.

2. Tobias Lear wrote State Department clerk Roger Alden on 12 Jan.: "I am directed by the President of the United States to transmit herewith to you, to be lodged in the office of State with other public papers under your care, and to be delivered to the Secretary of State whenever he may enter upon the duties of his office, the Form of the adoption and ratification of the constitution of the United States by the State of North Carolina, which has been officially communicated to him by the President of the Convention of said State; and likewise a letter which accompanied the above form of Ratification from Samuel Johnston President of the Convention of the State of North Carolina to the President of the United States" (DLC:GW).

To the United States Senate

United States [New York]
Gentlemen of the Senate,   January 11th, 1790.

Having advised with you upon the terms of a treaty to be offered to the Creek Nation of Indians,[1] I think it proper you should be informed of the result of that business, previous to its coming before you in your legislative capacity.

I have therefore directed the Secretary for the Department of War, to lay before you my instructions to the Commissioners, and their report in consequence thereof.[2]

The apparently critical state of the southern frontier will render it expedient for me to communicate to both Houses of Congress, with other papers, the whole of the transactions relative to the Creeks, in order that they may be enabled to form a judgement of the measures which the case may require.

Go: Washington

LS, DNA: RG 46, First Congress, Records of Executive Proceedings, President's Messages—Indian Relations; LB, DLC:GW.

1. See GW to the United States Senate, 22 Aug. 1789.
2. See GW to the Commissioners to the Southern Indians, 29 Aug. 1789. For the enclosures to GW's letter of 11 Jan. to the Senate, see *DHFC*, 2:202–41, or *ASP, Indian Affairs*, 1:65–80.

To the United States Senate
Answer to the Address of the Senate

Gentlemen,   [New York, 11 January 1790]

I thank you for your address, and for the assurances, which it contains of attention to the several Matters suggested by me to your consideration.[1]

Relying on the continuance of your exertions for the public good, I anticipate, for our Country, the salutary effects of upright and prudent Counsels.

G. Washington

LB, DLC:GW.

1. For the address of the Senate, see GW to the United States Senate and House of Representatives, 8 Jan. 1790, source note.

From Lafayette

My Dear GeneralParis January the 12th 1790
I Cannot let the packet Sail without a line from your filial friend, who, altho' He depends on Mr Short for your information, wants to Express you those Affectionate and Respectful Sentiments that Are Never So well felt as in UnCommon Circumstances—How often, My Beloved General, Have I wanted your wise Advices and friendly Support! We Have Come thus far in the Revolution without Breaking the Ship either on the Shoal of Aristocraty, or that of faction, and Amidst the Ever Reviving efforts of the Mourners and the Ambitious we are Stirring towards a tolerable Conclusion—Now that Every thing that was is No More, a New Building is Erecting, Not perfect By far, But Sufficient to Ensure freedom, and prepare the Nation for a Convention in about ten years, where the defects May Be Mended—I will Not Enter in all the details I Have Already Related—Common Sense is writing a Book for you—there you will See a part of My Adventures—I Hope they will turn to the Advantage of My Country and Mankind in General—liberty is Sprouting about in the other parts of Europe, and I am Encouraging it By all the Means in My Power—Adieu, My Beloved General, My Best Respects wait on Mrs Washington—Remember me to Hamilton, Harrison, Knox, Lear, and all our friends—Most Respectfully and Affectionately Your Most devoted and filial friend

Lafayette

I wish Mr Jay, John Adams, Wadsworth, and Doctor Franklin Could witness the difference Betwen this France, this Capital, and the once they Have Seen.

ALS, PEL.

To the United States Senate and House of Representatives

United States [New York] January 12th 1790
Gentlemen of the Senate, and of the House of Representatives.
I lay before you a statement of the south western frontiers,

and of the Indian Department which have been submitted to me by the Secretary for the Department of War.[1]

I conceive that an unreserved, but *confidential* communication of all the papers relative to the recent negociations with some of the southern tribes of Indians is indispensibly requisite for the information of Congress—I am persuaded that they will effectually prevent either transcripts or publications of all such circumstances as might be injurious to the public interest.

Go: Washington

LS, DNA: RG 46, First Congress, Records of Legislative Proceedings, President's Messages; LB, DLC:GW.

1. For the enclosures in GW's letter to both houses of Congress, see Henry Knox to GW, 4 Jan. 1790, and notes.

From Philemon Dickinson

Hermitage [N.J.] 13 Jany 1790.

Mr Philemon Dickinson's Compliments to the President of the United States of America, & begs his acceptance of an *American* Cheese, made by a Mr Capner, of Hunterdon County, State of New Jersey.

ALS, DNA: RG 59, Miscellaneous Letters.

Philemon Dickinson (1739–1809) had a distinguished military career during the Revolution in New York and New Jersey, earning GW's approbation on several occasions. During the 1780s he served in the New Jersey loan office and in 1782 was elected congressman from Delaware where he was a property owner. In 1790 he was elected to the United States Senate to replace William Paterson when the latter was elected governor of New Jersey.

From David Jones

Dear Sir   Lewisville [Ky.] January 13. 1790

when I saw you in augt[1] I informed you of my Intention of going to this Place where I arrived yesterday after a Tour thro' Kaintucke and the Miami Country. I find the Situation of each Place very different to the Common Representations in the old inhabited parts. The Truth is there is no Peace with the Savages; the Country bleeds in every Part. Many horred Murders have been committed since my arrival both at the Miamis & Kaintucke. I fear your Station prevents Information of Matters in their true Light; but I shall say no More on the Subject. these Hints may be useful. I wish to draw your attention a Moment to another subject. Judge Parsons is now Dead,[2] & I remember you said that you would fill up vacancies with the most worthy applicant. In the Present Case, Modesty will prevent any application from the most deserving. Permit me to mention William Goforth late of the City of New york, but now at Columbia between the Miamies. this gentleman is well known in New york, was in 75 appointed a Captain, went to Canady, but after his return in 76 resigned, being injured in Rank. since his return to york, he has been honored by being repeatedly appointed a Legislator; the war injured him & he has met with Losses in Trade, he has failed, & has time given him to discharge his Debts, which I beleive he will fully perform. he is truely a Man of superior abilities and is with his Family in the Country. this office would releive him & a worthy Family very much, & I think it cannot be confered on a more worthy Person. he has not solicited me to write.[3] A wish to help the worthy has been my Motive. with much respect I am your Excellency's most obedient & very humble Servant.

David Jones

ALS, DLC:GW.
  1. See Jones to GW, 20 Aug. 1789.
  2. For the death of Samuel Holden Parsons, see Winthrop Sargent to GW, 27 Nov. 1789, and notes.
  3. William Goforth did not succeed Parsons.

Clement Biddle to Tobias Lear

Tobias Lear Esqr.   Philadelphia 14th January 1790
  I have before me Your favour of the 6th & 10th Int. to answer which I could not do by last Post for want of the Necessary information respecting the Boulting Cloths.
  Mr Lewis says that he is at a Loss to put up the Boulting Cloth until he knows the size that will suit he says that a Reel which in the *whole length is ten feet* (the Common size here) requires a Cloth of 8 feet 3 Inches long and the remainder of the Reel is Covered with Strong Linen, the price for Such sized superfine

Cloth is £10 and as he expressed a Doubt from the words of your Letter I thought it best to wait your Answer by which I should only loose one post to the Southward & the Post Master will forward it with the Mail to the Nearest post Office to Mount Vernon, you will therefore please to mention if (as I suppose) the whole length of the Reel is only Nine feet two Inches,[1] I have Wrote to Mr Abraham Hunt at Trenton to procure the 200 Bushels of Buckwheat as he assured me he could get it[2] & I have desired his speedy Answer in Case of Failure that I might procure it in the Neighbourhood of this City in due season.[3]

C.B.

LB, PHi: Clement Biddle Letter Book, 1789–92.

1. On 10 Jan. Lear wrote to Biddle: "The President has directed me to write to you, requesting, that you will procure for him, & send to Mount Vernon by the first opportunity a superfine Boulting Cloth of the first quality, to suit A Reel which is nine feet two inches in length—and five feet six inches in circumference, You will be good enough to let the above mentioned Cloth be chosen by Mr Lewis or a skillful Miller" (ViMtV). GW needed the cloth to fit the reel of a bolting chest or flour sieve located at his sandstone merchant mill built in 1770 at the Mill plantation on Dogue Run Creek. Meal or flour was sifted from bran and other impurities through a firm fabric of transparent woven linen which came in various fine-meshed sizes and which was attached to the reel of the bolter. Lear answered Biddle's letter on 7 Feb.: "Major Washington has sent the following dimensions of the Bolting Cloth. 'The length of the Bolting Cloth, *now* in the Mill, is 8 feet 3½ inches; and the breadth 5 feet 7 inches. The length of the Reel is 9 feet 6 inches; and as Colo. Biddle observes has the difference between the Cloth and Reel covered with coarse linen.' The President would wish you to get one agreeable to the foregoing dimensions & send it to Mount Vernon by the earliest opportunity" (PHi: Washington-Biddle Correspondence). Biddle notified George Augustine Washington on 11 Feb. that he would ship the cloth in two pieces to Mount Vernon by that day's post (PHi: Clement Biddle Letter Book, 1789–92). See also Biddle to Lear, 24 Jan. and 10 Feb. 1790 (PHi: Clement Biddle Letter Book), and Lear to Biddle, 17 Jan. 1790 (PHi: Washington-Biddle Correspondence).

2. For GW's attempt to secure buckwheat for Mount Vernon, see Lear to Biddle, 21 Dec. 1789. On 24 Jan. Biddle wrote Lear that "Mr Abraham Hunt has agreed to Supply the Buckwheat (having abt 200 Bushels in Store) @ 2/8 —and I have the Bags in hand making & shall send them to Bring it Down in 2 or 3 Days and shall ship it by first Vessel for Alexandria" (PHi: Clement Biddle Letter Book, 1789–92). The buckwheat was shipped to Alexandria in early March on the sloop *Polly*, commanded by Captain Ellwood (Biddle to Lear, 6 Mar. 1790, PHi: Clement Biddle Letter Book). See also Biddle to Lear, 28 Jan., 9, 23 Feb. 1790, all in PHi: Clement Biddle Letter Book.

From the Marquise de Lafayette

Sir   Paris 14. January 1790.

   Amidst the agitations of our revolution, I have always participated in the pleasure which Mr de La Fayette found in following your footsteps, in observing, according to your example and your lessons, the means of serving his country, and in thinking with what satisfaction you would learn the effects and success of them. Permit me, to offer you the assurance of this sentiment and permit at the same time to request of you a favour which interests me sensibly. Mr Poirey the secretary of Mr De la Fayette[1] and who is at present that of our national guard, loaded with kindness by you in America where he has had the happiness of meriting your approbation has not ceased since that time, to give to Mr De la Fayette testimonies of attachment, and he has rendered to this cause important services and above all very affecting to him. His ambition is to obtain the glorious distinction of an American Officer, the Ribbon of Cincinnatus is the object of all his wishes, and Mr De la Fayette would think he could not refuse him the permission, if you would deign to confer upon him, a brevet commission. I set a great value upon obtaining for him this favour, and it would be to me a great pleasure if I owe it to your goodness for me, I should recieve almost as much pride as gratitude from it, ⟨and⟩ that it would be the means of acquitting a little what we owe to Mr Poirey, and which I believe due to him more than to any other person, persuaded as I am, that his vigilant cares have contributed very much in the midst of the Storms to the preservation of what I hold most dear in the world. Mr De la Fayette approves my request, and will leave to me I hope the pleasure and the glory of having obtained the success of it from you Sir, and of joining on this little occasion the hommage of my personal gratitude, to that of all his sentiments of admiration, attachment and respect, which I participate with him and with which I have the honour of being, Sir, Your very humble and very obedient servant

Noailles de la Fayette

   Accept I entreat you the hommage of respect of our little George and his Sisters, and permit that Mrs Washington receive here mine and those of all our family.

The Chr de la Colombe who has had the honour of serving under your orders,[2] and whose patriotism and sentiments for Mr De la Fayette have rendered eminent services to our cause as well in his province as in the parisien Army, in which he is Aid-Major, having known that I had the honour of writing to you wishes that I offer to you *his best respects*. Pardon my writing in french I intreat you, the occasion required it, and for six months since it is a great deal for me to recover my ideas in my own language. It is true that in writing to General Washington it is more my heart than my mind that dictates my expressions. This is my excuse, if I am indiscreet, this the justification of my confidence.[3]

ALS (photocopy), NIC; translation (photocopy), NIC. The text of this document has been taken from the contemporary translation.

1. Joseph-Léonard Poirey entered the French service in 1770 and later came to America with Lafayette in 1780 to act as his military secretary. Poirey served in the Virginia campaign and at Yorktown and returned to France with Lafayette. He was currently serving as captain secretary general of the French National Guard with the rank of major. In response to the request of the marquise de Lafayette, GW wrote the Senate in May 1790 asking that Poirey might, on the basis of his earlier service in America, be granted the brevet rank of captain. "I am authorised to add, that, while the compliance will involve no expense on our part, it will be particularly grateful to that friend of America, the Marquis de la Fayette." See GW to the United States Senate, 31 May 1790. The Senate confirmed the appointment on 2 June 1790 (*DHFC*, 2:71).

GW replied to the marquise's letter on 3 June 1790: "It gives me infinite pleasure, in acknowledging the receipt of your letter of the 14th of Jany last, to transmit the Brevet Commission, that was desired for Mr Poirey. Aside of his services in America, which alone might have entitled him to this distinction, his attachment to the Marquis de la Fayette and your protection added claims that were not to be resisted. And you will, I dare flatter myself, do me the justice to believe that I can never be more happy than in according marks of attention to so good a friend to America and so excellent a patriot as Madame la Marquise de la Fayette. Nor did she need any excuse for making use of her own language to be the interpreter of so much politeness & persuasion as she has found means to convey in one short letter. In truth that language, at least when used by her, seems made on purpose to have fine things communicated in it; and I question whether any other, at least in the hands of any other person, would have been equally competent to the effect.

"By some accident your letter reached me only a few days ago. This fact is the sole reason of your not hearing sooner from me, & must be an apology for any seeming neglect on my part. I request you will present my Compliments to the Gentleman who desired to be so cordially remembered to me. Mrs Washington and her two youngest Grand-Children (who live with us) join me in offering our affectionate regards to your family: in whose welfare, believe me Madame, no one is more deeply interested than he who has the honor to subscribe himself with the purest sentiments of respect & esteem Your Most obedient & Most humble Servt." The text of GW's letter, as far as the phrase "making use of her own language to be" is taken from a facsimile of an ALS in the Sotheby, Parke-Bernet catalog 4267, part III, Sang Collection sale. The remainder is taken from a copy in David Humphreys' writing in DNA: RG 59, Miscellaneous Letters.

2. Louis-Saint-Ange Morel, chevalier de La Colombe (1755–c.1800) came with Lafayette to America in 1777 to serve the marquis as an aide-de-camp. La Colombe later, in 1783, retired from the King's Dragoons with the rank of major. In 1791 he became colonel of an infantry regiment in France and in 1792 again served as Lafayette's aide. He was arrested during the French Revolution but escaped and came to the United States in 1794 where, except for a brief trip to France, he remained for the rest of his life.

3. The original French version of this letter reads: "Au milieu des agitations de notre revolution, j'ai toujours partagé les soucis que ⟨temoins⟩ Mis De la fayette, a suivre vos ⟨traces⟩, et devoir en vos exemples, en vos leçons, des moyens de servir sa patrie, et a songer, avec quelle satisfactions vous en apprendrais les ⟨illegible⟩, et ses Succés. permettés moy de vous offrir l'assurance de ce Sentiment, et permettés moy en meme tems de vous demander une grace qui minteresse sensiblement. Mis Poisey, Sécretaire de Mis De la fayette et qui l'est a présent de notre garde nationale; comblé de bontés par vous en amérique, où il a eu le bonheur de meriter votre suffrage; n'a cessé depuis ce tems, de donner a Mis De la fayette, des temoignages d'attachement, et il a rendu a cette cause, des services importans, et surtout trés ⟨touchans⟩ pour Lui. Son ambition est dobtenir la glorieuse marque d'officier américain, Le ruban de Cincinnatus, est lobjet de tous ses voeux; et Mr de la fayette ⟨coriroie⟩ pouvoir ne pas Lui refuser la permission de la porter, Si vous daignies lui accorder un brevet dofficier. je mets un prix extrême à Lui obtenir cette grace, et elle en auroie pour moy, un bien particulier. Si je la devois à votre bonté pour moy. j'en aurois presqu' autant d'orgueil que de recconnoissance, en meme tems que ce seroie un moyen d'accquitter un peu, celle que nous devons a Mr Poisey, et que je crois Lui devoir plus que personne, persuadée comme je le suis, que des soins vigilans; contribuere beaucoup au milieu des orages a la conservation de ce que j'ai de plus cher au monde. Mis de la fayette approuve ma demande, et me laissera j'espere le plaisir, et la gloire, d'en avoir obtenu de vous le succès, monsieur, et de joindre en cette petite occasion l'hommage de ma recconnoissance personele, a celui de tous Les sentimens, d'admiration, dattachement et de respect, que je partarge avec Lui, et avec Lesquels j'ai lhonneur d'être, monsieur, Votre très humble et très obeissante Servante

"noailles de la fayette

"agrées je vous en Supplie Lhommage du respect de nôtre petit George et de Ses Soeurs, et permettes que ⟨mme⟩ Washington recoive ici Les miens, et ceux de toute notre famille.

"Le Ch(er) de La Colombe, qui a eu l'honneur de servir Sous vos ordres, et dont Le patriotisme, et Ses sentimens pour Mis de La fayette ont rendus dé- minens Services, a notre cause, tant dans sa province que dans l'armée pari- sienne, ou il est aide major, ayans sue que j'avois l'honneur de vous ecrire, veut que je vous offre *his best respects.* pardonnés je vous en Supplie, Si jécris en françois, mais Loccasion ⟨prescrie⟩, et depuis Six mois c'est beaucoup pour moy, de retrouver mes idees dans ma propre Langue. il est vrai que pour ecrire au Gal Washington, c'est plus mon coeur que mon esprit qui dicte mes expressions, c'est mon excuse, si je suis indiscrete, c'est la justification de ma confiance."

From Beverley Randolph

Sir,   Richmond [Va.] January 14th 1790.

Since my letter of the 18th of December last General Wood at the request of the Executive went to Cape Henry to ascertain the present situation of the materials formerly placed there for the purpose of building a Light house.[1] I take the liberty to inclose to you his report upon this subject, and to offer the materials in their present situation so far as Virginia has an Interest in them, to the United States.[2] I shall immediately write to the Governor of Maryland to inform him of this measure and have no doubt but that state will unite with us in disposing of the whole.[3] If it should be determined not to accept the offer now made, I wish to be informed whether the purchase will be made upon any other terms.[4] I have &c.

Beverley Randolph

LB, Vi: Executive Letter Books.

1. For GW's concern about the material at the construction site for the Cape Henry lighthouse, see Thomas Newton, Jr., to GW, 17 July, 24 Oct. 1789, GW to Newton, 12 Oct., 23 Nov. 1789, and Beverley Randolph to GW, 18 Dec. 1789. See also Tobias Lear to Alexander Hamilton, 5 Jan. 1790.

2. Lieut. Gov. James Wood's report to Randolph stated that "in obedience to the advice of Council of the 17th ultimo, he had visited Cape Henry in order to ascertain the present situation of the material placed on the head- land of the Cape for the purpose of erecting a Light-House. He discovered from the books of the Commiss'r, and also from information of Col. Thos. Newton (one of them), that Virginia & Maryland had appointed the same commiss'rs; that they had rec'd from Virginia £5,418, 7s, 10½d, and from Maryland £2,489, 16s, 5½d, which sums were expended for stone, fr't to the Cape, Cartage to the spot which was intended for the sight of the Light-house,

and other necesssary expenses. Found the quantity of stone on the spot about 4,036 Tons, which was supposed to be sufficient for an octagon Light-House 72 f't high, diameter at base 26 f't, 9 inches, and at top 16 feet, 6 inches; walls to be 6 feet thick at the base, and 3 feet thick at the top; foundation to be 13 feet deep; the building to be divided into seven stories, besides the Lantern.

"The Stone was purchased at a quary on Rappahannock river at seven shillings the perch—Each perch estimated to weigh 3,004 lbs., fr't averaged 13s, 6d. per ton, and cartage to the spot fixed on for erecting the Light-House 6s, 2½d, so that Each ton stood the public where it now lies, 24s, 4d, Virginia Currency. Thinks that the same stone could not now be purchased and landed at high water on the Cape for less than 20s. per ton. There were 150 Hhd. of Lime placed with the stone, but they Appear to have been Carried off, or rendered useless by the Hhds. falling to pieces, or being buried under the sand.

"The Commissioners estimated the whole necessary expenses of building the Light-house, dwelling house, and Eight buoys to be placed in the Chesapeake at £13,000, Virginia currency. Thinks that nothing at present can be counted on but the stone. The buoys were provided by this state, but the copper was afterwards converted to other state purposes. The whole of the stone is covered by drifting sand 20 to 50 feet deep, & the digging out will probably amount to half its value in expense. He declined making any contract for recovering the stone, as it is not known whether the General Government will build with stone; thinks that an immediate attempt should be made to dispose of it to the Government as it now stands, or recovered from the sand, which Ever should be thought the more advisable" (*Calendar of Virginia State Papers*, 5:98–99).

3. Randolph's letter to the governor of Maryland, 18 Jan. 1790, is in Vi: Executive Letter Books.

4. GW replied to Randolph's letter on 29 Jan.: "I have been duly favored with your Excellency's letter of the 14th instant . . . and have put both the letter and report into the hands of the Secretary of the Treasury, who is authorized by Law 'to provide by contract, which shall be approved by the President of the United States, for building a Light-house near the enterance of Chesapeake Bay.' I have also directed him to write to your Excellency upon the subject, and to take such steps in the business as may tend to a speedy accomplishment of the desired object.

"In the first place it will be necessary that a deed of cession of the land upon which the Light-house is to be erected, should be executed from the State of Virginia to the United States; and when this is accomplished, as the building of the Light-house is to be done by contract, it is probable that the person or persons who may contract for the building of it, will make such agreement for the materials as to them shall seem proper; and in this case the expediency of their being purchased *immediately* by the United States will be superseded" (LS, Vi). Randolph's letter and the enclosure from Wood were submitted to Hamilton by Tobias Lear on 24 Jan. (DNA: RG 26, "Segregated" Lighthouse Records).

To the United States House of Representatives

Gentlemen   [New York, 14 January 1790]
    I receive with pleasure the assurances you give me that you will diligently and anxiously pursue such measures as shall appear to you conducive to the interests of your Constituents; and that an early and serious consideration will be given to the various and weighty matters, recommended by me to your attention.
    I have full confidence that your deliberations will continue to be directed by an enlightened and virtuous zeal for the happiness of our Country.[1]

                                          G. Washington

LB, DLC:GW; copy, DNA: RG 233, First Congress, Records of Legislative Proceedings, Journals.
    1. This document is headed: "Answer to the Address of the House of Representatives." See GW to the United States Senate and House of Representatives, 8 Jan. 1790, and notes. On 13 Jan. the House committee appointed to wait on the president and inquire when it would be convenient for him to receive the House's reply to his State of the Union address, reported that GW had designated noon on 14 Jan. as the time to receive the House's address "at his own house." The next day the Speaker, "attended by the House, then withdrew to the house of the President of the United States, and there presented to him the address of this House in answer to his speech to both Houses of Congress." GW then made the reply printed above (*DHFC*, 3:262).

To the United States Senate

Gentlemen,   [New York, 14 January 1790]
    I thank you for your address, and for the assurances, which it contains, of attention to the several matters, suggested by me to your consideration.[1]
    Relying on the continuance of your exertions for the public good, I anticipate, for our Country, the salutary effects of upright and prudent Counsels.

                                          Go: Washington

LS, DNA: RG 46, First Congress, Records of Legislative Proceedings, President's Messages.
    1. See GW to the United States Senate and House of Representatives, 8 Jan. 1790, and notes. On 12 Jan. the Senate ordered "that the address to the President of the United States, in answer to his Speech, be presented by the

Vice President, attended by the Senate, and that the Committee which re-ported the address [Rufus King, Ralph Izard, and William Paterson], wait on the President, and desire to be informed at what time and place, he will receive the same." GW designated Thursday, 14 Jan., at eleven o'clock, to re-ceive the Senate's address "at his own House, at which time he made the above reply" (*DHFC*, 1:221).

To Gabriel Dupare de Bellegard

Sir,   New York January 15th 1790

I have received your letter dated the 18th of September 1789; and in reply to it, must inform you, that so far from living upon terms of intimacy and friendship with the late General Ogle-thorpe, (as it appears by your letter you have understood that I did) I never was so happy as to have any personal acquaintance with that Gentleman, nor any other knowledge of him but from his general character. The distance of our places of residence from each other, which is near 1,000 Miles, and the different periods in which we have lived are circumstances which pre-clude the probability of our having been upon an intimate footing.

I have, however, directed enquiries to be made among the Gentlemen from the State of Georgia, who are now attending Congress in this place, respecting the affairs of the late General Oglethorpe, and am informed by them that they know of no lands belonging to him. One of the Gentlemen, a Senator from the State of Georgia, mentions his having been written to, some time since, by Mr Jefferson our Minister at the Court of Vers-sailles, upon the same subject, and in consequence thereof he made every enquirey in his power relative to the matter; but there were no lands in Georgia belonging to General Ogle-thorpe;[1] and he further adds, that if there had been property of that Gentleman's in Georgia in the time of the late War with Great Britain, so far from its having been confiscated, it would have met with singular protection, in consequence of the high estimation in which the character of General Oglethorpe stood in that State. I should have been happy, Sir, to have had it in my power to give you more pleasing information upon this subject. I am, Sir, Your Most Obt Servt

Geo: Washington.

LB, DLC:GW; Df, DNA: RG 59, Miscellaneous Letters.

Gabriel Dupare de Bellegard (1717–1789) was a prominent theologian, born near Narbonne, Languedoc. He studied at Toulouse and later at the Sorbonne. In 1757 he went to Holland and settled in Utrecht. Bellegard wrote and edited numerous works, among them the *Collection Général des Oeuvres d'Antoine Arnauld, Docteur de Sorbonne*, and *Supplementum ad Varias Collectiones Operum Zegem Bernard Van Espen*. In 1765 he wrote a history of the Catholic church in Utrecht. In 1771 he was named canon of a church in Lyon and acted as director of the Provincial Utrecht Society of Arts. Bellegard had died in December 1789.

1. Questions arose soon after Gen. James Edward Oglethorpe's death in July 1785 concerning the possibility that he still owned land in Georgia. In December 1785 Jefferson wrote to George Mathews, then governor of Georgia, and now one of its senators, stating that the death of Oglethorpe, "who had considerable possessions in Georgia, has given rise, as we understand to questions whether those possessions have become the property of the state, or have been transferred by his will to the widow, or descended on the nearest heir capable in law of taking them. In the latter case, the Chevalier de Mezieres, a subject of France, stands foremost, as being made capable of the inheritance by the treaty between that country and the United states. Under the regal government with us it was the practice, when lands passed to the crown by escheat or forfeiture, to grant them to such relation of the party as stood on the fairest ground." Jefferson informed Mathews that the chevalier de Mézières, Oglethorpe's nephew, was coming to America to press his claim and asked for Mathews's support for him "as presenting an opportunity of proving the favourable dispositions which exist throughout America towards the subjects of this country" (Jefferson to Mathews, 22 Dec. 1785, in Boyd, *Jefferson Papers*, 9:120–21). Jefferson wrote a similar letter to the Georgia delegates to Congress, 22 Dec. 1785 (ibid., 121–22). The Georgia delegates informed Jefferson, 21 Aug. 1786, that inquiries into ownership of land by Oglethorpe had indicated that "no land or any other property has been sold in that State as belonging to the late Genl. Oglethorp, nor can we hear of any Estate he had there" (ibid., 10:280–81).

From Andrew Ellicott

Sir   Philadelphia Jany 15th 1790

I arrived in this City the day before Yesterday, after a long and tedious journey from Fort Erie, and have the satisfaction to inform your Excellency that so much of the Survey on which I was employed, that fell within the Territory of his Britanick Majesty is compleated. I find the Geography of the Country about the Lakes very erronious, too much so to be even a tolerable guide. The south side of Lake Erie is laid down half a degree too far to the south, in the American Atlas published in 1776; and said to be corrected by Majr Holland, De Brahm and others.[1] The same Lake is by Hutchins, and Mc Murry, placed 20 miles too far North: Similar errors attend all that Country thro' which I passed.

A corrected Chart of the west end of Lake Ontario, the Strait of Niagara, and part of Lake Erie, comprehending the whole British Settlement of Nassau, shall be handed to your Excellency as soon as I come to New York.

From certain *data*, which cannot be materially defective, the sale of Lands made by the United States to the State of Pennsylvania, will not neat less than thirteen thousand pounds specie to the Union, rating Certificates at 4/6 to the pound.

On my arrival at the Garrison of Niagara on the 21st day of October last, I was introduced by the Officer of the day, in company with Gen. Chapen of Massachusetts, and Mr Joseph Ellicott of Baltimore, to the Commandant Lieut. Col. Harriss:[2] after the introduction I produced my Commission, which the Col. looked over; and then addressed himself to me in the following words—"Pray Sir what request have you to make from this paper?" (Meaning the Commission). To which I replied. "In order to execute the duties of my appointment, it will be necessary to go into the Territory of his Britanick Majesty; but as you may not be authorized to grant such permission, an express has been sent on by our Secretary of foreign affairs, to his Excellency Lord Dorchester Governor of Canada, to obtain this privilege: and if the express has not yet arrived, my present request is only, that myself, and party, may have the liberty of staying in the Country, with such privileges as are allowed to other Gentlemen from the United States, and wait his arrival." To which the Col. replied "You cannot have permission to stay in this Country, you must leave it Sir." I then informed him that our going away so precipitately must be attended with inconveniency to ourselves, and the present expence of the United States, sacrificed to no purpose; and as I was confident that the express would arrive with the first Vessel, and from a desire to have the business executed with all possible dispatch, I should not be very punctilious about the privileges; but would willingly be confined to one single Acre of Ground, or any other space, and under any restrictions which he himself should prescribe: to which he replied. "Your request cannot be granted Sir, you must leave this Country, and that with expedition." I then informed him, that myself, and companions were much fatigued with a long, and painful journey, and our Horses broken down with hard duty, and the want of food: and that our return home might be marked with some degree of certainty, I requested the privilege of continuing some few days in the Country to refresh ourselves, and recruit our horses. To which he returned "I cannot be answerable for your situation, you are not to continue in this Country, and if you stay any where in it, I shall hear of you, and will take measures accordingly." I then observed to him that I had some Gentlemen in my party, who were very desirous to view the falls of Niagara, and as this was the only probable opportunity which would ever fall in their way, I requested that their curiosity might be gratified; perticularly as the falls were not near any of their posts. To which he answered "Your Gentlemen cannot be gratified, they cannot see the falls, too many people have seen the falls already[.]" I then began to make some observations on the common usage of all civilized Nations with regard to matters of Science, and natural Curiosities; but was soon interrrupted by the Col., who desired that I "would not multiply words on that subject," that he "was decisive," and we "must depart." He then addressed himself to Col. Butler of the Rangers,[3] (who was present), as follows "Col. it is our *Luncheon* time, will you go and take a cut with us." Then turning to me he said "You may retire to the Tavern in the Bottom, and purchase such refreshment as you may want; in the mean time," (pointing to my Commission which lay on the Table,) "I will take a copy of that paper, after which the Adjutant shall return you the original[.]" We were then attended by the Officer of the day to the Tavern. After some consideration I thought it best to make one other request to the Commandant, which was; that myself, and party might have permission to go to the Indian settlement on Buffaloe Creek, which is 30 Miles from the Garrison, and in the Territory of the United States, and there wait the arrival of the express. This request was handed to Col. Harris by my companion Gen. Chapen; but shared the same fate with the others. Some time after dark, the adjutant waited upon us with the inclosed *pass*, without which we could neither get out of the

Garrison, nor pass the Indian Settlements in our own Country.[4] From the tenor of the pass it appears that the Military jurisdiction of the British Garrison at Niagara, is extended to the Jenesees River; but this in my opin[i]on is more full confirmed by their general conduct in that quarter.

After leaving the Garrison we had five miles to ride to join our party, on our arrival we gave immediate orders to have our Baggage prepared, and every measure taken for an early movment the next morning; but before we had time to leave the ground, a Leut. Clarke waited upon us, and renewed the orders of the Col. and added "that the Commandant desired that our departure might be attended with expedition." We left the ground about 9 OClock in the morning, and proceeded to the Jenesees River, a distance of near 100 miles, where we received Lord Dorchesters permission to execute any part of our business, which might fall in the Territory of his Britanick Majesty by an express sent on by Captain Guion, who had in the mean time arrived at Niagara from Quebeck. Although our Horses were unable to return, I was nevertheless determined to go on with the business. We then employed Canoes to carry our Instruments, and Baggage down the Jenesees River to the carrying-place, where we procured a Boat, and returned up Lake Ontario to Niagara. On our return we were treated with politeness, and attention. We entered immediately upon the execution of our business, which was attended with uncommon difficulty and hardship, no Horses were to be had in that Country at any price, we were therefore under the necessity of employing a greater number of men than would otherwise have been wanted, which has added considerably to the expence.[5] I have the Honor To be with the greatest Esteem Your Excellences Hbe Servt

Andrew Ellicott

ALS, DNA: RG 59, Miscellaneous Letters.

For background to this letter, see Andrew Ellicott to GW, 20 Aug. and 2 Sept. 1789, GW to Henry Knox, 4 and 5 Sept. 1789.

1. Thomas Jefferys, *The American Atlas; or, A Geographical Description of the Whole Continent of America. Wherein Are Delineated at Large, Its Several Regions, Countries, States, and Islands; and Chiefly the British Colonies.* By the late Mr. Thomas Jefferys . . . London, printed and sold by R. Sayher and J. Bennett, 1775. A revised version of the map was issued in 1776 by the same printers

with additional surveys by Samuel Holland, Lewis Evans, and others. There is no indication that Ferdinand Joseph Sebastian de Brahm was involved in the revised edition.

2. Israel Chapin (1751–1810), a native of Grafton, Mass., served as a brigadier general with a Massachusetts militia during the American Revolution. In 1789 he moved to Canadaigua, New York. In addition to aiding Ellicott in executing the boundary between the United States and the states of Massachusetts and New York in 1789, Chapin acted as United States interpreter to the Six Nations and by 1792 had become a well-known Indian negotiator. In 1792 and 1793 he served as United States agent to the Six Nations and by 1794 was acting as superintendent of Indian affairs in the Northern Department. His son, Israel Chapin, Jr., often assisted him in negotiations with the Indians. Joseph Ellicott (1760–1826), also trained in surveying, assisted his older brother with a number of surveys during the 1780s, including the 1789 survey of the New York–Massachusetts boundary with the United States. He later engaged in surveying for the city of Washington and in 1791 ran the boundary between Georgia and Creek territory. In 1794 he embarked on what was to become his real career—his lengthy association with the Holland Land Company in its expansion on New York's frontier. Lt. Col. John Adolphus Harris commanded the 1st Battalion 60th Regiment at Niagara.

3. John Butler (c.1728–1796) was lieutenant colonel and founder of Butler's Rangers which earned a bloody reputation on New York's frontier during the Revolution. After the war Butler and a number of his officers founded the settlement of Butlersbury (later Newark) on the Canadian side of the Niagara River opposite Fort Niagara. Butler remained in the area for the rest of his life.

4. The pass was issued by John Adolphus Harris to "Permit the Bearers Andrew Ellicott, Joseph Ellicott, Benjamin Ellicott, Jonathan Brown, Isaac Bornet, John Sullivan, Israel Chapen and Frederick Senton [Saxton] to pass from hence without delay, and by the *nearest Route*, to the Genecies [Genesee]" (DNA: RG 59, Miscellaneous Letters).

5. Ellicott and his party were back in Philadelphia by mid-January and had returned to the frontier by June 1790 in order to complete the survey. The mission was completed by October 1790 (Ellicott to Sarah Brown Ellicott, 11 Oct. 1790, in Mathews, *Andrew Ellicott*, 77).

From James Ewing

Sir,   Trenton [N.J.] Jany 15th 1790

Having had the honor of serving the State of New Jersey in different Appointments from the commencement of the late War until within the four last years in which I have served the United States as Commissioner of the Loan Office and Receiver of Continental Taxes in the State aforesaid, the Duties of which Offices are at present suspended. your Excellency will permit me to lay before you the inclosed Copies of Testimonials of my Conduct, and to solicit your favorable Remembrance of me when a reappointment to those offices shall take place, or to similar offices which may be created to supply their place.[1]

Presuming that the Weight of my Recommendation will not rest so much on Numbers as Respectability, I have not been solicitous to obtain a long list of Subscribers.

The Original I hope to have the honor of presenting in Person to your Excellency before the appointments shall take place. With Sentiments of the most perfect Respect and Esteem I have the honor to be Your Excellency's most obedient humble servt

James Ewing

ALS, DLC:GW.

James Ewing (1744–1824) served as a lieutenant and captain in the New Jersey militia during the Revolutionary War and in the New Jersey legislature in 1774 and 1778. He was New Jersey's commissioner of loans under the Confederation government from 1786 to 1789. In another letter, undated but probably written in the early summer of 1790, Ewing reminded GW of his earlier solicitation and his service as New Jersey commissioner of loans. "As I was obliged by the Regulations of the Office to give up my other business when I first accepted it and am in consequence out of employment it is to me an object of importance in my present situation" (DLC:GW). On 6 Aug. 1790 GW appointed him to the same position under the new government (*DHFC*, 2:89). In April 1791, upon the death of Nicholas Eveleigh, the comptroller of the treasury, Oliver Wolcott was appointed to the position, leaving vacant Wolcott's old post as auditor. On 14 July 1791 Ewing wrote GW applying for the position. "Col. Hamilton as he passed through this place this morning informed me that no appointment to the Office of Auditor of the Treasury of the United States had yet taken place; I presume there is no want of good Men offering themselves to fill that appointment yet as it will not probably be given to any person who does not apply, I have ventured to offer myself a Candidate—I have no extraordinary merit or services to boast of to entitle me to Notice—such services as have been in my Power the public have commanded from the commencement of the late War, and in such situations as the public favor has placed me I have the satisfaction to believe I have given general satisfaction—the examination and arrangement of accounts has always given me particular pleasure, and I have served the State of Jersey as their Auditor of Accounts for a number of Years with much satisfaction so that the employment is not new to me.

"With great Interest or warm Patronage I cannot pretend to come forward, yet with the Sentiments of the best Men in this State on the Subject of my conduct and abilities as an Officer your Excellency must be acquainted when you recollect the Testimonials given me in my application for my present appointment. I shall only say further that if you shall think proper to confer this second favor upon me, I shall endeavor so to act that no Person shall have reason to think less favorably than at present of that prudence and judgment which the whole World admits has governed the past appointments to Offices" (DLC:GW). Ewing did not receive the appointment.

    1. In his letter of 15 Jan. Ewing enclosed copies of testimonials signed by William Livingston, Robert L. Hooper, and other New Jersey citizens (DLC:GW).

From Clement Hall

Sir.   North Carolina Chowan County Jany 15th 1790
    This Letter with the Inclosed Recommendation will be handed to your Excellency by the honourable Samuel Johnston Esquire, who is appointed a senator for this State, in the Congress of the United States, It is Subscribed by several Gentlemen of Distinction amongst whom are the two Speakers of the General Assembly, and two of the Judges of the superior Court of Law and Equity in this state; Should their Recommendation Merit your Excellency's attention, and should ⟨I be⟩ considered Competent to the Trust of Surveyor for Edenton District, hope to Meet with your Excellency's Sanction to that appointment, In discharge of which important public Trust, should that Office be conferred on me, hope will be attended with General Satisfaction. I am Sir. respectfully your Excellency's Most Obedient Servant

                                      Clem. Hall

ALS, DLC:GW.
    Clement Hall was the son of Clement Hall, a prominent North Carolina clergyman and author. During the Revolution he served as a lieutenant, captain, and brevet major with North Carolina forces. After the war he received a military grant of 3,840 acres of land for his services and became a member of the North Carolina assembly in the mid–1780s. On 30 Jan. Hall wrote a second letter to GW explaining that "on the most accurate calculation I have been able to make, I find from a concurrence of Circumstances which attends our navigation to the Port of Edenton, the profits of the post for which I solicited in that Letter would be too inconsiderable to answer the purpose I had in view, viz., that of repairing a much diminished fortune during the absence of eight years in the service of my Country, so as to put it in my power to support genteelly an Aged Mother and two sisters who are now dependent on me. Permit me therefore to drop the first object, and to repeat my solicitation for the appointment of *Marshal* to the Federal Court, should your Excel-

lency think the recommendation which accompany'd my first letter entitles me to that place Otherwise I shall gratefully accept whatever else your Excellency shall think proper to confer in that way" (DLC:GW). Hall apparently received no federal appointment.

To Edward Newenham

Dear Sir, New York, January, 15th 1790

I have now before me your several letters of the 23rd of February, 24th of July, 14th of August and 10th of October 1789—the last of which but lately reached my hands.

I should feel myself guilty of a great impropriety in suffering your letters to lay so long without an acknowledgement, was I not conscious that the new and busy scenes in which I have been engaged for these 9 or 10 months past, by engrossing my whole attention, would excuse me in your mind from any apparent neglect—and I trust that the same cause will apologise for my not entering, at this time, into a particular response to the matter contained in your several letters.

I cannot however avoid observing that it must afford a most pleasing satisfaction to the friends of the human race to view the enlightened spirit of liberty which seems to have pervaded a great part of your European world, and, at the sametime the philanthropic mind cannot but feel anxious for the issue of those novel and patriotic exertions.

The government of the United States seems now to want very little more than the sanction of time to give it all that stability which can be expected from any human fabric—The people meet it with as much fondness as its most sanguine friends could anticipate, because they are convinced that it is founded in principles of national happiness—and the recent accession of the State of North Carolina (which has ratified the constitution of the United States with marks of peculiar good will) leaves the little State of Rhode Island by herself—how long she will be able to stand in that forlorn condition must depend upon the duration of that infatuation and evil policy by which she appears to have been guided.

I was pleased to hear of Mrs Montgomery's safe arrival, and the satisfaction which she enjoyed in her visit to Ireland[1]— Should she be in your neighbourhood when this letter gets to your hands, you will be good enough to present the best compliments of Mrs Washington and myself to her—and likewise make the same acceptable to Lady Newenham. With very great regard, I am &ca

G. Washington

P.S. In answer to your quere—why has Mr Thomson resigned? I reply—that it was his earnest wish to retire from the bustle of public life, and enjoy the evening of his days in domestic tranquillity, after having faithfully served his country for a series of years in an important station.[2]

The journals of Congress, which you request, will accompany this.

LB, DLC:GW.

1. See GW to Newenham, 29 July 1789. For Janet Montgomery's reception in Ireland, see Newenham's letter to GW, 10 Oct. 1789.

2. In his letter to GW of 10 Oct. Newenham asked why Charles Thomson had resigned as secretary of Congress. For Thomson's failure to secure a post under the new government, see his letter to GW, 23 July 1789, source note.

From George Augustine Washington

Honor'd Uncle   Mount Vernon Janry 15th 1790

On Saturday Your favor of the 28th Ulto[1] came here on which day I had left this for Loudoun to view a tract of Land about 8 miles above New Gate the property of Mr Theodorick Lee who I am endeavouring to make an exchange with for my property in Fredericksburgh the improvements on which, are so rapidly declining that I am anxious as there is a prospect of geting something for them[2]—Mr Lee goes to Fredericksburgh on Saturday next to examin my Lots and as my being with him to point out the advantages they possess and to fix the matter while he is in the humor will induce me I believe to attend him as it will require but a few days and may be of consequence to me.

I am pleased that You have dispensed with the cultivation of Pumpkins among Corn as I could not devise a probable mode by which it could be done without interuption to the Plows as our Corn requires late working which would allow too much time for the vines to spread before the working of it can be dispenced with, and I doubt not it will be found as You have directed that ground appropriated particularly for the purpose, will be most productive and attended with the fewest inconveniences and without some other mode more effectual than any we have tried should be discoverd more than will suffice for immediate use will be unprofitable—The ground under the New post and rail fence at the Mansion house is not now sufficiently enriched to lay down in grass next spring and as a fallow and coat of manure will prepare it for wheat and grass early in the fall it will I think be much preferable to takeing another crop of Tobacco from it—tho Fairfax says a second crop from manured ground generally succeeds best and by manuring of it again it would be in good order for Oats and grass seed the next spring—this if it has no other objection as it produces delay will have influence with You as the ground is designed to be got into Grass as speedily as possible it here occurs to me to suggest what I had in my last intended taking the liberty of doing which is that a crop of no kind should be designated to the hands of the mansion house, conceiving that the advantages arising from the speedy compleation of the post and rail fence which is to enclose Your Land will amply compensate for what might probably be raised by them; for the additional aid which this would afford from them would greatly progress the business—I am also induced from a belief that it will tend very much to the advancement of this work to mention another thing as it will be necessary previous to runing the Fence through the woods where the road is design'd to be open'd,[3] that the trees should be cut down to prevent injury to the Fence, which is to lay of the road mark such trees as will make posts and Rails and give the rest to any person or persons that will cut them down properly and remove them—Mason, Adams or any one convenient I am inclined to think would readily do it Mr Washington, Fairfax inform'd me had expressed a wish to be permited to remove some of the wood which has been cut down—I have said nothing respecting it to any of them least it should not meet your concurrence.[4]

I shall immediately apply to Mr Thompson for the deficiency of Buck wheat[5] and in case of disappointment You shall be immediately inf⟨orm'd⟩ I think that the Buck wheat may be got from Philadelphia without the expence of Bags or Casks, for I enquired of Capt. Elwood of the Packet from that place, and he informed me that for the quantity I mentiond 350 or 400

Bushels he would plank up a temporary apartment in his vessel and bring it in bulk, and deliver it here; and I do expect he will do the same for the quantity You have directed Colo. Biddle to send[6]—The Tobacco in the Mansion house Barn is not intirely striped but Fairfax seems still to have no doubt of its making 2 Hoggsheads I sent him to Alexandria the other day to examin at the warehouse the proper mode of presing &c. and hope it will be properly done.

I do not apprehend that any notice would be taken of the Gates proposed to be placed on the public roads unless by some of those who would be secluded from the advantages within them; I meant after informing you to apply to the Court for permission as I would not in that or any other instance designedly infringe the Laws[7]—I have once examind the Creek side, and will do it again but do not think it will answer to run the fence altogether below the bank as it will cause a very great increase of distance and in many places would be very liable to be washed up—I proposed after finishing the post and rail fence to the Millers Garden which will be tomorrow, to run a fence from the corner of the shed to the Mill, leaving a space for a Gate opposite the Bridge across the race, and then to run a temporary fence from the uper corner of the mill in a direct line to Frenches Fence to prevent the encroachment of horses and Cattle. The ditch is finished to the last bend in the fence next the Mill which is nearly opposite the post and rail by Berrys houses, but it cannot be well finished untill the ground & weather becomes more setled—I hope with care that the Corn made & the 150 Bls purchased will be sufficient untill we are supplied by the next crops. Corn I am told is now 12/ & 13/ and is supposed will be higher before spring—the Ground at D: Run adjoining No. 7 is too wet and rough to lay down in Timothy this winter I was thinking of taking a crop of Oats from it and laying it down next fall or plowing it during the Summer without a Crop which would not prevent the use of the pasture untill the fall—The mode You point out to me is certainly a great aid to the dispatch and accuracy of replying to Letters the want of time in replying to the Letters you mention arose from interuption which is sometimes unavoidable, tho' I endeavour to guard against it— the Mail leaves Alexandria twice a week on Mondays and Fridays at 3 oClock I shall as its agreeable to You write by the latter untill the next change—Fanny joins in best wishes for the health and happiness of Yourself my Aunt and the Children—and believe me to be Your truely affectionate Nephew

Geo. A. Washington

ALS, DLC:GW.

1. Letter not found.

2. Theodorick Lee (1766–1849) was the son of Henry Lee of Leesylvania and the younger brother of Light-Horse Harry Lee and Charles Lee.

3. For GW's new road through the Mount Vernon plantation, see References and Observations, 15 Dec. 1788.

4. George Augustine Washington is probably referring to Abednego Adams and George Mason, Mount Vernon neighbors, and Lund Washington, who was now living at Hayfield, 5 miles south of Alexandria.

5. Washington may be referring to Jonah Thompson, an Alexandria merchant and importer with a store on Fairfax Street.

6. For GW's attempts to secure buckwheat for Mount Vernon, see Tobias Lear to Clement Biddle, 21 Dec. 1789, and Biddle to Lear, 14 Jan. 1790.

7. See References and Observations, 15 Dec. 1788, source note.

Index